Formative Acts

Formative Acts

American Politics in the Making

EDITED BY STEPHEN SKOWRONEK
AND MATTHEW GLASSMAN

PENN

University of Pennsylvania Press

Philadelphia

Published by
University of Pennsylvania Press
Philadelphia, Pennsylvania 19104-4112

Printed in the United States of America on acid-free paper

10 9 8 7 6 5 4 3 2 1

Library of Congress Cataloging-in-Publication Data

Formative acts : American politics in the making / edited by Stephen Skowronek and Matthew Glassman.
    p.   cm.
  Includes bibliographical references and index.
  ISBN-13: 978-0-8122-4012-2 (alk. paper)
  ISBN-10: 0-8122-4012-X (alk. paper)
  1. United States—Politics and government. I. Skowronek, Stephen. II. Glassman, Matthew.
JK275.F67   2007
320.973—dc22   2006050032

Contents

Chapter 1

Formative Acts

Stephen Skowronek and Matthew Glassman

Political actors in America are a diverse lot. They operate inside and outside government and across the porous boundaries of government and society. What animates and engages them are the prospects for change. They are out to instigate or inhibit it, promote or deflect it, channel or absorb it. Their interactions keep the American polity suspended in a perpetual state of development, rendering it always to some degree imminent, unsettled, in the making.

The objective of this volume is to better understand these far-flung and multifaceted engagements as formative acts. Contributors assay various modes of action and various sites of interaction with an eye to their transformative potential. At issue from a normative point of view is the efficacy of political engagement. Our question is not simply how political actors in America behave, but how and to what extent their actions change the American polity itself. At issue from an analytic point of view is the largely unexplored terrain between macro- and micro-level theorizing about American politics. Our question here is not simply how to combine insights from actor-centered and polity-wide perspectives, but what new tools and concepts might be developed to more effectively address what each has missed.

It is no small irony that the study of political development in America has had more to say about the systemic factors that contain, regulate, and order political change over time than about those who act in the moment to change things. Against the appearance of uncertainty and flux, of relentless contestation and perpetual unfolding, analysis of American political development has favored the wide time horizons where embedded structures and operating mores are seen to set boundaries on change. The literature has in this way specified the operation of cultural frames, constitutional arrangements, regional cleavages, electoral alignments, modes of production, social stratifications, technical capacities—polity-level characteristics that situate actors and delimit their range. There is, of course, much to be said for accumulating knowledge of this sort. At the very least, it reminds us that political formation is a two-way street in which the larger whole being acted upon affects those who are acting upon it.

Nonetheless, the paradoxical nature of the enterprise is plain: to the extent that the study of political development in America becomes an inquiry into endogenous effects that illuminate the limits and regularities of change, it risks diminishing the significance of the subject itself, or worse, subsuming those who prompt and drive development in rarefied processes of political and cultural reproduction.

It is not as if students of American political development have been denied access to analytic approaches that are more strictly actor-centered; the larger discipline of political science has been generating such approaches since its inception. In fact, the earliest and most radical proposal was put forth in reaction to the study of political development as it was being pursued in America at the turn of twentieth century, particularly in reaction to its reliance on disembodied concepts, dynamics, and categories. Arthur Bentley's seminal work *The Process of Government* (1908) opened with a devastating critique of these abstractions—"mind stuff" he called it. He demanded that political science reconstitute itself as a rigorously empirical discipline and dedicate itself exclusively to providing unadulterated descriptions of people in motion, of political actors and what they are observed to do. No doubt, Bentley would have been suspicious of the more deductive and structurally attuned approach to action employed in today's rational choice scholarship. Nonetheless, the promise of building a universal theory of politics on the micro-level foundations of rational choice echoes Bentley's original insistence on a political science anchored in the constitutive acts of individuals.

The appeal of building an actor-centered theory of politics has gone hand in hand with a growing sensitivity to gaps in the macro-level mechanics of prior historical theorizing. There is little patience in any quarter today with explanations that invoke disembodied historical forces or political processes. But whether scholars interested in analyzing political change over time can simply piggyback on the actor-centered perspectives of others—whether the alternatives on the table will by themselves yield a satisfactory resolution of the cultural, temporal, and systemic issues that have traditionally animated research on American political development—these remain open questions. It is one thing to recognize the value of bringing micro-level thinking about action and macro-level concerns about the polity more directly to bear on one another; quite another to figure out how to do so. How to put the actor center stage and still keep open a view to the larger whole, how to assess changes effected in the moment against the standards of the longue durée—these are outstanding challenges. Two things seem clear at this point. First, simply cobbling together the perspectives at hand is unlikely to produce an effective synthesis. Second, as work elaborating extant theory proceeds apace, explorations of alternative conceptions of political action remain preliminary and scattered. For those attentive to the macro side of things in particular, bridging tools are at a premium.

To explore some of the options and open up some new possibilities, we asked leading scholars in and around the study of American political development to reconsider political actors and their formative effects more directly from a systemic and historical point of view. Recognizing that we are far from stipulating a theory of action of our own, we encouraged contributors both to consider those already available and to think about what they might be missing. While we did not stipulate a common program for these scholars to follow, we did suggest ways to orient this work. We pointed to three familiar but relatively undeveloped concepts, each of which seemed to illuminate a piece of that unattended ground between the micro- and macro-perspectives we have before us and each of which seemed especially promising in linking political actors in America to the polity-wide concerns of research on American political development (APD). One was political entrepreneurship, especially as it directs attention to ambiguity and malleability in the rules of action found in any complex institutional setting. Another was political leadership, specifically the conceptual conundrum of democratic leadership. The third was political agency, particularly the strongly voluntaristic construction of that concept found within American political culture.

Several features of a full-bodied approach to the study of political development emerge from these chapters. First is the animation of once-static categories. Rather than serving as a fixed boundary, political culture appears here as a set of contested categories, a repository of ideas and values that actors combine in new ways and redeploy on behalf of different political visions. Similarly with institutions: rather than treat them solely as a set of constraints, the authors approach them here as sites where the politically ambitious vent their creativity and redefine relations of authority. Even social conflict appears here to move out of the realm of embedded social structures to become the province of movements and actors whose transformative effects turn on their strategic placement with respect to cleavages among political elites, on interactions among their allied parts, and on the ties that bind leaders and followers.

Another, closely related feature of a full-bodied analysis of political development concerns the scope of the relevant action. Who the relevant actors are in the study of change is a normative as well as analytic issue, especially so in a democratic polity where public opinion looms large and re-actions are given wide berth. The term "collective action" is commonly used in social science to refer to a group of individuals mobilized on behalf of common purposes, but political formation comes across in these pages as collective action in another sense. As in theater, the relevant action often plays out in separate scenes featuring a variety of characters and subplots; often it encompasses people in very different situations who are motivated by very different concerns; often the formative effect is lodged in a contingent alignment or juxtaposition of actors, or in their reactions to one another in sequence over time. This is not to say that there is never a prime mover or a single locus of political creativity. The Radical Republicans of the Civil War era muscled through a constitutional amendment abolishing racial restrictions on voting, but in that case, as in others, new political formations giving meaning to the formal pronouncement of change emerged over time out of a wide and varied ensemble of interactions. As we see in these pages, change may rest on little more than a momentary accommodation among actors normally indifferent, if not hostile to one another. It may proceed in whipsaw fashion with concerted action in one direction catalyzing an even more radical reaction in the other. Ultimately, if not immediately, it will certainly provoke pervasive networks of actors interested in maintaining stability and restoring order.

A third feature of any full-bodied approach to political development follows from the present consequences of past actions. Because formative acts are durable, analysis of their significance is always in some measure historical, or to put it another way, because political actors work through and on the products of prior human construction, their efficacy must be continually reflected back in time upon the handiwork and intentions of others no longer on the scene. The particular consequences of prior formation may or may not be those envisioned by its creators, and prior formation may present opportunities as well as constraints. Either way, these path dependent effects lend the study of formative acts a temporal significance that extends far beyond the moment of formation itself. American political science is accustomed to thinking in this way about a Constitution which continues to function more than two hundred years after its framing, but students of American political development are apt to point as well to the operation of ascribed legal statuses carried into the Constitution from earlier times and incorporated into the operations of an otherwise liberal polity. As will be seen in these pages, the point may be elaborated further to include the political operation of physical structures, to the initial and supremely political decision to site the capital city away from the major commercial centers, or to the seemingly apolitical architecture of an arena in which a party convention is to be held.

All told, *Formative Acts* points to incongruity and incompleteness in temporal, structural, and ideological formations as a primary source of their political malleability. Instead of approaching these complications as problems that a theory of action must overcome, it suggests ways of building them into our conception of political action itself. When we begin with a culturally infused conception of the agent or an entrepreneurial conception of the office holder or a democratic conception of the leader, we are doing just that, orienting the study of action to the open-ended qualities of the situations political actors confront, exploit, and transform.

The essays in this volume speak to one another in in a variety of different ways, only one of which is suggested by our section divisions and order of

presentation. We begin with contributions that explore different conceptions of the political actor and of political action—the political entrepreneur, the political leader, the political agent. While the three conceptions
considered here do not exhaust the possibilities, each places the actor in a
dynamic political setting and relates action to its larger systemic effects. By
distinguishing the purview of each conception and considering its potential impact on new political formation, these essays serve as a reminder that
action is animated and motivated in a variety of different ways, each with its
own entailments, and that narrowing the study of formative actors to one
or another has both analytic and normative costs.

Adam Sheingate examines the domain of the political entrepreneur. He
locates political entrepreneurship in formal institutional settings and relates the self-activated, self directed, self-imposing character of this form of
action to the essential ambiguity of the rules of action in any complex institutional environment. Discussions of entrepreneurship are on the rise
in political science, he argues, not only because the concept comports well
with rational choice theorizing but also because American politics over the
years has itself become more highly institutionalized and thus more fully
permeated by a politics that turns on subtle shifts in the lines of authority.
Following up, Bruce Miroff argues that the current preference for the language of entrepreneurship in the analysis of political action bespeaks a narrowing of our conception of political possibilities and that the older, more
expansive notion of political leadership recaptures much of what has been
lost from view. Leaders imply followers, so this concept more naturally directs attention to political creativity as it is generated through interactive
dynamics and mutual exchanges. Accordingly, Miroff locates leaders in
webs of relationships between leaders and followers that are themselves
formative of political goals and strategies, and while he acknowledges that
leaders are hardly indifferent to the entrepreneurial arts, he suggests that
politically creative effects may be considered more democratic and consequential as they flow out of wider webs of mutual exchange. James Block
casts a wider net still. Taking up the concept of agency, he argues that political action in America, whether institutional or extra-institutional, is anchored in a culturally engrained conception of the individual actor. The
Protestant notion that each person is an agent of divine authority, duty
bound to realize God's will on earth, has, in Block's view, constituted America as "a nation of agents." A political culture infused with a Protestant conception of duty renders all earthly authority contingent and keeps actors at
all levels engaged in perpetual acts of institutional invention, dismantling,
and reformation.

Having begun with three essays that celebrate the transformative potential of political actors, we follow up in our second grouping with a closer
look at elements that order action and render its transformative effects
contingent. Each of the essays in this section is concerned with constraints

imposed by the larger environment in which political action occurs, and each puts an unusual twist on the familiar themes of structure and opportunity. Opportunities perceived and exploited by political actors can have real effects, but those effects are extracted from and remain embedded in aspects of the situation that are only more or less open to transformation.

Richard Bensel's analysis of the Democratic party convention of 1896 and Dan Kryder's analysis of police and organized protest in Washington, D.C., call our attention to the physical and spatial dimensions of political action. They show that political structure need not be a wholly analytic concept referring to some unseen constraint abstracted from the situation at hand, but that it can, and often does, take very concrete form—in the architecture of a convention arena for example, or in the geographic location and layout of the capital city. Richard Valelly considers changing configurations of political forces as they structure political possibilities over time. Examining the last major effort of post-Civil War Republicans to secure the voting right of the freedmen in the South, he elaborates upon the notion of a "window of opportunity." His analysis reminds us that a skillful exploitation of a contingent opening is no guarantee of success and also that exploiting such an opening may have a boomerang effect, bringing about exactly the opposite of what was intended.

Our third grouping of essays revolves around one of the less well attended ways in which actors reshape politics. Each examines the promulgation of new terms of governance, the establishment of new conceptual frames. While students of American political development have been quick to point out that ideas matter, they have had less to say about how actors generate new ideas and deploy them politically. Locating political creativity in the reworking of received values and ideas, these essays underscore the difficulties of dislodging extant political understandings and opening the polity to new possibilities. At the same time, they call attention to the contested character of cultural norms and to the formative effect of recombining norms in context-sensitive and strategic ways. The authors show that alternative conceptual frames often gain prominence in subtle ways, the processes often submerged by more visible displays of power in the moment at hand.

Nicole Mellow and Jeffrey Tulis offer a particularly striking case in point. Like Valelly, they break the equation of failure in the moment at hand with the absence of formative political effects, and they force to the fore the often-paradoxical consequences of the struggle for power. The political collapse of President Andrew Johnson in the battle over post-Civil War reconstruction stands out as one of the most colossal breakdowns in presidential history; yet, as Mellow and Tulis detail, Johnson was able to use the tools and resources of the presidency to articulate alternative conceptions of the meaning of the War and reunion. As things shook out over the next several decades, it was Johnson's terms for reunion—with their easy accommodation of white supremacy—that gained prominence, proving far more durable than those laid down by the party that destroyed him. An equally potent, if more momentary, conceptual breakthrough is featured in Eileen McDonagh's study of the women's suffrage movement. McDonagh eyes the limits of the liberal language of equal rights for addressing the political status of women and points out that the critical breakthrough for the political incorporation of American women—the attainment of suffrage—came when leaders of the women's movement combined arguments ventured on the ground of human political equality with arguments ventured on the ground of gender difference. McDonagh collects data to suggest that the failure to sustain this "combination argument," and the return to a more strictly liberal language for advancing women's rights, have been consequential, leaving the United States far behind other nations in representing women's interests. Finally, in a more general assessment of processes of conceptual reassociation and cultural dissemination, Victoria Hattam and Joseph Lowndes shed light on the question of why some ideational innovations become common parlance and find expression in durable features of state policy while others fail to take hold or achieve only momentary currency. Challenging the institutional and governmental focus of most scholarship on American political development and drawing on post-structural insights into the linguistic foundations of cultural norms and identities, they argue that the real work of political change—the work that has the most durable effects—is often accomplished prior to its expression in institutional politics and government policy. This is the work of breaking down and reconfiguring received cultural constructions. Hattam and Lowndes illustrate with three case studies of self-conscious efforts to redirect politics and change allegiances linguistically through the rearrangement of the chains of cultural association.

Our fourth grouping of essays examines the formative potential of one political engagement in particular: the engagement of large-scale social movements with the presidency. This relationship is pivotal given the national purview of the actors on both sides and their respective interests in setting the terms and conditions of change. The essays delve into the different motivations informing national action in these different spheres, their variable relationship to one another, and the different sorts of outcomes that might be negotiated through their interaction.

In its own way each of these essays disabuses us of the Progressive-era conceit that the presidency is inherently disposed to ally itself with movements for reform and liberation. The historical data collected by Elizabeth Sanders suggests, on the contrary, that the modern presidency's basic disposition toward popular mobilizations is set by its constitutional mandate to preserve, protect, and defend and by its particular orientation toward war-making. Thus, presidents are less interested in transformation than in the reestablishment of order. Daniel Tichenor's essay takes a closer look at the exceptional episodes, the ones in which the interaction between the presidency and large-scale movements have proven transformative on a grand scale. Examining the abolition movement as it came to bear on the presidency of Abraham Lincoln, the women's movement as it came to bear on the presidency of Woodrow Wilson, and the labor movement as it came to bear on the presidency of Franklin Roosevelt, Tichenor is able to point to general characteristics of the most productive interactions. These movements did not alter the presidential interest in reestablishing order, but they did possess a combination of radical and moderate wings that helped them insinuate their cause into the president's perception of how order might be most advantageously reestablished. Sidney Milkis picks up the doubly exceptional case of Lyndon Johnson. Not only did Johnson's interaction with the civil rights movement prove politically transformative but the president tried in this case to put himself out front of the movement as the leading champion of its cause. As Milkis shows, however, Johnson's early and earnest advocacy deepened his subsequent dependence on the movement for support of his other initiatives, initiatives that the movement itself was quick to perceive as a drain on and distraction from its core interests. There was, in the end, no submerging the very different interests structured into this relationship

A final set of essays returns to the emblematic mode of formative action in contemporary American government, the entrepreneurial mode. These essays confirm Sheingate's observation that the natural domain of the political entrepreneur is institutional and that individual creativity is cultivated in the ambiguous and malleable relationships that characterize all institutional authority. In each instance taken up here, strategic, self-activated incumbents, or cadres of incumbents, expand their authority against others who impinge on it, reshaping the contours of politics and policy in the process.

Recent theorizing has explained the development of the modern presidency with reference to the collective action problems that plague concerted congressional action and that advantage the president as a unitary actor. As Eric Schickler see it, however, this story is too simple and one-sided. Congress has not been rendered passive or defenseless in the face of entrepreneurial presidents who press their institutional advantages to fill in the Constitution's silences. Entrepreneurial congressmen, pursuing their own interests have, from time to time, used their powers of investigation to reassert their institution's prerogatives on basic matters such as war-making and control over the executive branch. That is why presidential dominance, while ever imminent, remains incomplete. In an analysis of bureaucratic entrepreneurship Andrew Rudalevige examines the history of the Bureau of the Budget and identifies several junctures at which the bureau's own leaders directed authorities in the constitutional offices to see their interests in a particular way; that is, bureau personnel framed the choices of their superiors to advance the bureau to prominence in the organization and operation of the modern executive establishment. Sharpening the point, he also shows how BOB officials muscled aside rivals less adept at making themselves indispensable. Finally, in an analysis of the promulgation and implementation of regulations for new drugs by the Food and Drug Administration, Daniel Carpenter and Colin Moore offer a different slant on the power-generating potential of ambiguity in institutional politics. In this study, ambiguity is not something given in the situation that skillful entrepreneurs can then exploit; it is, rather, something skillful entrepreneurs create of their own accord and introduce into the situation as a way of advancing their purposes and recasting relations of authority. Carpenter and Moore identify a new cohort of professionals recruited to the FDA after World War II, and follow their artful efforts to make new demands on drug companies while seeming all along to affirm the clear and restrictive limits of the legal authority under which they were acting. Deploying their own professional and scientific commitments in an apparent defense of established law, they pressed the boundaries between the drug safety standards which received law authorized and the new drug efficacy standards which they sought to impose. They built an inscrutable fortress of authority on the basis of strong signals and ambiguous claims, and when events prompted Congress to seek new standards, they were able to step in with a solution already at hand.

Elisabeth Clemens closes out our volume with a sober retrospective on these contributions. Contrasting the lessons learned about formative action in these pages with the celebration of individual actors to be found in contemporary biography and narrative history, she underscores the difficulty of attributing change to any particular individual, the broad compass of the explanatory field, and the often-paradoxical nature of the results of such far-flung interactions: "Formative action is not easily accomplished, particularly if we restrict such cases to those where the change produced roughly matches the intended outcome." Hard to sustain and replicate, buffeted by a range of intervening contingencies, narrowed by the thickening of the institutional universe of political action, formative acts are nonetheless always in the making all around us. The challenge at hand is to calibrate their potential with a view to change and development in the polity as a whole.

The editors wish to thank the Center for the Study of American Politics (CSAP) and the Institution for Social and Policy Studies at Yale University for support essential to bringing this volume to fruition. Special thanks go to Alan Gerber, Director of CSAP, for financial support of the conference at which these papers were first presented and to Pamela Greene and Stephen Engel for administrative support. We would also like to acknowledge the contributions of those who served as panelists and discussants at that conference: Ange-Marie Hancock, Jacob Hacker, Rose Razaghian, David Mayhew, Bruce Ackerman, Jim Morone, and Ira Katznelson.

Part I
The Actors

Chapter 2
The Terrain of the Political Entrepreneur

Adam Sheingate

Politics is marked by singular acts of individual creativity; at times it is supremely artful. Frequently, these "artists" are political entrepreneurs: strategic, self-activated innovators who recast political institutions and governing relationships. We can see the traces of political entrepreneurship across a wide array of institutions and political phenomena: in public policy, through the promotion of policy ideas and the redefinition of political issues; in Congress, during struggles over institutional reform or in the competitive dynamics of the committee system; and in the executive branch, from the innovations of enterprising bureau chiefs to the elaboration of presidential authority out of an ambiguous constitutional charter.[1]

Given the widespread nature of the phenomena, it is not surprising that political scientists have long recognized the role of the political entrepreneur in the process of development and change. Dramatic or important departures in politics understandably draw our attention toward the acts of extraordinary individuals who emerge at critical moments, when windows of opportunity suddenly open and political transformation becomes possible. However, my interest in the political entrepreneur is a broader one. Attention to entrepreneurship reveals more than a set of individual skills or an acute sensitivity to speculative opportunities; it focuses our attention on key features of American politics and the dynamics of development made possible through the routine functioning of complex institutions.[2] Put differently, the concept of political entrepreneurship can offer insights into the relationship between actors and institutions in American political development.

In the next section, I elaborate how institutional complexity contributes to political entrepreneurship. I pay particular attention to three features of institutional complexity: the heterogeneity of institutional components, the uncertainty of outcomes, and the ambiguity of rules. These features enable political innovation in distinct ways and prompt us to rethink how institutions shape actors' behavior. As I argue, institutions constrain actors, but they also empower them by providing a dynamic environment for the entrepreneurial pursuit of political goals.

In the second part of the chapter, I suggest several lines of research anchored in this view of political entrepreneurship and the creative dimensions of politics. In particular, I move from a discussion of *political entrepreneurship* to a focus on *entrepreneurial politics*. This move introduces an explicitly temporal dimension to the analysis and explores whether, over time, political innovations have transformed American institutions in a way that affords actors greater latitude in the operation and conduct of politics. Such a historical shift would account for the wide range and scope of actors working in and through politics today, often acting unilaterally or with little coordination. But if entrepreneurial politics captures a contemporary state of political affairs, then it raises important questions about the functioning of American institutions. For politics remains a collective enterprise; it requires cooperation across branches of government and the construction of coalitions for a variety of purposes. Attention to these collective enterprises, such as lawmaking, raises the enduring question of leadership, and in the conclusion I ponder whether developments in American politics have resulted in the pursuit of short-term entrepreneurial gains at the expense of long-term leadership goals.

Actors and Institutions: Rethinking Rules

Rules are a characteristic feature of political institutions. They govern the order and conduct of business within institutions and the distribution of power and authority among them. More important than the mere fact that rules form the basis of institutions is the way rules structure the behavior of goal-oriented actors. As noted in the introduction to this volume, rationalist approaches to the study of institutions have focused intently on so-called micro-foundations: the equilibrium outcomes that emerge from actors' goal-oriented behavior within a tightly specified set of rules. In this view, the analysis of actors and institutions proceeds through the identification and formalization of stylized game forms. Consider the following rationalist account of presidential power:

> This way of thinking about power shifts attention from the attributes of presidents to the characteristics of the games they play. Among these many games are the Supreme Court nominations game, the veto game, the executive order game, the treaty ratification game, the legislative leadership game, the staffing game, the executive reorganization game, the opinion leadership game, and the impeachment game. *Understanding the presidency means understanding these games.* I am tempted to add, "and that is all it means," but that would be too strong. Skill, personality, and charisma seem to matter, or so many people believe. But they always operate within the confines of specific games and strategic circumstances. Understanding the games presidents play is fundamental for understanding presidential power.[3]

It would be a mistake to reject out of hand the insights of such an approach. Attention to the veto power (and the supermajorities needed for an override) does capture an important feature of presidential-congressional relations, especially under conditions of divided government. But the translation of presidential power into game-theoretic terms misses an important fact. To extend the metaphor, the presidential "game" is, in fact, the *simultaneous play of multiple games*, each with its own set of rules, cast of players, and particular historical context. Put simply, presidents, as well as representatives and senators, bureau chiefs and department heads, aides, and staffers, issue advocates and lobbyists all operate within a complex institutional environment in which "single actions can be moves in many games at once."[4] Consequently, I argue that to apprehend the relationship between actors and institutions we must pay careful attention to the consequences of complexity and the opportunities it presents for innovation and creativity—in short, for entrepreneurship.

Consider in this regard the nature of political innovation within complex institutional environments. Echoing a view articulated most clearly by Joseph Schumpeter, John Kingdon writes that innovation is "usually recombination of old elements more than fresh invention of new ones . . . change turns out to be recombination more than mutation."[5] In the examples of creative recombination Kingdon explored, political entrepreneurs joined "solutions to problems, proposals to political momentum, and political events to policy problems."[6] Such combinatorial acts of innovation, I argue, are made possible by the complex characteristics of institutions themselves, or what March and Olsen describe as "a complicated intertwining of institutions, individuals, and events . . . nested within others with multiple overlapping connections."[7]

Three features of complexity are particularly important for understanding innovation. First, actors within complex systems confront multiple and heterogeneous components that can be combined and recombined in various ways. Accordingly, institutional complexity contributes the raw materials that make political innovation possible. Second, the manifold connections between system components make it difficult to predict ex ante how change in one component will affect other parts of the system. This uncertainty creates speculative opportunities. As the economist Israel Kirnzer put it, "the scope for entrepreneurship is provided by the uncertainty of the future."[8] Third, as complexity increases, it becomes more difficult to differentiate where the boundaries of system components end and others begin. Where "[b]oundaries abound," as William Connolly notes, "the function of boundaries becomes highly ambiguous."[9] But this also generates creative possibilities. Because boundaries normally demarcate the scope of formal authority, the ambiguity characteristic of complex systems enables actors to stretch, transform, or otherwise redefine boundaries in ways that create new understandings of political authority. In sum, the heterogeneity, uncertainty, and ambiguity of complex institutions provide actors with resources for creative recombination and speculative opportunities to redefine the scope of institutional authority.

We see an example of this process in Congress, where the complex and overlapping structure of committee authority generates resources and opportunities for battles over jurisdiction. As David King examined in his study of "turf wars," committees that sit at the intersection of multiple and overlapping policy domains afford entrepreneurial politicians the ability to combine existing responsibilities into new and expanded definitions of committee authority and to exploit ambiguous jurisdictional boundaries in justifying attention to previously unexplored areas of public policy.[10]

Sociologists too have explored how the complexity of social life—a heterogeneous set of rules, norms, and conventions that structure behavior—provide scope for innovation and creativity.[11] As Elisabeth Clemens and James Cook write, "change rests on an appreciation of the heterogeneity of institutional arrangements and the resulting patterns of conflicts or prospects for agency and innovation."[12] For example, writing in a different context, Clemens traced how leaders of the women's movement created new organizational forms from the intersection of multiple structures of class, gender, and politics. Tensions between middle-class traditions of civic voluntarism, a male-dominated public sphere, and growing anti-party sentiments enabled movement leaders to transform arguments for the exclusion of women from politics into a resource for their political mobilization.[13] Finally, similar claims about the temporal dynamics of politics and the possibilities for agency are found in recent work by Orren and Skowronek on the "tensions routinely introduced by the simultaneous operation . . . of different political orders." As Orren and Skowronek argue, developments in politics arise from "multiple orders . . . [and] the conflict and irresolution built into their reciprocal interactions."[14]

The relationship between complexity and innovation prompts us to rethink the place of rules in accounts of human behavior and institutional development. As mentioned above, rules provide a formal structure for strategic interaction; that is why they sit at the core of game-theoretic analyses of politics. But as game designers Frank Lantz and Eric Zimmerman point out, a set of rules is only one component of a game. In addition, rules of the game engender *play.* Whereas rules, "the laws that determine what can and cannot happen," are fixed and rigid, play is creative and improvisational, the human experience of a game "set into motion by the players' choices and actions."[15] As Lantz and Zimmerman describe,

Within the strictly demarcated confines of the rules, play emerges and ripples outwards, bubbling up through the fixed and rigid rule-structure in unexpected patterns. During play, relationships between parts becomes [*sic*] a complex system, capable of producing intricate patterns. . . . Uncertainty, produced by randomness or by a rich palette of strategic choice is a necessary ingredient of successful gameplay. Just try to imagine a game without the pleasurable suspense of an uncertain ending.[16]

Lantz and Zimmerman highlight the creative component of human action that occurs within the context of a tightly specified rule structure. Perhaps the best example of this creativity is in the game of chess, where a fixed and clearly delineated set of rules gives rise to an ever-evolving array of opening moves, attacks, defenses, gambits, and endgames.

An appreciation for the way static rules give rise to dynamic play suggests how creative acts contribute to a process of institutional development. Consider the example of campaign finance. One of the notable developments in American politics during the last quarter of the twentieth century surely is the exceptional growth in money in federal campaigns. Spending in presidential races alone increased more than three and a half times in real terms between 1976 and 2004.[17] More significant perhaps are the political and organizational developments that have accompanied this explosive growth: the full flowering of candidate-centered campaigns, the rebirth of parties as national clearinghouses for campaign contributions, the growth of Political Action Committees (PACs), the increasing prominence of legislative campaign committees in Congress, and the recent arrival of "527s" as major players in national campaigns.

Critically, each of these political and organizational innovations occurred under the rubric of campaign finance law and a regulatory regime that did not exist before the 1970s. The Federal Election Campaign Act (FECA) of 1971 and its various amendments (notably in 1974), the recent Bipartisan Campaign Reform Act (BCRA), and a host of court and administrative decisions together established a set of rules governing the conduct of federal campaigns. Within these rules, however, candidates, campaign professionals, party officials, and advocacy groups have devised a wide array of innovations that today are core features of the American political system. Frank Sorauf observes that "as the regulatory regime of 1974 aged, the major funders of campaigns discovered the loopholes and interstices of the regulatory structure. They began to see new opportunities for action and new ways of freeing themselves from the limits and constraints of FECA."[18] In each case, formal rules provided an institutional context for novel organizational forms or campaign practices that rapidly diffused through the political system. In the initial aftermath of FECA, the number of PACs multiplied from 608 in 1974 to over 4,000 ten years later. As political parties adapted to the new world of campaign finance, they developed the practice of raising soft money contributions, which grew from $40 million in 1988 to $495 million in 2000.[19] As soon as BCRA closed the soft money loophole in 2002, 527s emerged on the scene, spending more than $500 million on issue ads and other expenditures during the 2004 presidential campaign.[20] Campaign finance is so vexing from a reform perspective precisely because legal limits—the rules—engender novel practices that rapidly diffuse through the system. This diffusion, in turn, prompts new rules—and new practices that subvert them. It is the aggregation of these innovative cam-

[handwritten margin note: Action in Campaign finance]

paign practices, many of them with important organizational consequences for parties and interest groups, which has filled out the landscape of American electoral politics over the last thirty years.

There is an important distinction to be drawn between the election law game and games like chess: the formal rules of political games tend to be far more ambiguous. In chess, the rules are clearly delineated and known by the players. In politics, on the other hand, the rules are often vague and subject to multiple interpretations. It is precisely this ambiguity which fueled the campaign finance innovations described above. Indeed, ambiguity can be an important political tool, especially in the American political system, where fragmented authority creates numerous veto points and a bias in favor of the status quo. Vague or imprecise legislation defers conflict in the name of compromise and elides questions of enforcement that might otherwise threaten vested interests. Robert Lieberman's discussion of Dirksen's careful compromise in the 1964 Civil Rights Act, which embraced a broadly color-blind rather than specifically race-conscious approach to antidiscrimination policy and established a "hollowed out" enforcement authority for the new Equal Employment Opportunity Commission (EEOC), illustrates the political virtues, as well as the open-ended consequences, of legislative ambiguity.[21]

In the lead article of the inaugural issue of *Studies in American Political Development*, J. David Greeenstone wrote: "Because the rules are never complete and definitive, there is also an indispensable role for the individual. Verbal formulas can never state the rules unambiguously."[22] In Greenstone's case, it was Lincoln's creative exploitation of rule ambiguity that brought about a second American Revolution. Large and small, innovations by institutional actors who exploit ambiguous rules and relationships fuel political development. Courts are an integral part in this process: by adjudicating between competing interpretations of the law, they help to codify political or policy innovations in ways that facilitate their diffusion through the political system.

A vivid example comes from research in organizational sociology and sociolegal studies on the development and diffusion of personnel policies in the workplace. Although Title VII of the 1964 Civil Rights Act barred employment discrimination, it left unclear what constituted evidence of discrimination or which procedures should be adopted to protect against it. In response, corporations adopted job descriptions, performance evaluations, and salary classifications through "an iterative process in which the state creates broad rules about corporate behavior and then organizations experiment to find practical strategies that will be acceptable to the courts."[23]

Personnel professionals in newly established human resources departments played a critical role in this elaboration and adoption of workplace rules. By packaging their services in a way that met the new legal requirements of antidiscrimination policy, personnel professionals established their expertise over the growing sphere of human resources management[24] As Hwang and Powell explain, "the ambiguity of the laws and the lack of enforcement mechanisms created uncertainty about the proper means of compliance, opening space for personnel experts to be engaged in institutional entrepreneurship."[25]

A key insight of this literature is that this kind of organizational innovation reflects distinctive features of the American state. According to Frank Dobbin and John Sutton, "constitutional restrictions on federal power . . . cause Congress to issue complex and ambiguous regulations."[26] Moreover, because of the "structurally limited administrative capacity, dispersal of authority across levels of government, [and] decentralization of decision making at the national level . . . the state issues ambiguous mandates to organizations . . . and enforces its rules in a fragmented and indecisive way."[27] In other words, institutional and legal complexity gives rise to ambiguity and uncertainty, making possible entrepreneurial definitions of the law.[28]

In fact, this kind of entrepreneurship may be quite common. In her study of the diffusion of child care benefits, Erin Kelly found that entrepreneurial benefits consultants were able to generate uncertainty themselves about the meaning or interpretation of the tax code in such a way that not only sealed their claim to expertise but also enabled them to sell their services to firms more effectively.[29] In particular, benefits consultants devised alternative interpretations of the law. Bolstered by legal and administrative decisions that codified these novel interpretations, benefits consultants then linked their innovations to a package of services they sold to corporations. Kelly concludes that "uncertainty does not necessarily arise from ambiguity in the text of the law itself. Instead, uncertainty is often a by-product of actors using the law as a resource to pursue their own interests."[30] It is interesting to note that in Kelly's account the distinction between political and economic entrepreneurship begins to break down.

Other chapters in this volume offer similar insights into the dynamic of political entrepreneurship and institutional development. For example, Andrew Rudalevige describes how the Brownlow Committee set forth a broad mandate for executive reorganization and the enhancement of presidential administrative capacity. Yet beyond the oft-cited recognition that "the President needs help," key questions, such as the role of the Bureau of the Budget (BOB) within the newly formed Executive Office of the President "were far from settled." Rather like the entrepreneurial personnel professionals described above, BOB chief Harold Smith quickly realized that the uncertainty surrounding the expansion of presidential administration created, in his own words, "an opportunity for the Budget office to demonstrate in practical terms what it means to render assistance to the President in matters of management." Rudalevige shows how the entrepreneurial efforts of Smith and others helped the BOB emerge as a core administrative unit within the developing institutional presidency, beating out other potential rivals in the process. More than simply filling a need, however, I would suggest Smith and his successor James Webb created their own demand for the services they offered.

Victoria Hattam and Joseph Lowndes' chapter raises similar issues by drawing out the affinities between scholarship in American political development and the work of post-structuralists on the ambiguous, contested qualities of identity. Like workplace rules or child care benefits, Hattam and Lowndes show how subterranean policy decisions can have dramatic consequences for politics and policymaking. In one case, Statistical Policy Directive 15 of the Office of Management and Budget specifying the racial categories to be used by federal agencies in the collection and dissemination of data had far-reaching effects for the politics of race and ethnicity in the United States. What strikes me as distinctive about the politics of Policy Directive 15, and the virtues of casting a wide theoretical net as Hattam and Lowndes suggest, is the uncertainty that arises from efforts by the state to affix firm categories on what are dynamic and shifting conceptions of race and ethnicity. Although long-term social processes matter a great deal for understanding this dynamic, the narrative account of the Census Bureau's Race and Ethnicity Advisory Committee meetings also suggests that actors are keenly aware of both the political implications of racial classification and the opportunities to direct and shape them in a way that serves larger partisan concerns.

By rethinking rules, we begin to appreciate how actors routinely create and innovate new practices, and by doing so, drive political development. In some cases, the opportunities for this kind of entrepreneurship come from the ambiguous legal mandates that emerge out of the process of political compromise and the fragmented structure of American institutions. Other times, entrepreneurs generate their own opportunities by promoting alternative interpretations of the rules and then securing official recognition for their innovations before courts or agencies. Still other times, opportunities for entrepreneurship come from the tensions that arise when rules attempt to affix firm boundaries on what are essentially moving targets. What these examples suggest is that entrepreneurship is a routine feature of politics made possible by the heterogeneity, uncertainty, and ambiguity characteristic of complex institutions.

Rules are a key element of structure. Institutions are designed to impose order. However, the manifold connections and overlapping institutions of the American political system are far from orderly. It is this distinct lack of orderliness, the aggregate effect of complex authority, which makes political innovation possible. Consequently, a focus on rules as the formal structure guiding strategic action in fact tells us very little about the contribution of actors to politics. Rather, it is in the creative response to the rules that actors come to life. This, I argue, is the terrain of the political entrepreneur.

From Political Entrepreneurship to Entrepreneurial Politics

Political entrepreneurship captures the creative element in politics by focusing on the way actors exploit opportunities for innovation made possible by the routine functioning of complex institutions. In this section, I suggest how a focus on this creative element in politics opens up a broader understanding of American political development. In particular, I draw out several examples that illustrate how the capacity for actors to create or innovate has changed over the course of American history. The explicitly temporal component of this question shifts the focus from an inquiry into the nature of political entrepreneurship to what I will suggest is a broader trend toward entrepreneurial politics.

If political entrepreneurship describes a process of institutional development guided by individual acts of creativity, then entrepreneurial politics captures the cumulative effects of innovations that enhance the capacity for individual action in the operation and conduct of politics. In a way, these innovations are a consequence of fragmented authority and multiple veto points. By design, American institutions frustrate transformative action. Entrepreneurial politics, in this view, charts the effects of institutional innovations designed to overcome this frustration. Moreover, by focusing on the way complex institutions generate the potential for entrepreneurship, I highlight the way innovations that expand the range and scope of individual action are themselves the result of creative acts by presidents, members of Congress, and a host of political professionals working in multiple institutional venues.

It is no small irony that the proliferation of political entrepreneurs has accelerated the diffusion of authority in the American political system, exacerbating the effects of separated powers and institutional fragmentation. This has produced tensions between the pursuit of individual and collective political goals and points toward a paradox in contemporary political authority. As actors accumulate the capacity for independent action, they often weaken instruments of political coordination. Madison might have approved of this affirmation of his basic design: the entrepreneurial pursuit of innovations that promote individual action diminishes the capacity of any single entrepreneur to realize great ambitions. However, as I discuss in the conclusion, there are reasons to be less enthusiastic about the rise of entrepreneurial politics.

Consider the development of presidential power. The presidency easily lends itself to a notion of entrepreneurial politics because of the singular character of the institution. No other actor occupies such a central place in the American political system. Moreover, scholars have traced innovations in executive behavior that strengthen presidential capacity for independent or unilateral action, often as a device to overcome congressional obstruction or opposition.[31] Thus, it is common to view the contemporary

role of the president in the political system as a product of entrepreneurial innovations that transform an ambiguous constitutional mandate into
new understandings and practices of executive authority that advance the
pursuit of presidential goals.[32]

This articulation of presidential power resembles Joseph Schumpeter's
notion of creative destruction: new sources of extra-constitutional authority emerged from the partial destruction of previous modes of executive behavior. For example, Jefferson and other presidents of the Early Republic
invoked an eighteenth-century understanding of civic virtue to augment
their authority beyond the limited prescriptions found in the Constitution.
But presidents in the 1820s could no longer pursue political ends while
maintaining appearances "above party" in the face of nascent party organizations in Congress and the states. Andrew Jackson's multiple innovations—the claim of a popular mandate, a more robust policy-based veto,
and the aggressive use of patronage—all eroded the patrician mores that
guided his predecessors. But in doing so, these innovations catalyzed the
division of politics into two nationally competitive party coalitions and
placed the presidency in the pivotal political role.[33]

Eventually, the same patronage networks and partisan ties that served as
a powerful resource for party presidents became an instrument of congressional supremacy as presidential power reached its nadir during the Gilded
Age. During the first half of the twentieth century, presidents wrested political power away from Congress by building a new source of power and authority in an enlarged executive branch. In a sense, the "modern"
presidency that we associate with FDR was the culmination of more than a
half century of struggle, one that begins with Rutherford Hayes's battles
against the congressional party bosses and reaches its critical breakthrough
in Teddy Roosevelt's "stewardship theory" of the presidency. Successive
presidents hammered at the elements of the party state, such as patronage,
that had come to stifle the presidency during the late nineteenth century.[34]

The continued growth of government after World War II furthered the
expansion of presidential power and furthered the erosion of partisan constraints on executive action.[35] In time, however, presidents came to view the
federal bureaucracy as another source of inertia or obstruction, so incumbents found ways to operate on and apart from the executive branch they
ostensibly led. In particular, Johnson, Nixon, and Reagan built personal
parties they could direct from the commanding heights of an expanded
White House staff under their control—all to gain the freedom to act more
unilaterally.[36] In sum, presidential innovations have typically emerged from
political struggles that partially destroy previous sources of political authority such as patrician mores, party leadership, or bureaucratic autonomy. In
the process, presidents have released themselves from what had been
sources of constraint on the scope of executive action.

The fact that institutional change is partial, and that older systems and standards are never completely wiped away by innovation, is an important part of the story of presidential entrepreneurship.[37] The lingering presence of older forms of executive conduct offers a repository of roles on which an incumbent can draw at will. Because presidents are never locked into the use of one set of extraconstitutional resources at a time, they can combine multiple roles and functions in their pursuit of political ends. Consequently, we see presidents claiming mandates as party leaders, yet professing to operate "above" politics; one moment they repair to the executive power, posing as faithful administrators and duty-bound commanders in chief; the next, they lobby Congress hard on behalf of a partisan legislative agenda.[38] The centrality of the modern presidency is not only due to the resourcefulness of entrepreneurs who at critical moments changed the nature of institutional authority, but also due to the range of leadership postures available to present-day incumbents.

Like the presidency, institutional developments in Congress have enhanced the capacity of members in both chambers to pursue individual political or policy goals. In the House, for example, the 1970s reforms eroded the power of committee chairs and opened the door to congressional "enterprises" in which House members could employ enlarged staff operations to pursue various individual goals such as reelection, policy initiation, and chamber prestige.[39] Similar developments occurred in the Senate, where, until the 1950s, senior members enjoyed formidable powers as committee chairs while junior senators were expected to follow norms of apprenticeship and specialization if they wished to establish influence in the chamber. These norms eroded during the 1960s and 1970s as reforms distributed committee positions and staff more evenly and a "new Senate style" emerged in which senators became generalists better able to exploit the myriad opportunities for policy activism amid the diverse array of interests in Washington politics.[40] Describing this transformation, Burdett Loomis wrote, "What has changed within Congress is a context that fosters more entrepreneurial behavior from more legislators than ever before."[41]

Congressional developments suggest a general trend toward an increasingly entrepreneurial style of politics. However, innovations that expand opportunities for individual action do not obviate collective ambitions on the part of members for partisan control or institutional capacity. As Eric Schickler points out, multiple goals and member interests often drive congressional innovations. Indeed, Schickler demonstrates that successful reforms often require entrepreneurial House and Senate members to devise "common carriers" that appeal to a blend of individual and collective ends.[42]

More broadly, Schickler's work on congressional development highlights the interplay between institutions and entrepreneurship. As I described in the first part of this chapter, institutional complexity provides opportunities for innovation and creativity. Congress offers an illustrative example because the complex layering of rules and procedure and the multiple motivations of individual members create a structural context rich in opportunities for senators and representatives to innovate, often by employing existing instruments or institutions for new purposes and in ways that were unexpected or originally unforeseen. Over time, such innovations contribute themselves to the complex layering of congressional institutions, further expanding the range of possible action and, in the process, generating new tensions and uncertainties, and new opportunities for innovation.

The reforms of the 1970s that weakened committee chairs nicely illustrate how multiple motivations not only drive the reform process but also result in changes that increase the complexity of the institution. Recorded votes in committee, the referral of bills to multiple committees, and the strengthened role of subcommittees in the legislative process empowered rank-and-file members and also provided House leaders with new instruments for control. However, these goals often operated at cross-purposes: reforms that provided new opportunities for individual policy entrepreneurship also made coalition building and passage of a partisan agenda more difficult. Moreover, the tension between individual and collective goals combined with the complexity of congressional rules and procedures to generate a great deal of uncertainty in the post-reform House. This uncertainty was felt especially on the floor, where a sharp rise in amendment activity meant that "the range of possible policy outcomes increased while the ability of participants to anticipate outcomes decreased."[43]

Sitting at the crossroads of the legislative process, the House Rules Committee responded to this uncertainty in the late 1970s and 1980s by promoting the use of specially crafted rules that often restricted the scope of, or otherwise controlled, the amendments brought up for consideration on the House floor. These "special" rules imposed a measure of order and became a formidable tool for majority party control of the legislative agenda. Critically, the innovative use of special rules was almost entirely due to the efforts of Representative Richard Bolling, the Democratic chairman of the Rules Committee from 1979 to 1982. According to Stanley Bach and Steven Smith, Bolling "was an innovator" whose "unquestioned mastery of legislative procedure" enabled him "to develop an innovative repertoire of devices that has continued to evolve and expand since his retirement in 1982."[44] In particular, Bolling inspired successive efforts to craft new and increasingly esoteric instruments to control the agenda on the floor. More important, Bolling and the development of special rules illustrate the creative element in politics and the manner in which entrepreneurial innovations drive institutional development. Bach and Smith's description of Bolling's work on the Rules Committee captures this creativity:

In Congress, politics is neither art nor science, but craft. . . . Instead of choosing from among a few patterns for its special rules, the Rules Committee has demonstrated a willingness to create unique designs by recombining an increasingly wide array of elements, or by creating new ones as the need arises, to help leaders, committees, and members manage the heightened uncertainties of decision making on the House floor.[45]

Although the creative talents of a Richard Bolling may be rare, the contribution of such talents to congressional development is not an isolated phenomenon. In the Senate, for example, another formidable parliamentarian, Robert Byrd, developed the use of complex Unanimous Consent Agreements and a "track system" to consider multiple bills on the Senate floor in order to overcome the increase in obstructionist filibusters during the 1970s.[46] Finally, as Bruce Miroff describes in this volume, Newt Gingrich's rise to power illustrates the way entrepreneurial members can put existing rules and procedures to new purposes such as his innovative use of the ethics process to topple Democratic Speaker Jim Wright. These examples of congressional entrepreneurship stand in contrast to studies of how formal rules produce equilibrium outcomes among goal-oriented actors. It is interesting to note, however, that the analysis of micro-foundations has proceeded furthest in that institution of American government where the manifold complexities of procedures, practices, norms, and folkways are most pronounced.

Finally, developments in the presidency and Congress have taken place against the backdrop of important changes in parties and interest groups, changes that also reflect the dynamic of entrepreneurial politics. Reforms of campaign finance laws and nominating procedures weakened party organizations, transferred much of the responsibility for fund-raising and campaigning to individual politicians, and gave rise to candidate-centered campaigns for Congress as well as the presidency.[47] Meanwhile, there has been a profound expansion of advocacy organizations active in Washington politics. According to Theda Skocpol, the 1999 *Encyclopedia of Associations* listed more than 22,000 national groups, almost a fourfold increase since 1955.[48] Large umbrella organizations such as the Farm Bureau, the AFL-CIO, or the National Association of Manufacturers no longer dominate the interest group landscape by representing entire factors of production (land, labor, and capital). Instead, interest representation today is fragmented into groups of producers, sectors, and even single firms operating within narrow issue niches.[49] There has also been a significant expansion in the range of interests active in Washington politics. Although business groups remain the largest category of associations, public interest groups such as environmental organizations and groups advocating the rights of women, minorities, and other traditionally marginalized citizens have grown considerably.[50]

These developments in parties and interest groups accompanied many of the institutional changes described above that afforded presidents, senators, and representatives greater leeway in the pursuit of individual political goals. Indeed, the transformation of parties and interest groups has seen these organizations in some ways become the handmaidens of political entrepreneurship. For example, a major function of national party committees today is to coordinate the provision of campaign services to local candidates in need of polling, fund-raising, or advertising; parties operate something like general contractors.[51] Similarly, the vast array of associations active in Washington politics can operate as an extension of a senator or representative's enterprise, helping individuals to develop policy expertise, gather political information, and, of course, secure campaign contributions. The transformation of political parties into service organizations and the proliferation of advocacy groups are important developments in the shift toward a more entrepreneurial style of politics: a diffuse and decentralized system of electoral competition and interest representation that contributes means, motive, and opportunity for individual acts of political creativity.

In recent years, however, scholars have identified a resurgence of American party organizations: national party committees have grown considerably in staff and resources and today play a central role in the collection and distribution of campaign contributions. This has afforded parties greater capacity to conduct national campaigns; for example, by targeting resources to competitive races. Congressional parties also play key roles in campaign finance and election strategy through the House and Senate campaign committees.[52] Finally, affiliated political organizations, or 527s, now play an important role in fund-raising, voter mobilization, and issue advocacy after the BCRA banned soft money contributions to political parties. In 2004, groups like America Coming Together or Progress for America operated something like an auxiliary of the national party committees and provided a clearinghouse for liberal and conservative advocacy groups and activists to collect contributions and coordinate campaign activities. These developments may signal a more organized array of interests on both sides of the partisan divide.[53]

But these recent party-building efforts also bear the mark of creative individuals. The transformation of campaign committees in the House, for example, can be traced to Representatives Guy Vander Jagt and Tony Coelho, who each served as chair of the Republican and Democratic congressional campaign committees, respectively, during the late 1970s and 1980s. Vander Jagt and Coelho brought similar talents to their positions; notably, both proved particularly adept at devising new ways to raise money within the ever-evolving campaign finance rules. Coelho, in particular, perfected the collection of soft money. Their innovations had lasting effects insofar as both congressional campaign committees are today powerful instruments for the recruitment of candidates, the collection of campaign funds, and the coordination of campaign strategies. Moreover, Vander Jagt and Coelho helped make the chairmanships of the campaign committees important instruments of party leadership, as well as attractive paths for ca- *collective* reer advancement in the House.[54] A similar development took place in the *into ind.* national party committees through the efforts of Bill Brock, chair of the National Republican Committee and, later, of Ron Brown for the Demo- crats. Both men simultaneously built the organizational strength of the par- ties and increased the visibility of the committee chair in national politics.[55] As these examples illustrate, innovations that further collective goals can also provide new opportunities for the entrepreneurial pursuit of individ- ual rewards.

Recent developments in political parties and interest groups illustrate trends toward entrepreneurial politics in another sense: the steady advance of political professionals in American politics. Candidates for office are re- liant on a variety of experts skilled in the practice of direct-mail solicitation, media strategy, and speechwriting. Similarly, the advocacy explosion brought to Washington a new cadre of professionals adept at lobbying, lit- igation, and fund-raising. In fact, these professionals are themselves impor- tant entrepreneurs who have exploited opportunities created by the changed environment in Washington politics, notably the decline of tradi- tional parties and peak associations as well as the new campaign finance regime that emerged after the reforms of the 1970s. Their success is evi- dent in the widespread adoption of polling, fund-raising, and message- making in modern campaigns as well as the development of a campaign profession, complete with its own professional organization (the American Association of Political Consultants). Like the benefits consultants or human resources professionals discussed earlier, the entrepreneurial suc- cess of political professionals hinges on a specific claim of expertise over new technologies and an ability to persuade others that their services are indispensable to compete effectively on the complex terrain of American politics. As a form of business entrepreneurship, this expertise can be rather lucrative: a third of respondents to a 1997 survey of principals in po- litical consulting firms reported annual family incomes greater than $200,000.[56]

In sum, changes in American institutions have expanded the capacity of individuals to work in and through politics. Frequently, these changes are themselves the product of individual acts of creativity. The complex of rules that constitute American institutions offers a rich palette of opportunities for innovations that transform the boundaries of political authority. The traces of these innovations are evident across American politics, in the transformations of the presidency, Congress, political parties, and interest groups. These changes illustrate the creative elements in political action, and how they contribute to a process of institutional development.

More broadly, the dynamics of entrepreneurial politics have led to a pronounced diffusion of authority and a blurring of institutional bound-

Complexity offers opps.

aries over the course of American political development. During the early
Republic, for example, a relatively small cadre of actors participated in national politics. Politicians hewed closely to constitutionally defined boundaries that delineated legislative, executive, and judicial spheres of
conduct, boundaries that separated distinct Washington communities.[57]
Through some of the innovations I have described, these once distinct
communities became more and more internally differentiated, and in the
process, the boundaries between executive, legislative, and judicial tasks,
less and less clear.[58] Where the geometric simplicity of the "iron triangle"
once described a policy community in which the scope of membership was
clearly defined, the rise of "issue networks" marked a transition toward increasingly porous borders, loosely coupled coalitions, and more fluid participation.[59] Changes in public administration, especially the turn toward
privatization, outsourcing, and a consultant-inspired emphasis on performance and competition, blurred the distinction between public authority and private interest.[60] Hierarchical bureaucratic organizations
based on clear lines of authority and accountability have given way to a
new embrace of flexible "governance" based on flattened hierarchies,
public-private partnerships, and, interestingly, calls for a more entrepreneurial public sector.[61]

These characteristics of entrepreneurial politics are likely to persist. The
institutional conditions that make innovation possible are self-reinforcing:
successful innovations generate greater institutional complexity, more diffuse governing arrangements, and more resources and opportunities for
political entrepreneurship. Put differently, there is increasing entropy in
the American political system, a level of disorder that increases with the diversity of system components and the accumulation of institutional
arrangements.[62] In this regard, the dynamics of entrepreneurial politics recall Orren and Skowronek's focus on durable shifts in the pattern of governing authority as the hallmark of American political development.[63]

Entrepreneurship, Leadership, and American Political Development

What are the consequences of this shift toward an increasingly entrepreneurial politics of independent action and diffuse authority? According to
Samuel Kernell, this is a politics "constituted of independent members who
have few group or institutional loyalties and who are generally less interested in sacrificing short-run, private career goals for the longer term benefits of bargaining."[64] Put differently, institutional developments that
enhance the capacity for individuals to act in and through politics may undermine the prospects for collective action. Yet, many tasks of government
remain a collective enterprise: for example, lawmaking requires the construction of legislative coalitions and cooperation across government

branches. Indeed, as Bruce Miroff argues in this volume, such collective enterprises are the hallmarks of political leadership.

This suggests a tension between individual and collective ends inherent in the proliferation of entrepreneurial politics, a tension that political leaders must face as they attempt to overcome strong centrifugal tendencies in American politics. This is the world of "individualized pluralism" Kernell describes, where egocentric members "unsustained by collective rewards . . . must resort to their own devices to find their political fortunes." However, the uncertainty that attends this self-reliance "prompts many politicians to assume a permanent campaign footing. . . . Governing and campaigning lose their distinctiveness."[65] In this way, the pursuit of short-term entrepreneurial gains may undermine long-term leadership goals.[66]

More broadly, this trend toward entrepreneurial politics points toward a paradoxical nature of political authority today. Institutional developments in the presidency, Congress, interest groups, and parties have expanded the range and scope of political action, but often through the partial destruction of previous arrangements that had facilitated political coordination. In the case of the presidency, many incumbents still find themselves frustrated when political goals depend on the support of Congress or public opinion, despite the accumulation of extra-constitutional resources.[67] The development of an "institutional presidency" capable of directing sophisticated political operations and communications strategies from the White House can lead to organizational pathologies that isolate incumbents and make the coordination of policy initiatives more difficult. For all the advantages of unilateral action, contemporary presidents may appear more powerful, yet their success is also more precarious. They can do more, yet they may achieve less. It is not surprising that we see scholarly analysis of the presidency, and even single administrations, moving back and forth between views of an imperial and imperiled institution.[68]

Tensions between entrepreneurship and leadership are particularly vivid in the case of Congress. Although senators and representatives have accumulated staff resources and secured procedural changes that allow them to operate as semi-autonomous enterprises within a diverse Washington community, the successful pursuit of individual political goals in the House and Senate also requires that Congress retain a degree of power and prestige within the American political system as a whole. But this power and prestige requires the capacity to act collectively, either as an institution to defend encroachments from a robust executive or through a majority party to pass a legislative agenda. Although a well-known insight of congressional scholarship, this tension between individual and collective ends illustrates the way institutional innovations that facilitate political entrepreneurship risk undermining the capacity for collective action. Like the presidency, then, congressional reforms present a mixed legacy. Efforts to enhance the scope for individual action can, perhaps unwittingly, diminish older institutional forms, like the committee system, that facilitated political coordination.

Finally, the proliferation of advocacy groups and the growth of political professions that service a candidate-centered political system further illustrate a paradox of entrepreneurial politics. Even as parties and interest groups have become more central to the conduct of politics, particularly through their participation in the campaign finance system, both are less significant as organizations of mass mobilization and participation. As John Coleman puts it, parties may be "just busy" rather than resurgent.[69] Until parties claim a more central role in voter mobilization and political competition among a wider public (that is, beyond active partisans), Coleman argues that claims of party resurgence are dubious. Similarly, Theda Skocpol traces a decline in civic life that parallels the fate of federated mass membership organizations such as labor unions and farm groups that reached their zenith in both membership and influence during the mid-twentieth century.[70] Moreover, Skocpol points out that in the transition "from membership to management," many of the new advocacy groups created since the 1960s are, in fact, organizations without members. For Skocpol, this denotes the advance of "checkbook democracy" in which, for many Americans, civic engagement rarely goes beyond the provision of financial support for professional staffs of lawyers and lobbyists located in Washington.[71]

Leaders of advocacy organizations and in both major parties have adapted to this terrain in many ways. But the networks of activists, advocacy groups, and major contributors that constitute an "extended" party or political coalition nevertheless display an ephemeral quality. Powerful groups can enter and exit the coalition at any time, a lesson the Bush administration learned with the AARP between its enactment of a Medicare prescription drug benefit and its stillborn social security reform. Similarly, although 527s are particularly adept at channeling resources to competitive races or battleground states in ways that exploit the loopholes of campaign finance laws, they must still operate at arm's length from parties and candidates. Like the expansion in executive power that weakened ties between presidents and parties, or congressional reforms that deposed the committee barons, the rise of national party committees and the proliferation of advocacy groups occurred through the weakening of older organizational forms. And although 527s have emerged as an innovative device to mobilize partisan coalitions of like-minded activists and contributors, they apparently cannot replicate the success of a grass roots mobilization effort anchored in local or neighborhood networks, as the Democrats discovered in Ohio during the 2004 presidential election.[72] Even with their robust display in recent elections, parties and groups still appear something like a shadow of their former selves.

In fact, the battle for Ohio in 2004 offers a final illustration of my argument about political entrepreneurship and the uneasy contrast with political leadership. A number of factors contributed to the outcome in Ohio, the battleground state that delivered the reelection for George W. Bush. One view holds that victory hinged on the successful discovery of a new and highly effective means to identify and mobilize potential Republican voters through a network of volunteers. What was distinct about this network was its emulation of the kind of multilevel marketing scheme perfected by Amway distributors: a pyramid-like structure in which individual entrepreneurs sell products, channel profits higher up the pyramid, and recruit others to sell products on their behalf. Amway's success is based on the (often unfulfilled) promise of individual rewards and the successful marketing of instructional videos to new recruits. The Bush campaign adopted a similar strategy: the result was a new kind of mobilization effort that its advocates and admirers say was particularly suited to the contemporary terrain of American politics.[73]

This story illustrates the enduring quality of creativity and innovation in politics. Sophisticated polling technology and the pinpoint accuracy of direct mail played their parts in identifying potential supporters, but the key innovation was the creation of a novel political network able to make face-to-face contacts with voters in the suburbs of Ohio. This suggests that political success hinges, at least in part, on the capacity to innovate. As I have described in this chapter, the complex character of American political institutions provides resources and opportunities for this kind of political entrepreneurship. The diffusion of political authority, the blurring of institutional boundaries, and the proliferation of actors working in and through politics accentuates these features of American political development.

However, the trend toward entrepreneurial politics is also disquieting, and confirms some of Bruce Miroff's reservations about the substitution of entrepreneurship for leadership.[74] The expansion of opportunities for individual action contributes to the centrifugal forces in American politics and may compromise the connections between leaders and followers necessary for the kind of coordination effective governing requires. Such developments do not bode well for American democracy. After all, the source for the Republican innovation in Ohio was a pyramid scheme.

Chapter 3

Leadership and American Political Development

Bruce Miroff

"Leadership" is an ancient and familiar term in both political life and political science. Over the last several decades, however, many analysts of political action have come to substitute the figure of the "entrepreneur" for that of the "leader," or else to treat the two terms as interchangeable. Leadership, it appears, has increasingly been regarded as an old-fashioned and imprecise concept, one that, to make matters worse, seems humanistic rather than scientific. For many political scientists and other social scientists, entrepreneurship appears to be a more precise and parsimonious term, its conceptual appeal only enhanced by its derivation from economics. A number of outstanding recent works in the field of American political development (APD) reflect this trend, especially in employing entrepreneurship as a key concept.[1]

Entrepreneurship is a valuable concept in understanding political development. Yet it is my argument in this chapter that it should not be regarded as interchangeable with or assumed to cover the same phenomena as leadership, albeit in a more scientific fashion. The recent spate of writing about entrepreneurship, for all its insights, leaves unattended a large field of formative action that leadership occupies in democratic polities. I suggest that the two concepts can be distinguished across several dimensions, convey different assumptions about political change, and ultimately provide alternative understandings of the place of formative acts in American political development.

My ultimate goal in this chapter is to retrieve the potential of leadership as a conceptual tool in APD. To do so, I adopt an unconventional strategy. I do not simply rely on a definition of leadership, for one of the fundamental problems with this term has been the multiplicity of divergent definitions. Instead, I work with the contrast between entrepreneurship and leadership in answers to four questions about political change:

1. Who initiates a process of political change?
2. Who shapes the course of political change after it has commenced?

3. What kinds of relationships characterize the course of political change?
4. Whose intentions are reflected in the eventual outcome of the process?

By comparing how the concepts of entrepreneurship and leadership address these questions, the differences between them will be clarified. Even more important for my purposes, the political terrain depicted in the concept of leadership will be explored, at least for the context of American politics, from a new direction.

The chapter has three parts. In the first part, I contrast what the concepts of entrepreneurship and leadership have to say about political change. In the second part, I concentrate on leadership and highlight some of its conceptual utilities for APD. The final section of the chapter presents three brief case studies. Examining formative actors in three institutional settings—social movements, interest groups, and Congress—I illustrate the different work done by the concepts of entrepreneurship and leadership in analyzing signal episodes of political change in recent American history.

Formative Actors: Distinguishing Leadership and Entrepreneurship

If one of the difficulties in employing leadership as a conceptual tool has been an overabundance of definitions, one of the difficulties in employing entrepreneurship for purposes of political analysis is the paucity of definitions. "Entrepreneur" is a French term, absorbed into the English language perhaps because its closest English equivalent, "enterpriser," is more limited and less elegant. Dictionaries still define the term in its original context of business, and indeed the economic version of the term still predominates. I have not been able to locate any well-developed or widely cited conceptual formulation of entrepreneurship within the literature of political science. Consequently, in this chapter I elaborate the concept by drawing on three distinct sources:

1. the locus classicus for the concept in social science, Joseph Schumpeter's *The Theory of Economic Development*;[2]
2. the writings of political scientists who have explored entrepreneurship in specific American contexts, such as John Kingdon's *Agendas, Alternatives, and Public Policies*,[3] or have provided more general treatments of its innovative capacities and structural opportunities, such as Adam Sheingate in this volume;
3. common features extracted from historical case studies of American political entrepreneurs, especially Robert Dahl's account of Mayor Richard Lee of New Haven (in *Who Governs?*—the work that introduced "the political entrepreneur" to American political science),[4] Eugene Lewis's account of J. Edgar Hoover (in *Public Entrepreneur-*

ship),[5] and Daniel Carpenter's account of Harvey Wiley and Gifford Pinchot (in *The Forging of Bureaucratic Autonomy*, one of the most prominent recent books in APD scholarship).[6]

How does entrepreneurship as a conceptual tool address the four questions about political change?

Initiation of a process of political change. The hallmark of entrepreneurs lies in their origination of the process of political change. Schumpeter characterizes entrepreneurs with the words "initiative," "authority," and "foresight."[7] Entrepreneurial activity is often depicted as "creative,"[8] and the entrepreneur is often ascribed uncommon gifts.[9] Political entrepreneurs are thus self-activated, seeing and seizing opportunities that others in the same positions or offices would not have. The initiation of a process of political change is understood as a supply-side rather than a demand-side phenomenon, analogous to what Schumpeter depicts in his theory of economic development: "It is . . . the producer who as a rule initiates economic change, and consumers who are educated by him; they are, as it were, taught to want new things."[10]

Shaping the course of political change. Political entrepreneurs are more than merely "idea" men or women. They need to drive the change they initiate through the political process. And to stay atop the process of change they need access to institutional power and pertinent resources, along with personal qualities of energy, skill, and persistence.[11] The initial agenda for change has to be articulated, spread to important consumers, and pushed past obstacles put up by other actors. A would-be political entrepreneur can fail if his or her innovation receives a stony reception in the larger political world. But the political entrepreneur also can fail in less obvious ways, if other actors expropriate the agenda, dilute the innovation so extensively as to subvert its effects, or claim credit such that the entrepreneur is relegated to the sidelines. Case histories of American political entrepreneurs depict them in the driver's seat, as it were, dominating the course of political change from start to finish and identifying the change closely with their own names.

Constituting political relationships. Political entrepreneurship, I have written elsewhere, is highly individualistic.[12] Yet political entrepreneurs cannot make much of an impact unless they can attract substantial support. The historical case studies of political entrepreneurs are particularly valuable for gaining insight into the distinctive character of relationships between entrepreneurs and other political actors. What these case studies suggest is that political entrepreneurs, as initiators, assemble their own supporters, who can be divided into loyal subordinates and external support networks. Entrepreneurs recruit and socialize subordinates who become faithful and even zealous adherents of their institutional or policy innovations. Mayor Lee recruited a development administrator who became his "right-hand

Examples

man" on urban redevelopment in New Haven,[13] and Gifford Pinchot stocked the Forest Service with devoted practitioners of his brand of scientific conservation.[14] In an extreme case, J. Edgar Hoover staffed the FBI with "G-men" in his own image, even controlling the way they dressed.[15] Entrepreneurs also stitch together political networks beyond their offices or agencies that are particularly potent when they incorporate diverse and even discordant elements. The keynote of these networks lies in their supportiveness; impressed or even awed by the political entrepreneur, they do not challenge the entrepreneur's goals or press demands of their own. Mayor Lee's Citizens Action Commission for urban redevelopment was typical: "The members of these committees initiated no key decisions; they were auxiliaries. . . . [T]hey were counted on to form a group of loyal supporters who would help enlist a community following."[16]

Intentions and political outcomes. The ultimate payoff for the political entrepreneur lies in the outcome of political change. Business entrepreneurs seek monetary profits; political entrepreneurs also pursue self-interest, whether the profit they seek is power, policy accomplishment, or fame. Hence, successful political entrepreneurship requires not only that the process of change produce innovation in some portion of the political world but also that this innovation fulfill the original intentions of the entrepreneur. If the entrepreneur is interested in public policy, legislation or executive action must be in accordance with the entrepreneur's initial preferences. If the entrepreneur is an elected official, innovation should be a major basis for reelection. If the entrepreneur heads a bureaucratic agency, innovation should lead to autonomy, with the conventional relationship of deference to elected officials reversed. Particular interests or the public at large may or may not benefit from a process of change dominated by a political entrepreneur, but the entrepreneur is certainly a winner.

In contrasting leadership with entrepreneurship, I also draw on classic definitions, particular uses by political scientists, and a much larger set of historical cases. Although I suggested above that part of the problem with the term leadership is the multiplicity of extant definitions, I should clarify which ones strike me as relevant to the present discussion. For a minimalist definition, suitable to any polity, we can turn to Robert C. Tucker: "A political leader is one who gives direction, or meaningfully participates in the giving of direction, to the activities of a political community."[17] For a maximalist definition, signaling normative as well as empirical concerns, we can turn to James MacGregor Burns: "I define leadership as leaders inducing followers to act for certain goals that represent the values and the motivations—the wants and needs, the aspirations and expectations—*of both leaders and followers.*"[18] For the purposes of this chapter, perhaps the most useful is the middle-ground definition offered by John Gardner: "Leadership is the process of persuasion or example by which an individual (or leadership team) induces a group to pursue objectives held by the leader or shared by the leader and his or her followers."[19]

How does leadership as a conceptual tool address the four questions about political change?

Initiation of a process of political change. The concept of leadership is more indeterminate than the concept of entrepreneurship when it comes to initiating the process of change. A leader may originate some initiatives on his or her own and be propelled into action in other instances by the demands or pressures of formative actors with their own agendas. For example, Franklin D. Roosevelt was the originator of executive reorganization when he formed the Brownlow Committee, but he was responding to the initiatives of others when he endorsed the Wagner Act. Whereas entrepreneurship as a concept locates the single author who starts the process of change, leadership as a concept suggests that change can come from anywhere and have multiple authors. Indeed, it is probable that the more visible and powerful an office is, the more frequently it will be the focus of external demands for change.

Shaping the course of political change. In most cases, the course of political change will be more complicated and rockier for leaders than for entrepreneurs. Leaders may have a tough time staying atop the process of change, and there may be moments when the dynamics of the process are beyond their control. The process may be characterized by an ebb and flow between forces, with leaders sometimes in the driver's seat, sometimes compelled to respond to others' preferences, and sometimes battered and beleaguered by opposition they cannot subdue. To return briefly to my FDR example: FDR's reorganization initiative was derided and defeated by Congress in 1938 and passed in diluted form in 1939, incorporating congressional as well as executive prerogatives, while the Wagner Act, whether one credits its inspiration to a New York senator or a mobilized labor movement, reshaped the regime of American labor relations far more fundamentally than anything FDR had proposed. Neither sequence of change followed a course characteristic of entrepreneurial action. And had FDR simply been a loser in both instances, we might not want to talk about leadership either. But because he extracted important administrative and electoral assets in the end from a compromised executive reorganization and a more radical labor regime, because these accomplishments in fact came to be landmarks of his New Deal, we can count these processes of change as instances of his leadership.

Constituting political relationships. If any single characteristic is the hallmark of leadership, it is interaction: there are no leaders without followers. Entrepreneurs constitute their own support from loyal subordinates and wider external networks, and the resulting flow of political influence goes in one direction. Leaders, however, are defined by a two-way flow between themselves and their followers. Leaders move and are moved, react and act, learn and teach. They hold precedence over followers; that is what makes them leaders. But precedence does not mean dominance, and in a democratic polity the flow of influence between leaders and followers is always an empirical question. Moreover, the support of followers is generally less reliable than in the case of entrepreneurship and the domain of relevant political relationships is larger (a topic I take up in the next section). In those fields of action where political entrepreneurs prevail, formative action is individual; in those fields of action where political leaders operate, formative action is collective.

Intentions and Political Outcomes. Whereas the successful entrepreneur realizes his or her original intentions in the product of political change, the outcome of the process in the case of leadership will usually reflect a synthesis of intentions. The leader's own intentions matter of course; if they did not, one could hardly speak of leadership. But other actors will also realize some portion of their own intentions. In the dynamics of political action, the interplay of intentions between leaders and followers will produce outcomes that may not have been intended by anyone at the outset of the process. To count a leader as successful in a particular process of change, the outcome must be at least satisfactory to him or her, but it need not be maximal. Yet even unsuccessful leaders, as the chapter in this volume by Nicole Mellow and Jeffrey Tulis suggests, will play a significant role in shaping political change, a claim unlikely to be advanced in the case of entrepreneurs.

The contrasts I have drawn between the concepts of entrepreneurship and leadership in APD can be summed up in two visual images. We can visualize entrepreneurship as the drawing of a line. The entrepreneur is the drafter of the process, and while the line is seldom perfectly straight, we can follow the process of political change along this line from beginning to end. By contrast, leadership can be visualized as a web. Seen from the standpoint of formative action, the leader is located at the center of the web. But the strands of the web are many and may go off in varying directions in different cases. Other actors in the web operate more or less close to and more or less independently from the leader at the center, and it will often be hard to trace just who has done just what. Entrepreneurship is neater and more parsimonious to visualize in thinking about political causality; leadership is more tangled but may more often capture what happens in the course of political change.

Leadership in American Political Development

Up to this point, I have established that entrepreneurship and leadership are conceptually distinct in a number of important respects. To be sure, there are areas of overlap between the two concepts. Many of the same political skills are relevant for both entrepreneurs and leaders. Indeed, it is possible for the same actor to be an entrepreneur in one political context and a leader in another. One might even think of a continuum in which leadership, as the more extensive concept, can incorporate entrepreneurial elements. Nonetheless, when we conflate the two terms, we obscure the larger domain of formative action within which leadership operates.

If the concept of leadership is to be useful for students of APD in exploring this larger domain, several of its features need further elaboration. Since the hallmark of leadership is the leader-follower relationship, the question of who counts as a follower is vital to consider. Leader-follower relationships are generally more complex than entrepreneur-supporter relationships. In the web of leadership, other formative actors can be located at varying distances from leaders. Closest are active followers, who are influenced by—but also influence—leaders. At an intermediate distance are larger and more passive constituencies, whose backing is potential but cannot be obtained without successful persuasive efforts. At the farthest reach in the web are adversarial actors, whose objections may have to be assuaged or accommodated in the process of change.

Leadership's causal influence depends on persuasion rather than command, as Richard E. Neustadt famously observed about the American presidency. Leaders must move others to action, others who have the option of remaining passive. And if leaders hope to appeal to followers and motivate them to act, they must understand what those followers believe and value; the art of persuasion rests on the skill of interpretation. (Persuasion is also important for political entrepreneurship, but entrepreneurs push across their own ideas to supporters rather than interpreting and reshaping followers' views.) Successful leadership is neither too bold to be outside the web nor so dutiful that it lies on its periphery; rather, from a position in the middle, leadership must establish the persuasive connections that help political change to occur.

The interactions between leaders and followers may largely consist of exchanges of benefits—what James MacGregor Burns calls "transactional leadership."[20] But in cases of substantial political change, leadership ordinarily has to appeal beyond the range of benefits (and the domain of rational choice theories) to the realm of values. If institutional or policy changes are to be large-scale and durable, their promotion requires leaders to tap into the underlying values of followers. Rather than creating brand-new values, leaders tie proposed changes to traditional values, subtly transforming those values in the process. The transformation of values will seldom take place as a one-way flow of influence, with leaders couching their own objectives in a value-laden language that will direct followers wherever they wish. On the contrary, leadership is both constrained by existing values and informed by the new shapes of values that followers express in the process of change. This dialectic of values further helps to distinguish leadership from entrepreneurship.

Interactions between leaders and followers often have a more sustained life than do the activities of entrepreneurs. Some political entrepreneurs innovate through discrete actions in a particular policy area or institutional setting but in these cases they do not take on a long-term identity as an entrepreneur.[21] The exceptional case is the bureaucratic entrepreneur, whose attainment of agency autonomy allows for repeated innovations. By contrast, political leaders (at least successful ones) may establish lasting identities for themselves *and* their followers that are not reducible to particular actions or institutional settings. In this sense, leadership can be the basis for, and the subject of, a narrative. From a theoretical perspective attuned to the impact of political structures, Stephen Skowronek observes of presidents that "the first thing a leader does is to situate himself in a public discourse, and construct a narrative relating what has been done previously to what he proposes to do in the moment at hand."[22] From a theoretical perspective that prioritizes political psychology, Howard Gardner writes that "it is *stories of identity* . . . that constitute the single most powerful weapon in the leader's literary arsenal."[23] Such narratives of leadership are necessary to understand if we wish to capture the role of formative actors in American political development. It is not sufficient only to study what important actors did; it is also important to study what the political identities of a Hamilton, Calhoun, Lincoln, Bryan, FDR, Taft, King, or Reagan meant for themselves, their followers, and their successors throughout the course of political change.

Leaders of course try to dictate their own stories, but because they operate within complex political webs, they are not in the position of omnipotent narrators. The best biographies and analyses of American political leaders uncover the interplay of contextual forces and personal impulses that shape their public careers. If the concept of leadership sometimes seems to take us too far in the direction of literary or postmodern theories of narrative, its recognition of the political web brings us back to the social science language of structure and agency. Leaders can be studied in terms of the structures that pressure or constrain them. They can be studied in terms of the motives, visions, and agendas that they bring to or develop during their public careers. They should be studied in terms of both—as political actors whose activities reflect the shifting vectors of structure and agency that can be found during signal episodes of political development.

There are cases in American political history where a single figure has been so dominant that political change can be explained in strictly endogenous terms. But in most cases of political development, and especially where the change in question has been on a large scale, there are too many actors, institutions, and interests involved to ascribe change to an endogenous factor alone. Reflecting a dynamic balance of structure and agency, leadership bridges the endogenous and the exogenous. Unlike the concept of the entrepreneur, the concept of the leader can illuminate for the analyst the constraining forces (e.g., private or public organizations) and competing actors in a political sequence. Even more important, the concept of the leader gives priority to the interaction with followers that is the core of its definition. Leadership remains an indispensable concept for APD, for if we treat it as isomorphic with entrepreneurship, some of the most important features of political change will be lost from view.

The brief case studies that follow suggest how the concepts of leadership and entrepreneurship might be used in APD research. In the case of Martin Luther King, Jr., and the civil rights movement, we will see that just as leaders can create their own followers, so can followers create their own leaders; political creativity can be a mutual process. In the case of Bella Abzug and the National Women's Political Caucus, we will see that leaders can multiply the impact of their presence through a network of associates and subleaders whose own ties to other political forces in the web may be pivotal; even when an individual is the indispensable spur to change, the subsequent production of change may be a collective leadership project. And in the case of Newt Gingrich and the Republican Revolution in Congress, we will see that the qualities of entrepreneurship can transform a bounded institution but can then prove inadequate, or even counterproductive, in the larger political system, where the qualities of leadership are more valuable.

Leaders and Political Transformations: Three Cases

MARTIN LUTHER KING, JR., AND THE CIVIL RIGHTS MOVEMENT

Martin Luther King, Jr., is an important figure in American political development because he was the preeminent leader of the social movement that, more than any other, transformed modern American politics and society. King is an intriguing figure in American political development because he pioneered a new vocabulary and style of political action that became a counterpoint to, and a critique of, pluralist, interest-based American "politics as usual." Although his politics of social justice left him, at the end of his life, a marginalized figure, rejected both by the powers that be in the Johnson administration and their bitter opponents in the "Black power" movement, in his heyday the movement he led had rocked American politics to its core and engendered, with the Civil Rights Acts of 1964 and 1965, a profound legislative and administrative transformation of race relations.

King's leadership owed little to the then dominant modes of political action in the United States. His leadership was innovative in the substance and style of his oratory. Blending African American, Christian, and democratic images and traditions, he forged an interracial rhetoric that could inspire people of both races; his great speeches not only moved millions but mobilized many thousands of Blacks and whites (myself included) for civil rights activism. King was equally innovative in blazing the path for a new conception of social change that rested on nonviolence and sought racial reconciliation in the name of love. To a nation whose politics had largely revolved around interest and which was not unfamiliar with violence, he articulated an alternative path to political transformation. King was innovative, finally, in the tactics of political change. Rejecting the insistence that proponents of change must work through the official channels and stay within the boundaries of the law, he became the champion of civil disobedience, creating crises and compelling local and national officials to confront the most thorny racial conflicts by "filling the jails" with his followers.

King's creativity makes him an inescapable subject in contemporary scholarship on leadership—and an instructive example of what cannot be seen through the concept of entrepreneurship. To understand his transformative impact, it is necessary to see how much it depended on his interactions with followers. If King created a new kind of political following, his followers also created him as a political leader. Many of the innovations we associate with his leadership can be traced back to the efforts of his followers to make him the kind of leader that they needed.

King's emergence as a leader was not the result of ambition or even volition; he was never a political entrepreneur. To his surprise, he was tapped by other Montgomery, Alabama, black leaders to be the president of the Montgomery Improvement Association, formed to conduct the epic Montgomery bus boycott in 1955–56. Participants' accounts vary, but it appears that King was chosen because he was well educated and eloquent. Perhaps more important, he was a newcomer in Montgomery, neither identified with one of the competing factions in the Black community nor compromised by past favors from the white elite. At this initial point, and indeed for the remainder of his public career, King was something of a reluctant leader. Andrew Young, King's lieutenant in later years in the Southern Christian Leadership Conference (SCLC), once remarked: "I'm convinced that Martin never wanted to be a leader. . . . [E]verything he did, he was pushed into."[24]

The Montgomery bus boycott brought national attention to King as a leader. At the outset of the boycott, King articulated some of what would become his trademark themes of love and nonresistance to evil. But his philosophy of nonviolent political struggle was hardly well formed at this stage. Much of it would come from more veteran activists of a Gandhian persuasion, such as Bayard Rustin and Glenn Smiley, who traveled to Montgomery to assist this extraordinarily promising young leader. Discovering that King knew only the rudiments of the nonviolent philosophy, Rustin, who was Black, and Smiley, who was white, undertook to be his tutors. In progress reports to their pacifist organization, the Fellowship of Reconciliation, they charted King's alternative political education. Rustin thus noted that King "'is developing a decidedly Gandhi-like view. . . . He is eagerly learning all that he can about nonviolence.'"[25] The moral brand of politics that became synonymous with King's name was not his original invention; learning it largely from his followers, he moved it from the obscure fringes of American politics into the spotlight.

The tactics of mass civil disobedience were also the invention of followers. Until 1960, King's own sojourns in jail had always been involuntary. In the winter of that year, student activists in Greensboro, North Carolina, launched the lunch-counter sit-ins that began a new phase of the civil rights movement, and soon students throughout the South were deliberately "filling the jails." However, students in Atlanta, considered the most sophisticated Black center in the South, lagged behind. Atlanta student leaders, among them Julian Bond, were determined to catch up and make an appropriate statement, and so as they planned a sit-in campaign, they sought to recruit their city's most famous black leader, Martin Luther King, Jr. As Taylor Branch relates, the young activists emphasized to King that "his presence would boost their strength, guarantee headlines, and generate political pressure beyond the capacity of the students."[26] King was reluctant, understandably concerned about both his future political effectiveness and his personal safety. The students were unrelenting, even following King to the airport and pleading their cause with him on its concourse. Finally, he gave in to his youthful followers, and he was arrested with them at an Atlanta department store. Telling a journalist while in jail that "I had to practice what I preached,"[27] King joined followers who had moved ahead of him and then held him to his creed. It was only now that he could go on to become the exemplar of civil disobedience and the author of its great modern text, "Letter from a Birmingham Jail."

In responding to followers, King was never reduced merely to doing the bidding of others. Older black leaders picked him to lead the Montgomery bus boycott, but it was King's vision, eloquence, and courage that came to symbolize the Montgomery movement and brought to it national visibility and far-flung supporters. More experienced American followers of Gandhi schooled him in the philosophy of nonviolent change, but it was the version of nonviolent social transformation that King later developed which became the hallmark of the civil rights movement in its most successful era. Atlanta student activists first brought him voluntarily to the jailhouse, but it was King (and his SCLC lieutenants) who directed mass civil disobedience in shrewdly staged confrontations in Birmingham (1963) and Selma (1965) that compelled two reluctant presidents to introduce landmark civil rights legislation. The development of King as a political leader reflected an ongoing dialogue between him and his followers. Only the leader-follower relationship, central to the concept of leadership, captures King's part in a monumental episode in American political development.

BELLA ABZUG AND THE NATIONAL WOMEN'S POLITICAL CAUCUS

At the 1968 Democratic Convention in Chicago, 13 percent of the delegates were women and the party's platform did not discuss women's issues. Four years later, at the Democratic Convention in Miami, 39 percent of the delegates were women and the platform incorporated a fifteen-point Rights of Women plank, everything feminists had requested save a statement on reproductive rights.[28] This remarkably rapid increase in representation hardly proved that women had achieved full equality in the Democratic Party, as their experiences at the 1972 convention would painfully demonstrate. Nonetheless, the convention of 1972 was a watershed for women in American politics, an announcement that they had arrived as political players who could no longer be relegated to traditional, subordinate positions. This transformation of women's roles in American party politics was primarily due to one organization, the National Women's Political Caucus, whose formation and agenda, only a year before the 1972 convention, owed most to the leadership of Bella Abzug.

Between the two conventions, a vocal and militant women's movement had exploded onto the scene. The famous Atlantic City demonstration against the Miss America Pageant, which inaugurated the new public face of feminism (and gave rise to the myth of bra burning) took place only a month after the 1968 Democratic Convention. In this dawn of feminist assertion, the media were fascinated by the most militant groups and manifestos, highlighting the radicals (the Redstockings) and the anti-male separatists (including the colorful WITCH—Women's International Terrorist Conspiracy from Hell).[29] Less noticed was a more conventional political project: to adopt the methods of the pressure group for the goal of women's equal inclusion in electoral, legislative, and presidential politics. Bella Abzug, more than any other feminist leader, recognized that a portion of the surge of feminist energy could be captured for mainstream political purposes. Motivated not only by her fiery concern for women's equality, but by her passion, as a longtime peace activist, to end the war in Vietnam, Abzug mobilized more moderate feminists to turn their efforts to partisan politics.

The National Women's Political Caucus (NWPC) was founded in July 1971, as more than three hundred women assembled at the Washington Hilton to establish an independent political organization that would advance the causes of women. Many prominent women's leaders of the day (e.g., Betty Friedan, Gloria Steinem, Shirley Chisholm) were involved in forming the NWPC. But the group's creation and initial orientation were primarily the work of Representative Abzug. As Abzug relates, "In the spring of 1971, I began sounding out friends and coworkers on the notion of forming an independent women's political organization, and got a quick response of interest."[30] One of the founders and early activists of the

NWPC, Jane Pierson, comments on Abzug's creative role in establishing the organization: "So tenacious, so frustrated, and so driven," Abzug was "the engine behind a lot of it." Others were active too, Pierson explains, so as not to be left behind Abzug in leadership of the women's cause.[31]

Abzug was the mobilizer for the NWPC's political project, but as a member of Congress she could not be responsible for the group's day-to-day activities. These were the province of younger women activists, some of them recruited by Abzug for staff positions in NWPC. The group soon turned its attention to the reform process then underway in the Democratic Party, the McGovern-Fraser Commission. Here the NWPC won a swift, stunning victory, as Byron Shafer details in his comprehensive history of the Commission.[32] In November 1971, only four months after the organization came into existence, a delegation from NWPC met with Lawrence O'Brien, chairman of the Democratic National Committee, and secured his agreement to rewrite the McGovern-Fraser Commission's general language on representation for women, minorities, and youth so as to stipulate explicit numerical targets (representational quotas in everything but name). The tripling of female delegates from 1968 to 1972, and the advance in women's influence that it represented, can directly be traced to this agreement.

Abzug was a spokeswoman for the delegation that negotiated with (and pressured) O'Brien. Unlike the formation of the NWPC, however, its success with the Democratic Party leadership had less to do with her individual influence than with the importance of a political network in which she was only one participant. Some scholars in the field of APD have emphasized the role in political change of networks, loose coalitions of individuals who know and collaborate with one another in the pursuit of shared goals, and whose positions, as government officials, party officials, group leaders, academics, and journalists, link disparate institutions. Theda Skocpol has depicted the network of activist women and their reform allies that promoted a "maternalist welfare state" during the Progressive Era.[33] David Plotke has made network analysis central to his study of the New Deal political order, as has Julian Zelizer in his book on the congressional reforms of the 1970s.[34] In the case of the NWPC and the McGovern-Fraser reforms, network analysis is invaluable; indeed, in this instance the network was sometimes of the most intimate kind.

One of the charter members and activists of NWPC was Arvonne Fraser, wife of Representative Donald Fraser, by 1971 the head of the Democrats' reform commission. Byron Shafer detects her influence on her husband in the fact that the congressman, who before the formation of NWPC had opposed numerical targets in the selection of convention delegates, led the commission in favor of such targets shortly before the NWPC met with O'Brien.[35] An even larger role in the Democrats' adoption of numerical targets belonged to Phyllis Segal. As Shafer notes, "Segal had been the one to focus Abzug's attention on the possibilities inherent in delegate politics, through some early legal research."[36] Segal, who became the chief staffer of the NWPC in the area of delegate selection, had earlier done the critical research, on which the NWPC based its case, as a law student at Georgetown University. Her interest in the subject derived from the work of her husband, Eli, who was legal counsel to the McGovern-Fraser Commission.[37]

Flush with the unprecedented representation that women would enjoy at the 1972 Democratic Convention, NWPC activists arrived in Miami with high expectations. Establishing the first women's caucus at a major-party convention, they anticipated that they would have significant input into the presidential campaign of Senator George McGovern, whom most of them supported and who stood on the brink of his party's nomination. They were in for a rude awakening. On the first night of the convention, the McGovern staff violated a pledge of support and sabotaged the women's challenge to the gender composition of the South Carolina delegation, in order to avoid a parliamentary ruling on that challenge that could jeopardize McGovern's hopes in the upcoming credentials battle over the California delegation, on which his nomination hinged. The next night, McGovern staffers, concerned about the Catholic vote in November, undercut the NWPC feminists again when they sought adoption of a minority plank on abortion rights. Abzug and other NWPC activists were furious on both occasions, and they made their sense of betrayal plain. To Phyllis Segal, the feeling of betrayal was personal as well as political; Eli Segal was now a top McGovern campaign strategist. Networks have their strains as well as their solidarities.[38]

Despite these defeats, as the NWPC activists departed from Miami their sense of accomplishment began to return. Although they had learned that women would need to look out for their own interests and could not count on male allies to back them once pragmatic considerations pointed in the other direction, they were also aware that they had crossed a political threshold. To Doris Meissner, the first executive director of the NWPC, the rapid increase in the representation of women in the Democratic Party in 1972 (and to a lesser extent, that year, in the Republican Party as well) meant that women "didn't have to fight these kinds of battles anymore." From now on, "women had to be at the table"; from now on, campaigns would be expected to place women "in senior positions."[39] To Jane Pierson, the efforts of the NWPC in 1971–72 had made women a major new force in the Democratic Party. This was the "turning point for the women's movement," the moment in which it ceased to be a fringe group and became a prominent player in American party politics.[40]

If the change in gender politics we seek to explain is the formation of the NWPC, it is appropriate to depict Bella Abzug as an entrepreneur, self-propelled and creative in organizing feminists for political action. But if we seek to explain the entire process through which women swiftly increased their representation in the party system, we need to turn to the concept of leadership. Only the first of the four questions about political change can be answered in this case by describing Abzug's entrepreneurial activity. Answers to the other three questions require attention to leader-follower interactions. Abzug did not remain atop the process by which women obtained enhanced representation; other feminists, some of whom she had originally recruited, came to play at least as large a role as she in winning concessions from the Democratic Party. Abzug learned from her followers as much as she instructed them; the crucial idea of focusing on delegate selection through the McGovern-Fraser reforms primarily came from the research and advocacy of Phyllis Segal. What the NWPC ultimately accomplished reflected a synthesis of intentions: Abzug's broad objective that the women's movement be directed into mainstream politics made more concrete by others' insight that the point of entry for women as political players could be representation in the presidential selection process (and we might also add the impact of male actors from the McGovern camp who showed feminists the limits of the new power they had obtained). In sum, the larger story of women's representation in the party system is a story of a political web in which Bella Abzug, the figure at the center of the web, initiated the process of change and inspired other feminists to come to the fore in what became a collective leadership project.

Newt Gingrich and the Republican Revolution in Congress

Newt Gingrich was the most remarkable congressional innovator of recent decades. No other individual played such a large role in shaping today's Congress—not only its Republican majorities for the next dozen years but also its intensely partisan, polarized atmosphere. What was extraordinary about Gingrich was not only his historic impact on Congress but his dramatic rise and fall. The trajectory of Gingrich's congressional career can be explained as a case of successful entrepreneurship and failed leadership.

When Gingrich entered the House of Representatives in 1979, his Republican party had been in the chamber's minority for nearly a quarter of a century. House Republican leadership came primarily from moderately conservative pragmatists, in the mold of Gerald Ford and Robert Michel, from the party's traditional Midwest base. From the outset, Gingrich was restive at Republican complacency about minority status and determined to work for a Republican takeover of the House. In his very first year in the House, he gained appointment as the chair of a task force to develop a strategy for a GOP majority. Elected by a suburban Georgia district, it was Gingrich's insight that a new Sunbelt Republican party was emerging, more conservative and angrier than the party of Ford or Michel, and that this party could come to power in the House if it could accomplish two tasks:

displace the Republicans' moderate leadership and discredit the majority Democrats.

Gingrich's long road to power, from 1979 to 1994, fits well with the concept of political entrepreneurship. Whereas most congressional leaders accept the institutional context in which they find themselves and are strongly constrained by the needs of their rank and file, Gingrich set out from the first to transform the context and to develop new resources for himself and his party. Moreover, several of his innovations were introduced long before he won a formal leadership post. In at least five areas, Gingrich as political entrepreneur perceived opportunities that his colleagues missed and moved boldly to exploit them.

First, Gingrich recognized that a new Republican machine in the House could be built by sharpening ideological distinctions between the parties. In 1983, he formed the Conservative Opportunity Society in the House, a caucus of aggressive young conservatives who shared his belief in a frontal assault on the liberal welfare state. Initially, Gingrich attracted only about a dozen colleagues to his caucus, but he now had a conservative cadre around whom he could build. The growing Gingrich support network in the House would make ideology its standard against the pragmatic wing of House party leaders—a shrewd political move in the years in which President Reagan was constructing a highly ideological Republican regime.[41]

Second, Gingrich seized on new technological possibilities to publicize his group's ideology while delegitimizing the views of the majority House Democrats. He was the first House member to make imaginative use of the then-novel C-SPAN. Gingrich adapted the House's "special orders," which permit members to insert lengthy remarks into the Record at the end of the legislative day, to the age of television, delivering fiery expositions of his conservative philosophy and stinging denunciations of the Democrats before the cameras. In 1984, his televised assaults on the Democrats' alleged paucity of patriotism so provoked Speaker Tip O'Neill that he excoriated Gingrich on the House floor. But a Gingrich ally succeeded in having O'Neill's remarks stricken from the Record as out of order, embarrassing the Speaker and further burnishing Gingrich's reputation as a revolutionary.[42]

Third, Gingrich upped the ante in undermining the Democratic majority in the House by his innovative use of the ethics process. In Speaker Jim Wright, a bold leader himself, Gingrich perceived a greater threat to his long-term strategy than Tip O'Neill had represented. So in the spring of 1988, Gingrich harried Wright, accusing him of numerous ethics abuses (especially a suspicious book deal) and labeling him "the most corrupt Speaker of the twentieth century." Gingrich stood alone in this dangerous venture; while some House Republicans privately urged him on, none wanted to be publicly associated with him lest they share his exposure to the wrath of the powerful Speaker. But Gingrich triumphed, and when the

Gingrich vs. Wright

House Ethics Committee charged Wright with sixty-nine potential viola-
tions in 1989, the Speaker was compelled to resign. His replacement, Tom
Foley, was a more placid leader and presented less of a roadblock to Gingrich's revolution.[43]

Fourth, as the Democratic majority in the House became more vulnerable, Gingrich moved astutely to bolster the strength of his support network.
In 1989 he was chosen by his colleagues as House Republican Whip. Recognizing that it was not sufficient to win support for his strategy only from
current House Republicans, he set out to attract, socialize, and finance a
new generation of Republicans in Congress. Taking over a Republican political action committee, GOPAC, Gingrich converted it into the chief vehicle for stamping his influence on upcoming Republicans. As Ronald M.
Peters, Jr., has written: "He was actively involved in recruiting candidates
for office, he provided training for them through GOPAC workshops, he
articulated their campaign themes on audiotapes that most of them drew
upon, he planned campaign strategy for the party, he raised vast sums of
money for party candidates."[44] With the Republican caucus increasingly
taking on Gingrich's coloration, Minority Leader Robert Michel read the
omens and retired, clearing the way for Gingrich to head his party in the
House.

Fifth, Gingrich creatively seized on the moment of maximum Democratic weakness to stage his congressional revolution. His bid for taking
over the House would have been premature in 1992, when his party was
saddled with an unpopular incumbent in the White House. But by 1994,
with both a Democratic president and a Democratic Congress under a
cloud, especially with the collapse of health care reform, the time was ripe
for what Gingrich had been planning all along. His last entrepreneurial innovation on the long road to power was to nationalize the congressional
elections through a party platform, the "Contract with America." Having
tagged the Democrats and their leaders as weak, irresponsible, and corrupt, he marketed his party—and his leadership—as the visionary, responsible, and virtuous alternative. Although an analyst can point to several
exogenous factors that aided Republicans in capturing majority status in
Congress after so many years in the political wilderness, what happened in
the 1994 elections is primarily explicable in endogenous terms. As Peters
puts it: "Gingrich differed from all previous Speakers because he had created his own majority."[45]

However, with victory in the 1994 elections, and with the proclamation
of a Republican revolution in program and policy, Gingrich now had to
move beyond the House into larger arenas of political action. In particular,
his success would hinge on his efforts in two arenas that had been peripheral to his rise in the House: the realm of mass opinion and the system of
"separated institutions sharing power" (as Neustadt called it). Here, Gingrich's failures would be as stunning as had been his successes within the

House. The qualities and techniques that made him an exceptional entrepreneur in his rise to power did not help him when he moved onto a larger and more complex political field and tried to lead a Republican revolution in the nation. On the contrary, what made Gingrich a skilled entrepreneur also made him a flawed leader. Put differently, Gingrich reached the limits of entrepreneurship when he acted on a bigger political stage, and he lacked the qualities of leadership (persuasiveness, appeal to shared values, a compelling narrative) that he needed to thrive, or even survive, there.

Aggressiveness, the quality that had allowed Gingrich to dethrone both his own party's leadership and the Democratic majority in the House, came across to the larger public, as it first became aware of Gingrich after the 1994 elections, as abrasiveness. In a sense, the handwriting was already on the wall for Gingrich's public image as a leader even before he became Speaker in January 1995: the 1994 Christmas issues of *Time* and *Newsweek* caricatured him on their covers as Uncle Scrooge and the Gingrinch Who Stole Christmas, respectively. Things did not improve as Gingrich became a vivid television presence in the self-proclaimed "100 Days" of the Republican Revolution: by March 1995, polls showed him to be the least-liked political figure in the nation.[46] Gingrich's showy rhetoric, so effective in shaking up the House during his rise to power, now became a political embarrassment even to his loyal troops. During the budget showdown with President Clinton at the end of 1995, Gingrich's propensity for verbal excess led to the famous admonition from fellow Republicans: "Tell Newt to shut up!"[47]

Ideology, the basis for Gingrich's alternative political formation within the House Republican party, also became a detriment to leadership on the larger political stage. Gingrich's "Conservative Opportunity Society" was a magnet for congressional conservatives fired by dislike for the welfare state; it was a repellant to the majority of Americans, who had some stake in the welfare state. Sensing that Gingrich's revolution was outpacing public sentiment, Republican Senate leader Robert Dole and Democratic president Bill Clinton moved into its path; Clinton in particular ultimately blocked it with his vetoes. It would not only be the president's superior political wiles that allowed him to outfox the Speaker in the budget showdown; it would also be the ideological advantage of occupying the center and painting Gingrich as an extremist whose revolution threatened Medicare, Medicaid, education, and the environment. And when Gingrich, realizing that he was holding a losing hand politically, tried to compromise to reach a budgetary agreement with Clinton, his efforts were hamstrung by his own caucus; the new conservative generation he had created in the House would hold him to the ideology with which he had imbued them.[48]

Gingrich's entrepreneurial efforts at party building also backfired on him after he became Speaker. The ethics process that he had used to destroy a powerful Democratic foe was a two-edged sword, swiftly wielded by vengeful Democrats against their longtime tormentor. Ironically, having brought Speaker Wright low with his dubious book deal, Speaker Gingrich became vulnerable with a questionable book deal of his own with media mogul Rupert Murdoch. The book deal merely resulted in a reprimand; a more damaging ethics charge focused on Gingrich's financial methods in GOPAC. Finding that Gingrich had skirted the tax laws in the funding for a college course he had taught as part of his party-building enterprise, the House Ethics Committee fined the speaker $300,000. Impeaching the integrity of a revolutionary who had risen to power with a claim of purity, the incident left Gingrich weakened among his House supporters and further tarnished in the public eye.

Alienating the public, serving as ideological foil to a resurgent President Clinton, stigmatized by his own legislative chamber, Gingrich was on a downhill trajectory much more rapid than his protracted ascent to power. In the summer of 1997, he was almost toppled from power by an abortive conservative coup in the House. Just as he had driven the more moderate Michel out as House party leader, he was now threatened with his own displacement by his erstwhile followers on the right. As in the old saying that a revolution devours its children, Gingrich was now subject to a challenge from Tom DeLay, the Jacobin exterminator from Texas, who was more ruthless, and more comfortable operating behind the scenes, than the Speaker. Gingrich's ultimate fall from power came with the 1998 elections. Having nationalized the 1994 elections with the "Contract with America" and won, Gingrich nationalized the 1998 elections as a referendum on the impeachment of President Clinton and lost. Accepting the blame, before House Republicans could push him out, Gingrich resigned as Speaker and retired from Congress.

Within the institutional framework of the House, Newt Gingrich's entrepreneurship can be credited with profound political changes. He was the architect of the Republican takeover of the House in 1994, the creator of a majority that retained power for twelve years. He was the sponsor of a more ideological, unified, disciplined congressional party. He was the most important formative influence on contemporary congressional culture, including its most disturbing features of polarization and incivility. Yet in the larger political system, where Gingrich aimed at still grander political transformations, seeking a partisan and policy revolution that would demolish the liberal state and establish a "conservative opportunity society" in its place, his efforts largely ended in failure. Indeed, their short-term effect was to revive the presidential career of Bill Clinton and the political hopes of the Democrats.

The revolution of which Gingrich dreamed was doubtless beyond the reach of a single actor. Yet to accomplish even a significant share of his larger aspirations would have required qualities of leadership that were fundamentally different from the qualities of entrepreneurship that brought Gingrich to power in the House. Gingrich is, simultaneously, one of the most impressive cases for the conceptual utility of political entrepreneurship and the limits of such a self-propelled and self-focused conception of formative action.

Conclusion

These three case studies illustrate some of the distinct political landscapes inhabited by leaders and entrepreneurs. For analysts of political leadership in APD, they suggest the two-way flow of influence (King), the mobilization of networks to produce collective action (Abzug), and the necessity of persuasion and value dialogue in the largest political arenas (Gingrich). In figurative terms, all of these cases offer images of the web of leadership.

Leaders are more constrained than entrepreneurs, more dependent on the responses or initiatives of both followers and opponents. Leaders need not be self-starters, nor do they have to subordinate themselves to the initiatives of others; they operate within a web of political action in which both will and responsiveness are simultaneously in play. They may lack the creativity of entrepreneurs in imagining and launching processes of political transformation. Yet if they are to be effective, they need some creativity of their own in bridging the endogenous and exogenous forces of politics and in navigating complicated political processes to conclusions that mark significant change. In its grander instances, when far-flung followers assume political identities inscribed in the story of the most influential formative actors, leadership is a central feature of democratic life and a central force in American political development.

Chapter 4

Agency and Popular Activism in American Political Culture

James Block

An enduring question in the study of American political development, as in national studies generally, is how to strike a balance between what is unique to the context and what is typical of politics generally. Every nation in its quest for identity will emphasize—or overemphasize—its own special features, a tendency that those treating the United States call "American exceptionalism." For colonial societies like the United States, the pressures of establishing a separate nationhood have led, in the words of political scientist Louis Hartz, to inevitable "moral inflations and disguises." These are embodied in what historian Eric Foner calls our "master narrative" of freedom, exemplified in Seymour Martin Lipset's concept of the United States as "the first 'new nation'," whose achievement other "new nations" would be wise to "recapitulate" if they could.[1]

Comparative social science, by contrast, seeks to identify patterns that recur across time and place and relegates uniqueness of social groupings to specific combinations of general features. Similarities among nations take precedence in this frame over particular contextual considerations. Recent skepticism regarding exaggerated claims of American exceptionalism has prompted some to observe an emerging historiographic revolution in which American scholars spin out a comparative and "nonexceptionalist" history of the United States. For George M. Fredrickson, this more global focus should help counteract an "oversimplified and often idealized view" and provide greater perspective on the national experience. At the same time, Fredrickson stresses, because "national differences and identities" are crucial to "understand modern world history," the analyst must also remain open to multiple forms of exceptionalism, to what "makes every society distinctive . . . each exceptional in its own way."[2]

Given the similarities and differences evident among societies, a more balanced picture will move beyond the "equally dangerous presuppositions" of "total regularity" and "absolute uniqueness."[3] The effort undertaken in this volume to understand political action in America, specifically politically formative actions and the actors who undertake them, goes to the heart of the challenge of striking the right balance. Political action exists in all societies, and has, since the time of Machiavelli, been characterized according to typologies that offer no privilege to American or any other national experience. At the same time, the broadly recognized formation of the United States as one of the first popular societies necessarily speaks to new or at least more expansive conceptions of political action and the political actor. In *A Nation of Agents*, I tried to identify the cultural and theoretical traditions shaping the distinctive political practices in America; in this chapter I suggest how these traditions have manifested themselves in formative political action.

In claiming a significant extension in American popular culture of the conceptual reach of formative political action, the problem of accessibility immediately arises: how to render visible ordinary citizens' ideals about, and use of, political initiative broadly understood. A focus on large-scale institutional expressions of political action—within parties, governmental structures, NGOs, the mass media, coordinated leader-run insurgencies, organizational matrices for entrepreneurship, and the like—already presupposes an elite orientation rendering the American case equivalent to more traditionally hierarchical societies. This institutional approach is typically reinforced both by the scholarly preference for identifiable features and replicable results and by fears in periods of social upheaval and challenges to institutional legitimacy of what Samuel Huntington called the "democratic distemper" or "excess of democracy." Huntington's claim that the dangers of popular participation require participatory moderation reflects long-standing elite disparagement of local activism.[4] During the Revolutionary period, leaders such as Madison, Washington, and Jefferson similarly warned of its destabilizing impact, calling for greater institutional regularity and control.

Today, with public faith in institutional stability shaken by decades of insurgency—first from the left and then from the right—many seek refuge from the democratic distemper in the assurance that history is made by leaders and elites rather than by the more easily forgotten actions of ordinary people. This focus on famous figures, exemplified by massive and wildly popular biographies of great Revolutionary leaders, suggests that society could once again be free from popular meddling.[5] Such attitudes, bolstered in the media and complemented by political scientists' focus on institutions like Congress, the presidency, administrative structures, and elections, renders less institutionalized forms of political action ever less visible.

How, then, do we access this less institutionalized world of citizen political conviction and engagement? How are we to probe the deeper processes by which observable movements and institutions come into being, including the often wrenching mass movements that appear repeatedly as if from

54   James Block

nowhere to dramatically influence and at times reshape American life? Alexis de Tocqueville, an early visitor with an interest in social theory, realized that the expansive individualism of American culture in the early Republic meant that key personal decisions affecting social life at large were often being made in the "solitude of [one's] own heart."[6] He also noted how political elites cowered before the power of these unspoken popular values and choices. The periodic emergence and disruptive effect of ordinary citizens acting in political, religious, and social movements is only the most visible expression of this distinctive popular presence. It has exerted powerful and constant influence over the institutions closest to everyday life, shaping families, schools, and churches. In early America, it also helped to shape political, social, and economic norms and bore directly on governmental institutions and behaviors. As we shall see, uncertainty about its role in contemporary America raises questions about the direction of modern American liberalism.

The challenge, in other words, is to regain access to what Americans have always implicitly understood, the meaning of America as a "popular" society. This chapter lays out those distinctive underlying attitudes of citizens toward the value and validity of their own action and the novel cultural assumptions about institutional legitimacy that have infused American political practice and shaped its forms. Tracing the origins and development of these cultural-institutional conceptions will help us isolate the scope and role of its specifically American elements. In this volume, the Miroff chapter on leadership and Sheingate chapter on entrepreneurship invoke universal categories of action, focus on the most visible political manipulations, and facilitate thereby a broader comparative study of American politics. This chapter cautions against any too quick or too complete disregard of the culture in which all such action is anchored, and seeks to demonstrate the abiding value of balance.

The Limits of Formative Action Frameworks

Classic expression of formative action in America takes two forms. The first typically distinguishes the unprecedented levels of voluntary political and social action historically. One recent article began, "To understand America, it is necessary to recognize" the "luxuriant voluntarism that is its lifeblood," a propensity to participate in a "diverse network of local infrastructures" and a "complex welter of intermediate institutions."[7] Its distinctive character as a "nation of joiners," what Max Weber called this "association-land *par excellence*," was clear in the nineteenth century. William Ellery Channing noted in the 1830s a "most remarkable . . . energy" fueling the "disposition which now prevails to form associations," a "mighty engine" now "penetrating everywhere" to "accomplish all objects by organized means," such that "every thing is done now by societies."[8] The greatest observer of this tendency, and the source of most thinking on American activism, was Tocqueville. Noting in *Democracy in America* the "immense assemblage of associations"—that Americans "of all ages, all conditions and all dispositions, constantly form associations" of a "thousand" kinds, "religious, moral, serious, futile, general or restricted, enormous or diminutive"—he concluded that "in no country in the world has the principle of association been more successfully used, or applied to a greater multitude of objects, than in America."[9]

The second and more prominent expression, which in many ways stands opposed to the first, is what Louis Hartz called the uncontested "triumph of the liberal idea," its "dogmatic" commitment to "individual liberty." As explained by Jefferson in his First Inaugural, the "sum of good government" was to "restrain men from injuring one another, which shall leave them otherwise free to regulate their own pursuits."[10] Yet radical individualism with its emphasis on uncoerced private activity, though powerful as an ideal, has never been able to account for the full scope of formative action in America. It is woefully incomplete in describing the development of American institutions, how and why citizens, from the nation's founding and before, devoted themselves to making and remaking institutions. It fails in this regard to address the organization of villages, interdependent economic relations, state political structures, religious fellowships, school systems, and voluntary associations that transformed frontier settings into the networks of modern society. As we shall see, it similarly fails to capture the continuing vibrancy of social and political activism in movements of opposition and social change.

Collective action and the broad manifestations of mobilization that go beyond private initiative are blind spots in the national story of unencumbered individualism. The continuing dominance of this perspective in the social sciences is reflected in the pervasiveness of rational choice theory with its methodological individualism. Action in this framework is reduced to individual preferences or aggregates of individual preferences, with preferences arrived at by a conscious personal choice to weigh costs and benefits and maximize one's perceived self-interest. Yet, once intentionality is framed as private self-seeking, the entire dimension of formative public action toward a collective good is erased. Rational choice theory thus inevitably discounts the role of mass public action, stressing instead the benefits to ordinary citizens of nonparticipation and the interests of institutional elites in offering selective incentives for citizens to advance themselves.[11] By framing action formulaically as self-maximizing behavior by a "pseudo-universal human actor without a personal history or a gender, race, or class position within social history," it makes it impossible to gain insight into the different ways social members act within particular cultural contexts to shape their own destiny.[12]

Contemporary social theory, to counter the individualist bias, has evolved several alternative models for understanding mass action, models that move by degrees away from individualist categories to a more socially embedded approach. An early attempt, "collective behavior theory," by focusing on disruptive actions like insurgencies, protests, riots, and panics, arrived at psychological explanations of formative action such as "contagion" and "epidemic" that highlighted its "crudeness, excess" and "primitive character." Emphasizing general patterns of irrational mass action resulted in accounts that were neither culturally specific nor generally applicable.[13]

The widespread emergence of collective political action in the 1960s that, while disruptive, identified serious systemic grievances and expressed reasonable demands for social change and institutional reform led to "resource mobilization theory" (RMT). RMT treated formative action by institutional challengers and supporters alike as instrumental and purposive components shaping the political process. Relying heavily on rational choice assumptions, however, RMT normalized collective action as one variant of interest group mobilization. Available resources were identified not in terms of ideology or ideals but as organizational leverage to maximize individual ends. In so doing, RMT detached citizens from any independent normative stance, historical sensibility, or social networks and allegiances that might provide reference for goals of action beyond personal preferences. Much of the potential meaning and impact of the action was thereby neutralized. Moreover, RMT's focus on highly visible and resource-rich movements committed to maximizing their institutional access confined its reach to centralized organizations with elite leadership and hierarchy. Participants in this model were in turn reduced to a "mass market of isolated consumers" passively available as a "target for mobilization."[14] RMT thus could not account for the wide range of less mainstream, less visible expressions of public action or for the specific cultural and historical connections that precipitate them.

The value of a different sort of explanation for collective mobilization and the different cultural and national motivations driving it spurred the field of social movement analysis (SMA). Turning to social psychology, SMA looked to the efforts of individuals to interpret their condition through collective meanings, identities, affiliations, and expressions as a "more realistic" source of explanations for why they "care about *collective* goals" and why they act to further "values, norms, ideologies, projects, culture, and identity."[15] Attention to all forms of mobilization by SMA gave movements excluded from or challenging existing relations equal place with consensual movements, access-oriented groups, and institutionally legitimated behavior. The immediate benefit was to direct attention to an immeasurable array of far less visible kinds of action. SMA turned up local voluntary grassroots groups, typically decentralized, at times not even "entering the polity" but "reclaim[ing] private space."[16] Often tied to local communities or lower status "self-organized projects" and "special issues," such movements were embedded within "participatory environments," at times protean and temporary, oppositional and system sustaining, symbolic and nonutilitarian. They were often spontaneous and unpredictable as well, as if people had to "mobilize themselves," with leaders "trying to keep up."[17]

With the advent of SMA, national distinctions could be drawn from characteristic differences in cultural agendas and forms of solidarity as these were manifested in networks of informal social relations. In European societies, the traditional corporatist conception of formative action advancing the larger collective interest and the nineteenth-century emergence of "social class antagonisms" and "class consciousness" as the source of identity and action served to define public activism by its structural pursuit of state power and dominance. In America, by contrast, comparatively greater access to politically formative action framed a far more "open, fluid and decentralized" polity. At the same time, the tendency toward relatively flexible allegiances, along with the greater diversity and more limited nature of the agendas that rallied people to action, typically diverted the action from structural demands toward "equal opportunities" and "integration into established institutions."[18]

Still, the focus on mobilization as the central problematic of the new research program limited SMA to more visible manifestations. Though it was more sensitive to historical, cultural, and structural differences between groups and broadened to include "microevents [through] micromobilization," it provided no access to the underlying substrata of "social ties and networks linking people together in their everyday lives" within each culture.[19] The problem was that discrete examples of mobilization only represented particular instances that pointed to a larger cultural framework sustaining popular movements and citizen activism. Formal comparison of collective actors, whether groups or organizations, using broader historical and cultural settings as "a backdrop," failed to identify exactly which cultural resources provided the underlying ability to mobilize action in the first place.[20]

In the final analysis, the pervasiveness in America of fluid and shifting groups continually reshaped through the diversity of individual behavior and degrees of individual conviction testifies to cultural forces preceding and enabling formative action with which we have yet to come to terms. We have yet to confront the "*permanent* coexistence" of social movements and established institutions, of ordinary people in their myriad voluntary associations and informal conversations side by side with larger political formations, of a culture of action as it bears on regular political activity. By prioritizing group-level regularities and the group logic of action, social theory has been unable to account for the continuing influence of such cultural forces on individual citizens and the state.[21] As "active processors of meaning" and interpreters of the common good, Americans relate their

beliefs about power and legitimacy—about the right to determine outcomes for the larger community—to their own "*moral commitments*" and
sense of "social duty."[22] Access to the formation of these beliefs has to be
explained through an analysis not of visible activism but of the deeper cultural construction of action that lies behind it.

Beyond Mobilization: Grounding Action in American Civic Culture

Exceptionalist accounts of American political development fill in the lacu-
nae in more general social science treatments of popular political action
with reference to its civic culture. Acknowledging citizen activism in the
United States as a force for both constituting new communities and sustaining existing community institutions, these accounts credit a civic culture in
America that is distinctive for its dynamic associational and participatory attitudes. These attitudes are in turn responsible for constituting a realm of
civic life, civil society, whose vitality is often seen as the very measure of
America's political well-being. The claim to a civic culture issuing in a free,
democratic, participatory society is highly intertwined with the national
self-image as a "model . . . to be emulated," to the point of serving for many
as a normative basis of U.S. global intervention.[23]

Notwithstanding its often highly ideological and polemical claims, this
notion of an American civic culture does tap a vibrant tradition of popular
activism, and it does point toward the significant role of a pre-mobilization
milieu encouraging individuals' associational engagement. The capacity of
civic culture to provide significant resources for both individuals and more
visible leaders and groups helps to explain the prominence of a civil society of political organization and mobilization. Comprised of citizens acting
in associative networks but often less visibly as individuals, this pluralist and
conflictual domain of diverse and competing beliefs is the wellspring of
more visible types of formative action. More encompassing than the priva-
tized domain of family and friendship, less total than state citizenship, this
civil society is a middle "space of un-coerced human association." In these
informal networks of "contingent and unpredictable" participation and
group formation, "individuals form a multitude of associations and freely
move" among them, producing a vibrant domain of diverse and competing
beliefs.[24] In this realm, a veritable breeding ground for formative action,
citizens in fluid and mobile groups are schooled in promoting public goals,
and they obtain those activist skills and resources which sociologists call "social capital." Here they "acquire political competence, learn to win and
lose, learn to compromise, make friends and allies, explore oppositionist
ideas," develop a sense of social good, network building, decision-making
skills, and power.[25]

The preeminent role of civil society in the United States and the broad
distribution of social capital among its citizens are often attributed to the

demands of local institution building in the thinly structured society and state of colonial and early republican society. The theory of civic culture posits these early absences of settled elites and of the institutional structures of a strong state as the source of America's tradition of local mobilization, its ethic of voluntarism, and ultimately its "democratic civil society."[26] And yet, self-serving explanations aside, what explains the historical vitality of this civil society? Can we account for the development of something so distinctive solely with reference to institutional factors that were missing at the start? The lack of such vibrancy in other newly formed societies suggests that there was nothing inevitable about the development of American civic culture, that this unique repository of social capital did not simply emerge from the absence of traditional constraints.

The civic culture/civil society argument fails to account for its own emergence. It offers a version of American exceptionalism that is, on reflection, curiously ahistorical and noncomparative. The point of these arguments seems less to explain this culture than to celebrate it. What Americans created in fact was a complex new culture of popular activism that could sustain a variety of outcomes: pluralist openness, routinized institutional participation, even democratic intolerance. Tocqueville, above all others, knew that America's civic vitality did not preclude new forms of authority and compliance. He noted precious "little independence of mind" in the United States and alerted Americans to the slowly emerging—"invisible and subtle"—tyranny of the majority. His admission that he "cannot name" this emerging popular subordination nor identify its origins only emphasizes the abiding obscurity of the sources of formative action in America.[27]

Agency and Religion

Tocqueville's insight was that the scope of formative action in the United States encompassed not only oppositional mobilization but also collective participation in shaping and sustaining its unprecedented popular institutions. To neglect this central impetus to the constitution of institutions and collective forms of authority by emphasizing either individual freedom or protest movements leaves without explanation the steady, unremitting creation of a cohesive popular society in the nineteenth century and a vastly more organized and rationalized world power in the century thereafter. Such a broad application of formative action, Rhys Williams has argued, "must come from somewhere."[28] The historical frame for a political culture of citizen activism can be traced, I believe, through the concept of agency.

Contemporary theorists acknowledge the centrality of agency in Anglo-American political thought by defining the liberal moral subject as an agent. In this usage, dating from eighteenth-century English moral philosophy, agency reinforces the liberal bias that formative action is universal. The citizen in liberal society is a "*self-determining moral agent*" and is thus presumed to have not only "*autonomous*" choice over ethical decisions but also a natural capacity for realizing ethical decisions in action: "To act is therefore to determine, and the Agent is the determiner."[29] In rational choice theory, republican theory, communitarian theory, democratic theory, and contemporary moral philosophy, agency confirms formative action as a power intrinsic to individuals and foundational of liberal citizenship.[30]

Closer examination of Anglo-American traditions, however, reveals another well-developed understanding of agency quite distinct from individual autonomy. Agency at its origin, that is, well before it expanded to fuse with liberal ideology, was by no means either universal in its application or synonymous with the freedom and power to define and actualize one's own ends. It instead defined a limited and limiting human relation to authority, specified in the *Oxford English Dictionary* as "one who acts for another, a deputy . . . representative, or emissary" authorized by the "instigator" to "work . . . as a means" to their end as an "instrumentality." In this usage, agency describes an institutional role. It presumes specific qualifications and constraints for the performance of a set task. It derives from a commitment to undertake formative action in furtherance of goals taken from some authority distinct from oneself.

The notion of a "free agent" is a modern conflation with roots in ahistorical liberal theorizing. This conflation erases from memory the origin and meaning of agency as it informed the historical experience of American activism. More specifically, the abstract conflation of "free agent" severs liberalism from its roots in the Anglo-American religious tradition, which originated the culture of popular activism by conceiving the citizen as an agent at once possessing new powers of formative action while constrained by new theological and collective limits. This connection in American culture between formative action and religion is deep and enduring: religion today is "far and away the strongest resource available" to "voluntary actors," for "its own projects but [also] for many other kinds of voluntary efforts." At the same time, students of social movements in American history routinely note, but seldom explore, their strong connection with faith-based organizations.[31]

Historically, the link is inescapable. Stanford Lyman claims that "In virtually all of their manifestations in the United States, social movements have proclaimed a salvational message." Rhys Williams asks "why so many social change movements in American political history have been based in religious communities or have used religious symbols and rhetoric." Perry Miller identified the "dominant theme in America from 1800 to 1860" as the "invincible persistence" of "Revival," a "central mode of this culture's search for national identity." The fears expressed by Madison, Washington, and Jefferson of popular formative action all revolved around the "zeal for different opinions concerning religion" which might "shake the foundation" of "popular government" in fixed "religious obligation."[32]

To understand how the concept of agency gave rise to a popular culture of formative action, we must look to its origins in the "struggle for religious freedom" in England, consider how that struggle established a new concept of the individual's relation to divine and worldly authority, and follow the dissemination of this concept in England and the new world. Within this culture we find the makings of new forms of "expressive individualism" rooted in "personal meaning," forms that at once elevated collective responsibilities and constraints. It gave rise to an unprecedented ethos of institutional "voluntaryness" and participation founded upon "individual choice" and "consent" over the shaping of "policies" and managing of "affairs."[33] Introducing a new concept of formative action to the West, religious agency resulted in new models of both the individual and the nature of institutions and produced the first predominantly agency-driven nation, the United States.

Dissenting Protestantism and Formative Action: Origins

The agency roots of American political culture lie in the ferment attending English modernization in the century after 1550. As broad sections of the English middle estates played an ever-increasing role in the dramatic economic expansion of this period, they began asserting demands on traditional institutions commensurate with their ascending worldly importance. No longer content with political and religious subordination, they pursued release from caste hierarchies and institutional deference. Led by local ministers and religious activists dissenting from the Anglican establishment, aroused citizens throughout the nation pressed unprecedented claims on the organization and practice of religion and then on political, social, and economic arrangements as well.

Behind their specific institutional demands, these rising groups claimed the right to a more active and responsible role in the divine and secular worlds. Noting their contribution to England's ascendancy, they insisted that God had provided them with new and powerful capacities of personal judgment and effective action. Established institutions required restructuring to provide room for their participation in realizing the overarching ends of their God and contracted community. Crucially, exercise of this power by individual believers and citizens was not to freely define and realize wholly personal ends, but rather to fulfill as voluntary agents the goals theologically mandated and affirmed by the community of believers. Even as the responsibilities of formative action were for the first time willingly embraced and exercised throughout the community, the agent's performance was rigorously circumscribed by clear bonds and boundaries determining its role and duty.

The key doctrinal shift that was to mark dissenting English Protestantism and set in motion the ultimate transformation of Anglo-American civilization was the liberty of conscience. The advent of the believer's independent access to the divine presence with its firm truth and stiff requirements for action reconstituted the individual's relation to worldly activity and institutions alike. Because the human order was now the expression in time of believers' actualizations of transcendent goals, each Protestant dissenter was duty-bound as a "coworker" with God to act continually in furtherance of these goals. As a result, existing political and religious hierarchies, constituted on the basis of differential access to God, could no longer be sustained. Given the equal capacity of members to engage divinity, institutions were slowly evolving into voluntary and consensual associations whose legitimacy rested not with their leaders but with their constituents. Moreover, as evident in the increasing political fragmentation and religious sectarianism of ideas and institutions during this period, worldly organizations could no longer be accorded any permanent legitimacy. They were but so many contingencies, open to dismantling and reformation on the basis of new perceptions of God's will. Developing within this new culture therefore was a self-limiting public mandate: when institutions, inevitably fallible, failed to adequately fulfill theological prescriptions, believers had not only the right but the obligation to withdraw their consent and build anew.

Propelled by this new precept, churches and doctrines proliferated and claims of political entitlement expanded exponentially. Although agency powers did not specifically include the individual determination of ends (that being the prerogative of divine or collective authority), in practice the growing differentiation of beliefs among competing groups undercut the possibility of a common doctrine. Faced with this diversity, agents were increasingly thrust back on their own discretion regarding the choice of fellowships, means, and even ends. Even more dangerously, the continuing imperative to realize one's beliefs regarding the divine will as one understood it produced a *culture of formative action* which proceeded to generate continuous pressures for mobilization. The only way to accommodate this spreading dynamic of activism, absent elites with claims of transcendent priority, was institutional liberalization to accommodate multiple claims of truth, and universal exercise of the prerogatives of agency. The implications of this shift, only dimly perceived by the insurgents who challenged traditional society during the English Revolution, were to be played out most fully in America.

Dissenting Protestantism and Formative Action: The U.S. Case

This transformed and newly empowered conception of agency, first engaging radical dissenting Protestant leaders and in turn mobilizing a popular religious culture, catalyzed American national development. More than a doctrine, these were deeply experienced transformational imperatives that reshaped individuals in every aspect of their lives. Given that America began as a diverse set of imagined social projects that only slowly developed a political consensus and specific institutions to operationalize the goals of that consensus, these early efforts to realize the agency imperative infused all the sectors of the emerging nation, including the seemingly least "political." This is not to say that agency ideals gained unimpeded and uncontested ascendancy. A complete record would reveal continuing internal divisions and tensions as well as alternative and competing discourses. Nonetheless, the historic development and implementation of agency ideals played the central role in constituting America's civic culture.

Concentrating on the agency dimensions of this larger experience reveals how formative action in the new world involved from the outset not only opposition to established colonial society but also construction of institutions in the vast spaces beyond the settled order. Dissenting agency ideals were nurtured from the earliest colonial period in demanding religious insurgencies that challenged both Anglican and the established domestic denominations. Innovative processes of character replication, doctrinal dissemination, and institutional formation were first evolved and applied in the creation of voluntary religious fellowships and denominational organizations. In time, this culture of popular mobilization, driven by agency claims of a broad access to power and legitimacy, generated new structural practices. Institutional creation and re-creation through associational voluntarism by nonelite actors kept all authority contingent and resulted in the novel participatory institutions of modern society: market structures; communities of consensual norms and conforming membership; open and representative political processes; community education; and the post-traditional family.

While the immigrants to the colonies were primarily dissenters, the leadership of the early colonies hoped to reinstate modified forms of European corporate organization. Their efforts were defeated, however, by the refusal of many exiles, including radical sectarian dissenters such as Anne Hutchinson and Roger Williams, to submit to lifelong elite governance, strict property and social constraints, and caste distinctions. Among these Baptists, Anabaptists, Quakers, Gortonians, Fifth Monarchists, and other radical millennarians, doctrines of the personal indwelling of Christ, the precedence of "personal faith," and freedom from the illegitimacy of "Monarchie" and religious "Hierarchie" overwhelmed the indigenous religious leadership which had itself long opposed the clerical establishment in England with claims to universal religious agency.[34]

The recurring breakdown of local colonial authority amid proliferating religious, political, and economic differences sharpened the "centrifugal movement" toward religious separatism, sectarianism, and new settlements. Individuals, while seeking to live as members of communities, were driven to choose allegiances according to their own conscience and to voluntarily organize their own fellowships. The continual necessity of reestablishing one's institutions by formative action in turn reinforced that religious dissent which placed greater weight on personal faith and responsibility, accelerating the appeal of extreme forms of personal agency. Growing in confidence, colonists asserted the right of lay designation of pastors, making and enforcing church discipline, calling preachers, and, above all, defining conversion. As religious dissident Isaac Backus argued, given the "equal right" in "Christ's kingdom" for each "to judge for himself" on matters of conviction, the faith the "common man" was gaining to "trust his experience against the traditions, learning, and laws of his 'betters'" was producing the radical Protestant "priesthood of all believers." Indeed, the continual formation and reformation of congregations "all over the colonies" by "rich and poor, men and women, the schooled and the unschooled" was becoming the nation's "school of democracy."[35]

With local religious and democratic radicalism continually developing among obscure people "out of sight" and groups in "out-of-the-way corners" from Vermont to North Carolina, a culture of formative action began to consolidate its hold.[36] Despite the greater visibility of democratic insurgencies in their challenge to Puritan theocracy, to high church and elite social control over late colonial life, and then to the revolutionary leadership, the thrust of citizen activism in America was not primarily an adversarial one. In fact, the emerging convictions and practices guiding local formative action pressed for new institutional forms to replace the traditional hierarchical, pre-agency organization of colonial society. Thus, the First Great Awakening, a colonies-wide religious revival begun in the 1730s in an effort to return individuals to traditional piety, quickly ignited an outpouring of radical religious agency. Barnstorming religious itinerants "not confined" to but including "Men, Women, Children, Servants, & Negros" who "are now become . . . Exhorters" spread through the colonies to demand personal faith—"*their Right of private Judgment*"—and to incite massive attacks on religious establishment, instigating "convulsions into which the whole Country is thrown."[37]

This radicalized Awakening, creating a religious marketplace of countless sects with their "*Right of judging every one for himself in Matters of Religion,*"[38] permanently dashed any hope for religious consensus, and with it any hope for a political order that refused to acknowledge universal rights of individual judgment and formative action. Beginning in the 1740s, demands of ordinary dissenters for liberty of individual conscience and associational autonomy fueled ever increasing resistance to all ecclesiastical, political, and social establishment. This prepared colonial citizens to challenge both the tightening controls of the beleaguered British administration and the revolutionary elite's agenda of political monopoly. The "deep-lying connection between popular evangelicalism and patriot republicanism" has even led scholars recently to redefine the popular role in the Revolution. The participation of ordinary citizens, previously regarded as uniformly driven by the cause of the leaders, is now recognized as equally engaged in its own internal revolution for local religious autonomy and political freedom from elite control.[39] The Declaration of Independence itself, framed in liberal iconography as the immaculate conception of a secular nation from the state of nature, in fact arose from and embodied the values of Protestant dissent. The nation, its Founding Document declares, owes its very existence to the continuing right of all individuals and communities to engage in formative action, even to the extent of withdrawing legitimacy from existing institutions and reconstituting social order anew, and not merely as acts of political opposition but as principled acts of commitment to alternative values.

The popular revolution was propelled by "raging Republicanism," whose "evangelical fervor" spread egalitarian agency sects and demanded a "dismantling" of the remaining hierarchical "system that legitimated forms of deference." Anti-federalist agitation fought elite dominance at state constitutional conventions by advocating toleration and disestablishment, equal districting and broader suffrage.[40] Nearly defeating the newly proposed federal Constitution, these forces partially triumphed in the concessions of federal and state bills of rights. It was popular activism of this sort that brought about the collapse of the Revolutionary elite's Federalist party, empowered a more populist Jeffersonian majority, and gave rise to the novel post-traditional institutions of the agency republic in the nineteenth century.

The early national period from the Revolution to the Civil War was long misunderstood as the age of "independent American farmers" needing little government or community. With the modern revival of interest in the role of the frontier in American history, the "high degree of participation" and "political awareness" in the establishment of new communities has been more broadly recognized. But, as one scholar has put it, such "Grassroots social experience did not grow on western trees." The skilled application of "voluntary group action" to community building on the frontier presupposed a "society already accustomed to organizational activities," one nurtured in the "voluntary associations" of "popular denominations" which took responsibility in each location for establishing "broad social and quasi-judicial functions" on behalf of the community's "general welfare."[41]

Church building in new communities was only one manifestation of the religious activism that propelled a democratic culture of formative action in America. Long "fail[ing] to appreciate the influence of popular religion" or misreading it "as a conservative force," interpreters have neglected how, in this "unique spiritual hothouse," this society "Awash in a Sea of Faith" expressed new cultural and institutional claims. No mere "frontier phenomenon" but reaching far "backward to the East," the "unschooled and unsophisticated" demanded the authority to "*to think, but also to act for ourselves; to see with our own eyes.*" Individuals would now "*take all our measures directly and immediately from the Divine Standard.*" For "*as no man can be* judged *for his brother, so no man can* judge *for his brother,*" and as personal "*truth must sit in judgment upon all human organization,*" so the right to contest civil and religious elites at every turn and to shape the religious practices and institutions to community standards necessarily followed.[42]

Driven by a belief in the personal revelation of "things of a divine nature," commoners quickly brought an end to their deferential and outsider status: "Within a few years of Jefferson's election of 1800, it became anachronistic to speak of dissent in America—as if there were still a commonly recognized center against which new or emerging groups defined themselves." With hierarchies dissolved and "normative and institutional constraints . . . fallen apart," the door was now open to the widespread pursuit of local empowerment. There was "little to restrain a variety of new groups" claiming their own religious *and* secular legitimacy.[43]

In this new society, the now-legitimate capacity—indeed the theologically prescribed duty—to form and reform institutions became a primary cultural resource of both state building and social opposition. It infused the practices of nineteenth-century institutions themselves. Not only in religious and political institutions but also in the emerging voluntary market economy, participants drew on the "direction and discipline" of revivals and new religious practices to bolster individual responsibility and self-reliance. Beside these more evident dramatic shifts in public institutions is the increasingly acknowledged transformation of the once private sphere. The prominence of women and youth in the Second Great Awakening attested to their determination to reshape local patriarchy and institutional paternalism. In the church and family, awakened women "threatened to sunder the sexual hierarchy," demanding greater responsibility in religious practice and in directing the socialization of the young. Facing a large-scale, mobile, and urbanizing economy, communities hoping to prepare the young for new occupations began, with strong participation from women, a great public school movement that would reach into every locality. Youth for their part, now treated from infancy as "*moral agents* [who] possess *moral characters,*" expressed their new power by demanding the training and skills that would enable them to migrate toward centers of the new individualistic and competitive society.[44]

The religious origins of that "peculiar variety of political and social action" during the period we call Reform are selectively part of the nation's historical memory. In this era of popularly mobilized formative action featuring "great activity of thought and experimenting," this "spirit of protest" was, Emerson noted, the work of "the religious party." Generating myriad "projects for the salvation of the world" and instigating a "keener scrutiny of" and protest against "institutions and domestic life than any we have known," this activity was visible everywhere: in "temperance and nonresistance societies; in movements of abolitionists and of socialists; and in . . . very significant assemblies called Sabbath and Bible Convention" organized to "call in question the authority of the Sabbath, of the priesthood, and of the Church." "Even the insect world," Emerson quipped, far "too long neglected," was to be defended by a "society for the protection of ground-worms, slugs, and mosquitos." The theological core of this activity was an ever more sacralized personal agency, for whenever a "church censured and threatened to excommunicate one of its members" for acts of conscience, the "threatened individual immediately excommunicated the church, in a public and formal process."[45]

The ferocious grassroots activity of the many branches of abolitionism and women's rights movement strongly attests to the widespread conviction that individual citizens had a right to shape the common good. Ordinary women and Blacks joined men and often led the voluntary activities of publication and publicity, lecturing and preaching, petitioning and fundraising, creating organizations and recruiting members, and shaping protest agendas. Religious belief drove the organizers of the Underground Railroad to assist fugitive slaves, and the writing of that fire bell in the night, *Uncle Tom's Cabin*. Elizabeth Cady Stanton, drafter of the historic Seneca Falls Declaration, included the resolution propounding every woman's "sacred right to the elective franchise." Increasingly clear is the religious nature of the local "protest and resistance" that shaped antebellum workers' movements.[46]

One further outgrowth of the uniquely contingent foundations of American institutional legitimacy is the radical antebellum doctrine of civil disobedience, which along with "voluntary association" is "practically unknown anywhere else." With its assumption of universal agency powers and its qualified defense of extralegal action, civil disobedience is, according to Hannah Arendt, actually "compatible with the *spirit* of American laws." By limiting the legitimacy of a social contract over time through society's right of withdrawing consent, the Declaration implied limits to all government claims of moral validity. Emerson reasoned, "Every actual state" is corrupt and fallible. His resulting injunction that "Good men must not obey the laws too well" suggested to his student Thoreau the "obligation" imposed by "conscience" to hold "majority rule" accountable and to "do at any time what I think right." When the "higher law" directing one's agency requires one to "deny the authority of the State," as by exercising more than a "cheap vote" against the "*slave's* government," that dictate, that duty, must take precedence over the Constitution.[47]

Even preceding these philosophical elaborations, civil disobedience had emerged as a movement of radical pacifism and conscientious objection in both war and peace. Originating in colonial dissenting sects, it spread in the early Republic as diverse religious groups objected to participation in the War of 1812 and obstructed enforcement of slavery laws which were "clearly null and void in the court of conscience." Civil disobedience, emerging from a culture "dominated by religious concerns," lent further weight to the right to formative action within a liberal polity. As Michael Walzer has argued, in this tradition the "duty to disobey . . . arises when obligations incurred in some small group come into conflict with obligations incurred in a larger, more inclusive group, generally the state." In the case of such a duty, it is the "obedience to the state" itself that "must be justified." This enduring right to measure the actions of government by transcendent standards and to act on that judgment made "civil disobedience" in Arendt's words a "form of voluntary association" in "tune with the oldest traditions of the society."[48] The popular agitation that precipitated the Civil War and the great human rights movements thereafter are thus deeply embedded in the radical American culture of formative action.

The Crisis of Formative Action in Organizational Society

The continuing resonance of Frederick Jackson Turner's celebrated 1893 paper on the closing of the American frontier is a monument to the distinctive role of formative action in American history. Turner identified the vibrant culture of popular action as the core of its uniquely democratic, independent, and individualistic way of life, and the open world of the frontier as the ever-pressing catalyst "calling out new institutions and activities." His fear was that with its passing before an ever more "complex and representative industrial organization" the characteristic "fluidity of American life" would likewise recede. Absent this "wider field" for "continually beginning over again" through institutional creation, action would be forced henceforth into a merely oppositional stance against the restraints of "custom" and "older social conditions."[49]

As Turner predicted, the belief ordinary citizens once possessed that they could through their own engaged action significantly remake—or even influence—their dominant institutions has receded over time. From the institutional perspective, the rise and consolidation of an organizational society, complete with new justifications for hierarchy, eliminated the decentralized conditions that sustained agency convictions and practices. Narrowing the available channels for local institutional participation and self-reliant citizenship over the course of the twentieth century resulted in the declining efficacy and visibility of local activism. Citizen action, fueled by organizational imperatives and the popular drive for social integration, was in turn primarily redirected into system-sustaining behavior. In this view, the remaining expressions of critical activism, given the enhanced institutional mechanisms for incorporating the disaffected, were either directed toward obtaining institutional leverage or shunted to the margins.

Many developments of the last century support this analysis. Institutional growth led mainstream liberalism to adapt its agency foundations to organizational society. While preserving the Protestant commitment to individual agency, progressive thinkers like John Dewey recast responsible action as an expression of initiative within the channels of emerging collective structures. In this new pragmatic understanding, agency was any "purposive action people might employ to affect their fate," and as such was fully accessible within institutional settings. This institutionalization of the agent as an organizational actor was a realistic reflection of the new constraints being imposed on the rising industrial and bureaucratic middle class. It preserved popular belief that access to formative action remained undiminished in the new age, but only by framing agency functionally as institutional integration without any role in stipulating collective ends. In effect, this formulation undercut the historical role of agency in institutional and value formation. The implicit assumption was that American society had largely fulfilled its promise of full citizenship for all, and individual action could now safely be reduced to operationalizing existing collective priorities. Freedom was now compatible with voluntary institutional commitment; democracy with procedures for producing popular agreement on strategies; equality with a broadly disseminated opportunity for institutional success; and personal identity with the choice of productive roles within the organization.[50]

This narrowing of the channels for legitimate action squeezed the major late nineteenth- and twentieth-century movements for social change into a decidedly integrative stance. Dissenting visions of a radically more democratic and egalitarian society evident in the early phases of the labor, women's, and minority movements were, in the end, cast aside as unwarranted sectarian appeals for social restructuring and replaced by large-scale popular campaigns to expand citizenship within liberal society. This dynamic of organizational inclusion had become so prevalent by the 1950s, the high point of a purely functional agency, that social critics like Fromm, Riesman, and Whyte began to fear the decline of formative action within the settled procedures of a routinized, bureaucratic mass society. Such fears of the decline of civic and associational life persist in our own time in the influential work of Robert Putnam, Robert Bellah, Theda Skocpol, and others.

Given the continued vitality of local activism in our times, however, a more populist understanding of contemporary action and its formative effects remains a plausible alternative. The emphasis on the role of action within centralized and organized interest groups only focuses on the most visible dimension of agency. Increasing detachment from large institutions and disaffection with the need to submit value and lifestyle choices to an organizational society dominated by elite decision-making has shifted the focus of less visible activism from inclusion and system leverage. Pressures for institutionalization are thus being offset today by a continuously vibrant and widespread engagement in popular activism that is often unpredictable in its origins, decentralized in its expression, surprising in its agendas, and unusually disruptive in its cultural and social impact. The resulting turn by both progressives and conservatives toward experimental forms of mobilization, while not yet of system changing proportions, combines resistance to core liberal values and arrangements with bold innovation in the search for institutional alternatives.

This contemporary pattern of formative action was first manifested in the challenge to the meritocratic, bureaucratic, work-oriented organizational society in the 1960s. At that time, new social movements arose concerned less with institutional power and wealth creation than with diverse ethical, cultural, and lifestyle options. In an educated, prosperous, service-oriented society, many citizens believed that popular action should be freed from the increasing constraints on personally shaping ends and means, the circularity of endless work and consumption, and the embedded barriers to democratic community life. The early movements for institutional reform—the civil rights, student, and Vietnam protests—rapidly expanded this critique as they faced the society's lack of will to fulfill its now realizable "promises" to the people and thereby "complete its own agenda." Awakening the deeper cultural strains of individual conscience and institutional resistance, this pressure produced a widespread "questioning of authority," a "decline in public confidence and trust in political leaders and institutions," and ultimately delegitimation of the "moral authority" of the "major American social institutions: government, law, business, religion, marriage . . . the family" and the schools. This withdrawal of legitimacy in turn weakened the "obligation to obey."[51]

This burgeoning crisis, it was later recognized, reflected a long evolving cultural shift transforming "the way Americans relate to social institutions." The major factor was the emergence of an affluent, better-educated citizenry, with an increased knowledge of and scrutiny over society's operations. With their "heightened sense of democratic entitlement" and "commitment to participatory norms," they had higher expectations of effective formative action. Individuals now broadly asserted the right to contravene the "established political or legal frame" by undertaking principled action on behalf of more fundamental groups and ideals.[52] New progressive grassroots social movements, really loose associations of individuals, pursued qualitative and alternative "ideas and actions that were previously unthinkable," not as organizational goals but as anti-authoritarian values by which to live. What had happened? The deeply embedded agency belief in individual formative action to shape and realize common ends had become the "defining character" of popular "moral philosophy." Although unsettling in its institutional implications, this "new voluntarism" was nurtured by spiritual sources whose roots "lie deep in the heritage of religious institutions."[53]

What appeared as withdrawal was in fact a new form of engagement surging into arenas where its impact could more effectively call existing practices to account and alter institutional structures. The "forms, values, and arrangements of marriage" including who marries and for how long were transformed more in the "past thirty years" than in the "previous three thousand," as were the rights of once-subordinate partners and children within the family. Youth, women, and those with an alternative sexual orientation were playing an increasingly prominent role in culture and consumption practices and establishing distinct peer and lifestyle communities on the basis of these allegiances. Education was being widely reshaped by local initiatives to create charter schools, community schools, small and alternative schools, and home-schooling networks. Grassroots "neighborhood-based programs" and organizations for the "revitalization of democratic community" pushed for local public and commercial services, physical and cultural amenities, and alternative institutions and cooperatives.[54] Widespread movements coalesced to promote lifestyle issues like self-help, health, ecological, anticonsumer, antimaterialist, new age healing, and expanded consciousness initiatives.

This burgeoning spiritual "passion for asserting expressive individualism" has engendered a "structural transformation" of American religious institutions, with the "individual seeker and chooser" ever more "in control." Mainstream liberal denominations have been reshaping themselves by expanding the ministry; reconfiguring membership to include racial, ethnic, and lifestyle minorities and women; reconsidering the role of lay initiatives and activities; and advancing a social ministry concerned with community and neighborhood issues, with global justice work, and with a range of services for the needy.[55] New "seeker churches" are sprouting with an emphasis on personalized religion and the "quests of women, of minorities, of varying lifestyle constituencies, and the wisdom, the languages, and the experiences they bring with them." Vast constituencies who "move freely in and out, across religious boundaries" combine "elements from various traditions to create their own personal meaning systems." They are creating a seemingly inexhaustible proliferation of alternative, experimental, and multilayered religious and spiritual sects, theologies, and practices within small groups amounting to "new forms of community."[56]

This explosion of local formative action often surfaces in more visible progressive political activism. Rather than focusing on the "standard political process and the conventional methods of political pressure," much of this activism pursues new forms of "community building" and "radically egalitarian values" or forms of "moral witness" and "parabolic deeds" that "help bring about personal and social transformation" even as they challenge existing policies.[57] The recent defeat of mass mobilizations for Al Gore and especially John Kerry, together with the serious questions raised about systemic electoral, judicial, and political integrity, will likely sharpen the shift to non-system-maintaining forms of action.

Despite its different objectives, the increasingly dominant conservative movement also reflects these larger cultural shifts in popular activism. Disaffection over the liberalization of national policy, with its social experimentation and the seemingly boundless claim of cultural inclusiveness, has mobilized traditionalists. Ironically, traditional beliefs about strong institutional authority and controls now generate high levels of individual and grassroots activist commitment on the right to call their institutions to account. While professing a dedication to collective moral and religious certainty, these "seeming enemies of moral freedom" in fact now ground the "traditional way of life" in the radical agency "of a person's own decision" about values and institutional affiliations. Moreover, this "need of an individual to choose" by "following one's conscience" has as its goal the spiritual "self-improvement and self-fulfillment" of the individual.[58]

The institutional forms emerging from the conservative movement reflect this personal focus, even among the "most religiously orthodox and committed, the most alienated from secular American institutions and movements, and the most dedicated to seeing Christian morality and values influence American culture." While greater publicity and notoriety have accrued to mass political organizations, those citizens "most likely to be influenced by conservative Christian political groups" reveal upon examination an "individualistic, relationalist, and voluntarist mentality" quite inconsistent with a "mass-mobilized" approach. They may believe that "Christians should be involved in politics" by "taking a public stand" and using evangelism to "convert the nation," but they also mistrust large-scale activism, regarding it as "insignificant" in spiritual matters and unlikely to change people. This promotes a resolute localism: "one-on-one evangelism" and personal "witness" using the "free agency" that "God has given us" and appealing to the same "individual responsibility" of others "before God." The emphasis is on reform within such accessible and transformable settings as personal relationships, the family, schools, and the local community.[59]

Drawing on their "decentralized and voluntaristic organizational heritage" to reinvigorate conservative Christianity, conservative agents are establishing a "fragmented field of church groups and para-church organizations" rooted in individual "decentralized, voluntary associations." This "new organizational mode" dissolving hierarchies and centralized denominations into independent local congregations with strong lay initiative is producing new versions of the early "priesthood of all believers." This has led one scholar to regard them as "cultural innovators" rather than "backward-looking."[60] Even the more visible forms of conservative political mobilization have for the most part arisen in a "grassroots movement of the most genuine kind," as a "populist revolt" of "ordinary people" who were "driven into politics" by their fears for the country.[61] In these networks, centralized organization is undercut by incessant "internal controversy" and "multi-vocality" as citizens "agitate, educate, and organize with a conviction that anyone who believes in democracy has to admire." The result is a "Great Backlash," a crazy-quilt "movement culture" composed of myriad expressions of protest driven by a rebellious rage that "mounts and mounts" with hopes of reversing "national decline, epic lawlessness, and betrayal."[62] And yet, at the same time, precisely because large systemic solutions are often neglected by local activists, their passionate convictions about change and fears about the direction of society are easily mobilized and channeled by conservative elites in support of their own corporate and global agendas.

This is thus a fateful time in America's political development. On the formal institutional level, the system appears ever more consolidated in elite control and organizational regularity. The moderate liberals centered in the Democratic Party, facing increasing demands for inclusion from their historic constituencies and fearing terrible political fallout from any mention of structural reform, have turned sharply away from any connection with progressive grassroots or movement politics. Conservatives, sensing this weakening affiliation to party politics among progressives and the rightward assimilative drift of those gaining inclusion, have seized the initiative. Beginning with the Reagan insurgency, Republican Party and movement leaders have organized to capture political power for elite interests. Despite their reassuring rhetoric of populism and federalism, they have relentlessly pursued the consolidation of political and economic power in a corporate sector set loose from popular and administrative controls. The extraordinary success they have achieved in exploiting their own grassroots constituencies for the project of elite institutional dominance and for policies that further elite interests suggests the co-optation of conservative populism.

This story if complete would indicate a precipitous decline in the effectiveness of popular agency with the maturing of organizational society, providing as solace only the prospect of systemic stability. However, the centralization and growing elitism of both parties obscures the dissociation of mainstream political actors from popular priorities, producing constituencies increasingly unallied to the values of a centralized administrative liberal state. Popular polarization regarding national ends and a declining commitment to systemic procedures and leaders points to an underlying instability as yet unaddressed. Whether popular agency has lost its formative influence thus remains to be seen.

On the progressive side, the waning of expressive outlets for citizen empowerment and a personally directed life within an organizational framework has led not to passivity but to a restless search for alternatives. On the conservative side, the elite determination to inflame and mobilize popular reaction to secular society on behalf of a religious nation by promoting extreme views in every area of cultural policy involves the very real danger

that this "ferocious language" will be "turned on them." The inability to fulfill constituent demands for theocracy without fracturing the nation, together with the declining economic prospects of ordinary people, makes
for an increasingly volatile mix.[63]

Mainstream social theorists and public policy strategists have recognized
the dangerous juxtaposition of a mass society of passive, managed, atomized individuals on the one hand, and proliferating activism by polarized
groups exacerbating "social conflict" with "demands on state institutions
that are undesirable and unsustainable" on the other. Their response is to
call insistently for reforms to bolster our "civil society." These proposals to
strengthen civic engagement by revitalizing civil associations, civic education, and deliberative democracy would, it is argued, restore a culture of
formative action to "foster norms of reciprocity, citizenship, and social trust
and provide networks" that would facilitate efforts to "pursue shared goals
for the common good."[64] Yet the wish to garner the benefits of citizen activism without addressing the troubling "structural inequalities" that fuel
popular discontent or the ever-greater dominance of the process by
"middle- and upper-class citizens"[65] with the social capital available for civic
engagement is unlikely to be fulfilled. Such initiatives may in fact either reinforce the growing elitism of the present order or risk releasing more popular anger at organizational control.

The difficulties political experts are encountering in addressing the
strains in the American polity make the study of formative action more important than ever. The key question for our system of government is
whether this agency culture will continue, as it has in the past, to stir both
system-challenging and system-supporting engagements. Are we destined
to become passive members of an increasingly coordinated society producing elite actors and conformist citizens who awaken, as Tocqueville feared,
only to vote? Will fraying commitments to norms of the liberal project instead attract us to the fragmenting and system-challenging activism feared
by the designers of the Constitution? Or will these very dangers instead inspire Americans to restore the spaces for popular mobilization that shaped
this modern nation? As students of formative action with a window into the
center of America's distinctive agency culture, we have a privileged perspective from which to assess these alternate paths to the future.

Part II
Structure and Opportunity

Chapter 5

A Calculated Enchantment of Passion: Bryan and the "Cross of Gold" in the 1896 Democratic National Convention

Richard Bensel

On the third day of the 1896 Democratic National Convention, William Jennings Bryan of Nebraska delivered the concluding speech in favor of the majority report of the Committee on Resolutions. When he finished,

As if by magic touch of a wand delegation after delegation rose in solid phalanx and gave vent to the most enthusiastic demonstration in honor of the Nebraska orator. Everybody stood up, even the Eastern men, who at first were disposed to remain in their seats. Westerners shouted, waved handkerchiefs, hats, flags, canes, umbrellas and anything else conspicuous and portable. Deafening cheers rent the air and articles of every description were thrown high above the surging sea of humanity. The staffs bearing the names of the States were held aloft with flags and other things on top and waved to and fro. When that pastime became too tame, led by Mr. Galwood, of Texas, nearly all the silver States and Territories, and some gold States joined in a procession, bearing the State poles, and marched in triumph around the floor. Some of the Eastern States kept their sign staffs in their places and confined their expressions to standing up and giving a mild cheer as individuals. This furor continued for a quarter of an hour; and no effort was made by the chairman or sergeant-at-arms to check its tempestuous progress. Away to the west and north and south of the platform in the multitude of spectators the demonstration of the delegates was repeated. Hundreds of umbrellas were opened by the apparently crazed people. Harmless missiles of paper and other things were hurled through the air on the delegates' heads. The remarkable feature of this wild outburst was that its spontaneity was apparent, and it was so much a personal tribute to Mr. Bryan that Eastern delegates who differed with him caught the infection and joined in moderately. Nebraska's delegation was the cynosure of observation and [the] smooth-faced silver champion who had electrified the Convention sat unmoved in his seat at the edge of the aisle opposite his opponent from New York—Senator Hill.[1]

Bryan's oratorical defense of the platform became known as the "Cross of Gold" speech and propelled him into serious contention for the presidential nomination. When the convention opened in Chicago on July 7, Bryan was not ranked among the leading candidates for the nomination. In fact, most observers did not consider him anything more than the favorite son of his home state's silver delegation. When he spoke to the convention, Bryan was defending the free coinage of silver as a plank in the national platform. His speech had little or no effect on adoption of the plank because the votes for and against silver had been strongly committed even before the convention came together.[2] Nonetheless, Bryan's oratory, widely viewed as one of the most stirring and effective political addresses in American history, figuratively and almost literally brought down the house. The next day he was awarded the presidential nomination on the fifth roll call.

The purpose of this study is to explain how structure and agency came together to produce the uncontrollably passionate demonstration which transfixed the delegates following Bryan's speech. The structure can be broken down into two parts: the parliamentary rituals that created the procedural foundation for the convention proceedings and the physical setting that determined how delegates and spectators could monitor each other's reactions to those proceedings. The structure of the proceedings defined the limits and opportunities of his agency, as it did for all of the participants. And the most skilled of all those agents was Bryan, who managed to exploit an opportunity that he, almost alone of all the professional politicians in the convention hall, recognized existed. I begin by explaining how the ritual structure of the convention shaped the situation in which Bryan gave his speech. I subsequently examine the ritualized proceedings up to and including Bryan's speech. I then discuss how the physical structure of the convention hall focused attention on the podium and the galleries, compelling the delegates to take their cues from Bryan and spectators. With the ritual and physical structure set up, I turn to an exploration of Bryan's agency, including how he maneuvered himself into the situation within which he delivered his speech. In the actual event, Bryan's oratorical talent was at least matched, if not exceeded, by the creative imagination with which he anticipated the course of the proceedings.

The Structure of National Party Conventions

National party conventions are among the most ritualized settings in American politics, so much so that modern conventions, with their perfunctory addresses and foregone conclusions, are extremely monotonous. Convention rituals include the order in which presiding officers are appointed, contests between rival delegations are resolved, the platform is adopted, and nominees are selected. This ritual sequence produces collective expectations as to how the convention will proceed and, as such, frame the strategies and tactics of the participants. Underlying all of these settings are the "parliamentary rules" which control, often in minute detail, how delegates are recognized and what they may do.[3]

This ritual structure arises out of a clear conception of the convention in its relationship to the national party. In the nineteenth century, the national convention was a quadrennial convocation of the almost entirely autonomous state party organizations. Once a convention adjourned, the only remnant of this gathering was the national party committee, composed of one representative from each of the states and territories. This committee was empowered to set a date and choose a location for the next convention but otherwise played little more than a caretaker role for the national party. When the next convention met, the national party emerged anew as a collective assembly of the respective state delegations. This emergence in many respects mimicked the traditional myths describing the creation of government out of a "state of nature." From this perspective, the major problem was to provide just enough order for the convention to open without impairing the unfolding discovery of an unconstrained "democratic will."

At the very beginning of the convention, the presiding officer was the chairman of the outgoing national party committee. His primary responsibility was to open the proceedings and immediately move to the election of a temporary chairman (see Table 1). The outgoing national party committee nominated a candidate for temporary chairman who, in the normal order of things, would be ratified by the delegates. Since the outgoing committee, including its chairman, might not reflect the collective will of the new convention, the election of a temporary chairman was an interim arrangement through which the committee yielded control to the delegates. Since there was still a possibility that these opening moves might prejudice the proceedings (in the sense that the outgoing national party committee might be out of sympathy with a majority of the delegates), the duties of the temporary chairman were more or less restricted to completing the initial tasks associated with opening the convention: the adoption of rules of procedure for deliberations and the construction of an official roll of delegates. Adoption of rules of procedure was usually a mere formality.

The construction of a permanent roll for the convention, however, was usually more contentious because it involved resolution of contests over the right of competing delegations to represent their state or territory. Because the permanent roll named the delegates who would represent their respective states and territories, the list determined who could rightfully participate in the proceedings. For that reason, resolution of delegation contests had to precede the election of a permanent chairman of the convention, because only legitimate delegates could select the officer who presided over the regular convention proceedings. Election of a permanent chairman completed the preliminary organization of the convention and, thus, the transition from a "state of nature" to a formally organized political community.

TABLE 1. STRUCTURE OF NATIONAL PARTY CONVENTIONS

Task	Function	Originating body	Possible alternatives
Election of Temporary Chairman	Presides over proceedings until permanent chairman is elected	Nominated by majority of the outgoing national party committee	Nominations of other candidates by a minority of the outgoing national party committee
Adoption of rules of procedure	Provides parliamentary order as frame for for proceedings	Individual delegate recognized by temporary chairman	Amendments offered by other delegates
Resolution of contests over state delegations	Determination of the official delegate roll	Proposed by majority of the Committee on Credentials	Support of contesting delegations by a minority of the Committee on Credentials
Election of Permanent Chairman	Presides over proceedings for remainder of the convention	Nominated by majority of the Committee on Permanent Organization	Nominations of other candidates by a minority of the Committee on Permanent Organization
Adoption of the party platform	Declares party position on major policy issues	Proposed by majority of the Committee on Resolutions	Amendments to platform planks offered by a minority of the Committee on Resolutions
Nomination of the presidential candidate	Selects the party nominee for president	One or more candidates nominated by one or more state delegations	Individual delegates may vote for other candidates who have not been formally nominated
Nomination of the vice-presidential candidate	Selects the party nominee for vice-president	One or more candidates nominated by one or more state delegations	Individual delegates may vote for other candidates who have not been formally nominated

While each of these steps was intended to facilitate the uncovering of a democratic will (as the collective desire of the newly assembled delegates), all of them were vulnerable to abuse. For example, the outgoing national party committee could nominate someone who was out of sympathy with a majority of the delegates. This actually happened in 1896. Here, however, we are not so much interested in the possibility of abuse as in the logic underpinning the order in which these things were decided, because the ordering of these decisions became the first part of the ritual backbone shaping the expectations and strategies of the delegates.

The other part of that ritual backbone was composed of three decisions. First, the delegates were to consider and adopt a national platform on which the party would conduct a campaign. Second, the delegates were to select a presidential nominee. Finally, when both of these decisions had been made, the delegates would select a vice-presidential nominee. Here too, the order in which these decisions were made possessed a certain logic. Before a presidential candidate could be named, the party had to construct a platform defining the policy positions on which the nominee would run. Because, at least in theory and more or less usually in practice, the principles on which the party stood were more important than the charismatic qualities of the candidates, the platform influenced how candidates were evaluated as viable contenders. The important point for our purposes is that the platform was constructed first, and then a candidate was nominated, not the other way around. In addition, the vice-presidential running mate was always named last because he had to be personally compatible with the presidential candidate. Another consideration was whether or not the vice-presidential nominee would "balance" the ticket, something which could only be determined once the presidential candidate had been chosen.

The ritual backbone to the convention presented situations in which contestation could take place and, as such, structured the expectations of the delegates and the strategies of their leaders. Some of these situations actually produced competing alternatives and generated formal roll calls which tested the relative strength of the rival factions. Others, for one reason or another, gave way to consensual decisions (see Table 2). That part of the ritual backbone leading up to and including the adoption of the platform was dominated in 1896 by the overarching division between the gold and silver factions.

The opening contest between the gold and silver wings occurred at the very beginning of the convention when the outgoing head of the national party committee, William Harrity of Pennsylvania, submitted the name of Senator David B. Hill of New York as the nominee for temporary chairman. The outgoing national party committee still held a narrow majority for gold over silver and was thus out of sympathy with the almost two-thirds majority for silver among the delegates to the convention. In nominating Hill,

TABLE 2. CONTESTATION AND STRUCTURE IN THE 1896 NATIONAL DEMOCRATIC CONVENTION

Task	Gold faction alternative	Silver faction alternative	Outcome
Election of Temporary Chairman	Senator David B. Hill of New York, nominated by majority of the out-going national party committee	Senator John W. Daniel of Virginia, nominated by minority of the out-going national party committee	Daniel is elected, 556 to 349 as some silver delegates defect
Adoption of rules of procedure	No proposal	The 1892 convention rules along with those of the House of Representatives, moved by Senator Stephen M. White of California	Unanimously adopted
Resolution of contests over state delegations	Seating of gold delegates in the Michigan delegation	Seating of silver challengers to gold delegates in the Michigan delegation	Challengers seated, 558 to 368, as some silver delegates defect
Election of Permanent Chairman	No candidate	Senator Stephen M. White of California	Unanimously elected
Adoption of the party platform	Minority amendment endorsing the gold standard	Platform plank endorsing the free coinage of silver	Silver plank prevails, 626 to 303
Nomination of the presidential candidate	Governor Pattison of Pennsylvania	Several candidates, among them Richard Bland of Missouri, Bryan, Horace Boies of Iowa, and John McLean of Ohio	Bland leads on first three votes, Bryan leads on the fourth and wins nomination on the fifth
Nomination of the vice-presidential candidate	No candidate	Several candidates, among them Bland, Joseph Sibley of Pennsylvania, McLean, and Arthur Sewall of Maine	Sibley leads on first vote, Bland on second and third, McLean on fourth; Sewall is nominated on fifth

the committee chose one of the most prominent and personally popular of all the gold Democrats in the nation. In addition, they stressed the traditional nature of their role and prerogatives (that a nomination for temporary chair made by the national party committee had never been overturned in a Democratic convention) and the certainty (conceded by most silverites) that Hill would be a fair and efficient presiding officer. For their part, the silver delegates named Senator John Daniel of Virginia as their choice (which took the form of a minority report from the committee to the convention). The silver wing contended that the majority of the convention should control the organization of the proceedings. Equally important, they contended that the opening address of the temporary chairman, perhaps his most important duty, should reflect the sympathies of the convention majority. And from that perspective they wished to prevent Senator Hill from making a strong defense of the gold standard in what would be the opening speech of the convention. The silver wing knew there would be gold speeches at the convention, but they wanted them to be minority protests, not the formal declarations of an elected presiding officer.

While the election of a temporary chair was not a pure test of delegate strength for the gold and silver factions, the monetary alignment still dominated the voting. Daniel prevailed by a large majority and proceeded to deliver a fairly conventional speech in defense of the free coinage of silver. After he was finished, the convention adopted rules of procedure.

The next task was the construction of a permanent roll. This meant settling contests in which more than one delegation competed for the right to represent a state. In the end, most of these contests were abandoned, leaving only two contests to be settled. One of these was the Nebraska case in which the silver delegation was led by William Jennings Bryan. For a number of reasons, the gold delegation was on very weak footing in this contest, clearly representing but a minority of Nebraska Democrats when it had staged a separate state convention and sent a gold delegation to Chicago. Although the outgoing national party committee had originally ruled in its favor and thus allowed it to vote on the roll call electing a temporary chairman, the Nebraska gold delegation was more or less deserted by the gold faction when the permanent roll was constructed and Bryan's silver men took over their seats without a floor fight.

One of the reasons the gold faction gave way on Nebraska was that they chose to devote their energy to the Michigan case. Although only four of the twenty-eight delegates were at stake, these four held the balance of power between the silver and gold factions in the state delegation. And, thus, under the unit rule, the Michigan contest was really about control of all twenty-eight votes, not just the four which were formally contested. Another reason this contest became a focal point between the gold and silver wings was that Michigan held the key to whether or not the silver wing would hold a two-thirds majority in the convention. If Michigan's twenty-eight votes went over to silver, the gold wing could not block the nomination of a silver presidential nominee no matter what they did. By the time the Michigan contest came to the convention floor, the possibility that the gold wing might try to stonewall such a nomination probably seemed remote to most delegates, particularly since the two-thirds rule could be abrogated if necessary. Just the same, the Michigan contest became a second opportunity for the silver faction to demonstrate its mastery of the convention.

With the permanent roll now in place, the convention moved to the election of a permanent chairman. By this time, the silver delegates controlled a majority of the Committee on Permanent Organization, and that committee nominated Senator Stephen M. White of California, a prominent silver leader who had removed himself from presidential contention, for the post. The gold faction chose not to present an alternative candidate, and White was elected by acclamation.

With a permanent roll and a chairman, the convention now turned to what was both the most climactic and most foreordained part of the proceedings: the adoption of a national party platform. Almost all the state and territorial conventions had strongly endorsed either silver or gold when they adopted their own party platforms. Most of those conventions had then pledged their delegates to support that position in Chicago, leaving little room to maneuver even if those delegates had wanted to change sides. An overwhelming majority for silver in Chicago had become a certainty even before the last state conventions adjourned. All the silver men had to do was to formally count their votes.

Adoption of the silver plank, however, would irreversibly split the party and was thus fraught with tension and angst. During the weeks preceding the opening of the convention, the eastern gold men had repeatedly presented the gold case to their southern and western brethren. How could the silver wing break what had been a fruitful and durable detente between the sections? For decades, this detente had permitted congressional Democrats to stake their positions on silver while allowing the national party to nominate gold presidential candidates on platforms that evaded positions on money. The formula for national victory in the presidential race had been New York, New Jersey, and one or two other small northern states plus the South. The formula for congressional majorities had been huge, almost solid delegations from the South and New York City with a scattering of representatives and senators from the remainder of the country. The price exacted by the eastern states for their electoral votes in the presidential race was the practical (but not explicit) endorsement of the gold standard (and, invariably, the nomination of a New Yorker as the presidential candidate). Congressional Democrats simply divided along sectional lines when the monetary issue surfaced in Congress.[4]

An open and unequivocal endorsement of silver would destroy this detente with nothing but disaster looming before the eastern gold men. To them, the relative insulation of the southern wing of the party from the monetary issue, arising out of the growing utility and popularity of "white supremacy" as a Democratic campaign theme, seemed to make southern insistence on a silver declaration a rather gratuitous assault on the eastern wing. And easterners repeatedly reminded that their unflagging support for "home rule" had brought an end to Reconstruction, thus returning the Democratic party to power in the South. How cruel, the easterners lamented, that this region should turn on their protectors, destroying them in pursuit of the silver grail. The pathos of this struggle was thus deeply embedded in the history of the party, in the manifold alliances and understandings of the past, in the careers and futures of the party's most prominent leaders, and in the interpersonal relations of men who had known each other for many years. When they passed each other in hotel corridors or on the convention floor, there was bitterness in their glances, sadness in the words they exchanged, and poignancy in their mutual recognition that the party was now destined to go separate ways.

For all these reasons, the struggle over the silver plank was the most climactic event of the convention, a crossing of the Rubicon which abandoned to their fates many of the party's most revered national leaders. This, the personal dimension of the struggle over money, was of course what the gold faction had hoped to expose and exploit when it had nominated Senator Hill as their candidate for temporary chairman. Now, when the platform itself came before the convention, the last stage at which rupture might be avoided loomed before the delegates.

The Committee on Resolutions was assigned the task of drafting the platform and, like all the committees at this point, had a large silver majority. Because many of the state conventions had adopted silver planks which could serve as models for the national platform, the silver plank was fairly easy to write. As placed before the convention, the most salient section of this plank read: "We demand the free and unlimited coinage of both silver and gold at the present legal ratio of 16 to 1 without waiting for the aid or consent of any other nation."[5] While there were other issues to be resolved, they were clearly secondary to the monetary issue.

The gold minority on the committee dutifully filed a minority report and the battle was joined. By agreement, two hours and forty minutes were allotted for debate, an hour and twenty minutes to each side. The opening and closing speeches were to be made by the majority, with the minority addresses sandwiched in between. Senator Benjamin "Pitchfork" Tillman of South Carolina would start the debate, followed by Senator Hill of New York, Senator William Vilas of Wisconsin, and former Governor William Russell of Massachusetts. William Jennings Bryan was to close with a speech supporting the majority report. All of the speakers were interrupted by demonstrations coming from the delegates and the spectators in the public galleries, so much so that the debate ran on far longer than the allotted time. Senator Tillman was frequently hissed by the gold wing of the party and became entangled in a "dialogue" with his opponents at several points in his address. In fact, Tillman made statements which the silver leaders judged to be so damaging to their cause that Senator James Jones of Arkansas, the chairman of the Committee on Resolutions, asked Hill if he might briefly address the convention before the New York Senator took his turn at the podium. Jones then publicly repudiated Tillman's charge that the silver plank was, and was intended to be, "sectional" in nature.

From the gold standpoint, this repudiation of the lead address in defense of the silver plank was a splendid way to introduce the chief spokesman for their side. As Senator Hill left his place in the New York delegation and walked to the dais, the gold men launched into a prolonged demonstration which was in part a personal tribute to Hill and in part a poignant celebration of their own lost cause. Hill was frequently interrupted by demonstrations of approval from his allies, and another large demonstration followed the conclusion of his address. Senator Vilas spoke next and was heard with respect, but there were only a few moments of polite applause during his speech. Russell was welcomed much more vigorously by the gold money faction and delivered a passionate address in which sad resignation was the dominant theme.

When Bryan moved to the podium for the closing defense of the silver platform, the gold leaders had clearly won the debate thus far, even if they had failed to change any votes. Tillman's speech had been a disaster which occasioned an apology, and that apology came on the charity of the gold wing when Hill had yielded time to Senator Jones. Hill himself may have been ill during the convention and had faltered a little in his delivery. However, the gold delegates and spectators made up for his abnormally weak performance with enthusiastic demonstrations before and after he spoke. Vilas had delivered a workmanlike, if forgettable, address but had not done any harm to the gold cause. And Russell, a popular favorite among all factions of the party, had given the crowd a moving evaluation of what the silver declaration meant to the eastern wing of the party.

For years, Bryan had traveled around the country as one of the leading spokesmen for silver and was thus well known among the silver delegates as an accomplished orator. Although the silver men knew they would prevail on the approaching roll call, they nonetheless needed someone to tell them—and the gold men—why they must enshrine silver at the heart of the platform. As the gold delegates had done for Hill, the silver delegates were prepared to make Bryan look good in this, their final moment of truth. And, unlike Hill, Bryan was in fine health, fully prepared to take advantage of their enthusiasm.

Cheer after cheer went up as Bryan of Nebraska, tall, smooth-faced, youthful-looking, leaped up the platform steps, two at a time, to close the debate. Banners waved from the free coinage delegations and handkerchiefs, newspapers, hats, fans and canes were brought into play by the enthusiastic crowd. . . . When quiet had been restored Mr. Bryan began speaking clearly and deliberately.[6]

Bryan started by subordinating his own pride to the silver cause:

I would be presumptuous indeed to present myself against the distinguished gentlemen to whom you have listened if this were but a measuring of ability, but this is not a contest among persons. The humblest citizen in all the land when clad in the armor of a righteous cause is stronger than all the whole hosts of error that they can bring.

As the *Detroit Free Press* reported, this opening passage "struck a keynote which sounded to the rafters."[7] The next line also drew loud applause: "I come to speak to you in defense of a cause as holy as the cause of liberty, the cause of humanity."

Having deftly captured the attention of his audience and impersonally placed himself at the head of the silver column, Bryan momentarily calmed the crowd by reviewing the history of the silver movement. He ended this account by denying that the silver wing bore any hostility toward the gold men. Then came the first of several passages which affirmed the honorable intentions and worthy standing of the common citizens whose cause the silver men espoused:

We stand here representing people who are the equals before the law of the largest cities in the State of Massachusetts.[8] When you come before us and tell us that we shall disturb your business interests, we reply that you have disturbed our business interests by your action.[9] We say to you that you have made too limited in its application the definition of business man. The man who is employed for wages is as much a business man as his employer.[10] The attorney in a country town is as much a business man as the corporation counsel in a great metropolis. The merchant at the crossroads store is as much a business man as the merchant of New York. The farmer who goes forth in the morning and toils all day, begins in the spring and toils all summer, and by the application of brain and muscle to the natural resources of this country creates wealth, is as much a business man as the man who goes upon the Board of Trade and bets upon the price of grain.[11] The miners who go a thousand feet into the earth or climb 2,000 feet upon the cliffs and bring forth from their hiding-places the precious metals to be poured in the channels of trade are as much business men as the few financial magnates who in a back room corner the money of the world.[12]
    . . . It is for these that we speak. We do not come as aggressors. Our war is not a war of conquest. We are fighting in the defense of our homes, our families, and posterity.[13] We have petitioned, and our petitions have been scorned. We have entreated and our entreaties have been disregarded. We have begged, and they have mocked when our calamity came. We beg no longer; we entreat no more; we petition no more. We defy them![14]

From this point forward, Bryan was cheered at almost every pause in his delivery. As he worked his way through the platform, succinctly outlining po-

sitions on the income tax, national banks, and the federal courts, Bryan left
the monetary standard to the last.

Now, my friends, let me come to the great paramount issue. If they ask us here why
it is that we say more on the money question than we say upon the tariff question,
I reply that if protection has slain its thousands the gold standard has slain its tens
of thousands.[15] If they ask us why we did not embody all these things in our platform which we believe, we reply to them that when we have restored the money of
the constitution all other necessary reforms will be possible, and that until that is
done there is no reform that can be accomplished.[16]

At this point, Bryan launched his one attack on the Republicans, embracing McKinley's image of himself as Napoleon and then noting that he had
been "nominated on the anniversary of the battle of Waterloo."[17] But he
soon dropped that theme and returned to the task of explaining to the
gold men why the party must endorse silver. The silver delegates were now
in an almost continuous uproar. Even so, there were two more passages
where the display of passion was greater than the rest. The first arose when
Bryan again stressed the equality of agrarian producers with those who inhabited the nation's cities:

You come to us and tell us that the great cities are in favor of the gold standard. I
tell you that the great cities rest upon these broad and fertile prairies. Burn down
your cities and leave our farms and your cities will spring up again as if by magic.
But destroy our farms and the grass will grow in the streets of every city in this country.[18]

The second marked the very end of his speech.

If they dare to come out and in the open defend the gold standard as a good thing,
we shall fight them to the uttermost, having behind us the producing masses of the
Nation and the world. Having behind us the commercial interests and the laboring
interests and all the toiling masses, we shall answer their demands for a gold standard by saying to them, you shall not press down upon the brow of labor this crown
of thorns.

As Bryan uttered the last phrase, he first raised his hands and then brought
them down as if to place a "crown of thorns" on his own head. Then came
the closing line: "You shall not crucify mankind on a cross of gold." For this,
Bryan stepped back from the podium and stretched his arms in the form
of a crucifix, symbolically sacrificing himself for the cause. There was an almost imperceptible moment of silence, a pause while the delegates and
spectators came to fully appreciate the image which had just been placed
before them. And then bedlam broke throughout the hall.

This demonstration lasted between fifteen and twenty-five minutes.
Bryan was carried on the shoulders of other delegates back to his seat in
the Nebraska delegation. The standards of many of the states and territo-

READY FOR THE WORD "GO" IN THE GRAND DEMOCRATIC FREE-FOR-ALL SWEEPSTAKES

Figure 1. Ready for the word "Go" in the Grand Democratic Free-for-All Sweepstakes. *Chicago Tribune*, July 5, 1896.

ries collected around him and then moved in procession around the convention hall. At this point, the transfer of sentiment from silver as a policy to Bryan as a possible presidential candidate took place. In terms of its ritual role, his speech had been a formal, impersonal defense of the silver plank. And it was in this role—a role in which Bryan purposely cloaked himself—that the silver delegates could unreservedly display passion for their cause. Going into the speech, almost all the delegates had either committed themselves to, or were leaning toward, one of the other candidates for the nomination (see Figure 1).[19] Recognizing this, Bryan had opened his address by disarming those who might otherwise have seen Bryan as a threat to their favored candidate. Putting the cause before his pride, he first released and then harnessed the tension which had been accumulating as the party moved toward an open disruption over silver.

The awkward element in all this, from the perspective of Bryan and his newly won supporters, was that his speech and this demonstration occurred well before the voting could begin on the nomination. In fact, when the demonstration ended, several more hours were consumed in roll calls which first defeated the minority report on gold, turned back an amendment which would have endorsed the Cleveland administration, and, in the third and last vote, finally approved the platform in its entirety. By that point, the delegates and spectators were much less excited than they had been at the end of Bryan's speech. Still, the managers of the other campaigns were so concerned that they lobbied—and lobbied successfully—for a recess. The convention met again in the evening, heard speeches formally offering candidates for the nomination (including several for Bryan), and then, once more at the behest of these campaign managers, adjourned.

The next day the voting began on the nomination. Richard Bland of Missouri led the pack on the first three roll calls, but Bryan was always in second place and steadily gained on the front runner. The other candidates who were expected to mount competitive challenges rapidly faded away, leaving Bland and Bryan the only obvious contenders. On the fourth ballot, Bryan moved past Bland, and on the fifth a bandwagon gave him the nomination.

Maneuvering behind the scenes delayed the vice-presidential contest until the following day, and although the voting revealed surprising movements among the delegates, the convention was very calm and deliberate. Arthur Sewall of Maine was finally nominated on the fifth roll call and the 1896 National Democratic Convention was over.

The Physical Setting in Which Sentiment and Preferences Are Displayed

As we have seen, the ritual structure of the proceedings created the context within which Bryan delivered his speech, including the crucial role in which he could formally pose as the spokesman for the silver faction while implicitly offering himself as their standard bearer in the election. The transfer of sentiment from the faction's commitment to silver to Bryan as their charismatic champion could never have taken place if, first, the convention ritual had not prescribed such a role in the form of a speech for the majority silver plank (structure) and, second, Bryan had not maneuvered himself into the role of delivering that speech (agency). However, before discussing how Bryan came to give his speech, we should take a look at the way the physical setting of the convention shaped the emotional response Bryan was able to elicit from the delegates and spectators who heard him speak.

When the Democrats gathered in Chicago in 1896, the Coliseum was a fairly new building, constructed at what had been the entrance to the fair grounds of the 1892 Columbian Exposition. Proclaimed the "Largest Permanent Convention Hall in the World," the Coliseum was some 700 feet long by 300 feet wide. The interior ground floor was thus about five acres in size. For the convention, the hall had been divided into two sections by a canvas wall composed of gigantic flags. The smaller of these was set aside for a large restaurant, telephone booths, refreshment stands, and a typewriter office. Although this section took up almost a third of the space in the Coliseum, none of the newspaper reporters seem to have filed a story from this space; from their perspective, at least, we can surmise that almost nothing of interest occurred in this area.

The larger portion of the hall had been fitted out for the public sessions of the convention. This space was roughly 400 feet long by 250 wide (see Figure 2). The dais was constructed at the center of one of the long sides of the building, facing west. At the rear of this platform, running along the wall, was a large section in which seven hundred seats were reserved for members of the national party committee and other dignitaries. Just in front of this section was the podium where the presiding officer and those who addressed the convention took up their positions. Slightly lower than the podium and stretching out on either side were four hundred seats set apart for reporters.

The space reserved for delegates was divided by aisles into five sections. Each state was assigned its own area, with the spaces arranged alphabetically (see Figure 3). In the far right of the five sections, Alabama was seated at the front, nearest the podium. In back of that state was the Arkansas delegation, followed by California, Colorado, Connecticut, and so on until the Illinois delegation was reached. Then the seating arrangement jumped an aisle, placing Indiana at the rear of the second section, with Iowa just in front and so on until Massachusetts was assigned the section nearest the podium. The small contingents from the territories and the District of Columbia were given spaces at the very rear of the delegate sections. Altogether 930 delegates occupied this level rectangular space facing the podium.

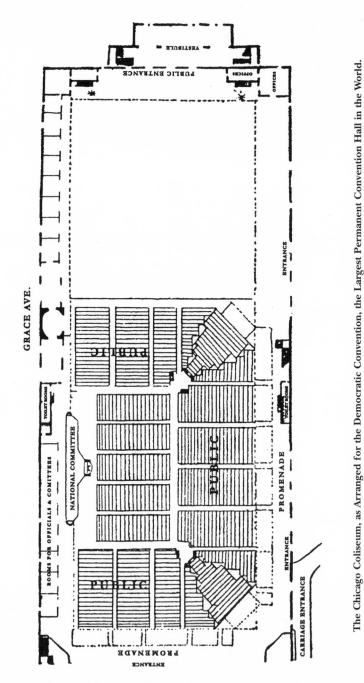

Figure 2. Seating arrangement of delegations. Edward B. Dickinson, *Official Proceedings of the Democratic National Convention* (Logansport, Ind.: Wilson, Humphreys, 1896), front matter.

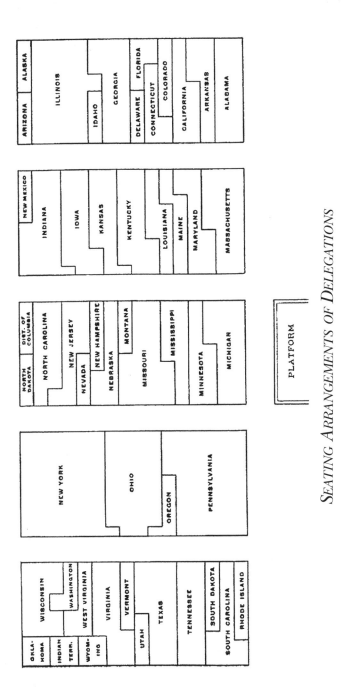

Figure 3. Interior design of the convention hall. *Boston Globe* (Extra), July 6, 1896.

One of the consequences attending this arrangement was that the gold and silver delegations were intermixed on the convention floor. While the far right section toward the north end of the hall was predominantly composed of silver delegations, the Connecticut and Delaware gold men occupied the center rows of the column. New Jersey and New Hampshire were similarly marooned in the center column while the gold men, with the huge New York and Pennsylvania delegations, dominated the column just to the south. Observers looking down on the convention floor could, of course, locate each of the state delegations by finding its standard. And when the silver and gold factions took turns displaying sympathy for their respective leaders and principles, these observers noted the checkered pattern the seating arrangement produced. When the silver men stood and cheered, the gold men usually sat on their hands and vice versa. This meant that, in some instances, these partisans were taking their cues as much from their opponents as their allies. For example, the Ohio and Oregon silver men, almost surrounded by gold delegations from New York, Pennsylvania, and Vermont, were much more isolated from their allies than most of the other silver contingents. For them, displaying support for the cause was not so much an act of solidarity as an act of defiance, because those most closely observing their enthusiasm were their archenemies.

Another consequence was that those delegations at the front of each column found it much easier to interact with those speaking from the podium than those seated to the rear of the delegate space. For example, Michigan was seated in the front row of the middle column, squarely in front of the podium. During debate over the unseating of the gold men in that delegation, Michigan's proximity allowed delegates on the floor to directly engage speakers as they made their speeches. These exchanges became public dialogues which would have been much more difficult to mount if the Michigan delegation had been farther away.

Surrounding the convention floor on three sides were the tiered galleries for public spectators (see Figure 4). Row upon row of chairs gradually ascended the hall until they were much higher than the podium. The fifteen thousand spectators in the galleries outnumbered everyone else in the hall (including delegates, alternates, guests, and reporters) by about five to one. They were also in an asymmetrical position with respect to the delegates' public displays of sentiment. Because of their tiered seats, spectators could easily view, albeit from a distance, both the delegates and other spectators throughout the Coliseum. They were also easily seen by the delegates and these other spectators. But the delegates themselves had a better view of most of the spectators than they had of each other. This meant that, during a demonstration, the delegates could more easily watch those spectators who were throwing their hats and newspapers into the air than they could view their colleagues on the floor who might or might not be doing the same thing.

Figure 4. Interior of the Coliseum showing the scheme of decoration and seating arrangements. *Detroit Free Press*, July 5, 1896.

If we treat these passionate displays as signals which encourage others to join in their collective expression, the physical arrangement of the convention hall begins to appear a little odd. When, as in Bryan's speech, a massive demonstration changes the preferences of the delegates and spectators as to their favorite for the nomination, the preferences of the delegates are the only ones that are formally important to the party's decision because the spectators cannot vote. So, from the perspective of the delegates, it is the display of sentiment by other delegates that matters, not the vocal and physical expressions of the spectators. But the delegates had a better view of the spectators because the level field on the floor hampered their ability to monitor each other. Not only that, but the spectators outnumbered the delegates by fifteen to one, so that in terms of the noise they could generate, they simply overwhelmed anything the official participants might do or say. Thus, if the intention of the convention organizers had been to facilitate the emergence of a collective opinion among the delegates, they might have inverted the arrangement of seats and the ratio of spectators to delegates. Two thousand spectators would have sat in flat space just in front of the podium while fifteen thousand delegates and alternates occupied the tiered rows arranged in an amphitheater style around the southern, northern, and western walls of the convention hall.

It is not surprising that this inverted design was never conceived as an alternative to the traditional arrangement actually constructed. The purpose of a large number of spectators was to raise money for the party (if they paid for their tickets), to reward party loyalists (if the spectators received their tickets from party members who used the tickets as a form of patronage), and to demonstrate the popular appeal of the party (by allowing thousands of interested spectators to be drawn into the proceedings). Thus, the ratio of spectators to delegates was traditionally quite large. That meant, in turn, that only a thin band of delegates would have inhabited the far reaches of the convention hall if the arrangement were inverted. In this era before microphones could bolster a speaker's voice, many of the delegates would not have been able to hear the proceedings if they had been seated in this outer band up under the rafters. And, since the proceedings were of greater significance to the delegates (who, after all, were supposed to listen closely to debates attending the major decisions facing the party), placing them in this outer band would have seriously impaired the deliberative aspect of the convention. In terms of mutual consultation and informal exchange of views between delegates, distributing them throughout the far precincts of the hall would have been counterproductive as well.

Bryan as Agent

Because the physical structure of the convention hall conformed to a traditional pattern (albeit on a very large scale), Bryan's long experience as a public speaker would have accustomed him to the setting. He also had ample opportunity to study the hall after the Nebraska delegation had been seated on the second day of the convention. He would have observed the success and failure of the speakers who went before him, including the fact that many of them had been unable to project their voice throughout the immense space. From where he sat, their performances would have been measured by the size and intensity of the demonstrations they had been able to elicit from their respective factions. He would have studied that as well, noting that the silver faction had become quite accustomed to vigorously displaying the intensity of its devotion to the soft money cause. As Bryan wrote his speech, he would have incorporated symbols and a cadence which he believed would enchant the hall, transfixing spectators and delegates into a frenzy. There is agency in all these things, but it is the agency of an intuitive political performer in the possession of a very great talent. He could not have articulated just how he wove these preparatory observations into the performance he intended to deliver.

But other aspects of what he did can be analyzed. For example, Bryan anticipated that delivering the closing speech on the silver plank would be the optimal situation in which to exercise his oratorical talents, and he did his best to maneuver himself into that position. As a start, he intentionally discouraged early endorsements of his candidacy because these would have made him a visible presidential possibility. For example, when the North Carolina delegation appeared to be on the verge of endorsing Bryan on July 8, a message was sent to his supporters that "Mr. Bryan would prefer that his friends give Bland the North Carolina delegation on first ballot. He does not care to show Presidential strength that early in the fight."[20]

In his postconvention account, Bryan claimed to have deliberately downplayed his availability as a candidate because that strategy promised the best chance of delivering the last speech in support of the silver plank. In order to win this spot in the proceedings, he had to be, on the one hand, too prominent as a candidate to be considered for the posts of temporary or permanent chairman. On the other hand, he could not be so prominent as to preclude his delivering a major address before the convention.[21]

Because he had to wait until the Nebraska silver delegation had unseated the gold men, Bryan joined the Committee on Resolutions too late to play more than a minor role in its deliberations. He had, however, a well-deserved reputation as an orator, and when the time came to decide who would defend the silver plank, he was a natural choice. As Bryan himself reported, "Just before the platform was reported to the convention, Senator Jones sent for me and asked me to take charge of the debate."[22] Because Bryan wanted Tillman to go first, he offered the South Carolina senator more time if he would open the debate. While Bryan may have thought Tillman would undermine the silver cause with his speech, his desire to close the debate was a more important factor in this offer.

From Bryan's perspective, Tillman's performance was thus icing on the cake. Clark Howell, editor of the *Atlanta Constitution* and one of the leaders of the Georgia delegation, was seated just in back of the podium as Tillman spoke. Howell was just as disappointed in the senator's address as the rest of the silver faction but saw something else as well. Realizing that Tillman "had not met the expectations of the friends of silver," Howell dashed off a note and sent one of the assistant sergeant-at-arms scurrying down to the Nebraska delegation in search of Bryan. Howell wrote,

You have now the opportunity of your life in concluding the argument for the majority report. Make a big, broad, patriotic speech that will leave no taste of sectionalism in the mouth and which will give a sentiment that will touch a responsive chord in the heart of the whole country. You can now make the hit of your life.

Bryan immediately replied with a note of his own. "You will not be disappointed. I have had little or no preparation, but I will speak the sentiment of my heart and I think you will be satisfied with it."[23] Bryan, of course, was vastly misstating the amount of work he had put into his speech. While some of what he was to say would be extemporaneous, Bryan had long anticipated and prepared for this very moment.[24] In setting him up, "Pitchfork Ben" had done just fine.

As for the speech itself, Bryan said that he had

never addressed an audience which seemed to act in such perfect harmony; it reminded one of an immense chorus trained to sing in concert. The applause broke out simultaneously in all parts of the hall, and ended as simultaneously when the next sentence began. The intense interest depicted upon the faces before me presented a picture never to be forgotten.[25]

The close coordination of speaker and audience was "spontaneous" in that they had never rehearsed their respective roles. But Bryan had manufactured much of the setting in which they performed. One of the most important elements, for example, was the uninhibited displays of the delegates and spectators. Because they did not regard Bryan as a serious presidential contender, his audience responded to him solely as the agent of their cause, and the resulting demonstrations were unalloyed exhibitions of enthusiasm for silver. Tillman had unwittingly done his part as well. Because of him, the silver men were focused on demonstrating to the gold men that they had a champion as worthy as the best they could put forward. Because the gold men were the intended recipients of these demonstrations, the inhibitions of the silver men were even further reduced.

Bryan thus recognized the situation in which he could best exercise his oratorical powers, worked instrumentally to place himself in that situation, and then performed magnificently. In all of this, Bryan displayed a very high level of political skill. The night before he delivered his speech, Bryan was eating supper with his wife, Mary, and a friend in a restaurant on Dearborn Street. As they ate, they watched noisy processions of men supporting the two leading candidates, Richard Bland and Horace Boies. Looking out the window, Bryan said,

These people do not know it, but they will be cheering for me just this way by this time tomorrow night. I will make the greatest speech of my life tomorrow in reply to Senator Hill. . . . I will be at my best. Hill is the brains of the opposition, and when I have answered him, it will dawn on the convention that I am a pretty good man to lead the fight.

Mary turned to their dinner companion and asked, "Don't you think that Mr. Bryan has a good chance to be nominated?" Before he could respond, Bryan stepped in, "So that you both may sleep well tonight, I am going to tell you something. I am the only man who can be nominated. I am what they call 'the logic of the situation.'"[26]

And so he was . . . the product of logic and luck.

Agents and Agency in the 1896 National Democratic Convention

Agents initiate significant actions by authoring or supporting alternatives from which the convention chooses. Such actions can be influential addresses, public endorsements of one of the presidential candidates, tactical agreements between leaders, or visible displays of enthusiasm or hostility toward another agent's declarations. The ratio of "agents" to participants is extraordinarily high in a national party convention for a number of reasons, including the large proportion of professional political leaders among the delegates and the fact that the political stakes are often very high for these professional leaders.[27] From this perspective, we should always remember that every silver delegate would have fervently desired to have had made the kind of speech which Bryan delivered. The competition for the opportunity, if only those delegates had realized that it existed and had the talent to exploit the possibility, would have been unimaginably intense.

Placing Bryan's speech in a "structure-agency" framework requires clarification of these terms. "Structure" is composed of those durable elements of a social setting which provide meaning to an agent's actions but cannot themselves be altered by that agent. This is a very narrow definition in that those features of a social setting which are not consciously apprehended are excluded. Those elements might not be apprehended, for example, because of incomplete or incorrect understanding of the causal relations into which they enter (for example, an illness might be ascribed to witchcraft as opposed to a pathogen) or because they are so pervasive and immutable that they constitute an unconscious backdrop when an agent makes a decision (much as the longue durée of Mediterranean geography underpinned the region's politics and economy without being explicitly recognized by agents in their daily lives).[28] One of the structural backdrops in the national convention was the procedural backbone against which agents played out their roles. Another was the physical arrangement of the convention hall as a stage on which agents pursued their goals.

Within this procedural and physical setting, delegates became agents when they made choices, choices which were limited to alternatives that were feasible and meaningful within that setting. "Agency" is the possible and actual making of such choices, including activities directed toward fulfilling the purpose of the choices which are made. As Jon Elster put it,

When collective action is explained by its goal or purpose, this must either be understood distributively, in the sense that each actor in the group acts for the sake of that goal, or with reference to the goal or purpose of leaders who are able to induce or compel others to execute their policy. The crucial step in an intentional explanation is the specification of the goal—the future state of affairs for the sake of which the action is undertaken.

The demonstrations during and following Bryan's speech do not meet Elster's conditions because the participants neither articulated a goal as individuals nor shared a purpose as a collective. In addition, the demonstrations were neither "led" by recognized leaders nor orchestrated in accord with a preconceived elite design. Fritz Wilhelm Scharpf's assumption that "social phenomena are to be explained as the outcome of interactions among intentional actors" (which he presents as the foundation of his "actor-centered institutionalism") fails to encompass the demonstrations for similar reasons.[29]

Bryan's speech was able to elicit a passionate display precisely because he implicitly persuaded the delegates and spectators to cheer on the silver cause and thus redeem their self-image before the gold men. However, once the demonstration was underway, it was far beyond his (or anybody else's) control. He could only wait for the outpouring of emotion to work its magic, transferring sentiment from the silver cause to his own candidacy. And this is precisely the point at which the dichotomy of structure and agency fails us.

The dichotomy fails us even though the vast majority of the people in the convention hall, even the spectators, were in some sense agents. The spectators could not vote, but they could nonetheless instrumentally pursue their goals by collectively cheering and stomping their feet. Because delegates could vote, their participation in such displays was even more instrumentally effective. Here we may embark on a discussion of whether and how an individual's decision to cheer or hiss might be instrumentally rational. To do this, we must first examine the qualities of a such acts as individual and collective performances. A cheer or a hiss, for example, indicates an attitude toward whatever individual or event is presently at the center of the audience's attention. These vocalizations, by their volume and persistence, also indicate the depth of a person's feelings on the matter at hand. Cheers and hisses are also profoundly democratic acts. In a political setting devoid of drama, angst, and uncertainty, a political convention will traverse traditional rituals under the command of party leaders. It is these leaders who decide who may or may not address the convention, what will be in the platform, and so forth. It is the leaders whose movements and pronouncements are avidly monitored by the news media. And it is the leaders to whom the delegates turn for signals as to how to act or vote.

But in a political setting riven by drama, angst, and uncertainty, political leaders lose much of their agency. They lose agency not because they themselves do not attempt to influence the proceedings but because the delegates literally lose sight of the leaders as they engage in collective displays of sentiment. The prolonged demonstration following Bryan's speech, for example, was far beyond the control of the party leaders. This is what reporters meant when they described the demonstration as "spontaneous." And when the delegates stood on their chairs, threw newspapers into the air, and yelled themselves hoarse, each of their displays was the equal of any attempted by one of the leaders. In fact, most party leaders restrained their displays in order to maintain a dignity they felt should accompany their status. All of this meant that the most insignificant delegate could merge into a collective display in which his contribution and role was at least the equal of the most powerful leader. The cacophony of sound and motion thus profoundly leveled the playing field because individual contributions were impossible to distinguish within the demonstration.

The vast majority of the delegates must have had very modest ambitions within the convention. They knew they were not to have an opportunity to address their colleagues. And they knew that, even if they did have an opportunity, their lack of standing in the party would have meant that their fellow delegates would probably have ignored them. In fact, the background noise of the convention was great enough that delegates and spectators had to make a special effort to quiet themselves so that a speaker could be heard. And speakers who lacked a reputation at the beginning of their address could not earn that reputation through their oratory because the audience would not be quiet. But these delegates of modest reputations and ambitions did have their votes and their throats. And they realized that, collectively, they could determine outcomes.

And this is what makes "agency," with its emphasis on individual action and goals, inadequate as a description of what happened in the 1896 convention. The great mass of silver delegates was passionately committed to an "imagined collectivity" arising out of the silver movement within the Democratic party and the nation at large. They were constantly told that this movement existed, and they often credited their own presence in the convention to its support. But the convention itself was the first setting in which this silver movement, within the party, could be evidenced as a tangible force. Their passionate commitment to silver led these delegates to subordinate their personal autonomy with respect to the formation, expression, and realization of individual goals (which would have been out of reach anyway) in favor of collective demonstrations which, from one perspective, appeared to validate the existence of this movement and, from another perspective, created that movement, as a national force, on the floor of the convention. These collective demonstrations melded the individual delegates from the separate states and territories into a collective whose identity owed everything to the contest over silver. As long as it was the policy issue of silver and the organizational issues associated with that policy issue that were before the convention, the silver leaders were able to direct the course of the convention without restraining the spontaneous display of emotion among fellow delegates and spectators. Since these collective displays were perfectly consistent with the instrumental goals of the leaders in executing the silver program at the convention, there was no reason to control them.

As in most political settings, two kinds of leadership can be distinguished in the 1896 convention. The first we might term "entrepreneurial" and entails the detection and shepherding of followers who already hold preferences favoring the goals of the leaders. Most rational choice approaches stress this form of leadership as that normally encountered in legislative settings.[30] The silver leaders, for example, themselves constantly described their roles as merely coordinating the wishes of the silver delegates. That service, they said, was made vitally necessary by the plots and machinations ascribed to the gold faction, which was ostensibly committed to frustrating the silver cause. The second kind of leadership we might call "charismatic," and it entails the changing of preferences among followers such that they come to favor the goals of a leader. In guiding the silver faction toward passage of a silver platform, the leaders were acting in an entrepreneurial role. And, when Bryan delivered his "Cross of Gold" speech, he too was posing as an entrepreneurial leader whose role was to facilitate the translation of preexisting preferences favoring silver into votes for the silver plank. However, Bryan's (albeit disguised) intention was to charismatically change the preferences of the delegates with respect to the presidential nomination. He thus played out both types of leadership roles at the same time.

The magic, in the sense of an apparently agency-less collective response, arose when the silver faction melded its collective expression for silver into an affectionate appreciation of Bryan's personal performance. We could call this charisma, following Weber, and attribute it to a conflation of man and cause. Whatever we label it, it occurred during the displays of enthusiasm which continually interrupted and followed Bryan's address. Bryan had almost no formal campaign organization at this point and what he had was almost entirely limited to the small Nebraska delegation. When delegates stood and cheered, there were no hirelings scattered about the convention floor to give them cues. And they could not have spontaneously co-ordinated their actions by signaling one another. Most delegates could not even see each other on the flat plain of the convention floor. Even if they could have seen one another, they would not have known what to signal because they came to support Bryan for the nomination through (by means of) the demonstration itself. Their preferences for the nomination formed within an ostensibly neutral display of passion for the silver cause.

Hundreds upon hundreds of delegates and thousands upon thousands of spectators rose en masse and cheered. Each of their cheers was certainly an individual act, a choice made by an agent within the convention hall. But what they collectively created was much more and much less than an agent. Each of the delegates and spectators could literally feel the emotional reaction of the others. As the newspaper correspondents reported, the floor and rafters were physically shaken by the demonstration. And, of course, the noise was deafening. This vibrating spectacle of sound produced sensory perceptions which had no focus in terms of individuals. Without a focus, the participants had to imagine what the other delegates and spectators were intending as they stomped and cheered. At first, and perhaps until the end of Bryan's speech, this intention was almost purely an expression of silver sentiment. But somewhere in the demonstration the delegates and spectators began to impose another interpretation on this sentiment, one that conferred a special honor on Bryan as the man who had created the occasion for this demonstration. Given the absence of a consensus choice for presidential candidate, the transformation of this honor into the shaping of a preference for Bryan as the nominee was fairly simple (and what Bryan had intended to have happen all along). But these shifts were made without explicit communication between individual delegates and spectators. Such communication was simply impossible unless you shouted something to your neighbor on the convention floor. In some sense, each individual was an observer with respect to this demonstration, absorbing information from the others. In another sense, each individual was a participant whose personal identity was drowned in the collective demonstration. Their agency, such as it was, could only be pursued through this collective, and the possibilities they came to imagine unfolded within that collective.[31]

Conclusion

The 1896 National Democratic Convention was one of the great turning points in American political development. Southern and western insurgency triumphed over the patricians of the East. Lower-class immigrants and urban workers gained influence, if not outright control, over the party throughout the industrial belt. And the Populists were doomed to extinction by the impending merger with the Democrats under William Jennings Bryan. Pathos is produced in almost all such turning points. As a traditional coalition shatters, personal ties and alliances are torn apart. This rending takes place under conditions of great uncertainty, an uncertainty which colors the choices as much more personal in nature than would otherwise be the case. To understand just how pathos emerges in such a context, "passion" must be constructed as an element orthogonal to the structure-agency dimension. The origins of passion in the 1896 convention were the anxiety arising out of the uncertainties attending the momentous choice before the party and the personal feelings implicated in the disruption of long-standing interpersonal friendships and associations. In other venues, passions are aroused for very different reasons, one of the most dependable being religious belief.[32]

Demonstrations have occurred in all national party conventions. In recent years, they have had an artificial quality, as if they were stage-managed in conditions of great certainty in which important policy disputes and competitive candidate races were absent. For its part, the 1896 Democratic convention had hired bands and marching clubs. But most of the noise and commotion was, again in the words of the newspaper correspondents, spontaneous. Pathos begat passion in 1896 as the party turned to silver and away from the patricians of the East. And the displays of passion in Chicago meant just what they implied: that the delegates and spectators strongly felt their preferences. And passion, working through those demonstrations, created William Jennings Bryan as one of most important political leaders in American history.

Organizing for Disorder: Civil Unrest, Police Control, and the Invention of Washington, D.C.

Daniel Kryder

Though in politics the concept of "agency" is usually associated with change, a large share of significant and purposeful political activity is system maintaining rather than system transforming. Human agency is involved in system maintenance in several different ways. Many of the structures that control potentially transformative action were themselves designed and built with that purpose in view. For example, it is difficult to imagine a structure as set in stone as the monumental buildings and avenues of Washington, D.C. But the capital's durable and structured setting was originally, and has always been, itself the product of purposeful human design and political struggle. Those who did so engaged in a politically "formative act," perhaps, given the enduring impact of this structure on opportunity, the most formative of all. Second, those who police the actions of others on behalf of the state and seek to contain popularly driven transformations are important and innovative agents. The often heated reactions of police to confrontational demonstrators are thus very striking examples of such order-maintaining human agency. In practice police may shape the course and outcome of mobilized protest as much as the protesters themselves. Thus two primary goals here are simply to justify the study of the police as politically relevant agents and the streets of the capital as a politically relevant site. Oddly political scientists have given little scholarly attention to the police, despite the fact that historically oriented social scientists have grounded their conception of the state in Weberian social theory, highlighting coercion and order maintenance within a defined space: "states are compulsory associations claiming control over territories and the people within them. Administrative, legal, extractive, and coercive organizations are the core of any state."[1]

To bring to the fore these neglected aspects of agency in politics, this chapter considers police agency in relation to formative structure, here conceptualized as the location and design of the national capital. Because it involves enduring as well as contingent factors, an analysis of capital policing must be layered, and it must be dynamic to reckon with the effects of structure on agency, and of individual actors on short-term outcomes as well as on structure over time. The primary advantage of a layered analysis is the ability to delineate analytically separate spheres of politics, to trace each sphere's unique temporal logic or evolution, and to demonstrate how, at any particular moment, politics involves the interaction of these conceptually distinct layers. The bedrock level for this analysis is geographic placement, which typically and in the American case, once Congress lodged it on the Potomac River, is a settled matter lacking a temporal order. The placement of this invented federal district outside of the jurisdiction of preestablished state and local governments produced two important effects: local police forces' chronic lack of resources and their peculiar administrative fragmentation. Constructed "atop" this factor on an agency-structure spectrum is the design and layout of the city, which is more amenable to human agency over time (see Figure 1). In effect, attending to two factors closely associated with agency and two with structure isolates dissimilar factors in pursuit of conceptual clarity and ignores many important factors "between" them, including political parties and socio-economic patterns, for example. Within this structured setting, police administrators work to organize, supply, and deploy units to master various forms of disorder, including criminal and political disorder generated by the political economy of the city and the nation. Finally, the top graphic marker in the diagram represents specific episodes of policing. Here we find human agency in its most contingent form, as decision making at crisis points. This "least determined" aspect of capital protest, which represents police struggling operationally to control disruption as it unfolds, is the most uncertain and rapidly changing. While the spatial terms of the diagram provide a heuristic framework for the remainder of this text, the challenge here is to move beyond conceptualization to generate relational and causal propositions that clarify the effects of a capital's spatial qualities on the outcomes of protest events.

National capitals are crucial sites for resolving political conflicts through informal as well as formal means. By inventing a rural capital the Framers set American political development on a distinctive path, particularly as it concerns the nature and resolution of protest. Separating the capital from the social networks of the largest cities, for example, ensured that American demonstrators were usually travelers, and that such travelers could not hope to disrupt the nation's primary trade, transport, or financial hub. Thus central state institutions would evade direct assaults from the poor laborers and unemployed masses concentrated in larger cities. Built to monitor a medium-sized city, the local police always lacked the standing personnel necessary to patrol large parades. Taken together, the analysis suggests, these placement effects limited the number of confrontations be-

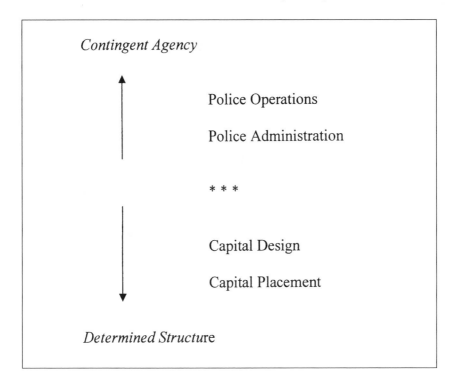

Figure 1. A structure-agency continuum: selected factors influencing the policing of protest in capital cities.

tween challengers and authorities in the American capital. When one erupted, however, it often overwhelmed local forces. Also, because they sought to recapture the grandeur of history's great imperial cities, the city's designers provided both the symbolic sites later demonstrators found attractive and the broad avenues amenable to police and military movement. Thus marchers returned to a small set of ritualized paths and sites, such as the stretch of Pennsylvania Avenue between the Capitol and the White House, and into the collection area provided by the National Mall. This second dimension of structure as setting seems to have had the unintended effect of favoring police by standardizing their work to some degree. Thus, the analysis specifies structure as physical setting, and investigates the way that urban design overlays geographic placement to create a specific political topography that governed the maneuvers and interactions of police and protesters.

This chapter seeks to specify the mechanisms linking these various layers. The familiar examples reviewed here include a suffrage parade led by Alice Paul in 1913, which organizers carefully planned to exploit several physical sites, to the befuddlement of police. The relatively disorganized invasion of the capital by bonus-seeking veterans in 1932 led to a series of scattered and disorganized actions that posed a very different set of problems for authorities. In the absence of the channeling by monumental routes and sites, police and military operations decisively determined outcomes. Less than ten years later, in 1941, when several thousand black Americans planned to descend on the capital, the Roosevelt administration was so uncertain about the city's police capacity that it offered a substantial concession to prevent the march altogether. In the case of the 1963 March on Washington, the protest leadership was so keen on creating new cooperative relations with the White House that it provided its own auxiliary police to help ensure a peaceful outcome. In all of these cases, the immediate problem of police operations was influenced by and in turn reverberated downward through a spectrum of structural factors. Put simply, both the administrative capacity and the size of the deployable force of the police were influenced by the placement of the city outside of extant states and cities. Specific police operations were also directly shaped by design factors channeling the physical movement of the protesters. In each case these factors combined to create and end crises which decisively affected presidential reputation and decision making, with enduring results. These illustrations suggest the gradual mastery of the problem of civil unrest by capital authorities over the long term.

I begin by attending to the concept of agency in American political history. Because mass protest was, in the colonial era, a very effective form of participation outside of formal institutions, and because American rebels had used crowds to help launch the rebellion, the analysis reviews early American elite thinking concerning both social order and the capital's placement and design. In fact, the invention, placement, and design of the capital involved several principles that were foundational to the American constitutional system. Thomas Jefferson, for example, offered good republican reasons for moving the capital out of the great commercial centers. After considering the roots of physical structures in human design, the study considers the consequences of these formative decisions over the long haul, in particular their effect on the shape and direction of police response to collective action. Setting constrained not only crowds of challengers and claimants but also police deployments against challengers; in short, it affected the appearance and resolution of mass protest. Finally, I offer some provisional conclusions about the relationship between structure and agency found in this type of informal political conflict in America.

Two Faces of Agency

As Almond and Genco put it in "Clouds, Clocks, and Politics," a social science solely concerned with the search for structured regularities misses the distinctively human aspect of politics, which is our effort to escape from constraints, or to discover value-optimizing solutions to social problems in the context of constraints.[2] Protest is one form of contingent human agency that aims at resisting or changing structural constraints. In proposing that a consensus exists on this point I risk a platitude: agency takes its life from economic, institutional, and spatial structure. Institutions, for example, can create severe and certain constraints that prompt resistance by agents. Authoritative institutions can create and deploy loyal agents to defend rules and arrangements. Or potential agents may grow emboldened when they sense moments of structural instability. Thus theories of leadership and entrepreneurship, as Adam Sheingate argues, must focus on the agent's strategic evaluation of certainty within prevailing economic and social structures. Certain endogenous characteristics of institutions—mainly their complex, changing, and overlapping jurisdictional authority, as in the American constitutional system—can enable creative institutional politics. Particularly helpful is Sheingate's suggestion that officials use "multiple goals and the resultant ambiguity of actors' intentions" to cobble together disparate groups into formidable change-oriented coalitions. Although such heterogeneous coalitions are difficult to achieve, certain institutions provide more of the opportunities, resources, and assets that innovators need to pursue and consolidate reform. Given that the Framers created ambiguous and overlapping jurisdictions to check ambitious centralizers, however, some consideration of the competitive system-maintaining response of jealous authorities and rivals is also essential. And the exclusive focus on uncertainty among and within institutions neglects what is arguably an equally important cause of institutional innovation, namely uncertainty in society, and the ability of skilled agents to exploit that uncertainty.[3]

If structure breeds agency, the reverse is also true. In most historical social science, an agent is generally simply "one who acts or exerts power," and agency simply "the capacity of an agent." Madison deploys this meaning when, in Federalist no. 10, he compares liberty to air, which "imparts to fire its destructive agency." But James Block reminds us that the word "agent" is a contronym, a concept with another, opposite meaning: one who acts for another. "Agency," he writes, "exists only with reference to a principal, a designator, an author/ity." This dual sense is suggested in Thomas Jefferson's letter of dismissal to Pierre L'Enfant: "I am instructed by the President to inform you that nothwithstanding the desire he has entertained to preserve your agency in the business, the condition upon which it is to be done is inadmissible & your services must be at an end."[4] This complex concept was a core cultural mechanism at the time of the founding of the American republic and thus deserves further attention.

Block denies that insurgents launched the Revolution to create a regime built solely or even primarily on self-government and personal liberty.[5] Agency principals—"individuals participating actively in shaping the

worldly means to be employed for realizing divine and collective purposes"—instead provided the transcendent ends motivating both elites
seeking national authority and a populace rejecting social hierarchies.
While the masses fought against class privilege and domination as well as
imperial authorities, rebel elites hoped to defend a hierarchical republic
based on differential personal attributes of virtue, reason, and ability. Given
these very different interests, leaders promoted a radical Declaration "to
mobilize and co-opt the popular revolution on behalf of a moderate revolution for national separation—not universal liberty—that would legitimate their political leadership and buttress their commercial position in
society."[6] In fact, no revolutionary group found motivation in radical Lock-
ean conceptions of a liberal republic or of "free" or rational citizens; most
dreamed of creating communities of voluntary agents of a single transcendent Author. But the Declaration, the new touchstone of national political
culture, promoted an unobtainable conception of personal rights through
which free, individual citizens imagined ever more expansive democratic
claims. Madison's "trick" agency system appeared to be a federal structure
in popular control, but in fact it directed people's participation into institutions that would consume their passions, displacing individual authority
consensually onto a collective author "by the memory of the participatory
Founding."[7] Thus the idyllic language of the Revolution contained a crippling contradiction: "the unresolvable tension between the 'free society'
placing authority in the majority and the 'free individual' which contests all
forms of authority."

Block's nuanced conception of agency emphasizes the paradox at its
core. An agent may relate to authority as a challenger and as an executor.
Agents are not only subjects performing "independent" or free acts, but objects of an authority which is directing them and aggregating them. A successful authority, whether secular or spiritual, dispatches effective agents.
One problem, therefore, is to consider the logic by which one's agency as
an object creates or relates to one's agency as a subject.[8] Put another way:
how do certain agents manage to turn their location in authoritative structures into obedience or into choice? Some forms of agency, like the American rebels' intellectual justifications of an isolated capital or of
constitutional consolidation, purposefully create stabilizing structures.

Formative Agency: Inventing a Capital City

The writers of the Constitution, like all nation builders, encountered a vari-
ation of this problem of dual agency in their attempt to balance mechanisms of authoritative social order maintenance with mechanisms
promoting individual participation and freedom. This is a fundamental
problem of liberal political development, and to allow for both liberty and
authority, the Federalists created a large republic based on representation

rather than a democracy, and divided the national government into three competitive and collaborating branches. They admitted that governing by force would sometimes be necessary, but since policing had not yet developed to a practicable level, the Framers did not yet have a notion of how to control the masses through anything other than a very clever institutional design to filter and contain their passions, for most of the time, and a strong, decentralized volunteer militia, for those moments when such institutions failed. Debates about the capital city reflected these concerns. The Founders undertook this novel task with very little preparation, for they "had no feeling for cities at all, little sense of what a city was, and little experience of what urban life meant." Prior to the settlement of "new worlds," authorities rarely invented cities, much less capitals; these simply evolved from prior sites of trading and protection. Most radically, the capital's founders intentionally sought to exclude commerce.[9] The London metropolis—distant, congested, and corrupt—was what they hoped to avoid.

Their deliberations on this issue rapidly produced a consensus, and a powerfully formative outcome. When the Federal Convention of 1787 considered a permanent capital, a temporary one had been installed in New York City for three years. Many delegates feared the issue would "excite . . . hostile passion against the system," particularly from representatives of cities that lost out. Virginia's George Mason proposed that the Constitution bar the national capital from any state capital site, since it would produce jurisdictional disputes and since the "intermixture" of the two legislatures would lend a "provincial tincture" to national deliberations. Others worried that a state might move its capital to a new site once the decision had been made. Elbridge Gerry of Massachusetts described "the general sense of America, that neither the Seat of State Government nor any large commercial City should be the seat of the General Government."[10] James Madison believed that lodging it in a central location was now more necessary, since the new government would wield more diverse powers, and would thus generate more government officials and petitioners, more often drawn from the interior. The convention altered his proposal to prevent the federal authority from "awing" any state by buying its territory and constructing forts and arsenals within it. The final text in Article I, Section 8, postponed the final choice of location, merely describing the legislative authority over territory not to exceed ten miles square.[11]

The Federalists noted that the exclusive authority the Constitution granted to the Union on this matter was rare but justified, since the system required a setting that cultivated independence for the national government. All state governments, indeed all national governments, exercised such powers; otherwise, local interests could interrupt the functioning of the institution, or local authorities could make national officials dependent on them for protection. In addition, the public works projects necessary for a capital would simply be too costly for a single state. Although most national politicians favored creating an independent capital city, Thomas Jefferson drove the negotiations which finally placed it. Having spent several years reflecting on the problem—and designing the capitol building—for Virginia, he reconciled Hamilton's northerners keen for the federal assumption of state debt with Madison's southerners, who favored an invented capital. The First Federal Congress passed the Residence Act on July 1, 1790, empowering the president to appoint and direct a three-man commission to oversee the purchase and development of a "Potowmack" site. The statute also moved the capital to Philadelphia for an interim ten-year period.[12] Jefferson's commitment to the location stemmed from his vision of what this city would represent. To be a place of moral influence that would escape the corruption fostered by an "overgrown commercial city," the site should be rural, rendering it at best a "secondary place of commerce." Jefferson also favored certain design features, including building codes to encourage a gracious uniformity, and a system of boulevards to carve out spacious parks and open squares. He hoped his instructions would help planners create a city that would portray "both republican dignity and elevation of spirit in every phase of design and construction . . . making the Federal City a fit expression of America's aspirations." To insulate the design process from new local interests, he insisted that the president govern street layout and public architecture and regulate the construction of private houses. Necessary funds would come only from the profits of District land sales, for involving Congress might reopen the question of placement. New Yorkers and Philadelphians still saw their cities as natural capitals, and he sought to minimize their influence.[13] The Founders' decision to bypass these cities elevated a popular set of Jeffersonian values of "rural prosperity and peace" that had little use for big cities.[14]

A properly designed capital was now essential. When George Washington fired Major Pierre Charles L'Enfant in 1792 after only a year's work on site, the president still celebrated and retained most of his design, including the wide avenues radiating across a grid of narrower streets which the engineer created to promote rapid and even settlement.[15] Capitol Hill's planned mansions and public squares would provide the common space necessary for a well-functioning capital and suited Washington's vision of making the District into "the seat of an empire as great as Rome." According to James Young, the capital's "community plan of 1791" better previewed an image of the new government as seen by the men who planned it than did the "constitutional plan of 1787." Force was not to be a source of its greatness. Absent were battlements, stockades, or protective barriers, which ill-suited a community imagined as open to interchange from all sides by wide routes.[16] Nearly empty, isolated from the nation's major activities, the location was not immediately popular. Sales of lots proceeded embarrassingly slowly. A disputed bridge over Rock Creek collapsed. When Jefferson solicited designs for the president's mansion in newspaper advertisements, months passed before two arrived.[17] Little changed for decades, but some observers viewed the idea's sluggish reception as appropriate for a relatively stateless polity.

"America has no great capital city," Tocqueville wrote some forty years later, "whose influence is felt over the whole extent of the country; this I hold to be one of the first causes of the maintenance of republican institutions in the United States." Cities, he reasoned in a Jeffersonian vein, resemble large impulsive assemblies that excite members to conspire and pursue "sudden and passionate resolutions," or influence administrators selfishly, and thus unjustly influence national politics.[18] Serious riots had recently struck Philadelphia and New York, but since these cities exercised no power over other districts or states, the unrest had no effect on the nation.[19] Indeed, it was fortunate that the new nation had no real metropolis since the American rabble—mainly free Blacks and undesirable Europeans lacking all civil rights—was even more threatening and formidable than in Europe, in part because the nation was underregulated. Murders and vigilante justice were relatively common, and states lacked laws against fraud and duties on alcoholic beverages. For all these reasons, Tocqueville feared the residents of American cities as threats to the security of the regime's democratic principles. The government needed an armed force, under the control of the majority, "to repress its excesses" and "to intimidate a discontented minority."[20]

This would rarely be necessary, he argued, since the American system promoted social order in a peculiar way. The states rarely attempted any "general police regulations," and American authorities lacked the administrative capacity, such as state police or passports, necessary to investigate crime. Still, criminals rarely eluded punishment because "everyone conceives himself to be interested in furnishing evidence of the crime and in seizing the delinquent." American criminal justice was mild and hardly dependent on capital punishment due to the moral legitimacy of its laws. Tocqueville used the example of policing to argue that the American spirit of civic enterprise, while imperfect, was superior to centralized administration.[21] The tension in his work—between some reasonable and even productive level of creative disorder, and the self-reliance and opportunities it engendered on the one hand, and the danger of excessive state centralization and repression on the other—again reflects the contradiction at the core of American agency concerning the terms by which citizens can reconcile their agency in pursuing individual goals with their agency as servants of a higher authority. Despite their anxieties concerning the resolution of this tension, and in part because they lacked a sophisticated sense of how to regulate the masses, the Founders chose to place their invented capital in unsettled land. The placement and design of the capital city was a quintessential formative act, and would significantly shape the nature of local challenges to order as well as the options of police administrators and reformers in responding to them.

Police played no role; despite their creativity in designing new and complex government machinery, the Framers had no sense of police forces, for they had not yet been invented in modern form.

D.C. Police as Dual Agents: Administration and Operations

Since police in capital cities, unlike most municipal police, regularly face large, politically motivated crowds, such police may execute the will of national as well as local authorities. Thus we can imagine how authoritative political structures may be both a cause and an effect of police behavior during protest events. Protesters, however, generally seek to destabilize authority and generate trouble, or uncertainty. Police agency in turn creates two forms of uncertainty: on-the-job trouble (the disruption protest causes, which demands instant and discretionary operational reactions) and in-the-job trouble (the authoritative and administrative pressures brought down from superiors).[22] Police attempt to reduce uncertainty in confrontations with protesters through spatial strategies; for example, by "taking the ground," that is, capturing territory and effectively turning public space into "police property." Police also use physical or human barriers to restrain marchers from deviating from an agreed-upon route or to channel them into public parks; they also neaten marches by assisting protesters and observers or by stopping stragglers.[23] Complicating matters over time, protesters have learned more about police tactics and the rights provided to them by law. Police, in turn, have learned to try to draw protesters into the task of pursuing the consensual value of public safety. For example, authorities now require protest organizations to provide them with a planned route for marches, and can insist on changing the route to address security concerns or traffic congestion. Such police tactics can be seen as a general effort to shift events from the realm of uncertain operations toward planned administration.[24]

The fact that police work seeks to control space justifies a closer look at how the capital's built structure—conceptualized here as Jeffersonian placement and design—directed demonstrators and police toward certain kinds of engagements. First, the effect of geographic placement is most apparent in a chronic lack of local police capacity. Since the Founders purposefully separated the capital from New York City and Philadelphia, and thus the administrative capacity of those cities and their state governments, District police administrators lacked what would have been a large force rooted in state and local institutions and parties, one capable of patrolling a vast metropolis.[25] Second, over time, separate units emerged with narrow missions to patrol particular turf: Capitol, Park, Metropolitan, Secret Service, and White House police units did not train or patrol together as an integrated urban police force.[26] Third, the District's placement between Virginia and Maryland meant that local policemen held relatively "southern," or antidemocratic attitudes toward Blacks and women, or at least that federal authorities and marchers often believed they did. Finally, the District territory was governed by an aberrant system of federal and congressional oversight—in effect by part-time residents. The system generally lacked the electoral mechanisms by which city residents normally hold local authorities accountable for underperforming municipal services like the police. It also enabled a president to intervene directly in local police operations when his political standing was at risk. These four factors repeatedly, if indirectly, influenced police administration as it prepared for protest events. Most obviously, undermanned metropolitan forces continually struggled to control large crowds. This incapacity repeatedly forced administrators to prepare for large crowds by patching together a force from a variety of specialized units, by temporarily deputizing "special" policemen, and by borrowing forces from surrounding towns and cities.

The design and layout of the city shaped both the course of specific events and police operations as well. Most organizers of demonstrations planned their marches to exploit the symbolism of certain routes and features of the built environment. When marchers chose not to channel themselves along lines suggested by the built environment, they appeared radically disorganized and disorderly to police. Even a disciplined and ritualized march could be threatening, however, if authorities believed that the social and racial attitudes of the police might lead to excessive force. Eventually authorities learned to collaborate directly with march leaders to control and channel rallies onto harmless ground, namely the Mall. Police chiefs and presidents contended with a local force that occasionally seemed both incapable of controlling—and capable of overreacting to— any serious confrontation. In sum, the effects of the city's design varied across these cases, as a product of the particular choices protesters made about engaging the environment.

Difficulties in successfully organizing and deploying the city's police force were apparent from the beginning. In August 1861, Congress, concerned about pro-Southern feeling in the District, established the Metropolitan Police Department, supervised by a Police Board consisting of local mayors and presidential appointees, who were required to take a loyalty oath.[27] The Board struggled with staffing, salary, and morale problems, and in 1878 Congress abolished it, shifting responsibility directly to city commissioners appointed by Congress. The force always lacked funding and personnel.[28] At the turn of the century, local observers believed D.C. to be America's "most inadequately policed city." In 1908, Superintendent Richard Sylvester admitted that he lacked the resources necessary to root out "the hold-up evil," and like all subsequent chiefs he called on Congress to fund additional police officers.[29] His force was incapable of controlling even peaceful gatherings. Facing the crowded Grand Army Reunion of 1902, Sylvester secured reinforcements of 350 special policemen,

150 citizen assistants, and 75 detectives from other major cities. To keep residents off the streets, officers used heavy cables to rope off Pennsylvania Avenue from the Capitol to the Treasury Building for three days. This route immediately became the most popular for parades. L'Enfant's artful design had anchored a sense of the separation of powers by placing the buildings housing the executive and legislative branches at opposite ends of a grand, central axis, one of many named after a state of the Union. As crowds gathered along the same avenue for the inauguration of President-elect William Howard Taft in 1908, Congress again temporarily augmented Sylvester's force with approximately five hundred "special policemen," who wore nickel-plated badges to make themselves more noticeable.[30] Again and again in subsequent episodes, over-matched police forces struggled to gain control of events shaped in varying ways by physical layout.

When Alice Paul and the National American Woman Suffrage Association led five thousand demonstrators on March 3, 1913, the built environment helped determine the behavior of both protesters and police. Because Washington was "primarily" a southern city, organizers downplayed calls for an interracial march. Paul planned a dramatic procession and pageant to "co-opt the symbolic grandeur of the increasingly monumental capital" and take full advantage of the national attention focused on the inauguration of Woodrow Wilson to be held the following day. Such events had become elaborate demonstrations of presidential and governmental pomp and power, and the inaugural committee had refused to allow women to participate in the procession. For all these reasons, Paul sought for her march the now-familiar route from the Congress to the White House, and planned a silent, dramatic pageant for the front steps of the Treasury Building. When petitioned for permission, Police Superintendent Sylvester thought Pennsylvania Avenue—and its bowery district of bars and flophouses—improper for the women; he proposed that the march follow Sixteenth Street, known as "Executive Avenue" for its large mansions housing respectable city elites. Paul rejected this proposal as confounding her plans "to use the central and most potent national spaces of the nation." The downtown area had recently grown more visually impressive. A city beautification campaign had removed railroad tracks from Pennsylvania Avenue; workers had recently completed the House and Senate office buildings, a National Museum on the Mall, and the West Wing of the White House.[31] Organizers formed the event to benefit from the city's built structure in other ways. Modeled on an inaugural or military parade, the march began in disciplined rows. At the Treasury Building, marchers would meet a separate group staging an allegorical pageant in the plaza fronting the classically designed structure. Evoking the stone statutory that graced the city, female figures robed to represent Columbia, Liberty, Charity, Peace, and Hope silently personified the ideals which men and women would join together to achieve.[32]

With personnel levels inadequate to patrol such an extraordinary event, Sylvester again augmented them with temporary deputies. Despite deploying the largest force ever arrayed against a public event in Washington, D.C., and despite fronting the march with a unit of police vehicles, Sylvester and his men rapidly lost control of the crowd, which closed in on the suffragists, throwing stones and jostling and cursing at them. When it became clear that the more than seven hundred regular and special policemen either could not or cared not to impose order—New York City by comparison fielded nearly 11,000 police officers in 1913—Sylvester called on U.S. Army cavalry to assist them in clearing the streets. A Congressional investigation concluded that "the District government needed more control over the streets." In the end, the disruption allowed advocates of suffrage to argue its necessity: "everything that was in the hands of women on Monday was a success; the one thing in the hands of men went to smash."[33] Most importantly, the unexpected violence introduced many Americans to the goals and arguments of the suffrage movement.

When National Women's Party suffragists returned to Washington after the 1916 elections, Paul chose to picket the White House. Again staking out a symbolic space, the marchers again confronted a fragmented and ineffective force. Sylvester's successor, Raymond W. Pullman, called in visiting detectives and even incorporated five hundred Boy Scouts into a security detail to assist police along the march line. At the time of the U.S. entry in the World War, the government had little capacity for self-protection: in the Treasury Department, a small Secret Service force handled counterfeiting, a small group of men guarded the White House, a force of mostly political appointees patrolled the Capitol, and a small Bureau of Investigation supplemented these deployments. The circling protesters ignored a June 1917 order to disperse from the White House, and on August 14, an angry crowd of sailors and workers attacked them. Police did nothing to stop this, and the unrest continued for four days. In October, officers arrested Paul for carrying a sign using one of Wilson's slogans: "The Time Has Come to Conquer or Submit." From solitary confinement in a psychiatric ward, she managed to communicate with her supporters and gain public sympathy as a political prisoner. In November, Wilson acted to free Paul, and when informed of his support for the federal suffrage amendment, she halted the pickets. Paul's very public and irritating tactics confounded Wilson, who began to actively support the amendment. He could not countenance the obvious contradiction produced by fighting a war for democracy while repressing political speech and resisting women's suffrage. Paul's tactics and the police response to them, combined with the lobbying of Carrie Chapman Catt, clearly helped convince Wilson to support suffrage.[34]

Police administrators seemed to gain mastery over demonstrations as

time passed, in part due to new equipment, legal authority, and tactics, including force. They also benefited from the increasing routinization of
marches. The next two superintendents, Harry L. Gessford and Daniel Sullivan, still lacked the resources to control disorder. Crime in the District
reached such alarming proportions by the summer of 1919 that both government officials and local citizens demanded military police patrols until
Congress provided adequate funds.[35] Prompted in part by the Paul
episode, Sullivan helped craft legislation which created a special White
House police force. Although this freed thirty-three men for other duties,
a Shriners meeting in June 1923 still forced Sullivan to augment his forces
with borrowed officers. In August 1925, when acting superintendent
Charles A. Evans granted the Ku Klux Klan a parade permit, he required
the marchers to forego their hoods, and insisted that the Klan's application
include $1,000 to cover the cost of lining Pennsylvania Avenue with cables
to contain up to 150,000 onlookers. For the first time in decades, Evans ordered his force to deploy with "full equipment"; officers, poised for emergency, discarded their white gloves and carried batons. Other "warlike
preparations" included calling out all active and reserve force members
and assigning nearly three hundred patrolmen to cover the cables. Once
the Klansmen reached the monument grounds, where the police had
roped off a separate collection area for them, U.S. Marines assumed monitoring duties. The parade produced no violence, but the public, concerned with the repression of legitimate political speech, criticized Evans
for his severe methods.[36]

As police superintendent Edwin B. Hesse assumed office, he faced additional criticism of excessive force. Residents complained that the police
fired recklessly while chasing rumrunners' cars on busy streets; others complained of brutality and illegal searches. A crime wave in 1926–27
prompted him to request appropriations for new automobiles, motorcy-
cles, armored cars equipped with machine guns and tear gas bombs, and
radio and teletype systems. In 1926, 75,000 KKK demonstrators again
marched down Pennsylvania Avenue from the Capitol to the Treasury Department. A year later when 100,000 people gathered to honor Charles A.
Lindbergh, Hesse placed approximately 500 policemen along the cabled
route. Both parades unfolded without incident.[37]

Seeking to readjust the balance between social control and free assembly, administrators lessened the department's reliance on force just as the
Depression began. In 1930, District commissioners sought to address the
department's corruption and brutality problems by selecting a police superintendent, Major Pelham Glassford, who had no prior police experience. Two years later, when waves of veterans descended on the capital, the
protest appeared benign enough. Their original petition asked for permission for only one thousand veterans to parade on Pennsylvania Avenue,
meet the president, and be provided with food and shelter. With President

Herbert Hoover's cooperation, Glassford, who had served as an officer in the Expeditionary Force of 1918, first sought to accommodate them with a tolerant policy that granted demonstrators relatively free access to the capital and provided them with tents and rolling kitchens. When asked to help maintain order, the Bonus Expeditionary Force (BEF) cooperated and ejected suspected agitators from its ranks.[38] But unlike previous marchers, the participants installed themselves in ramshackle encampments scattered throughout the city, and more continued to arrive. As estimates of attendance reached 50,000 in early June, the city commission claimed that Glassford's friendly stance only attracted demonstrators.[39]

An undermanned force again lost control of a political demonstration using the capital territory in an unorthodox manner. Violence erupted on July 28, 1932, after one veteran threw a brick at a police officer, who shot him dead. Federal troops under the command of Chief of Staff Douglas MacArthur responded to orders from Secretary of War Patrick Hurly to join with the Metropolitan Police, and "surround the affected area and clear it without delay." Federal soldiers invaded the city's numerous camps and with tear gas and bayonets forcefully drove the BEF across the Anacostia River. This encounter took the life of one man and injured sixty. While President Hoover had seemed reluctant to approve MacArthur's orders, and his uninspired and maladroit response to the Depression had probably already sealed his fate, this tragic outcome effectively doomed his presidency.[40] It was, as Rexford Tugwell remarked years later, Hoover's "final failure—the symbolic end." David Kennedy considered the debacle "the lowest ebb of Hoover's political fortunes."[41]

New itinerant and indigent groups caused police administrators to invent new crowd control methods to maximize the power of their limited personnel. Glassford's replacement, Ernest W. Brown, promised Washington a "sane and unspectacular police administration," but the Depression activated new claimants. Rejecting the Framers' vision of an accessible capital space, the District Commission hoped to prevent another deadly debacle by controlling entry to the city. If any group arrived without a clear purpose, a police officer was to stop it until officials could determine its motives. For a hunger march of 10,000 participants, Brown equipped all divisions of the police with an ample supply of gas bombs, ordered a close watch on all "local agitators," and refused to provide protesters with food or shelter. Brown dealt with a second hunger march in early December 1932, when five hundred farmers called for financial relief. Residents and officials alike asked whether the police had the authority to bar such groups from entering the capital. After meeting with the D.C. Commission and the U.S. attorney general, Brown announced that the farmers could enter the city if they did not form a parade. Numerous civic and business associations supported his policy of warning protesters to turn back unless they were financially self-sufficient.[42] Despite these warnings, some 4,000 men, women, and children entered the city to discover 1,700 policemen awaiting them. With 10,000 marines standing by, the police surrounded the protesters as they marched. Brown created what the *Post* referred to as a "concentration camp" on New York Avenue, where protesters slept, surrounded by a wall of officers five deep, reinforced by soldiers directly behind them with tear gas bombs. Only individuals or pairs of people could leave the camp, effectively preventing any organized demonstration in another area. Brown also placed detachments of guards at strategic points: the White House, Capitol, Treasury, electric and gas plants, and Marine and National Guard arsenals. He cited such new tactics and technologies when noting that crime fell to "one of the lowest ebbs" in 1933.[43]

But authorities understood that these new techniques of physical monitoring and containment might actually spark violence. In the spring of 1941, A. Philip Randolph announced a call for ten thousand Blacks to converge on the capital to demand equal access to opportunities in the defense mobilization. Throughout May and June, various associates of President Roosevelt, including Eleanor Roosevelt and NYC Mayor Fiorello LaGuardia, tried to convince Randolph to cancel the march, set for July 1. Administration loyalists worried that it would occur during a time of great international instability and—due to yet another apparent crime wave in Washington—local instability and police incapacity. At a June 13 meeting between Randolph, La Guardia, Walter White, and others, Eleanor Roosevelt explained that while she fully supported the movement's goals and ideals, "the attitude of the Washington police, most of them Southerners, and the general feeling of Washington itself are such that I fear there may be trouble if the march occurs." Randolph replied that "there would be no violence unless her husband ordered the police to crack black heads." LaGuardia warned that the South-leaning police force would not look kindly upon the protesters: "You are going to get Negroes slaughtered!" Randolph simply maintained that the marchers, which he now estimated at 100,000, would be orderly. The Metropolitan Police were known to use brutal tactics on Black residents, and responded grudgingly to the organizers' permit requests. The president, too, feared violence. On June 18, when FDR met with civil rights leaders and defense officials, he warned that "somebody might get killed" if the march proceeded as planned. The following day, LaGuardia recommended that the president approve an executive order that would render defense contract hiring nondiscriminatory and notify unions and agencies of their obligation to halt unfair practices. On June 24, Randolph negotiated the final language of the order and canceled the march. The next day, President Roosevelt signed Executive Order 8802, establishing the Committee on Fair Employment Practice to "'receive and investigate' complaints of discrimination."[44] In this case, presidential uncertainty regarding local police capacity was the primary cause of an unprecedented and substantial policy concession to African Americans, the first decisive break from a decades-long tradition of federal indifference to racial inequality.

In the 1960s, federal authorities developed new approaches to the problems of police incapacity and protest that exploited symbolic space. In the spring of 1963, when Martin Luther King, Jr., and a variety of civil rights groups agreed that a march on Washington should focus on economic inequality, authorities and protesters collaborated to pursue their mutual interest in demonstrating the legitimacy of the movement's ideals. When asked about it in July, President John Kennedy praised the movement's "cooperation with the police" in pursuing the "great tradition" of marching on the capital. Such protests, a policeman noted, had become a "national habit." A. Philip Randolph, directing the march, and his several co-chairs all agreed at the urging of the White House that marchers would not engage in civil disobedience or lobby members of Congress, despite the recent effectiveness of coercive direct action in Birmingham, Alabama. The White House, sympathetic to the movement's claims and sensitive to international opinion, hoped to gain momentum from the event for its civil rights legislation pending in Congress. The executive and the marchers shared an interest in preventing violence at all costs, and an orderly demonstration broadcast nationally and internationally would help frame the reformers' claims as legal and wholly American. While many politicians feared violence, once President Kennedy publicly endorsed the rally, the Metropolitan Police Department worked with the administration and the march leadership to develop a plan for maintaining order. The Metro Police planned to keep all officers on duty on August 28, and to supplement them with firefighters and police reservists. The administration mobilized two thousand National Guardsmen, called out every Capitol, White House, and Park Police officer, and added three thousand additional soldiers to the one thousand already in the area. The White House actively aided the marchers and monitored preparations. A Justice Department staffer, for example, worked full-time on logistics, while the Voice of America planned to broadcast reports in thirty-six languages. The organizers also sought to gain credit for a peaceful protest by policing themselves; a large deployment of black New York City police officers would marshal the parade.[45]

March organizers made critical concessions concerning the route of the event. While Bayard Rustin's original plan placed the marchers—estimated at 100,000—directly in front of both the Capitol and the White House, later negotiations moved them out of these areas. The Kennedy administration did not want the group to mass near the Capitol, agitating members of Congress, nor did they want their energies aimed at the president. Organizers conceded that the scale of the demonstration made the traditional Pennsylvania Avenue route unworkable. The new plan concentrated them at the Mall, where they would stream in two columns along Constitution and Independence Avenues toward the Lincoln Memorial. With its museums and monumental vistas, the Mall "posed fewer security challenges and less general disruption to the city or the federal government." The committee worked hard to exclude radical sentiments from the event, supplying all signs to the marchers with approved messages. As some 250,000 marchers descended on the Mall, John Lewis agreed to soften the rhetoric of his speech, and the march and rally proceeded entirely peaceably, amplifying and propelling Rev. King's remarkable oration worldwide. Police found themselves directing traffic and parking, and caring for lost or fatigued visitors. Organizers even addressed the problem of travelers laying over. Unlike previous demonstrators, these marchers departed promptly "because of the decisions about security and layout made by the organizers and authorities."[46] Although this fusion of challenger and authority interests remains rare, structured police agency continued in later decades to develop toward the more complete pacification of capital protest, through the accumulated wisdom gained from numerous discrete episodes of policing. Challengers would never again exercise as much leverage over the police as they had in the early decades of the twentieth century, when they developed new forms and techniques of mass mobilization and participation to demand civil rights, to question the rise and nature of new forms of central state administrative capacity, and to help steer the gradual nationalization of American politics. The capital, by the time of the Civil Rights Movement, was becoming a safe setting for the cooperative staging of planned encounters between protesters and authorities. The Framers had only a dim view of this eventuality; police administrators and officers were primarily responsible for the outcome.

Structure and Agency in Resolving Episodes of Capital Protest

Currently, the three primary branches of the Washingon, D.C., police—Park, Metropolitan, and Capitol—manage between fifteen hundred and two thousand protests each year.[47] Over the course of the twentieth century these institutions have refined their strategies and tactics by repeatedly fitting their discretionary operations to crowds channeled by enduring built structures. Several analytic tendencies of historical institutionalism enable it to address such examples of the interaction of agency and structure in political change. First, it takes structure seriously, grounding analysis in macroanalysis of the evolution of institutions, or constellations of institutions, over substantial periods of time, given certain material and ideological foundations. Thus, the work takes large-scale structures as foundational. Second, most historical institutionalists recognize how particular historical moments and particular institutional arrangements offer individuals and organizations specific—even unique—strategic opportunities, as well as a range of political mechanisms and tactics to pursue them. Temporal sequence is of course central to such explanations. Thus, such work takes each particular context seriously. Finally, the careful reconstruction of very short-term political processes allows analysts to gauge the independent effects of nonsystemic factors, including what appear to be accidents of history, such as the path of an assassin's bullet, or a leader's choice between two equally reasonable strategies. Thus, historical insitutionalism can recognize contingency, discretion, and the absence of likelihood within particular events. In sum, a layered analysis of longue durée factors, intermediate political organizational and institutional factors, and short-term contingent events allows us to perceive the distinctive contributions of agency within consequential political movements to reform or police structures of authority and power. Such work can point scholars toward critical political junctures—at which human agency, channeled by structures to be sure, constrains, affirms, or shifts subsequent political change and development.

Given the centrality, and tenuousness, of basic physical security in transitional democracies today, it is important to use such frameworks to investigate the problem of policing disorder through formative acts, and then along the trajectories of political development they launch. From its earliest conception, the capital has functioned as a site for collisions between historical agents bent on change and historical agents charged with maintaining order. It should not surprise us that paths set in stone should have structured and constrained the agency of both authorities and challengers. But clearly agency has shaped those same structures in turn, in a variety of ways. Indeed, the largest share of agency in American politics is system-maintaining. Some forms of this conserving agency purposefully create system-maintaining or -stabilizing structures, like Jefferson's push to separate the capital from urban social forces. Other forms of agency, like police agency, directly aim at controlling challengers to the established order, through both individual choice and by executing the will of a structuring authority. In doing so, they personify Block's dual agency.

The analytical challenge is to use categories and concepts drawn from the structure-agency continuum to consider causal mechanisms connecting the various tiers. The mechanisms posited here focus first on the relationships between the contingent formative actions of Thomas Jefferson and his allies and the enduring placement and design of the American capital. Second, the analysis describes the effects of placement on administration, and of design on operations (see Figure 2). The figure depicts the longer-term social and political mechanisms by which individual agency generated enduring structures that shaped the preparation or stance of the police responding to protests. To the extent that authorities have bureaucratized and routinized such operations, they have managed to shift much of their operational work toward the less discretionary realm of administration, reducing uncertainty in this type of political contestation.

The Federalists' fear of insurrection driven by faction or inequality compelled them to build institutions for a mass polity that was not fully or

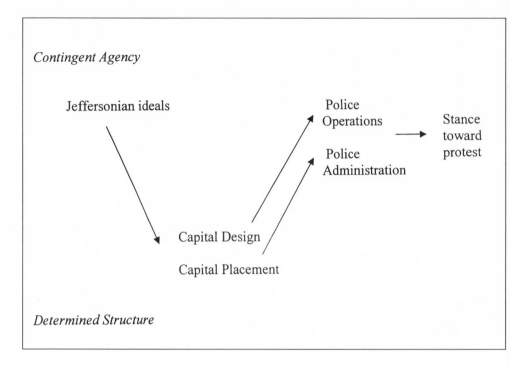

Figure 2. Structure engaging agency: posited causal relationships among selected factors influencing the policing of protest in Washington, D.C.

evenly enfranchised.[48] In part because of this, they imagined and invented an independent, uncorrupted capital. The effects of this decision were manifold. The scale and intensity of collective protest aimed at federal authorities and representatives, the response of local counter-demonstrators, and the capacity of local police would have all been greater had the capital been placed "naturally" in New York. The creation of a new city and the physical separation of the city from the social forces animating protest meant that marchers would almost invariably be travelers, fewer in number and separated from social and organizational sources of support. In addition, the decision meant that the police, unable to draw on the deep resources of a major metropolitan police force, would continually lack capacity. Other placement effects included the city's relatively "southern" cultural atmosphere, and the administrative fragmentation of the police force. Taken together, these effects seem to have operated as Jefferson intended, to invent a city somewhat drained of the passions and interests of a metropolis. The capital's quasi-imperial urban design seems to have primarily favored authorities, although the effects of built structure varied across cases as a product of the degree to which the protesters conformed to the environment in their planning. Wide boulevards and monumental buildings suited the needs of challengers for symbolic display, but at the same time, by leading to the development of ritualized routes, especially the one connecting government branches along Pennsylvania Avenue, the design made the work of the police more predictable and systematic. Police clearly helped determine the outcomes of several critical demonstrations in the capital streets concerning female suffrage, the rights of the poor, and race equality. Since they valued stability, the Framers were wise to embrace the plans of Washington and Jefferson. Their favored bulwarks against a rapidly spreading organized movement—the fragmentation of authority through various vertical and horizontal institutional firebreaks—have made it more difficult for factional interests to build national coalitions. But these secondary mechanisms, the placement and design of an isolated, monumental capital, have functioned as they had hoped. The police, mastering their work over time, guard not only the streets but Jefferson's vision of a stable, republican capital city.

Chapter 7

Partisan Entrepreneurship and Policy Windows: George Frisbie Hoar and the 1890 Federal Elections Bill

Richard M. Valelly

The rise, fall, and aftermath of the 1890 Federal Elections Bill demonstrate that entrepreneurial defeat, not just accomplishment, has politically formative effects. Little known and poorly understood because it was never enacted, the Elections Bill and its history nonetheless carry an important lesson: failure's repercussions can be pronounced when talented politicians pushing a transformative idea nearly pull it off—the materialization of a grave threat to one side can incite an even more radical reaction. When Senator George Frisbie Hoar (R-Mass.) led the Republican Party's 1889–91 effort simultaneously to revive African American voting rights and the Southern Republican parties, he built on existing law and exceptionally favorable (if today obscure) Supreme Court precedents. Impressed and alarmed by the boldness of his stroke, Democrats struck back. Indeed, they repealed the Reconstruction-era federal elections statutes altogether.

The cycle began in 1888, when the Republican presidential platform began with a call for "effective legislation to secure the integrity and purity of elections. . . . We charge that the present Administration [the Cleveland Admistration] and the Democratic majority in Congress [the House] owe their existence to the suppression of the ballot by a criminal nullification of the Constitution and laws of the United States."[1] Then, during the 51st Congress, 1889–91, when Republicans exercised unified control of national government for the first time since 1883, Hoar, a longtime advocate of black voting rights, coordinated the Republican party's consideration of the Elections Bill. The measure implemented Article I, Section 4 of the Constitution, granting Congress the authority to manage its own elections. The bill transferred the administration of U.S. House elections from the states to the federal judiciary, bypassing Southern Democratic governors and state elections officials.

After House passage on July 2, 1890, the Republican elections initiative triggered a Senate showdown in late 1890 and early 1891—a thirty-three-day filibuster—that is still studied for its political lessons. The Democratic filibuster cracked the Republicans' cohesion, leading a silver Republican bloc to hijack the floor for a full nine days to enact a silver coinage measure. When Republicans regained control they sought to abolish the filibuster. But the bill instead died on January 26, 1891, when a silver Republican exploited the absence from the floor of a fifth of the Republican caucus. He adroitly moved that the Senate consider new business, a motion that carried—after a dramatic delay of several days to verify the count, which was 35 to 34. Table 1 shows the vote on whether to continue debate (that is, to table the motion for new business).[2]

TABLE 1. SENATE VOTE OF JANUARY 26, 1891, TO CONTINUE DEBATE ON THE FEDERAL ELECTIONS BILL

Party	Yeas	Nays	Not voting	Total
Republican	34	6	11	51
Democrat	0	29	8	37
Total	34	35	19	

Source: Xi Wang, *The Trial of Democracy: Black Suffrage and Northern Republicans, 1860–1910* (Athens: University of Georgia Press, 1997), 249, table 6.3. Note that the actual date of the vote was January 26, 1891, but Senate procedure produced a vote on the "*legislative* day" of January 22.

End of story? Not quite. Democrats might have moved on to other issues, such as monetary and tariff policy. But they chose differently. Despite the passage of eighteen months time, Democrats actually ran against the Federal Elections Bill in 1892. The national 1892 platform of the Democratic party denounced the Harrison administration's "tendency to centralize all power at the Federal capital" and immediately turned in the first sentence of the platform's second paragraph to "*the policy of Federal control of elections, to which the Republican party has committed itself*" (emphasis added), warning that it was "fraught with the gravest dangers, scarcely less momentous than would result from a revolution . . . establishing monarchy on the ruins of the Republic." For their part, Republicans did back off a bit, putting the issue lower in the platform. Nonetheless the GOP platform proclaimed, "We demand that every citizen of the United States shall be allowed to cast one free and unrestricted ballot in all public elections . . . the party will never relax its efforts until the integrity of the ballot . . . shall be guaranteed and protected in every State."[3]

The issue of Southern elections administration defined national interparty conflict in 1892. As matters happened, Democrats gained unified control from 1893 to 1895 (previously achieved during the antebellum Buchanan administration.) They promptly used *their* window of opportu-

nity to repeal the federal elections statutes that enforced the Fifteenth
Amendment. A House committee report demanded that "every trace of reconstruction measures be wiped from the books." If the Republicans were
going to trot out a new statute, then Democrats were simply going to get
rid of federal election statutes.[4]

The cycle that stretched from 1888 to 1894 in the end resembled a
"boomerang"—to use Theda Skocpol's term from a different policy context.[5] Hoar's policy entrepreneurship had supremely high stakes. If the bill
had passed—again, it failed by only one vote—then the formal-legal disenfranchisement of Black Southerners might have stalled. Instead, Hoar and
his copartisans touched off a Democratic drive to dismantle the federal
elections statutes—thereby destroying much of what Hoar and many other
Republicans had long fought for. The damage to African American interests was incalculable. Not until the 1957 Civil Rights Act did Congress reen-
ter the field of voting rights for blacks.

How best to dissect this remarkable sequence of political events?[6] My
contribution is to apply John Kingdon's idea of a *policy window*, from his
classic analysis, *Agendas, Alternatives, and Public Politics.*[7] The "Republican
policy window" from the 1868 through the 1888 presidential elections
shows that the window for Hoar was relatively large. I frame who Hoar was
and what he brought to the Federal Elections Bill, the statutory and judicial precursors that augmented its threat to the Democratic party, and the
regulatory scheme it envisioned—built on a system the Supreme Court had
emphatically approved. The impact of the bill on Southern politics alone
would have been zero-sum for the Democratic party, but it had other bleak
implications as well for Democrats. These events illustrate my primary concern: what can happen to an entrepreneur's goals when she or he engages
zero-sum party conflict.

The Size of the Policy Window

To measure Reconstruction and post-Reconstruction policy windows—as
they might have been perceived—I devise two scores (see Table 2). The
first score sums the *change* in Republican strength, positive or negative, in
the Electoral College vote (expressed as percentage points), the positive or
negative *change* in the numerical spread in the Senate, and the positive or
negative *change* in the numerical spread in the House, and then divides by
100 to yield a figure between 0 and 1. The second score comes from sum-
ming the *margins*, expressed in percentages for the Electoral College vote
and numerical spreads for the Senate and the House, and dividing by 100.
Both measures show that there was a substantial jump in the party's electoral vitality between 1884 and 1888. Substantial policy opportunities occurred for the first time since Reconstruction.

TABLE 2. REPUBLICAN POLICY WINDOWS, 1868–88

	1872	1876	1880	1884	1888
Size of change	.64	.17	.31	.15	.52
Size of margin	1.95	-.14	.5	-.43	.57

Source: Patricia Heidotting Conley, *Presidential Mandates: How Elections Shape the National Agenda* (Chicago: University of Chicago Press, 2001), 58–61, table 4.2; Kenneth C. Martis, *The Historical Atlas of Political Parties in the United States Congress 1789–1989* (New York: Macmillan, 1989), 127–43.

Who Hoar Was

What personal intellectual and political history did George Frisbie Hoar bring to this policy window? Although it was not obvious until late in the game, Hoar's factional influence peaked before the 1889–91 period. High noon had come for Hoar when he led the Half-Breed Republican faction that organized the 1880 Republican national convention and influenced the Garfield-Arthur administration.[8]

Nonetheless, going into the 1889–91 cycle Hoar was a formidable player. For one thing, his unswerving support for high tariffs and protection of home industries—and his slashing attacks on the Mugwumps in 1884—made it far easier for his colleagues to entertain his preoccupation with African American rights. Hoar stood for a happy harmony of interests. Without strong Southern Republican parties, the Republicans could never really be certain of the regular electoral and legislative majorities necessary for tariff legislation and revision. High tariffs, industrialization, partisan strength, and Fifteenth Amendment enforcement all went together.[9]

Hoar also knew more than most about election law. He was one of the House Republican appointments to the special electoral commission set up by Congress in 1877 to resolve the crisis of the 1876 presidential election. He chaired the Senate Committee on Privileges and Elections from 1881 through the 51st Congress. During his Senate career, 1877–1904, he "served as bill manager for numerous important measures," including shepherding the Electoral Count Act of 1887 (the measure that affected the 2000 election crisis in Florida) across three Congresses.[10]

Finally, Hoar never got ahead of his colleagues philosophically. He expressed, and may have actually held, a belief in so-called Anglo-Saxon superiority. But he also publicly insisted that white status resulted solely from favorable historical circumstances. Racist feelings were also socially dysfunctional: "in all these race difficulties and troubles, the fault has been with the Anglo-Saxon. . . . The white man has been the offender." For Hoar, the whole point of American fundamental law and democratic principles was inclusion and political progress for all citizens.[11]

Statutory and Judicial Precursors of the Federal Elections Bill

Hoar had yet another major advantage: the availability of potent electoral-regulatory tools that could be turned toward the effective protection of Black voting rights. The conventional wisdom is that all hope for Black suffrage succumbed to the overthrow of the Reconstruction governments, the apparent hostility of the Supreme Court to elections statutes targeted at the South, and, of course, the Compromise of 1877. But in actuality rich possibilities for Black voting rights survived.[12]

STATUTORY FOUNDATIONS

Woodrow Wilson's *Congressional Government* unwittingly describes the devices that had this potential. Wilson rails against "The federal supervisor who oversees the balloting for congressmen," a form of electoral regulation that for Wilson "represents the very ugliest side of federal supremacy."[13] This now cryptic literary relic offers a startling window into a once thriving legal-electoral reality. Federal supervisors? Of House elections? When did all this happen? Why?

The so-called very ugliest side of federal supremacy had three statutory foundations: the Immigration and Naturalization Act of 1870 and two federal elections bills enacted back-to-back in 1871 and 1872. It also had extremely strong support from the Supreme Court, something Wilson did not mention in *Congressional Government*. Let us briefly examine each statute, and the Court decisions that strengthened these federal laws.

Reacting in 1870 to the largest fraud ever devised in American electoral history—the production by Tammany Hall of sixty thousand naturalization papers a month before the 1868 elections in New York state, which tainted 16 percent of the state's presidential vote[14]—a Republican Congress placed federal elections administration in cities under direct national control with the 1870 Naturalization Act. It criminalized fraud in the naturalization and citizenship process. Under this statute, federal judges could also, in response to citizen petition, provide (in cities with upward of twenty thousand inhabitants) for bipartisan temporary federal supervision of elections to the House. In such cities, furthermore, Congress authorized the U.S. marshal for the district in which the city was located, "to appoint as many special deputies as may be necessary to preserve order at any election at which representatives in Congress are to be chosen . . . to preserve order . . . and to arrest for any offense or breach of the peace committed in their view."[15]

Then, in the 1871 Federal Elections Act, Congress judicialized the new regulatory scheme. Any two citizens of a city with a population in excess of twenty thousand could petition a federal judicial circuit for special bipartisan supervision of the House election in the district where the city was located. The federal supervisors were authorized to assure that no eligible person was omitted from the rolls and to strike the names of unauthorized voters. They were also permitted to assemble and maintain their own registration lists. On election day they and their deputies, as appointed by the U.S. marshal, physically surveilled the polling places from the time they opened until they closed, and could personally inspect and count ballots as they chose. Anyone caught interfering with any voter's right to vote could be brought immediately before a federal judge or commissioner.[16]

In about two years, then, midway through Reconstruction, Congress established an electoral-regulatory structure for U.S. House elections in urbanized districts. It did not operate everywhere; it affected (at most) about 14 percent of U.S. House districts.[17] With the 1872 Civil Appropriation Act, Congress subsequently extended the urban regulatory scheme to rural House districts—if only in part. Under Chapter 1425 of the Civil Appropriation Act of June 1872, any ten citizens of any congressional district could petition for federal *observers* (as opposed to the supervisors provided by the 1870 and 1871 statutes).[18]

JURISPRUDENTIAL FOUNDATIONS

This largely Northern system of federal electoral regulation received genuinely emphatic Supreme Court approval. In *ex parte Siebold*, 100 U.S. 371 (1879), the Court dealt with a case in which Baltimore elections officials physically prevented federal supervision of the federal elections in Baltimore in the fall of 1878. In *ex parte Clarke*, 100 U.S. 399 (1879), a companion to *Siebold*, the Court dealt with the prosecution of a Cincinnati city councilman who flagrantly mishandled ballots in violation of both Ohio and U.S. law during these federal elections. What the Court did was stunning: *it denied writs of habeas corpus in both cases.* The regulatory jailing of state and local elections officials was perfectly constitutional.

To accomplish this breathtaking result, the Court rested these 7-2 decisions on a centralizing and muscular reading of Article I, Section 4, of the Constitution, which states that "the Congress may at any time by law make or alter" regulations for the "times, places, and manner of holding elections for Senators and Representatives." Consequently, the Enforcement Act of May 31, 1870, and the supplement passed February 28, 1871, regulated "elections of members of the House of Representatives and were an assertion, on the part of Congress, of a power to pass laws for regulating and superintending said elections, and for securing the purity thereof, and the rights of citizens to vote thereat peaceably and without molestation." In violating these statutes, the petitioners violated the Constitution.

Several things were claimed by counsel for the Baltimore city elections judges (or so the opinion said). But all were wrong. The false propositions were the following: Congress had to completely superintend national elections or not at all, since "concurrent sovereignty" in electoral regulation was intrinsically impossible; it could not punish state and local elections officers for interfering with federal officials because the former were not required to protect federal interests; punishment of state and local officials amounted to double jeopardy; federal marshals could not act in states or cities, because law enforcement was a state and local prerogative; and Congress could not require federal circuit courts to appoint elections supervisors, who were executive, not judicial, officers. The opinion for the Court denied all of these propositions.

Article I, Section 4, had a "natural sense" that was "the contrary of that assumed by the counsel of the petititoners." Specifically, Congress could legislate as it saw fit, and if that resulted in "concurrent sovereignty" then the "paramount character" of the federal regulations "has the effect to supersede those made by the State, so far as the two are inconsistent, and no farther." The opinion went to on to add, "Let a spirit of national as well as local patriotism once prevail . . . and we shall hear no more about the impossibility of harmonious action between the national and State governments in a matter in which they have a mutual interest." As for prosecution of state and local elections officials, the United States had a constitutional interest in "the faithful performance . . . of their respective duties. This necessarily follows from the mixed character of the transaction, State and national. A violation of duty is an offence against the United States, for which the offender is justly amenable to that government. No official position can shelter him from this responsibility." After putting to one side the issue of double jeopardy, the majority opinion then exploded: "It seems to be often overlooked that a national constitution has been adopted in this country, establishing a real government therein, operating upon persons and territory and things." Thus it was "an incontrovertible principle, that the government of the United States may, by means of physical force, exercised through its official agents, execute on every foot of American soil the powers and functions that belong to it. . . . Why do we have marshals at all, if they cannot physically lay their hands on persons and things in the performance of their proper duties?" The alternative was to "drive the national government out of the United States, and relegate it to the District of Columbia, or perhaps to some foreign soil. We shall bring it to a condition of greater helplessness than that of the old confederation." As for the appointment of an elections supervisor by a federal circuit court, Congress could properly lodge that power in a federal circuit court.

The opinion for the Court in *Siebold* ended on a strongly nationalist note: "The true doctrine . . . is this, that whilst the States are really sovereign as to all matters which have not been granted to the jurisdiction and control of the United States, the Constitution and the constitutional laws of the latter are . . . the supreme law of the land; and when they conflict with the laws of the States, they are of paramount authority and obligation."[19]

It is hard to imagine a stronger endorsement of the federal electoral-regulatory scheme than the one which the Court provided. *But could these ideas help Black voters in Southern congressional districts?* If they did not, then there could never have been a Federal Elections Bill. The missing link is the remarkable 1884 case *ex parte Yarbrough*, 110 U.S. 651.

The case facts were unhappily familiar. Jasper Yarbrough, several kin, and other white males were involved in a Klan-like conspiracy to intimidate black voters in a U.S. House election in Georgia. The defense argued that there was no valid indictment or process under two former pieces of the federal elections acts (by then placed in the *Revised Statutes*, per the code revision of 1874). One section criminalized any conspiracy against a citizen's enjoyment of any right under the Constitution; the other criminalized conspiracy to obstruct voting in national elections. These sections of the code, the defense claimed, were simply unconstitutional.[20]

The defense's position was legally quite promising. Several Court decisions seemed to advantage it. These decisions came from black voting rights cases that got to the Court during and after the collapse of Reconstruction.[21] But in *Yarbrough* the Court broke free from these earlier cases, taking its cue instead from the ideas in *Siebold* and *Clarke*. The Court in fact *strengthened* Fifteenth Amendment enforcement by fusing it to the congressional regulatory power contained in Article I.

Speaking for a now unanimous Court, Justice Miller denied the defense's petition for a writ of habeas corpus. At stake was whether Congress could constitutionally protect the national electoral processes that selected representatives to Congress. Article I of the Constitution gave it ample authority to do so, and it was power that Congress had repeatedly exercised. "If this government is anything more than a mere aggregation of delegated agents of other states and governments, each of which is superior to the general government, it must have the power to protect the elections on which its existence depends, from violence and corruption. If it has not this power, it is left helpless before the two great natural and historical enemies of all republics, open violence and insidious corruption." To then draw the inferences that followed from this point, Miller took two tacks: description of how Congress always protected federal officers in the conduct of their duties, and of how Congress came to protect the elections which gave it form.

With respect to the protection of federal officers, Miller noted that Congress early on criminalized "offenses against person and property committed within the District of Columbia, and in forts, arsenals, and other places within the exclusive jurisdiction of the United States," but that "it was slow to pass laws protecting officers of the government from personal injuries inflicted while in discharge of their official duties within the states. This was not for want of power, but because no occasion had arisen which required such legislation." Miller then went on to trace congressional action to "protect government officers while in the exercise of their duty in a hostile community," touching on federal legislation to strengthen customs enforcement in the wake of the "nullification ordinance of South Carolina," and legislation to protect enrolling officers who enforced conscription during the Civil War.

With respect to congressional protection of the institution's electoral foundations, Congress had, similarly, "been slow to exercise the powers expressly conferred upon it in relation to elections by the fourth section of the first article of the Constitution. . . . It was not until 1842 that Congress took any action under the power here conferred" (a reference to the federally established requirement that each member of the House "should be elected by a separate district"). In February 1872, Congress again acted under its Article I, Section 4 power to require "all the elections for . . . members to be held on the Tuesday after the first Monday in November in 1876, and on the same day of every second year thereafter." Congress also required the two chambers of state legislatures to meet in joint convention and to continue meeting until they successfully chose a U.S. senator. Similarly, Congress "fixed a day, which is to be the same in all states, when the electors for president and vice-president shall be appointed."

Miller then asked, "Can it be doubted that Congress can, by law, protect the act of voting, the place where it is done, and the man who votes from personal violence or intimidation, and the election itself from corruption or fraud?" He added that "it is only because the Congress of the United States, through long habit and long years of forebearance, has, in deference and respect to the states, refrained from the exercise of these powers that they are now doubted." But if Congress needed "to make additional laws for the free, the pure, and the safe exercise of this right of voting, they stand upon the same ground, and are to be upheld for the same reasons."

Miller then turned to the right to vote—as distinct from the prior topics of congressional protection of federal officers and federal elections. Could the right to vote be federally protected? This was an obvious and necessary move for Miller to make; after all, the Constitution placed the power to set suffrage qualifications in the states. But Miller emphasized that matters had changed. "The fifteenth amendment . . . by its limitation on the power of the states in the exercise of their right to prescribe the qualifications of voters in their own elections, and by its limitation of the power of the United States over that subject, clearly shows that the right of suffrage was considered to be of supreme importance to the national government, and was not intended to be left within the exclusive control of the states." He then quoted the entire amendment, including Section 2, which reads "The Congress shall have power to enforce this article by appropriate legislation." Miller thus suggested that the Fifteenth Amendment was part of the general pattern of growing federal control which he had just described, and which dated to the United States' response to the nullification ordinance.

Miller agreed that the amendment "gives no affirmative right to the colored man to vote," but then announced that "it is easy to see that under some circumstances it may operate as the immediate source of a right to vote." After giving an illustration involving Delaware (where the Fifteenth Amendment automatically invalidated the state's constitutional "whites only" restriction), Miller held that "In such cases this fifteenth article of amendment does, *proprio vigore* [with its own force], substantially confer on the negro the right to vote, and congress has the power to protect and enforce that right."

Furthermore, the Fifteenth Amendment affected all national electoral processes.

> This new constitutional right was mainly designed for citizens of African descent. The principle, however, that the protection of the exercise of this right is within the power of Congress, *is as necessary to the right of other citizens to vote as to the colored citizen, and the right to vote in general as to the right to be protected against discrimination.* The exercise of the right in both instances is guarantied by the Constitution, and should be kept free and pure by congressional enactments whenever that is necessary. (emphasis added)

In a concluding passage, Miller sounded a warning: "If the recurrence of such acts as these prisoners stand convicted are too common in one quarter of the country, and give omen of danger from lawless violence, the free use of money in elections, arising from the vast growth of recent wealth in other quarters, presents equal cause for anxiety. If the government of the United States has within its constitutional domain no authority to provide against these evils . . . then, indeed, is the country in danger." Miller ended by writing, "The rule to show cause in this case is discharged, and the writ of habeas corpus denied."[22]

It is essential to step back and fully recognize the result: a *unanimous* Court ruled that in order to protect the electoral processes that made it a national representative assembly, Congress could protect the right to vote of any citizen, Black or white. Congress could therefore directly criminalize any *individual* behavior—not just the state and local official behavior of *Siebold* and *Clarke*—that tainted the integrity of national elections. To enforce such criminal law, the United States could constitutionally deploy and protect federal officials in the states and localities.

In 1888, just before the 51st Congress took up the Federal Elections Bill, one final signal came from the Court—and it too was unambiguously nationalist. In *ex parte Coy*, a 7-2 majority held that the United States properly fined and jailed elections officials in Indianapolis and elsewhere in Indiana for interfering with the U.S. House electoral process. The state and local elections officials claimed that they were immune from punishment under the federal statutes because their admittedly corrupt handling of ballots was intended only to influence the results of state and local elections, not the House election. The Court dismissed the claim, and it did so on the ground that during the elections the state and local elections officials had, for all intents and purposes, become officers of the United States and were subject to the jurisdiction of the United States.[23]

By this point it should be obvious how potent the Federal Elections Bill's constitutional, statutory, and judicial antecedents were. The first was an Article I, federal electoral-regulatory system devised by the Republican party during the Reconstruction. The second was strong Supreme Court approval for this Article I system—approval which it reiterated in 1888, just before the 51st Congress. The third antecedent was Supreme Court endorsement of a conceptual and legal fusion of the Article I system to the Fifteenth Amendment's implications for the protection of voting rights for African Americans. For some time a majority of the Court had been quite uncomfortable with federal electoral regulation to protect black voting rights that was based on the Civil War Amendments. But the entire Court appeared quite certain, some six years before Congress considered the Federal Elections Bill, that the United States could criminally enforce the Fifteenth Amendment against private action in U.S. House elections under Article I. The possible consequences for Southern election administration were striking. It is time now to turn to the Federal Elections Bill itself—and Hoar's role in its creation.

The Federal Elections Bill Itself

The idea for an elections bill, in Hoar's mind, dated to the aftermath of the 1884 elections. Hoar determined to introduce some sort of new national elections bill. Doing so must have meant admitting two things to himself: that the Supreme Court had broken beyond repair the Reconstruction elections statutes that directly implemented the Fourteenth and Fifteenth Amendments, and that previous post-Reconstruction Southern strategies— counting on Southern promises (President Hayes's approach) or building independent party movements (President Arthur's approach)—were insufficient.

Speaking to the Commonwealth Club of Boston on December 27, 1884, Hoar announced a decision to "consecrate" himself to the "cause" of erecting a "system of laws, institutions, and administration under which . . . millions of men will represent the Black race in the manhood and citizenship of this republic."[24] During the 50th Congress, the Senate Committee on Privileges and Elections, chaired by Hoar, reported on its investigation into the 1886 elections in Washington County, Texas, which left three African Americans dead from lynching. In a dress rehearsal for the epic conflict to come, Democrats prevented a vote on the main recommendation, "that the Committee on Privileges and Elections be directed carefully to revise the existing laws relating to elections of members of Congress, with a view of providing for the more complete protection of the exercise of the elective franchise." Hoar got to work anyway on drafting a bill.[25]

When the policy window opened during the 51st Congress, the *Siebold-Yarbrough* jurisprudence immediately influenced how Republicans addressed federal electoral regulation. It encouraged Hoar and others to take the implications of Article I, Section 4, to the next step, a fully national approach. Hoar did not start out by building on the regulatory system just described, but instead worked up a new system of dual registration and elections for national elections that was initially roughed out by Senator John Sherman. Many other—particularly Southern and African American—Republicans were interested in such a fully national system.[26]

The alternative, though, was building on and extending the existing supervisory system that so exercised Woodrow Wilson. Worried about administrative feasibility and cost, Hoar and most Republicans soon fell back on this option. Working with the newly arrived Senator John Coit Spooner, Hoar abandoned Sherman's fully national scheme and proposed having "National officers . . . present at the registration and election of Members of Congress, and at the count of the vote, and who should know and report everything which should happen." Hoar opted, in short, for building on the existing hybrid system of "concurrent sovereignty."[27]

Elsewhere in the Capitol, the House Republican caucus wrestled with both approaches, but it too settled on enlarging the existing system of "concurrent sovereignty." A lengthy bill, over seventy pages long, was reported to the full House by a select House committee chaired by Hoar's protégé, Henry Cabot Lodge. After brief and tightly controlled debate, the House passed the Lodge version of the elections bill on July 2, 1890. Every single Democrat who voted on the bill cast his ballot against it. Only two Republicans voted with them.[28]

When the House bill got back to the Senate, Hoar, as chair of the Committee on Privileges and Elections, took custody of it. He sought to make it more palatable to his colleagues by stripping out provisions for military enforcement and the detailed criminal regulations the House had put into the bill. He also watered down the fee schedule for the supervisors, and dispensed with federal juries that would regulate indictment and trial for bribery, intimidation, and fraud. In his opinion, the end result "was a very simple measure. It only extended the law which . . . had been in force in cities of more than twenty thousand inhabitants, to Congressional districts, when there should be an application to the Court, setting forth the necessity for its protection. . . . We added to our Bill a provision that in case of a dispute concerning an election certificate, the Circuit Court of the United States in which the district was situated should hear the case and should award a certificate entitling the member to be placed on the Clerk's roll, and to hold his seat until the House itself should act on the case."[29]

This was not quite the full story. Hoar might have added that during the

51st Congress Republicans had begun a drive to modernize the federal circuit courts—what eventually became the Evarts Circuit Court Bill of 1891 (in the 52nd Congress.) Remodeling the federal judiciary was certain to improve the Elections Bill's impact.[30]

Also, a chief federal election supervisor would in fact already exist for each national judicial circuit.[31] Once appointed, the supervisor's role in regulating the congressional electoral process could be activated by a petition of one hundred citizens in a House district. Regulation by the supervisor was not, in other words, automatic; it had to be activated. Once the supervisor's role was set in motion by the citizen petition to the supervisor, the supervisor could then appoint two deputy supervisors, one from each major political party. Prior to election day, the federal supervisors could screen registration lists. On election day they could observe the balloting.

After election day, the federal supervisors were entitled to offer certifications of the count and of the winner of a House election in parallel with that offered by state elections officials. These certifications would be forwarded by both sets of officials to a three-person U.S. Board of Canvassers appointed by the circuit court.

If the Board of Canvassers found that a federal certificate agreed with a state certificate, then a House candidate with congruent certificates would be elected from the congressional district. If the two certificates disagreed, the Board would vote on whether the federal certificate trumped the state certificate. If the Board decided, by majority vote, that the federal supervisors' certificate was more accurate than the state certificate—something it would know from registration and citizenship data previously collected by the supervisors—then the federal certificate prevailed. The decision could be appealed directly to the circuit court, and that court had authority to reverse it. But the circuit court's decision was final whatever the outcome, reversal or affirmance of the U.S. Board of Canvassers, unless the House itself reversed the court in hearing a contested elections case from the losing candidate.

Whatever the precise details of a finally enrolled statute, its purpose would have been clear: to impose effective federal regulation over all House elections in the South. Before 1890, the Article I system covered less than a fifth of U.S. House districts. The shift envisioned by Hoar and other proponents was therefore huge.[32] The *Siebold-Clarke* doctrine, which protected federal elections supervisors in House districts and allowed them to operate freely there as law enforcement officials—able to actually sanction irregularities—could in principle extend to all U.S. House elections.

As a result of *Yarbrough*, furthermore, federal supervisory officials in the South would have been able to inhibit and sanction behavior by private citizens who attacked black voters as they exercised Fifteenth Amendment rights. Not only would the supervisors have been immune from arrest by state and local officials; indeed, the implication of *Coy* was that these state and local officials were themselves federal officials with federal responsibilities, if only temporarily. These federal supervisors could themselves arrest and process private individuals who operated in Southern congressional elections to intimidate black voters before, on, or after election day.

Finally, challenge in the federal courts to any new system created by the Federal Elections Bill would face a great obstacle. During the Reconstruction the federal elections statutes that enforced the Civil War Amendments had been implemented for several years in the South *before* the Supreme Court reviewed them. The Federal Elections Bill, in contrast, would be implemented *after* the Court had already reviewed and approved of the plan's various components.

In short, the Federal Elections Bill was a very serious proposal. Its enormity was heightened, furthermore, by highly dramatic circumstances—what Kingdon aptly calls "focusing events." One was the assassination of a Republican candidate from Arkansas, murdered while collecting evidence for his contested elections case. Another was the assembly of Mississippi's famous constitutional convention for the purpose of legally disenfranchising African American voters. America was manifestly at a political crossroads.[33]

Reconstructing the Reconstruction?

What about the Federal Elections Bill's result on the ground? What would it have done to Southern politics? Would it have forestalled Black disenfranchisement, and, if so, how? There are two answers. First, the prospect of a new federal elections bill had a clear effect before the bill reached the Senate. Second, we can fruitfully speculate about its possible impact had it passed and been implemented.

All over Dixie, Republican and independent parties called for fair elections during the 1888 state conventions. In Mississippi, for instance, Republicans ran a statewide ticket in 1888, their first since 1875, with former Confederate general James Chalmers running for governor. The party ran on a platform attacking the "present State Government" for relying on a "fraudulent and violent suppression of free suffrage." The ticket functioned, more or less, until violence forced its cessation. The party then issued a statement that "our candidates are not safely allowed to discuss or protest. We refer not only to such well-known slaughters as Kemper and Copiah. . . . Yazoo City and Leflore, but the nameless killing by creek and bayou." Mississippi Republicans thus urged a federal elections statute.[34]

The Alabama Republican party called for a "national law to regulate the election of members of Congress and presidential electors"; the Arkansas Union Labor party, representing the Agricultural Wheel, the National Farmers Alliance, and the Knights of Labor, fused with the state Republican party and called for the "consolidation of the elections, State and national"; the North Carolina Republican party called for protective state legislation that would assure "free and just exercise of the elective franchise"; the South Carolina Republican party asked "Congress to enact such legislation as shall secure a fair election at least for members of Congress and presidential electors"; and the Waco gathering that fused the State Alliance, Knights of Labor, Union Labor, Prohibition, and Republican parties of Texas called for a "free ballot and a fair count."[35]

In short, the anti-Bourbon forces anticipated a federal elections bill. Thus, in Southern House districts, black citizens would probably have quickly organized themselves to petition the federal courts. During and after the Civil War, when promising political opportunities opened up, Black Southerners regularly displayed capacities for action and organization through an intricate matrix of social networks, associations, institutions, and small business. The Election Bill's design invited such self-organization among black voters and cooperation with Republican candidates and party organizations. That process would have stimulated the rebuilding of Southern Republican party organizations.[36]

The protections afforded by the bill would also have brought talented politicians, both black and white, out of the woodwork. Because federal officials regulated House elections, maintained physical surveillance on them, kept their own records, and could criminally sanction intimidation and fraud, the incentives to join the Republican party—or the largely white but pro-voting rights populist third parties—would have been strong. It was the candidate certified by federal officials, after all—not state and local officials—who would travel to Washington for the next session of Congress. Losing candidates could certainly launch an election contest. But the burden of proof for a contest would rest on them, not on the federally certified winner—and it would have to be carried after an adverse determination by a federal circuit.[37]

What House Republicans Got—As a Party—Out of the Elections Bill

The Elections Bill had great potential, in short, to recast Southern politics. There was another vital sense in which the Federal Elections Bill would have altered the course of Gilded Age politics: it would have increased the national policymaking capacities of the Republican party. The Elections Bill would have augmented the Republican party's policy-making capacities in two ways. It would have brought back a large number of Southern House districts for the Republicans. Also, it institutionally relocated the contested elections process, freeing up legislative time and energy.

To appreciate these two points—(1) that the Federal Elections Bill meant better outcomes for Republicans in Southern House elections; and (2) that the bill freed up scarce legislative time for the majority in the

House—it helps to look more closely at the characteristics of Southern House elections, the contested elections process, and the conflict between that process and growing pressures on legislative time and energy.

Panel A in Table 3 shows that Republicans continued to compete in Southern House elections in the period between the Compromise of 1877 and the introduction and consideration of the Federal Elections Bill. (It is interesting to note, in panel A, that *Yarbrough* may have induced a sharp increase in the supply of Republican candidates in 1884—all the more striking since the number of Southern House districts increased from seventy-three to eighty-five between 1880 and 1882.) But as panel B shows, very few Republicans won House elections.

TABLE 3. HOUSE RACES IN THE FORMER CONFEDERACY, 1878–90

Panel A: Extent of competition						
Election	1878	1880	1882	1884	1886	1888
Percent of districts with competition	85	94	94	91	67	92
Percent of competitive elections with Republican candidates	48	76	61	91	52	86
Panel B: Relative success						
Congress	46th	47th	48th	49th	50th	51st
Total Southern Republicans	3	12	9	8	9	14
Percent of all Southern seats held by Republicans	4	16	10	9	10	16

Sources: *Congressional Quarterly Guide to U.S. Elections* (panel A); Jeffery A. Jenkins, "Partisanship and Contested Election Cases in the House of Representatives, 1789–2002," *Studies in American Political Development* 18 (Fall 2004): 112–35; table 11: "Election Contests and Republican Seats in the Former-Confederate South, 1867–1911" (panel B). States are Alabama, Arkansas, Florida, Georgia, Louisiana, Mississippi, North Carolina, South Carolina, Tennessee, Texas, and Virginia.

What made the Republicans' lack of success palpably galling was the fact that *about a third of Southern House districts were majority African American.*[38] Thus the Southern Democratic war of attrition against the voting rights of Black Southerners—through fraud, intimidation, and violence—cost the Republican party a great deal. Imagine how Democrats today would react if, during several presidential elections in a row, the Republican governors of key, battleground states and their secretaries of state delivered the Electoral College to the GOP by adopting irregular administrative tactics. For the Republicans of the Gilded Age, something rather similar was happening to them—to say nothing of black Southerners who wanted national representation.

Republicans were apparently "cheated" *of about 15–19 seats per Congress*—or so they could understandably conclude.[39] As Table 4 shows, during the post-Compromise Congresses in which Democrats controlled the House, that number of 15–19 seats was a huge percentage of the number necessary to instead give Republicans control of the U.S. House. Small wonder, then, that the administration of national elections in the former Confederacy preoccupied Republicans. Indeed, the day after the House passed Lodge's version of the elections bill, the *National Republican* (edited by New Hampshire Republican Senator William Chandler, the only member of the Senate who knew as much as Hoar did about Southern elections) optimistically predicted that over half of the ex-Confederacy would become Republican, replacing a dozen Democratic senators and twenty Democratic members of the House. Undoubtedly this was too hopeful. But the prediction speaks volumes about Republican expectations.[40]

TABLE 4. DIFFERENCE MADE TO REPUBLICANS BY SOUTHERN HOUSE ELECTIONS ADMINISTRATION

Congress	46th	48th	49th	50th
GOP "Southern Deficit" as percent of margin of control exercised by Democrats in Democratic controlled Houses	166	49	90	190

Source: Jerrold G. Rusk, *A Statistical History of the American Electorate* (Washington, D.C.: CQ Press, 2001), 219, and author's calculations.

There was a second way in which the Federal Elections Bill would have helped Republicans. It was not an issue in debate, but it is hard to believe that no one noticed the matter. The Elections Bill would have meant an abandonment of any further reliance on the existing contested elections process—freeing up legislative time at the margin for policy making. Due to the bill's impact on Southern elections, that benefit would immediately accrue to Republicans.

The existing contested elections process had become something of a burden on the House by this point.[41] Further, because so many contests involved Southern House elections, there was little prospect of the burden becoming lighter if no change was made. In the 46th Congress, 45 percent of the 11 cases were Southern; in the 47th, 84 percent of the 19 cases were Southern; in the 48th, 54 percent of the 13 cases were Southern; in the 50th (there were no Southern cases in the 49th), 25 percent of the 8 cases were Southern. Yet only about 25 percent of House seats were Southern. Most of the time, then, the politics of contested elections was disproportionately Southern.[42]

Leading Republicans interested in streamlining the House—principally Thomas Brackett Reed of Maine, Speaker of the House in the 51st (and later the 54th and 55th) Congress(es)—were eager for change. Speaker Reed considered the existing contestation process

a tremendous waste of resources for the committee members, who had to read thousands of pages of testimony, as well as the House, which had to spend an often significant amount of time considering arguments and rendering decisions. His principal concern was the Republican party agenda, which was often put on hold for contested elections cases. As Reed stated, elections contests "consume the time of the House to the exclusion of valuable legislation."[43]

Reed was right. Congress was busier than it had ever been by the 51st Congress. As Table 5 shows, the overall size of the congressional agenda expanded sharply between the 46th and 50th Congresses. In the face of this conjunction of scarce time and constant elections contests, the Federal Elections Bill offered a welcome solution.

TABLE 5. EXPANSION OF THE CONGRESSIONAL AGENDA IN THE GILDED AGE

Measures introduced					Measures enacted		
Congress	Years	Total	Bills	Joint resolutions	Total	Public	Private
46th	1879–81	10,067	9,481	586	650	372	278
47th	1881–83	10,704	10,194	510	761	419	342
48th	1883–85	11,443	10,961	482	969	284	685
49th	1885–87	15,002	14,618	384	1,452	424	1,028
50th	1887–89	17,078	16,664	414	1,824	570	1,254

Source: Erik W. Austin with Jerome M. Clubb, *Political Facts of the United States Since 1789* (New York: Columbia University Press, 1986), 47, table 1.18.

The Federal Elections Bill's Impact on Party Conflict

To sum up, the word "ingenious" nicely describes the Federal Elections Bill. It had reinforcing complementarities. In strengthening Black voting rights, it increased the number of Republicans likely to take seats in every House—and in doing that it portended more frequent Republican control of the House, and conceivably more frequent unified Republican control of the national government. By transferring to the courts the process of handling contested elections cases at a time when these were frequent, the Federal Elections Bill also freed up scarce legislative time and energy just when agenda control was becoming a more serious problem for parties-in-Congress. Due to the efficiencies of the Federal Elections Bill, the party likely to make the most of this increase in legislative capacity—at least in the short run—was the Republican Party. Finally, the federal regulatory sytem that created these changes was likely to survive judicial review.

In an important sense, though, the bill was *too* strong. Its partisan implications were not just zero-sum; they were transparently and palpably zero-sum. Hoar had devised and championed the party systemic equivalent of an atom bomb.

Furthermore, in a little-known but vital facet of the whole struggle, Speaker Reed had shown what the bomb could do. Before his ascension in the 51st Congress, Speaker Thomas Brackett Reed expected to streamline House procedure—that is, to impose the famous Reed Rules lowering the size of the House quorum—*in order to pass the Elections Bill* (as well, of course, as other major pieces of legislation.)[44] Reed's imposition of his eponymous reform allowed him to demonstrate why Republicans would benefit from the Elections Bill. The House GOP had begun the 51st Congress with just a one-vote majority. But the House Republican majority quickly grew once the Reed Rules allowed the Speaker and his copartisans to resolve a large crop of contested elections in their favor, thereby sweeping in a more comfortable majority early in the session. It would have been hard for rational politicians to miss the obvious lesson of how Reed smartly increased his majority. The contested elections cases which Reed rapidly sorted out were overwhelmingly from the South. More than one of them involved a black Republican candidate running in an overwhelmingly African American district who nonetheless lost to a Democrat when the state's governor certified the election. By providing for a judicially controlled certification process, the Elections Bill leveled the playing field for Southern Republican candidates and their electoral supporters—thereby obviating the kind of ex post restoration which Reed so briskly supplied.[45]

Reed's real-time demonstration of what an Elections Bill might do to Southern House elections enormously raised the stakes for Democrats. Democrats also came to strongly believe that they had public opinion on their side. In the 51st Congress, Republicans enjoyed a majority of 179–152; in the 52nd, Democrats would enjoy a stunning 238–86 majority, having crushed Republicans in the 1890, off-year elections. Democrats interpreted the House elections as a popular revolt against "Reedism" meant to check the entrenchment of one-party government.[46]

Under the circumstances, were Senate Democrats to let the Elections Bill pass (during the imminent, short session of the 51st Congress, after the 1890 elections), then they had only themselves to blame for whatever the bill did to the Democratic Party. Democratic resistance in the Senate during the short session was tenacious, coordinated, and relentless. Indeed, Democrats displayed perfect cohesion during all of the Senate roll calls related to the Elections Bill.[47]

The Elections Bill's supporters nonetheless fought a remarkably fierce action, coping ably with the problem of only tepid support from Western Republicans and hostility from silver Republicans. President Harrison, a consistent advocate for the measure, lobbied his Senate colleagues. Vice President Levi Morton, also a supporter, entered the process as presiding officer, and worked with Rhode Island Senator Nelson Aldrich (who had taken over for an exhausted Hoar) to abolish the filibuster altogether—choosing what today, thanks to Senator Bill Frist's similar interest, is called "the nuclear option."[48]

Together, Morton and Aldrich actually won a historic vote, 36-32, to abolish the Senate rules that permitted a filibuster. But lacking the parliamentary touch possessed by Speaker Reed, the vice president failed to immediately clinch the results of the vote, paving the way for the disastrous vote of January 26, described at the beginning of this chapter.[49]

TABLE 6. SENATE VOTE, JANUARY 22, 1891, TO ABOLISH THE FILIBUSTER

Party	Yeas	Nays	Not voting	Total
Republican	36	4	11	51
Democrat	0	28	9	37
Total	36	32	20	

Source: Voteview for Windows v. 3.0.3; roll call no. 423, Senate, 51st Congress.

Even the January 26 vote just might have been reversed. A bitter dispute broke out when silver Republican Senator William Stewart claimed that the absent Senator Leland Stanford was actually paired with the one-vote majority. While not a strong supporter of the Elections Bill, Stanford had previously announced he would vote both for changing Senate rules to gain cloture and for the bill. The historian Daniel Crofts has shown, in his unpublished dissertation, that Stewart's apparently fantastic "inside" account in his memoir of how he then got Stanford to back him up was in fact true. According to Stewart's memoir, he inadvertently learned of a plan by Aldrich to rush to New York City to get Stanford's vote. Stewart accompanied Aldrich on the train to New York, taking pains to treat his presence as nothing more than a coincidence, but then gave Aldrich the slip in the middle of the night to take an express stagecoach to Manhattan, getting to Stanford's hotel before Aldrich did. In his memoir, Stewart wrote, "we met Senator Aldrich at the elevator on his way to visit Senator Stanford. I told him he was too late." Had Stewart not "happened to be in the cloakroom," and overhead "one of the . . . messengers remark that Senator Aldrich was going to New York that night," Aldrich might have gained Stanford's vote and thus forced a tie that the vice president would have decided.[50]

TABLE 7. PRIORITY INDEX OF EQUAL SUFFRAGE FOR MAJOR PARTY PLATFORMS

	1868	1872	1876	1880	1884	1888	1892
Republicans	0.93	1.0	0.89	0.14	0.04	0.85	0.76
Democrats	0.37	0.93	1.0	0.72	0.45	0.00	0.96

Source: Kirk H. Porter and Donald Bruce Johnson, comps., *National Party Platforms, 1840–1956* (Urbana: University of Illinois Press, 1956).

Democrats did not rest easy, though, after the Republican drive collapsed. Consider Table 7. Based on a measure devised by Carmines and Stimson, it displays scores for the parties on the salience of black suffrage and Southern elections administration.[51] The score is calculated as 1.0 minus the *ratio* of (a) the number of the quadrennial party platform paragraph (counting from the top of the platform) that contains the first clear discussion of African American voting rights and (b) the total number of paragraphs in the party platform. The higher the number, the greater the importance, and vice versa.

As one reads Table 7 from left to right, one sees sharp conflict between the parties during most of Reconstruction. After Reconstruction, however, the parties do not match each other in taking the issue seriously, yo-yoing back and forth. In 1880 and 1884, Republicans hardly treat the matter; Democrats, in contrast, show some concern over black suffrage and Southern elections administration. Then, in 1888, Republican concern shoots back up. But Democrats drop the subject altogether. In 1892, in the wake of the elections bill crisis, Republicans draw attention to the issue. But here we get to the outlier in the series: Democrats rocket from 0 in 1888 all the way up to .96. This is far and away the largest jump in either party for the entire period from 1868 to 1892.

Such a single-minded issue focus did not emerge automatically. Lawrence Grossman has shown that Northern Democrats were racially moderate before the Elections Bill standoff. Their stance on race relations was meant to capitalize on the discontent with the Republican Party that circulated among a small part of the black Republican base in the North and to thereby attract enough black votes to cost Republicans across a variety of Northern state and local elections. The Southern wing enabled this Northern strategy by avoiding open rhetorical pressure for white supremacy. But the Elections Bill brought out full-throated white supremacism among Southern Democrats—not least to break the Populist wave coursing among white Southerners. The Northern Democrats could fight the Southern wing's white supremacist stance, or adopt it. An energetic faction of Northern Democrats pressured Grover Cleveland, the 1892 candidate, and other racial moderates, to rhetorically line up with Southern white supremacy. Eager to return to the White House, they complied.[52]

As the elections turned out, Democrats scored very big: they established unified control of the national government *for the first time since before the Civil War.* Had the racially moderate Northern Democrats successfully resisted the intraparty turn to white supremacy, and had the party done as well as it actually did, the new Democratic administration would very probably have left the federal statutes alone. But Democrats instead regained unified control—after 36 years—through making federal regulation of elections the paramount national issue. The implications for the federal elections statutes could not have been clearer.

In September 1893, House Democrats proposed to repeal *all* of the Reconstruction-era federal elections statues. On October 10, the House passed a repeal, 201-102. The majority was entirely Democratic; the minority entirely Republican. The Senate did not consider the repealer until December. But on February 7, 1894, the Senate repealed the elections statutes 39-28—and, quite significantly, *without a Republican filibuster.*[53]

That Senate Democrats won a filibuster-free repeal revealed much about what the Southern Democrats had accomplished by then. The Democratic majority numbered forty-four, the Republican minority forty. Nevada's William Stewart, erstwhile adversary of the Elections Bill, had returned to the chamber as a "silver" independent. Three Prairie Populists from South Dakota, Nebraska, and Kansas rounded out the chamber's independent/minor party contingent. So the numbers hardly precluded a filibuster. Stewart and the Populists would certainly have cooperated with the Democrats to try to impose cloture. But a Republican filibuster was quite possible.

Why, then, was there no such obstruction? In his memoirs Hoar supplied the vital clues:

The last vestige of the National statute for securing purity of elections was repealed in President Cleveland's second administration. . . . I have reflected very carefully as to my duty in that matter . . . such legislation, to be of any value whatever, must be permanent. If it only be maintained in force while one political party is in power, and repealed when its antagonist comes in, *and is to be a constant matter of political strife and sectional discussion,* it is better . . . to abandon it than to keep up an incessant, fruitless struggle. (emphasis added)[54]

The point seemed to be that Democrats had introduced an alarming new uncertainty into national party competition. They appeared willing and able to indefinitely make electoral regulation *the* issue in American politics. The choice for Republicans was clear. They could subordinate all of their other policy goals in favor of Black voting rights, opting instead for "constant . . . political strife." Or they could call off the fight.

They called off the fight. African Americans were now on their own. Construing the new reality in words that must have had his mentor Charles Sumner spinning in his grave, Hoar later wrote, "So, after [the] repealing act got through the Senate, I announced that, so far as I was concerned, and so far as I had the right to express the opinion of Northern Republicans, I thought the attempt to secure the rights of the colored people by National legislation would be abandoned until there were a considerable change of opinion in the country, and especially in the South, and *until it had ceased to become a matter of party strife*. . . . So far as I know, no Republican has dissented from it."[55]

The political progression that stretches from 1888 to 1894 looks very much like a "boomerang" (Skocpol's apt term for cycles such as this).[56] Leveraging both Republican interest in a renewal of the party's Southern strength and the party's announced concern over Southern elections and African American voting rights, George Frisbie Hoar comes very close to an extraordinary feat: he nearly reconstructs the Reconstruction. Ratcheting up the conflict, the Democrats respond by placing the issue of federal electoral regulation at the very center of national party competition and dare Republicans to keep it up. Brought to the brink of "incessant . . . struggle," the Grand Old Party backs off.

Policy Entrepreneurship, Policy Windows, and Party Showdowns

The dramatic conclusion to the two-party standoff over Hoar's proposal underscored how much rode on the 1890 Federal Elections Bill. Several things had been in play: the basic interests of the two parties as vote-getting, office-seeking organizations; sectional conflict and the continuing red glow cast by the Civil War on national life; the voting rights of African American voters in the South, and thus the actual status in American political life of the Fifteenth Amendment; the filibuster and whether it would persist; the relationship between the federal circuit courts and national electoral administration; and the consequences of Article I, Section 4, for electoral administration. Contrary to the bulk of scholarly opinion, the Federal Elections Bill was by no means an irresponsible, misguided, or futile project. Instead, the bill seized and fortified precisely the ground that was still available to the Republican party for protecting African American voting rights.[57]

As is already apparent, concepts and terms from Kingdon's classic analysis of policymaking clarify this pivotal sequence. For Kingdon, policy change is neither incremental nor rational-comprehensive. Instead, it results from a partly random, disjointed coupling of "three major process streams . . . (1) problem recognition, (2) the formation and refining of policy proposals, and (3) politics." He adds, "These three streams of processes develop and operate large independently of one another." When opportunity knocks, the kind of action undertaken by Hoar connects these three streams.[58]

Kingdon's perspective highlights at least two essential things about the cycle. First, because consideration of the elections bill happened during a window of opportunity, the effort stood a serious chance of success. Indeed, history could easily have turned out differently. Second, and relatedly, because entrepreneurship was the factor that connected the trio of (1) political change, (2) problem definition, and (3) refinement of relevant proposals, George Frisbie Hoar's considerable expertise and creativity bore fully on the situation and aroused the energies of many partisan colleagues in both houses of Congress.

The story also teaches a great deal about the role of policy entrepreneurship when it intersects with sharp partisan conflict. Party divergence plays little role in Kingdon's analysis. Instead, he tacitly assumes partisan convergence or inaction as constant and background features of policymaking dynamics. Kingdon treats a party platform, for instance, as "a grab bag of mostly very vague concerns." He adds, "While differences between the two platforms are obvious, and while the agendas of the parties are different and reasonably clear, the party position could not possibly constitute a serious guide to policy making once the party is in power."[59]

In contrast to Kingdon's premise of party irrelevance, party divergence and conflict were critically defining elements of Federal Elections Bill politics. Hoar's plan had zero-sum implications for the party system: one party would lose; another party would win by as much as the other party lost. The results were explosive. Hoar's party-centered policy entrepreneurship had effects that lasted well beyond the opening of the 51st Congress policy window.

Partisan, zero-sum policy entrepreneurship will feed back into politics, palpably and right away. All that is in question is the direction of the feedback—in a forward cycle, toward the entrepreneur's goals, or in a reverse cycle that will unexpectedly damage, even tragically postpone, those goals.

Part III
Resetting the Terms of Government and Politics

Chapter 8
Andrew Johnson and the Politics of Failure

Nicole Mellow and Jeffrey K. Tulis

Andrew Johnson is generally regarded as one of the worst presidents in American political history. It would be hard to think of a clearer example of failed leadership. His vision and his specific plans for bringing the South back into the Union were rejected by Congress. He aggressively opposed the major Reconstruction agenda, which was legislated over his vetoes. Amendments to the Constitution that he opposed were passed by Congress and ratified by a northern national majority. The victorious opposition against him included leaders of Johnson's own governing coalition, and they grew to detest him. Johnson's extraordinary string of political defeats culminated in the first impeachment of a president. He escaped conviction by the narrowest of margins and left office politically defeated and disgraced.

Yet it was Andrew Johnson's vision, not that of Reconstruction, which reconstituted American politics. Policies similar to those he had advanced as president quickly replaced those that constituted the Reconstruction agenda, evidencing such a powerful hold on the polity that they made a mockery of the amended Constitution. Johnson's vision was woven into the very fabric of American political life for a century. Less than a handful of presidents have been as successful as Andrew Johnson in advancing their political project.[1]

That Andrew Johnson failed to legislate his vision, and that American political development subsequently came to be characterized by policies close to those he preferred, are facts that would be difficult to contest. It is therefore surprising that it is so difficult to find major studies of American politics that conjoin the two. Perhaps this reflects social science's discomfort with the ironic. Our central argument, however, goes beyond reflection on the ironic conjunction, and it is contestable. We claim that these two facts are connected historically, that Andrew Johnson's political failures were themselves instruments for the later success of his policies. It can, of course, be argued that policies like those Johnson preferred later prevailed for reasons having nothing to do with him, that these sorts of policies would have been developed whether or not Johnson had been president.

It is impossible to know whether or not Andrew Johnson's actions were *necessary* conditions for the later emergence of policies that resembled his vision. But one can never prove that any leader was necessary for the articulation and success of policies that he or she advanced. While it is impossible, methodologically, to demonstrate that a leader was indispensable, one can make plausible cases that leaders affected the changes that they preferred. Here we muster substantial evidence that Johnson's actions *facilitated* the establishment of policies that bore the stamp of his vision. This lineage was anticipated by Southern elites in the nineteenth century, for example.[2] Our best evidence, however, comes from an interpretation of Johnson's actions themselves, from the logic and character of his distinctive brand of leadership. When one looks anew at Johnson's political "failures" one can see that their meaning and effects extended well beyond the Washington community to incipient coalitions in the nation at large and especially among the defeated elites of the South.

When he assumed the presidency upon Lincoln's assassination, Andrew Johnson adopted a style of leadership that is hard to understand in conventional terms. As leader of the Union's governing party, Johnson was in a position to use his inherited authority to seize on efforts by the Congressional leadership to reach an accommodation with him regarding the shape of Reconstruction. The record of the period is replete with opportunities (some of which we describe later) for Johnson to very substantially moderate the Radical Republican agenda and to reintegrate the South into the Union on terms that at the time would have been satisfactory to much of the South and that were consistent with the core principles of the party of which he was the purported leader. Instead, Johnson chose to advance a program contrary to the core principles of the coalition he inherited from Lincoln, and he attempted to block every major policy initiative for Reconstruction that would have been supported by a large Union coalition. We describe this leadership style as preemptive and obstructionist.

Because preemption and obstruction were so unsuccessful during Johnson's term in office, and because more conventional approaches would have won him legislative accomplishment and perhaps even election to the office he inherited, one might conclude that Johnson was mentally deranged, or at least politically tone-deaf. His failures and that characterization call to mind Woodrow Wilson's obdurate fight for a League of Nations.[3] But, like Wilson's defeat, Johnson's political tactics were more rational than conventional accounts suggest. Johnson was a semiliterate man, not a sophisticated thinker like Wilson. Yet he developed an unusually powerful political sense while schooled on the stump in Tennessee. If he could not outline his political understanding for university press publication, he could feel it instinctively and act on it in the heat of political battle. Johnson's political moves formed a remarkably coherent pattern, albeit one that reverses most conventional understandings of effective leadership.[4]

Johnson's politics of preemption and obstruction can be usefully categorized in two ways. First, Johnson used the resources of the executive office
to rebuild the capacity of the South to politically engage the North on its
own terms. He preempted Congress with his lenient "restoration plan" for
the South and later willfully mis-executed the less forgiving plan of Congressional Reconstruction; through these actions, Johnson provided the
South with time to rebuild its social, economic, and, most important, civil
infrastructures. Johnson also began to build new political coalitions and to
link political allies outside the dominant party apparatus. The strategic sub-
versions of "office" and "party" allowed Southern elites the opportunity to
regroup and to develop the networks necessary for reframing their political battle to preserve their racial-economic hierarchy. Second, Johnson disrupted the ideological frame that the politically and militarily successful
Republican Party was intent on establishing. To the victor in politics typically goes the opportunity to establish the political narrative that will prevail.
Because of the complex constitutional process by which Reconstruction Republicans were attempting to change the polity, Johnson was able to exploit
the pulpit of the presidency to launch an alternative narrative. In doing so,
he disrupted the Republicans' frame and constructed ideological space for
the South to inhabit in defining the nation's political future. Each of these
dimensions, capacity building and ideological construction, is considered
in turn.

Capacity Building Through Preemption and Obstruction

At the time of his assassination in 1865, President Lincoln had not yet committed himself to a particular path by which Southern states were to be
reincorporated into the Union. During the war, Lincoln was largely conciliatory. Lincoln's Ten Percent plan, which would have readmitted
Louisiana, Tennessee, and Arkansas once 10 percent of voters eligible in
1860 (prior to the war) had taken an oath of loyalty and voted new state
representation, would have excluded former slaves from political participation. His vice presidential choice of Andrew Johnson, a Southern Democrat who stayed loyal to the Union, is further evidence of his willingness to
accommodate the South in hopes of a speedy restoration. Yet just prior to
his death Lincoln was seriously considering a reintegration plan that would
be more demanding, requiring, for example, at least limited African American suffrage. The upshot is that Johnson assumed the presidency without
inheriting a clear plan of action from his predecessor.[5]

Radical Republicans in Congress and their supporters were initially optimistic that Johnson would impose an aggressive reconstruction plan on the
South.[6] They were quickly disabused of this expectation. Johnson's first
move was to institute a "restoration plan" for the South that was far more
lenient than that desired by congressional Republicans. Reminiscent of

Lincoln's assertion of executive authority at the outset of the Civil War, Johnson enacted his plan while Congress was in recess. Because the war was over, Johnson could easily have chosen to reconvene Congress for the purpose of establishing a jointly negotiated postwar agenda. He chose, instead, to preempt it.

The essence of Johnson's plan is contained in an Amnesty Proclamation and an accompanying program for the reintegration of North Carolina. Amnesty was granted upon the taking of an oath of loyalty to all who had participated in the rebellion, with the exception of former civil and military officers of the Confederacy and ex-Confederates who owned more than $20,000 worth of property. With amnesty came the restoration of all confiscated property except former slaves. The North Carolina Proclamation, subsequently extended to all other unreconstructed states, allowed loyal citizens (that is, those granted amnesty) who had been eligible to vote before the war to elect delegates to a convention at which a new state government would be formed and representatives to Congress chosen. The new state governments were obliged only to abolish slavery, repeal the secession ordinances, and repudiate their war debts.

Johnson's plan for "restoration" was lenient in that it enfranchised only white Southerners. It also did not redistribute land to former slaves or attend to their welfare as other policy proposals at the time did.[7] Congressional Republicans, on the other hand, favored at least limited African American suffrage (ranging from moderate proposals to extend the vote to those who had served in the Union Army or were literate to radical proposals for universal manhood suffrage), and they advocated policies that would reconstruct Southern civil society in a way that would make freedom for former slaves politically meaningful and economically viable. Johnson's Proclamation would make eligibility for future electoral participation the determination of individual states. This would, of course, leave the decision about black political rights in the hands of white Southerners. Additionally, in his Amnesty Proclamation, Johnson made available the possibility of individual pardons for those not included in the general amnesty. The president then proceeded to grant clemency to 13,500 of 15,000 applicants, thus restoring citizenship and property rights to a large portion of the former Confederate elite.[8]

By preempting Congress with his restoration plan, Johnson strove to put the white South back on its political feet as quickly as possible. This would ensure that the region had the normal tools of political contestation, including congressional representation and some version of state sovereignty, with which to settle the terms of the postwar era. Short of the reinstitution of slavery, Southern elites could not ask for better terms. Not only were Johnson's conditions generous, the process would be quick. Indeed, Southern representatives were presenting themselves to be seated in Congress by the time it reconvened in December 1865. True, the war effort in the South had cost $2.3 billion (far more than in the North, proportionate to resources), and repudiation of the debt left many without the opportunity to reclaim their former wealth. But the quicker they could restore their fields and resume economic production, the sooner they would return to prosperity.[9] Most important, having been defeated militarily, a quick restoration of political representation in the national government was essential if white Southerners were to restrain (or reverse) policy initiatives of Northern lawmakers. With a Democrat, albeit a Union loyalist, in the executive office, particularly one making overtures to the region, and sympathetic fellow Democrats still retaining a foothold in the North, a legislative remedy for some of the ails of defeat was entirely feasible.[10]

By attempting to expedite the return of the Southern states to the very national government against which they had just revolted, Johnson's plan gave the ambitions of the former Confederate elite not just new institutional footing but constitutional grounding as well. The premise on which Johnson developed his position was the supreme authority of the Constitution and the Union it created. Reflecting on his wartime loyalty to supporters in February 1866, Johnson said, "I said then that I was for the Union with slavery— or I was for the Union without slavery. In either alternative I was for my government and its Constitution."[11] It was this loyalty that had prevented him from joining his regional brethren in secession and motivated his denouncements of their treason. But because the Constitution provided no avenue by which states could withdraw from the Union, it was, in his logic, only traitorous individuals who had engaged in rebellion. Having quashed their efforts, the imperative was now to restore to the loyal citizens residing in the South the republican form of government constitutionally promised to them. Since the war had been fought over secession and the supremacy of the constitutional order had been vindicated, all that was needed from the defeated was a renunciation of their efforts to withdraw and evidence of renewed loyalty to the Union; there was no reason to extract additional concessions, such as Black suffrage. With the war question settled, the South should be free, according to Johnson, to return to the constitutional exercise of self-governance.

In addition to returning the South to national government, Johnson's plan recognized the integrity of the states and their sovereignty as decision-makers. Entwined with his fealty to the Constitution were his beliefs in states' rights and white supremacy, products, in part, of his Southern heritage. His emphasis on the primacy of states, as the locus for suffrage decisions and, more generally, in ordering affairs and protecting citizens, was consistent with his reading of the Constitution. He had no interest in maintaining the strong centralized national government that had been so necessary to winning the war—he was a self-proclaimed "Jacksonian Democrat." While Johnson had eventually supported the abolition of slavery, his racism combined with his suspicion of federal dominion led to his belief that the states should be left free to reconstruct their racial hierarchies on their own.[12] Thus, virtually every component of Johnson's plan was designed to protect the former Confederacy from the congressional action of Northerners and to give the South the institutional and jurisdictional capacity to author its own rebuilding.

Beyond official proclamations, Johnson promoted his goals through other unilateral actions, taking quick steps to restore to the South a proximate version of the antebellum economic and social order. Not only did he liberally pardon ex-Confederate leaders, he also directed that land confiscated by the Union Army be returned, rather than redistributed to former slaves, as leading Radicals such as Thaddeus Stevens wanted. He prioritized the use of civil government, particularly courts, over military government and tribunals, which had the effect of placing the old Confederate elite and their sympathizers in positions of civil and juridical authority. In defiance of a legislative act, Johnson refused to collect a levied cotton tax so as not to additionally burden economically struggling Southerners. To the extent possible, he removed black Union troops, and separately, he allowed for the organization of white Southern militia in order to maintain order, overruling the orders of his own generals in some cases to do so.[13]

The president's actions created opportunities for the former rebels to assert control over the economic and racial reconstruction of their states, and they endowed the actions taken by local elites with legitimacy. For example, by insisting only on loyalty to the Union and by reinstating many former Confederate leaders, Johnson's restoration policy sanctioned the adoption of Black Codes, the state and local laws enacted to regulate the movement and employment of freedmen. Requiring blacks to carry written permission from employers to move about, imposing curfews, regulating social and civic gatherings, restricting access to certain trades, and outlawing "vagrancy," the Black Codes returned African Americans to virtual enslavement.[14] As one Republican touring the South at the time put it, Black Codes made clear that "although the former owner has lost his individual property in the former slaves, the Blacks at large belong to the whites at large."[15]

The Black Codes were the first articulation of the South's vision of a postslavery world, and congressional response to the readmittance of the states hardened in response to the enactment of the Codes. While the laws outraged many in the North and caused Johnson some political discomfort in Washington, they were nonetheless accommodated by his policy and by his strong defense of states' rights. Still less legitimate hallmarks of the Jim Crow South began to emerge at this time as well, most notably the reign of terror and violence by which whites enforced social, economic, and political domination of blacks. Riots, organized white militias, and the activities of the newly birthed Ku Klux Klan and similar organizations formed the informal police state that enforced white supremacy. Johnson's 1866 proclamation halting military tribunals and restoring civil court proceedings not only undermined military rule in the South but meant that many offenders faced sympathetic juries of white peers. Despite reports of escalating violence, Johnson did not back down from his stance, thus implicitly condoning the South's informal methods of state-controlled reconstruction.[16]

More than simply setting the agenda for postwar politics, the net effect of Johnson's actions in this regard was to place in the hands of the just-defeated rebels the tools for financial rebuilding, the means, including arms, for management of the social and racial order, and the sanctioning power of political authority. By facilitating the South's quick rejuvenation of its desired racial-economic order and civil infrastructure, Johnson's actions enabled his Southern contemporaries to begin building the region's capacity for political engagement with the North on its own terms.[17] More significantly, Johnson signaled his endorsement of Southern priorities and his willingness to use the national government to further regional goals. In this sense, Johnson established the grounds of a long-term agenda for American racial politics.

An Obstructionist Politics to Preserve the South on Its Own Terms

Though many in the North had been initially willing to give Johnson's restoration plan a chance, by the time Congress had reconvened in the fall of 1865, the rejuvenation of the South under the region's former political and military leaders was sufficiently evident for opposition to crystallize. When Southern representatives, elected under Johnson's scheme, presented themselves to Congress, their readmission was denied. Under the guidance of leading Radicals, Congress in December of 1865 organized the Joint Committee on Reconstruction to survey conditions in the South and to develop a Congressional Reconstruction plan as an alternative to the president's. The poles of the conflict were already clear; if Johnson was going to use the presidency to aid the South, Congress would deploy its resources to ensure that the victory of the Union was not squandered.

The result of these efforts was the series of legislation associated with Congressional Reconstruction, including the Freedman's Bureau Bill, the Civil Rights Bill, the Fourteenth and Fifteenth Amendments, and the several Military Reconstruction Acts. The gist of this legislation was to provide legal and material assistance to former slaves transitioning to freedom, to extend citizenship rights to blacks and suffrage to black males, and to eliminate race-based discrimination. The Military Reconstruction Acts, which were administered by district commanders and troops occupying the South, enfranchised black males (prior to ratification of the Fourteenth and Fifteenth Amendments) and disfranchised many former Confederates. They further stipulated that states, to be readmitted to the Union, had to adopt new state constitutions granting universal male suffrage and had to ratify the Fourteenth Amendment. The three states of Texas, Virginia, and Mississippi, all of which lagged in this process, also had to ratify the Fifteenth Amendment before being readmitted.

When Johnson's effort to preemptively restore the South to its antebellum status was threatened by congressional action, he turned to a politics of institutional obstruction. As Congress first began to pass Reconstruction legislation, many lawmakers were still interested in working with the president.[18] His immediate and forceful vetoes of their legislation soured this prospect, however, and drove moderates toward the Reconstruction agenda of the Radicals.[19] A veto-proof majority was formed in short order, thus securing Congressional Reconstruction and making Johnson irrelevant to the process of policy production. Yet by responding with an obstructionist politics—including vetoes, reactionary speeches, and disruptive execution of the laws passed by Congress—Johnson continued to advance his aims. He signaled his enduring commitment to the Southern cause, an act not insignificant for a region that had just been militarily defeated. He bought more time for the South to regroup and forced Northern lawmakers into an increasingly uncomfortable defense of their actions to a war-weary Northern constituency. Last, Johnson's obstructionist politics functioned as a model of opposition strategy for the South. Whether these actions were political miscalculations, as many scholars claim, or components of a conscious strategy, Johnson's obstinacy, provocation, and subterfuge did function to provide support and legitimacy to a desperate and defeated region. As we argue below, Johnson's actions were not simply futile efforts of an impotent president but rather sustaining signals from a movement's leader.

Johnson's leadership of the South in opposition to Congressional Reconstruction relied heavily on the weapon of administrative obstruction—a strategy that was hampered by the threat of impeachment but a type of defensive leadership nonetheless. While his earliest executive actions, including those described above, were designed to rejuvenate the politics and economy of the white South, his actions as Congressional Reconstruction progressed focused on subverting the political project of the North. For example, when Northern Republicans, invigorated by successes in the 1866 elections, demanded that Southern states ratify the Fourteenth Amendment, Johnson encouraged Southern leaders to adopt a position of "masterly inactivity." If they refused to cooperate with Reconstruction, he argued, the Republican Party would not press the issue further, and if they did, the unconstitutionality of their actions would be grounds for the president and the courts to intervene. Southern states proceeded to reject the Amendment.[20]

Similarly, in the winter of 1866–67, Congress, dissatisfied with conditions in the South and continued obstruction in the region, imposed military Reconstruction, vesting responsibility for its implementation in the hands of district commanders. Johnson was authorized to select the commanders, and he made appointments that were acceptable to Congress; yet soon after the lawmakers adjourned, he began to replace the more radical commanders with more conservative ones. In addition, the president made an amnesty proclamation in September of 1867 that restored the vote to many former Confederate supporters disfranchised by the congressional acts.[21]

More than just signaling support of the Southern cause, Johnson's vetoes and his execution of the laws exercised Northern lawmakers and forced them to rely on ever-greater legislative instruction and military implementation. This required continued justification to a Northern populace that believed the war had been won in 1865 and were generally not keen on black suffrage. Republican setbacks in the 1867 elections and the repeated failure of black suffrage referendum votes in Northern states was evidence of a growing intolerance in the North for lawmakers' continued efforts on behalf of blacks. And it demonstrated to some, Johnson included, that Northern political will, ultimately dependent on popular support, was capable of being worn down.[22] In this way, the president's actions, while often unsuccessful in the short run, nonetheless modeled the potential long-term benefits of obstructionist behavior for the South.[23]

With the increase in the conditions attached to readmittance, the South, too, began to engage in obstructionist behavior. Buoyed by Northern Democratic electoral victories, white Southern conservatives began in late 1867 to organize and discipline their efforts to defeat ratification of the new state constitutions and thus repudiate Congressional Reconstruction. In Alabama, for example, conservatives encouraged a boycott of the election in the hopes that the necessary majority of registered voters would not be convened and the vote on the constitution would be nullified.[24] While their efforts failed, they nevertheless are part of the lineage of post-Civil War Southern political strategy that extends from "masterly inactivity" in the 1860s to "massive resistance" in the twentieth century.

As African Americans began mobilizing throughout the South, white Southerners' informal yet increasingly systematic methods of opposition to Reconstruction—violence, intimidation, and fraud—increased. Because the exercise of political control by the military had ended with the resumption of the states' civil operations, the army in the South was again under Johnson's full control. With violence escalating, he deferred to local commanders on when and how to respond to state requests for troops to maintain order. Southern Republicans charged that, because the commanders tended to share Johnson's conservative views, they did not provide the degree of support necessary; some even demanded that Congress reconvene earlier than planned to pass additional Reconstruction legislation.[25] Again, Johnson's actions led to leniency and, in effect, unofficial endorsement of the emerging system of racial order maintenance in the South.[26]

With Grant's election in 1868, Johnson's preemptive and obstructionist efforts in determining the Reconstruction of the South ended, but the struggle to determine the interior life of the South was not over. What had been fought out at the national institutional level was moved to the state level, as the terms to which the South had been forced to agree were now subject to interpretation on implementation. White conservatives moved quickly to enact economic policies that would ensure continued control over labor under conditions closely approximating plantation life. Some imposed penalties in ways akin to the earlier Black Codes, while others tilted the benefits of the contractual relationship between landlords and sharecroppers squarely toward the planter elite. This economic control continued to be accompanied by violence and the threat of violence.[27] Over the ensuing decades, as the South's racial caste system was reestablished, the effort by the Reconstruction Congress to reverse Johnson's policy was revealed to be nothing more than an interruption in the enactment of his vision.

REBUILDING POLITICAL INSTITUTIONS AND FORTIFYING ALLIES

Providing the South with the opportunity to rebuild its racial-economic order was a key element of Johnson's policy agenda. Yet it would be meaningless if the region did not have the capacity to sustain itself in the political arena. One way that Johnson sought to ensure this was, as described earlier, through the quick recognition of the Southern states and the facilitation of their speedy return to representation in national government. At the same time, Johnson took advantage of the political ambiguity of postwar politics to begin building new political coalitions and networks of allies.

Andrew Johnson was a Southern Democrat who assumed office as the result of the assassination of a Northern Republican president in the waning moments of the Civil War, and his political position was precarious. On the one hand, Johnson had no natural base of support. Southerners initially viewed him suspiciously because of his wartime loyalty to the Union, and Northern Republicans, especially Radicals, were wary of his regional and party roots.[28] On the other hand, with precariousness comes potential. Johnson's ambitions were focused on the presidency in 1868. Unfettered by party constraints, he was free to build his own coalition to help him in his quest. Given the unique politics of the time, this was an attractive option. Republicans were, for the moment, dominant, but theirs was a new party, tested only on the issue that birthed it: opposition to slavery and secession. A speedy resolution to war issues might sap the wind from the party's sails. Quick restoration of the South would also return that region's Democratic constituency to participation in national government elections. And there were enough Democratic and conservative Republican constituencies in the North that the possibility existed of constructing a new, national, moderate coalition that would return him to the presidency in 1868.

Johnson turned to Secretary of State Seward to help him cultivate this new base of support. Seward was anxious to steer the Republican Party away from the influence of the Radicals and in a more conservative direction, and this would be a central and legitimating part of the coalition in the North. To this end, the president curried favor with other conservative Republicans as well by distributing among them such patronage-laden posts as the collector of the Port of New York. At the same time, Johnson met and made overtures to top Democrats, in both North and South. In addition to granting clemency to many of the former elite of the South, Johnson sent his political loyalists throughout the region to oversee his restoration efforts and establish contacts. For his efforts, he received assurances from party leaders that the Democratic Party "is today a Johnson party; that the South just as rapidly as his reconstruction plans are carried out, will be a Johnson party."[29]

By 1866, in the face of an increasingly assertive oppositional Congress, Johnson intensified his efforts to build a new coalition by championing the National Union movement, made up of supporters of his restoration policy including Democrats, conservative Republicans, and conservative Southerners. That summer, a National Union convention was held; it was nicknamed the "arm-in-arm" convention after Massachusetts and South Carolina delegates entered the hall in pairs. At the same time, he purged his cabinet of those who did not support this effort (of these, only Secretary of War Stanton, who was sympathetic to Congressional Reconstruction, remained) and in their place appointed conservative Republicans.[30] The movement was defeated in the fall elections that year, but Johnson's political linkages and patronage laid the groundwork on which his allies could continue to build their political network.

This did not stop when Johnson left office. During the 1870s, Republicans were beset by Democratic and Southern conservative gains in state governments, usually accomplished through voter intimidation and fraud.[31] Organized intimidation in Alabama in the 1874 election was then successfully copied by other Southern states, resulting in the election of Redemption governments throughout the region. By 1876, Redemption governments were sufficiently ensconced in the South to affect the outcome of the presidential election, disputing returns and forcing the compromise that resulted in the selection of Republican Rutherford B. Hayes as president and the official end of Congressional Reconstruction.[32]

With the withdrawal of military troops, the South achieved the final terms of the settlement it had sought, and it was free to exercise unencumbered control over its political-economic and racial orders. Within fifteen years, this regional order, enforced informally since the end of the Civil War, acquired legal form with the adoption in the 1890s of Jim Crow segregation and restrictive voting laws.[33] The political networks and protocoalitions spawned by Johnson in the immediate aftermath of the war authorized and legitimated the Southern racial order and were, in turn, buoyed by that order. Both had the opportunity to reemerge because of Johnson's early and sustained leadership.

Ideological Disruption and the Provision of New Frames for the South

Johnson's strategy to provide the South, through preemption and obstruction, with the capacity for rebuilding its institutional and political infrastructure was made all the more powerful because he articulated the righteousness of this cause in plausible, sometimes compelling, constitutional arguments. To use language not normally attributed to the post-Civil War white South, Johnson's rhetoric, especially as it developed in opposition to Congressional Reconstruction, were part of his leadership of the politically dispossessed. Johnson was able to position the "dispossessed" South on the side of the Constitution. Because Congress was engaged in a constitutional revolution, arguably in substance and especially in form, Johnson could ally himself and the South with the cause of the original Constitution. As defenders of the Founders' Constitution, Johnson and the South could more easily claim legitimacy. This then lent authority to his interpretation of the Constitution.

Johnson's first veto was of the Freedman's Bureau Bill, passed by Congress in early 1866. The bill extended the life of the wartime agency and authorized its provision of legal and economic assistance (including land and funds for education) to former slaves. In his veto message, Johnson argued against the bureau on the grounds that it would enlarge the scope of the national government and alter the traditional, appropriate balance of federal and state governments. He claimed that the legislation's promotion of the interests of a specific group, former slaves, was unfair because whites had never received such support and that it was unnecessary because Blacks now possessed the same economic opportunities as any other group. Last, he argued that the very passage of the bill was illegitimate, because it targeted states that were not yet represented in Congress and so had no say in making the law. These themes—a defense of states' rights and limited government and a heralding of race-neutral individual rights over group rights—dominated Johnson's rhetorical battles with Congress in the ensuing years; they also became the ideological backbone of Southern conservatism for the next 150 years.

Though this was only the first of his many vetoes, Johnson used the moment to adopt his famously bellicose stance toward Radical lawmakers and Congress' attempts to legislate Reconstruction. A few days after the veto, the president responded to criticisms of his action in an impromptu speech to a crowd of his supporters. In what became known as his "Washington's Birthday Speech," Johnson linked his administration's policy to his staunch support of the Constitution and the Union—the preservation of which was the sole reason for fighting the war. Affirming the necessity of putting an end to Southern treason, Johnson then positioned the actions of Radicals, particularly the creation of the guiding hand of the Joint Committee on Reconstruction, as traitorous in its own right:

One struggle was against an attempt to dissever the Union; but almost before the smoke of the battle-field has passed away—before our brave men have all returned to their homes, and renewed the ties of affection and love to their wives and their children, *we find almost another rebellion inaugurated.* We put down the former rebellion in order to prevent the separation of the States, to prevent them from flying off, and thereby changing the character of our Government and weakening its power. . . . we find now an effort to concentrate all power in the hand of a few at the Federal head, and thereby bring about a consolidation of the Government, *which is equally objectionable with a separation.* We find that powers are assumed and attempted to be exercised of a most extraordinary character. It seems that Governments may be revolutionized—Governments at least may be changed without going through the strife of battle. I believe it is a fact attested in history that sometimes revolutions most disastrous to a people are affected without the shedding of blood. The substance of your Government may be taken away while the form and the shadow remain to you.[34] (emphasis added)

Johnson asserted that the actions of the Joint Committee and the legislation passed without representation of the South were equally a rebellion against the Constitution as the decision to secede. This did not simply claim for him the righteous action of Constitutional preservation against all enemies—though it did do that—it simultaneously pulled the South out of its status as conquered foe, giving to it instead the opportunity for redemption as the new defender of constitutional propriety. Cloaking narrow Southern goals in the language of the Constitution, Johnson's argument made the North the region behaving out of synch with constitutional mandates. Making this point more explicit are Johnson's remarks later on in the speech:

When those who rebelled comply with the Constitution, when they give sufficient evidence of loyalty, when they show that they can be trusted, when they yield obedience to the law that you and I acknowledge, I say extend to them the right hand of fellowship, and let peace and union be restored. I fought traitors and treason in the South; I opposed the Davises, the Toombes, the Slidells, and a long list of others, which you can readily fill without my repeating the names. Now, when I turn round and at the other end of the line find men—I care not by what name you call them—who still stand opposed to the restoration of the Union of these States, I am free to say to you that I am still in the field.[35]

Note that Johnson moves directly from a defense of the loyal citizens of the South to an accusation of treasonous separatism on the part of Northern leaders and an indication of his unfinished battle task (the seamlessness of being "still in the field"). In this and in other messages of the time, including the speeches of his "swing around the circle" tour in the North, Johnson's goal was to put Radicals on the defense and rally popular support behind his course of action. While there were some indications in both the Northern and Southern press that this was initially successful, by the time of the fall elections, Northern voters were rejecting Johnson's program.[36]

Northern rejection, however, is an indication of Johnson's success in signaling to the South his discontent with Congressional Reconstruction and his willingness to work on the region's behalf—a demonstration of sorts of the adage, "my enemies' enemy is my friend." His speeches decrying Congress's constitutional transgressions were heralded in the South as of "historical" significance.[37] Johnson's vetoes and speeches provided rhetorical legitimacy to the Southern cause, and he used his position of national institutional authority to sustain that side of the ideological dispute.

This was important because Southerners were willing to concede the loss of the secessionist idea as a result of Northern military victory, but the accompanying ideas surrounding race and economy had not, for them, been equally vanquished. Writing in 1866, Southern historian Edward Pollard acknowledged Johnson's role in sustaining Southern ideas: "The doctrine of secession was extinguished; and yet there is something left more than the shadow of State Rights, if we may believe President Johnson, who has recently and officially used these terms, and affirmed in them at least some substantial significance."[38]

Even after Johnson left office, Southerners continued to rely on his ideological provisions. When, in the aftermath of Reconstruction, the South moved from relatively informal, local efforts at race control to systematic control fully backed by the legal apparatus of the states, the evolution was justified through the same prism on national politics and constitutionality that Johnson had used. For white Southerners, the abolition of slavery and Congressional Reconstruction did more than simply impose objectionable conditions—it bred chaos and "mob rule." White elites argued for racial solidarity in reclaiming Southern politics on the premise that Reconstruction was, in essence, a Northern-fostered slave revolt. The establishment of African American political equality was seen as fundamentally illegitimate for a constitutional order premised on white male citizenship. This argument, which justified white Southerners' resistance to Reconstruction and reestablishment of white rule, continued the logic of Johnson's argument about Northern unconstitutionality. By ascribing to their actions a constitutional vigilance, Southern elites maintained the ideological space for their laws and their "order-maintaining" use of violence that was created earlier by Johnson's rhetoric.[39]

Southerners continued to echo Johnson when they made arguments that elided differences between the regions in order to justify increasing race control and race separation. By the 1890s, for example, Southern leaders in Congress were recalling the Black Codes and similar laws as efforts not to monitor blacks but to control labor, comparable to Northern vagrancy and apprenticeship laws.[40] Making arguments for race regulation in terms of labor and class may have been a strategy to appeal to Northern audiences; it was also a way of insisting on cross-regional solidarity, much as Johnson's efforts to rally Southern and Northern loyalists and "friends" against traitorous Radical lawmakers had done. In other words, constructing similarities became a strategy by which Johnson and subsequent Southern leaders could legitimize race policies and ward off attention to questionable Southern practices.[41]

This method of masquerading differences became a trademark of voting restriction legislation. Just as Johnson had argued for race-neutral individual rights over group rights in opposing Reconstruction legislation, arguments were now made in favor of race-neutral educational and property tests for voters. In 1890, Mississippi became the first state to codify an education qualification in its constitution, and it received the support, not just of Southerners, but of press and politicians from throughout the North as well.[42] That these sorts of laws also disfranchised many poor whites does not diminish the fact that, particularly when deployed in the context of the full range of Jim Crow laws, blacks were primary targets for disfranchisement.

When Northerners in Congress first began their task of Reconstruction in the 1860s, they were under the sway of an influential Republican lawyer from Boston, Richard Dana, who argued that the North should use the instrument of national government to hold the South "in the grasp of war" until it had extracted from the vanquished region all that it justly deserved as the fruits of its victory.[43] This justified an expansion of the capacity of the national government and its reliance on the military until the South had submitted to Northern demands. This Northern plan for Reconstruction was ultimately unsuccessful. Whether out of a sense of moral justice or out of an interest in securing the region politically, the North's demand that the South reconstitute its social, economic, and political order to give Blacks a fair and equal place failed. Indeed, bolstered by Andrew Johnson's leadership—his legitimating rhetoric, his strategic lessons, the capacity-building space he cleared, and the lifeline to national government he provided while the region was disfranchised—the South more effectively executed Dana's strategy. With Johnson's early encouragement, the South held the North in "the grasp of war," a guerrilla war to be sure but a war nonetheless, until it wearied of the effort of attempting to impose its will. Analyzing the class politics of the time, Eric Foner has written that Reconstruction began with the South trying to adjust to the North's system of free labor and ended with the North accepting the South's understanding of labor-capital conflict.[44] The same could be said of the evolution of the regions with regard to race relations: the attempts to impose a more egalitarian racial politics on the South ended with the North's acceptance of the other region's system of racial order management.

Though Johnson's actions toward this end were often thwarted and though they led to his impeachment, they are not simply indications of his failure as a president. What he did successfully with his preemptive efforts on behalf of the South, his obstructionist politics, and his dogged rhetoric was to lay the groundwork for and guide Southern states toward ultimate victory: a return to the Union with the freedom to determine their own socioeconomic order. Southern conservative leaders acknowledged the defeat of slavery, but they refused to accommodate in any but the most superficial of ways the additional demands placed on them by Northern lawmakers. And in the end, they prevailed—for over one hundred years. The collapse of Congressional Reconstruction in the 1870s removed the last barrier to the institution of the Jim Crow South, complete with the political disfranchisement, economic subjugation, and social segregation of African Americans that white Southerners had been seeking since the end of the war.

Reflections on the Politics of Failure

The birth of the Jim Crow South may well have resulted absent the actions of Andrew Johnson. But the shape and the character of the South, and of American politics more generally, was surely facilitated by Johnson's unconventional leadership. We offer this claim as a useful counterpoint to a dominant theme in the literature of American political development that stresses the structure and direction of Northern capitalism as well as Republican political miscalculations as the principal cause of the end of Reconstruction.

Tocqueville reminds us that, just as regimes have their characteristic vices, so do the historians who write within them. Democratic historians diminish the significance of "great men" while overemphasizing the role of impersonal laws or underlying social forces. Aristocratic historians overemphasize the significance of individuals and neglect the role of social forces. For Tocqueville, the truth of history always lies somewhere in the middle, in some combination of general causes and individual interventions. However, he stresses that, for democracies to approach the truth of their histories, they need to confront and counteract their own worst tendencies, such as their neglect of the significance of individual agency, of leadership, of human intervention in the course of affairs.[45] One cannot understand the development of American politics from the end of the Civil War through the middle of the twentieth century if one does not comprehend the leadership of Andrew Johnson.

Yet to think of Andrew Johnson as a "democratic" leader raises its own set of questions about the meaning and nature of leadership on the one hand, and of the character of the polity he led on the other.

The Johnson case illustrates the fact that skillful and creative leadership may be deeply problematic. It may frustrate the deeper aspirations of democracy, or depending on one's understanding of democracy, it may advance democracy at the expense of other constitutional values. The concepts of agency, entrepreneurship, and leadership are too narrow to capture the political direction of change because they are neutral or value free. These terms are better discussed in tandem with a notion like statesmanship, because taken together, one can elucidate the content and direction of the change being sought as well as the strategy and tactics deployed. Johnson was an exceptionally effective leader. But in considering what he accomplished, we realize that the more effective he was as a leader, the more he failed as a statesman.

Our account also uncovers and illustrates a design flaw in the logic of American constitutionalism. Much like a hacker whose virus exploits the operating system of a computer, Andrew Johnson exploited and successfully subverted a basic attribute of the constitutional order. In the understanding of *The Federalist*, for example, the Constitution will be effective to the extent that it is able to institutionalize hypocrisy. Political self-interest is translated into action for the common good by the creation of incentives for ambitious politicians to defend their actions with publicly justifiable reasons. In this view, the injustice or prejudice of individual motives become politically irrelevant to the extent that politicians feel constrained to justify their actions with good reasons—though these reasons may not have actually been their motivation. As long as politics trades on the plane of these public-regarding rationalizations, liberal constitutionalism will have worked.

Now one might have thought that this attribute of American politics would have precluded manifestly unjust policies like those that paid little heed to the needs of former slaves. But the circumstances of constitutional failure surrounding the Civil War forced those who would rid the Constitution of slavery to adopt means and arguments that went beyond the Constitution. Thus, Radical Republicans imposed a settlement on the South, violated the terms for amending the document, adopted military tribunals in the place of civil courts, and more generally, allowed abstract notions of justice to trump settled legal practice. Most important, the partisans of the Northern vision of Reconstruction argued that all these policies were legitimate because they were constitutional. Few, if any, Republicans argued that necessity required extra-constitutional emergency measures for Reconstruction. They pretended to operate under a constitution, while they actually operated outside it. In this circumstance, the logic of constitutional hypocrisy might not work as intended. Andrew Johnson was thus sometimes able to construct better constitutional arguments than his opponents could. Johnson covered his narrow and unjust sectionalist motives with plausible, sometimes sound constitutional argument, whereas his opponents distorted the Constitution, however sound their political motives. By exploiting the logic of constitutionally induced argument, Andrew Johnson reveals a limit of the political architecture—a point at which the Constitution fails.

Chapter 9

Forging a New Grammar of Equality and Difference: Progressive Era Suffrage and Reform

Eileen McDonagh

The Grammar of Liberalism

The "grammar" of liberalism directs all claims of access to politics through the same channel: individual equality. It is this principle that informs the two main components of political citizenship: voting and office-holding. Analysts of politics in the United States, beginning with Alexis de Tocqueville and including Gunnar Myrdal, Louis Hartz, and Samuel Huntington, describe a polity founded on and dominated by this liberal principle. Rebelling against a feudal world defined politically and socially by static identities and ascribed group differences, the fledgling nation declared as a self-evident truth that all were "created equal." In principle, ascriptive group difference was deemed to be irrelevant as a qualification for access to political participation and governing authority.

It goes without saying that there was at the outset an enormous gap between liberal theory and practice. Not only did slavery remain intact as an institution for almost a century, but so, too, did coverture marriage, an institution annihilating the civil identity and basic legal rights of married women. Well into the nineteenth century, common law tradition as codified by William Blackstone was the rule: "by marriage, the husband and wife are one person in law: that is, the very being or legal existence of the woman is suspended during the marriage, or at least is incorporated and consolidated into that of the husband."[1] By these terms, married women in the United States were legally restricted from owning property, inheriting property, claiming their wages as their own, or even signing contracts. In addition, married women had neither authority over their children nor custody rights for them should marriage terminate. In addition, a husband possessed a form of ownership right over his wife that legally entitled him to her services and to compensation for the loss of her services should she be injured in an industrial accident or should she run away and be sheltered by another person.[2]

What is more, at the founding of the American state, the very ascriptive group differences liberal theory deemed irrelevant to political citizenship—such as class, race, and sex—were used at the state level to define voting qualifications. At the outset all states invoked some form of property qualification for the franchise, seven states explicitly used racial qualifications to define their electorates, and by 1807 all states explicitly limited the vote to men. Rationalization of these exclusions generally relied on negative depictions of subordinate class, racial, and gender groups: the propertyless were too unreliable to exercise voting rights, racially subordinate groups insufficiently prepared for political citizenship, and women lacked independence of judgment necessary to vote by virtue of being too dependent on others, such as their parents or husbands.

However, if the case of women stands out, it is because the group difference that rationalized their exclusion also emphasized their positive virtues. For example, as historian Linda Kerber has shown, women as an ascriptive group were viewed as making invaluable contributions to the public sphere from their position in the home as mothers and nurturers of children, the citizens-to-be. Women's socialization of children took on special political relevance in the United States because in addition to its liberal heritage, the Founders established a republican form of government based on popular sovereignty. In this type of state, the assumption that the people are sovereign as free and equal participants in political governance requires the people to have imbibed civic virtue in childhood if they were later to be capable of governing effectively. The paradox is that at the founding of the American state, the unique maternal capacities associated with women as a group became the very basis for their exclusion from the public sphere in order to facilitate their contributions as "Republican mothers," who were viewed by the Founders and the populace as essential to the state though not included in it.[3]

Thus, the grammar of individual equality would in fact become a double-edged sword for women as they struggled for access to voting and office-holding rights in the liberal American state. Those who would claim access to the public sphere in America were encouraged to argue that they were the *same* as others "in spite of" their ascriptive group differences. In other words, the task for those individuals excluded "because of" their race, class, or sex was to convince others that their *group differences were irrelevant* to the public sphere of voting and office-holding. This is the grammar that worked for class and race in dramatic and startling ways.

However, the grammar of equality *alone* did not work—and perhaps cannot—for women, whatever their class or race. How can a group, such as women, argue that their maternal group difference is irrelevant to the public sphere of political rule in a liberal, republican state when good citizenship required for participation in such a state depends on women's social maternalism. True, men can "mother," that is, nurture and socialize children to be good citizens as well as women, but traditionally, men do not. What is more, even were there to be "mothering equity" between men and women, there is still women's biological maternalism to consider. Though, of course, the capacity to give birth is not an essentialist distinction common to all women as individuals; nevertheless, given even today's reproductive technology, it is still necessary for at least some "individuals" from the group "women" to be pregnant and to give birth, if society and the state are to continue, whatever the form of governance.

Thus, in distinction to other ascriptive groups, women do—and, I argue—must retain a positive and an intractable group difference in relation to the state, even when claiming equal rights as individuals who are the same as men. Women's necessary and positive group difference, therefore, limits the degree to which it makes sense for political reformers to claim that the *only* aspect about women that is relevant to their participation in political governance is their "sameness" with men. To the contrary, it is precisely women's maternal group difference from men—social and biological—as well as women's sameness with men, that is not only relevant to the public sphere of governance, but essential to it.

Women's political citizenship, therefore, in contrast to other ascriptive groups, advances most effectively when women's identities as individuals who are the same as men are *added to, not substituted for,* their identities as maternalists who are different from men. Consequently, in contrast to other ascriptive groups, women's political citizenship advances on the basis of a different grammar than that of equality alone. It advances on the basis of a grammar of equality *and* difference.

The Grammar of Equality *and* Difference

I argue here that, although the grammar of equality and difference potentially was available from the very inception of the American state, it was not developed by woman suffrage reformers until the early twentieth-century decades of the Progressive era. Prior to this time, the dominant grammar used to advance women's political rights was the same as that used for other ascriptive groups, namely, the grammar of individuality alone. This, as the nineteenth century illustrates, resulted in political failure for women.

I contend that the reason reform agents could articulate a new grammar of equality *and* difference in the Progressive era is because this was a time period when the American state itself endorsed a set of public policies representing these dual principles. That is to say, state action expanded at the state and national levels to include social and economic legislative provisions for those at the mercy of the newly industrializing American society. The incipient American welfare state that was founded in the Progressive era, therefore, represents "maternalism" as socially defined, that is, as the provision of social and economic assistance to those in need. At the same time, however, the basic liberal structure of the American state remained intact in the Progressive era as is evident from very language of the Nineteenth Amendment, which guarantees women's right to vote as individuals "in spite of" their sex.

When the state performs by means of its political institutions and public policies in ways that represent women's dual identities, such state performance teaches the public, so to speak, that the sphere of political governance is "like women," that is, the public sphere is one that embodies the dual principles of individual equality and maternal group difference. State performance that represents women's dual identities, therefore, generates public attitudes that view women as more suitable as political leaders, thereby opening the door to agents of political reform to capitalize on these public attitudes by developing a rhetorical grammar of equality *and* difference as justification for expanding women's political citizenship. This I argue, was what happened in the United States in the Progressive era, as Figure 1 illustrates.

The State Performance Mechanism

Social policies create citizens. Political scientist Theda Skocpol and others make a persuasive case that "structure matters." In Skocpol's foundational work on American political development, for example, she demonstrates how the structural location of women in the Progressive era as voteless citizens claiming identities as moral, maternal caregivers, combined with their federally structured voluntary organizations, spearheaded the establishment of an American maternalist state, defined by the passage at the state level of mothers' pensions prior to such developments in comparable Western democracies.[4] Building on her work, others such as Suzanne Mettler, Andrea Campbell, Robert Lieberman, and Jacob Hacker argue persuasively that the structure of state social policies, particularly the way their content and their administration includes or excludes segments of the

POLITICAL STRUCTURE	PUBLIC ATTITUDES	REFORM AGENTS	POLITICAL CITIZENSHIP
State Performance - - ->of Equality and Difference	Public Attitudes - - - - ->Supporting Women as Political Leaders	Grammar - - - - - ->of Equality and Difference	Women's Right to Vote

Figure 1. Equality and difference model of women's right to vote.

mass public, affects the degree of civic engagement of the recipients.[5] As
Suzanne Mettler argues, the inclusion of mass publics, such as African
American men, in social programs, such as the G.I. Bill, had an impact on
their subsequent civic engagement. By extension, exclusion from social
programs had the reverse impact; that is, exclusion reduces subsequent
civic engagement.[6]

State performance creates citizens. I agree, but extend attention to the way social policies set parameters for civic engagement of mass publics to the way
state performance sets parameters for the expansion of *women's political citizenship.*[7] I argue here that it was the state performance in the Progressive era
of women's dual identities as individuals who are the same as men, and as
maternalists who are different from men, that provided the structural context that enabled the agency of woman suffrage reformers to develop a
public grammar of equality *and* difference that facilitated support among
the public and political elites for expanding the right to vote to include
women.

After the Progressive era, however, reformers in Congress and the presidency failed to sustain this combination in public policies at the national
level. I argue that it is this failure that explains why today the contemporary
United States is such a laggard among the world's industrial, Western
democracies in terms of the other component of women's political citizenship: office-holding.

We can discern the efficacy of the grammar of equality *and* difference as
advanced by political reformers in conjunction with the state's public policies by examining how equality alone failed to secure women's political citizenship in the nineteenth century, how equality and difference succeeded
in the Progressive era, and how the American state's laggard status in relation to women's national office-holding patterns results from the failure of
the United States to support both principles of equality and difference in
its current public policies.

The Nineteenth Century: The Grammar of Equality and Political Failure

State performance in the nineteenth century. Foundational documents of the
American state, such as the Declaration of Independence and the Bill of
Rights, attest to its liberal heritage based on the principle that what is relevant to the public sphere of governance is the equality of all individuals "in
spite of" their ascriptive group difference. The national government even
at its founding, and after the Civil War, did provide social benefits to a select group of Americans, namely, veterans who had served their country in
military combat. As political scientist Laura Jensen has shown, the American government as early as 1776 used federal pensions and land entitlement as incentives to encourage participation in the accomplishment of

America's national goals.[8] Similarly, as Theda Skocpol has demonstrated, Civil War pensions in the late nineteenth century expanded to provide "disability, old-age, and survivors' benefits for anyone who could claim minimal service time on the northern side of the Civil War."[9]

However, it was not until the Progressive-era decades of the twentieth century that the United States developed social and economic regulatory and economic provisionary policies sufficient to constitute the claim that the American state was a "welfare state," be it ever so fledgling. Hence, in the nineteenth century, the all-but-dominant norm acted out by the American state by means of its political institutions and public policies was the liberal prinicple of individual equality.

Equality and political reform. It was the grammar of individual equality on which reforms to enfranchise propertyless white men in the early nineteenth century were successful. So, too, did abolitionist reformers in the early nineteenth century invoke liberal claims that all individuals are created equal to challenge the presence of the institution of slavery in the United States. It was the use of the grammar of individual equality in the context of abolition, in fact, that first triggered for American women recognition of the blatant sexism that existed alongside blatant racism.

Many women joined abolitionist organizations in the early nineteenth century, which typically were segregated by sex. Thus, when a World Anti-Slavery Convention was held in London in the summer of 1840, the American delegation included representatives from both male and female abolition associations. However, after heated debate, Convention officials refused to recognize the women from the American delegation, ruling that only the men could be seated.[10]

Lucretia Mott and Elizabeth Cady Stanton were two of the women excluded from the American delegation. Mott, in particular, was already a public persona in the abolition cause. She had dedicated her home in Philadelphia as a center of the Underground Railroad, founded the first Female Anti-Slavery Society, and had become a gifted public speaker advocating abolition. Stanton was a young woman whose father had been a judge. Her sensibilities about the need for women's rights had been developed by the many hours she had spent as a child crouched in the corner of his study, listening to the frantic stories of women who had no legal recourse in response to abusive and dominating husbands. Elizabeth had just married Henry B. Stanton, a leading abolitionist noted for his courage and skill in facing down mobs of angry protestors, and she was primed to expand her sensibilities about injustice, as tutored by the seasoned and sophisticated Lucretia Mott. The refusal of the Convention to allow these two women to participate solely because of their sex galvanized their attention to the pressing concern of sex discrimination. The result eight years later was the Seneca Falls Convention.[11]

Drawing on the grammar of individual equality as exemplified in the American Declaration of Independence, these early feminists drafted a Declaration of Sentiments. The document used language parallel to Jefferson's Declaration of Independence to reject men's tyranny over women and impress upon their countrymen how this tyranny was analogous to King George's tyranny over American colonists. The Declaration of Sentiments proclaims:

When, in the course of human events, it becomes necessary for one portion of the family of man to assume among the people of the earth a position different from that which they have hitherto occupied, but one to which the laws of nature and of nature's God entitle them, a decent respect to the opinions of mankind requires that they should declare the causes that impel them to such a course.

We hold these truths to be self-evident: that all men and women are created equal; that they are endowed by their Creator with certain inalienable rights; that among these are life, liberty, and the pursuit of happiness, that to secure these rights governments are instituted, deriving their just powers from the consent of the governed. Whenever any form of government becomes destructive of these ends, it is the right of those who suffer from it to refuse allegiance to it, and to insist upon the institution of a new government . . . when a long train of abuses and usurpations [by government] . . . evinces a design to reduce them [the people] under absolute despotism, it is their duty to throw off such government. . . . Such has been the patient sufferance of the women under this government and such is now the necessity which constrains them to demand the equal station to which they are entitled.

The history of mankind is a history of repeated injuries and usurpations on the part of man toward woman, having in direct object the establishment of an absolute tyranny over her.

The Declaration of Sentiments then identifies a wide range of policies that subordinate women in relation to men, including the right to vote; coverture marriage (in which married women had no civil identity, meaning no right to their own property, right to sign contracts, and so on); women's lack of employment opportunities, including prohibitions against women entering the Church; lack of educational opportunities for women; double standards for men and women in morality and sexual experience; and women's deprivation of psychological resources, such as self-respect and independence.[12]

The debate at Seneca Falls was a preview for what would be the debate over voting rights for African Americans and women in the aftermath of the Civil War. Women should be given equal rights "despite" their group difference; group difference does not establish a basis for unequal treatment. The responses in Congress to such a claim when applied to African Americans and women were equally parallel. That is, Congressional debate on voting rights during Reconstruction pitted reformers using individual rights rather than group differences as an argument for expanding political citizenship, against those wishing to bar African Americans from the right to vote by depicting their group difference as a rationale for their continued exclusion. Senator Davis argued,

It is nothing but a form of demagoguery to say that every man is entitled by nature to the right to hold office or to vote. . . . They do not exist as natural rights. They ought not to exist as universal rights, because the intelligence, the circumstances, and the condition of all nations differ. . . . Gentlemen, concede that idiots and lunatics have not either a natural or an artificial right to vote or to hold office. I ask them how they can give this right to a race of men [African Americans] who throughout their whole history, in every country and condition in which they have ever been placed, have demonstrated their utter inability for self-government.[13]

In the case of women, exactly the same tactic was used by those who opposed woman suffrage. That is, opponents used the language of *group difference* to argue for the *political exclusion* of women from the electorate. Senator Williams argued, for example, "When God married our first parents in the garden according to that ordinance they were made 'bone of one bone and flesh of one flesh'; and *the whole theory of government and society proceeds upon the assumption that their interests are one* . . . the woman who undertakes to put her sex in an adversary position to man, who undertakes by the use of some independent political power [such as the vote] to contend and fight against man, displays a spirit which would, if able, convert all the now harmonious elements of society into a state of war, and make every home a hell upon earth."[14]

   To combat arguments about group difference as a reason for political exclusion, others in Congress advanced arguments about the *sameness* of Blacks and whites and of men and women. That is, they invoked the grammar of individual equality to argue for the political inclusion of individuals subordinated by their ascriptive characteristics. As Representative Logan stated in the case of race, "What we should do, in my judgment, is to give all men without regard to race or color the right of suffrage."[15] Senator Welch stated that it is an "absurd position, contrary to all true philosophy, that a man cannot hold office in this Republic, not because of what is in him, but because he belongs to a certain race, because he has a skin not colored like our own."[16] Similarly Senator Anthony made the same individual equality argument for women, stating that "The true basis of suffrage of course is intelligence and virtue . . . [and] it will not be contended that there is such a difference in the intellectual capacity of the sexes as that alone should be a disqualification from the exercise of the right of suffrage."[17]

   For women, however, the "in spite of" argument, *in and by itself*, was an especially hard sell. As women's difference was deemed essential to the state, a plain assertion of their sameness threatened to rob the state of a resource vital to its very survival. Rail as they might against the nonsense of their inequality, women were in a sense arguing against themselves, cutting themselves off from a palpable, valuable, politically potent sense of their difference. Consequently, the nineteenth-century grammar of equality failed miserably, as no women—whatever their class or race privilege or liability—secured voting rights comparable to men's.

In the end, the language of equality worked for men but it did not work for women. Thus, by the end of the nineteenth century, no states invoked property or race as voting qualifications in contrast to 91 percent of the states that used sex as a qualification for voting. The grammar of individual equality alone, therefore, was insufficient for expanding women's political citizenship in the nineteenth century. Women would advance only when they used their group difference as an additional rationale for their inclusion. Moreover, the transformative political implications of women's inclusion in the state, the reconstruction of authority attendant on this shift in authority, would only be manifested to the extent that this alternative argument could take hold in the Progressive era, a time period when the state itself became representative of women's dual identities.

The Progressive Era: Equality and Difference and Political Success

It was not as if the people of the Progressive era discovered for the first time that it was women, not men, who became pregnant and bore children, or that it was women, instead of men, who did most of the care-work in society. Nor was it novel to place such maternal contributions in a positive framework. To the contrary, it was common to attribute the very stability of society as resting on the foundation of the family, and within the institution of the family, on the maternal roles of women. In this respect, therefore, women were a unique subordinate group, one viewed positively by society, even though excluded from political citizenship.

It was only until the Progressive era, however, that women were able to capitalize on this difference to advance their role *in* the state. This was a time of acute sensitivity to the threat of rampant industrialization to the welfare of people. It was easy to understand how the working conditions of children and other people caught up in the factory system might be dangerous to their health and well-being. Reformers of all stripes sought to use the power of government as an instrument for promoting the welfare of people. Those seeking to expand the role of government in the service of people's welfare, therefore, saw women as a group as their allies.

Even without the right to vote, many viewed women's involvement in the public sphere as volunteers as already changing it for the better. Paula Baker and others have argued that women's voteless activities in the public sphere in the late nineteenth and early twentieth centuries were effective in "domesticating politics."[18] Elizabeth Clemens and Michael McGerr point to the development by women of distinct political styles, presaging those of our contemporary period.[19] Seth Koven and Sonya Michel depict women's voteless activities as producing "federal maternalists," such as Julia Lathrop and Grace Abbot, who were able to "translate the ethos of the settlement house into a distinct political mode and agenda."[20] Kathryn Kish Sklar stresses the state-building effects of women's voteless activities in the Progressive Era, claiming that "gender did the work of class in shaping the welfare state."[21] And Theda Skocpol has established the power of women's voteless agency prior to obtaining the right to vote as responsible for establishing mothers' pensions legislation across the states.[22]

Thus, reformers in the Progressive era had every reason to believe that if women could accomplish so much in the way of welfare reform without the right to vote, how much more would they be able to do with the right to vote. Reformers envisioned that enfranchising women "because of" their maternal group difference would add to the electorate more voters who supported the types of welfare legislation needed to protect the multitudes of people at the mercy of unregulated industrial capitalism.

The claim that women should be added to the electorate "because of" their maternal group difference has been the subject of considerable scholarship. Pioneering work by historian Aileen Kraditor finds this rhetorical mechanism to have been so dominant as to replace the reliance of nineteenth-century woman suffrage reformers on liberal arguments that women should have the right to vote "in spite of" their group difference from men.[23] Other historians, such as Alexander Keyssar, attribute women's acquisition of the right to vote in the Progressive era as primarily based on twisting the meaning of women's group difference from a reason to be politically excluded to a reason to be politically included.[24] The emphasis on the "difference" argument for the success of woman suffrage, therefore, has many proponents.

Other scholars, however, attribute the success of woman suffrage to the continuation and development of liberal arguments pressing for incorporation "in spite of" differences. Carol DuBois, for example, brilliantly analyzes how Elizabeth Cady Stanton's nineteenth-century legacy is continued in the Progressive era. She refers to Stanton's daughter Harriott Stanton Blanch, a noted woman suffrage activist in the state of New York, to document these ideological continuities. These scholars argue that it was "sameness" "in spite of" arguments that tipped the balance for achieving passage and ratification of the Nineteenth Amendment.[25]

It is true that difference arguments were traditionally employed to justify women's subordination and exclusion. The fact that liberal arguments about individual equality also remained as a component of the narrative was critical in inverting the political implications of difference. What is most remarkable and unique in the feminist movement of the Progressive era is neither the advance of difference arguments nor the advance of sameness arguments. It is the way suffrage reformers *combined* arguments about women's maternal group difference for the right to vote with arguments about women's individual equality. This was their formative act. It founded women's right to vote on the dual ground of maternalism and individualism, and did so in full view of the politically transformative implications of that combination. In so doing, the efficacy of reformers' use of a grammar of equality and difference stemmed from the way that grammar complemented the state's performance of equality and difference vis-à-vis its public policies in the Progressive era.

State Performance in the Progressive Era: Equality and Difference

The American heritage is complex, but a consistent characteristic is its emphasis on liberal individual equality. What is remarkable about the Progressive era, however, is the way the American state expanded its public policies to include a positive recognition of group difference, at least in the issue area of economic assistance through regulatory policies and even to some degree redistributive polices.

Mothers' pensions. Legislatively, the Progressive era is remarkable for passing mothers' pensions legislation at the state level. As Theda Skocpol has shown, this legislation authorized states to provide funding to women to support their roles as mothers to children.[26] Thus, mothers' pensions legislation exemplifies a policy authorizing the state to give women privileges, benefits, and protections "because of" their ascriptive group difference from men in contrast to treating women equally "in spite of" their ascriptive group difference. Skocpol has argued that the establishment of mothers' pensions in the United States in the early twentieth century marked the United States as a pioneer nation in establishing social provision benefits for women's maternal role. From the perspective of American liberalism, mothers' pension legislation is equally remarkable as an example of the state's provisions of benefits "because of" a positive, ascriptive group identity.

Sheppard-Towner Act. Jeannette Rankin was elected to the House of Representatives in 1917, thereby becoming the first woman to serve as a member of Congress. The next year, in 1918, she introduced a bill to provide federal funds for the protection of mothers and infants. In the 66th Congress, Senator Morris Sheppard (D-Tex.) and Representative Horace Towner (R-Iowa) reintroduced Rankin's bill as the Sheppard-Towner Act. The Sheppard-Towner Act, though modest in its provision was nonetheless the first to provide federally funded benefits to mothers and children. As a result, during the period of implementation, the infant death rate dropped from 75 per thousand live births to 64 per thousand, and the maternal death rate dropped from over 67 per thousand to 62.3.[27]

Protective labor legislation for women. The Progressive era is a time period in which female workers also received special policy benefits "because of" their ascriptive maternalism. As Susan Lehrer puts it, night work and long hours deemed unhealthy for men were considered especially dangerous for women, because "women's physiological makeup differed from men's and rendered them more susceptible to injury," and because "women had household responsibilities in addition to their wage labor" that might be handicapped by adverse work demands.[49] Working on the assumption that after work, women would return to a home that expected and required the services of a wife and mother, "no-night work laws were linked with the hours limitation" laws for women.[28]

The Supreme Court endorsed special benefits for working women, though not for men. For example, when asked to consider whether it was a valid exercise of the police power of the state to limit work for bakers to no more than ten hours per day or a sixty-hour week, the Court ruled in *Lochner v. New York*[29] in 1905 that a state statute limiting the number of hours of work for bakers "necessarily interferes with the right of contract between the employer and employees . . . [and that] The general right to make a contract in relation to his business is part of the liberty of the individual protected by the Fourteenth Amendment of the Federal Constitution."[30] However, when the same type of legislation came before the Court in the context of women workers in *Muller v. Oregon*[31] in 1908, it was upheld, precisely on the basis of women's ascriptive maternalism. The Court stated:

> We held in *Lochner v. New York* . . . that a law providing that no laborer shall be required or permitted to work in bakeries more than sixty hours in a week or ten hours in a day was not, as to men, a legitimate exercise of the police power of the state . . . and as such was in conflict with, and void under [the Fourteenth Amendment of] the Federal Constitution. That decision is invoked by plaintiff in error as decisive of the question before us. *But this assumes that the difference between the sexes does not justify a different rule respecting a restriction of the hours of labor* . . . [however] health[y] mothers are essential to vigorous offspring, [so] the physical wellbeing of woman becomes an object of public interest and . . . *she is properly placed in a class by herself, and legislation designed for her protection may be sustained, even when like legislation is not necessary for men, and could not be sustained.*[32]

Woman Suffrage Reformers: Equality and Difference

The way woman suffrage reformers successfully forged a language of equality and difference in the Progressive era that complemented the state performance of these dualities is evident in their justifications for women's right to vote. We can see the way woman suffrage reformers solidified a new grammar of equality and difference by examining the justifications for women's right to vote in the speeches of two major figures in the Progressive era, Carrie Chapman Catt and Jane Addams.

Carrie Chapman Catt. The major social movement organization behind the drive for women suffrage in the Progressive era was the National American Woman Suffrage Association (NAWSA). In 1916, Carrie Chapman Catt took over as president of NAWSA, and it was she who saw the suffrage amendment through to the end, including its passage by Congress and ratification by three-fourths of the states. Mainstream suffrage reformers, such as those involved in NAWSA, are dubbed by some historians as "social feminists," meaning that they argued that women should have the right to vote "because of" their maternal group difference from men.[33] However, when we examine how Carrie Chapman Catt constructed arguments for woman suffrage, we see that what she really did is to combine difference arguments with sameness arguments, that is, to use a rhetorical form of maternal individualism to expand women's political citizenship. To document this combination, I will draw on fifteen speeches and fourteen articles included in the Carrie Chapman Catt papers at the Schlesinger Library at Harvard University.

Carrie Chapman Catt expressed women's difference in a variety of ways, including reference to innate character difference between women and men. She held firmly that "men must climb up and that women must always refuse to go down."[34] She also stated that the government "continues to make and to enforce laws not only without regard to the wishes or opinions of its women citizens but often in direct opposition to the known views of the majority of them," implying that women's wishes are different than men's.[35] She also ascribed different capabilities to women and men, saying that women are used to taking "half a loaf" and can do much more with it than men can.[36] In addition, she stated that "the virtues of women are assets worth having in a government," implying that women's virtues are different than men's and are not already represented in the government.[37]

Practically, these virtues and differences between women and men meant a difference in behavior, both with the vote and before it. Without the vote, women were led toward charitable works. "The best types of [rich] women . . . have engaged their activities in good works. The land is covered with the institutions which such women have built and are maintaining. Along a thousand avenues their hands are outstretched to uplift the fallen, to guide the erring, to help the weak, to strengthen our entire social machinery."[38] Unfortunately, this was at the time the only way that these issues could be addressed. With the vote, however, women would feel the need to enact humane and decent legislation attentive to the needs of all women and children, and to the degradation of the state by rampant corruption and poverty. As she stated, "For years women have labored to secure the vote as a tool with which to build a better nation."[39]

In the following passages, Catt suggests that it precisely because women are different from men that they can be counted on to build a different nation. In particular, as she argued, the inclusion of women in the electorate would clean up corruption in government. "When American women secure their vote, corruption must depart. I personally believe that the first great effort made by voting women will be to reestablish the sanctity of the ballot, to elevate our political campaigns from the mud and mire of control by money and conspiracy to a plane of argument, reason and persuasion."[40]

Catt also stressed the way women would provide civic improvement in general, were they to be enfranchised. She said, "The women voters of the world, and they number millions, united, insistent, can do for the women of those struggling new republics what no man ever has done for them. . . . place the ballot in the hands of women and make them responsible citizens. In the Public Schools, the Sunday Schools and the Settlements, women will undertake with a new understanding and a new zeal the task of the 'Melting Pot'."[41] "They and they alone can train in the souls of the young of our country the kind of patriotism and honor that will guard our nation in the time of peril."[42]

Importantly, however, the difference argument did not stand alone. After all, the difference argument had been used throughout the nineteenth century to cut women off from the public sphere. To prevent the positive valuation of their difference from continuing to justify their exclusion, women needed sameness arguments as well. Claims of individual equality permeate the speeches of Carrie Chapman Catt. Echoing the nineteenth-century Seneca Falls Declaration of Sentiments, she equates woman suffrage with the Declaration of Independence: "woman suffrage became an assured fact when the Declaration of Independence was written . . . woman suffrage rests exactly upon the same basis as man suffrage. Women ask for it because it is the right of a citizen of a Republic to express a ballot's share in the making of the law the citizen is expected to obey."[43]

If anything, the onset of World War I intensified Catt's reliance on arguments about democracy and the equality of all citizens in terms of why women should have the right to vote. Thus, all in all, we find that in a wide range of speeches delivered by Carrie Chapman Catt, she used sameness arguments twice as often as different arguments, as Figure 2 indicates. Even *within* the NAWSA, a mainstream organization that exemplifies the maternalist "because of" argument in the Progressive Era, suffrage leaders characteristically combine difference, "because of" arguments for woman suffrage with sameness, "in spite of" arguments.

Jane Addams. Many associate Jane Addams with the application of social reform policies in the context of her establishment of Hull House in Chicago; her tireless efforts to improve the economic, political, and cultural position of immigrants; and her centrality to the Progressive Party.[44] However, when we look at the writings of Jane Addams, we find she used an astute construction of difference and sameness principles to advance not only the political incorporation of immigrants but also the political citizenship of women. Through an examination of fifty-eight of her articles, all taken from the Jane Addams Papers on microfilm at the Schlesinger Li-

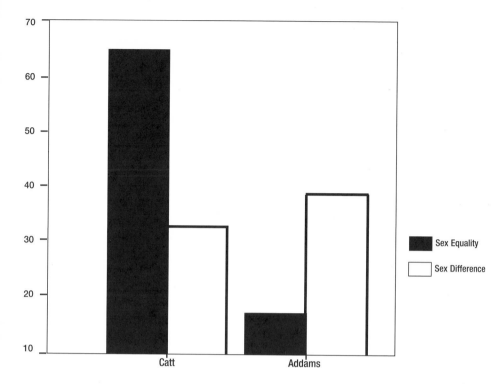

Figure 2. Percent equality and difference arguments for woman suffrage used by Carrie Chapman Catt and Jane Addams in the Progressive era, based on analysis of all the papers of Carrie Chapman Catt and Jane Addams archived at the Schlesinger Library.

brary, Harvard University, we can see the way in which she constructed a new grammar of political citizenship, one based on combining women's political identities as maternalists who were different from men and as individuals who were the same as men, that is, combining maternalism and individualism, for advancing the cause of women's right to vote.

Jane Addams, like others in the Progressive era, advanced difference arguments for suffrage, referencing women's abilities as mothers. Addams believed that both experience and an innate motherly instinct makes them more willing and more capable of dealing with humanitarian issues such as poor conditions for workers, unclean food, and unclean housing for the working class. She said in a speech, "All legislation that pertains to children, whether educational, industrial or corrective, relates to the chief occupation of women. Men can never feel so intense an interest or have so large a part in the training of children as do women."[45] In an article, she recognizes the importance of having diverse opinions in order to deal better with societal problems:

In a complex community like the modern city all points of view need to be represented; the resultants of diverse experiences need to be pooled if the community would make for sane and balanced progress. . . . After all, woman's traditional function has been to make her dwelling place both clean and fair. Is that dreariness in city life, that lack of domesticity which the humblest farm dwelling presents, due to a withdrawal of one of the naturally co-operating forces?[46]

Addams amplifies this point by describing what a society in which gender roles were reversed would be like. She asks us to imagine "a hypothetical society solely organized upon the belief that 'there is no wealth but life' . . . let us further assume that the political machinery of such a society, the franchise and the rest of it, were in the hands of women, because they had always best exercised these functions."[47] In such a society, it would be men who would be petitioning for the right to be included in the electorate, not women. And the question is: what would be the grounds for and against the enfranchisement of men? Addams suggests that women would say, "Our most valid objection to extending the franchise to you, is that you are so fond of fighting—you always have been, since the dawn of history. You'd very likely forget that the real object of the State is to nurture and protect life."[48]

Another important place where positive difference comes up in Addams's writing is on the issue of peace. Addams feels that women are more sensitive to the importance of peace and the repercussions of war, while men are inherently aggressive and quick to engage in violence. She writes, "Women always pay the great costs of war, not only during the conflict but in the years of suffering and privation which succeed it. Because of this it is not only just and fitting but necessary that women should have a large share in proposing peace and a great voice in determining what shall be the agreements of peace, a voice which shall demand that permanent peace shall be the aim and end of all negotiations."[49] Similarly, "As women we feel a peculiar moral revolt against both the cruelty and the waste of war. . . . We demand that our right to be consulted in the settlement of questions concerning not alone the life of individuals but of nations be recognized and respected, that women be given a share in deciding war and peace."[50]

As we can see from Figure 2, Jane Addams used difference arguments to advance women's political citizenship twice as often as sameness arguments. Yet, like Catt, the more notable feature is the way she used both. That is, Addams and Catt combined liberal individualism and ascriptive maternalism as a foundation justifying women's entry into the electorate. Advancing a sameness argument for expanding women's political citizenship, Addams stated: "As the governing classes have been increased by the enfranchisement of one body of men after another, the art of government has been thus enriched in human interests and at the same time, as government has become so much more humanized, it has inevitably become further democratized through the accession of the new classes who represent those interests."[51] Or consider this passage: "As Mazzini once said we have no right to call our country a country until every man has a vote, and surely no logical mind can stop at sex in granting suffrage."[52] She also quotes a declaration from The Hague that "the exclusion of women from citizenship is contrary to the principles of civilization and human right."[53]

The Demise of Equality *and* Difference in the United States

In the aftermath of the Progressive era, however, advocates for women's rights who had come together under one umbrella for the woman suffrage cause now began to split apart and to fight with one another. Yes, advocates of working women's rights, such as Florence Kelley, continued to push for protective labor legislation for women on the grounds of their maternal difference. However, Elizabeth Cady Stanton's grand-daughter, Nora Blatch Barney, was keenly uncomfortable with what she considered to be "state maternalism" and ridiculed laws that "classed women with children as the 'industrial and political wards of the state.'"[54]

In November 1923, on the seventy-fifth anniversary of Elizabeth Cady Stanton's writing of the Declaration of Sentiments, for example, women rights advocates gathered in Seneca Falls, New York, and commemorated the anniversary by launching another legislative initiative, the Equal Rights Amendment (ERA). It declared that "Men and women shall have equal rights throughout the United States and every place subject to its jurisdiction."[55] Woman suffrage leader Alice Paul introduced the ERA into Congress in December of 1923 on the grounds that the right to vote was not enough to guarantee women's incorporation as full participants in American society. Others sensitive to the drift of the debate were less enthusiastic. Historian Mary Beard, for instance, worried at that time that such a constitutional amendment could harm women by making protective labor legislation for women unconstitutional.[56]

The struggle for suffrage in the Progressive era is, as historian Nancy Cott notes, a prototype for achieving political unity, for incorporating women of diverse class, race, religion, ethnicity, social, cultural, and economic interests. Women, she says, achieved cohesion, not merely coalition, because they could support the Nineteenth Amendment for different reasons, yet remain united on this collective goal.[57] However, after passage of the Nineteenth Amendment, there remained no single legislative goal that could serve to unite women's disparate interests. Hence, the legislative goals of some seemed nothing more than fatal for achieving the legislative goals of others. Thus, women's rights organizations became fragmented and torn by strife within and between themselves. Lost in this strife was the *combination* of maternalism and individualism, difference and equality, as a viable strategy for further expansion of women's rights.

Another factor weighing on the demise of the combination of maternalism and individualism was the failure to connect these arguments to partisan politics. The maternalism argument had worked in the Progressive era because it corresponded to reformers' agendas, enabling women with the vote to be seen as allies for promoting a regulatory state that would intervene on behalf of economically disadvantaged groups. Ultimately, however, electoral politics requires partisan politics, including allegiances to political parties. As it turned out, most women's rights advocates were reluctant to connect themselves with party politics, idealizing instead nonpartisanship as the preferred norm. The National American Woman Suffrage Association, for example, morphed into the League of Women Voters after the Nineteenth Amendment was added to the Constitution. The goal of this new organization was variously described as nonpartisan, unpartisan, or pan-partisan.[58] The League could not endorse political candidates and soon became associated with a "strong critique, if not an outright rejection, of the party system."[59] The opportunity to press a combination of maternalist and individualist arguments for the passage of legislation by way of partisan politics was lost as newly enfranchised women voters were urged by major women's rights organizations to stay away from partisan activities.

Finally, not only did women stay out of the political parties to a large degree, but too many stayed out of the voting booth as well. That is to say, the promise of the power of the "women's vote" failed to materialize after the Nineteenth Amendment. Not only was there no coalescing issues on which women could agree to vote as a bloc, there was not even complete agreement that women should exercise the right to vote at all. While it is true that most newly enfranchised groups fail to go to the polls the first chance they get, in the case of women this reluctance was compounded by internalized normative attitudes *among women* that it was improper for them to do so.

It was not merely antisuffrage sentiment that was at work, but also the problem of associating the act of voting with masculinity. For this reason, even women who thought they should have the "right" to vote were not sure about exercising that right on the grounds that they had not yet adjusted themselves to the "idea of women voting." As political scientist Kristi Andersen notes, researchers found in their study of Chicago voting wards in 1920 that women internalized a belief that they should not vote that ranged from "an attitude of mild indifference toward women's civic responsibilities" to a "confirmed conviction that women should keep out of politics altogether."[60] Absent a women's voting bloc, attention to women's maternal identities on the part of political parties and candidates waned.

At bottom, however, one senses that strong undertow of America's pervasive liberalism that makes it difficult to sustain the positive valence of group difference arguments in American political culture, and of the unique circumstances accounting for the Progressive era's temporary breakthrough.

In the end, it is principles of individual equality that prevailed in the United States after the Progressive era, and principles of maternal difference that were rejected as a platform for further expansion of women's social, civil, and political citizenship, as T. H. Marshall would term them.[61] In 1971, the Supreme Court, in *Reed v. Reed,* established that the Fourteenth Amendment guarantee of equal protection of the laws applies to sex discrimination as well as race discrimination.[62] In 1973, the Supreme Court ruled in *Roe v. Wade* that an individual's due process constitutional right to liberty and privacy is broad enough to include a woman's right to choose an abortion, for any reason prior to viability, and after viability if her health or life is endangered.[63]

Congress included "sex" in Title VII of the 1964 Civil Rights Act, thereby making it a federal crime to discriminate against women "because of" their sex in the area of employment. In 1972, Congress passed Title IX of its Educational Act, thereby making it a federal crime to discriminate on the basis of sex in educational programs. And, finally, after decades of hard work, every state in the country now recognizes marital rape as a crime.

All these "liberal" accomplishments are invaluable to women for guaranteeing their more equal access to opportunities in society. Yet there is reason to believe that liberal individualism, while *necessary, is not sufficient* for expanding women's political citizenship to include national office-holding. Women's access to political rule as voters was produced in the Progressive era by a rhetorical version of maternal individualism, which combined liberal individualism with ascriptive maternalism. However, that combination failed to be institutionally sustained in subsequent decades. I argue that it is this failure that accounts for the severe underrepresentation of women in national office today in the United States. We can see the dramatic relationship between constructing the state on the basis of maternal individualism and women's access to national office-holding by a cross-national comparison of women's office-holding patterns in relation to forms of state construction.

Office-holding. The right to vote is but one dimension of political citizenship. The other crucial component is office-holding. When we turn to women's cross-national office-holding patterns, we find a striking peculiarity. Despite the status of the United States as one of the world's most industrialized, literate, and long-standing democracies, the American state lags far behind other comparable political systems in terms of the election of women to national political leadership positions. Today, for example, some national legislatures are composed of nearly 50 percent women, such as Rwanda (48.8 percent) and Sweden (45.3 percent). A total of fourteen additional nations have at least 30 percent of their national legislatures composed of women; ten additional nations have at least 25 percent; and an additional twenty nations have at least 20 percent. However, in 2004, the American House of Representatives was composed of only 14.3 percent women, ranking the United States a lowly 73rd among the world's nations in terms of the percentage of women elected to national legislative office.

Thus, far from having percentages of women in office comparable to our Western industrial counterparts—such as Sweden (45.3 percent), Denmark (38 percent), Finland (37.5 percent), Netherlands (36.7 percent), Norway (36.4 percent), Spain (36 percent), Belgium (35.3 percent), Austria (33.9 percent), Germany (32.3 percent), Iceland (30.2 percent), New Zealand (28.3 percent), Bulgaria (26.2 percent), Switzerland (25.0 percent), Australia (24.7 percent), or our next-door neighbor Canada (21.1 percent)—the United States has a lower percentage of women in its House of Representatives than do the geographically, economically, and culturally different states of Vietnam (27.3 percent), Namibia (26.4 percent), Turkmenistan (26 percent), Uganda (24.7 percent), and Suriname (17.6 percent).

State performance of equality and *difference.* Many scholars have sought to explain what accounts for the contemporary laggard status of the American state when it comes to women's national office-holding patterns. Most importantly, scholars point to the power of political structures—such as proportional representation, parliamentary systems, and multiple parties—for enhancing women's election to national legislatures.[64] My research supports those findings, but also adds another crucial mechanism: *state performance* that represents women as both maternalists who are different than men and individuals who are the same as men.

State Performance and Women's Political Citizenship

Not essentialism. Scholars note the dangers in assigning to any ascriptive group, including women, universal traits or characteristics, such as maternalism. In invoking the term "maternalism" here, however, I am *not* asserting that maternalism is an "essential" characteristic of all women everywhere; rather, I am observing empirically that it is the most stable social construction of what constitutes women's group difference and that it has proven the most politically transformative construction the women's movement has thus far promulgated. Throughout all historical periods, in every political system of which we have records, the dominant social construction of women as a group has associated them with the capacity to be pregnant and to bear children, and with the disproportionate care and nurturing of people once they are born—what sociologists refer to as biological and social reproductive labor respectively. So, too, in the American case do we find women associated with biological and social maternalism. Hence, I adopt this definition of women's group difference from men not because it is necessarily true, but because it is historically stable and highly salient politically.

State performance. In the Progressive era, the state acted vis-à-vis its political institutions and public policies in a way that represented women's dual identities as maternalists who are different from men and individuals who are the same as men. This state action—that is, state performance of women's dual identities—created a new view of the public sphere, one that embodied both maternalism and individualism. Woman suffrage reformers were crucial agents in the Progressive era for capitalizing on the way the state itself represented women's dual identities by forging a new, *complementary grammar* that used the same combination as justification for why women had the right to vote. We examined this political grammar by reference to the arguments used by suffrage reformers to sway public attitudes and political elites to support the enfranchisement of women.

When we turn to cross-national comparisons of women's office-holding patterns in contemporary political systems, we do not have a comparable set of political reform agents for each country to examine how they have developed of a grammar of equality and difference reflecting state performance mechanisms representing women's dual identities. However, we do have at the level of the mass citizenry measures of public attitudes about the suitability of women as political leaders. Thus, when we turn to a contemporary examination of women's office-holding patterns, we can show that state performance of women's dual identities affects public attitudes about women's suitability as political leaders, and in turn, how both state performance and public attitudes affect women's election to national office-holding positions, as Figure 3 indicates.

Although the United States failed to sustain the institutionalization of both difference and equality—maternalism and individualism—as a foundation of its political institutions and public policies, other contemporary political systems are notable for doing just that. They institutionalize a principle of individualism as the foundation of their states by "Bill of Rights" guarantees and political policies that guarantee civil and political rights to

POLITICAL STRUCTURE	PUBLIC ATTITUDES	POLITICAL CITIZENSHIP
State Performance ----------> of Equality and Difference	Public Attitudes ---------> Supporting Women as Political Leaders	Women's Election to Legislatures

Figure 3. Equality and difference model of women's election to national legislatures.

all individuals "in spite of" their ascriptive group differences. They institutionalize a principle of maternalism as the foundation of their political systems in at least one of three ways, corresponding to the three ways
maternalism can be defined: (1) sex classification that is female, where female refers to the sex that bears offspring; (2) as a verb, as in "to mother,"
meaning to nurture or care for people once they are born; and (3) as a noun,
as in to be a "mother," that is, a woman who has given birth to offspring,
thereby generating family-kinship networks. The three corresponding ways
a political system can institutionalize a *principle* of maternalism, therefore,
are (1) to institute gender quotas, which give preference, though no guarantee, to women's election to national legislatures "because of" their classification as female; (2) to institutionalize welfare provision, which makes
women's care-work the work of the state; and (3) to fuse the state with a
family-kinship network generated by women's capacity to be pregnant and
to give birth, such as instituting a hereditary monarchy where individuals
have access to political rule "because of" their family-kinship status.

My argument is twofold. First, I argue that state performance of maternalism and individualism that thereby corresponds to women's dual identities generates *public attitudes* that view women more favorably as national
political leaders. I then argue that public attitudes about women's suitability as political leaders, in addition to state performance of women's dual
identities, affects the actual election of women to national leadership positions, as Figure 3 indicates.

State performance and public attitudes. When we assess from a cross-national
perspective women's contemporary leadership patterns, we find confirmation that state structures and policies that represent women's dual identities do, indeed, increase public attitudes favorably inclined toward women
as political leaders as well as the election of women to national political office, such as national legislatures. I find evidence for this by reference to
the World Value Surveys, which include this question: "Do you agree
strongly, agree, disagree, or strongly disagree with the following statement:
'Men make better political leaders than women'?" We would expect the respondents' answer to vary with their sex and age, with females and younger
respondents disagreeing more than men and older respondents. However,
we might also expect people living in a political system that represents
women's dual identities as individuals and as maternalists to be more favorably disposed to viewing women as suitable political leaders, and hence to
register greater disagreement with the above state.

As we can see from Table 1, this is indeed the case. Controlling for sex
and age, there is a positive (partial) correlation between individualism and
all three forms of institutionalized maternalism. In addition, there is a positive (partial) correlation between the combination of maternal-individualism and public attitudes supportive of women as political leaders. These
findings also hold when the Nordic nations are omitted.

TABLE 1. CORRELATION BETWEEN STATE PERFORMANCE MECHANISM AND PUBLIC
ATTITUDES, CONTROLLING FOR AGE AND SEX OF RESPONDENTS, 2004 ($P = 0$)

	State performance mechanism				
	Equality	Difference (maternalism)			Equality-difference combined
	Individualism[b]	Gender quotas	Welfare provision	Hereditary monarchy	Individualism-maternalism[c]
Public attitudes: women are suitable as political leaders[a]	.290[d]	.156	.143	.257	.261
	.285[e]	.139	.141	.208	.229

a) Question from World Value Surveys, 2004
b) measured as "free" or "not free," Freedom House scores
c) additive scale 0-3, measuring presence of gender quotas, welfare provision, or hereditary monarchy open to women in conjunction with presence or absence of individualism
d) partial correlation coefficient, controlling for sex and age, all nations
e) partial correlation coefficient, controlling for sex and age, Nordic nations omitted, in italics

State performance and women's election to public office. We also see confirmation that women's election to national legislatures is enhanced by the state performance of women's dual identities. This holds even when controlling for the impact of public attitudes and other features of political systems that previous scholarship has also found to be important for explaining women's recruitment to national political office, such as political structures and economic characteristics. When state performance represents both equality and difference by means of its policies and political institutions, women's election to national legislatures increases by 5.5 percent, as model I of Table 2 indicates. When public attitudes are favorably disposed toward women as political leaders, women's election to national legislatures increases by .44 percent, as indicated by model II. This increase would represent the election of two more women to the House of Representatives in the American case. When a political system has a presidential system, the increase in women elected to national legislatures is 4.3 percent; it is 4.5 percent for a parliamentary system, and 3.6 percent for a multiparty electoral system, as indicated by model III. Of the economic features of a political system, the percent female labor participation increases the percent of women elected to national legislatures by .43 percent and the degree of urbanization by .1 percent, as indicated by model IV.

When we compare the relative impact of maternal-individualism, public attitudes, political structures, and economic features on women's election to national legislatures, we find confirmation that of all the characteristics of a political system, it is the state's performance of equality *and* differ-

TABLE 2. REGRESSION ANALYSES, PERCENT WOMEN ELECTED TO NATIONAL
LEGISLATURES, 2004, AS PREDICTED BY STATE PERFORMANCE, PUBLIC ATTITUDES,
POLITICAL STRUCTURE, AND ECONOMIC FEATURES

	Model I	Model II	Model III	Model IV	Model V
	State performance	Public attitudes	Political structure	Economic features	All
Maternalism[b]	1.045 (.086)[a]				-3.699 (-.333)
Individualism[c]	-.780 (-.039)				-2.977 (-.164)
Maternal-individualism	**5.546 (.474)****				*8.554 (.726)* **
Public attitudes toward women as political leaders[d]		**.440 (.570)*****			*.470 (.539)* **
Presidential system			**4.302 (.178)****		-.416 (-.022)
Parliamentary system			**4.475 (.223)****		.533 (.031)
Electoral system			**3.583 (.324)*****		-.439 (-.041)
Female labor force				**.429 (.292)*****	.228 (.160)
Urbanization				**.102 (.240)****	-.094 (-.232)
Industrialization				.126 (.096)	*.620 (.417)* **
Gross domestic product				-.000 (-.048)	.000 (.016)
Population				.000 (.013)	-.000 (-.204)
Constant	**9.886*****	**8.699*****	**7.121*****	**-10.449***	*-4.966*
R-squared	.271	.325	.165	.129	*.519*

Regression analyses assessing impact of maternal-individualism, public attitudes, political structures, and demographic variables on percent women elected to national legislatures, 2004. Bold highlights statistically significant components of regression analysis, $p \le .05$.
a) Regression coefficient; standardized regression coefficient in parentheses; b) additive scale 0–3, measuring presence of gender quotas, welfare provision, or hereditary monarchy open to women; c) measured as "free" or "not free," Freedom House scores; d) question from World Value Surveys, 2001.

TABLE 3. REGRESSION ANALYSES, PERCENT WOMEN ELECTED TO NATIONAL LEGISLATURES, 2004, AS PREDICTED BY STATE PERFORMANCE, PUBLIC ATTITUDES, POLITICAL STRUCTURE, AND ECONOMIC FEATURES, NORDIC NATIONS OMITTED.

	Model I	Model II	Model III	Model IV	Model V
	State performance mechanism	Public attitudes	Political structure	Economic features	All
Maternalism[b]	1.045 (.090)[a]				-6.296 (-.665)
Individualism[c]	-.368 (-.020)				-5.2398 (-.295)
Maternal-individualism	**4.508 (.395)****				*8.230 (.949)***
Public attitudes toward women as political leaders[d]		**.406 (.411)****			*.372 (.346)**
Presidential system			**3.748 (.166)****		*1.295 (.066)*
Parliamentary system			**3.877 (.208)****		*2.596 (.231)*
Electoral system			**2.937 (.285)****		*2.596 (.231)*
Female labor force				**.354 (.253)****	*.283 (.189)*
Urbanization				**.008 (.193)****	*.062 (.134)*
Industrialization				.126 (.096)	*.099 (.066)*
Gross domestic product				-.000 (-.030)	*.000 (.002)*
Population				.000 (.014)	*.000 (.156)*
Constant	**9.886*****	**9.192*****	**7.605*****	**-6.407**	*-10.706*
R-squared	.208	.169	.131	.093	*.385*

Regression analyses assessing impact of maternal-individualism, public attitudes, political structures, and demographic variables on percent women elected to national legislatures, 2004 (Nordic nations omitted). Bold highlights statistically significant components of regression analysis, p=.100 at least.
* p =.100; ** p =.05, *** p =.001.
a) regression coefficient, standardized regression coefficient in parentheses; b) additive scale 0–3 measuring presence of gender quotas, welfare provision, or hereditary monarchy open to women; c) measured as "free" or "not free," Freedom House scores; d) question from World Value Surveys, 2001.

ence—as corresponding to women's dual identities—that has the most powerful and positive impact on the election of women to national legislatures. State performance of equality *and* difference increases women's election to national legislatures by 8.9 percent, as model V in Table 2 indicates. In the American political system, this would mean the election of 37 more women to the House of Representatives. These findings hold when the Nordic nations are omitted, as indicated in Table 3.

Thus, our findings confirm and extend the research of others. Yes, multiparty electoral systems benefit women; yes, proportional representation benefits women; and yes, women's entry into the paid labor forces increases women's access to national electoral office-holding. In addition, however, we have found a new component of the state that enhances women's political recruitment in elective national office: a state construction that combines the institutionalization of women's individual sameness with men with the institutionalization of women's maternal group difference. Just as it is this combination that provided access to women as voters in the Progressive era so too is it this combination that provides access to women as office-holders in contemporary political systems.

Conclusion

Structure and agency. Clearly, for there to be social and political reform, there must be agents of change with the will, the resources, and the organizational networks to instigate such change. However, agents do not, and cannot, operate in an institutional vacuum. On the contrary, reformers always find themselves situated in particular historical contexts defined by structural contingencies of the moment. Important work by Theda Skocpol has demonstrated that one of the most crucial features of the relationship between structure and agency is the degree to which there is a "fit" between the federal structure of the American political system and the federated structure of social movement organizations seeking to promote significant reforms. As she has shown, the federated structure of women's reform organizations in the Progressive era was a perfect "fit" with the federated structure of the American state, and it is this correspondence between state structure and social movement structure, she argues, that accounts for what might be thought of as the establishing of a "Golden Age" of a maternalist welfare state. As she puts it,

The institutional arrangements and electoral rules of a national state and party system affect which of the society's groups become involved in politics, and when. Given that certain social groups do become politically active, moreover, some of them achieve more political leverage than others. Much of the reason has to do with the "fit," or lack thereof, between a nation's governmental institutions at a given time and the goals and organizational capacities of the various groups and alliances that seek to influence policymaking.[65]

My findings expand the way we may evaluate the "fit" between political structures and social movement agency. On the basis of an historical look at the expansion of women's political citizenship rights to include the right to vote in the United States and a cross-national look at women's office-holding patterns, we see a new view of what makes or breaks the power of reform agents to promote the political inclusion of women, namely, state performance that represents women's dual identities.

Two-dimensional "mixed" mechanism. My identification of the representative state as a two-dimensional mechanism brings together disparate areas of scholarship. Yes, welfare states have been described as "woman friendly," and it goes without saying that we would assume that gender quotas are also "woman friendly." However, I have done something more with the identification of the state performance mechanism. I have shown how a principle of maternalism underlies welfare provision and gender quotas, and that what enhances women's political citizenship—that is, women's political inclusion in the state—is a state mechanism that represents women both as maternalists who are different from men and as individuals who are the same as men. In addition, I have identified a third way the state can represent women's maternal group difference from men, through hereditary monarchies.

Thus, I have done more than merely identify three ways the state can represent maternalism. I have identified the maternalist category to which all three modes belong. In addition to this category, as I established, the state must also perform in ways that correspond to women's sameness with men, that is, to individualism. Thus, the mechanism is two-dimensional, one defined by both maternalism and individualism as the definition of state action.

Understanding how state performance representing women's dual identities is a structural mechanism fostering the agency of those seeking to advance women's political citizenship as voters and as office-holders clarifies "what's wrong" with the American state, both historically and in contemporary times. Historically, what's wrong is that this mechanism did not surface in the United States until as late as the Progressive era, despite the concerted efforts of agents seeking to expand women's political rights in the nineteenth century. Thus, it is the lack of this representative state performance mechanism until the early twentieth century that explains why women's voting right guarantees in the United States trailed behind those of unpropertied white men and newly freed African American men by decades and decades of time.

In terms of the contemporary period, what's wrong with the United States is the failure to sustain this mechanism of representative state performance beyond the Progressive era. Today, the United States is one of the very few industrial, Western-oriented democracies that does not act out, in its political institutions or public policies, principles of individual equality combined with at least some form of women's maternal group difference. Demonstrating that this is what explains the laggard status of the American state today when it comes to women's election to national leadership positions provides new perspectives for academics and activists alike seeking to understand if not to improve women's inclusion in political governance of the American state.

Chapter 10

The Ground Beneath Our Feet: Language, Culture, and Political Change

Victoria Hattam and Joseph Lowndes

For almost a decade now, scholars have been interrogating the notion of order as an organizing concept for political analysis. Forceful critiques have been offered by Karen Orren and Stephen Skowronek and Rogers Smith showing that historical periods and political regimes are marked by multiple institutional orders and conflicting traditions. Notions of coherence that underlie earlier arguments by Louis Hartz, Walter Dean Burnham, Robert Wiebe, to name only a few, have been criticized for ignoring, or more actively minimizing, institutional and ideological divisions within periods and regimes. Political ascendance, these critics have shown, is more tenuous and contested than earlier scholars allowed. Adam Sheingate has extended the critique of periods and regimes to institutions per se when he contends that organizations are not as coherent or homogeneous as many have assumed and that attending to the internal fissures within them allows us to rethink agency and change.[1]

These post-order institutionalists, for want of a better name, have related the analytic precedence of order to truncated conceptions of political agency. Arguments about American exceptionalism, party systems, and path dependence, different as they are from one another, tend to conceptualize politics in Rokkanian terms of punctuated equilibrium. Within this frame, normal politics is bounded by ordering routines and significant change is exogenously generated, coming as a response to external shocks or crises that provide temporary openings in which institutions might be reconfigured. These moments of openness, or "critical junctures" as they are called, provide only intermittent expressions of transformative agency. In contrast, the critics of order have pushed agency front and center in a veritable celebration of the ever-present endogenous possibilities for reconfiguring the parameters of political authority and power. For Sheingate, political entrepreneurs are the agents of change, exploiting the complexities built into the routines of modern institutional life. Analytically speaking, then, agency has been allowed to flourish to the extent that order recedes.

Though it is by no means clear just how far it can be extended, this critique of order has already provided a much-needed corrective to more mechanistic models of political change and remains a continuing provocation when reflecting on the operating assumptions guiding historical work. We sense, however, that disaggregation has its limits, since it fails to distinguish flux from more enduring political change. This omission is especially telling in the current moment when the Republican Party has been able to reconfigure American politics in such a bold fashion. How might we reconcile this innovative new work on agency with Republican power? We need to rethink issues of aggregation without simply resuscitating older conceptions of order by finding new ways to distinguish flux from durable change. We explore this problem in four parts. We begin by considering parallels between political order and identity advanced over the past three decades, attending to the ways both schools have foregrounded issues of agency in new ways. In the second part, we address the problem of significance and argue for the importance of cultural analysis as the marker of durable change. We elaborate the importance of culture by examining three moments of change: the rise of the modern Right, the invention of ethnicity, and contemporary efforts to reconfigure Republicanism and race. We conclude with brief reflections on the implications for political research in the years ahead.

Deconstructing Order on Two Fronts

A stunning parallel is evident between institutional critiques of order and poststructuralist critiques of identity that offer new opportunities for fruitful engagement across this longstanding scholarly divide. Judith Butler, Michael Warner, Denise Riley, and numerous others have challenged unitary treatments of identity in ways eerily similar to the historical institutionalist assault on the iconography of order.[2] Identity politics of the 1960s and 1970s was premised, many poststructuralists have argued, on a false sense of coherence in singular and discretely bounded identity claims. No sooner had second wave feminists stood up for women's rights, than their African American counterparts quickly objected to white women speaking on their behalf. Black feminists' critiques were quickly joined by dissenting voices from lesbians, transsexuals, and transgender activists, as one group after another objected to being spoken for by others.[3]

By the late 1980s, leading feminist theorists, most visibly Judith Butler but others as well, began to argue that the problem was not simply one of inadequate political representation; rather the difficulty lay in the inherent limitations of signification and identification. Drawing on the work of Derrida, Lacan, and Foucault, scholars began to theorize a very different conception of identity and power than that embodied in the various social movements of the 1960s. Those earlier claims to freedom and liberation were seen as belying a political imposition that failed to recognize the intricate relationship between subjectivity and subjugation. Identity politics, whether for Blacks, women, or gays, were declared fantasies of coherence, ruses of power that obscured the inherent heterogeneity entailed within groups organized under any sign. By the late 1980s, scholars had pushed this critique to its logical conclusion by declaring all identity politics to be always already failed, compromised from the outset by the reduction of complex subjectivities to unitary subject positions. The very act of speaking on behalf of others, Butler argued, actually *generated* internal dissent and division. The way forward was not to seek new terms under which to organize, since they too would fall prey to the same limitations. Instead, many began to advocate a politics of *dis*identification in which one disrupted the discursive regime by refusing to be "hailed" under any sign.[4]

The parallels between entrepreneurial and poststructuralist arguments are telling. Both attend to heterogeneity, multiplicity, and complexity, challenging prevailing assumptions about the stable, coherent, and unitary nature of power. The common claim is that taking order and coherence at face value obscures the regulatory force inherent in such claims and as such blinds us to vital sources of agency as well.

For the past twenty years there has been little or no traffic across the institutionalist-poststructuralist divide. To the extent that political science has engaged poststructuralism at all, it has been political theorists who have done so—most of the discipline has largely ignored these ambitious efforts at rethinking power. Both sides have been diminished by the separation. But the intellectual terrain is changing; we see an opening at hand, an important opportunity for fruitful exchange. The possibilities are especially promising right now because poststructuralists have begun to engage issues of persistent identification—or structure if you will—while institutionalists, as this volume attests, have begun to consider agency and change.

Distinguishing Flux from Significant Political Change

Institutionalist and poststructuralist critiques of order generally juxtapose order and change. On both sides, order is repeatedly linked to structure, stability, coherence, and equilibrium and then contrasted with certain allegedly more change-friendly words—uncertainty, ambiguity, contingency. This oppositional framing leads to a presentation in which order and change are placed in a zero-sum relation; securing more of one leads to a diminution of the other. But this formulation leaves much of the relationship between the two unexplored. We do not know much about the importance of reaggregation as a source of change. Poststructuralists certainly allow for processes of resignification, but do little to explore their dynamics. The emphasis remains on *dis*identification, on refusing rather than reconfiguring identification. Similarly, post-order institutionalists highlight political disaggregation, with accounts of institutional reconfiguration either absent or top-down. Considering the limits of both perspectives not only links them more closely, it also identifies a missing element critical to their mutual advance.

If deconstructing order has placed issues of agency center stage, it has done so in ways that make it difficult to weigh the significance of any particular change. How are we to determine whether a given set of entrepreneurial manipulations will secure enduring shifts in policy and power? How much of this agitation is just tinkering around the edges of power? As Bruce Miroff suggests, notions of entrepreneurship have an individualistic cast that make it difficult to detect and distinguish pervasive change.[5] Something similar might be said of poststructuralist accounts of identification. Critiques of unitary identity claims are powerful, yet we cannot simply dispense with identification. The issue at hand is not whether to identify, but in what ways to do so. How might we advance identifications that avoid the pitfalls of reifying identity claims?

Orren and Skowronek's *The Search for American Political Development* might be read in this way, as "troubling" the opposition between order and change. Development, in their lexicon, is a notion of political change located *between* older conceptions of systemic coherence, or order, and the constantly churning and often-fleeting actions of political agents. Allowing for the essential heterogeneity of political formations, Orren and Skowronek nevertheless seek to establish a means of distinguishing agency effects from meaningful political change. They define "development" as "a durable shift in governing authority," making it a "distinguishable event, one that can be established empirically" and "a phenomenon worth studying in its own right."[6] Focusing on shifts in authority, for Orren and Skowronek, is what secures American Political Development (APD) as a distinctive intellectual endeavor. Defining the research enterprise in these terms, Orren and Skowronek reposition notions of order and change in much less either-or terms; they make analytic space for more carefully specifying political changes of different kinds and degrees. Herein lies a means of breaking into the constant flux of political life—an essential task if we are to assess the significance of change.

Although we find Orren and Skowronek's deconstruction of order compelling and their search for a new metric of significant change central, their formulation strikes us as too narrow. The focus is almost exclusively on government. Consider the central propositions of their argument as they unfold in turn: political development is a durable shift in governing authority; no change reorganizes all governing authority relations at once; what distinguishes more from less durable change is the extent to which existing authority is rearranged to accommodate it; rearrangements that cut deeper and wider through surrounding authority are more likely to endure, and to have greater transformative effect than changes that fail to rearrange surrounding authority or simply fill a niche without much im-pingement on anything else; given the limited nature of all change, how-ever, the polity will always be a composite of different and often incongruous orderings of authority. Even if one grants that change may, in this formulation, gestate beyond governmental institutions, and that extra-institutional politics may be credited as a source of and contender for significant political change, the telltale action all takes place within the gov-ernment—in contests among institutional actors. In the end, "develop-ment" is determined in a top-down fashion by state actors. We find this conception of the political too circumscribed. Foucault was right to cut off the king's head; it is a mistake for APD scholars reattach it.[7]

We share Orren and Skowronek's interest in specifying durable political change, but look to language and culture rather than to governance as the locus of significant "transformation." We follow poststructuralists into the lin-guistic turn, embracing their more capacious conception of power in which subjugation, and resistance to it, is diffused through discourse of all kinds. But not all linguistic change carries with it the same order of significance; some innovations are fleeting, momentary examples of word play, while others enact more durable shifts in meaning that reverberate through political iden-tifications and alliances in the most profound fashion. Language is critical, but we too want to distinguish between flux and more significant discursive change. We do so by attending to issues of circulation and to the patterning of linguistic associations. Drawing on the work of Ernesto Laclau, we pay par-ticular attention to the linkages or associations at work within the discursive field; these "associative chains" establish the topography of the political broadly conceived. Linguistic innovation is always at work, but only some shifts rearrange the social cleavages and political alliances of the day. It is to these profound discursive reconfigurations that we attend.[8]

Whatever the drawbacks of poststructuralism, it provides the theoretical underpinnings for a broad conception of politics and power. Institutional change alone, even when broadly conceived, cannot account for many shifts that are demonstrably durable and significant. Nor do we think it suf-ficient to argue that durable change will be achieved by changes in govern-ing authority. This is not always so. The three examples elaborated below identify moments of change that were secured long before any shift in gov-erning authority was apparent. Limiting the evaluation of significance to moments of "development" as Orren and Skowronek define it generally relegates cultural change to a prefigurative status, always preparatory to the real business of institutional change. Doing so, we argue, misspecifies both the nature and timing of change. A broader conception of politics, one that extends beyond governance to power in all domains, may encompass these "developments" with little risk of returning us to the overarching no-tions of coherence and essentialism that scholars on both sides have done so much to set aside.

Language, Culture, and Change

Arjun Appadurai frames issues of language and politics elegantly when he identifies a heterodox scholarly tradition preoccupied with examining the relationship between "the word and the world."[9] To be sure, approaches vary and disputes abound, but there is a common intellectual project in which language is seen as key to understanding political subjugation and change. We draw on this heterodox tradition when we consider the words used, the political appeals made, and the identifications evoked to be *the* ground of politics, *the* site of change in which otherwise disparate elements are recombined into apparently coherent political positions. Changes in governance are often crucial, but are themselves nested within a broader context of cultural change. Interests and identities are not given in advance, with politics relegated to the task of distribution. Rather, who we are, what we want, and how we might satisfy our desires are produced and reproduced discursively over time. If we want to understand political change, we need to attend to discourse, since this is where political identifications and social cleavages are made and remade.[10]

We have found time and again that political positions that seemed to rest on natural affinities in fact were established slowly over decades during which otherwise disparate elements were hitched together through associative chains. The principal task of cultural analysis, as we understand it, is to denaturalize the prevailing associations by recouping the acts of cultural suturing that linked social and linguistic fragments into seemingly coherent political positions. Political agency and formative change lie in these acts of *recombination,* in the rearrangement of often disparate social and ideational fragments into vital associative chains. Political elites play a central role in offering up new associations, but they do not have a monopoly on linguistic innovation. Everyday speech practices also serve as sites of invention. As Miroff points out, relations between elites and followers are reciprocal, with interactions between them often mutually transformative.[11]

In many ways our work might be seen as reconceptualizing the act of coalition building. If new movements, institutions, political parties, and regimes are to endure—if they are to be more than strategic alliances or marriages of convenience—they need to generate new identifications through which adherents understand their social location and interests therein. Significant political change, as we understand it, is achieved through circulation and the taken-for-grantedness of the discursive linkages that follow. Each of the examples below—the rise of the Right, the creation of American ethno-racial categories, and Condoleezza Rice's efforts to reconfigure Republicanism and race—all are fascinating moments of political change. Each began small; only two thus far have reached a level of significance in which new associative chains have been naturalized through widespread circulation. The third example offers a moment of cultural change where the issue of significance is not yet settled. The specific moment when and where new linguistic innovations gain circulation might be disputed; but in each of our examples there is no doubt that the discursive changes occurred long before formal shifts in governing authority. From our perspective, governmental change often codifies transformations that have already occurred. More important than the issue of timing is the fact that discursive innovations entail rather different processes of change than those evident in shifts in governing authority. Micro speech practices are placed center stage: how words are used, and which terms are linked together, are of the utmost importance. Beginnings, innovations, and linguistic recombinations mark the frontiers of change; they are tremors indicating the potential power of broad-based discursive change. Significance will be determined by circulation. *Political formation is best discovered through an analysis of words in motion.*

The Rise of the Right: Charles Wallace Collins and the Dixiecrat Revolt of 1948

Our first example is drawn from Lowndes's work on the rise of the Right, specifically from the constitutive power of political discourse in the Dixiecrat Revolt of 1948. We choose it because by Orren and Skowronek's yardstick this political event would not be seen as a political development. It fell so short as an electoral event, a bid for entry into the institutional contest, that it would, by their standard, appear an utter failure. And yet the language of the leadership of the Dixiecrat Revolt and the new associative chains that were forged there proved critical to the rise of modern conservatism in the United States.

Scholars and popular writers have generally located the origins of the rise of the modern Right in the late 1960s. These accounts rest on a story of backlash against the excesses of liberalism endemic in that decade, excesses that naturally played into the hands of conservatives generally and the Republican Party in particular.[12] But the major themes of the national Republican message in 1968 and thereafter, including law and order, opposition to civil rights advances, federalism, and a commitment to economic conservatism, did not come together naturally, reflexively, or organically. They had to be combined in a coherent discourse and form of political subjectivity. Such combining was a long-term, contingent process that had to be worked out by political actors on the ground. It began long before the "backlash" of the 1960s, and would not bear institutional fruit until 1980.

In 1948, J. Strom Thurmond led a bolt from the national Democratic Party and ran for president on the States' Rights Democratic ticket to protest Truman's support of federal civil rights legislation. Although the Dixiecrat Revolt is generally depicted as a regional protest sidelined by an emergent racial liberalism in the national party, attention to the discursive strategies of Dixiecrat leaders reveals another dynamic. By looking at the writings of the movement's most influential intellectual and strategist, Charles Wallace Collins, we can see how issues of race began to get linked to economic conservatism in a strategy meant to make the southern revolt national.

Charles Collins was an attorney from Alabama's black belt whose career encompassed work in government, private legal practice, and continual political writing on economics, constitutional law, and states' rights. He directed the Economic Section of the Legislative Reference Service at the Library of Congress, and went on to become the librarian for the Supreme Court, the law librarian for the U.S. Congress, and adviser to numerous congressional committees.[13] He also worked for the Treasury Department and was counsel to numerous financial institutions and holding companies. This background was instrumental to perception and articulation of the new linkages. Collins's experiences in government, banking, constitutional law, and southern politics are all reflected in his political writings, particularly his 1947 book *Whither Solid South? A Study in Politics and Race Relations.*[14] The book, which served as lodestar for the Dixiecrat Revolt, combined institutional, linguistic, legal, and strategic analyses in an argument for a marriage of economic conservatism and white supremacy.

In *Whither Solid South?* and elsewhere, Collins urged a realignment of U.S. politics that would conjoin Southern Democrats and conservative Republicans in one party, and New Dealers and racial liberals in the other. As Collins understood it, creating an effective opposition to the New Deal would involve two achievements: severing the identification between voters and the national Democratic Party in the South, and making effective links to other New Deal opponents across the Mason-Dixon Line.[15] This was no mean feat. White southerners had been fiercely devoted to the Democratic Party since the Civil War. Indeed, the Republican Party barely existed below the Mason-Dixon Line. Moreover, having benefited greatly from the New Deal, most southern voters were committed to its economic ends.[16] Enormous governmental projects such as the Tennessee Valley Authority, which brought electrification to many parts of the South for the first time, were central to New Deal liberalism and cherished in the nation's poorest region. And the most important New Deal opponents *outside* the South were small-government economic conservatives in the Republican Party.

Conservative Republicans were antilabor and opposed to state intervention in the economy, but they had no political dedication to the South or to Jim Crow. If anything, the South was seen as underdeveloped, dependent on federal largess, and a poor place to do business. Thus, changing the political commitments of white Democrats in the South and economic conservatives outside the South required a reinterpretation of the political interests of both groups. It was this task that focused Collins's political energy.

Collins made the case for a new political identity merging racial and economic concerns prior to the Dixiecrat Revolt by claiming that the New Deal itself had threatened the nation's very identity. As he put it, "The people of the United States have been pushed to the left of their accustomed position. In high places only lip service is now given to States Rights, local self government and individual initiative. The institution of private property itself is on the defensive. . . . A question mark now faces everything that has made America great."[17] Collins argued that this "question mark" should form the basis of an historic realignment of the two major parties. "There is a grim and bitter struggle ahead which bids fair to shake both the Democratic and Republican Parties to their foundations."[18] He went on to discuss how this split in the parties would be the basis of new "associations":

This political cleavage across party lines . . . is an illustration of a national condition under which men and women are seeking new affiliations for self-expression. The old associations are losing their meaning in the face of a determined move toward complete stateism on the one hand and a desperate attempt to hold on to the old values of personal freedom and local self-government. Among the latter will be found practically all Southerners.[19]

Collins predicted that this shake-up in politics could unite Southern Democrats and conservative Republicans in the North and West into "the strongest party in the country, provided that the issue of Negro equality was left to the sponsorship of a new Liberal Party."[20]

A speech by Truman in January 1948 endorsing the findings of his civil rights commission became the triggering event in the process of partisan dissociation Collins had hoped for. Said Mississippi Senator James Eastland, "The South we know is being swept to its destruction. It is a real danger—it is an imminent danger."[21] Committed segregationist political elites and intellectuals began to mobilize in response with the blueprint closest at hand, *Whither Solid South*.[22] For many involved in the Revolt, the issue was purely the protection of southern white supremacy within the Democratic order. But others envisioned a national movement committed to racial supremacy *and* economic conservatism. Campaign chairman Merritt Gibson announced during that election season that the Dixiecrats "could be the core of a new conservative party which would attract the conservative elements from both major parties."[23] Another Dixiecrat leader wrote that the States' Rights movement could only be successful by "winning . . . conservative sentiment outside the South and the sentiment of those who fear the results of the encroachment of the federal government upon states' rights and the rights of the individual."[24] The Dixiecrats did not win support outside the South, nor did they lead their own region on an exodus from the party of their fathers. In the election, Thurmond came in a distant third to Truman, receiving only one-fifth of the popular vote even in the South, where 98.8 percent of his total vote was from.

The defeat at the polls was a serious blow to both popular and financial support for the Dixiecrat movement, and the Democratic Party punished participants.[25] Thurmond himself abandoned the Dixiecrat strategy after the election. But for Collins and others, particularly those who hoped to connect white supremacy to economic conservatism, this was just the beginning of what they hoped would be a long-term struggle. For these political actors the struggle would involve building both a southern and a national movement, linking them through a commonly held set of political ideas. Northerners would have to come to understand the fundamental principles at stake in the southern defense of Jim Crow, and white southerners would have to come to see the New Deal state as a threat to their fundamental commitments. While the white North was not currently allied with the South, Collins argued in a letter to Gibson, it would be when the South organized itself for itself, when it sharpened its arguments and began to wage a war not just in the political sphere, but in the cultural as well—through southern literature, art and philosophy.[26] And "When those on the other side of the Mason and Dixon Line, who love the Constitution, see the quality of the fight the South is making, they will respond with respect and admiration." But in order for this to happen, a "way must be found to educate the North on the issues in this fight. They must be given the information and the arguments to enable them to understand."[27] Building such a political alliance, then, would necessitate not just a sense of political expediency on behalf of northern conservatives, but a deeper identification with the white South—its perspectives on race and state sovereignty, but also its heritage and cultural values.

Attempting to pursue their national vision, some Dixiecrat leaders established a nonprofit institute in Washington "for the purpose of spreading, nation-wide, the principles on which the States' Rights campaign was founded" and with an eye toward passing a states' rights amendment to the Constitution. The proposed amendment linked racial and economic concerns in numerous ways. Its first provision, for instance, was that "Congress . . . make no law . . . that conflicts with a state law pertaining to education, elections, qualifications for suffrage, civil rights of individuals, racial relations, labor, zoning, [and] transfer and ownership of property."[28] Here states' rights, an open defense of Jim Crow, and an opposition to state intervention into the economy were brought together in an associative chain to rally various elements into one political identity.

Dixiecrat organizers attempted to build a grassroots movement across the South as well, focused on pressuring Democratic members of Congress not to vote with the national party on liberal initiatives. However, southern racial politics and free-market conservatism had no real connection for many former Dixiecrat supporters. One example is John Temple Graves. Graves, a *Birmingham Post* columnist, was a major voice in southern politics and had been a noted New Dealer.[29] He became an active supporter of the

States' Rights Revolt, but for him the issues were solely state sovereignty and the protection of southern customs. In a letter to Thurmond following the 1948 election, Graves wrote that he could not support the new states' rights organization "because I have some doubts about letting any group like this hold itself forth in the coming years as inheritors of the movement you led." If the movement were to be a successful and positive development, Thurmond had to regain control, Graves told him, "because you stand for a liberalism . . . that set[s] you apart from most of the leadership."[30] Like Graves, Thurmond had been considered a liberal political figure prior to his increasing involvement in racial politics in South Carolina.

Indeed, Collins did his best to bring old allies like Graves along toward conservatism, arguing that the defense of states' rights and economic conservatism was one and the same. In June of 1951 he wrote to him that, "I think your 'genuine liberal' and my 'genuine conservative' will turn out to be the same man. The leftwing political element in this country has taken over the word 'liberal' and has squeezed the original meaning out of it. This new liberal is in fact a rank reactionary. He stands in the shoes of the old conservative who used the power of the federal government to promote his personal ambition. . . . I therefore classify everyone a conservative who fights on our side to conserve those basic principles of government upon which the Republic is founded."[31] In order for Graves' liberal and Collins' conservative to become the "same man," a champion of the NIRA and the TVA had to be sutured to an enemy of all the New Deal stood for.[32]

Evidence of the success of this strategy began to emerge as early as 1951, when Dixiecrats began to get recognition from the national Republican Party. In the run-up to the 1952 election, conservative GOP leaders met with Dixiecrats and spoke at meetings of Democrats in Deep South states. In one of these gatherings in Jackson, Mississippi, for instance, Senator Karl Mundt (R-S.D.) was met with great enthusiasm when he endorsed cooperation between Democratic states' righters and Republicans. This was "not mere applause," editorialized the *Jackson Daily News*, "but ear-splitting Rebel yells the kind heard at political gatherings in this State three score years ago."[33] This eagerness to embrace northern allies prompted greater attention from the Republican leadership. Speaking at a Lincoln Day rally for Alabama Republicans in February 1952, chairman of the Republican National Committee Guy Gabrielson announced, "We want the Dixiecrats to vote for our candidate. The Dixiecrat party believes in states' rights. That's what the Republican Party believes in."[34] Such an unabashed bid by the top Republican Party official in the country demonstrates the impact that these southern battles were having on the nation. Never had the party of Lincoln committed itself to the racist vote in such a manner.

In the years following, conservative intellectuals and writers, as well as GOP political operatives outside the South, began to take notice of the opportunities afforded by this initial discursive linking below the Mason-

Dixon Line. Thus began an exchange carried out in the pages of conservative magazines like the *National Review*, in efforts to organize a conservative
GOP base in the South, and later in the Goldwater, Nixon, and finally Reagan campaigns. But the central features of modern conservatism were not
produced by Nixon's victory or the Reagan Revolution. The political
change had been introduced and consolidated discursively decades earlier.
Only once the associative chains had been articulated and the identifications reconfigured could the more formal rewards of change be secured.
The case of the Dixiecrats confirms a view of politics as an incongruous mix
of elements arrayed against one another; but in doing so, it reveals reorder-
ing as something that occurred in the very midst of liberalism's hegemony
and outside the corridors of government.

The Office of Management and Budget and American Race Categories

On May 12, 1977, the Office of Management and Budget promulgated Statistical Policy Directive 15, an obscure two-page document that mandated
the categories to be used by all federal departments and agencies when collecting and disseminating data on race and ethnicity. Although formally
limited to the federal bureaucracy, the Directive's categories were quickly
adopted by state governments and most private sector institutions so that
the OMB categories now serve, in slightly revised form, as the official ethnic and racial categories for American society at large. When you enroll a
child in school, read a newspaper, or hire someone at a university, the
chances are that the racial and ethnic categories used will be those stipulated under Directive 15. Moreover, since the Directive also establishes
Census Bureau categories, which in turn provide the denominator for all
ethno-racial data in the United States, the Directive might be considered
one of the most formative and neglected legacies of the civil rights era.[35]

The impetus for the Directive lay in the need for standardized ethno-
racial categories when implementing civil rights laws. The Civil Rights Act
of 1964, the Voting Rights Act of 1965, the Fair Housing Act of 1968, the
Equal Credit Opportunity Act of 1974, and the Home Mortgage Disclosure
Act of 1975 required the federal government to monitor ethnic and racial
discrimination in a variety of policy domains. In order to assess discriminatory practices, agencies first had to specify the relevant protected groups,
which, in turn, required stipulating ethnic and racial categories. Initially,
dispersed government bureaucracies established their own categories so as
to comply with these new legislative mandates. However, this multiagency
process of data collection proved unwieldy, prompting efforts to standardize the collection and dissemination of federal race and ethnicity data by
way of Directive 15.[36]

The Directive specified that the American ethno-racial taxonomy included four races (black, white, American Indian or Alaskan Native, and Asian or Pacific Islander) and one ethnicity (Hispanic). According to the Directive, Hispanics can be of any race; their Spanish origins and culture, rather than their race, unites them as a social group. Although many scholars have analyzed the race categories in Directive 15, little has been written on the race-ethnicity distinction that the Directive institutionalizes. When and why did the federal government begin to classify Hispanics as an ethnic group rather than a race? What are the political consequences of distinguishing the two?

In the middle of the nineteenth century there was *no* category of ethnicity; rather, experts and laymen alike used a broad conception of race to refer to a wide range of differences that we would generally distinguish today. Nationality, culture, religion, and language were encompassed in earlier, more expansive conceptions of race. Between 1880 and 1945, the social topography of racial classification changed as scholars, intellectuals, and some state officials began to distinguish ethnicity as a separate social formation from race. In May of 1977, when the federal government institutionalized the race-ethnicity distinction in Directive 15, it was ratifying this change, a change which, with minor revisions, remains the classificatory scheme in the U.S. federal government today.

How should we understand this shift from an omnibus category of race to our more familiar categories of race, nation, and ethnicity? How might we understand this process of category formation as an instance of political change? In many ways, it is a classic case of institutional "development" in which governing authority shifted to accommodate the civil rights revolution. Indeed, this is precisely how key participants understood their actions; Grace Flores and Juanita Tamayo Lott both described themselves as agents of important change.[37] Flores and Lott both were members of the critical advisory committee that drafted the post-civil rights ethno-racial categories in the United States. But accepting their description of the process, and their role in it, is misleading; it obscures the extensive cultural work needed to establish ethnicity as a distinct social category from that of race. Research by Victoria Hattam makes clear the deep roots of Directive 15. Rather than specifying state actors as the agents of change, Hattam suggests that OMB unwittingly institutionalized shifts that had been secured decades earlier beyond the arms of the state. Scholarly debates over the nature of heredity in the last quarter of the nineteenth century, along with New York Zionists' debates over the nature of Jewish identity in the second and third decades of the twentieth century, were crucial to establishing the categories.[38]

Between 1880 and 1945, changing conceptions of heredity along with New York Zionists' views of Jewish difference established the race-ethnicity distinction as a meaningful one in the United States. They did so by generating new associative chains that linked certain characteristics with ethnicity and others with race. By observing how the terms race and ethnicity operate in a wide variety of texts, Hattam reveals the associative chains at work as one author after another began to connect ethnicity with culture, plurality, malleability, and equality while race was seen as homogeneous, fixed, and hierarchical—as tied to body and blood.

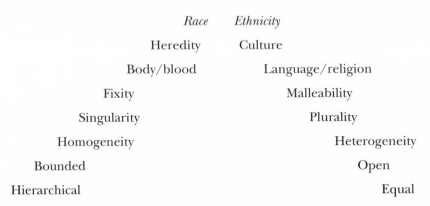

	Race	*Ethnicity*
	Heredity	Culture
	Body/blood	Language/religion
	Fixity	Malleability
	Singularity	Plurality
	Homogeneity	Heterogeneity
	Bounded	Open
	Hierarchical	Equal

Figure 1. Associative chains: discourses of difference in the United States.

The associative chains specified above certainly are not exhaustive; linguistic inventions are not so tightly bound. But even as new associations proliferate, the constitutive distinction between race and ethnicity has remained. By World War II, the omnibus nineteenth-century language of race had gone, replaced by a language of difference in which the race-ethnicity distinction was commonplace.

Moreover, the race-ethnicity distinction was consequential. By repeatedly establishing ethnicity as different from race, these early architects of ethnicity produced a distinction between ethnic and racial identifications that continues to divide immigrants and African Americans today. Horace Kallen is a classic case in point. Perhaps the premier theorist of American ethnicity, he was certainly one of the progenitors of the modern usage of the term. In his pathbreaking two-part essay "Democracy Versus the Melting Pot," published in *The Nation* in February 1915, Kallen lays out his antiassimilationist account of American ethnicity in which he celebrates immigrant difference as the vital force of American democratic life. Rather than succumbing to pressures to Americanize, Kallen called for immigrants to hold onto their folk ways in order to withstand the stultifying effects of industrialization and assimilation.[39]

Kallen's principal metaphor for his pluralist vision was that of the orchestra in which each musical instrument had it own timbre and tonality; yet when played together the object was to achieve a harmony and not a unison. So too with groups of immigrants; distinctive immigrant cultures might be harmonized into a new, more vibrant American nationalism that welcomed the profusion of immigrant cultures in gateway cities like New York.

While Kallen's essay is widely known for his celebration of ethnic difference, the ways in which he established the contours of ethnicity have not been sufficiently explored. Attending to Kallen's textual deployment of the term ethnic allows us to see how the meaning of ethnicity is secured by contrasting ethnicity with race. Throughout the essay Kallen elaborates the benefits of ethnicity by contrasting it with the deleterious effects of race.

Kallen sets up the comparison by limiting his discussions of race to the colonial past and to the South, both of which he suggests suffered from an unhealthy unity—a like-mindedness—that we would do well to avoid now. Note how Kallen links whiteness and uniformity in the following passage:

In 1776 the mass of white men in the colonies *were* actually, with respect to one another, rather free and equal. I refer not so much to the absence of great differences in wealth, as to the fact that the whites were *like-minded*. They were possessed of ethnic and cultural unity; they were homogeneous with respect to ancestry and ideals.[40]

Similarly, see how Kallen designates the South as degenerate and backward, and identifies the source of the problem in the homogeneity of southern cities which lack the cosmopolitanism of their northeastern counterparts:

South of Mason and Dixon's line the cities exhibit a greater homogeneity. Outside of certain regions in Texas the descendants of the native white stock, often degenerate and backward, prevail among whites, but the whites as a whole constitute a relatively weaker proportion of the population. They live among nine million negroes, whose own mode of living tends, by its mere massiveness, to standardize the "mind" of the proletarian South in speech, manner, and the other values of social organization.[41]

Why exactly "nine million negroes" served to standardize the southern mind is not clear. There is nothing inevitable about the linkages being made here. We can easily imagine a different way of putting the elements together. But Kallen quite clearly began to articulate new associative chains in which ethnicity is positioned as plural and malleable and race as singular and fixed.

Kallen was not alone in positioning ethnicity as tied to language and culture, and race to body and blood. Many New York Jewish intellectuals began to elaborate the race-ethnicity distinction. A rather spectacular collection of such writings can be found in the pages of the *Menorah Journal* which was dedicated, as the masthead stated, "to the study and advancement of Jewish culture and ideals." The list of contributors in the interwar years is impressive: Mary Antin, Israel Zangwill, Louis Brandeis, Felix Frankfurter, Roscoe Pound, John Dewey, Charles Beard, Randolph Bourne, Louis Mumford, Edward Sapir, Alfred Kroeber, Norman Hapgood, Julius Draschler, and Isaac Berkson, among others, all wrote for the journal in an effort to spell out the basis of Jewish identity. All tried to stipulate what it was that made Jews Jews. Although not all agreed, several began to define ethnicity quite explicitly as different from, and not reducible to, race.[42]

Between Reconstruction and the end of World War II, then, the topography of racial discourse changed. But these changes were not secured through governmental authority. Rather, the shift was well established as a cultural norm long before passage of civil rights laws and promulgation of Directive 15. Most institutionalists, by definition, would specify the ideational and discursive changes associated with changing conceptions of heredity and New York Zionists' writings as *precursors* to changes in formal categories promulgated by OMB. But these cultural shifts were not merely preparatory for the real business of institutional change. The ideational and discursive changes that preceded Directive 15 did not just clear the way; they filled the ground. They established the very meaning of race and ethnicity in the United States that Directive 15 then ratified.

Civil Rights and Foreign Invasion: Condoleezza Rice and Discursive Intervention

Finally, we turn our attention to a more current moment—2005—to show how cultural analyses might be used to flag early signs of potentially significant change. Over the last two years, conservatives have been reconfiguring Republican ideology by questioning Democrats' presumptive claim to civil rights reform. Condoleezza Rice, G. W. Bush's Secretary of State, is a prime case in point; she has been offering up new associative chains in which the relation between civil rights and foreign policy are being realigned. As yet this reconfiguration has not taken hold; the new associations still surprise and unsettle our assumptions about how disparate political elements might fit together. But jolting our sensibilities only suggests that the proposed reconfiguration has the potential to cut wide and deep. The issue to watch is whether these new chains of equivalence gain circulation—that will be the mark of significant change. Attending to this moment of associative recombination brings our analytic tools to bear on transformation in the making.[43]

In October 2005, Condoleezza Rice took the United Kingdom Foreign Secretary, Jack Straw, on a southern tour of the United States. One of their stops was the 16th Street Baptist Church in Birmingham, Alabama, where they attended a commemorative ceremony for the four African American girls who had been killed twenty-two years earlier when a bomb was detonated in the church basement to protest civil rights reform. Rice's speeches and press conferences during the tour are remarkable: we see Rice linking foreign intervention in Iraq today with earlier civil rights reform. Where the Johnson administration was torn apart by the competing demands of civil rights and Vietnam, and where Martin Luther King, Jr., had struggled to hold peace and civil rights together, Rice tries to reconfigure old political elements into a new associative chain. As previous tensions and inconsistencies are eschewed, violence, and one's reaction to it, is used to reposition bombings in Baghdad and bombings in Birmingham as two sides of the same coin.[44]

On Rice's telling, if one supported civil rights in the past, then one ought to support a belligerent foreign policy now; both, Rice argues, require fortitude against political resistance from an old guard. In speech after speech, Rice links the two by analogizing violence in the South with violence in Iraq. In putting these two previously incongruous elements together, Rice tries to reclaim civil rights politics for Republican foreign policy now. Gone is the presumed alliance between civil rights reform and the Democratic Party; gone is the coupling of civil rights at home and peace abroad; gone is the association of civil rights advocacy and nonviolence. When reading Rice's speeches, the political terrain begins to shift beneath one's feet as old antagonisms dissolve and new affinities appear.

The Birmingham bombing on September 16, 1963, provides a crucial pivot for the political transformation at hand. Rice knew one of the four girls who had been killed in the 16th Street Baptist church—Denise McNair, who had been a kindergarten classmate and friend. Rice uses this personal connection as the hook with which to equate Birmingham and Baghdad. Her 2004 commencement address at Vanderbilt University is instructive. Rice begins on familiar terrain:

I grew up in Birmingham, Alabama, before the Civil Rights movement—a place that was once described, with no exaggeration, as the most thoroughly segregated city in the country. I know what it means to hold dreams and aspirations when half your neighbors think you are incapable of, or uninterested in, anything better.

I know what it's like to live with segregation in an atmosphere of hostility, and contempt, and cold stares, and the ever-present threat of violence, a threat that sometimes erupted into the real thing.

I remember the bombing of that Sunday school at 16th Street Baptist Church in Birmingham in 1963. I did not see it happen, but I heard it happen and I felt it happen, just a few blocks away at my father's church. It is a sound that I will never forget, that will forever reverberate in my ears. That bomb took the lives of four young girls, including my friend and playmate Denise McNair. The crime was calculated, not random. It was meant to suck the hope out of young lives, bury their aspirations, and ensure that old fears would be propelled forward into the next generation. But those fears were not propelled forward into the next generation.

But those fears were not propelled forward. *Those terrorists failed.*[45]

For the most part, the speech is quite familiar, not very different from many other reflections on civil rights reform. But the last sentence shifts the ground. When Rice claims, "Those terrorists failed," something new is at work. Here begins the new associative chain in which Iraqi resistance and southern segregationists are joined, with Rice the Black Republican stand-ing steadfast against both. We have moved from familiar affinities onto new political terrain. Republican opposition to 1960s civil rights reform has dis-appeared. The elision is established through personal biography in which Rice herself brings civil rights aspirations and Republican internationalism together.

At the end of the commencement address the new linkages between civil rights and Republican foreign policy are made explicit. Rice concludes by suggesting that the privilege of higher education comes with three obliga-tions: to be optimistic, to work to close cultural gaps that divide our nation and our world, and to promote democratic progress here and abroad. When laying out these obligations, Rice further underscores the parallels between Birmingham and Baghdad:

In my professional life, I have listened as some explained why Russians would never embrace freedom, that military dictatorship would always be a way of life in Latin America, that Asian values were incompatible with democracy, and that tyranny, corruption and one-party rule would always dominate Africa.

Today we hear these same doubts about the possibility of freedom in the Middle East. We have to reject those doubts. Knowing what we know about the difficulties of our own history, knowing the history of Alabama and Mississippi and Tennessee, we should be humble in singing freedom's praise, but our voice should never waiver in speaking out on the side of those who seek freedom. And we should never in-dulge in the condescending voices that allege that some people are not interested in freedom, or aren't ready for freedom's responsibility. *That view was wrong in 1963 in Birmingham, and it's wrong in 2004 in Baghdad.*[46]

In one speech after another, Rice takes us from Birmingham and civil rights to invasion in Iraq. One begins on familiar territory, with familiar al-lies, and ends at quite a different political location, having crossed silently over a deep partisan divide. The object in each speech is to align civil rights reform with foreign invasion, so that if one was against the bombings in Birmingham, then one should be for war in Iraq. Nonviolence is dimin-ished and liberation cast in high relief, thereby aligning civil rights and the supposed fight for freedom in Iraq.

Once made aware of the new linkages being offered, they appear time and again, even in the smallest phrases such as "the empire of Jim Crow" and "home-grown terrorism." Moreover, political commentators are quite alert to the discursive innovation; several have asked Rice point blank whether the analogy she draws between Birmingham and Baghdad is a valid one. Take Rice's interview with Mary Orndorff of the *Birmingham News*, con-ducted during the southern tour. Orndorff's very first question probed this new linkage between civil rights and foreign invasion. "In your speech yes-terday (October 21, 2005) you compared the civil rights movement in the

American south to America's foreign policy goal of promoting democracy in Iraq and the Middle East. Is that a fair comparison given one was initiated by individual citizens and the other by military invasion?"[47] After Rice replied by invoking the importance of individual capacity to fight for freedom and liberty, Orndorff pushed harder, trying to reveal the depth, or lack thereof, in the Bush administration's commitment to civil rights:

Obviously, this trip has a very strong civil rights theme, as we saw today with that very moving ceremony (at 16th Street Baptist Church). But now, the part of the Voting Rights Act, which is a by product of this movement, is up for reauthorization and some parts of it are due to expire. My question to you is this: Should states like Alabama be free to change their election laws as they choose without checking with the federal government?[48]

Rice responded: "Well, this is something that I know my good friend, Attorney General Al Gonzales is considering—I'll let him consider it because he's the Attorney General and he and others in the Administration will have to deal with the determination." Throughout the interview Orndorff pushed on the apparent contradiction between Republican rhetoric and action. Rice gave little ground. Steve Weisman of the *New York Times* probed the new political configuration more gently by asking Rice when she began "fusing" her own past with the political present.[49] Throughout the southern tour, Rice willingly spelled out the reconfiguration, using her own biography to realign civil rights, violence, and Iraq. The sense of novelty is politically telling; it signals that the political configuration has not yet taken hold, has not yet been naturalized as a presumptive affinity. The linking of civil rights and foreign invasion still requires explanation.

What should we make of Rice's efforts to connect the Iraq war with 1960s civil rights reform? Do such speeches signal significant political change? Taken alone there is no way to judge their impact—circulation is the issue at hand. We need to assess whether Rice's efforts at discursive recombination are part and parcel of a more general trend. There is some evidence that Rice is not acting alone; other Republicans can be seen reconfiguring conservative ideology and its relation to race. Recently, the Republican National Committee chair, Ken Mehlman, linked the Republican Party to civil rights reform. In July 2005, he told the African Methodist Episcopal Church Convention in Houston that, "The civil rights movement was led by the faithful, whose fierce sense of justice was rightly offended by an institutionalized, legal bigotry. . . . A century before that, the Republican Party was born amidst the abolitionist movement, another creation of the faithful who were fighting for justice."[50] Mehlman no longer distances the Republican Party from civil rights politics, as did the architects of modern Republican hegemony thirty years earlier. Instead, he draws on the moral symbolism the civil rights movement provides for the nation at large to strengthen the links between the Party of Bush and the Party of Lincoln.

This twinning of religious faith and a moral commitment offers a template and justification for Bush's foreign policy. Speaking to the National Association of Black Journalists, Mehlman echoed Rice's words:

Millions of African Americans share key values with the Party of Lincoln. If you believe that every man, woman and child on this earth is endowed by their creator with certain unalienable rights, then it is wrong that women do not have the right to vote in so many places in the Middle East and elsewhere. Let's work together with President Bush and Condoleezza Rice's initiative to spread democracy to all people.[51]

To the degree that the civil rights movement's broad aims have been embraced, they provide a rich source for the Bush administration's defining mission—the war in Iraq.[52]

It is by no means certain that this associative chain will gain currency; Condoleezza Rice is not a popular figure among the civil rights leadership in the U.S., and Black sentiment toward the Bush administration suffered a severe blow after its response to Hurricane Katrina. Moreover, support for the war in Iraq continues to decline among all Americans. The agency of Rice, Mehlman, and others is embedded in circumstances not of their control, and thus their prospects for success remain open. But it is precisely this openness that must be grasped if we are to understand the possibilities of change.

The difficult task for cultural analysis is to assess the weight of particular discursive innovations. How do we know whether this is a singular act or the beginning of a new associative chain? There is no solace to be found in clearly measurable assessments of cultural change. The problem is not one of insufficient institutionalization, but identifying the new associative patterns and assessing degrees of circulation. The new linkages are now visible in several locations, but it is still too early to tell whether these particular discursive chains have gained traction. Attending to Rice's speeches alerts us to the front lines of change.

Determining issues of circulation is an art rather than a science. Nevertheless, there are telltale signs of significant and durable change. A taken-for-grantedness, a naturalness, to the speech-acts is a sure sign that the discursive associations have gained traction. When new associative chains appear, as they did with interventions by Charles Wallace Collins, Horace Kallen, and Condoleezza Rice, we see that each went to considerable lengths to explain the new combinations. There is a way in which the texts themselves signal the *labor of rearticulation* that alerts the reader to the changes at hand. Similarly, once the discursive links have been accepted, they take on a common-sense quality, a naturalism that elides their constructed character. We have seen with the Rice example above that the linkages have not yet reached the status of familiar assumptions. Rather, the incongruities and newness of the linkages Rice offers continue to startle, making plain the newness and potential reach of the associative chains.

Whether this will continue to be the case a decade from now is unclear—that will be the critical test of this bold linguistic innovation. The cultural work accomplished by the likes of Collins and Kallen read quite differently; it no longer requires explanation. The analytic task for the political historian is to recover the political work that has long since been absorbed into the familiarity of everyday life.

Transgressing Disciplinary Boundaries and the Future Directions for APD

Throughout this essay we have rather strongly distinguished between language, identity, and culture on the one hand, and institutions and governance on the other. Such a distinction, however, perpetuates a split that we would rather avoid. We have maintained it here in order to highlight the importance of culture in a way that is largely absent in institutionalist literature. Ultimately, however, we would like to transcend this split so as not to perpetuate notions of culture and institutions as separate spheres of inquiry, or to suggest that culture should simply be added as a variable.[53] Rather, we understand institutional action at every level, from individual entrepreneurs to broad state imperatives, as expressive of norms, values, beliefs, and interests—in other words, of culture. This is not to say that institutions do not matter; on the contrary, they matter a great deal insofar as they represent organized articulations of power. But we cannot understand these articulations—how they emerge, congeal, change, or erode—without attending to issues of language and culture and the identifications that linger therein.[54]

   As with institutions and culture, so too with the boundary between history and political science; we want to traverse both. For us, the promise of the historical turn in political science, and the torrent of new research that was produced in its wake, lay in the blurring of disciplinary boundaries that such research often entailed. We want to foster that interdisciplinary impulse now when APD scholars are turning to issues of agency and change. Rather than limiting the purview of APD to issues of governance and development, we want to open up APD to broader conceptions of politics by drawing more self-consciously on the reconceptualization of power offered by poststructuralists over the past half century. A common assault on the iconographic status of order and identity provides the critical common ground. Pursuing it may make it more difficult to justify or defend APD as a distinctive research enterprise, but it will have important advantages as well. It will bring political science in general and APD in particular into conversation with other disciplines that have long grappled with more capacious conceptions of power. APD could serve as an intellectual crossroads for those interested in power and politics without regard to old disciplinary divides.[55]

Part IV
At the Interface of Movements and the State

Chapter 11

Presidents and Social Movements: A Logic and Preliminary Results

Elizabeth Sanders

Presidents and Social Movements

Social movements have long been major vehicles for political reform.[1] They are important mechanisms—more targeted, more inclusive, and less constrained by time than elections—through which the ills of democracy are addressed and the grievances of marginalized sectors and interests are brought into the public forum for consideration. If they are successful and achieve some positive result, it is usually through a fortuitous combination of political opportunity, astute movement leadership, and clever adaptation.[2] One of the conditions of success, particularly after the early twentieth century, has been assistance, or at least tolerance, from the president. After all, over the course of that century, the president became the main publicizing agent in American politics and increased the office's control over the national policy agenda. Through his "bully pulpit" and executive branch resources—appointments, propagation (and framing) of information, influence over enforcement in the courts and bureaucracy, and the power to recommend and veto legislation—he has been able to mobilize public opinion for or against social movements and greatly affect their chances of winning a positive response to their goals.

The common portrait of the president as a "purposive, active, power-wielding, yet benevolent chief executive," an "engine for the pursuit of [a] liberal agenda," a champion of reform and a spokesman for the hopes and dreams of the disadvantaged, has survived cycles of disillusionment and recurring bad examples.[3] With the administrations of Lincoln, the two Roosevelts, Truman, Wilson, and Lyndon Johnson in mind, public and academic expectations that the president has been (and should be) a prominent spokesman and legislative advocate for the major reform movements of American history have not been systematically challenged. Americans are inclined to view the president as an agent for the public at large, and as a voice for the marginalized, be they African Americans, women, farmers, workers, immigrants, gays, or lower middle-class religious traditionalists offended by the advance of secular culture . . . and even for the unborn.

This analysis of presidential interactions with social movements cuts the other way and takes a more skeptical view. It posits an institutional logic that inclines the presidency in a conservative direction—a direction perfectly consistent with the intentions of those most responsible for Article II of the Constitution. The logic behind this conservative disposition has been reinforced by the president's modern responsibilities for economic management, by the rise of global capitalism, and by innovations in methods of candidate nomination and campaign finance. In foreign policy, there has been a more pronounced shift toward presidential preoccupation with war making.[4] After 1945, the initial power endowments and historical affinities of the institution of the presidency were overtaken by a profound transformation of the president's role and resources as the chief executive assumed worldwide leadership of both economic recovery and a "war on communism." These tendencies were spurred further in the 1950s–1970s by changes in communications systems and in presidential recruitment methods that rewarded raw personal ambition and personalized coalition building.

The effect of these developments on presidential affinity for military policy and the disposition of the presidency toward social and economic reform movements remain to be explored. With regard to presidential interaction with social movements, these are the central hypotheses of the larger work in which the present research is positioned:

• In domestic politics, presidents have played a more reactive than leading role in the construction of the institutions of the modern regulatory and welfare state. In both policy arenas, presidents have usually been less favorable to social movements of the disadvantaged than their party majorities in Congress.

• The president's support for social movements is almost always based on either (a) electoral calculations; (b) foreign policy needs; or (c) the necessity for preserving or restoring tranquility in a situation of increasing social disorder caused by protests of disadvantaged groups—disturbances that local elites have difficulty containing, and/or disorder that threatens the president's international goals.

• Absent the latter conditions, the president will probably not take the lead in positive government response to social movements, particularly if they (a) have goals that appear to demand economic redistribution; or (b) challenge the president's war-making powers. When the president *does* agree not to oppose the goals of social movements that have won substantial congressional support, he will make his support contingent on enforcement by an administrative agency with considerable discretion to interpret the new law in line with presidential preferences (thus expanding presidential power in an important policy arena). The president will *never* acquiesce to peace movements and agree to end a war he has begun or expanded *absent* strong congressional and elite support for ending the war. His control of information related to his reasons for, and uses of, military force will further limit the ability of peace groups to organize around their goals.

• The presidency is logically dependent on a favorable investment climate for reelection, and on business organizations and wealthy individuals for campaign contributions and executive branch staffing (especially in an era in which campaign finance needs are great and not centered in party organizations). Executives of advanced, large, internationally competitive firms are also the social sector most likely to support his interventionist/expansionist military policies. Thus the president will in most circumstances be reluctant to support the redistributive demands of labor or other working class organizations, or the inflationary demands of low-wage or high-debt economic sectors.

• Presidential support for the domestic goals of labor and other organizations of the disadvantaged, and also for trade and labor protection from international competition, will lag that of his party in Congress; the latter is more closely linked to labor, farmers, and less-competitive industry.

• The president will act in support of disadvantaged groups abroad only if they are linked to domestic constituencies in his party coalition that demand such action, and the action demanded allows him to exercise his military powers at low cost (in terms of casualties, financial expense, or potential alienation of large domestic firms).

These are broad-ranging hypotheses, rooted in assumptions linked to the president's institutional position in modern American government and its web of incentive structures. They are conjectures that can be supported with a good bit of historical case citation, but which, of course, remain to be categorically specified and subjected to rigorous empirical testing. They do call into question the popular notion, to which generations of political scientists have subscribed, that the presidency is a unique institution for incorporating the disadvantaged when the other branches of national government are ambivalent or hostile, a "place of heroic achievement."[5] Has the president indeed acted historically as an agent of incorporation and progressive amelioration of social ills? Or is he first and foremost a political entrepreneur whose vision is fixed by his institutional position and its incentive structures, and who is driven by electoral and power needs that only incidentally coincide with the needs and demands of the weak or marginalized? Are the reform roles attributed to Lincoln, the two Roosevelts, Wilson, and Lyndon Johnson exaggerated? Or could they be aberrations?

If presidents are in fact slow to take up the causes of large and important social movements, if the historic actions for which they are admired in fact lag behind the responses of other national political institutions and are more often reactive than proactive—whether because presidents in fact tend to envision their roles as profoundly conservative, as "nation keepers," in Russell Riley's argument, or for other reasons (like those posited in the propositions listed above)—then we have assigned the presidency far too much credit for social change.

Designing a Study of President-Movement Interaction: Group Selection

The data analyzed in this chapter are organized into a rubric of president-social movement interactions that permits a systematic assessment of presidential support for social movements in the United States. A social movement is defined here as "*an organized and sustained pressing of demands on the state by people outside formal centers of power.*"[6] To create a case universe of social movements, I use the list of "organizations with political goals" enumerated in Theda Skocpol's *Diminished Democracy.*[7] Her criterion for inclusion on the list, it should be noted, is a conservative one. It includes only groups whose membership reached, in enumerated years, at least 1 percent of the adult population; or, if a single-gender group, 1 percent of the targeted sex. Although 1 percent of the population may seem a modest membership, it represents an impressive achievement in the history of social organizations. These are movements that have somehow managed to overcome the notorious "free rider" effects that discourage collective action, and have attained an unusual degree of mobilization, sufficient to command the attention of the news media and at least some national politicians at the time. Usually organized in federated networks, these organizations have been "at the heart of local as well as national civil society."[8]

Like the seminal social movement work of William Gamson,[9] Skocpol's list includes organizations we would normally refer to as "interest groups," as well as social movements that conform to the above definition. The distinction between interest groups and social movements is, of course, not easy to pin down, and social movements that achieve some modicum of success often "age" into interest groups and/or become durable party factions. In its social movement (henceforth SM) phase, it is usually assumed that the organization has a newer and more fluid organizational and membership structure, and less secure acceptance by, and access to, political elites than does an "interest group." A reasonable expectation is that a genuine social movement must be "moving"; that is, it must be expanding, reaching outward, putting considerable effort into member recruitment, and making alliances that will help to overcome the inherent weakness of marginal groups. Whether an SM must also involve (a) some specified degree of face-to-face interaction and member participation in goal and strategy determination (that is, not just existing as a mailing list of check writers whose perceptions and actions are structured by the national leadership); and (b) whether it must employ at least some "unconventional" protest activities (like marches, boycotts, strikes) are questions on which social movement theorists have reached no consensus. For the purposes of this chapter, such distinctions are not critical.

Membership figures for both SMs and interest groups are often unreliable, but particularly so for SMs, in view of their greater dynamism, lax dues collection, and haphazard record keeping. One of the notable absences from Skocpol's list of "1 percent" groups is the Farmers Union (FU), organized in Texas in 1902, not far from the birthplace of the nineteenth-century Farmers Alliance. The FU was an important reform organization in the South, West, and Midwest in the Progressive Era. It was involved in several major legislative campaigns in the 1940s and remains a liberal farmers' organization to this day, albeit with a much smaller membership.[10] The FU did not meet the 1 percent cutoff required by Skocpol, even in its Progressive Era heyday, but a fourth to a third of its membership was female, and women were generally not required to pay dues.[11]

The National Association for the Advancement of Colored People (NAACP), and the principal SMs of the later civil rights movement are also missing from the Skocpol list, not having amassed sufficient documented membership to reach the 1 percent cutoff. Because of the significance of the FU and the NAACP from the Progressive Era forward, and on the assumption that the former membership was undercounted, and the latter constrained by its minority base, I have added these two organizations to the analysis.

The portion of the study presented here extends only from 1897 to 1932, beginning with the administration of the first twentieth-century president, William McKinley. The larger project will extend the analysis to at least 2004. Examining the period prior to the categorical transformation of the president's role that attended the New Deal and World War II, when the presidency's claim to a national stewardship role was just beginning to expand and anticipate its modern form, will provide a limited but more elemental view of the interactive dynamics at issue. The list of organizations that met the 1 percent standard during the years of a particular presidential administration, beginning with the first year of the McKinley administration, and with the addition of the FU and NAACP, are listed in Table 1. Except for the two added groups, the organizations are those listed in Skocpol's *Diminished Democracy* that are described as having political goals (in other words, merely social or fraternal organizations are excluded here).

TABLE 1. LARGE ORGANIZATIONS WITH POLITICALLY RELEVANT GOALS, BY PRESIDENTIAL ADMINISTRATION

William McKinley (March 4, 1897–September 14, 1901)
    Young Men's Christian Association
    Grand Army of the Republic
    Modern Woodmen of America
    American Federation of Labor
    General Federation of Women's Clubs
    Fraternal Order of Eagles
Theodore Roosevelt (September 14, 1901–March 4, 1909)
    Young Men's Christian Association
    Grand Army of the Republic
    Modern Woodmen of America
    American Federation of Labor
    General Federation of Women's Clubs
    Fraternal Order of Eagles
William Howard Taft (March 4, 1909–March 4, 1913)
    Young Men's Christian Association
    Grand Army of the Republic
    Patrons of Husbandry (National Grange)
    Woman's Christian Temperance Union (WCTU)
    American Red Cross
    Knights of Columbus
    Modern Woodmen of America
    American Federation of Labor
    National American Woman Suffrage Association (NAWSA)
    General Federation of Women's Clubs
    Fraternal Order of Eagles
    German American National Alliance
Woodrow Wilson (March 4, 1913–March 4, 1921)
    Young Men's Christian Association
    Junior Order of United American Mechanics
    Patrons of Husbandry (National Grange)
    Woman's Christian Temperance Union (WCTU)
    American Red Cross
    Knights of Columbus
    Modern Woodmen of America
    American Federation of Labor
    National American Woman Suffrage Association (NAWSA) (**until 1920**)
    General Federation of Women's Clubs
    National Congress of Parents and Teachers (PTA) (**last 2 months**)
    Fraternal Order of Eagles
    German American National Alliance (**until 1920**)
    American Automobile Association (**last 2 months**)
    Ku Klux Klan (Second) (**last 2 months**)
    American Legion (**last 2 months**)
    Farmers' Union*
    NAACP*
Warren Harding (March 4, 1921–August 2, 1923)
    Young Men's Christian Association
    Junior Order of United American Mechanics
    Patrons of Husbandry (National Grange)
    Woman's Christian Temperance Union (WCTU)

American Red Cross
Knights of Columbus
Modern Woodmen of America
American Federation of Labor
General Federation of Women's Clubs
PTA
Fraternal Order of Eagles
American Automobile Association
Ku Klux Klan (Second)
American Legion
American Farm Bureau Federation
Farmers' Union*
NAACP*
Calvin Coolidge (August 2, 1923–March 4, 1929)
Young Men's Christian Association
Junior Order of United American Mechanics
Patrons of Husbandry (National Grange)
Woman's Christian Temperance Union (WCTU)
American Red Cross
Knights of Columbus
Modern Woodmen of America
American Federation of Labor
General Federation of Women's Clubs
PTA
Fraternal Order of Eagles
American Automobile Association
Ku Klux Klan (Second)
American Legion
American Farm Bureau Federation
Farmers' Union*
National Association for the Advancement of Colored People (NAACP)*
Herbert Hoover (March 4, 1929–March 4, 1933)
Young Men's Christian Association
Patrons of Husbandry (National Grange) (**until 1930)**
Woman's Christian Temperance Union (WCTU)
American Red Cross
Knights of Columbus
Modern Woodmen of America
American Federation of Labor
General Federation of Women's Clubs
PTA
Fraternal Order of Eagles
American Automobile Association
American Legion
Old Age Revolving Pensions, Ltd. (Townsend Movement)
Congress of Industrial Organizations (CIO)
Farmers' Union*

Group list taken from Theda Skocpol, *Diminished Democracy: From Membership to Management in American Civic Life* (Norman: University of Oklahoma Press, 2003), table 2.1, 26–28. The NAACP and National Farmers' Union, identified with asterisks, did not have documented membership that met the 1 percent standard employed by Skocpol, but have been added to the list for presidential administrations in which they were most active to give representation to these two very important social movements. Bold specifies the particular period when the 1 percent standard was met.

Modes of Interaction

The next task is to develop an inclusive scheme of interactions linking presidents to social movements, on a scale from least to most supportive. The posited gradation of interactions is shown in Table 2. The six categories in the table represent a plausible continuum from weakly to strongly supportive presidential involvement. But there are three additional modes of interaction that should be considered in an inclusive list. Rather than responding to an existing and presumably growing social movement, a presidential administration may actually *start* a group or movement—an organization that may subsequently, of course, develop a life of its own. In "The Origin and Maintenance of Interest Groups in America," Jack Walker demonstrated the significance of government patronage to a substantial number of organizations, both in their instigation and their continued maintenance.[12]

Two examples stand out in the contemporary period: the National Organization for Women was formed as a result of a 1966 conference instigated by officials in the Equal Employment Opportunity Commission who hoped to maintain and expand the influence of their own offices and mission. They anticipated that a women's movement would provide a broader clientele for the agency and support the desire of activist commissioners to pursue with much more vigor the new rights won for women as a matter of strategic accident in 1964. The Moral Majority—forerunner of the Christian Coalition—was formed in 1979 at the instigation of three Reagan Republican activists who arranged a meeting with religious broadcasters in Virginia. They promised White House support for conservative Christian goals in return for the electoral support of the evangelicals in 1980.

Looser examples might include President Kennedy's appointment of an assistant for women's affairs and his support for an equal pay act *before* there really was a women's movement worthy of the name,[13] and Richard Nixon's active support for environmentalism when the "environmental movement" was still in its formative stage. In both cases, reform was spurred and legitimated from the top, by presidential anticipation of the need for and benefits of new government programs, and his actions handed women and environmentalists important legislative victories. The absence of such goals in previously announced presidential agendas or personal experiences leads one to suspect that these are cases of electorally vulnerable presidents in search of potentially popular issues and new constituencies to shore up their fragile political claims.[14] This "inverse" president-movement relationship is not included in the Table 2 rubric. That schema displays the range of more common interactions suggested by the democratic theory that underlies the questions examined here, in which mobilized sectors of the population outside formal centers of power press their demands on the president and he responds in some fashion, or does not.

TABLE 2. MODES OF PRESIDENTIAL-SOCIAL MOVEMENT INTERACTION

1. The president receives members of the group at the White House (or other residence), giving them symbolic access and acceptance, without promising anything specific. Examples: Teddy Roosevelt receiving Booker T. Washington at the White House; Taft receiving labor leaders and agreeing to look at their proposals.[a]
2. The president publicly voices support, conditional or not, for the group's work or a particular organizational goal. An example of conditional approval is Wilson's announcement that he supported woman suffrage but believed that only the states, not the federal government, should confer it. Unconditional approval occurred when Wilson later voiced support for the national woman suffrage amendment to the Constitution.[b]
3. The president goes to meet with the group at an annual convention or like forum, and voices support for the group or its goals (example: Wilson becoming the first president to attend the annual AFL convention).
4. The president appoints a member of the organization to a committee, commission, or official governmental position relevant to the group's goals (example: Harding responding to demands of farm organizations by appointing a dairy farmer to the Federal Reserve Board).
5. The president endorses the group's goal(s) in a State of the Union speech or other message to Congress.
6. The president has introduced or supports a bill or amendment, or issues an executive order to achieve a major goal of the group (examples: Lincoln backing the abolition of slavery in the District of Columbia, or issuing the Emancipation Proclamation; Teddy Roosevelt backing railroad legislation demanded by farmers' organizations; Lyndon Johnson calling for passage of a Civil Rights Act; George W. Bush signing a partial-birth abortion ban).

a) Washington was at the time president of the National Negro Business League, an elite Black organization he founded. It was too small to be included in the Skocpol list, and is mentioned here only as an example of such symbolic interaction. For Taft, see "Taft Hears Pleas of Labor Leaders . . . Gives No Pledge to Them," *New York Times*, April 17, 1909.
b) Eleanor Flexnor, *Century of Struggle: The Women's Rights Movement in the United States* (Cambridge, Mass.: Harvard University Press, 1975), 288–89, 301, 320–22; *New York Times*, May 21, 1919.

There are two other categories of interactions that beg inclusion in the president-movement rubric, however. The president may publicly *oppose* the major goals of a social movement (examples include vetoes by Presidents Coolidge and Hoover of bills around which major farm organizations and the congressional "farm bloc" mobilized in the 1920s). Lastly, whatever his relationship had been to the movement earlier, the president may attempt to enlist the group's support for *his* agenda, particularly in time of war. The path of influence here runs in the opposite direction to that assumed by the first six categories. Rather than autonomously pressing their demands on the president, existing groups are (at least temporarily) coopted and made instruments of the president's goals. As Theda Skocpol and her coauthors have shown, groups that furnish the requested cooperation with the president's war efforts usually expand their membership and institutional strength.[15] However, one suspects that they may thereby also cease to perform the essential function of these critical intermediate associations—to press on the state member interests that have been marginalized—since, as a result of the formal cooperation with the government, groups may be pressed to water down or ignore goals important to the membership in order to maintain access and presidential support (as well as the heady experience for group leaders of being in the chief executive's inner circle).[16]

Including these final two categories in the typology of interactions in Table 2 yields:

7. The president communicates with a group in order to gain support for his own policies or goals.
8. The president publicly condemns or opposes the group's goal.

All eight interactions should be affected by partisanship, of course (both the party ideology and coalition interests of the president, and the group's own strategic choices about party support); and by the electoral cycle. Social movements consider a range of political choices—from selective candidate endorsements to close alignment with one party. In the past, it was not uncommon for movements also to pass through a stage of independent party activity, sometimes on the way to fusion with one or the other major party (for example, the Antimonopolists, Greenbackers, Populists, various independent labor parties, and Alice Paul's Woman's Party, which splintered from the more conservative NAWSA).[17] Many successful SMs "die" in the embrace of a party—that is, they cease to manifest the traits of independent SMs and become long-term factions of one major party (as, one may say, did the abolitionists, AFL-CIO, religious right, feminists, gay rights movement, and environmentalists after the late 1970s). It is reasonable to expect a president to pay most attention to groups whose goals do not conflict with those of existing coalition members, and that furnish, or are expected to furnish, his party with strong electoral support. However, in the early years of a group's mobilization it may be unclear where its members' support will ultimately fall, and so agents of both parties may be attentive (as was the case with women's organizations and environmentalists before the late 1970s, and with labor before the New Deal).

Our questions in analyzing the data are these: How were presidential interactions with groups structured and patterned in the early twentieth century? Which groups received the most, and the most supportive, presidential attention? Was there an electoral cycle effect? Did these interactions change over time as presidents became less dependent on their parties, and more like individual entrepreneurs, constructing their own, more *personal* electoral coalitions in an increasingly "plebiscitary" presidency?[18]

Data and Methodology

Using the ProQuest historical newspaper collection, the names of the groups, and other key words indicative of group membership (for example, "labor," "women," "Negroes") were combined with the name and dates of service of presidents. The relevant *New York Times* articles were collected and dates of interactions fitting the Table 2 typology were entered in an Excel file. Then the number and types of president-movement interactions were counted for groups, presidents, parties, and categories of interaction. Notwithstanding the early and limited periods for which these data have been gathered and analyzed to date, over 350 articles of relevance were found and categorized. As will be seen, these seven presidencies reveal interesting dynamics that are in important respects quite "modern."

Findings

The interaction data for the first seven presidents of the twentieth century are summarized in Table 3. The growth of large national organizations and president-group interactions in the Progressive Era (and particularly during World War I) can be seen in Table 1 and the third column of Table 3. This growth evidences the common view of historians that the Progressive Era witnessed a great expansion of collective action. The ratio of groups with whom the president interacted to all groups meeting the one percent threshold (column 1) hardly changes, however, so the increasing frequency of presidential involvement with organizations must be attributed not so much to presidential initiative (which is most affected by his war needs) as to the expansion of collective action itself. In domestic politics, it is citizen organizations who command the attention of the president, and not vice versa.

The rise of "patriotic partnerships" in World War I, noted by Skocpol and her colleagues, is reflected in the increased presidential attention to civic associations like the Red Cross both during and after the war (Table 3, column 4).[19] But the effects of war on president-group interaction had been anticipated by the significance of the Grand Army of the Republic (GAR, made up of Civil War veterans) organization to Republican presidents. In the McKinley administration, the GAR accounted for eight of the president's fifteen positive interactions, and it was the only one of the six large movements of the McKinley years to merit the highest level (level 3, in this case) of presidential attention: McKinley personally attended the GAR annual meetings and even rode at the head of its parade.[20]

Organizations like the Red Cross and YMCA had been presidential favorites even before World War I (Table 3, column 5 registers their popularity with Roosevelt and Taft), but these groups, along with the Knights of

TABLE 3. PRESIDENTIAL INTERACTIONS WITH LARGE ORGANIZATIONS

President (yrs. in office)	Organization/ all[a]	Interactions[b]	Most frequent[c]	Highest level[d]	Election year (pr.)[e]
McKinley (5)	3/6	15	(13) GAR	(3) GAR	1 (1)
T. Roosevelt (7)	3/6	24	(10) AFL	(3) YMCA, GAR	15 (1)
Taft (4)	7/11	25	(8) Red Cross	(3) YMCA, GAR, RC, KC, NAWSA	14 (2)
Wilson (8)	9/18	80	(24) Red Cross	(6) FU, Grange (5) NAWSA[f]	50 (10)
Harding (3)	8/17	37	(11) Red Cross	(6) FU, AFBF	18 (-)
Coolidge (5)	10/15	69	(24) Red Cross	(6) AFL	30 (7)
Hoover (4)	8/15	42	(11) Red Cross	(6) AFBF	17 (6)

a) Number of groups in presidential interactions/all large organizations at that time.
b) Number of positive presidential interactions with groups (1–6 scale; excludes opposition, or president asking the group for its support).
c) Groups with which president interacted most frequently (number of interactions with that group).
d) Group with which president had highest level (positive) interactions (6 = highest level).
e) Number of interactions that took place in election years (number in *presidential* election years in parentheses).
f) President Wilson pressed hard to get the suffrage amendment passed and then ratified in the states. Since the president plays no formal role in constitutional amendments, 5 is the highest level possible here; thus NAWSA is included in the "highest" cell.

Columbus and Salvation Army, were especially valued by presidents for their work with U.S. troops—both active duty soldiers and the wounded and POWs. Their association with patriotism and assistance to soldiers helped them to grow and raise funds; presidents themselves often aided the organizations with fundraising, and even served as officers.[21]

Awareness of the benefits of wartime service also inspired the leaders of the AFL and National American Woman Suffrage Association to offer the president their support during World War I.[22] Wilson had been lukewarm toward suffrage, and even less enthusiastic about labor legislation before 1916.[23] But in both cases, the turn in presidential support came in a year when he faced a difficult reelection, and at a time when he was increasingly leaning toward involvement in the European war. As he prepared to take the United States into the war, Wilson needed votes and support from both women and labor organizations for a host of discretionary and controversial actions. The president even touted the constitutional amendment for women's suffrage as a measure that could (by raising morale) help the allies win the war[24]—not the first, or the last, occasion on which presidents would support social movements of the disadvantaged in the service of foreign policy goals.[25] As Daniel Tichenor indicates in his essay in this volume, Wilson may also have been embarrassed (he was clearly annoyed) by the persistent public demonstrations of the radical faction of the suffrage movement (led by Alice Paul), some of which resulted in harsh treatment by the police, and caused a public outcry.[26]

For a Democratic president who had won election narrowly in a four-candidate race, there was keen awareness, as 1916 approached, of the need to expand his base. Women enfranchised in a block of western and midwestern states; farmers (including midwestern farmers who usually voted Republican); and organized labor, which had heretofore been an unreliable Democratic ally, were the most available and likely targets. Still, Wilson's reluctance to antagonize business in the recession triggered by the war in Europe (and aggravated, his opponents claimed loudly, by the surge of tariff, monetary, antitrust, and other regulatory reform pouring out of Congress in 1913–15), made him hesitant to endorse the unprecedented government credit programs demanded by farmers. Wilson was even more timid where labor was concerned. Though he did appoint William Wilson, the highly respected leader of the mine workers' union, to be the first secretary of labor, he held out stubbornly against the relief of labor unions from antitrust prosecution, resisted both a child labor act and a seamen's protection act, and blocked immigration restrictions desired by labor (but opposed by business).[27]

While Wilson did eventually take the lead on women's suffrage, which had fewer economic implications (beyond its expected impact on the liquor industry), it was *congressional* Democrats who led the response to farmer and labor movements. Only in the critical election year of 1916 did the president finally take the advice of congressional party leaders and shed his opposition to several farmer and labor measures, like the child labor law, an eight-hour day for railroad workers, and the Farm Credit Act he had opposed in 1913–15.[28] And to build up his electoral base in October of 1916 (as well as to prepare the public for entry into the European war), he courted AFL president Gompers with a prestigious appointment to a Defense Advisory Board.[29]

The president's generosity did not extend to blacks, who lived mostly in the South, and whose progress his white constituents there steadfastly opposed. Wilson ordered the segregation of black federal employees in 1913 and forced others out of their offices.[30] Yet when it served his international interests, he was willing to demand an end to lynching; the Germans, Wilson reported in making this plea in 1918, were using it in propaganda against the United States. The country must, he pronounced, show the world that "while it fights for democracy on foreign fields, it is not destroying democracy at home."[31]

After the war was over, the AFL found itself less popular at the White

House than it had been during wartime.[32] Women's organizations, having won the vote with a wartime president's help, were free to return to a goal that had more uniform support among their members, the campaign for peace and disarmament.[33]

Farmers and workers experienced far fewer legislative victories in the Republican administrations that preceded and followed Wilson's eight years. Though most trade unionists were probably voting Republican in the McKinley, Roosevelt, Taft, Harding, Coolidge, and Hoover administrations, the extent of Republican presidential interaction with labor leaders seldom went beyond receiving them at the White House and promising to think about their grievances.[34] President Hoover did address an AFL convention in 1930, when it happened to take place at the same time as the American Legion's annual meeting. Coolidge signed a bill restricting the interstate transportation of convict-made goods (which accounts for the "highest positive interaction" designation for the AFL in the Coolidge row of Table 3); it was a goal long sought by labor but also popular with manufacturers.[35] Likewise, the 1926 Railway Labor Act (for voluntary bargaining to avert strikes) had been worked out in joint meetings between the Railway Brotherhoods and the CEOs.

But as the fifth row (Harding) in Table 3 shows, the farm groups in one policy arena did compel presidential attention to a rather remarkable degree in a GOP era. The postwar farm depression spurred great militancy on the part of farm organizations. First, they called for an end to the Federal Reserve Board's deflation policy and demanded that the president appoint a farmer to the board. When President Harding responded only with cabinet meetings and studies, the three main organizations, the Grange, the Farm Bureau, and the Farmers' Union, pressed Congress for a new law requiring a farmer appointment, and a bevy of policy changes in monetary policy. Harding then agreed not to reappoint a conservative board member to the Federal Reserve Board, and finally reached a compromise with Congress: he would back monetary easing and appoint a farmer to the Fed if Congress gave up the idea of forcing him to do so by statute. His two sequential farmer appointees were hardly militants, but the Fed got the message and began to ease monetary policy after 1923.[36]

Calvin Coolidge was an economic conservative par excellence, and he carried the notion of public-private economic partnership to a peacetime high. He helped to raise money for the Red Cross and approached the AFL and Chamber of Commerce to help find jobs for the war wounded.[37] The government, he argued (in a speech to the American Legion!), had spent quite enough on veterans,[38] and to drive home his point, he vetoed the soldiers' bonus bill passed by Congress in the 1924 election year. (They passed it over his veto.)[39]

Coolidge praised the expanded Red Cross and encouraged it to help the victims of floods, storms, and other disasters at home, even while continuing its relief work abroad.[40] It was funded by private charity and did work that would eventually gravitate to the government, but which Republican presidents preferred to keep in private hands. The Coolidge experience underlines a function of social organizations not explored in the work of Skocpol et al. on "patriotic partnerships" in wartime, but recalled by the policies of the GOP in the contemporary era: whether for reasons of limited governmental capacity due to fiscal stringency, or inspired by an antistatist ideology that has characterized Republican administrations in particular since the early twentieth century,[41] GOP presidents appeal to private groups to take on functions for which there is an increasing public demand. Such delegation permits the president to respond to that demand at low economic and political cost.

Given his strong preference for a government with as few responsibilities as possible, it was inevitable that Coolidge would veto the innovative agricultural reform program developed and advocated by the "farm bloc," a coalition of major farm organizations and the members of Congress closest to them. The Republican Congress, determined to aid the deeply distressed countryside, passed the McNary-Haugen bill embodying that program a second time. Coolidge vetoed it again (as did Hoover after him).[42] However, not all market intervention was anathema to Republican presidents in this era. In September of his reelection year, Coolidge met with AFL representatives to remind them of the benefits to labor of high tariffs and the immigration restriction bill he had signed a few months before.[43] Just before leaving office he handed the AFL a more substantial victory by signing the bill banning goods produced by convict labor from interstate commerce. However, the new law was not scheduled to take effect for five years.[44]

Another large membership organization, one enjoying a remarkable rejuvenation in the 1920s, caught the attention of President Coolidge. Although he did not mention it by name, the president publicly condemned organizations that furthered intolerance, and it was clear to his audience that he was speaking of the KKK.[45] In the 1920s, the GOP was seriously debating a momentous reorganization of the Southern Party, to push aside the "black and tan" Republican state organizations that its white elites saw as corrupt and, because of the votelessness of Black southerners, inconsequential. The plan was to move strongly to recruit middle-class white southerners.[46] Still, backpedaling on Republican commitments did not imply condoning racial terror.

In the expanding regime of White House-social movement interactions, the presidency of Herbert Hoover is the exception that proves the rule—the rule that presidents cannot afford to antagonize most large groups when times are very, very hard. Hoover's group interactions are lower than his closest predecessors, and while he signed off on a modest farm relief bill that won the praise of farm organizations early in his first year, he went on to veto major farm bills as the Depression deepened in 1930.[47] His positive responses to social movements were mostly symbolic. He made a large number of appointments of group representatives to conferences and advisory committees but seldom took their advice.[48] The Hoover column under the category "president supports a bill to achieve a goal of the group" was virtually empty, save for his strong support for Prohibition.

Table 4 summarizes presidential interactions with the major social movements of the early twentieth century. It provides one measure of the relative importance of women, veterans, farmers, and workers. Veterans' votes were very important to Republican presidents in the early twentieth century, and they could count on an open White House door and the presence of their commander in chief at ceremonial parades and annual conventions. However, once veterans became, in the aftermath of World War I, major claimants on the public purse—a purse now filled by the income tax, not the tariff, and hence more tightly drawn by conservative Republicans—they could not count on much sympathy from the president. That is a surprising finding in view of the centrality of the presidency's war role, but it is a relationship that, one suspects, will hold in contemporary times as well. Just because presidents count on soldiers to execute their war policies does not mean (apparently) that, once they are mustered out, the veterans' sacrifices and debilities will be sympathetically received by the commander in chief. Congress is apt to be much more forthcoming (and that was true of the long campaign for a Veterans' Bonus from the Harding through the Roosevelt administrations).

TABLE 4. NUMBER (AND HIGHEST LEVEL) OF POSITIVE INTERACTIONS WITH MAJOR SOCIAL MOVEMENTS

President	Military	Women	Labor	Farmers	Blacks
McKinley	13 (3)	1 (1)	1 (1)	—	—
T. Roosevelt	8 (3)	0	10 (2)	—	—
Taft	5 (3)	3 (3)	5 (1)	1 (1)	—
Wilson	4 (2)	24 (5)	11 (5)	13 (6)	1 (2)
Harding	5 (3)	5 (2)	3 (3)	11 (6)	1 (2)
Coolidge	11 (3)	11 (1)	6 (6)	15 (3)	1 (1)
Hoover	6 (4)	11 (2)	5 (3)	9 (6)	0

Dash indicates no active major organization during the administration.

The totals for women in Table 4 are boosted by the extraordinary level of interactions in the Wilson administration, when the peak of suffrage agitation found a president in desperate need of new votes. Once enfranchised, women were major activists in the movement for national Prohibition, and, subsequently, its enforcement (which fell to Republican presidents). The overwhelming majority of interactions between presidents and women's groups after 1920 concerned Prohibition. Farmers had a wider range of goals, and when they were highly mobilized and relatively unified in organizational goals (as was the case from the 1880s to the mid-1940s), farmers' organizations achieved sufficient congressional support to generate legislative initiatives to which presidents had to respond. Labor had a harder time in this era, but its diverse organizations were also less cooperative with one another, and less committed to politics than farmers' or women's movements. In peacetime, labor needed strong congressional support to overcome the president's reluctance to respond to their more controversial and redistributive demands.

The time of the Black civil rights movement was still decades away. Republican presidents were at least willing to condemn violence against African Americans in peacetime, but offered little in the way of positive response and became committed, in the 1920s, to gaining a white base in the South at the expense of executive appointments and party leadership positions for southern blacks. Democratic President Wilson segregated and excluded black office holders in Washington, and only came out against lynching in the service of his war goals. African American numbers were still too concentrated in one region where local officials would spare no effort to keep them in subservience. They had as yet few friends in high places, and too few votes to matter to national politicians.

Conclusion

Social movements in the twentieth and twenty-first centuries need the president's support, or at least acquiescence, if they are to attain their goals. If they cannot persuade the president to support their interests in legislation or its enforcement in the courts or bureaucracy, they at least need his agreement not to veto the measures that Congress sees fit to pass. If they demonstrate or strike, they need assurance that the president will not call out troops, or urge the Washington police to deal harshly with their collective actions. If he is sympathetic, that may trigger other elite endorsements, or at least discourage opposition. If opponents threaten violence, and local governments side with the opponents, the president can commit troops to the movement's protection (a very uncommon action in the period under examination here).[49]

In the nineteenth century, some groups (farmers and workers, in particular) advanced without significant presidential support, sometimes winning action by states, or from a sympathetic Congress. With the coming of the twentieth century's more active presidency and the centralization of policy-making initiative in the national government, it became very difficult to accomplish much without some degree of presidential help. The analysis of president-movement relationships presented here, though limited to the period between 1897 and 1932, suggests that help is forthcoming only when it is in the president's political interest to give it; or, if the movement is large enough, rowdy enough, or has sufficient support in Congress to win significant compliance there, he might act on their goals defensively, in order to prevent more radical legislation. Such was the case in the Harding administration when farmers agitated over monetary policy, and later, in the mid-1930s, when Franklin Roosevelt finally agreed to a conservative federal insurance program for old age pensions at a time when the Townsend Movement for check-in-the-mail redistribution had gained many adherents in society and in Congress.[50] The interactions between presidents and social movements were, throughout the early twentieth century, tense and fluctuating. However, there were highly significant reforms that originated with social movement agitation—new legislation that responded to unmet needs and promoted some incorporation of once-marginalized groups into more complete citizenship (even while one group, African Americans, were further marginalized). At the least, several new players in national politics gained recognition and access. However, at no time in this period was the president the leading voice of reform or at the cutting edge of change in causes championed by social movements.

Chapter 12
Leaders, Citizenship Movements, and the Politics Rivalries Make

Daniel J. Tichenor

Notwithstanding pervasive evidence of what James Block has called America's "agency culture," organized efforts to secure basic human, political, and economic rights for excluded categories of people fail far more often than they succeed. Citizenship movements routinely encounter stiff resistance from government and the mass public alike. But these campaigns are not always quixotic. Consider three rare yet monumental transformations driven by citizenship movements in different eras of U.S. history: the abolition of slavery during the Civil War, the extension of voting rights to women in the early twentieth century, and the creation of new economic protections for industrial workers during the New Deal. Each of these reform campaigns overcame daunting cultural and institutional impediments, decades of official repression or indifference, and fierce popular resistance. Why did these movements secure large-scale changes that have eluded so many others? My aim in this essay is to trace the transformative effect in each instance to creative tensions among different sets of political actors in and outside the government. These exceptional moments when durable forms of exclusion were dismantled turned on conflict, negotiation, and accommodation among multiple sets of leaders and followers.

Presidents and social movements have been especially important in these successful struggles for greater inclusion. This is hardly surprising given that presidents and social movements share the frustration that comes from grappling with a governmental system that is designed to thwart concerted action. Yet, the alliance of American chief executives and American social movements, citizenship movements in particular, is neither natural nor instinctive. Indeed, there are good reasons to expect this to be an antagonistic relationship. As most presidents set about to remake the political order on their own terms and for their own purposes, the contentious reform agendas of strong insurgents threaten to interrupt, if not ruin, the best-laid executive plans. Charismatic movement leaders occasionally enjoy a "bully pulpit" as commanding as that of the rhetorical presidency, competing with the White House to shape public discourse and opinion (consider, for example, the immediate impact and now iconic status of Martin Luther King, Jr.'s "I Have a Dream" speech). Moreover, movement leaders have strong incentives to exploit disorder and governmental vulnerabilities, especially during domestic and international crises, to advance their goals; presidents, meanwhile, want to meet national emergencies with a firm hand and to restore a modicum of social order and economic tranquility. Finally, presidents and movement leaders speak to different constituencies; they have their own sets of followers, and they must respond to their different and divergent demands. Figure 1 illustrates different dispositions between order and change as they normally set the distance between presidents and movements. The constituents (or at least enfranchised majorities) that presidents serve are normally hostile toward reforms advanced by "citizenship movements," defined by James Jasper as efforts "organized by and on behalf of people excluded in some way from full human rights, political participation, or basic economic protections, such as racial and ethnic minorities, women, gays and lesbians, immigrants, and lower-class workers."[1] Rank-and-file movement activists, in turn, tend to embrace conceptions of social justice far more radical than the mainstream and to assail moderate movement leaders for their political expediency.

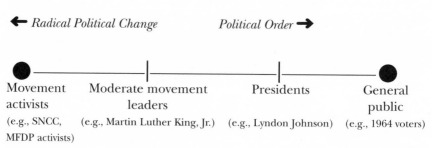

Figure 1. Two leader-follower relationships.

Given these different interests, presidents typically have had strong incentives to minimize, disregard, or even repress the demands of citizenship movements. (The previous chapter by Elizabeth Sanders elucidates well the logic of executive resistance.) As shown here, breakthroughs were reserved for movements that were capable of waging effective "insider" and "outsider" political strategies. And more than that, a fundamental, if fleeting, disruption of ordinary White House perceptions was necessary for a partnership between presidents and movement activists in service of abolition, woman's suffrage, and the rights of industrial workers. In each case of success, an unprecedented national security or economic crisis proved critical in altering executive incentives and warrants governing organized struggles for democratic inclusion. As I will show in the pages that follow, this un-usual coincidence of factors provided conditions essential for rival political actors to collaborate in the construction of unprecedented new rights for African Americans, women, and working-class laborers.

Citizenship Movements: Patterns of Repression and Indifference

Government indifference and repression have been politics as usual for citizenship movements during most of American history. Beginning in the 1830s, for instance, abolitionists of the American Anti-Slavery Society (AASS) tried to sway public opinion by distributing antislavery literature. It was a desperate strategy, but, as the abolitionist William Jay explained, one of the few available to antislavery activists within a polity structured to protect property rights and frustrate significant reform: "Constitu-tional restrictions forbid all other than moral interference with slavery in Southern States."[2] But even that was too much. The Jackson administra-tion suppressed their efforts by permitting local postmasters to destroy abolitionist mailings and to reveal the names of southern subscribers. In addition to facing regular bursts of mob violence and local sanctions, then, abolitionists faced what even the pro-administration *New York Evening Post* called "a censorship of the press in its worst possible form, al-lowing every two penny Postmaster . . . to be the judge of what species of intelligence is proper to circulate, and what to withhold from the peo-ple."[3] This was but one of many efforts initiated by presidents and other political actors in the decades before the Civil War to impede the designs of abolitionists.

The woman's suffrage movement confronted its own set of prominent ideological and institutional barriers. Three decades after organizing the women's rights convention at Seneca Falls in 1848, the suffragist leader Elizabeth Cady Stanton ruefully noted that her movement was hamstrung by indifference, ridicule, and outright antagonism on the part of govern-ment officials and ordinary citizens. "Looking back over the past thirty years," she lamented, it "taxes and wearies the memory to think of all the conventions we have held, the legislatures we have besieged, the petitions and tracts we have circulated, the speeches, the calls, the resolutions we have penned."[4] Little changed after the turn of the century. When the leader of the National American Woman Suffrage Association (NAWSA), Carrie Chapman Catt, successfully generated wide national media atten-tion for the suffragist cause with a transcontinental whistlestop train cam-paign in 1905, President Theodore Roosevelt dismissed the movement. "The President of the United States does not absent himself from the coun-try during the term of the Presidency; it is his domain," he declared. "So it will be with the woman; she is queen of her empire and that empire is the home."[5] When suffragists pursued more confrontational forms of protest

244 Daniel J. Tichenor

in later years, their demonstrations were repeatedly suppressed by local police and federal troops.

American government responded to the labor movement with decades
of hostility. Official repression of the labor unrest was both fierce and complete in the century preceding the New Deal. At the same time as the legal
code routinely enervated labor organization prior to the 1930s, U.S. companies employed their own spies, police, and armies to derail unionizing
through blacklists, firings, and violence. During rare episodes when private
repression faltered, governmental coercion typically quieted working-class
agitation. "On the political surface, the state backed private power with
public violence," James Morone explains. "When company troops failed,
local police and state militia were dispatched; if they were unwilling or unable to end strikes, federal forces were called."[6] The Pullman strike of 1894
is instructive. Begun by employees of the Pullman Palace Car Company
who were disgruntled by severe wage reductions, the strike eventually was
joined by workers associated with the American Railroad Union led by Eugene Debs. When 150,000 striking railroad workers in Chicago threatened
to grind the nation's railway system to a halt, Grover Cleveland ordered federal troops to the city with instructions to end the strike forcibly. In the violence that followed, thirty workers were killed, union leaders were
arrested, and workers were compelled to return to work. "The United
States government was at the beck and call of the railroad corporations,"
Debs later complained. "These corporations, with the Federal Courts and
troops to back them up, had swarms of mercenaries sworn in as deputy
marshals to incite violence as a pretext for taking possession of the headquarters of the American Railway Union by armed force, throwing its leaders into prison without trial and breaking down the union."[7] The
governmental response to the Pullman strike was especially dramatic, but
its resistance to extending basic economic protections to unskilled laborers
was par for the course. Backed by a restrictive legal code and violent government repression, American labor policy was clearly biased against working-class insurgency over more than a century.

Patterns of Breakthrough: Crisis, Leadership Rivalries, and Creative Tensions

For the most part, then, ending slavery, winning access to the ballot box for
women, and extending basic economic security to industrial workers
proved elusive goals that ran up against strong ideological and institutional
obstacles. Significantly, these reform causes only became realistic possibilities during rare moments of U.S. history when crises of the first order
threatened the nation. This is not to say that exogenous events or shocks
by themselves served as the primary catalyst for dismantling long-standing
exclusions. Rather, the Civil War, World War I, and the Great Depression

challenged government officials with new imperatives; it altered their strategic environments and calculations. By virtue of their disproportionate responsibility to manage crises, presidents at these moments shouldered especially profound burdens. But they were also armed with extraordinary prerogative powers. Abraham Lincoln, Woodrow Wilson, and Franklin D. Roosevelt were not unconstrained in dealing with crises, but they were empowered by events to deal with crises in a new way.

For the insurgents, in turn, the crises provided a critical opportunity to exploit the elite's search for a new orientation and to overcome the normal cultural, institutional, and majoritarian impediments to egalitarian reform. This was, however, no guarantee of success. It is telling that many of the citizenship movements afoot during these crisis moments failed, including organized efforts on behalf of women's enfranchisement and Chinese rights during the Civil War, on behalf of African American civil rights and the rights of new immigrants in World War I, and on behalf of migrant workers, tenant farmers, and southern Blacks during the Great Depression. Why did some movements for contentious democratic inclusion succeed where others did not?

We can gain some analytical purchase on how breakthroughs for citizenship movements have occurred by considering the role of conflict, negotiation, and accommodation among multiple leaders and followers. In particular, I argue that two forms of leadership rivalry during times of crisis helped achieve nonincremental reforms for advocates of social justice and broader inclusion. The first is to be found in the divisions within social movements between moderate and radical leaders. The second is that between presidents and key movement figures. Let us consider each of these in turn.

Abolitionists, suffragists, and labor activists all disagreed fervently among themselves over political strategies and tactics. Whereas some movement leaders and their followers favored relatively conventional political methods such as electoral mobilization, conciliatory or "globalizing" publicity, lobbying, litigating, and coordinating with allies within government, others championed disruptive protest and militancy as the surest path to success. Interestingly, one can detect similar divisions among social movement scholars. For example, Frances Fox Piven and Richard Cloward contend that poor people's movements achieve success mostly when they employ highly disruptive tactics and that more conventional organizational efforts are doomed to fail.[8] In turn, Ann-Marie Szymanski's superb study of temperance campaigns of the nineteenth and twentieth centuries highlights the promise of moderate mobilization strategies and the limitations of radical activism for securing movement ends.[9] Still other social movement scholars have recognized the efficacy of what Sidney Tarrow has labeled "multiform" movements that blend "institutional and noninstitutional politics." Along these lines, Herbert

Haines has analyzed the positive and negative effects of radical flanks on mainstream movement efforts.[10]

Taking a cue from Tarrow and Haines, consider how conventional (institutional) and disruptive (extra-institutional) political capacities of social movements might affect patterns of success and failure. Social movements are usually characterized as efforts sustained by ordinary people who put pressure on government officials or other powerful opponents by disruptive, unconventional means.[11] They are commonly assumed to exert power in the streets, pursuing tactics such as large public rallies and marches, boycotts, labor strikes, occupation of key sites, provocative verbal or visual rhetoric, destruction of property, and planned violence. But a more complete inventory of movement resources and activities would include conventional political methods of pressing demands on the state; many movements have pursued the standard repertoire of lobbying, electioneering, and litigation, as well as nurturing alliances with politicians at the centers of power.

As Table 1 illustrates, the political efficacy of social movements is best grasped by taking into account their capacities along two dimensions: their ability to disturb social, economic, or political order through disruptive tactics and their conventional political leverage. It would seem that movement success in terms of transforming public policy, government structures, or the political culture is all but impossible in the absence of either conventional political leverage or the capacity to disrupt domestic order.

Government officials have all the advantages in responding to movements that fall short on both counts. These *marginalized movements* are easily dispatched. Indifference is the typical state reaction and it can be exercised with impunity. Repression is always an option. Consider two examples: the anti-imperialist movement of 1898–1900 and the Poor People's Campaign of 1968. The Spanish-American War of 1898 galvanized peace activists and isolationists to coalesce within a new movement led by the Anti-Imperialist League (AIL). Activists organized public meetings and publicity efforts demanding withdrawal of U.S. troops from the Philippines and raised various constitutional, racial, and economic objections to imperialist policies. Given the movement's limited capacities for both conventional and contentious politics, national foreign policy-makers simply ignored the anti-imperialists. Movement activists failed in their efforts to block the ratification of the Treaty of Paris in 1899 that granted U.S. control of the Philippines, Puerto Rico, and Guam, and permitted a military occupation of Cuba. Lacking resources to influence the election of 1900, the AIL and the movement it led faded after William McKinley's decisive reelection.[12]

The Poor People's Campaign of 1968 offers a similar illustration of the marginalized state of movements that are unable to marshal either institutional or extra-institutional pressures on the state. Initiated by Martin Luther King, Jr., in the spring of 1968, the campaign hoped to compel Con-

TABLE 1. MOVEMENT EFFICACY: LINKING CONVENTIONAL AND DISRUPTIVE CAPACITIES

	Significant challenge to social, economic, or political order	*Insignificant challenge to social, economic, or political order*
Significant conventional political leverage	**CONTENTION**	**COOPTATION**
	Formidable reform movements	**Captured or incremental movements**
	Official response: *Repression, breakthrough reform*	Official response: *Institutionalization, incrementalism, gradual retrenchment*
	-Civil Rights Movement, 1950s/1960s -AIDS Activism, 1980s	-Labor Movement, 1917–28, 1941–present -Religious Right, 1984–present
Insignificant conventional political leverage	**MILITANCY**	**WILDERNESS**
	Pariah movements	**Marginalized movements**
	Official response: *Repression*	Official response: *Indifference or repression*
	-Industrial Workers of the World, 1910s -Militia Movement, 1990s	-American Anti-Imperial League, 1890s -Poor People's Campaign, 1968

Challenge to social, economic or political order refers to credible disruptive threat via protest, violence, strikes, etc. Conventional political leverage refers to lobbying access, formal institutional allies, public opinion support, etc.

gress to enact new programs alleviating poverty in America. To pressure lawmakers, the campaign mobilized thousands of indigent people to camp out in shanties on park land next to the Lincoln Memorial. Just weeks before the campaign began, King was assassinated and a less prominent civil rights leader assumed leadership of the protest effort. Days of torrential rains drenched the campsite, many of the fragile wooden shanties fell apart, trash piled up, violence broke out among protestors, and most activists went home. Only six weeks after its start, the Poor People's Campaign fell apart. The few indigents who remained at the campsite at the end of June were evicted or arrested.[13]

Of course, many social movements command considerable attention from state actors. Radical movements that do not exhibit mainstream proclivities and are perceived by officials as posing a credible threat to social, economic, or political order typically elicit harsh forms of government repression. The antebellum abolition movement, the German-American antiwar efforts during World War I, and the Black Panthers are all examples of *pariah movements* perceived by state officials as threatening to the social order and thus necessary targets of repression. Two movements generations apart—the Industrial Workers of the World (IWW) of the 1910s and the militia movement of the 1990s—capture this pattern well. The IWW was founded in 1905 to organize unskilled, factory, and migrant workers ignored by other unions. Its leadership included militants who embraced radical visions of class struggle and revolution. Many of its campaigns, like the "free speech fights" in Spokane (1909–10), relied on nonviolent resistance. Yet the provocative rhetoric and labor unrest associated with the IWW disquieted various employers and officials. During World War I and the First Red Scare, the state took vigorous action. Federal agents raided IWW offices nationwide, searching for treasonous materials. The raids were followed by mass arrests charging all movement leaders and numerous members with various crimes. Deportations and imprisonment soon followed after 1918, leading to the IWW's ultimate collapse.[14]

The citizen militia movement of the 1990s illustrates similar patterns. Movement activists subscribed to right-wing conspiracy theories that portrayed the federal government as tyrannical and warned of an impending takeover of the country by the United Nations. Organized in rural areas, citizen militias focused their energies on paramilitary training in preparation for an eventual federal or international assault on their freedoms. In 1995, the bombing of the Murrah Building in Oklahoma City resulted in 168 deaths at the hands of two domestic terrorists with ties to the militia movement. The response at all levels of the government was swift. Militia groups and their members became the target of intense government surveillance, infiltration, and arrests. Both radical left-wing and right-wing movements inspire intense government crackdowns when perceived as threatening the social, economic, or political order. Movement militancy may draw governmental attention, but disruptive capacities alone are hardly the means to favorable breakthroughs.[15]

Social movement organizations that enjoy significant conventional political leverage but pose little challenge to domestic tranquility usually have notable strategic advantages not shared by their marginal and militant counterparts. These *captured* or *institutionalized movements* enjoy political recognition, access to the centers of power, and a secure role in mainstream policy making. In contrast to those lacking conventional political clout, these movements may win incremental policy gains, but they are unlikely to shatter the status quo in favor of sweeping reforms. The bureaucratization of the American labor movement during World War II is instructive. In 1940, labor leaders of the Congress of Industrial Organizations (CIO) elected to discard earlier militant tactics in favor of a more refined role in Washington and a firmer alliance with Democratic leaders. CIO "labor statesmen" like Sidney Hillman forged close ties with the Roosevelt White House and oversaw the creation of the CIO's political action committee, which cemented ties between organized labor and the Democratic Party. After Pearl Harbor, war imperatives called for extraordinary industrial production and coordination. Labor leaders such as Philip Murray, the new CIO president, and Walter Reuther of the United Auto Workers (UAW) proposed "industrial councils" that would facilitate efficient wartime production while giving organized labor real influence—along with business and government—in supervising industries and the workforce. The Roosevelt administration eschewed such ideas. In the end, the AFL, the CIO, and other unions agreed to a "no-strike pledge" during the war and grew dependent on the war agencies to exercise their power over industrial workers benevolently.[16] "Instead of an active participant in the councils of industry," historian Alan Brinkley notes, "the labor movement had become, in effect, a ward of the state."[17] Co-optation was the price of labor's programmatic collaboration, as union militancy and independence gave way to a moderate, bureaucratic style of labor organization. Incremental gains or gradual retrenchment are the likely responses of the national state to institutionalized movements. Breakthrough politics are animated by very different movement orientations and capacities.

The exceptional breakthroughs won by the abolitionist, woman's suffrage, and industrial workers movements turned on a paradox: insurgent goals were well served by internal leadership rivalries that produce strong moderate and militant wings. While internal divisions may weaken a movement in normal times, they can also position a movement to take advantage of extraordinary circumstances. Rival militant and moderate leaders, when they inspire distinct repertoires of collective action and organization, equip *competitive movements* with essential, though different and often competing, capacities—capacities that make them political forces with which governing elites must contend during crises. More precisely, citizenship movements have proved most viable in their pursuit of contentious breakthroughs when they have combined mainstream political leverage with credible disruptive threats to orderly politics.

A second form of leadership rivalry, however, has contributed to winning the elusive reforms advanced by citizenship movements. During rare periods of acute crisis, all three of our citizenship movements worked to press American presidents into service of their political goals. They did so not because they viewed the presidency as heroic. Each movement enjoyed more intimate alliances with other government officials, first scored political victories in other formal institutional settings (such as Congress or the states), and historically faced resistance if not active suppression from the nation's chief executives. The reason movement leaders courted, pressured, and provoked the White House was precisely because of the exceptional power and opportunity afforded the presidency in times of crisis. Initially, Abraham Lincoln, Woodrow Wilson, and Franklin D. Roosevelt each proved reluctant to serve as an agent of sweeping reform on behalf of Black freedom, woman's suffrage and labor rights. But in each case, the reform movement insinuated itself into their perceptions of how best to achieve their own goals, and for a moment, the movement became instrumental to their desire to restore order on new terms of their own.

Despite unmistakable conflicts, the creative tensions between American presidents and social movement leaders during extraordinary times have played a pivotal role in advancing breakthroughs for political inclusion and in shaping their form and substance. Absent pressure from insurgents, presidents and other elected officials would have little incentive to dismantle durable structures of repression. Without the agency of prerogative presidents or the assistance of other government officials, social movements would struggle to secure their ends on the periphery of power. In turn, for all the acrimony they yield, internal leadership rivalries have the potential to empower movements with conventional and disruptive political capacities that increase their chances of winning political breakthroughs. Save for the disruptive protests and confrontational tactics of militants, moderate social movement leaders would have little leverage in their negotiations with government officials. And in the absence of mainstream movement leaders and activists to impress elite officials with the opportunities presented by the movement to realize their own goals, radical insurgents would more likely provoke repression than win lasting concessions, let alone a permanent seat at the table. Significantly, it is the struggle and interplay of these various political actors in exceptional circumstances that proved instrumental in achieving the abolition of slavery, voting rights for women, and the establishment of a new labor regime.

Rivalry and Breakthrough I: Lincoln, Abolitionists, and Emancipation

Although the campaign against slavery can be traced back to the earliest days of the American republic, abolitionists agitated at the fringes of American politics for decades. It was not until 1833 that a national organization, the American Anti-Slavery Society (AASS), was founded by William Lloyd Garrison with support from relatively well-educated and prosperous abolitionists to pressure state legislatures and Congress for reform.[18] Garrison and his supporters focused their efforts on producing and distributing confrontational antislavery literature designed to evoke moral outrage toward slavery in both the North and the South.[19] However out-of-step abolitionists were with both the nation's dominant political leaders and its enfranchised majority, their spirited activism helped AASS membership rolls to swell to over 250,000 by 1838. The Jackson administration's open suppression of AAAS efforts to distribute provocative antislavery materials captures how much it viewed the abolitionist movement as a potent threat to social and political order.

INTERNAL CONFLICT AND MULTIPLE CAPACITIES

Rivalry within the abolitionist movement emerged early on. Garrisonian abolitionists were hostile to conventional forms of political activism, devoted to the purity of their principles, and unwilling to compromise. Their hostility toward a constitutional system they viewed as explicitly supportive of slavery heightened their disdain for mainstream politics.[20] Many abolitionists disagreed with the Garrisonian disavowal of mainstream politics. At the close of the 1830s, a sizable wing of the abolitionist movement parted ways with Garrisonian radicals in the belief that a conventional strategy of advancing their cause through elections and party politics was most likely to secure meaningful legal change.[21]

During the 1840s, two old friends who were prominent abolitionist leaders, Wendell Phillips and Charles Sumner, engaged in a heated debate that captured the creative tensions within the movement. A staunch Garrisonian and electrifying orator, Phillips told audiences that America and its constitutional system was so riddled with sin that Christian reformers had little choice but to "seek to be in this country like an alien, like a traveler."[22] Sumner responded by scolding Phillips for such utopian thinking. The only solution to evils like slavery, he averred, was to boldly enter the political fray: "Take your place among citizens, and use all the weapons of a citizen in this just warfare."[23] Phillips fired back that even when a person of impeccable ethics, such as Sumner himself, entered conventional political life, the reformer would be corrupted by a thousand political maneuvers and compromises.[24]

Over the next two decades, antislavery activists gained increasing influence in party politics, elections, and ultimately the composition and work of Congress. The number of northern lawmakers opposed to slavery grew markedly in these years. Harriet Beecher Stowe's *Uncle Tom's Cabin*, a bestseller that illuminated the evils of slavery by portraying a slave family torn apart, created a national sensation. More than 300,000 copies of the book were sold in 1852 alone. Amid this restiveness, a succession of presidents who followed Jackson tried mightily to keep slavery off the public agenda. When Franklin Pierce entered the Oval Office in 1853, for example, he offered hollow assurances that the controversial Compromise of 1850 and vigorous enforcement of fugitive slave laws would quiet the slavery controversy. "I fervently hope the [slavery] question is at rest," he declared in his inaugural address. Yet as Pierce spoke wistfully of the virtues of national harmony, the electoral environment and the legislative branch were being transformed by the abolitionist movement. As historian David Potter writes of this period, "the antislavery bloc in Congress, strengthened by militant recruits like Sumner and [Benjamin] Wade, was no longer a little handful of isolated men.[25] While Garrisonian abolitionists continued to agitate outside the traditional institutional arenas of American politics, other abolitionists were advancing a promising "insider" strategy that won them increasing clout in the nation's capital, and especially within the halls of Congress. Diversity in the movement was accentuated further by a consequential split among militant insurgents loyal to Garrisonian nonviolence and those committed to far more aggressive confrontations, as John Brown and his followers dramatically illustrated in their raid at Harper's Ferry. Militant antebellum abolitionism ensured that the slavery conflict dominated the public agenda, despite the best efforts of political leaders like Pierce, Stephen Douglass, and James Buchanan to change the topic. In turn, moderate abolitionists were gaining Northern support and electing allies to Congress who would be well positioned to assist the cause when the time was ripe.

CRISIS, MOVEMENT ACTIVISM, AND PRESIDENTIAL RESISTANCE

The crisis of the Civil War provided abolitionists with unprecedented opportunities. Abraham Lincoln's victory in 1860 brought to the executive office for the first time a politician hostile to the institution of slavery and dedicated to halting its expansion into new territories, itself a partial triumph of abolitionist electioneering. Yet Lincoln's inaugural address reaffirmed his opposition to any efforts "to interfere with the institution of slavery in the states where it already exists."[26] The new president believed that the "only substantial dispute" was whether slavery could be extended to new territory. On this score, he asserted that the dispute over slavery's extension could not be settled by the *Dred Scott* ruling, but that it was a matter to be decided by ordinary voters and their representatives.[27]

The day after the North's surrender of Fort Sumter, the White House and Congress were flooded with abolitionist petitions, letters, and personal confrontations demanding immediate emancipation. Abolitionists understood well that the crisis of Southern secession presented openings for reform that were almost unimaginable in quieter times when American constitutional democracy regularly frustrated ambitious reform. "If slaveholders had staid [*sic*] in the Union they might have kept the life in their institution for many years to come," one prominent abolitionist observed. "That what no party and no public feeling in the North could ever have hoped to touch they had madly placed in the path of destruction."[28] Lincoln, however, was unwilling to abolish slavery by executive action. The use of the broad prerogative powers of the presidency during wartime, he argued, could only be justified by the exigencies of war and not as an instrument of either his party's or his own personal policy preferences. If Lincoln resisted sweeping action, his own moral aversion to slavery and his eagerness to assuage moderate abolitionists in Congress did lead him to distance himself from the proslavery positions of earlier presidents. In defiance of the *Dred Scott* decision, Lincoln signed legislation barring slavery from all the national territories. He also supported a new treaty with Great Britain aimed at better attacking the Atlantic slave trade, and at the urging of the abolitionist senator Charles Sumner of Massachusetts, he refused to commute the death sentence of the first American convicted of participating in the slave trade. But he remained unwilling to endorse "radical and extreme measures." On July 4, 1861, Lincoln again assured the nation that he had no intention to disturb slavery in the states; three weeks later he told Congress that "this war is not waged . . . for any purpose . . . of overthrowing or interfering with the rights or established institutions of . . . Southern states."[29] Militant and moderate abolitionists alike were undaunted, pressing strongly for a decidedly bolder course.

RADICAL AGITATION

Movement radicals launched provocative publicity campaigns and rallies meant to unravel Lincoln's gradualism. They firmly rejected Lincoln's claims that national preservation, principles of popular rule, and constitutional requirements trumped emancipation. "The conviction that *Slavery Is A Sin* is the Gibralter of our cause," declared Phillips.[30] Garrison himself made this point graphically by publicly burning the U.S. Constitution for shielding slavery. In November 1861, an Emancipation League was formed by Phillips, Garrison, and Frederick Douglass to coordinate a vigorous publicity campaign of public speeches, writings, and demonstrations aimed at "urging upon the people and the Government emancipation of the Slaves, as a measure of justice, and military necessity."[31] Garrisonian abolitionists saw their militancy as playing a critical role. "I do not believe that [Lincoln] has the boldness to declare an emancipation policy, until, by a pressure which we are to create, the country forces them to do it," Phillips reasoned. "I must educate, arouse, and mature a public opinion which shall compel the administration to adopt and support [abolition]. . . . My criticism is not, like that of the traitor presses, meant to paralyze the administration, but to goad it to more activity and vigor."[32] Their efforts drew unprecedented attention. The New York *Tribune* estimated that during the winter and spring of 1861–62 more than five million people heard or read antislavery speeches of Phillips and other Emancipation League agitators.[33] "Keep pounding the rock," Douglass urged his colleagues, while his own speeches assailed Lincoln's "vacillation, doubt, uncertainty, and hesitation."[34] The League was not alone in its efforts to instigate change. The White House also was beleaguered by a steady stream of antislavery petitions, letters, and delegations of indignant abolitionists.[35]

Moderate abolitionists at the centers of power recognized the moral and practical strains that these publicity and protest activities placed on Lincoln, and they sought to capitalize on them in two ways. First, reform-minded lawmakers and cabinet members, most notably Senator Sumner, conferred with the President several times a week on how to address both abolitionist demands and the moral obligations to end slavery.[36] Sumner and others also gave a more respected voice to militant arguments that freeing slaves served an immediate military purpose. Second, abolitionists in Congress (including prominent members of the influential Joint Congressional Committee on the Conduct of the War) worked to force the president's hand amid the constant drumbeat of external abolitionist criticism.[37] This was especially evident in how Congress responded to the issue of thousands of slaves who fled behind the lines of Union armies in pursuit of freedom. Some Union officers followed the Fugitive Slave Act and permitted slave masters to reclaim these fugitives, while others refused to return the slaves on the grounds that they were contrabands of war. Lincoln made no public comment on the subject in the summer of 1861, but he privately resolved that these fugitives ought not be returned to bondage.[38] Still, he faced a nettlesome dilemma: most people living in border states crucial to the Union cause supported the return of these fugitives and those in Northern states resisted the resettlement of large numbers of freed slaves in their territory.[39] As the White House responded slowly, movement allies in Congress seized the initiative. When numerous fugitive slaves sought haven at a Union fort in Virginia, abolitionists in Congress persuaded their colleagues to adopt a Confiscation Act in the summer of 1861 that allowed Union forces to seize all property used to aid the Confederacy. The measure was carefully designed to provide relief for fugitive slaves behind Union lines. Lincoln reluctantly signed the legislation.[40]

To resolve the puzzle of what to do with fugitive slaves who escaped into Union encampments, Lincoln considered colonization and instructed administration officials to investigate the prospects of resettling runaway slaves overseas. He also developed an emancipation plan intended to address abolitionist demands for dismantling slavery without alienating the majority of citizens in both border and Northern states. Unveiled in his annual message to Congress in December 1861, Lincoln's proposal called for abolition to be voluntary on the part of loyal slave states, for compensation to be made to the slave owners, and for freed slaves to be colonized.[41] It was meant to be a compromise plan that spoke to abolitionist demands. "If the President has not entered Canaan," Phillips proclaimed, "he has turned his face Zionward."[42] Other abolitionists castigated the president's blueprints as "diluted milk and water gruel." Lincoln's careful designs for compensated emancipation ultimately went nowhere as none of the loyal slave states agreed to the plan. But his efforts speak to abolitionist influence both inside and outside the councils of government.

THE FINAL PUSH: SUSTAINED PRESSURE AND EXECUTIVE ACTION

Despite border-state recalcitrance, militant and moderate abolitionist pressures had an unmistakable impact on the White House. Lincoln warned centrists in his own party that antislavery sentiment in the North "is still upon me, and is increasing."[43] Early in 1862, the abolitionist leaders of the Emancipation League noted a significant change in how Northern audiences greeted their fiery demands for immediate emancipation. Douglass marveled that earlier jeers and mob violence against abolitionist speeches had been replaced by hearty applause and cheers from packed audiences, but he was quite certain that the change in public sentiment was driven by the belief that abolition would hasten Union victory rather than any faith in racial justice.[44] Abolitionists also grew adroit at framing the abolition of slavery as consistent with Lincoln's self-proclaimed duty to do whatever was necessary to preserve the Union. That is, abolitionists themselves took great care to cast emancipation as a crucial war measure in line with two executive and popular goals: swift victory and enduring peace. As one movement leader strategically put it, an emancipation order by the President "would compel every fighting [Confederate] man to remain at home and look to their negroes instead of going into the army to kill our friends." Senator Sumner pressed very much the same point in his speeches and consultations with Lincoln. "It is often said that war will make an end of Slavery," he said. "This is probable. But it is surer still that the overthrow of slavery will make an end of war."[45] In March, Phillips brought his rhetorical campaign directly to Washington, where "he took the town by storm." Phillips's celebrity as an eloquent agitator led Lincoln to grant him an interview during the trip, during which he counseled the president on his moral duty to liberate slaves. While militants like Phillips were gaining mainstream appeal and recasting Northern views, Sumner and other abolitionist insiders advanced the League's arguments through private lobbying and public action.

In Congress, Radicals derailed readoption of the so-called Crittendon Resolution that originally disavowed the abolition of slavery as a central war aim of the Union. They subsequently won passage of an article of war prohibiting U.S. troops from returning fugitive slaves to slaveholders, followed by legislation in April 1862 that abolished slavery in the District of Columbia. Congress then enacted a new Confiscation Act that featured provisions freeing slaves of every person found guilty of treason after its passage.[46]

Against this backdrop, Lincoln consulted with various confidantes, including moderate abolitionists, about issuing an emancipation proclamation as a military measure liberating slaves behind Confederate lines. A draft of a proclamation was soon prepared and locked in his desk drawer. When Sumner persistently urged Lincoln to issue the proclamation, the president firmly explained, "We *mustn't issue it* till after a victory." To begin preparing Northern sentiment for such an order, he resuscitated his colonization proposal as a way of assuaging popular fears that emancipation would lead freed slaves to resettle en masse in Northern states.[47] He also issued his famous public response to Horace Greeley's New York editorial, titled "The Prayer of Twenty Millions," that criticized the president's lethargy on emancipation. Lincoln's open letter clarified what he saw as his official obligation to subordinate the slavery question to preserving the Union. If carrying out these official duties frustrated the abolitionist cause, they represented "no modification of my oft-expressed *personal* wish that all men every where could be free."[48] His open letter was designed to reassure Northerners "who did not want to see the war transformed into a crusade for abolition," and alert "antislavery men that he was contemplating further moves against the peculiar institution."[49] Lincoln wavered in coming days about whether the emancipation order was too radical for public opinion or might drive border states into the Confederate fold. He confessed to a delegation of Chicago abolitionists that it was his "earnest desire to know the will of Providence in this matter." To his cabinet, Lincoln explained that he had "made a vow, a covenant, that if God gave us a victory in the approaching battle," he would consider it "an indication of Divine will" that he issue the proclamation. When military victory finally came at Antietam in September, Lincoln issued a "Preliminary Emancipation Proclamation" followed by a permanent proclamation a few months later. The centerpiece of the executive order was its declaration of presidential intent to emancipate all slaves in areas failing to return to the Union by January 1, 1863. Using language consistent with his constitutional role as commander in chief, Lincoln defined emancipation in terms of military imperative; the proclamation was to be applied essentially in unconquered sections of the Confederacy. Slaves also were described in martial terms as commodities of war; their freedom was "not a question of sentiment or taste, but one of physical force, which may be preserved and estimated as horsepower, and steampower, are measured and estimated."[50]

Despite the limited scope of the proclamation's language and spirit, abolitionists regarded it as a breakthrough. "We shout for joy that we live to record this righteous decree," Douglass proclaimed. Greeley hailed the president's order as "the beginning of the new life of the nation," and Garrison described it as "an act of immense historic importance."[51] Yet both militant and moderate antislavery leaders soon urged more sweeping emancipation. Throughout his presidency, Lincoln insisted that full emancipation of slaves could only be achieved by constitutional amendment, and not by executive fiat. Nonetheless he had come to sense a historic opportunity to secure the nation on new foundations. With pressure from both abolitionists and Lincoln, the Republican platform of 1864 endorsed a constitutional amendment banning slavery nationwide. More than three decades after Garrison had founded the AASS, complete abolition of slavery finally was achieved with congressional passage and ultimate ratification of the Thirteenth Amendment in 1865.

"Viewed from genuine abolition ground," Douglass observed, "Mr. Lincoln seemed tardy, cold, dull, and indifferent; but measuring him by the sentiment of his country, a sentiment he was bound as a statesman to consult, he was swift, zealous, radical, and determined."[52] Douglass clearly overstates the case, but he aptly highlights the competing pressures to which Lincoln was subjected, and the importance of his efforts to prepare public opinion. At a time of extraordinary crisis, the friction and abrasion between the leadership pursuits of Lincoln and his abolitionist counterparts produced an unprecedented transformation of the American constitutional and social orders. The form, substance, and timing of sweeping emancipation was ultimately a shared, albeit contentious, leadership enterprise. Militants kept abolitionism on the nation's front burner and ultimately reshaped public debate over slavery during the war. Sumner and other abolitionist "insiders" capitalized on the political strains and ideas posed by militants, but repackaged them in congressional legislation and private deliberations at the White House. Finally, Lincoln's strategic choices and actions were profoundly influenced by both militants and moderates, and his exercise of executive powers was ultimately decisive in winning large-scale change.

Rivalry and Breakthrough II: Wilson, Suffragists, and Enfranchisement

The woman's suffrage movement languished at the periphery of American politics for far longer than the abolitionist campaign. Born in the 1840s, the suffragist cause was not a mainstream issue until the Progressive Era. At the heart of the movement's growing prominence was the development of strong conventional capacities by the National American Woman Suffrage Association (NAWSA) led by Susan B. Anthony and her protégée, Carrie Chapman Catt. It formed a vanguard of trained activists to direct state amendment campaigns, built suffragist organizations in every state, dramatically expanded the number of local clubs, and established a leadership committee to coordinate national, state, and local suffrage efforts. It also launched a Congressional Committee to lobby federal legislators and a Press Committee to garner publicity for the cause. Speaking tours, conventions, petition drives, and direct lobbying became regular activities of the movement.[53]

During the first decade of the twentieth century, Catt and other NAWSA leaders recognized that their national reform campaign faced formidable obstacles. Suffragists launched a legal campaign in the 1870s that ended with a decisive Supreme Court defeat, and the federal courts remained inhospitable to their goals. Despite pioneering lobbying efforts in the nation's capitol, the federal woman's suffrage amendment was tabled by hostile congressional committees. Although suffragists were intrigued by the energy of Theodore Roosevelt's "stewardship" presidency, the White House left little doubt that it opposed universal suffrage. When Catt garnered extensive media attention in 1905 by undertaking an ambitious transcontinental speaking tour, Roosevelt used his "bully pulpit" to lash out against her and the movement.[54] Roosevelt's successor, William Howard Taft, was equally opposed to "as radical a step" as extending voting rights to women.[55] Given these constraints, NAWSA activists set about to capitalize on the one key opening afforded by the American polity, namely, a federal structure that allowed them to pursue suffrage victories in the states. This was a strategy that yielded considerable success for suffragists in the West.

Moreover, suffragists pressed their cause in electoral and partisan politics. The 1912 election marked a small yet important shift in the national electoral clout of the movement. Although the Democratic and Republican Parties—along with their presidential candidates—rebuffed the suffragist cause, the Progressive Party platform and its candidate, Theodore Roosevelt, endorsed voting rights for women. The Progressives also invited Jane Addams and other prominent women reformers to hold important positions in the party. As the gestures of a third party whose political influence would wane steadily in following years, the endorsement was of marginal importance. Far more promising for the movement, however, was the fact that Roosevelt and a notable party embraced woman suffrage "to capture the votes of Western women."[56] Over several decades, suffragists had fought to win voting rights in various states by lobbying state legislatures and mobilizing support for prosuffrage state referenda. Many prominent movement leaders believed that a tipping point existed for the nationalization of women's suffrage; once enough women acquired access to the ballot box in certain states, they hoped that national politicians and parties would curry favor with these women voters by advocating universal woman suffrage.[57] When asked in in 1908 what was required to win presidential and congressional support for woman suffrage, Roosevelt advised the movement to "Go, get another State."[58] His Progressive Party's efforts to court suffragists four years later suggested to movement leaders that women voters were beginning to have an impact on politicians' electoral calculations.[59]

At the same time, the 1912 election also gave suffragists reason for pessimism. Among the presidential aspirants, the winning Democratic candidate, Woodrow Wilson, was the most elusive on the suffrage issue. In the campaign, Wilson evaded suffrage questions from journalists and NAWSA delegations by asserting that it was not an appropriate matter for presidential candidates or incumbents to address. "Suffrage is not a national issue," he insisted. "It is a local issue for each State to settle for itself."[60] While quietly pressuring the platform committee to reject a prosuffrage plank, Wilson disingenuously told suffragists during the election that his hands were tied by a Democratic platform opposing their goals.[61]

Internal Rivalry: The Rise of a Radical Flank

Significant organizational and leadership rivalries emerged within the suffrage movement during the early twentieth century. In particular, younger suffragists grew increasingly impatient with the movement's focus on securing voting rights in individual states. As state campaigns were stymied in one contest after another, this new generation of suffragists grew to advocate direct pressure on the national government. Alice Paul, a young activist schooled in militant tactics by British suffragists, led the way in 1912 when she won NAWSA's blessing to initiate a new federal amendment campaign in the nation's capital. But to the dismay of moderate leaders, Paul and her followers made their presence known in dramatic fashion. Soon after opening a Washington office, she organized a confrontational suffrage parade of eight thousand women through the streets of Washington in protest of Wilson's 1913 inauguration. The provocative act of street theater drew violent reactions from crowds assembled for the ceremony. "No inauguration has ever produced such scenes," a Baltimore newspaper reported, "which in many instances amounted to nothing less than riots." Federal troops were eventually summoned to restore order. The incident was an ominous sign for Wilson, who would be hounded by militant and moderate suffragists throughout his presidency. Dozens of moderate suffragist delegations called on Wilson in office, while radical activists pursued more disruptive forms of protest outside the White House gates. Paul in particular was convinced that winning the services of the energetic presidency established by Roosevelt, "and perhaps it alone, would ensure our success."[62] Yet Wilson continued to tell reformers that he was bound by his party's platform to remain impartial on the suffrage issue. "I am not a free man," he explained to NAWSA activists. "I am not at liberty until I speak for someone else besides myself to urge legislation upon the Congress."[63]

NAWSA leaders concluded in 1913 that the roadblocks to a federal amendment were insurmountable, and they refocused on grassroots organizing in state referenda struggles. Paul and her followers disagreed sharply with this strategy, choosing instead to step up pressure on the Wilson administration by exercising overt electoral pressure and disruptive civil disobedience. In the midterm election of 1914, Paul and other militant suffragists decided to campaign fiercely against Democratic candidates.

These tactics forced a rupture between Paul's supporters and NAWSA, which saw itself as scrupulously nonpartisan. Paul quickly formed the radical Congressional Union and later the National Woman's Party. Now two rival organizations were trying to lead the suffragist crusade: NAWSA's moderate wing and Paul's militant groups.[64] Internal conflict proved instrumental to the movement. In coming months, Paul's disruptive tactics regularly made headlines for the suffragist cause while Catt's quiet grassroots organizing and mainstream Washington lobbying earned key victories at the state level and new allies in Congress and the executive branch.[65]

During the 1916 election, the movement won a key endorsement of its cause from the Republican presidential nominee, Charles Evans Hughes. His eleventh-hour decision was no doubt informed by hopes of making inroads against Wilson in western states where women voters were consequential.[66] Softened by Hughes's prosuffrage stance and NAWSA's restrained lobbying, Wilson agreed to address the association's national meeting during the campaign. His speech stopped well short of endorsing the suffragist agenda. Instead, he reminded NAWSA activists that his presidential duties made him accountable to democratic majorities opposed to equal suffrage. "It is all very well to be ahead and beckon," he lectured them, "but after all, you have got to wait for the body to follow."[67] Despite his continued resistance, Wilson's appearance indicated some measure of accommodation to the movement. The principal reason, NAWSA leaders argued, was state-level victories. "Eleven states had been won to full suffrage and the argument that was bearing down with the most force upon the passage of the Federal Suffrage Amendment," Catt noted, "was the number of western women who were voting for the President of the United States."[68]

Even with these momentous electoral shifts, NAWSA's lobbying efforts in Washington made little headway in 1917. Moderates redoubled their efforts to win new state referenda battles.[69] Mounting grassroots organization and publicity drives, suffragists won presidential suffrage in Ohio, Indiana, Nebraska, Michigan, and Ohio in 1917. However, the most crucial triumph was in New York the same year, where suffragists had lost a grueling campaign just two years earlier. National politicians, including the president, took notice.[70]

Disruptive protests by militants applied additional pressure on the White House to address the proposed national amendment. Shortly before the United States declared war on Germany in 1917, Paul and her supporters initiated daily pickets of the White House. After American entrance into World War I, protesters employed provocative rhetoric, visual images, and demonstrations to challenge the hypocrisy of "Kaiser Wilson" in fighting for democracy abroad when so many were denied basic political rights at home.[71] At one White House demonstration, picketing suffragists were attacked by angry crowds as unpatriotic and then arrested. The abuse by prison officers of well-connected suffragists and their subsequent hunger strikes made national headlines that embarrassed the Wilson administration. When the protesters were jailed, their abuse at the hands of District of Columbia prison officials and a subsequent hunger strike made national headlines.[72]

Catt and NAWSA members preferred conventional political tactics over the antagonistic methods of Paul and her followers. Yet they also recognized after the onset of World War I that Paul's disruptive protests provided incentives for a beleaguered Wilson administration to embrace the movement's moderate wing. Through gentle lobbying, Catt and one of her confidantes, Helen Gardener, cultivated good relations with White House advisers. They began communicating directly with Wilson, reminding him that NAWSA "refrained from forcing the issue" because they understood his enormous wartime duties. Catt also agreed to a White House request that she serve on the Women's Committee of the Council of National Defense."[73] Calculated restraint, Catt believed, would pay political dividends. Against the backdrop of NAWSA's quiet diplomacy and distracting protests of Paul supporters, Wilson finally endorsed a national suffrage amendment in January of 1918. He justified reform as a necessary war measure. His public reasoning reiterated arguments made by Catt in letters to the president that disenfranchisement "aroused in patriotic women a just suspicion that men and women are not co-workers for world freedom," and that political inclusion would serve for women as "an incentive to better and more work."[74] "The effort of the women lies at the very heart of the war," he told Congress. "I tell you plainly that this [suffrage] measure which I urge upon you is vital to the winning of the war and to the energies alike of preparation and of battle."[75]

After lobbying by both movement activists and the White House, Congress eventually affirmed the federal suffrage amendment. Suffragists then turned their attention to winning state-level approval. Only a year and a half after its victory in Washington, the Nineteenth Amendment was ratified. Based on his private views on the subject and his political agenda, it seems highly unlikely that Wilson, not to mention most other elected officials, would have taken steps to win voting rights for women in the absence of militant and mainstream political pressure from suffragist leaders and activists. The efficacy of the suffragist crusade, in turn, hinged on the combination of disruptive and conventional political weapons forged by leadership and organizational rivalries within the movement.

Rivalry and Breakthrough III: FDR and the Industrial Workers Movement

At the time of the crash of 1929, the dominant organization of the labor movement, the American Federation of Labor (AFL), was nearly a half-century old. Largely a federation of national craft unions, the AFL and its

leadership traditionally made little effort to organize vast numbers of industrial workers. Tellingly, even during the Great Depression, AFL leaders
saw little reason to alter their emphasis on craft union membership, its governing structure, or its preference for conciliation over militancy. As a
restive industrial labor force endured economic hardships and public officials worried aloud about worker revolts, national union membership stood
at a low of 9 percent of the workforce (2,126,000).[76] While the entrenched
leadership of the AFL was unwilling to depart from moderate craft traditions, the ambitious leader of the United Mine Workers (UMW), John L.
Lewis, had other designs. A man of great political cunning, Lewis hoped to
take advantage of the political opportunities presented by national crisis
and exceptional presidential activism to advance transformative ends. He
eagerly welcomed openings to affirm and participate in the formation of
the New Deal regime if it would enhance the fortunes of the union movement. In particular, he hoped to organize the millions of unskilled industrial workers long neglected by AFL oligarchs.

In 1933 the Roosevelt administration invited a large number of organized interests—including many business and labor groups—to help in
shaping the National Industrial Recovery Act (NIRA). Although Roosevelt
permitted labor leaders to participate in designing the NIRA, he did so
more out of a desire to conciliate disparate political interests than out of
any enthusiasm for the union movement. Indeed, he initially envisioned social programs and government standards as the crucial means of enhancing basic protections for America's working class, not as an opening for
greater self-empowerment through unions. Nonetheless, prominent New
Dealers such as Labor Secretary Frances Perkins persuaded the president
that key union leaders ought to join their business counterparts in the
drafting of recovery legislation. Lewis saw to it that his lieutenant and chief
economic adviser, W. Jett Lauck, was part of the labor delegation that had
a hand in molding the NIRA.[77]

At the persistent urging of Lauck and other labor activists, New Dealers
reluctantly included a provision in the NIRA, section 7(a), that recognized
the right of workers to bargain collectively. "Before the [NIRA], industry
leaders had bridled at the least hint of legitimacy accorded to the union
movement," Morone observes. "But in the context of national crisis . . . and
in the relative safety of a program that granted employers new powers without imposing state sanctions, they accepted section 7(a)."[78] Labor scholars
suggest that Lewis and Lauck had more to do with the incorporation of section 7(a) into the emergency law than anyone else.[79] Corporate giants were
reassured by their lawyers that the provision was a toothless tiger because it
contained no administrative mechanisms for enforcement and that the
courts would strike down any rigorous enforcement. Lauck, however, assured Lewis that Section 7(a) "will suit our purposes." The NIRA sailed
through Congress.

Lewis hailed the NIRA provision as labor's "Emancipation Proclamation" and threw all of the UMW's resources into a massive organizing campaign. Fanning out across the Appalachian fields, UMW activists capitalized on the popularity of FDR and the NIRA to attract miners. "The President wants you to join the union," proclaimed UMW speakers and literature. Tens of thousands of miners signed union cards and formed lodges with names such as "New Deal" and "Blue Eagle." After one year of invoking the hallowed names of Roosevelt and the New Deal, UMW membership soared from 150,000 to 650,000. A handful of other unions, such as the Amalgamated Clothing Workers and International Ladies Garment Workers Union followed the organizing strategy that Lewis employed so effectively, swelling their ranks to record levels.[80]

These aggressive organizing efforts promised new rivalries within the labor movement. The staid labor barons of the AFL held fast to organizing workers according to craft, a method simply ill suited for unionizing the new mass-production industries of rubber, auto, and steel. Lewis and his supporters had a decidedly different vision for the labor movement, and they scored AFL leaders for preferring control in an enervated organization over subordination in a strong one. At AFL executive council meetings and on the convention floor in 1933 and 1934, Lewis pleaded with his fellow labor leaders to accept new realities and to embrace industrial unionism. But his efforts were opposed by the leaders of large unions in the federation, as well as AFL President William Green.[81]

MILITANCY AND CONVENTION IN THE INDUSTRIAL WORKERS MOVEMENT

If the NIRA and Lewis's organizing campaign raised the hopes of rank and file laborers for union representation, they were largely frustrated by a combination of fierce resistance by employers, AFL inertia, and government passivity. The response was rising militancy among industrial workers: industrial disputes reported by the Labor Department increased from 841 in 1932 to 1,695 in 1933 and 1,856 in 1934. Especially foreboding to political leaders was the fact that few of the more than 1.5 million rank-and-file workers involved in strikes during 1934 were under the control of established union leadership. Many of the strikes degenerated into violent confrontations with industry. During the spring and summer of 1934, a series of dramatic struggles between workers and employers riveted the nation. In the "Battle of Toledo," strikers at the Electric Auto-Lite Company engaged in several days of bloody clashes with company police and the Ohio National Guard. After Guardsmen were unable disperse crowds, Auto-Lite owners closed the plant and agreed to federal mediation lest a general strike broke out. Workers won a 22 percent wage increase and recognition for their union. When a "Citizen's Alliance" of employers in Minneapolis tried to crush efforts by truck drivers to unionize, four months of strikes and violence ensued that culminated with the state's governor declaring martial law and the Teamsters Union winning the right to represent truckers. In San Francisco, a prolonged strike by longshoremen was eventually put down by force. At the behest of the city's business community, police officers charged the picket lines, causing hundreds of injuries and two deaths among the strikers. The funerals of the slain picketers provoked anger and sympathy among city workers, and the first general strike in fifteen years was organized. New Dealers like General Hugh Johnson worried about "civil war" in San Francisco. The general strike collapsed after four days, but longshoremen won many demands from employers including union recognition.[82]

Lewis recognized the potential political leverage that this rising militancy of rank-and-file workers might provide for winning significant policy change. What was desperately required, he believed, was a strong, mainstream organizational voice that could channel the energies of aroused industrial workers into tangible programmatic gains.[83] At the 1934 AFL convention, Lewis publicly pressed federation leaders to organize industrial workers while quietly lining up support from sympathetic unions for a future break from the federation. One year later, Lewis held the AFL convention floor for an hour, assailing AFL leaders for abandoning millions of industrial workers that they once pledged to unionize. Neither the UMW nor American workers, he declared, could abide AFL intransigence while "our people are suffering."[84] The next day, Lewis assumed the helm of a new Committee on Industrial Organizations (CIO). His CIO would deftly portray itself as a militant force within the labor movement, and as a mainstream political partner of the New Deal outside it.

Both Congress and the Roosevelt administration were rattled by labor agitation that raged across the country in the spring and summer of 1935. A year earlier, Senator Robert Wagner (D-N.Y.), a strong ally of labor, had introduced a bill to establish a new labor relations board with strong enforcement powers to protect unionizing efforts. At the time, business leaders and conservative lawmakers denounced the measure as Stalinist, and Roosevelt refused to support it. During labor turmoil the following summer, however, the Senate passed the legislation by an overwhelming margin. The White House only tepidly endorsed the initiative, which subsequently passed in the House easily. Although FDR understood that the labor movement was a crucial element of his electoral and governing coalitions, he took pains to publicly assert his independence of both labor and business interests. During major strikes, for example, Roosevelt was known to tell reporters that labor activists "did silly things," and he often sounded centrist tones in urging employers and disgruntled workers to embrace "common sense and good order."[85] FDR's labor secretary, Frances Perkins, later noted that the president never grasped that unions provided workers with "unbreakable bonds which gave them power and status to deal with their employers on equal terms."[86] Lewis privately distrusted FDR, but he instinctively gave public support to the president's efforts to lend democratic durability to the New Deal's transformative aims. In the end, the Wagner Act of 1935—hailed as labor's "Magna Carta"—placed the authority of the national state behind the right of industrial workers to form unions and to bargain collectively.

Lewis clearly understood FDR's lack of enthusiasm for union radicalism, but he also recognized that the labor movement could make the most of what Alonzo Hamby called "the New Deal's general endorsement of social change and fair play for the underdog."[87] In 1936, Lewis envisioned an electoral marriage of convenience between the CIO and the Democratic Party to reelect Roosevelt. Forming the Labor Nonpartisan League, Lewis hoped that union votes could be marshaled in future elections to support whichever party or candidate best served the interests of the CIO's membership. At the same time as donations to the Democratic Party from business leaders plummeted between 1932 and 1936, CIO unions contributed $770,000 to the president's campaign coffers. The $469,000 raised by Lewis's UMW made it the party's largest single benefactor. Equally important, Lewis mobilized the CIO and called on his own formidable rhetorical skills and status in the movement to lionize FDR and his party as the champions of unions and their membership. As one working-class voter declared during the election, "Mr. Roosevelt is the only man we ever had in the White House who would understand that my boss is a son-of-a-bitch."[88] Lewis and CIO supporters were widely credited with turning the tide in states like Ohio, Illinois, and Indiana, and in making Pennsylvania Democratic. "Never before had union leaders done so effective a job of mobilizing the labor vote in a national campaign," writes William Leuchtenburg.[89]

Lewis soon cashed in on the electoral debt Roosevelt owed the CIO in major strikes in 1936–37. When auto workers loyal to the CIO refused to vacate General Motors plants in Flint, Michigan, for instance, the White House refused to permit troops to remove the strikers. Roosevelt and Perkins then successfully pressured auto executives to enter direct negotiations with the CIO. The United Auto Workers, now affiliated with the CIO, soon represented 350,000 laborers. A few months later, the industrial workers movement scored another major victory when U.S. Steel opted to cease costly union-busting efforts in favor of compromise with Lewis and the UMW.

Despite White House assistance in Flint, it soon became clear that Roosevelt had his own vision of the new order and that he expected the labor movement to follow *his* lead, not the reverse. Like other presidents who have dominated the policy process, FDR intended to dictate the terms of any alliance with organized interests. Amid labor confrontations with "little steel" companies in 1937–38, FDR stunned Lewis and militant labor activists with his public commentary on the killing of ten steelworkers during a demonstration in Chicago against Republic Steel Corporation. Denouncing management and unions alike as sponsors of senseless violence, Roosevelt declared "a curse on both your houses." In a Labor Day address to millions of listeners, Lewis rebuked the President: "It ill behooves one who has supped at labor's table and who has been sheltered in labor's house to curse with equal fervor and fine impartiality both labor and its adversaries when they become locked in a deadly embrace."[90] By the end of the 1930s, Lewis and sympathetic labor militants were convinced that the administration was limiting the labor movement's larger aims. During the 1940 election, Lewis worked in vain to derail FDR's reelection, fearing that it would bring about U.S. entry into war and the concomitant demise of labor's agenda for progressive change. After unsuccessful efforts to launch a third party challenge and then to back the Republican candidate Wendell Wilkie in 1940, Lewis stepped down as CIO president.[91]

For most of the 1930s, the militancy, electioneering, and lobbying of the labor movement produced a powerful combination of disruptive labor unrest and mainstream political pressure that spurred sweeping changes in national labor policy. The architectonic conflicts between Roosevelt and Lewis were equally important to the production of large-scale change. Each viewed the other as a dangerous rival: whereas Lewis feared movement capture, FDR worried about labor dominance.[92] Yet Lewis and Roosevelt ultimately used one another during critical moments of political construction, as evidenced by Lewis' union organizing during the early New Deal and by Roosevelt's efforts to establish a lasting electoral coalition during the 1936 campaign. In the end, the labor movement benefited from its ties to a president who had been granted broad authority to advance major policy changes.

Conclusion

After decades of struggle and frustration, the abolitionist, suffragist, and industrial workers movements won political transformations of monumental proportion. In this essay, I have suggested that these innovations were assisted by major crises that provided unusual openings for reformers to transcend the routine inertial power of political culture and institutions in America. Crises can alter the strategic environment of government officials. They grant presidents, in particular, special warrants to exercise prerogative powers to meet the emergency. Presidents will not alter their preference for order, but they may gradually see how a disruptive movement, previously resisted, might be instrumental to reestablishing order. Movements with the ability to exercise conventional political leverage and to disturb the social and political order are especially well positioned to capitalize on this new strategic environment and prod presidents to embrace new possibilities. Abolitionists, suffragists, and industrial workers were all perceived as important forces in presidential elections shortly before their breakthroughs. Successful citizenship movements also demonstrated considerable aptitude at mainstream lobbying, winning support in Congress or in state legislatures and referenda campaigns even before securing presidential endorsements. These conventional forms of political influence were especially potent when combined with contentious protest politics that posed a credible threat to social order. As Sidney Milkis shows in the next essay, the postwar civil rights movement follows this same logic.

For all of the striking similarities in breakthrough politics across our cases, the leadership rivalries at the heart of these political transformations were ultimately shaped by distinctive human interactions and creative motivations. Consider, for example, Lincoln's personal moral connection with the aspirations of Phillips and Sumner, and their eventual collaboration in remaking both American constitutional structures and the political culture. By contrast, Wilson exhibited little if any genuine devotion to gender equality throughout the process, and his role in the production of sweeping reform was more marginal than that of the other presidents examined in this essay. Indeed, it can be argued that the creative tensions between Catt and Paul within the woman's suffrage movement served as much more of a catalyst for change than those between movement leaders and the White House. Finally, the rivalry between Roosevelt and Lewis was so profound that neither was ever truly willing to accommodate the other. In the end, one of these rivals had to dominate, and it was ultimately FDR who set the terms of a long-term alliance that sapped the movement's disruptive capacities. The human element of presidential-movement interactions guarantees that none of these transformative episodes can be carbon copies.

Tellingly, the impressive advances won by abolitionists, woman suffragists, and industrial workers did not culminate in full and lasting inclusion of those disempowered people they championed. African Americans encountered new forms of invidious disenfranchisement only a few years after the Emancipation Proclamation and the ratification of the Thirteenth and Fourteenth Amendments, reinforced by Jim Crow institutions, southern white terror, economic marginalization, and federal governmental retreat. The women's movement languished for decades after gaining access to the ballot box, and its efforts to secure an Equal Rights Amendment and stronger descriptive and substantive representation remain frustrated. For its part, the labor movement could point to a large body of tangible, long-term policy benefits gained from its alliance with the New Deal regime and its Democratic successors, but the reaction against organized labor came swiftly with enactment of the Taft-Hartley Act, and the movement's decline in both membership and power over the years has had deleterious effects for today's working class. The politics of retrenchment is often not far behind large-scale change. At the end of the day, we are left with the sobering conclusion that the governmental structures, processes, and ideals that define the American political system are well suited to fortify the existing social, economic, and political order and to routinely frustrate advances in racial, gender, and class equality.

Chapter 13

The President in the Vanguard: Lyndon Johnson and the Civil Rights Insurgency

Sidney M. Milkis

Presidential Ambition and Social Movements

Lyndon Johnson's relationship to the civil rights insurgency of the 1960s presents itself as an exception to all the rules. It breaks the general norm of presidential resistance to the demands of insurgent groups, a norm Elizabeth Sanders roots in the president's constitutional duty to preserve, protect, and defend. Its also breaks the corollary rule discussed by Daniel Tichenor: even when, in the exceptional circumstance, presidents do accommodate insurgent demands, they do so as laggards who have belatedly come to recognize accommodation as the expedient best suited to fulfilling their underlying interest in the restoration of order. In contrast, LBJ put himself out front on civil rights, seeking from the start to lead the movement toward its goals, tap its energy, and manage its unfolding. Tying his presidency to this cause from the start, Johnson defied the structural logic that has traditionally kept insurgent movements and presidents at arm's length.

The progressive vision of the "modern presidency" reached its fullest expression in this defiance. Until the Johnson presidency, the idea that the presidency might act as a spearhead for social justice—a rallying point for democratic reform movements—had proven more a dream than a reality. Anticipated but not fulfilled by Teddy Roosevelt's Bull Moose campaign in 1912, that vision, as Tichenor shows, was only partially and haltingly expressed in the relationship between Woodrow Wilson and the movement for women's suffrage and between FDR and the labor movement. Only with Johnson was the full panoply of modern presidential powers—political, administrative and rhetorical—deployed on behalf of insurgent interests and demands. In turn, Johnson's inability to sustain that vanguard role exposed more fully than any other example the unresolved constitutional tensions at the heart of the progressive vision. Indeed, it may be said that the modern presidency imploded upon the unraveling of Johnson's relationship to the Civil Rights Movement.

Johnson's predecessor John F. Kennedy conformed closely to the
Tichenor model in his relationship to the Civil Rights Movement. Civil
rights was one interest among others for Kennedy. Seeking to protect and
nurture a fragile liberal consensus and riveted by the heightened tensions
of the cold war, he kept his distance from the movement and acted only
when highly incendiary and well-publicized clashes between activists and
the guardians of Jim Crow allowed him to pursue reform as a matter of national necessity. Johnson was contemptuous of this course, and his trumpet-
ing of a Great Society signaled his intention to push the reform capacities
of the modern presidency to their limit.[1] The "liberating" potential Johnson and his aides spied in the modern presidency dovetailed with the political climate of the 1960s. Johnson and his political allies saw the social
movements of the 1960s, especially the Civil Rights Movement, as evidence
that America was on the threshold of a bold new era of reform. To them,
the civil rights revolution exposed not only the power and possibility of organized protest, but also the unsuspected fragility of resistance in America
to liberating changes. Indeed, the Civil Rights Movement established the
model for other social movements that grew out of the 1960s—the feminist
movement, consumerism, and environmentalism. In the relatively calm
early days of LBJ's leadership, aides such as Bill Moyers and Richard Goodwin, and Johnson himself, envisioned these new social forces as potent
agents of change that the president might spearhead to great effect. The
way Johnson joined with Civil Rights leaders in pushing through the 1964
and 1965 civil rights legislation appeared to justify this vision.[2]

To be sure, Johnson also sought to "manage" the new social forces of the
1960s. Like FDR, he was a presidentialist: the thrust of his approach to social agitation was to strengthen the managerial tools of the presidency with
a view to enhancing the programmatic reach and energy in the executive
branch. But Johnson badly misjudged the managerial difficulties of expanding the liberal coalition and keeping its new social elements aligned
with its other supporters. As James Block's chapter in this volume argues,
American social movements embody the nation's "agency culture," which
celebrates "the right of all individuals and communities to withdraw legitimacy from existing institutions and reconstitute social order not as acts of
mere opposition but as principled commitments to alternative values." The
Civil Rights Movement, a fissiparous mixture of interest-oriented organizations that sought traditional rights long denied African Americans and militants intent on recasting the very framework of political life, perfectly
expressed this agency culture and the uneasy relationship it was bound to
have with its self-proclaimed ally in the White House.

Ironically, the liberating energy that LBJ and his political allies valued in
the Civil Rights Movement made a firm bond with its leaders impractical.
By the middle of his second term, Johnson had been forced to retreat from
the notion that he was a leader of the movement; indeed, the growing mil-

itancy of the movement abetted the rise of antiwar activism that viewed Johnson as the hated symbol of the status quo. Like every other president, Johnson had many interests to attend to, some of which competed with those of the movement to which he had tied his reform aspirations. Ironically, by supporting programs such as the War on Poverty, Johnson unwittingly bestowed legitimacy on an insurgency that far outstripped the managerial capacities in which had placed his faith. Johnson's effort to apply "leverage" over the civil rights movement and to make his own distinctive mark on the American reform tradition set loose forces that ultimately diminished his legacy, weakened the executive office, and exposed the limits of the modern presidency.

Seizing the Moment: Lyndon Johnson and the Politics of Race

When Johnson assumed the presidency, he had substantial reasons for taking a strong civil rights stand. By this time, the Solid South was no more, as Eisenhower and Nixon had won substantial support below the Mason-Dixon line. The best hope for shoring up the national Democratic party lay in expanding the black vote. Black voters were suspicious of a southern president, as were many northern liberals who had become strongly committed to the civil rights cause after the demonstrations in Birmingham, Alabama, and the March on Washington in 1963. Johnson felt the need to prove himself to the growing civil rights movement by carrying out—indeed surpassing—the civil rights program of the Kennedy administration.

Johnson's militant liberalism with respect to civil rights first came into view during his vice presidency, when as Paul Conkin notes, "Blacks became his primary constituents."[3] Against the advice of his friend and former Roosevelt aide James Rowe, who warned LBJ that he was becoming involved in an explosive situation, the vice president accepted the role of chairman of the President's Committee on Equal Employment Opportunity, where he began a quiet and unpublicized campaign for a strong civil rights program.[4] Viewing the growing Civil Rights Movement as an opportunity for the White House to take bolder action, Johnson became scornful of the Kennedy administration's cautious moves toward new federal intervention, even as it pushed unsuccessfully for a major civil rights bill in 1963.[5]

As the congressional fight over the civil rights legislation intensified, Johnson gave a Memorial Day speech at Gettysburg, Pennsylvania, to recognize the centennial year of the critical Civil War battle that took place there and the famous address that sanctified it. Expressing some of the same sentiments that would elevate Martin Luther King, Jr.'s "I Have a Dream" speech a few months latter, Johnson called on Americans to honor the still unfulfilled promise of Emancipation: "One hundred years ago, the slave was freed. One hundred years later, the Negro remains in bondage to

the color of his skin. The Negro today asks justice. We do not answer him—
we do not answer those beneath the soil—when we reply to the Negro by
asking, 'Patience'." America would never live up to the honor of those who
died at Gettysburg or the words Lincoln spoke there, LBJ insisted in a dramatic peroration, "Until justice is blind to color, until education is unaware
of race, until opportunity is unconcerned with the color of men's
skins....To the extent that the proclamation of emancipation is not fulfilled, in fact, to that extent we shall have fallen short of assuring freedom
to the free."[6]

Soon after his Gettysburg address, LBJ spoke privately but no less passionately to Kennedy aide Theodore Sorenson about the urgency of civil
rights, telling him that "the Negroes are tired of this patient stuff and
tired of this piecemeal stuff and what they want more than anything else
is not an executive order or legislation, they want a moral commitment
that he's [Kennedy] behind them." Johnson recalled FDR's failed attempt to "purge" conservative Southern and border state Democrats in
1938 and to replace them with 100 percent New Dealers who were committed to economic reform. He prescribed a different approach. The
president's moral commitment to civil rights, LBJ believed, should not be
expressed in an effort to purge southern Democrats, but rather, in an appeal to their consciences: "I think the President could do this in North
Carolina or some place. I'd invite the congressmen and senators to be on
the platform. . . . I'd have him talk about the contributions that they had
made and then I'd say, 'Now, we have a problem here. No Nation—a hundred years ago in the Lincoln-Douglas debate, Lincoln said, No Nation
can long endure half slave and half free. Now no world can long endure
half slave and half free and we've got to do something about it in our own
country'."[7]

During the early days of his presidency, Johnson practiced what he had
preached. In May 1964 he gave two courageous speeches in Georgia, one
before the state legislature where he declared unequivocally that the time
had come for "justice among the races." "Heed not," the president urged
the southern lawmakers at a breakfast meeting in Atlanta, "those who seek
to stir old hostilities and kindle old hatreds, who preach battle between
neighbors and bitterness between States." Johnson insisted that he would
never feel that he had done justice to his "high office"—the national constitutional office—so long as those old hatreds continued to rend the country. He would not fulfill his responsibility as president "until every section
of the country is linked, in single purpose and joined devotion, to bring an
end to injustice, to bring an end to poverty, and to bring an end to the
threat of conflict among nations."[8] Johnson did not scold or preach; his
tone was one of gentle persuasion rather than threat of coercion. The president sought to stir the conscience of his southern audience—to moderate
their racial prejudice with an appeal to their "bias" for law and the Consti-

tution: "In your search for justice, the Constitution of the United States must be your guide. Georgians helped write the Constitution. Georgians have fought and Georgians have died to protect that Constitution. . . . Because the Constitution requires it, because justice demands it, we must protect the constitutional rights of all of our citizens, regardless of race, religion, or the color of their skin."[9]

Johnson's campaign to take his civil rights fight into the Deep South was a great triumph, one that reverberated far beyond Georgia's borders. In going before the legislature of a southern state to make an unflinching statement on civil rights, he gained the hard-won respect of northern liberals and civil rights leaders. It was "becoming of the President of the United States," a *Washington Post* editorial declared, that he should make such a "forthright statement" below the Mason-Dixon line. Johnson's words were not novel; he and other presidents had said as much before. "But said in this setting," the *Post* recognized, "the words have special impact, special meaning. They throw down the gauntlet of a challenge: they say to the South—in part because they are spoken by a president of the United States who is himself a Southerner—'Remember that you are Americans; remember that you belong to a Union, not a confederacy'."[10]

The reaction to Johnson's moral appeal was hardly less impressive in the South than it was in the North. To be sure, he did not overcome all resistance. At the breakfast meeting in Atlanta, which also included Governor Carl E. Sanders and Senator Herman Talmadge, the audience applauded the president on several occasions, but not when he spoke of equal rights.[11] Similarly, when he thumped the podium at his second stop in Georgia, the town of Gainesville, and shouted that "the Constitution of the United States applies to every American of every race, of every religion, of every region in this beloved country," there was no applause from the large and otherwise enthusiastic audience. Nonetheless, as the *Richmond Times Dispatch* admitted, "despite his uncompromising civil rights stand, the President's public appeal made its impact." No major Georgia official, save the unreconstructed states' rights senator Richard Russell, boycotted LBJ's visit. Moreover, although there were notes of disagreement among the huge crowds that greeted the president in Atlanta and Gainesville—white workers wearing coveralls held up a sign along the Atlanta motorcade that read "Kill the Bill"—the overwhelming response to Johnson's visit was remarkably positive, an indication, LBJ insisted, that a "new South" was ready to turn the page of racial intolerance.[12] As an editorial in the *Atlanta Constitution* put it, "It was typical of the President's directness that he came South to state the case for racial justice, to say that 'no one is fully free until all of us are fully free'. . . . But it was also very much in his style that he said the words not as a hickory-stick teacher but rather as a compassionate friend. . . . It was as though he were placing a fatherly hand on the shoulders of the South and saying: 'Look, I am of your same soil. I understand. But it is time to put aside this stultifying issue of race and get on with the business of the nation'." Reminding its readership that Franklin Roosevelt had once visited Gainesville in the cause of economic justice, the editorial concluded: "Georgia and the nation responded with deep enthusiasm for FDR. And if the surging crowds in Atlanta and Gainesville . . . were any measure, they are doing the same for LBJ."[13]

Johnson's remarkable and widely praised trip to Georgia strengthened his resolve to see civil rights legislation enacted that would eliminate the legal barriers to Black equality and end Jim Crow in the South. Much is made, and rightfully so, of Johnson's skill in moving legislation through a recalcitrant Congress; what is often overlooked is how the fight for civil rights legislation saw Johnson's mastery of the legislative process joined to moral leadership. LBJ's greatest strength as majority leader of the Senate had been personal persuasion, a talent he now used to convince the Senate Republican leader, Everett Dirksen, to endorse the 1964 Civil Rights bill and enlist moderate Republicans in the cause. Johnson's success with Dirksen, however, was greatly aided by the senator's perception, confirmed by the president's triumphant southern tour, that the public's support for civil rights was building in the country. Investing the prestige of his office in a cause and a movement, Johnson persuaded Dirksen and most members of Congress that civil rights reform could no longer be resisted. As Dirksen put it, paraphrasing Victor Hugo's diary: "No army is stronger than an idea whose time has come."[14] Dirksen's support sounded the death knell for the conservative coalition of southern Democrats and Republicans against civil rights. For the first time, the Senate voted cloture against a southern filibuster designed to thwart a civil rights bill, and did so by a considerable margin of seventy-one to twenty-nine. Congress passed the bill, with no crippling compromises or amendments, and Johnson signed it on July 2, 1964. Throughout the fight for this legislation, Johnson drew strength from and collaborated with civil rights leaders, even seeking their support for his decision not to delay signing the bill until Independence Day.[15]

Having gained credibility with civil rights activists during the first critical year of his presidency, Johnson solidified an alliance with them during the dramatic prelude to the enactment of the 1965 voting rights legislation, which would enfranchise millions of African Americans. On January 15, 1965, Johnson put in a call to Martin Luther King, Jr., on the occasion of the civil rights leader's thirty-sixth birthday. The president found King in Selma, Alabama, where the Southern Christian Leadership Conference (SCLC) had just launched a bold voting rights project. LBJ urged the Reverend King and the grassroots organization he headed to put pressure on Congress by dramatizing "the worst conditions [of blacks being denied the vote] that you can run into in Alabama or Mississippi or Louisiana or South

Carolina. . . . If you can take that one illustration and get it on the radio, get on the television, get it in the pulpits, get it in the meetings—every place you can—than pretty soon the fellow who didn't do anything but drive a tractor would say, 'Well, that is not right—that is not fair.' Then that will help us in what we are going to shove through in the end."[16]

In the days that followed, Johnson might have had second thoughts about this importunity, because King and civil rights activists would take direct action in Selma that aroused massive resistance from local police and state troopers, as well as national demonstrations in support of the marchers, some of which were directed at the president for not taking immediate action to avert the violence in Alabama. But when King sought his public endorsement of the Selma campaign, Johnson, rejecting the advice of White House aides who sought to shield him from public involvement in the crisis, read a prepared statement at a press conference on February 4 that acknowledged the civil rights demonstrators' cause and pledged to do something about it. "I should like to say that all Americans should be indignant when one American is denied the right to vote. The loss of that right to a single citizen undermines the freedom of every citizen. That is why all of us should be concerned with the efforts of our fellow Americans to register to vote in Alabama . . . I intend to see that the right [to vote] is secured for all our citizens."[17]

The following month, as the crisis in Selma worsened, Johnson lived up to this promise. On March 15, 1965, for the first time in nineteen years, a president appeared before a joint session of Congress to present a legislative message. Sensing that America was at a pivotal moment in its long and tortured history of slavery and discrimination, hoping to seize the opportunity presented by the brave civil rights demonstrators, Johnson spoke with unusual feeling about the voting rights bill. Although he had privately fumed about the outbreak of protests in cities across America, especially those demonstrations in front of the White House, Johnson now embraced the swelling tide of emotion instigated by the civil rights movement. "The real hero" of the struggle for voting rights, "was the American Negro. His actions and protests, his courage to risk safety and even to risk his life, have awakened the conscience of the nation. His demonstrations have been designed to call attention to injustice, designed to provoke change, designed to stir reform. He has called upon us to make good the promise of America. And who among us can say that we would have made the same progress were it not for his persistent bravery and faith in America." Johnson's speech warned that the enactment of the voting rights bill would not end the battle for civil rights; rather, it was but one front in a larger war that must include not just federal laws to throw open the "gates of opportunity" but also affirmative action against ignorance, ill health, and poverty that would enable individual men and women to "walk through those gates":

What happened in Selma is part of a far larger movement which reaches into every section and State of America. It is the effort of American Negroes to secure for themselves the full blessings of American life.

Their cause must be our cause too. Because it is not just Negroes, but really it is all of us, who must overcome the crippling legacy of bigotry and injustice.

And we shall overcome.[18]

Johnson thus adopted as his own rallying cry a line from an old hymn that had become the slogan of the civil rights movement. "Much of his audience," Conkin has written, "was in tears, for he had succeeded in doing what he had asked Kennedy to do in 1963—use the presidency as a moral platform."[19] LBJ had not won over southern congressmen, most of whom slumped in their seats as the joint session erupted in applause. Nonetheless, he had triumphed where FDR failed—without embroiling himself in an enervating purge campaign, he joined civil rights activists to discredit southern resistance to liberal reform. As Johnson embraced the ringing anthem of the civil rights movement, Dr. King, watching the speech on television in Montgomery, Alabama, was moved to tears. John Lewis, president of the Student Nonviolent Coordinating Committee (SNCC), was surprised to see King so moved, for he had always been a man in careful control of his emotions. Lewis, too, was moved. More suspicious than was King of the president, whom he had always dismissed as a "politician," Lewis acknowledged that on this night LBJ was "a man who spoke from his heart, a statesman, a poet."[20]

Johnson recognized that his alliance with the civil rights movement was fraught with political risks. The Democrats had depended on their southern base to win national elections. "He knew very well what the impact would be of an all out Civil Rights program," White House aide Harry McPherson related many years later—that "he would be considered a traitor."[21] Johnson's triumphant visit to Georgia gave him hope that he would be forgiven by white southerners; this was the very purpose of his appeal to conscience. "I can't make people integrate," he told Richard Goodwin, "but maybe we can make them feel guilty if they don't."[22] The elections of November 1966, however, revealed the South was not in a forgiving mood. Three segregationist Democrats—Lester Maddox in Georgia, James Johnson in Arkansas, and George P. Mahoney in Maryland—won their party's gubernatorial nomination. In Alabama, moreover, voters ratified a caretaker administration for Lurleen Wallace, since her husband, George, was not permitted to succeed himself. George Wallace, dubbed the "prime minister" of Alabama, had by 1966 emerged as a serious threat capable of consummating the North-South split in the Democratic Party, either by entering the 1968 presidential primaries or running as a third-party candidate. What happened in the 1966 gubernatorial race in California, where former movie star Ronald Reagan handily defeated the Democratic incumbent Edmund G. Brown, revealed that conservative insurgency was not limited to southern Democrats.[23]

The prospect of losing the White House in 1968 made certain members of the administration nervous, if not completely repentant, about Johnson having alienated southern Democrats. A few days after the midterm election, one aide, Ervin Duggan, urged immediate attention to the problem: "Bill Moyers once [said] that Lyndon Johnson's mission might be to 'free the white South from itself....' If President Johnson is to accomplish that, he'd better get busy. Bitterness and resentment and outright hatred for the President in the South are bad—and getting worse. If they are to be moderated, if Wallace is to be stopped and the South saved for the President's party, we should start developing a Southern strategy now."[24]

The fear of "white backlash"—the new phrase for white resentment of black gains through political action—did not shake Johnson's determination to obtain civil rights progress through legislation and executive action. Johnson had no stomach for a "southern strategy" that retreated from civil rights. The defense of this cause above all was how he intended to make his mark on history, and Johnson's place in history meant more to him than serving another term as president or the standing of the Democratic Party. Moreover, the civil rights movement had become far too powerful and the issues it raised too riveting for a return to relatively "safe" New Deal issues such as economic security and educational opportunity. Johnson believed that as long as the economy remained strong, the Democrats "could still squeeze through." "But whatever the consequences," McPherson has insisted, LBJ "was determined to make major advances in the area of civil rights."[25]

To Johnson's deep disappointment, however, the growing militancy of the civil rights movement gave further impetus to "white backlash." Although Johnson, with the help of Democratic National Committee deputy chairman Louis Martin, was able to maintain an alliance with civil rights leaders, King and other moderate activists faced constant pressure not only to take more aggressive direct action against southern segregationists like George Wallace, but also against important northern authorities like Chicago Mayor Richard Daley.[26] Tensions within the civil rights movement threatened to sever its critical but uneasy ties with the Johnson White House. Indeed, no sooner had Johnson invested his presidency in the cause of civil rights, than radical dissidents who scorned White House leadership gained greater influence over the movement. Johnson's voting rights sermon won little praise from militant civil rights activists in Alabama like James Foreman, the field secretary for the Student Nonviolent Coordinating Committee (SNCC); as far as radical SNCC dissidents were concerned, the president had "ruined a good song."[27] As the schisms in the civil rights movement deepened along with the administration's involvement in Vietnam, Johnson became the target rather than the ally of civil rights activists.

Social Protest and the Limits of White House Leverage

Toward the end of 1965, the energy and resources committed to the Great Society began to suffer, threatened more and more by Johnson's preoccupation with the Vietnam War. From Franklin Roosevelt and subsequent occupants of the modern White House, LBJ inherited not just domestic responsibilities but also international commitments that pulled him away from the liberal activists to whom the early days of his presidency were dedicated.[28] African Americans were among the first to sense this change, and even moderate civil rights leaders, such as Martin Luther King, Jr., became visible participants in the antiwar movement. In late November, Hayes Redmon lamented these efforts of civil rights activists. "I am increasingly concerned over the involvement of civil rights groups with anti-war demonstrators," he wrote in a memo to Moyers. "The anti-Vietnam types are driving the middle class to the right. This is the key group that is slowly being won over to the civil rights cause. Negro leadership involvement with anti-Vietnam groups will set their programs back substantially."[29]

Johnson had tried to renew ties with King a few months earlier. In August, soon after race riots broke out in Watts, he called the civil rights leader to express his continued, indeed strengthened support for civil rights and to question him about rumors that he was opposed to the administration's actions in Vietnam.[30] Johnson feared that the Watts riot was but the most dramatic episode in what was becoming a routine conflagration, a pattern of lawlessness that would defy his hope to exert leadership in the cause of an enduring civil rights program.[31] Trying in vain to meet the demands of spiraling civil rights militancy, the president urged King to take seriously and help publicize a recent commencement address the president had given at Howard University, with which Johnson sought to burnish his credibility as an ally of the civil rights movement, and indeed lead it in advancing the cause of poor African Americans.[32] Explicitly linking civil rights to the great expectations of the Great Society, Johnson's Howard speech singled out African Americans for special attention: insisting that "Negro poverty was not white poverty," Johnson told the students and their families that "deep, corrosive, obstinate differences" distinguished the economic deprivation of black Americans—differences "radiating painful roots into the community, and into the family, and the nature of the individual." The Howard University address, LBJ told King, proclaiming that "freedom was not enough" and that the time had come to "seek . . . not just equality as a right and a theory but equality as a fact and as a result," demonstrated his administration's commitment to treat the most stubborn forces that sustained racial inequality.[33] He also urged the civil rights leader to support the administration on Vietnam, telling King: "I want peace as much as you do if not more so," because "I'm the fellow who had to wake up to 50 marines killed."[34]

King acknowledged that Johnson's Howard University speech was "the best statement and analysis of the problem" he had seen and that "no president ever said it like that before."[35] Indeed, Walter Fauntroy, director of the SCLC's Washington Bureau, had told White House aide Lee White that Johnson's address had inspired King to take his civil rights campaign north, with the purpose of gaining "a deeper insight into the more complex problems facing the Negro community."[36] Nonetheless, King saw himself, and not the president, as the leader of the Civil Rights Movement. Moreover, he feared that tying himself too closely to Johnson, in an atmosphere of mounting racial tension, would weaken his standing in the civil rights community. As David Carter has written, "in this period of growing polarization it had become increasingly clear to civil rights leaders, and ultimately even to the President and his staff, that a White House blessing of a leader was tantamount to a curse."[37]

In truth, King was the least of the administration's problems. More troublesome was the emergence of a new generation of black leaders dedicated to "Black Power," a militant, more threatening type of activism. As the civil rights movement trained its eye on the poverty-stricken ghettos of large northern cities, King, although still a giant of the movement, lost influence to more militant leaders who were better attuned than he to the frustrations and rage of young urban blacks.[38] People like Stokley Carmichael, newly elected head of SNCC, and other angry young civil rights leaders such as Floyd McKissick of the Committee of Racial Equality (CORE), were not only dissatisfied with the achievements of the Johnson administration's civil rights program, but also were contemptuous of its objective of racial integration. The growing militancy of black America erupted during the summer of 1966 as urban riots swept across the nation. In the wake of these developments, the moderately conservative middle class, as Redmon had feared, grew impatient with reform. The administration's string of brilliant triumphs in civil rights was snapped. Its 1966 Civil Rights bill, an open housing proposal, fell victim to a Senate filibuster. Johnson's leadership of the civil rights movement was a great asset to him in 1964; it had become something of a liability by the summer of 1966.

As Bruce Miroff has pointed out, presidents with reform aspirations had sought to find a "symbolic point," where they appeared "to cooperate with a social movement for noble purposes" while retaining their "special commitment to law, order, and the general good."[39] Even as he made unprecedented overtures to social activists, Johnson managed to maintain this "balance point" between the White House and the civil rights movement during the first two years of his presidency. For example, he effectively intervened in civil rights matters during the summer of 1964, the first of the long hot summers. Riots erupted in July of that year, soon after the Republican National Convention nominated conservative Arizona senator Barry Goldwater for president. Although proclaiming himself an opponent of discrimination, Goldwater had voted against the recently enacted Civil Rights Act; his acceptance speech denounced it as unconstitutional and prescribed a reliance on the states for the advancement of constitutional protections owed blacks. As the rioting spread and civil rights demonstrations continued in 1964 after the passage of the Civil Rights Act, the administration feared that racial unrest would turn white voters against a president identified with the cause of African Americans. In July of that year, at LBJ's request, leaders of major civil rights organizations, including King, held a meeting in New York, where they called for a moratorium on black unrest.[40]

Johnson also actively intervened a month later in the struggle over the seating of the Mississippi delegation at the 1964 Democratic Convention. A Mississippi Freedom Democratic Party (MFDP) challenged the "regular" delegation, on the grounds that the Democratic Party in the state excluded blacks from membership. The conflict confronted Johnson and the Democratic Party leaders with a dilemma, since they risked antagonizing the civil rights forces if they banned the Freedom Party delegation and much or all of the South if they seated it. To avoid these unpalatable prospects, Johnson, with considerable help from Minnesota senator Hubert D. Humphrey and the leader of the United Auto Workers, Walter Reuther, worked assiduously behind the scenes to achieve a compromise. The compromise plan included the seating of the regular Mississippi delegation, provided its members signed a loyalty oath that pledged them to support the presidential ticket; the symbolic gesture of making MFDP delegates honored guests at the convention, with two of its members seated as special delegates at large; and a prohibition of racial discrimination in delegate selection at the 1968 convention, to be enforced by a special committee to assist state parties in complying with this expectation.

Johnson's intervention in these two episodes was resented by more militant civil rights leaders. John Lewis of SNCC and James Farmer of CORE dissented from the moratorium on demonstrations, signaling their commitment to "direct action" as a critical method of civil rights progress. Moreover, SNCC and CORE rejected the White House negotiated compromise at the 1964 Democratic Convention and bitterly criticized Johnson for his willingness to sacrifice the MFDP's moral cause on the altar of expediency. But the MFDP, through its lawyer, Joseph Rauh, accepted the compromise, which was adopted by the convention without notable objection.[41] In fact, most civil rights activists, including King, accepted the White House's leadership on these two occasions. King joined Whitney Young (executive director of the National Urban League), Roy Wilkins (executive secretary of the National Association for the Advancement of Colored People), and A. Philip Randolph (chairman of the Negro American Labor Council) in signing the moratorium statement. Johnson's heroic support for the Civil Rights Act and Goldwater's opposition to it, they believed, put a special premium not only on the election but also on the need to cultivate a climate in which racial progress could continue. As the declaration read, "Our own estimate of the present situation is that it presents such a serious threat to the implementation of the Civil Rights Act and to subsequent expansion of civil right gains that we recommend a voluntary, temporary alteration in strategy and procedure."[42]

Similar considerations persuaded most civil rights leaders to swallow the MFDP compromise, albeit not without creating a great "sense of distress" in King and other moderate activists.[43] Not only were southern states threatening to walk out of the convention if the regular Mississippi delegation was purged, but Johnson and Democratic leaders also warned civil rights leaders that an unruly convention would cost the party the support of several border states and deprive Democrats of a chance to win a historic landslide—and a mandate for further reform.[44]

Just as important, LBJ helped to diffuse the Mississippi controversy by championing a fundamental reform of convention rules that would have enormous long-term consequences for the Democratic Party. Previously, state parties had sole authority to establish delegate selection procedures. Johnson's proposed solution to the MFDP compromise established the centralizing principle that henceforth the national party agencies would not only decide how many votes each state delegation got at the national convention but also enforce uniform rules on what kinds of persons could be selected. As the president told Reuther, "We don't want to cut off our nose to spite our face. If they [MFDP protesters] give us four years, I'll guarantee the Freedom delegation somebody representing views like that will be seated four years from now."[45] Contrary to conventional wisdom, LBJ made it clear to all parties—civil rights reformers and regular southern delegates alike—that he did not propose this compromise merely as a short-term, stopgap measure to ensure peace at the 1964 convention. Rather, he viewed the new nondiscrimination rule as a justified extension of the national party's power over state delegations that carried on discriminatory practices, a commitment to reform that was an important prelude to the 1965 Voting Rights Act and the banning of segregated delegations at the 1968 Democratic Convention. As Humphrey confirmed with Johnson in a telephone conversation soon after the compromise plan was accepted, the MFDP representatives should "be heralded not as delegates from the state of Mississippi," but, rather, "as an expression of the conscience of the Democratic Party, as to the importance of the right to vote, political participation by all peoples in this country, and that we, in this historic period when we passed a civil rights act, which establishes a whole new pattern of social conduct in the country, that we're prepared to make official recognition of the all-important right to vote and of active participation in political affairs."[46]

The leadership Johnson displayed during the Selma crisis, which led to the enactment of the Voting Rights Act, seemed to confirm, even in the eyes of skeptics like John Lewis, the critical role of the White House as the steward of reform. Significantly, White House aides, acting on Johnson's instructions, were able to work with King and other moderate civil rights leaders to ward off the efforts of militant activists who hoped to instigate a more violent clash between demonstrators and Alabama state troopers.[47]

One year later, Harry McPherson, who played an important role as a White House liaison with the civil rights community, urged Johnson to intervene once again in racial politics—in the civil rights crisis of 1966.[48] He suggested that the president call an immediate meeting of civil rights leaders to address the Black community's demand for further advances. Once eager to take steps that would solidify his personal ties with the civil rights movement, Johnson hesitated this time. He referred McPherson's recommendations to Attorney General Nicholas Katzenbach. Katzenbach agreed with McPherson that the racial situation had taken a disturbing turn, but in a memorandum to the White House aide he opposed the suggestion for an immediate meeting between the president and civil rights leaders. Underlying Katzenbach's objection to holding such a meeting was his disagreement with McPherson's characterization of Johnson as a "civil rights leader," the attorney general's view that there were inherent tensions between a movement dedicated to challenging the establishment and an institution inextricably linked to it. Johnson was and would continue to be a leader working toward racial progress. But to consider Johnson a civil rights leader was to assume falsely that the civil rights movement was constrained by its association with the White House—that it was a loyal part of a presidential coalition. In fact, Katzenbach observed, "one of the principal difficulties of established Negro leadership has been and will continue to be taking positions that are at the same time responsible, practical—and clearly independent of the Administration."[49]

In the end, Johnson did not meet with civil rights leaders, even as he refused to sound a full retreat from civil rights reform. He followed Katzenbach's advice to send a number of his younger aides to various cities to meet with young black leaders. The attorney general's suggestion was the origin of ghetto visits that White House aides made throughout 1967; a dozen or so visited troubled black areas in more than twenty cities, including Chicago, Philadelphia, New York, Detroit, the District of Columbia, Los Angeles, and Oakland. On the one hand, the ghetto visits revealed the extent to which the modern presidency had become the principal agent of popular government, how the White House had assumed so many of the more important tasks once carried out by intermediary political associations like political parties. Instead of relying on local party leaders for information about their communities, Johnson asked his aides to live in various ghettos for a time and then to report directly to him about the state of black America. Local public officials and party leaders, even Chicago's powerful boss Richard Daley, were not told of the ghetto visits, lest they take umbrage at someone from the White House rooting about their home territories.[50]

At the same time, these visits marked the declining significance of the modern presidency as the leading agent of liberal reform—a symptom of its "extraordinary isolation."[51] This isolation was accentuated by the evolution of the civil rights movement, whose more militant leaders, representing an agency culture that tended to withdraw rather than bestow legitimacy on reigning institutions, gained ascendancy in urban ghettos. Johnson and other members of the White House were left to figure out why young urban Blacks, as one aide put it, "were against just about every leader (Negro and white) . . . except [Black Power advocates like] Stokely Carmichael."[52] The awkward presence of these Johnson aides—mostly white, mostly from small towns and cities in the Midwest and Southwest—spending a week, sometimes a weekend, in volatile ghetto environments such as Harlem and Watts was, as a leading participant put it, a "unique attempt by the President to discover what was happening in urban ghettos and why."[53] Aides were not sent to organize or manipulate or steer, but solely to gain a sense of the ideas, frustrations, and attitudes at the basis of the riots.[54]

The lengthy reports that White House aides prepared for the president appeared to vindicate the objectives of the Great Society. The volatile conditions in the ghetto did not stem from material deprivation alone, these reports argued; rather, as one White House aide put it, the most serious and common problem was that "the ghetto Negro lives in a world which is severed from ours." Sherwin Markman, who organized the White House ghetto visits, wrote in his summary report that the first essential key to understanding urban America was "'alienation'—of the ghetto Negro from the mainstream of American life, and of white America from the ghetto Negro." Although housing, education, and employment varied from city to city, the "disconnection" blacks felt from the rest of America was "not limited to one city or region, but [was] nation-wide in its pattern, and growing." Markman related that as he left the comfortable parts of downtown and suburban U.S. cities, he had the "same feeling in the ghetto as I did when I visited the poverty stricken areas of South America a year ago. It was almost like visiting a foreign country—and the ghetto Negro tends to look on us and our government as foreign."[55]

Markman sought to persuade LBJ that the severe alienation that afflicted urban America both explained and perhaps justified the Black Power movement. The "dramatic growth" of Black Power had become the "rally cry in the ghetto," he reported after a return visit to Chicago in February 1968. "Power" should not be confused with violence, Markman insisted, even though "some advocates of the philosophy preach violence." After talking with intellectuals like Charles Hamilton, who had just written a book with Stokely Carmichael on Black Power, as well as militant black nationalists who championed the idea from the pulpits and in the streets, Markman concluded that this vague concept most essentially meant "an increase in race consciousness and pride." In their early visits to urban areas, White House aides had discovered, as one report put it, that "perhaps the most significant symbol of the ghetto is the *absence of proud men*." Black Power, Markman told LBJ, would bring "positive results" by filling that terrible void: "It is my judgment that the increased pride in race must inevitably lead to strong racial motivation for better social organization, better education, and better jobs. This motivation can, at least, serve the same purpose for Negroes as ethnic history has served for other minorities which have successfully made it in our society."[56]

By all accounts, Johnson was deeply moved by these reports. The president carried one of Markman's reports on the Chicago ghetto around with him and read it to members of the Cabinet, Congress, and the press, with the hope that it would persuade them to accept the White House's position on civil disorders.[57] LBJ condemned the riots, declaring in a nationwide address of July 1967, "There is no American right to loot stores, or to burn buildings, or to fire rifles from the rooftops. That is a crime—and crime must be dealt with forcefully, and swiftly, and certainly—under law." At the same time, he insisted, "This is not a time for angry reaction. It is a time for action: starting with legislative action to improve the life in our cities. The strength and promise of the law are the surest remedies for tragedy in the streets."[58]

The ghetto reports apparently were pivotal in persuading Johnson to respond to the riots by redoubling his efforts to expand civil rights and the war on poverty programs. The administration continued to push for an open-housing bill, and in the aftermath of King's assassination, one was passed in 1968. That year, LBJ also submitted, and Congress passed, the most extensive and most expensive public housing legislation in American history. Finally, Johnson continued to support the war on poverty's Office of Economic Opportunity, the White House office charged with administering poverty programs, even though its sponsorship of Community Action Programs (CAPs), requiring "the maximum feasible participation of residents of the areas and groups involved," was reportedly having a disruptive influence in many cities and was the target of bitter complaints from local party leaders.[59] As Frances Fox Piven and Richard Cloward have shown, the idealistic thrust of community action quickly gave way to the more practical objectives of enabling poor people to obtain welfare benefits.[60] But the Community Action Program gave institutional support to social activists who defied direction from the White House Office of Economic Opportunity.

The president seethed privately about the "revolutionary" activity that some CAPs were fomenting. Nonetheless, encouraged by the ghetto reports of their valuable work in ameliorating the alienation of urban dwellers from American society and government, he never repudiated them and continued to support federal funds for neighborhood organizations. As Markman concluded dramatically after a visit to the California east bay communities of Oakland, Berkeley, and Richmond: "The only way the Negro can identify with the [War on Poverty] is by being an integral part of it. The War on Poverty is the great bulwark against the total disaffection of the ghetto Negro, which in the long run can lead only to guerilla warfare. The Poverty program succeeds by involving the Negro totally in the dreams and destiny of this Nation."[61] By the same token, the War on Poverty's Community Action Program was the Johnson administration's final, frail hope that it could benefit from the transformative energy of a movement over which it was rapidly losing influence.

The Johnson Presidency and Community Action

Johnson's relationship with the War on Poverty helps explain how he both extended the reach of the modern presidency and built the skids for its diminishing influence. In part, the Johnson White House's delegation of administrative responsibility to these local citizen groups was intended to be an extension of the modern presidency. LBJ and his aides viewed state and local governments, and the party organizations that influenced them, as obstacles to good government, to the "enlightened" management of social policy. They conceived of CAPs as a local arm of the Office of Economic Opportunity, thus enabling the Johnson administration to bypass local governments and the entrenched, usually Democratic political machines.[62] Federal guidelines, in fact, stipulated that the community action program had to be conducted by a public or private nonprofit agency (or some combination thereof) other than a political party.[63]

At least in part, then, the communal concerns of the Johnson presidency were closely connected to administrative invention, a bold new initiative that embodied, in Nathan Glazer's words, "the professionalization of reform in modern society."[64] Moreover, for all its confidence in presidential guidance and governance, Johnson's invention never fulfilled its stated objective of popular participation. Under the banner of community control, Daniel Patrick Moynihan observed, "the essential decisions about local affairs came increasingly to be made in Washington via the direct CAP-OEO line of communication and funding."[65] Especially after 1967, following the recommendations of the Heineman task force on government organization, Johnson tried to tighten White House management over the CAPs.[66] The following year, George Nicolau, head of the Harlem Community Action Agency (HARYOU-ACT), declared himself "a victim of that process which in the space of three short years created and has almost been overwhelmed by its own complexities and its own bureaucracy."[67]

The administrative innovation that gave rise to the War on Poverty was an attempt to respond to real problems, albeit problems that could not be readily addressed by executive administration. Moynihan argued that the Johnson administration had blundered into the Community Action Program and that the phrase mandating "maximum feasible participation" was a shallow rhetorical bow to the Jeffersonian tradition of local self-government. Yet the ideas that informed the creation of the Community Action Program were not so distinctive from certain aspects of the New Deal, to more communal reform ideas and practices that Johnson understood well as a result of his experiences as the Texas director of the National Youth Administration (NYA), the New Deal agency that Roosevelt created in 1935 to rescue young people from ignorance, unemployment, and enduring hardship. The NYA, headed by the militant southern liberal, Aubrey Williams, was both more idealistic and less bureaucratic than most other New Deal agencies. Its programs were administered from state offices and under state relief administrators, who were encouraged to develop innovative grassroots reforms that would provide meaningful work for young people and help keep them in school long enough to become self-sufficient.[68] The 1943 report of the National Resources Planning Board (NRPB), a planning agency Roosevelt created in 1939 as part of the newly formed Executive Office of the President, singled out the NYA for avoiding bureaucratic inertia; it was as one of the few New Deal agencies, the NRPB found, that did not "divorce the average citizen from participation in the problems involved in public-aid policy and administration."[69]

The Johnson White House's sponsorship of the Community Action Program represented another attempt to reconcile the New Deal state with the historical antipathy in the United States to centralized power. LBJ's experiences as director of the Texas National Youth Administration, no doubt, gave him a practical sense of the prospects and difficulties involved in accomplishing this objective. The NYA's steadfast commitment to local self-determination, the 1943 NRPB report claimed, was its greatest strength but also the source of some concern among New Deal planners:

The present arrangement has made for adaptability of the program to local conditions and community needs and has permitted experimentation in methods and techniques. . . . On the other hand, it has resulted in a marked lack of uniformity in program and methods and techniques and a wide diversity of achievement. The situation would appear to be particularly serious in view of the national significance of the problems of unemployed youth, and the fact that so large a proportion of the young unemployed population is concentrated in areas where both social and economic conditions are likely to inhibit the development of appropriate projects if reliance is so largely placed upon local initiative.[70]

The cultural changes and social circumstances of the 1960s greatly aggravated the tension between enlightened administration and community control. After reading his White House aides' accounts of the conditions in the ghetto, Johnson developed a deeper appreciation of the limits of executive administration in fighting a war against racial discrimination and economic deprivation. More important, the riots and the White House aides' reports of them confirmed the Johnson administration's view that "community action" was a critical element of their program to establish a post-New Deal version of the welfare state. The architects of the Great Society were well aware of the political risks involved in delegating administrative responsibility to community action agencies; however, these risks were taken in the hope of revitalizing, indeed surpassing, the militant side of New Deal liberalism. Interestingly, the evaluations of the task forces charged by the Johnson White House with the responsibility to investigate the administrative problems of the War on Poverty are strikingly reminiscent of the NRPB's critique of the NYA. Although it described problems of administrative fragmentation and uneven performance standards, the Task Force Report on Intergovernmental Program Coordination noted in a typical analysis that the decentralized management of the Office of Economic Opportunity should not be condemned out of hand:

Administrative tidiness is not the only test of effective government. In truth, some Federal programs operating from new and revolutionary postulates (e.g., the Community Action Program) may have to measure their success, in part, in terms of what they temporarily disrupt. Furthermore, total program coordination can be bought at too high a price: the imposition of "commissar" sanctions by one agency or one level of government over other agencies, levels, and jurisdictions, and a deadening multiplication of paper work and inter-agency clearance.[71]

Johnson's surprising patience with the CAPs, his continuing, albeit certainly not unqualified, support of the War on Poverty, in the face of blistering criticism from Congress and local government officials, suggests that he did not disagree with this assessment.[72] He did not appreciate fully the tension between executive management and local self-determination. Nor did he sufficiently appreciate that the civil rights movement was a catalyst for a "new" politics that was inherently suspicious of presidential leadership. As one policy analyst has written, "It was precisely because the civil rights movement had already built organizations and mobilized community resources that 'maximum feasible participation' was translated so quickly from abstraction to reality."[73] The community action agencies took on the energy and aspirations of the civil rights movement and refocused it, thus giving a new generation of black leaders entrée into local and administrative politics. As a 1967 Senate investigation of the War on Poverty put it: "The Office of Opportunity policies and programs have produced a cadre of citizen leadership, heretofore neither seen nor heard in the community arena." They have brought "to the fore a sizeable cadre, for the first time in the Negro community, especially, of young energetic and striving leadership."[74] That "cadre of striving leaders," instrumental in the increasing election of black mayors in American cities, the number of African Americans employed directly or indirectly by the government, and the enhanced influence of civil rights groups on social policy during the late 1960s and 1970s, developed political bases that were not tied directly to the Democratic Party or the White House. Nonetheless, having invested his immense ambition in the Great Society, having staked his political fortunes in the social movements that it empowered, Johnson had little choice but to support the Office of Economic Opportunity and the community organizations it spawned, even as he grew increasingly aware of the fact that it aroused leadership and social forces that he could not control, that had come to view him "as part the white apparatus which created and fostered the perpetuation" of racial injustice.[75]

Lyndon Johnson's Legacy for the Modern Presidency

Unlike Eisenhower, who treated racial strife in the South as a matter of domestic order, or Kennedy, who tried to keep civil rights a legal issue, Johnson understood the inequality between black and white Americans as a ringing moral cause, one worthy of a deployment of the full powers of the modern presidency.[76] But this singularly determined fusion of presidential power to a movement for social justice imploded on two fronts.

It imploded first in the effort to manage all the other commitments the modern presidency pulls in its train. Johnson's decision to expand America's involvement in Vietnam, in particular, stemmed in part from his firm belief that nothing could be accomplished unless certain received commitments were steadfastly affirmed, and in this he unwittingly confirmed the view of civil rights activists that the presidency could not be trusted with the mantle of leader of their cause. Johnson was far from indifferent to this indictment of the administration's foreign policy; indeed, his commitment to bold domestic reform strongly influenced his decision to refrain from any full-scale mobilization of the Vietnam conflict. On the one hand, he feared that too much forbearance, let alone withdrawal, would allow the Right to use anticommunism to subvert domestic change, just as the "loss of China" had weakened liberalism on Truman's watch.[77] On the other hand, the distractions of this limited war soaked up resources and exposed the president's attachment to received commitments to the social activists' charge that he was, after all, a trimmer.

Second, Johnson's attempted fusion imploded upon the modern pretension that the managerial capacities and administration mechanisms of executive leadership could serve as instruments of community control and social justice. The Community Action Program, resulting from an effort to wed to this end administrative invention with a rejection of centralization, perfectly captured the paradox of Lyndon Johnson's Great Society. There is a real sense in which this program, the signature innovation of the Great Society, marked a serious, if flawed, effort to routinize the intense emotion of the Civil Rights Movement. Harry McPherson attempted to express the essence of this effort to reconcile executive leadership and community control at the twilight of the Johnson presidency. Notes he prepared in November 1968 for a presidential address (never given) on intergovernmental relations disavowed the conservative view "that Washington was somehow wholly separate from (and an ominous threat to) the grass roots." But the draft address also rejected "the liberal dogma that the Federal government had all the answers." And then, in a revelation of the full scope of the dilemma, McPherson expressed the concern that the newfound celebration of "participatory democracy" and the recent denigration of "enlightened administration" had left the country without a national purpose; the Great Society, McPherson lamented, had helped to bring to power issue-oriented independents who failed to acknowledge a transcendent public interest. "Does this lack of a central core," a fellow White House assistant asked McPherson, "explain the emptiness we all sense...as Peer Gynt discovered when he peeled the onion."[78]

LBJ's abdication on March 31, 1968—his announcement that he would not seek or accept the nomination of his party for another term as president—signified a failure of his ambition to keep himself and the powers of the modern executive aligned with the carriers of a new politics—civil rights activists, consumer and environmental advocates, and those fighting for women's rights. But it also exposed something deeper. It showed that just as the modern presidency had become swept up in the expectations of a society mobilized for great reform achievements, so it had become vulnerable to the expanded responsibilities of its stewardship across a vast and varied set of policy domains. By 1968, Johnson, the self-fashioned agent of a political transformation as fundamental as any in our history, had become a hated symbol of the status quo, forced into retirement lest he contribute further to the fast unraveling of the liberal consensus. As he told Hubert Humphrey in their private meeting of April 3, 1968: "I could not be the rallying force to unite the country and meet the problems confronted by the nation abroad and at home in the face of a contentious campaign and the negative attitudes towards [me] of the youth, Negroes, and academics."[79]

Part V
Insiders Out to Change Things

Chapter 14

Entrepreneurial Defenses of Congressional Power

Eric Schickler

There are good reasons to expect the president and executive branch to steadily gain power at the expense of the Congress. The twentieth century witnessed the decline of numerous elected legislatures, leading some observers to expect the U.S. Congress to suffer a similar fate.[1] Although congressional dominance was a staple of much early rational choice theorizing,[2] recent models have suggested that Congress suffers from debilitating collective action problems that pave the way for the steady accretion of presidential power and the relative decline of the legislative branch.

Terry Moe has stated the argument most forcefully.[3] Moe observes that scholars are wrong to reify Congress, treating it as an institutional actor capable of battling the president. Instead, "Congress is made up of hundreds of members, each a political entrepreneur in his or her own right, each dedicated to his or her own reelection and thus to serving his or her district or state."[4] Moe acknowledges that each member shares a common stake in the institutional power of Congress, but "this is a collective good that . . . can only weakly motivate their behavior."[5] Thus, "presidents have both the will and the capacity to promote the power of their own institutions, but individual legislators have neither and cannot be expected to promote the power of Congress as a whole in any coherent, forceful way."[6] Similarly, in *Power Without Persuasion*, William Howell emphasizes individual members' primary focus on reelection and claims that the "job of attending to constituent interests rarely overlaps with that of protecting Congress's institutional integrity."[7] As a result, "the institutional power of Congress steadily wanes, while that of the president, with each unilateral action taken, expands further and further."[8] Howell's innovative study of executive orders finds that it is extremely rare for Congress to enact legislation reversing presidential decisions. The transaction costs of putting together a coalition to fight the president are simply too great for individual members to bear, given that the benefits are shared by all members, regardless of their contribution to the collective good.

The Moe-Howell thesis captures an important element of congressional-presidential relations. It cannot be assumed that members of Congress will defend their institution against presidential encroachments. Yet Congress has not simply surrendered its authority to the executive branch, and current scholarly interest in explaining "presidency-centered government" as the distinctive institutional formation of modern American political development misses as much as did earlier work that fixated on Congress. Existing theories do, however, provide some leverage for understanding the congressional response to external challenges. The potential for a single institutional innovation to serve as a common carrier for multiple member interests helps explain how members can overcome the collective action problem highlighted by Moe. While changes to defend congressional capacity and power provide benefits that are shared among all 535 members, it is possible to frame innovations that simultaneously offer additional benefits to a narrower subset of members, thereby motivating those members to bear the costs of providing the collective good.

For example, when Nixon's budget impoundments and attacks on Congress's fiscal mismanagement threatened the legislative branch's role in the budget process, members responded with the Congressional Budget and Impoundment Control Act of 1974. The act provided a more centralized budget process that allowed Congress to set broad priorities, even when confronted with a hostile president.[9] Support for the act, however, was not simply based on broad institutional interests. Instead, budget reform also served majority party Democrats' interest in defending their party's reputation against Nixon's rhetorical attacks, along with the policy goals of conservatives seeking mechanisms to limit spending.[10] Furthermore, by superimposing the new budget committees on top of the preexisting system of authorization, appropriations, and revenue committees, the Budget Act mitigated the potential opposition of turf-conscious members. While this layering made the Budget Committees' task more difficult, the act nonetheless had a substantial impact, providing Congress with an important new resource in budget battles with the White House.

Yet this begs the question of how such common carrier changes are devised in the first place. One possibility is that entrepreneurs play a critical role in aligning member interests on behalf of changes that defend Congress's institutional position. Thus, in a recent study of congressional development, entrepreneurs were involved in nine of the eighteen cases of significant institutional innovation in which Congress-centered (or chamber-centered) interests were either a primary or secondary motivation, as opposed to just five of twenty-four cases that did not promote Congress-centered interests.[11] Most members can perceive the immediate benefits of changes that promote policy, personal power, or partisan goals.

But the benefits of Congress-centered changes are typically more distant. Entrepreneurs can help craft reforms that will also appeal to other, more tangible member interests.

Nonetheless, important questions remain about the conditions under which Congress will succeed in responding to executive aggrandizement, and about the role played by entrepreneurship in shaping the congressional response (or lack thereof). One need look no further than the current War on Terror and the Iraq War to find clear evidence that Congress does not necessarily mount a response when the White House attempts to dictate U.S. foreign and military policy. To say the least, the dearth of aggressive congressional investigations of the intelligence failures, reconstruction setbacks, alleged profiteering by politically connected contractors, and prison abuse scandals in Iraq are precisely what a believer in presidential dominance would expect. Observers in the press—and some prominent senators from both parties—have lamented Congress's feeble response to these developments, but the bottom line is that the White House has largely been free to set United States policy largely on its own terms, subject to only limited congressional questioning.[12] For example, the House Government Reform Committee, which has the broadest executive oversight jurisdiction in the chamber, issued no subpoenas to the executive branch from 2001 to 2003.

The Iraq experience, however, stands in sharp contrast to congressional behavior during several earlier military conflicts. This chapter focuses on the period during which Congress faced perhaps the most serious challenge to its position vis-à-vis the White House: the late 1930s and 1940s. Franklin Roosevelt's commanding performance in responding to the Great Depression and in leading the United States in World War II suggested to many observers that Congress was in eclipse.[13] The greatly expanded federal role in economic management and world affairs seemed to require vigorous centralized leadership, which only the president could provide, and this relegated Congress to a subordinate role. However, instead of deferring to the president, members of Congress undertook a concerted and reasonably successful effort to rein in the executive branch and to reassert their own authority. While this effort did not overturn the modern presidency, it ensured that the president would continue to be heavily constrained by Congress, among other institutional competitors for power.[14]

This chapter traces the congressional response to Roosevelt, focusing in particular on the role played by investigations targeting the executive branch. While Moe emphasizes the costs confronting members seeking to battle the president, such entrepreneurs as Martin Dies (D-Tex.) and Howard Smith (D-Va.) proved the potential electoral and personal power benefits of spearheading investigations of executive branch actions. Entrepreneurial members used investigations as a common carrier to promote their individual careers and conservative policy goals while simultaneously reining in the executive branch. Since the lead sponsor of resolutions authorizing special investigative committees is generally named the chairman of the committee, there was ample motivation for individual members to undertake the work involved in initiating investigations.[15] While some of the entrepreneurs—such as Dies—appear to have been driven almost entirely by personal electoral and power goals, others, including Smith, were at least partly motivated by concerns about executive power. The cumulative impact of the investigations was to greatly complicate the political challenges confronting the executive branch. As David Mayhew argues, investigations are a potent tool used by members to shape the contours of political debate and to do battle with the White House.[16]

In addition to investigations, the congressional response to executive aggrandizement during World War II included appropriations riders and other legislative maneuvers reversing key administration decisions, as well as the Legislative Reorganization Act of 1946 and the Administrative Procedures Act of 1946. The Reorganization Act streamlined the congressional committee system, provided professional staffing for committees, and attempted to systematize oversight of the executive (see below). The Act's passage was facilitated by entrepreneurs who aligned members' personal interest in improved pay and perks with their broader institutional interest in defending congressional capacity and power.[17] Similarly, the Administrative Procedures Act (APA) was the culmination of a series of efforts to rein in agency discretion. Starting with the Walter-Logan bill of 1939—which FDR vetoed—Congress sought mechanisms to accommodate the need for delegation to expert agencies with the goal of maintaining legislative control. By bringing legislative values into administration—such as openness and formal rule-making processes—the APA helped ensure that agencies would confront dueling legislative and presidential controls, rather than be simple tools of the White House.[18] Subsequent empirical analyses have demonstrated that legislators tend to write more detailed laws that delegate less discretion to the bureaucracy when Congress and the White House are controlled by different parties, while providing more discretion when the legislative majority shares the same partisan (and, presumably, policy) interests as the president.[19] These mechanisms clearly are also important ways in which Congress defends its institutional position. During World War II, however, investigations were the most visible congressional response, and by highlighting numerous cases in which agencies disregarded Congress's wishes, they paved the way for the postwar effort to institutionalize greater legislative control through the Reorganization Act and Administrative Procedure Act.[20] In addition, the potential for such investigations to promote individual member careers while also reining in the executive makes them a particularly useful window into entrepreneurial politics.

The investigations boom counters the notion that Congress simply abdicated power to the White House, but it by no means indicates that Congress "won" and the president "lost." These were formative acts. Rather than substitute a Congress-dominated set of arrangements for the executive-led model sought by Roosevelt, the result was a highly contested, ongoing struggle for control, in which both ideological and institutional interests were at stake. One systemic effect of this struggle was to greatly complicate bids for coherent, executive-led planning and coordination of the postwar economic order. The same agencies that might have formed the core of efforts to develop a more corporatist, planning-oriented system—such as the National Resources Planning Board and Office of Price Administration—confronted the greatest congressional resistance. The notion of executive-led economic planning ran afoul of a congressional majority determined to challenge administrative centralization. Congress did not stop the development of the administrative state, but it did ensure that the president would lack the power to direct and coordinate its myriad operations.

After analyzing the role of investigations in fighting the executive branch during the Roosevelt years, the conclusion of this essay considers the conditions under which members successfully challenge executive aggrandizement. The crucial question today is whether the conditions allowing the entrepreneurial response in the 1940s were an aberration, and thus whether the weak congressional supervision of the wars on Terror and in Iraq are characteristic of member behavior. The existence of a weak and divided majority party in the 1940s provided a context favorable to entrepreneurial initiatives to rein in the executive, notwithstanding Democrats' nominal control of both branches. With southern Democrats most concerned with blocking any policies that they believed threatened their system of racial subjugation and low-wage production, Democrats were in little position to exert party discipline.[21] By contrast, the recent context of strong parties and unified control of Congress and the White House greatly reduced the space for such entrepreneurial initiatives. But under divided government, strong parties offer an alternative mechanism to solve the collective action problems highlighted by Moe, without reliance upon individual entrepreneurship. The strength and internal unity of the parties, combined with the presence or absence of unified control of the branches, helps determine whether members' partisan, policy, and personal power interests are likely to reinforce or run afoul of their shared stake in congressional capacity and power.

The Investigative Boom of 1937–46

Congressional investigations are by no means strictly a twentieth-century phenomenon. The first investigation was authorized by the House of Representatives in 1792, examining Major General Arthur St. Clair's embarrassing military setbacks in the Northwest Territory. The initial proposal called for the president to carry out the inquiry, but James Madison and other members successfully proposed that the House instead appoint a special committee to conduct the investigation.[22] Despite these early origins, congressional investigations were relatively uncommon for much of congressional history. Congress conducted approximately 185 investigations from 1789–1918.[23] After World War I, the House and Senate launched a series of investigations into the war effort, followed by a spurt of investigations of corruption in the Harding administration, culminating with Senator Thomas Walsh's (D-Mont.) famous investigation of the Teapot Dome scandal. The wave of investigations receded in the late 1920s, but soon "began to build up into the surge that by the 1950's established the investigative function as a major activity of Congress . . . and one of the most potent forms of control over the executive departments."[24]

The sheer volume, scope, and diversity of investigations starting in 1938, and accelerating once the United States entered World War II, was unprecedented. As late as 1940, the Senate spent only $170,000 on all of its investigations. By 1952, the Senate was spending $1.63 million annually on investigations. Spending continued to increase rapidly in the 1950s, topping $5 million annually by the end of the decade.[25] A similar increase occurred in the House. Mayhew's count of significant investigative actions by members of Congress also reveals a big increase in the 1940s, accelerating into the 1950s.[26]

Beyond the increase in the frequency and expense of investigations, there was a noteworthy shift in targets starting in the late 1930s. In the early to mid-1930s, there were few investigations of the executive branch. Instead, the most prominent investigations focused on targets such as corruption on Wall Street (the Pecora investigation, 1932–34) and anti-union activities by corporations (La Follette's "civil liberties" investigation). Future Speaker John McCormack (D-Mass.) led a 1934–35 inquiry into subversion, but the investigation was restrained in its approach, did not target governmental actors, and was modest in its recommendations.[27]

By 1938, however, as conservatism began its resurgence in Congress, and as members became increasingly concerned about executive power grabs amid FDR's court-packing bid, executive reorganization proposal, and attempted party purge, investigations were transformed into an instrument of the bipartisan conservative coalition and of members seeking to redress the institutional balance of power. The context of a weak and divided majority party, along with widespread distrust of the executive branch and conservative control of key power bases, such as the House Rules Committee, encouraged ambitious individual members to put forward new investigative initiatives. While individual entrepreneurs paved the way by demonstrating the potential personal power and electoral benefits of investigations, it is important to emphasize that the surrounding political context was conducive to the spread of this approach.

The resulting boom in investigative activism occurred in three stages. The first, from 1938–41, featured a handful of high-profile, innovative investigations that illustrated the political dividends to conservatives of harnessing Congress's oversight powers to challenge the executive branch and its interest-group allies. Political entrepreneurs, most notably Martin Dies (D-Tex.), played a prominent role in proving the political benefits of these investigations. The second stage, starting soon after the onset of World War II and lasting through 1946, was characterized by over one hundred investigations in the House and Senate. The executive branch was the most common, but by no means the only, target. The net result of this investigative activism was that federal agencies were constantly forced to answer to special committees on Capitol Hill that were specifically charged with limiting their arbitrary decision making. The investigative activism offered an outlet for ambitious individual members, while restraining executive branch autonomy and, at times, serving conservative electoral and policy goals. Finally, the third stage began in 1946, with adoption of the Legislative Reorganization Act (LRA). Congressional reformers sought to systematize the oversight that had flowered during the war, shifting primary responsibility from temporary special committees to well-staffed, permanent standing committees. Instead of relying on entrepreneurial individual members to propose ad hoc investigations, the LRA sought to encourage the standing committees to exercise "continuous" watchfulness over the executive branch.

Stage 1: The Dies Committee and Loyalty Investigations

A new type of investigation entered the scene in 1938, with Martin Dies's Special Committee on Un-American Activities, which probed the loyalty of left-leaning federal workers, activists, union organizers, and celebrities. The Dies Committee was not the first congressional investigation into subversion, but its systematic grilling of reluctant witnesses and its ability to garner headlines were new. As Edward Schneier observes, "whether or not Martin Dies was the first to sense the almost boundless possibilities opened by this tactic, it was he who set the pattern."[28]

Members initially supported Dies because he promised to investigate both fascist groups and communists. Liberal Democrat Samuel Dickstein (D-N.Y.) had repeatedly sought an investigation into Nazi influence in the United States and enthusiastically endorsed Dies's proposal for a special committee on "un-American" activities. Given the immense 334-88 Democratic majority in the 75th Congress (1937–38), Dies needed to enlist New Dealers concerned about fascism. Although a few liberals expressed concern that the committee would attack the Left, Dies appealed to a broad range of members interested in attacking political extremists at either end of the spectrum.[29] The resolution to create the committee passed easily, 191–41.

Once the investigative committee was created, however, Dies essentially ignored the Nazis, and instead molded his committee into a potent weapon for attacking liberal causes by associating the New Deal and its supporters with communism.[30] In this case, an institutional change adopted to serve members with diverse ideological viewpoints ended up serving conservatives alone. By early 1939, Dickstein had changed sides, calling for abolition of the Dies Committee.[31] But the positive publicity generated by Dies's efforts to expose communists protected the committee from such attacks, even though Dies had effectively dropped fascists as a target. Polls confirmed the popularity of the loyalty investigations: 74 percent of those Americans who had heard of the Dies Committee approved of its work.[32] The investigation, however, generated considerable consternation in the executive branch. The Dies Committee charged in January 1939 that Secretary of Labor Frances Perkins and Secretary of the Interior Harold Ickes had sought to cripple its activities. Meanwhile, FDR was reported to object to continuance of the committee.[33] But Democratic leaders responded that attempting to block its renewal would be "politically dangerous."[34] The Dies Committee continued to plague the administration for the next six years, and even gained standing committee status in 1945.[35]

Dies's fame and popularity demonstrated to individual members the personal political payoff for undertaking investigations. The principal loyalty investigators were hardly team players in the manner of Sam Rayburn, who famously advised members that "to get along, go along." Dies, Joseph McCarthy (R-Wis.), Pat McCarran (D-Nev.), and Richard Nixon (R-Calif.) adroitly used the press to gain attention for themselves and for their causes. Dies's intense ambition is suggested by his sponsorship of numerous unsuccessful resolutions in the 1930s proposing investigations of a wide array of targets, including lobbying by international bankers and administration tactics to "shackle" the press.[36] When he finally succeeded in gaining approval for an investigation, he used it to impress his constituents as well as a national audience, and to carve out a powerful niche for himself.[37] Similarly, McCarthy and Nixon used their investigative activism to enhance their personal power and electoral prospects. As such, the loyalty investigations were a common carrier for political entrepreneurs' career interests and for an ideological faction.

Although Dies's investigation was the most famous of the early conservative coalition probes, it was not alone in targeting the executive branch and its political allies. For example, following allegations that the WPA had been used as an administration tool to promote the election of New Deal supporters in the 1938 campaign, House and Senate committees conducted investigations targeting the agency. The Senate Campaign Expenditures Committee issued a scathing report in January 1939, demonstrating that the WPA had diverted funds to help New Deal Democrats in several states. As Arthur Krock noted in the *New York Times*, the effect of the report was to "sweep away all the defenses of the agency."[38] The Senate Committee recommended tight restrictions on government workers' campaign activities, generating pressure that helped lead to the Hatch Act of 1939.[39] Congress thus used the combination of aggressive, high-profile investigations and legislation to curb the executive branch tactic of using its personnel and resources to sway election results. In the contemporary context, it is especially striking that congressional Democrats were willing to highlight their own administration's political use of government workers to elect New Deal Democrats.

The House investigation of the WPA went even further. Appropriations Committee member and "economy bloc" leader Clifton Woodrum (D-Va.) worked with Rules Committee conservative Eugene Cox (D-Ga.) to push for the investigation, notwithstanding administration and leadership opposition.[40] The Rules Committee has jurisdiction over proposals for investigations in the House, and thus the conservative coalition's control of the committee was especially valuable in promoting investigations of liberal targets. The WPA investigation won approval from the Rules Committee in a 7–4 vote pitting Republicans and conservative Democrats against the administration's defenders.[41] Democratic leaders then dropped their opposition, knowing they had little chance of prevailing on the floor. Once the investigation was authorized, Woodrum took some pages from Dies's playbook. Past Appropriations Committee investigations had been conducted behind closed doors, and the press initially expected Woodrum to follow this practice.[42] But Woodrum instead led a series of open hearings in which the committee accused various WPA officials, as well as the main lobby for WPA workers, of Communist Party ties. The hearings garnered repeated front-page headlines and led to legislation requiring WPA workers to sign a statement saying that they did not belong to the Communist Party and pledging loyalty to the U.S. government.[43] In implementing the new law, the administration compared the affidavits with the lists of communists in the files of the Dies and Woodrum Committees.[44] The Woodrum Committee also found evidence of waste and inefficiency in the WPA, and used this to promote the chairman's goal of cutting relief spending.[45] Indeed, Roosevelt's budget proposal for 1940 included dramatic cuts in the WPA.[46] The economy bloc had succeeded in using investigations to undercut the political credibility of one of the centerpieces of the New Deal.[47]

A third major pre-World War II investigation targeted another mainstay of the New Deal, the National Labor Relations Board. Rules Committee conservative Howard Smith proposed and led the investigation of the labor board, which began in 1939. The administration and a majority of northern Democrats opposed the investigation, but southerners and Republicans joined forces to approve it on the House floor.[48] With the House Labor Committee firmly in the control of liberal Democrats, Smith and his conservative allies viewed the investigation as an opportunity to build opposition to the labor board and to frame legislation to scale back recent union gains. Smith's committee received frequent front-page coverage of its accusations that the NLRB was controlled by communists, biased in favor of the CIO, and hostile to employers.[49] Much like Dies, Smith connected communist subversion to the executive branch. Unlike Dies, Smith used his investigative committee to devise specific legislation targeting the NLRB and its union allies. The Rules Committee paved the way for this legislation to reach the floor, notwithstanding the Labor Committee's opposition.[50] Thus, Smith's investigation contributed to the growing movement to redress the NLRB's pro-union tilt, which eventually culminated in the Smith-Connally Act of 1943 and the Taft-Hartley Act of 1947.

By the early 1940s, Dies, Woodrum, and Smith had established investigative committees as a potent tool for undermining the Roosevelt administration's policy goals and political coalition. Furthermore, the publicity and personal power achieved by the individuals leading these investigations suggest how individual entrepreneurial action could overcome the collective action problems that supposedly incapacitate Congress in its battles with the executive branch. In the course of pursuing initiatives to promote their individual careers and ideological agendas, members such as Dies, Woodrum, and Smith devised investigations that simultaneously challenged executive primacy and reinforced congressional prerogatives.

Stage 2: World War II and the Investigations Boom

Although Dies, Woodrum, and Smith's high-profile investigations were signs of increased congressional aggressiveness in challenging the executive branch, it was the onset of World War II that triggered the most dramatic expansion in oversight. There is nothing inevitable about the relationship between war and investigations. In his classic account of Congress during World War II, Roland Young contrasts the flurry of investigations in the 1940s to the lax oversight during World War I and to the single, powerful Joint Committee to Investigate the Conduct of the War created to help manage the Civil War.[51] But soon after U.S. entry into World War II, Congress began to take on an active role in supervising the executive branch's conduct. Floyd Riddick, who published an annual review of each congressional session in the *American Political Science Review*, took note of the investigations boom. Starting with his review of the second session of the 77th Congress (January 6, 1942–December 16, 1942), Riddick included

a separate section in each session summary on "investigating committees."[52] The new section described the most prominent investigations and
included footnotes listing each investigation authorized by the House and
Senate in that session.[53]

Drawing on Riddick's annual session summaries, Tables 1a and 1b present a list of investigations authorized by the House and Senate from 1941
to 1946. The chief sponsor of each investigative resolution, along with
that member's party and state, is also included in the tables. The sheer
number of investigations is impressive. The House voted to authorize
seventy-three investigations from 1941 to 1946, while the Senate authorized an additional fifty-three inquiries.[54] While not all of the investigations targeted the executive branch, a close examination of the list
suggests that a clear majority involved Congress questioning policies or
decisions made by executive agencies, or otherwise challenging executive
influence over policy making. Examples include the investigations of the
war effort by the Military and Naval Affairs Committees, which found evidence of wasteful spending and production inefficiencies. Another example, though not directly targeting a single executive agency, was
William Colmer's Post-War Economic Policy Committee, which sought to
ensure that Congress would help direct the economic transition following the war instead of deferring to the administration. Colmer's investigation was inspired by member fears that the administration would use
the postwar transition as an opportunity to institute greater executive-led
economic planning.[55] An example of an investigation that appears not to
have targeted the executive branch is the creation of a select committee
to study the problems of small business.

When one examines the data, a handful of patterns emerge. First, the
number of investigations, particularly in the House, accelerated as the war
progressed. The House authorized thirteen investigations in the 77th Congress (1941–42), compared to twenty-nine in the 78th Congress (1943–44)
and thirty-one in the 79th Congress (1945–46). This suggests that members
became increasingly aggressive rather than muted in their criticism during
the war. The GOP gains in the 78th Congress, which left an extremely slim
Democratic margin, likely enhanced the prospects for investigations. Senate investigations also increased in frequency toward the end of the war,
though the pattern is less clear than in the House.

Second, investigative activism in the House appears to have been driven
to a greater extent by the conservative coalition than in the Senate. In both
the House and Senate, Democrats accounted for the vast majority of proposals. However, fully 57 percent of the investigations approved in the
House were sponsored by southern members. In the Senate, just 20 percent of the investigations had southern sponsors. Table 2, which compares
the median ideology score of investigation sponsors to the full membership
of the chamber, also indicates a greater role for the conservative coalition

TABLE 1A. INVESTIGATIONS AUTHORIZED BY THE HOUSE, 1941–46

Congress	Investigation	Sponsor	State	Party
77	Merchant Marine and Fisheries to investigate national defense program as it relates to the committee	Bland	Virginia	Dem.
77	Continue Special Committee to Investigate Un-American Activities	Dies	Texas	Dem.
77	Interstate and Foreign Commerce to continue investigation of petroleum industry	Kelly	Illinois	Dem.
77	Public Buildings Committee to investigate defense housing program	Lanham	Texas	Dem.
77	Rivers and Harbors to investigate feasibility of St. Lawrence Waterways project	Mansfield	Texas	Dem.
77	Create a Select Committee to Investigate Air Accidents	Nichols	Oklahoma	Dem.
77	Authorizing an investigation of the national defense program in its relation to small business	Patman	Texas	Dem.
77	Extend Phosphate Supply Investigation	Peterson J.	Florida	Dem.
77	Continue Special Committee to Investigate Replacement and Conservation of Wildlife	Robertson	Virginia	Dem.
77	Public Lands investigation of national parks system	Robinson	Utah	Dem.
77	Continue Select Committee Investigation of Interstate Migration of Destitute Citizens	Tolan	California	Dem.
77	National Defense Investigation by Military Affairs and National Affairs Committees	Vinson C.	Georgia	Dem.
77	Continue Special Committee on Campaign Expenditures	Whittington	Mississippi	Dem.
78	Continue Special Committee on Campaign Expenditures	Anderson	New Mexico	Dem.
78	Investigation of the program for the planting of guayule as a domestic source of crude rubber	Anderson	California	Rep.
78	Insular Affairs to investigate the political, economic, and social conditions in Puerto Rico	Bell C. J.	Missouri	Dem.
78	Continue Merchant Marine and Fisheries national defense investigation	Bland	Virginia	Dem.
78	Interstate Commerce investigation of matters related to air commerce and air navigation	Bulwinkle	North Carolina	Dem.
78	Appropriations Committee to investigate budget estimates and administrative expenditures	Cannon C.	Missouri	Dem.
78	Appropriations Committee to examine the fitness of certain Government personnel	Cannon C.	Missouri	Dem.
78	Create a Special Committee on Postwar Economic Policy and Planning	Colmer W.	Mississippi	Dem.
78	Select committee to investigate the activities of the Farm Security Administration.	Cooley	North Carolina	Dem.
78	Expand Farm Security investigation to include the Farm Credit Administration	Cooley	North Carolina	Dem.
78	Special Committee to Investigate Federal Communications Commission	Cox	Georgia	Dem.
78	Continue the Special Committee to Investigate Un-American Activities	Cox	Georgia	Dem.
78	Select committee to investigate seizure of Montgomery Ward	Dewey	Illinois	Rep.
78	Investigation of the present system of distribution of farm products.	Fulmer	South Carolina	Dem.
78	Interstate Commerce to investigate plans for government regulation of product labels	Halleck	Indiana	Rep.
78	Labor Committee to investigate government aid to the physically handicapped	Kelley A.	Pennsylvania	Dem.
78	Committee on Public Buildings to investigation Defense Housing Program	Lanham F.	Texas	Dem.
78	Continue Commerce committee investigation of petroleum situation	Lea	California	Dem.
78	Education Committee to study war effects on higher education	McCormack	Massachusetts	Dem.
78	Continuing for 90 days the Select Committee to Investigate Air Accident	Nichols	Oklahoma	Dem.
78	Creating Select Committee to investigate small business conditions	Patman	Texas	Dem.

Congress	Description	Name	State	Party
78	Committee on Public Lands to study the use of public lands in rehabilitation of veterans	Peterson J.	Florida	Dem.
78	Civil Service Committee to investigate various activities in the civil service	Ramspeck	Georgia	Dem.
78	Continue Special Committee to Investigate Replacement and Conservation of Wildlife	Robertson	Virginia	Dem.
78	Committee on Roads to investigate the Federal road system, and for other purposes	Robinson	Utah	Dem.
78	Select committee to investigate acts of executive agencies beyond the scope of their authority	Smith H. W.	Virginia	Dem.
78	Judiciary to investigate the official conduct of two district court judges	Sumners H.	Texas	Dem.
78	Establish a Select Committee on Postwar Military Policy	Wadsworth	New York	Rep.
78	Committee on Irrigation and Reclamation to study plans for improvement of the Columbia River	White	Idaho	Dem.
79	Investigate supplies and shortages of food, particularly meat	Anderson	New Mexico	Dem.
79	Continue investigation of political, economic, and social conditions in Puerto Rico	Bell C. J.	Missouri	Dem.
79	Continue Merchant Marine and Fisheries investigation of defense program	Bland S. O.	Virginia	Dem.
79	Foreign Affairs Committee to do investigations of all matters within its jurisdiction .	Bloom S.	New York	Dem.
79	To continue investigation of government plans for product labeling regulations	Boren L. H.	Oklahoma	Dem.
79	Interstate Commerce to study commerce outside the U.S.	Bulwinkle	North Carolina	Dem.
79	Appropriations Committee to conduct examinations of executive agencies	Cannon C.	Missouri	Dem.
79	Continue the Special Committee on Postwar Economic Policy and Planning	Colmer W.	Mississippi	Dem.
79	Committee on Immigration and Naturalization to study postwar immigration and naturalization	Dickstein	New York	Dem.
79	Special committee on congressional campaign contributions and expenditures	Domengeaux	Louisiana	Dem.
79	Judiciary to investigate FBI handling of espionage cases	Dondero	Michigan	Rep.
79	Ways and Means investigation of expansion of Social Security	Doughton	North Carolina	Dem.
79	Agriculture to investigate marketing, transportation, and distribution of farm products	Flannagan	Virginia	Dem.
79	Labor Committee to continue investigation of government aid to the physically handicapped	Kelley A.	Pennsylvania	Dem.
79	Committee on Public Buildings to continue investigation of defense housing program.	Lanham F.	Texas	Dem.
79	Continue investigation of Petroleum situation	Lea	California	Dem.
79	Authorize the investigation of the transportation situation	Lea	California	Dem.
79	Rivers and Harbors to investigate Shore and Beach Erosion	Mansfield	Texas	Dem.
79	Committee on Military Affairs to study the progress of the war effort	May A. J	Kentucky	Dem.
79	Education Committee to continue study of War Effects on Colleges and Universities	McCormack	Massachusetts	Dem.
79	Continue select committee on small business	Patman	Texas	Dem.
79	Continue Public Lands Committee study of use of lands for veterans' rehabilitation	Peterson J.	Florida	Dem.
79	Civil Service to continue investigation of Civil Service System and Civilian Employment	Ramspeck	Georgia	Dem.
79	Committee on World War Veterans' Legislation to investigate the Veterans' Administration	Rankin J.	Mississippi	Dem.
79	Continue the Special Committee to Investigate Replacement and Conservation of Wildlife	Robertson	Virginia	Dem.
79	Continue Committee on Roads investigation of the Federal road system	Robinson	Utah	Dem.
79	Investigation of the operation of the program for the disposition of surplus property.	Slaughter	Missouri	Dem.
79	Continue Committee To Investigate Acts of Executive Agencies Which Exceed Their Authority	Smith H.W.	Virginia	Dem.
79	Continue Judiciary investigation of two federal judges	Sumners H.	Texas	Dem.
79	Naval Affairs Committee study of progress of the war effort	Vinson C.	Georgia	Dem.
79	Select Committee on Postwar Military Policy	Woodrum C.	Virginia	Dem.

Table 1B. Investigations Authorized by the Senate, 1941–46

Congress	Investigation	Sponsor	State	Party
77	Interstate Commerce to investigate telegraph industry	Wheeler	Montana	Dem.
77	Special committee to investigate need for balanced budget	Tydings	Maryland	Dem.
77	Investigate Ross Eakin, the superintendent of Great Smoky Mountains National Park	McKellar	Tennessee	Dem.
77	Continue investigation of airplane crashes	Clark	Missouri	Dem.
77	Special committee to investigate operation of old-age pension system	Downey	California	Dem.
77	Continue La Follette Civil Liberties investigation	La Follette	Wisconsin	Ind.
77	Continue investigation of administration of public lands	McCarran	Nevada	Dem.
77	Study Irrigation and development of Missouri River	Bulow	South Dakota	Dem.
77	Truman Committee to investigate the national defense program and the handling of contracts	Truman	Missouri	Dem.
77	Byrd Committee on Non-Essential Activities (1941 Revenue Act)	Byrd	Virginia	Dem.
77	Development of Mineral Resources on public lands	O'Mahoney	Wyoming	Dem.
77	Special committee to investigate Gasoline and Petroleum Shortage	Maloney	Connecticut	Dem.
77	Agriculture Committee investigation of wool situation	Gillette	Iowa	Dem.
77	Continue Special Silver Committee	McCarran	Nevada	Dem.
77	Special committee on Senatorial Campaign Expenditures	Green	Rhode Island	Dem.
78	Use of Fuels West of the Mississippi River	Clark J.	Missouri	Dem.
78	Special committee on Post-War Economic Policy	George	Georgia	Dem.
78	Centralization of Heavy Industry in the United States	McCarran	Nevada	Dem.
78	Petroleum Resources	Brewster	Maine	Rep.
78	Special Committee on Presidential and Senatorial Campaign Expenditures in 1944	Green	Rhode Island	Dem.
78	Investigation concerning the disclosure of information obtained through censorship	Reed C.	Kansas	Rep.
78	Investigate whether rayon and synthetic products can be used as a substitute for cotton and wool	Bankhead	Alabama	Dem.
78	Investigate matters relating to the manufacture and distribution of farm machinery	Clark J.	Missouri	Dem.
78	Investigate the legal authority for Executive orders and departmental regulations	McCarran	Nevada	Dem.
78	Adjustment of Veterans into Civil Life	Clark J.	Missouri	Dem.
78	Investigation of the alcoholic-beverage industry	Scrugham	Nevada	Dem.
78	Investigation of Termination of Government Contracts	Murray	Montana	Dem.
79	Continue investigation of legal authority for Executive orders and departmental regulations	McCarran	Nevada	Dem.
79	Continue investigation of the use of public lands	McCarran	Nevada	Dem.
79	Continue investigation of silver situation	Thomas	Oklahoma	Dem.
79	Continue investigation of international communications by wire and radio	McFarland	Arizona	Dem.

79	Continue study and survey of the problems of American small business enterprises	Murray	Montana	Dem.
79	Continue investigation of the supply and distribution of hydroelectric power	McFarland	Arizona	Dem.
79	Continue special committee on Postwar Economic Policy and Planning	George	Georgia	Dem.
79	Investigate activities of the Securities and Exchange Commission and the Post Office in Florida	Pepper	Florida	Dem.
79	Continuing the Special Committee on Petroleum Policy	Brewster	Maine	Rep.
79	Continue the Special Committee to Investigate the Conservation of Wild Animal Life	Bailey	North Carolina	Dem.
79	Continue the investigation of war mobilization problems and war contracts matters	Kilgore	West Virginia	Dem.
79	Naval Affairs Committee to inspect naval establishments in Western Hemisphere	Walsh	Massachusetts	Dem.
79	Continue the investigation of the war program	Lucas	Illinois	Dem.
79	Continue the investigation of production, transportation, and marketing of wool	O'Mahoney	Wyoming	Dem.
79	Continue the investigation of airplane crashes	Bailey	North Carolina	Dem.
79	Continue study of distribution and use of health, personnel facilities, and related services	Pepper	Florida	Dem.
79	Investigate treatment by the Japanese of prisoners and civilians in the Philippines	Wilson	Iowa	Rep.
79	Investigate the disposal of the Government's interest in the *Nashville Tennessean*	Mckellar	Tennessee	Dem.
79	Investigate certain matters relating to food production and consumption	Thomas	Oklahoma	Dem.
79	Investigate economic and other conditions in the Philippine Islands	Tydings	Maryland	Dem.
79	Investigate the disposal of surplus government property and related problems	O'Mahoney	Wyoming	Dem.
79	Create special committee to investigate problems relating to atomic energy	McMahon	Connecticut	Dem.
79	Investigate matters relating to the handling of insolvent railroads	Wheeler	Montana	Dem.
79	Special Committee on reorganization of the Legislative Branch	La Follette	Wisconsin	Ind.
79	Special Committee on senatorial Campaign Contributions and Expenditures in 1946	Green T.	Rhode Island	Dem.
79	Investigate all phases of Social Security	Vandenberg	Michigan	Rep.

A handful of investigations had more than one sponsor; the table includes only the first sponsor in the *Congressional Record Index.*

TABLE 2. MEDIAN IDEOLOGY SCORES OF INVESTIGATION SPONSORS COMPARED TO FULL CHAMBER, 1941–45

	House investigation sponsors	House as whole	Difference between investigators and House median	Senate investigation sponsors	Senate as whole	Difference between investigators and Senate median
First NOMINATE Dimension (common space scores)	-.12	-.01	-.11	-.04	-.04	.00
Second NOMINATE Dimension (common space scores)	.57	.01	**.56**	.25	.18	**.07**

NOMINATE scores place members in two-dimensional space, with high scores representing greater conservatism. Common space scores are designed to place senators and representatives in a common ideological space, so that one can compare scores across chambers. A handful of Senate investigations had more than one sponsor. In computing descriptive statistics, each investigation has the same weight. Thus, if two senators cosponsored an investigation, each cosponsor has a weight of .5, so together they contribute the same amount in computing the descriptive statistics as does a single senator who solely sponsors an investigation.

in the House. Investigation sponsors in both chambers were relatively similar to their chamber as a whole on the first NOMINATE dimension, which taps into economic issues central to interparty divisions. Yet House investigation sponsors tended to be much more conservative than the House as a whole on the second NOMINATE dimension, which taps into civil rights and related sectional issues. By contrast, Senate investigation sponsors were representative of their chamber on the second dimension. In other words, knowing a representative's region and ideology (particularly the second dimension score) helps predict the likelihood of his or her sponsorship of a successful investigative resolution in the House, while the same information has little predictive power in the Senate. This evidence hints that there was a stronger policy basis for the House investigations than for those in the Senate. One possibility is that the conservative coalition—through its control of the Rules Committee—helped ensure that investigations sponsored by conservatives received favorable treatment in the House, while the more open Senate process afforded opportunities to a wider range of members. Another hypothesis is that individual senators' personal power interests were sufficient to encourage even liberal Democrats to undertake aggressive investigations during the war years, while representatives launched investigations of the executive branch only when their personal power goals coincided with their policy interests.

A comparison of the most wide-ranging wartime investigations in each chamber reinforces the quantitative evidence suggesting that ideological interests played a more prominent role in spurring House action to curb the executive branch than in the Senate. The Senate's leading investigation of the war effort was the Truman Committee. Chaired by loyal New Dealer Harry Truman (D-Mo.), the committee earned positive publicity for uncovering poor administrative practices.[56] Beyond seeking to defend Congress's institutional position, Truman was eager to undertake the inquiry because he saw an opportunity to promote sectoral and sectional interests important to his state: Truman argued that big eastern corporations had received a disproportionate share of contracts, and he used the committee to encourage a fairer distribution of the economic benefits from the wartime mobilization. While greatly bolstering Truman's national profile, the committee conducted its deliberations in an impartial, nonpartisan manner.[57] It challenged decisions by the executive branch, but did not seek to tarnish the administration's reputation or to convert its specific recommendations into a broad, ideological critique. As such, the committee's work received considerable praise from members of both parties.

By contrast, the leading House investigation of the war effort had an explicit ideological agenda, revealed even in its name: the Committee to Investigate Acts of Executive Agencies Beyond the Scope of Their Authority. The committee originated in late 1942 when conservatives Cox and Woodrum joined with GOP leader Joseph Martin (R-Mass.) in selecting

Howard Smith "to impugn bureaucratic excesses."[58] Smith drafted a resolution so broad that it "would throw open to inquiry any action, rule, procedure, regulation, order or directive taken or issued by any department or agency."[59] Republicans unanimously voted to establish the Smith Committee, as did ninety-two of ninety-seven southern Democrats, while northern Democrats were evenly divided on the proposal. As one might expect, analysis of the roll call reinforces the importance of conservatives' policy interests: conservatives were much more likely to support the investigation than were liberals.[60]

Driven by both an ideological and institutional agenda, the Smith Committee sought to show that executive agencies routinely abused their power and ignored the wishes of Congress. The committee conducted several damaging investigations, particularly of the Office of Price Administration, which conservatives disliked because it limited profits and was unsympathetic to rural interests.[61] Young argues that "it was not always clear whether the [Smith Committee] investigators wished only to improve OPA procedures by exposing delinquencies or whether they wished also to undermine confidence in the agency so that it might be the more readily scuttled."[62] Thus, the leading House investigators of the war effort used their committee power bases to undermine public support for key elements of the emerging wartime state. Senate investigations, by contrast, appear to have had a less clear ideological agenda, while still challenging executive dominance.

A final point worth emphasizing is that the wartime investigations garnered considerable public attention. From 1941 to 1945, a total of 208 front-page stories in the *New York Times* mentioned a proposed or ongoing congressional investigation.[63] There were 30 front-page stories in 1941. Coverage of investigations rose during the first two years of the war, reaching 48 front-page stories in 1942, and 46 the following year. Coverage dropped off in 1944—perhaps reflecting a shift in attention during the presidential election year—to a total of just 25 stories. But in 1945, the number of front-page stories mentioning a congressional investigation reached a high-water mark of 59. While the investigative topics varied across years, approximately 85 percent of the probes discussed in the *Times* involved oversight of executive agency operations or challenges to administration claims or policies.[64]

Stage 3: Systematizing the New Investigative Activism

The investigations boom during World War II was fueled by ambitious individual members seeking to make a name for themselves while challenging the executive branch and, often, promoting an ideological cause. As noted above, many of the investigations were conducted by temporary special committees. Although these investigations forced executive agencies to constantly look over their shoulders, critics within the Congress charged that reliance on ad hoc special committees resulted in duplication and inefficiency. Once the war had ended, reformers sought to systematize Congress's approach to executive oversight. Instead of relying on entrepreneurial individual members to launch investigations through the creation of new committees, the authors of the Legislative Reorganization Act of 1946 hoped to make oversight a permanent responsibility of House standing committees.[65] The act instructed each congressional standing committee to exercise "continuous watchfulness" over the agencies in its jurisdiction and provided each committee with professional staff.

The hearings conducted by the La Follette-Monroney Committee, which framed the Reorganization Act, suggested that members of both parties and all ideological stripes shared the belief that vigorous oversight was essential to maintaining Congress's institutional role. Liberal Democrat Jerry Voorhis took the lead in advocating more concerted oversight.[66] Voorhis initiated the act's provision assigning increased investigative responsibilities to each standing committee, arguing that "Congress should know from day to day whether powers granted by it are being properly used."[67] Voorhis testified before the La Follette-Monroney Committee that "conservative and progressive Members alike" agreed on the need for closer scrutiny of executive actions.[68] The subsequent testimony of Republicans Edward Rees and Homer Capehart and conservative Democrat William Poage echoed Voorhis's arguments about the need for better oversight.[69] Given such bipartisan support, the Reorganization Act's oversight provisions were adopted without controversy. Democratic Whip Robert Ramspeck (D-Ga.) summed up the consensus that Congress must transform its institutions to preserve its coequal role when he noted that "we are trying to keep up with this great, colossal executive government that we have expanded all over this country."[70]

The Reorganization Act was successful in shifting investigations from select committees to standing committees. Nonetheless, individual initiative continued to play an important role. The standing committees now had greater resources for oversight, but it was up to the individuals on each committee to make use of those resources. With the Democratic party still deeply divided and weak in the postwar years, Congress continued to undertake an array of aggressive investigations of the executive.[71] Important investigations during this period included the Senate Committee on Expenditures in the Executive Department's investigation of influence peddling by the White House staff (the "five percenters" investigation of 1949–50), the Senate Banking Committee investigation into corruption in the Reconstruction Finance Corporation (1950–51), the Senate Armed Services and Foreign Relations Committees' joint investigation into the Truman administration's handling of the Korean war, and Senator Joseph McCarthy's (R-Wisc.) probe of the State Department and Army. One can view the Reorganization Act as reducing the costs that individual members had to bear to launch investigations: well-staffed standing committees, often with subpoena power, afforded ambitious members numerous platforms from which to challenge the executive branch.

The postwar adoption of the Reorganization Act exemplifies the potential for Congress to respond creatively to presidential aggrandizement. Rather than defer to the expertise and capacity of the immense executive bureaucracy that had developed during the Depression and the war, Congress reformed its own structure to enhance its oversight of executive agencies and improved its access to internal sources of expertise. The collective action problems identified by Moe as a key source of the president's advantage in battles with Congress were overcome by entrepreneurial members motivated by both broad institutional concerns and individual ambition. These entrepreneurs packaged a pay raise and a new pension system along with the reorganization proposal in order to defuse opposition from members who stood to lose existing committee power bases. Reformer Mike Monroney (D-Okla.) liked to point out that the 1946 Act had been approved partly because of the "ice cream" provisions which made its "spinach" more palatable.[72] Along with the Administrative Procedure Act, the 1946 Reorganization underscored Congress's commitment to limiting executive discretion and defending its power in the postwar era. These formative acts did not undo the growth in the administrative state, but they did ensure that agencies would be subjected to dual, competing controls. Over the next several decades, presidents would undertake formative acts of their own, seeking to gain a degree of control of the bureaucracy commensurate with their political responsibility to ensure effective performance.[73] Neither branch has consistently emerged victorious in these institutional battles. The upshot has been a political formation characterized by two creative forces at either end of Pennsylvania Avenue, at times cooperating with one another but often wrestling for control of both policy formation and administration. The president's unilateral powers and influence over the legislative agenda afford far greater influence over policy content than any view of congressional dominance would allow; yet Congress is not debilitated by collective action problems, and has the resources to intervene aggressively in the administrative realm.[74] The critical question, taken up below, is when one can expect members of Congress to capitalize on these resources to challenge the executive.

Conclusion

What explains the difference between Congress's response to executive aggrandizement during World War II and its response in the current era? Why did individual members prove so effective in launching aggressive investigations in the 1940s, while Congress has shown far greater restraint today?

The potential intersections among members' multiple interests may illuminate this question. In the 1940s, conservative policy goals fused with individual members' power and electoral goals to fuel the numerous investigations of the executive branch. At the same time, the majority party during this period featured deep ideological divisions and weak leadership. As a result, the Democrats' formal party leaders lacked the resources to counter the ambitious entrepreneurs who sponsored the attacks on the executive branch. By contrast, in the current period, which has featured strong parties in Congress and (until recently) unified control of the branches, members' stake in congressional capacity and power has run afoul of majority party members' interest in fostering a favorable party reputation. Congressional Republicans have seen their ability to retain majority status as dependent on the White House's success, and as a result, they were loath to challenge the president publicly. Since the GOP's formal party leaders in Congress have had considerable tools for influencing rank-and-file behavior, this partisan interest has essentially trumped members' shared stake in defending congressional power.

But in the present context of strong legislative parties, divided control of the branches will likely once again give rise to aggressive efforts by Congress to check the executive branch. In this scenario, the majority's partisan interests reinforce members' broader interest in defending congressional power against executive encroachments. However, in contrast to the 1940s, one could expect the formal leaders of the majority party and senior committee chairmen, rather than backbenchers, to spearhead these efforts to check the executive branch. In the current centralized Congress, under divided party control, the majority party's formal leadership has both the incentives and the resources to mount substantial challenges to the executive branch. The Clinton years offer a case in point. After 1995, Republicans launched numerous investigations of executive branch wrongdoing. While individual investigators—such as Representative Dan Burton (R-Ind.) and Senator Fred Thompson (R-Tenn.)—played a prominent role, the investigations appear to have been part of a concerted party strategy, rather than bubbling up from the machinations of ambitious individual entrepreneurs.

These comparisons suggest two different modes through which members of Congress can solve the collective action problems highlighted by Moe, as well as the conditions under which each mode is likely to be adopted (see Table 3 for a summary). When parties in Congress are internally divided and weak, this affords space for individual entrepreneurial members to devise common carrier changes that challenge executive dominance. Consistent with Mayhew's study of postwar investigations, the presence of unified as opposed to divided control of Congress and the White

TABLE 3. HYPOTHESIZED RELATIONSHIP BETWEEN PARTY STRENGTH, OVERSIGHT, AND DIVIDED GOVERNMENT

	Divided party control	Unified party control
Strong formal party leadership in Congress	Party leadership-based oversight (e.g., 1995–2000)	Little oversight of executive (e.g., 2003–6)
Weak formal party leadership in Congress	Entrepreneur-based oversight (e.g., 1947–48, 1955–60)	Entrepreneur-based oversight (e.g., 1937–46)

House has little or no impact on the degree of investigative activism in this context because the majority party lacks the resources to block ambitious members who propose investigations.[75]

But in recent years, the majority party in Congress has gained firmer control of the committee system, particularly in the House. With the erosion of the seniority system, committee chairs are now much more dependent on formal party leaders for their positions. As a result, individual members are unlikely to be able to initiate successful investigations that are not part of their party's program. In this context, the presence of unified party control is likely to have a substantial impact on Congress's aggressiveness in overseeing the executive branch. The combination of strong parties and unified control of Congress and the White House generates minimal congressional oversight and maximal freedom for the president. Although some may interpret this as congressional abdication, it is worth noting that the dearth of oversight is rooted in the overlapping goals of the congressional majority and the White House, rather than in a debilitating collective action problem. Indeed, as the Clinton years demonstrate, divided party control in the present context of polarized parties is likely to result in much more aggressive oversight.

These comparisons suggest that entrepreneurs have played a significant role in defending congressional power, but that entrepreneur-based defenses are more likely in the context of weak parties. By contrast, in the present context of congressional centralization and fierce interparty warfare, the ability of members of Congress to challenge executive decision making rests much more heavily on the calculations of formal party leaders. It may well be that congressional investigations will have different systemic impacts depending on whether they are entrepreneur-driven or party leadership-driven. Entrepreneur-based defenses allow Congress to challenge the executive on numerous specific fronts, but may not be particularly good at offering a coherent, alternative policy vision. Party leadership-based defenses are more likely to offer a coordinated, alternative policy direction, but dependence on formal party leaders is also more likely to generate oscillation between periods of congressional assertion and abdication. The deepest challenge to congressional power today appears rooted not in collective action dilemmas, but instead in the close alignment between the congressional majority party and the White House when centralized party leadership, partisan warfare, and unified government coincide.

Chapter 15

Inventing the Institutional Presidency: Entrepreneurship and the Rise of the Bureau of the Budget, 1939–49

Andrew Rudalevige

Today the Office of Management and Budget (OMB) is the single largest agency in the Executive Office of the President (EOP), with more than five hundred staffers and an annual budget of about seventy million dollars. OMB is responsible for producing the president's budget proposal each year; for broad fiscal analysis; for policy advice and "central clearance" of proposed legislation, executive orders, enrolled bills, and draft regulations; and, more generally, for serving as the president's eyes and enforcer across the executive branch. Indeed, if presidential power is defined in terms of control over governmental outcomes, OMB is "a unique bulwark for the presidency."[1]

Yet midway through Franklin Roosevelt's administration, OMB—then known as the Bureau of the Budget (BOB)—hardly factored in the president's arsenal. The bureau had been created in 1921, but nearly two decades later it was, in the words of one long-time staffer, "a very small, very hidebound organization which viewed its main function as a . . . sort of green eyeshade manipulator of the figures in the budget book."[2] In 1939 it had barely forty professional employees, with little capacity to monitor executive branch activity and even less to change it. In fact BOB could only awkwardly be described as a presidential agency at all, housed as it was in the Treasury Department and led by an acting director who also served in that department.

By 1949 the picture had changed dramatically. The BOB appropriation had increased more than fifteenfold (see Figure 1); its staff levels had risen past five hundred; and it was housed in the Executive Office Building next to the White House. More important still, this expansion in personnel reflected a newly expansive role for the bureau within the presidential orbit. Many of the responsibilities for coordination, legislation, and management had already shifted to BOB. In acquiring them, BOB had displaced potential staff rivals and, as one observer put it in 1946, "grown into the most vital part of the Executive Office."[3]

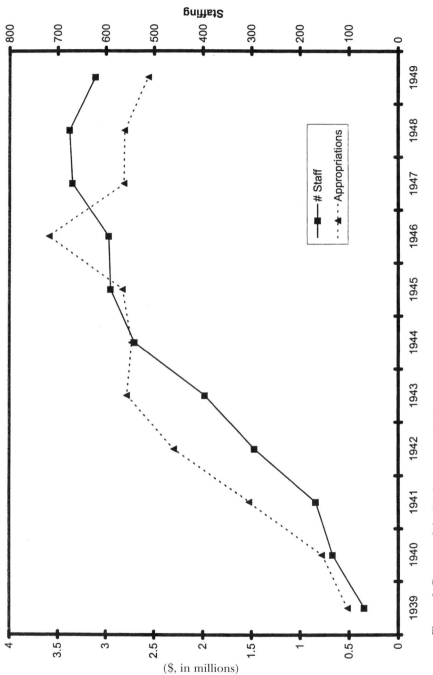

Figure 1. Bureau of the Budget appropriations and staffing, 1939–49, OMB records, National Archives.

How did this happen? And did it—and does it—matter? My point of departure in this chapter is an explanation offered by Ira Katznelson and his collaborators, who argue that the congressional coalitions of the 1930s and 1940s chose a "fiscal" over a "developmental" approach to the management of the national economy, and that BOB was the clear institutional winner in that choice.[4]

My argument here does not contradict that account, but complicates it in order to spotlight the actors it left offstage and their role in formulating consequential change. Congress's preference for "fiscalism" is, indeed, a necessary component of BOB's ascent. But it is not, in my view, sufficient in itself to explain the bureau's success or the products of that success. After all, BOB's own statecraft had a role in framing Congress's choices. No less significant is what the bureau provided the president as an institutional actor. Presidency-side variables were central in at least two senses: the growth of government during the Depression and World War II had created new demands for presidential management of bureaucracy; and the fortuitous placement of BOB astride the executive's one inescapable annual process gave it an indispensability not enjoyed by its bureaucratic competitors.

Even these factors, however, leave room for another explanatory element. If, as the Brownlow Committee famously declared in 1937, "the President needs help," the kind of help he was to receive was far from settled. Thus we must also pay attention to the bureau itself, and more specifically, to the actors within the bureau. These political entrepreneurs sought out ways the bureau could be of use to the president, and they shaped the development of the institutional presidency in the process. At the center of the action were two men, Budget Directors Harold D. Smith and James E. Webb, who between them ran the BOB from spring 1939 through early 1949. Smith guided the BOB's transformation into a full-blown presidential staff agency. Webb, later steward of NASA's race to the moon in the 1960s, made a nearly equivalent contribution in broadening BOB's utility to a new president in the postwar period.[5] Both proved dexterous in responding to the changing constraints and incentives they faced, whether imposed by history or Congress, and persistently sought to impress the presidency with the usefulness of their agency.

The consequences of their success go beyond fiscalism, though some are functions of it. Indeed, thriving in part because of opposition to state-driven development, the BOB's operations also reinforced that choice: the mechanisms of short-term budget cycles, not long-term industrial planning, were the tools future policy-makers had at hand. Another tool was the bureau's managerial reach into the executive agencies. When the political environment, and the consensus surrounding fiscalism, began to unravel in the late 1960s, the BOB could bolster the efforts of the "administrative presidency" to control bureaucratic processes and outcomes through management rather than via budgeting per se. The 1970 change from "Bureau of the Budget" to "Office of Management and Budget" presages President George W. Bush's Presidential Management Agenda, the most recent incarnation of a reinvention that has shaped the very ways in which presidents relate to the executive branch.[6]

Instrumental in all this was the conceptual design of the BOB as it facilitated strategic repositioning. It was to be an office of "the presidency," not "the president." But there was considerable room for creative manipulation of that boundary. The agency that resulted from Smith and Webb's exertions was not, as many more recent accretions have turned out to be, a pure staff extension of the White House. Nor did they foster the kind of nonpolitical, think-tank atmosphere that came to dominate the Council of Economic Advisers. These design alternatives are manifest in the EOP's varied staffs today, as is the unique position of OMB among them. In practice, positioning shapes both the kinds of advice presidents receive and the resources presidents have for projecting their authority across the interstices between the White House, the bureaucracy, and Congress.

I begin by briefly laying out existing accounts of BOB's ascent, making the case for using the lens of political entrepreneurship, and introducing Smith and Webb as the key entrepreneurs. Subsequent sections discuss the development of the agency in terms of the marketplace in which it found itself: the needs it observed, the products it provided, and the competition it faced. The conclusion highlights how individuals can operate creatively within a complex institutional context—and how their choices affect the development of American politics.

Political Entrepreneurs at the BOB: Formative Actors

What does it mean to call someone a political entrepreneur? Adam Sheingate suggests the term refers to self-motivated individuals within institutions whose "creative acts have transformative effects on politics, policies, or institutions." Such individuals exploit ambiguities in organizational mandates—both their own and those around them—to expand their authority and enlarge their horizons. Given the uncertainty fostered by a multifaceted institutional environment, different outcomes may be equally plausible a priori. Thus, as Sheingate notes in this volume, knowing the rules is not enough: understanding how (and how well) entrepreneurs play a given game provides important leverage on the specifics of the change that unfolds, and how this change might occur even in the absence of exogenous shock. As in the business setting where the terminology of entrepreneurialism arose, one can specify the market, the products offered those "customers," the competition among "sellers," and finally, as Sheingate puts it, how and whether actors manage to "consolidate [their] innovations into lasting change," forging a new institutional equilibrium.[7]

As noted earlier, one way to view the BOB's development is to stress external forces, if not from outside the government at least from outside the executive branch. Katznelson and Pietrykowski argue that the crucial question during the "long 1930s" was not whether the state should be strong or weak, but what approach the newly strong state should take to the federal role in the economy. One option, relying on fiscal or budgetary instruments, focused on the mechanisms of taxing and spending. "Developmentalism," on the other hand, was far more planning-oriented and interventionist in markets and manpower policy. Though the latter probably flowed more naturally from the New Deal, Congress chose the former, driven by a coalition of Republicans and Southern Democrats eager to undercut the potential power of organized labor or wall off government interference in labor markets that might intrude on the South's racial caste system. Thus BOB prospered, while developmentalist agencies like the National Resources Planning Board (NRPB) were starved and ultimately displaced. Furthermore, within BOB, the Fiscal Division gained prominence, staff, and an increasing share of spending.

Because the Katznelson and Pietrykowski account highlights the nexus between organization and policy outputs, it is most interested in BOB looking *outward*, as a policy instrument for the state. The divergence of BOB and NRPB, for example, is put "in terms of an understanding of the alternative kinds of state-market transactions that each agency embodied in administrative terms."[8]

Such an approach, though, downplays the perspective of BOB looking *inward*—the relationship of BOB to the president as part of the president's staff in a burgeoning "institutional presidency." Presidency-centered literature on the development of the executive office argues that to understand the dynamics of presidential leadership it is vital to see the "presidential branch" as distinct from the wider executive branch.[9] Key decisions about that branch's design and operation were made at both ends of Pennsylvania Avenue. Those decisions were not entirely exogenous: the BOB worked hard to shape legislators' choices about its competitor organizations, even as it benefited from their default preferences. Moreover, with a mandate and a structural position at the center of relations between the president, Congress, and a sprawling bureaucracy, it offered its leaders ample leverage to expand their domain on all fronts. Entrepreneurial directors offered presidents in particular an ever fresh and attractive series of options, keeping them supplied with the tools to strengthen their hand against the wider bureaucracy and Congress. As the bureau saw things, it was not a proxy for congressional policy but an instrument in its own right, one with a different major player as its principal. Examining the match between presidential needs and the bureau's internal (and interbureaucratic) efforts helps explain why the bureau grew so much before 1943, when NRPB was dismantled, as well as its tra-

Inventing the Institutional Presidency

jectory after the war. As Webb's successor reported happily to his senior staff in 1950, "President greatly pleased. . . . President's reliance on the Bureau constantly increasing."[10]

This suggests the utility of using the entrepreneurship framework to analyze the impact of Harold Smith and James Webb on the development of BOB and the presidency. Smith and Webb assessed the market for their agency's staff services and the structure of the marketplace in which they operated. They observed disequilibria in what we might term the president's bargaining market and tailored those services to the varying needs of the presidential office. As a 1948 BOB memo observed, "Authorities and prerogatives among staff units are meaningless if the President finds the services rendered unsatisfactory and must turn elsewhere for assistance."[11] Smith and Webb dreaded that outcome, and avoided it.

The two men were different enough from one another that they might not appreciate our pairing them. Smith was both a scholar and practitioner of public administration. He entered the Roosevelt administration not as a New Deal partisan, but as a registered Republican, having served as an elected county supervisor and in other municipal posts before becoming budget director for the state of Michigan. Nor did he seem much of a salesman. Indeed, with his subdued, "rather plain" personality and cheap suits, Smith seemed in some ways an unlikely entrepreneur. His passion was seemingly for process, not people: "The individuals come and go," Smith wrote in his diary, "but the organization remains."

Webb, on the other hand, was extraordinarily energetic: "trying to make conversation with [him] is like trying to drink out of a fire hydrant," noted one contemporary. He came from partisan politics, the private sector, and the Marines; at the time of his appointment he was working as executive assistant to Treasury undersecretary Max Gardner, former governor of North Carolina. Treasury chief John Snyder, partly to forestall another Cabinet member's favored candidate, recommended Webb to President Truman.[12]

But despite their divergent backgrounds and personalities, the two men shared the key goal of strengthening the presidency. For Smith, public administration empowered democratic governance by allowing government to fulfill the public good. Since Congress had too little information and too few incentives to overcome its parochial limitations, only the presidency could make government work in the national interest. To do otherwise was simply dangerous in light of the massive challenges facing the United States and the world. To "atomize Presidential authority," Smith wrote to Roosevelt, would "render the Government impotent to plan and coordinate the vast adjustments in policy and operations that postwar conditions will require."

Likewise, for Webb, "for democracy to work, bureaucracy had to function." That meant effective use of presidential resources—resources he felt he could provide. Webb was personally ambitious, managerially astute, and politically deft, a student of both organizations and power. "He consciously thought about how to strengthen the capacities of his organization to do its job," noted one biographer—and for Webb, "his organization" was both the bureau and the presidency. Thus one priority would be to lower the barriers between the two.[13]

With these goals in mind, Smith and Webb sequentially took the Bureau of the Budget from a small accounting arm of the Treasury Department to the heart of the institutional presidency. As we shall see, both developed their brand of staff help to make it indispensable under changing circumstances and presidential needs.

The Presidential Market for "Machinery"

To consider how their contributions mattered we must start by considering those needs. The answer might begin with Franklin D. Roosevelt in 1919. That year, FDR, as assistant secretary of the Navy, testified to a House committee that departments should have a central "inspection force . . . that we could send first to one bureau and then to another, with authority to . . . dig out the facts for us." The same principle applied "in the case of the next higher step, the President," who needed "machinery which he has not got at the present time." For example, "he ought to have . . . someone who could come into my department at any time and see how I am running it, for his own satisfaction" as well as some means of overseeing legislative and spending proposals produced by the bureaucracy. "No President of the United States, as an individual," FDR observed, "has time to coordinate the hundreds of items of the different departments before they are sent to Congress."[14]

As Roosevelt's comments imply, at the time, the chief executive had little to say about the execution or even the formulation of the federal budget. Individual agencies sent requests directly to Congress, blissfully isolated from one another and from any sense of how initiatives might fit into national (or presidential) priorities. Two years later, in 1921, the Budget and Accounting Act gave the president annual responsibility for preparing a unified executive budget and provided the Bureau of the Budget to help him do it. The bureau was placed within the Treasury Department, though it reported to the president and its director was to be appointed without Senate confirmation. It had the authority to "assemble, correlate, revise, reduce, or increase the estimates of the several departments or establishments" and to study executive branch organizations in order to make them more efficient. The idea, as one journalist put it, was to give the president "the instruments with which to work" as he surveyed "the biggest business in the world."[15]

Even so, BOB was widely viewed not as truly presidential but as an adjunct of Treasury. Many agencies never realized for whom the bureau was supposed to speak. This confusion was reinforced by the organizational stance of the bureau itself. When BOB's first director, Charles G. Dawes, announced "The Basic Principles of Budget Operation in the United States" in June 1921, first on the list was that "The Budget Bureau must be impartial, impersonal, and non-political." BOB's job, Dawes argued, was to efficiently implement received policy, not to make policy, and he explicitly offered Congress its services in so doing.[16]

The BOB continued in this vein through the 1920s and 1930s, focusing nearly exclusively on cost-cutting throughout the government and never using its authority to conduct management or organizational studies.[17] The bureau rarely spent the entirety of its own appropriation, never grew beyond forty-five professional staffers, and as late as 1939 owned a total of one ancient adding machine and one calculator. With business booming, the "normalcy" presidents wanted little else. "I am for economy," intoned Calvin Coolidge in 1924. "After that I am for more economy."[18] This remained the focus of the bureau as boom became bust and then Depression, and even as the party of the presidency changed after 1932. Franklin Roosevelt, it should be recalled, was elected on a platform that urged reductions in expenditures and government waste. He saw little immediate need to change the institutional character of the BOB; his request for an Economy Act, for instance, cutting a wide array of appropriations, was largely written by new BOB head Lewis Douglas.

By September 1934, Douglas had resigned, angry at FDR's embrace of expensive relief programs. His replacement, Treasury career civil servant Daniel Bell, was less vitriolic about deficit spending but would make few structural or functional changes. Indeed, Bell served as acting director for the next five years while continuing to serve as assistant secretary of the Treasury. The dual roles did little to sort out bureaucratic confusion over the BOB's role. Nor did the agency involve itself much in substantive disputes. As Labor Secretary Frances Perkins asked the president at a meeting in late 1935, "should one refer to the Bureau of the Budget a question of policy? It seems a peculiar thing to do. . . . You say the Director of the Budget passes upon the question as to whether the project is worth the price?" Roosevelt demurred: "He gives me factual information about finances, that is all."[19] As this colloquy suggests, budgetary tracking remained BOB's focus.

Yet by now FDR was beginning to worry that the BOB's historical emphasis on cost-cutting left it too narrowly focused. He told Louis Brownlow it "had never exercised its functions with respect to continuing examination of the organization because it had been led astray by General Dawes' decision . . . [to] keep a small staff and thereby be an example of economy to other bureaus," a "precept . . . followed by other budget directors."[20]

Presidents, including Roosevelt, had encouraged that precept. But the administrative and budgetary landscape had been dramatically changed by the Depression and New Deal. The bureau's chief customer thus wanted new tools. And by 1939 the bureau was, at least in theory, in a position to provide them. In 1936, worried that the proliferation of agencies and program responsibilities threatened to overwhelm the presidency's administrative capacity (and were a political liability, besides), Roosevelt had assigned a small panel under Brownlow to find a means to enhance that capacity. The Brownlow Committee soon urged strengthening the president's hand toward the executive branch by giving him formal control of independent agencies and commissions and federal personnel, creating an Executive Office of the President (EOP) to serve his political and managerial staff needs. In the fall of 1939, by reorganization plan and executive order, Roosevelt created the EOP. The White House Office (WHO), BOB, National Resources Planning Board, and Office of Emergency Management were its key elements.[21]

It is worth noting that the Brownlow recommendations, entangled as they became in Roosevelt's efforts to "pack" the Supreme Court, were denounced in Congress as a new bid for dictatorship. The 1939 Reorganization Act was a shadow of the original draft and limited presidential authority on congressional terms, truncating executive power over personnel and independent agencies.[22] But that fact made the president's need for the tools the EOP *could* provide all the more pressing. Roosevelt craved information and coordination, the "machinery" to unite the executive branch behind his priorities and preferences. Four services in particular were required:

1. Enhanced budgetary analysis, rather than simple compilation of agency requests, to provide both information about what the departments were up to and a substantive sense of the worth of those endeavors: to determine, that is, whether the "project was worth the price."
2. Organizational analysis, to reorganize agencies and organize new ones effectively (in a way that enhanced executive capacity), as well as to advise agencies on how to manage everything from procurement to personnel.
3. Policy and program analysis and advice independent of departmental viewpoints.
4. Central clearance of legislation, enrolled bills, and departmental testimony, to provide a chokepoint over transactions between "his" executive branch and Congress.

The relative weight of these needs would vary over time: what Roosevelt sought in 1939 differed from his requirements at the height of World War II, and from Truman's in facing an opposition Congress in 1947-48. But all shared the same basic function of providing presidents with a government-wide view and ability to coordinate a wide-flung bureaucracy. In 1946, Harold Smith summed up:

> To help [the president] work out the program of the Government . . . [it is] absolutely necessary to have a separate staff operating in a detached, objective atmosphere to supply him with information and to check all information that came in. . . . [Where Cabinet officers are concerned] neither their judgments nor their facts can be altogether trusted—not because they are in any way dishonest men, but because their facts and their judgments are colored by personal ambitions and their operating experience in only a segment of the government. [The president] must be so well-equipped that [he] can direct the heads of departments and say, "here's what I want done and here's what I do not want done."[23]

The Bureau of the Budget Product Line

Enabling the president to be "well-equipped" to manage and lead, Smith and Webb realized, meant developing BOB not as budget staff per se but as staff for a new presidency that was to be organized, in no small measure, around the budget.[24] Upon taking office in 1939, therefore, Smith immediately set out to expand the bureau's functionality, formulating reorganization plans that built BOB around the ability to perform the four sets of tasks above. Webb further expanded the bureau's repertoire in ways that reflected the postwar political environment and shaped how presidents would receive advice—and exercise power—to the present day.

Budget analysis. The Estimates Division, charged with formulating the executive budget, remained the heart of the bureau. Smith, though, gave it more and better-qualified people, less routine paperwork, and a new structure, grouping analysts around the functional tasks of government (military affairs, social welfare programs, and so forth). Four new bureau field offices, intended to keep BOB "in closer touch with the major administrative and social problems growing out of Federal programs throughout the country," also gathered intelligence on public opinion and the like. Abroad, bureau staff conducted field surveys of the various theaters of military operations during World War II.[25]

The war, of course, greatly increased the division's workload. By fiscal 1940, defense expenditures hit $5 billion, more than the entire budget when Roosevelt took office. A series of executive orders assigned the bureau responsibility for functions ranging from personnel classification to public works planning. FDR did not want to spend money on pork projects irrelevant to the war; this set off an impoundment battle between the president and Congress, with the bureau used (as by President Nixon much later) as Roosevelt's main weapon.[26]

After the war, many aspects of the EOP were (to use BOB staffer Richard Neustadt's phrase) "frantically uncertain," and the president desperately needed reliable information.[27] Under Webb, even more than under Smith, the bureau would leverage the budget process both to garner intelligence and as a positive function for policy formulation through the fortified process of central clearance discussed below.

Organizational analysis. Smith and Webb realized that reorganization and management issues affected presidential power stakes. Aggressive study of administrative management across the entire executive branch became a mechanism by which presidents could increase control over department and agency behavior. As Webb told Navy Secretary James Forrestal, "We are not interested in having you organize the President. The President will organize *you.*"[28]

BOB's managerial authority traced back to the Budget and Accounting Act, but had lain dormant since 1921. One of Smith's first moves was to hire public administration specialist Donald Stone to head a new Division of Administrative Management (DAM) and direct it into that potential growth area. An early problem with one New Deal agency struck Smith as "an opportunity for the Budget office to demonstrate in practical terms what it means to render assistance to the President in matters of management." Being able to do so, he thought, "may mean the difference between success and failure in this new function." Soon Smith started drumming up additional business for the new division, asking Roosevelt in 1939 to tell the executive agencies "he desired the Budget Office to assist with their problems." This included not only long-term study of broken organizations, but also timely efforts to defuse departmental turf feuds. Such delegation became a given during the war, which, Pendleton Herring wrote, "posed the most stupendous set of problems in the management of public activities that the country has ever faced."[29] The DAM staff grew from zero to seventy-seven by 1942 and to more than a hundred at the height of World War II. With a new BOB Defense Projects Unit created in 1941 to optimize governmental management of its new agencies and tasks, BOB was charged both with conversion to a wartime footing and (in conjunction—and competition—with OWMR, as discussed below) with reconversion to peace. Its stature was enhanced by its staff's near-monopoly on detailed knowledge of the rapidly expanding federal government.[30]

As the war faded, so did BOB's proactive influence over management issues. In 1949, however, a President's Management Program launched through BOB was charged to improve program analysis and review and "strengthen agency management practices and provide for continuous review and improvement of federal programs and operations." An advisory committee on management was created along with a fund for financing private-sector research on specific management issues.[31]

Program analysis and formulation. In the original Brownlow conception, policy formulation was vested not in EOP but in the departments. But under Smith—"rather covertly," in Neustadt's view—BOB began to build a policy and program staff.[32] One means was the Fiscal Division, created in

1939. As Katznelson and Pietrykowski note, Fiscal was a staff "charged with placing budgeting in the context of larger economic and financial trends."[33] But it served purely presidential ends as well. Its expertise in revenue projection helped Smith give Roosevelt, unhappy with Treasury's consistently low revenue estimates (which raised deficit projections), an alternate source of credible data. The division also worked to "sell" budget policy to the public, analyzing media reaction to budget messages and calculating how presidential budget requests compared to congressional spending. A third task was analysis of specific government programs' economic impact to provide the president with guidance about programmatic alternatives and specific budget decisions. In all, as Alfred Dick Sander argues, the division "enhanced the sophistication of the budget messages and the bureau's policy recommendations."[34]

Central clearance. With the creation of the Council of Economic Advisers (CEA) in 1946, the rationale for a separate economic team in BOB faded, and by 1952 the Fiscal Division was largely defunct. However, the bureau remained actively involved in policy advising through the mechanism of central clearance, managed by the Legislative Reference Division (LRD). LRD replaced the Division of Coordination, which in 1938 had inherited the clearance function housed in, but only sporadically used by, the cabinet-level National Emergency Council. Smith saw the potential behind the drab exterior. He thought "Legislative Reference" sounded prudently non-threatening to legislators, but the idea was for the new LRD to be more powerful, not less. In 1939 it processed departmental comments on some 2,400 pending bills (up from 300 in 1935), and on more than 400 drafts of proposed legislation (up from 170).

Even so, departments often evaded its reach. As Smith told President Truman, as late as 1946, "clearances—if at all—were more by accident than by design." The exception was in the area of enrolled bills awaiting presidential signature or veto. Gathering comment on these provided the bureau with a wealth of information across different policy areas and helped forge new departmental contacts. Smith strove to have LRD, working with Estimates staff, present a view that gave Roosevelt an objective analysis of projects' pros and cons. Pressures to downgrade "mathematical considerations" in favor of "political and psychological factors" were strongly resisted. Political factors were not excluded, however, but were the icing on the analytical cake. Since the president had personal staff at hand for political advice, Smith felt his special advantage lay in making the substantive case for and against a bill. At that point the president could make his own decisions, weighted by whatever considerations he saw fit.[35]

Under Webb the bureau modified and expanded the clearance process to identify, develop, and promote a priority set of presidential legislation: in short, to manage a presidential program. Two developments made such a program desirable. The 1946 Employment Act required the president to present an agenda for governmental action across the economy—which had to be harmonized with the State of the Union and Budget messages. And the 1947 Republican takeover of Congress made the GOP's purported "do-nothing" record fair game for the 1948 campaign. To take advantage of this, the president would need a wide-ranging and detailed legislative program of his own.[36]

Who would provide such a program? BOB was not the only possibility, so this topic provides a useful case study of the competition in which Webb and BOB were engaged within the EOP. Detailed discussion comes below, but it is worth noting here that Webb won the battle by taking advantage of BOB's previous connections across the bureaucracy and linking his staff directly to the president's personal staff in ways that made the bureau a crucial underpinning for White House operations.

Bringing the machinery to life. By 1945, an internal BOB memo observed that the "Bureau is essentially a management arm of the president. While it prepares an annual budget . . . those functions account for only a minority of its functions."[37] That could not have been said in 1939. Webb would soon add a process of formulating, refining, and promoting a presidential legislative program. All told, the machinery available to the president within the EOP had been dramatically upgraded.

In this vein, it is important to note that the organizational changes described here were only skeletal instruments: they needed to be given life by personnel able to make function follow form. Smith, especially, took great pains in choosing staff who would meet these criteria, even hiring outside the civil service "to try them out" before making them careerists. He did not want accountants as examiners, or staff with myopic "technical training"; he sought instead policy analysts, "people with sufficiently broad background and experience, who at the same time have balanced outlook and judgment concerning governmental problems," people with "training in the social sciences" and "planning type of minds." And he demanded too the *cultural* depth he associated with public administration: "how narrow are the interests of some of these young people," he complained. "They read almost nothing but the newspaper, take part in no outside organizations." As Smith added his kind of people, the culture of the bureau began to change; he gave "the Bureau a tone—an elite quality."[38]

Webb stirred that mix vigorously. BOB's new energy in the late 1940s, one observer has noted, "came largely from contagion," as its director's enthusiasm for what the agency could do spread through the divisions. Webb made sure the White House itself was infected as well. BOB's Elmer Staats would recall, "Given the close adjunct relationship . . . with the [White House] counsel's office . . . we were never quite sure who were working for, the budget director or the counsel. But that didn't really make too much difference."[39] Webb had made personnel a product in itself.

Indeed, many bureau staffers eventually made a formal move to the

White House—a direct result of Webb's desire for better connections with the two key WHO power centers, led by Truman aides John Steelman and Charles Murphy. David Stowe recalls that Webb complained that "'Steelman's getting into some of my business.' So I went over [to work at the White House]," and successfully defused the situation. Murphy, recounting how he came to hire David Bell, recalls that

> Jim then started, I think, figuring that . . . he might get things done better in the White House if he could sort of guide them. It wasn't long before I was getting pretty busy, and he offered—said I should have an assistant. And I said, "I don't need an assistant." Well, he insisted that I needed an assistant and . . . he said "I'll give you anyone in the BOB that you want."[40]

As this sequence suggests, Webb was sensitive and responsive to Truman's political interests—positioning BOB in ways that made it indistinguishable at the edges from Truman's White House staff. This marked a shift in administrative philosophy and agency strategy from the Smith years. It succeeded, as Smith's strategy had, in large part because it provided new tools of practical utility to the president. Prior to the revamped LRD function, for example, the White House had no way to control systematically what was being designated "in accord" with the President's program; this had been left up to the career budget examiners. Thus over time, BOB's new functions added a layer of responsiveness and presidential control to bureaucratic management, broadly defined, giving the president a structural underlay linking budgetary, legislative, and political advice. Smith and Webb had fashioned a product they felt presidents would want to buy, indeed, one that they could not resist.

Fending Off the Competition: NRPB, OWMR, CEA

Still, it was not always clear that BOB would be the purveyor of that product. The bureau was just one actor in an organizational and political marketplace. To emphasize the point (though at the risk of oversimplifying), this section will focus on three agencies that contended with BOB for presidential primacy: the National Resources Planning Board (NRPB, 1933–43), the Office of War Mobilization and Reconversion (OWMR, 1943–46), and the Council of Economic Advisers (CEA, 1946–). How did the agency fare vis-à-vis these competitors? And what did Smith and Webb add to BOB's assets in the competition? Putting the question this way helps isolate the role of entrepreneurship in what was, after all, a complex sequence of events; answering it requires setting the narrative above in a richer context.

BOB started play with at least three circumstantial advantages over its rivals. One was its institutional placement, firmly astride the routine of budget formulation. As the 1921–39 period showed, BOB could survive simply as compositor of the executive budget, "the prime general-purpose,

decision-and-action-forcing process" in government.[41] (Even a developmentalist state needs a budget.) However, the mechanics of preparing that
document could also, if utilized creatively, enable BOB to provide the president with a wide range of useful information on policy proposals and
agency maneuverings; Smith once told Webb that "the Bureau has survived
because its name concealed its function." It did not hurt that President Truman, especially, appreciated the minutiae of budgeting. Webb took full advantage of that in his personal dealings with the president.[42]

Second was the situation abroad. Hitler invaded Poland even as the EOP
was taking organizational form. American involvement in the hostilities
portended both more tasks for the federal government and less attention
from the president to domestic requirements. Smith claimed that in late
1944 he was delegated near total authority to compile the upcoming
budget, effectively moving into a policy-making role. The onset of total war
ratcheted up the need for both budgetary and organizational analysis, expertise the BOB was well positioned to provide.

Third was the general attitude of Congress toward the various EOP agencies and what they represented. The triumph of fiscalism noted above was
made possible by the coalition of convenience formed by Republicans and
Southern Democrats around issues involving enhanced government intervention in labor markets.[43] That alliance was strengthened dramatically in
the 1942 elections, when Republicans netted more than forty seats in the
House and nine in the Senate, mainly at the expense of northern, liberal
Democrats. It is not obvious that this was good news for BOB, which represented a general instrument for the presidential authority also under fire
by the right. But it was certainly bad news for agencies like NRPB.

These contexts bound the field of play, affecting the terms on which
BOB and other agencies competed. Yet they do not seem to have themselves dictated the outcomes.

NRPB. The NRPB was created as the National Planning Board in 1933.
After various organizational shifts it became a founding member of the
EOP, headed by a three-member "citizen board" and chaired by President
Roosevelt's uncle, Frederic A. Delano. It had a professional staff of administrators and planners and responsibility for long-term planning and policy
development as well as project coordination. Over ten years it published
some 370 reports on subjects ranging from natural resources to housing
and welfare to income and interest rates.[44] In 1943, however, NRPB was liq-
uidated by Congress.

BOB largely appears to have been the default beneficiary. Its relations
with the board were proper, if sometimes distant, though other agencies in
the wider bureaucracy with strong ties to Congress, such as the Corps of En-
gineers, were NRPB's active enemies. Within the EOP, BOB did gain a leg
up over NRPB during the war as a coordinator and purveyor of organizational advice to the president. Given the war's demanding immediacy, long-

term planning seemed superfluous, especially when significant victories had yet (as of early 1943) to be achieved.[45] If BOB was less controversial than NRPB, it also leveraged its options more effectively to appear more useful: thanks to Smith's efforts, it was active, directive, and efficient. Even before the war, there is little evidence that NRPB did much in the way of instrumental advising: "in general," Marion Clawson concludes, FDR "did not rely much on the Board as an action arm of his office." By 1943, with much else on his mind, the president was unwilling to commit much political capital to the Board's defense.[46]

And a vigorous defense would have been required. NRPB had very vague statutory authority, which had troubled its appropriations process since 1939. Its plural structure made unified action difficult, and its most vigorous member (Charles Merriam) despised not only Congress but, unhelpfully, his own staff director. Congress, as noted, had shifted to the right after 1942 and was inclined to resist any real or imagined abuses of executive authority.[47]

More broadly, as Katznelson points out, the very notion of national planning on a grand scale could not command a legislative majority. Wartime planning had been sold as an emergency, something apart from the regular economic order. Planning's opponents drew on a fear of centralized control with deep roots in American political culture, exacerbated by the nature of the governments with whom the U.S. was at war. NRPB's well publicized 1943 reports on postwar policy, envisioning as they did an expansive social agenda for peacetime, focused that fear on the agency.

The Board did itself no tactical favors in its legislative dealings. Relations with Congress were "simply awful," one study concludes; another finds that NRPB's "lack of support [was] not entirely to be laid to the unpopularity of its work. The board failed dismally in its lobbying obligations," refusing to engage Congress and then insulting it. By contrast, Smith was constantly before legislative committees, cleverly playing down his organization's new expansiveness by playing up its traditional ethic of economy. "Department heads are aggressive and imaginative and it is their job to spend money," he told appropriators; thus he required "sufficient staff to know in detail what those agencies are doing and what they propose to do. . . . [T]o do this would mean saving many times the cost."[48] But of course the mechanics of discovering "in detail what those agencies are doing" dramatically extended BOB's reach and utility. One scholar has speculated that different leadership might have done the same for NRPB, at least if a skilled bureaucratic infighter like Harold Ickes had maintained his centrality to the planning board's work.[49]

OWMR. The rise of the Office of War Mobilization, led by just such an infighter—FDR confidant James Byrnes—presented a new and more direct competitor to BOB, for both coordination and policy development. A 1943 executive order gave OWM sweeping responsibilities for "develop[ing] programs and establish[ing] policies for the maximum use of the nation's . . . resources for military and civilian needs" and, in so doing, for "unify[ing] the activities of the Federal government." In 1944 Congress would put OWM on a statutory basis, and add "Reconversion" to its title and authorities (hence "OWMR"). Since Roosevelt had assigned BOB many reconversion tasks as well, bureau staffers resented this intrusion into a battle they thought was already won.[50]

Smith had not hated NRPB, though he was happy to have BOB pick up some of its policy coordination functions. But Smith despised OWMR as an "abortion," as duplicative of BOB and far less effective. And he clashed frequently with Byrnes, who, in Smith's view, saw himself as "assistant president" and thus treated BOB as a subordinate staff agency, not as an equal institution. The structure of OWMR did effectively grant its director powers over the operating agencies, creating what one academic observer called "a monster from its inception." Worse still, to Smith's mind—and perhaps ultimately to Truman's—it was a congressional monster. As V. O. Key observed at the time, OWMR represented an entity "vested by statute with broad powers of direction essentially presidential in character, to be exercised, not in the name of, and by delegation from, the President, but in its own name by authority of Congress."[51]

Despite this, during the war OWMR won the battle to become the presidency's policy staff, handling the Atomic Energy Act and other legislative priorities. BOB provided presidents with a well-structured institution for management advice and general coordination. But while OWMR was never very organizationally coherent, Don K. Price pointed out it could do "enterprising and even brilliant work" that enabled the president to take on "current policy problems in a . . . selective and flexible way."[52] The agency provided presidents with an early version of today's Office of Policy Development—that is, with a White House staff. And by 1945 Truman desperately needed one. Smith constantly railed against Truman's aides, and while this viewpoint may have been embittered, it was not unfounded. Years later Richard Neustadt would remind an old colleague who had complained about the Kennedy inner circle that "You've mercifully forgotten the state of Truman's staff work circa 1945–46. . . . How could anything be worse than that?!"[53]

Such disequilibrium created its own opportunities. On the White House side, it was exploited by Clark Clifford, who became Truman's special counsel. But Smith was unable to make BOB the institutional beneficiary. Truman feared Smith had been too close to FDR to serve a new president well, and that his unsuccessful effort to merge CEA with BOB (see below) was simply a power grab. By early 1946, the bureau's status was at low ebb.

Webb's arrival turned the tide. Ironically, he was at first seen by bureau staff as an instrument for subordinating BOB to OWMR: Webb's patron, Treasury Secretary Snyder, had previously headed OWMR, and while there had wondered loudly "why policy is any business of the Budget Bureau." Webb was aware of OWMR's ambitions, but he had other ideas.[54]

One was to provide the small White House staff with reliable help. In December 1945, Truman had asked OWMR "to coordinate the whole administration program on legislation," but the assignment was fumbled. OWMR was not designed for the systematic and diplomatic clearance the task required.[55] Webb made sure to let the president know, through Clifford, that BOB could do the job. To prove it, in late 1946, Budget careerists were dispatched to work on the labor relations proposals in Truman's State of the Union address. When Congress began debating the Taft-Hartley bill, one of those staffers recalled, "Clifford used us as his personal staff to keep track of the progress of the legislation, and to analyze the various provisions. . . . And then we assisted him in drafting the veto message after the bill was enacted." "My dear Jim," Clifford wrote Webb, "the efforts of these men were of great value."[56] At the same time, as noted below, Webb began to build other legislative links that OWMR could not match.

By then, OWMR had been dismantled. Truman aide Charles Murphy later credited Webb specifically with this development. Webb, in interviews, suggested that John Snyder was its engineer—that Snyder, now at Treasury, did not want OWMR to remain in place as a power center for Steelman. But even if so, Webb was close to Snyder, and may have lent the Treasury secretary some useful talking points.[57] It did not help OWMR's cause that it had muffed its audition for building a legislative program in 1945. V. O. Key did not believe the agency "could be used to make a genuine difference in actual departmental operations"; Browlow Committee member Luther Gulick agreed that it fell short in developing a systematic positive program.[58] BOB had shown itself to be simply more useful, especially in a peacetime setting.

CEA. But BOB was still not the uncontested keeper of the president's program. The Council of Economic Advisers, created by the Employment Act of 1946, had responsibility for the Economic Report presenting the administration's agenda for economic growth and stability—potentially a large proportion of the overall program. CEA still exists, but it has remained a small unit specializing in an academic approach to economic analysis. One reason is that that CEA was the weakest alternative for economic planning offered during debate on the Employment Act. Its structure as a "detached group delivering learned reports" to both Congress and the president from an Olympian height of economic expertise tended to make it a less-than-fully presidential resource in the political and policy fray.[59] If nothing else its triple-headed nature would have made it difficult to exert a coordinative function effectively.

In the end, CEA proved more complement than competitor to BOB.[60] But at the time Smith read the similarities as a threat. "There can't be two Budgets," he told Commerce Secretary Henry Wallace, and lobbied to be-

come chairman of CEA while still directing BOB. This move was institutionally self-serving, certainly, but consistent with Smith's administrative philosophy and with his efforts (dating at least to 1944) to get Roosevelt to pay
renewed attention to EOP organization. An independent CEA, he argued,
would undercut a unified presidential planning and management capacity;
combining them would give the president new tools for executive effectiveness and force the EOP speak with one voice.[61]

When this failed, BOB adopted a strategy of killing with kindness. Indeed, CEA's continuity with BOB reflected the bureau's affirmative choice
to infiltrate and influence council decision-making. In 1946, with legislative
clearance still underpowered, Webb worried that CEA had real potential
for an active role in what might be termed a presidential growth industry.[62]
While the bureau officially took a "hands-off" position, Webb offered to
render whatever assistance CEA wanted, while gathering detailed intelligence about its intentions, motivations, and capacities, down to the ré-
sumés of its potential hires.[63] While CEA resisted BOB's efforts to have CEA
use Fiscal Division staff rather than hire its own economists, and to combine the Economic Report with the Budget Message, these Pyrrhic victories
meant it spent its budget hiring professional economists (some, in fact,
from the Fiscal Division). That, in turn, allowed BOB to provide the staff
necessary to expand its role in program coordination. It was able to make
the case, for instance, that "the President's program and budget recommendations must be equivalent" and, naturally, centered in Budget. CEA
and bureau calls for legislative proposals for 1947 were combined, but coordinated by BOB: "this discussion," a BOB memo cautioned, "should not
be taken to imply that the Council's staff will consider agency recommendations *de novo* or *in vacuo*." The bureau was to control that flow. Soon Legislative Reference Division staff sought to expand their role in evaluating
those proposals for the White House as well, calling it "the only way to do
a good job on this thing and keep our own hand in properly."[64]

A postscript. BOB likewise moved to forestall any role by CEA or any other
competitor in the other side of the clearance process: the link between
president and Congress. After the 1946 elections Webb named Republican
BOB careerist Roger Jones the bureau's legislative liaison. Since no White
House legislative affairs staff yet existed, Jones and other LRD staff expanded the bureau's ability to track program items' status, learn of forthcoming congressional plans, and mobilize what one staffer called "spot
salvage operations" on troubled proposals. It was even suggested that BOB
work to place candidates in congressional committee staff positions to give
the president better legislative connections, though "the initiative will have
to, at least, have the appearance of coming from Congress."[65]

In 1948, bureau efforts enabled the White House to "have a special message ready to go to Congress every Monday morning"; as the campaign progressed, LRD produced a checklist of items to be considered by the drafters

of 1949 messages even before the agency programs arrived. As assistant director Elmer Staats told the divisions, the bureau needed to give the president advice not only on the issues themselves (which of course needed to be "thoroughly canvassed") but on the "scope and relative emphasis in the messages on program, timing of introduction, relative administration priority, form of and responsibility for Congressional presentation, and possible upward or downward effects on budget allowances." This meant that even Budget careerists had to be sensitive to Truman's political interests when identifying items as part of the president's legislative program. By fall 1949, the large briefing book assembled for the White House compiled the proposals made by each department and gave both substantive and political assessments of each.[66]

Thus, a decade after the Coordination Division's creation, legislative clearance was institutionalized in departmental and presidential expectation. It connected the president to the bureaucracy, on the one hand, and to Congress, on the other.

The relationship of the bureau to Congress had moved even farther from Dawes's original conception. Smith had hoped to overcome the separation of powers by appealing to legislators' rationality, showing them the high caliber of information they could get if they relied on bureau staffing; indeed, he chided his staff for wasting time and effort on gathering intelligence about political doings in Congress. Webb, by contrast, saw Congress as predatory, to be placated where possible and defeated where not. Such an approach was a better fit with the presidential vantage, especially in 1947–48 but even during periods of unified government.[67]

All this made BOB a more political institution. Smith believed in service to the institution of the presidency, staying far away from temporary partisanship. He felt that the director should be the only political appointment in the bureau, and "something of a political eunuch." While Smith sometimes took on partisan assignments personally, he took care to distinguish them from his agency role. He met with Roosevelt alone and shielded the rest of the staff from temptation.[68]

Webb, dynamic where Smith was dry, instead saw the director's role as mobilizing the bureau as a whole to serve the "President's needs in all areas including political needs." Webb brought staff to meet with Truman, which helped acquaint the president with a wide range of BOB personnel and made him comfortable giving broader responsibility to the agency. He was also very willing to pass along political advice to the president. And in sharp contrast to Smith, he encouraged an upward flow of political advice within the bureau, which resulted in a stream of suggestions in various policy domains.[69]

There was a consequence here: while the bureau remained respected for its analytic capacity, by the late 1940s it was clearly seen at the other end of Pennsylvania Avenue as "the president's man." As a Congressman told the

BOB's Fred Lawton, "We can not consider your judgment wholly objective. We are willing to take facts, but when it comes to the interpretation of the facts . . . we get a little suspicious because you do represent the President."[70]

The Rise of the Bureau: Causes and Consequences

As we have seen, BOB *did* represent the president. Its ascent flowed from a combination of factors. It had procedural advantages, especially its placement with respect to the annual budget cycle and the legislative links it fostered. It had not just legislative history, but legislators' bias on its side, as Congress shaped even the presidential bargaining market by bounding the competition within the EOP and, at times, the EOP's very structure. Other agencies' missteps in navigating legislative and executive minefields also helped the bureau's cause. But BOB's leaders' concurrent skill at making the budget staff an indispensable underpinning for the broader White House operation must be considered as well. Roosevelt did not fight for NRPB, nor Truman for OWMR or CEA; they did fight for a larger and more authoritative Budget Bureau.

We must understand, then, not just the overarching regime but the shorter-term tools of organizational development sought by the presidency versus the bureaucracy, and versus Congress itself. The narrative above suggests the utility of using an entrepreneurial lens in so doing. We often speak of institutional evolution, but economics trump genetics, at least metaphorically, when it comes to explaining BOB's decade-long "golden age." What took place in the EOP was not natural selection, at least in the purest sense: there were not a thousand Budget Bureaus with distinct DNA and pursuing distinct strategies, the winner managing to reproduce. Instead, each director made choices that developed new attributes for the bureau. Those choices mattered for the sort of agency BOB became. BOB would have survived as an agency for budget compilation regardless, but its exercise of additional functions was hardly a matter of chance. Smith and Webb were the doctors Frankenstein who gave the organism brains, then legs.

We would not much care, if all that emerged was short-term bureaucratic advantage. But that short term had an impact on the long. Nearly six decades later, the bureau's successor agency remains a critical part of the president's staff resources. The maneuverings of Smith and Webb matter today for the kinds of tools presidents have at hand, and the kinds of advice they receive or do not. BOB was a particular *version* of the "president's man."

For instance, OMB capacity today flows from a key, indeed, perhaps the most basic, choice: endorsement of the view that "the President's program and budget recommendations must be equivalent." This was a triumph for BOB. But it was probably a defeat for broader analysis of national priorities outside the sphere of a balance sheet. Because the annual budget process is so complex and time-consuming—three fiscal years' worth of monitoring and preparation are ongoing at any one time—other functions are naturally subordinated to its demands. Scoring can outweigh substance. With the demise of NRPB, the Executive Office permanently lost its long-term planning capacity: the bureau was never well suited to moving outside the budget process to a broader view unobstructed by the pressing deadlines of the fiscal calendar.

Along these lines, it is worth noting that not all the functions and routines Smith and Webb established were equally consolidated. A key reason, perhaps, is that while those directors sought primarily to appeal to a market of one—the president—their institutional innovations also affected other players in government, and succeeded to the extent that those players accepted the changes. For example, the executive branch agencies and Congress both cared deeply about the president's capacity for control of administrative management and the development of legislative clearance into a process for formulating a presidential program. The latter quickly took hold: Webb's new product proved useful to those other players as well. Both legislators and bureaus found that the routinization of a presidential program served their own organizational needs. But bureaucracies have long resisted, and Congress often resents, presidential "control." The managerial capacity Smith built has thus been more difficult to sustain.[71]

Management functions have nonetheless been a vital component of the BOB legacy. Through the next two decades, the bureau continued to tinker with its management arm, successfully fending off outside efforts to create a separate Office of Administration and creating a new Office of Executive Management after an in-depth self-study. As the fiscalist consensus and the New Deal regime began to splinter in the 1960s, the bureau provided presidents with tools to traverse the new institutional landscape under their own power—without relying on congressional or bureaucratic assistance. Roy Ash, the architect of the 1970 reorganization into OMB, and later its director, argued that the bureau must "adequately enabl[e] the President to gain control of the vast Federal establishment." The tools of the new administrative presidency—asserting unilateral authority over governmental structures, personnel, processes, and thus outcomes—would have been recognized by the old Division of Administrative Management. But they became increasingly important to presidents. In 1981 central clearance was extended to departments' proposed regulations. In 1994 OMB created "resource management offices" designed to link management and budget more closely. In 2001 George W. Bush announced OMB would oversee a "President's Management Agenda" to systematically review federal programs for managerial effectiveness and put thousands of government jobs out to bid against the private sector. As Sheingate notes in a related context, "American institutions frustrate action. Entrepreneurial

politics . . . charts the effects of institutional innovations designed to overcome this frustration." Presidents' administrative strategies have relied on
BOB/OMB to do just that.[72]

Still, as suggested above, the agency has rarely given presidents all they
wanted in this area. This is itself an important piece of the BOB's legacy. In
part, it shows that the day-to-day demands of the budgetary process can
drive out even management concerns. But it also flows from the very nature of OMB. While BOB moved to a distinctly presidential position under
Webb, it retained the "neutral competence" so valuable to effective administration: that is, it saw its role as serving primarily the office of the presidency, as opposed to any particular president. That made it different from,
say, OWMR, with concurrent trade-offs. OWMR provided flexibility in discrete areas of policy formulation, but little systematic overview. BOB was excellent at coordination and at aggregating legislative policy proposals into
a comprehensive and consistent presidential program. But it was rarely a
generator of innovative policy ideas, nor was it a partisan tool. It made firm
legislative connections, but was unwilling to become the "stop on the lobby
trail" (in the LRD's phrase) that full-blown legislative liaison functions
would have required.[73]

Presidents, though, came to want these functions, to favor responsiveness over competence. As a result, over time the agency's pride of place as
the "president's man" lost ground to other institutional incarnations of that
role, largely to an increasing staff in the White House proper. President
Eisenhower created a White House legislative office. Policy-making assistants began to flourish in the West Wing, and by 1970 the Domestic Council was formally created to enhance centralized support for policy
development. The concurrent reorganization of BOB into OMB reflected,
as one 1967 internal memo put it, that new managerial demands would
"extend beyond the traditional role of the Bureau; nearly all of them are
opposed to the Bureau's traditional style."[74]

During this period many of the tools the "traditional style" Budget Bureau could provide presidents seemed less useful. For Roosevelt and Truman, bureaucratic coordination was politically beneficial. Facing the
nation's vast problems in the 1930s and 1940s required not only moral sua-
sion—not fearing fear itself—but also the translation of grand ideals into
effective organizations. But Nixon and his Republican successors more
often viewed government programs as problems in themselves. Presidents'
strategic reality also changed: in a time of (largely) unified government,
the legislative process was an attractive option; in a time of government retrenchment and economic stagnation, top-down budgeting and administrative control seemed more useful. As Sidney Milkis notes, presidents
sought to escape the bonds of their parties, to become independent actors.
Samuel Kernell nicely captures the broader shift in his description of "individualized," as opposed to "institutionalized" pluralism, where skill in a

permanent campaign became vital in fashioning coalitions from an atomized political populace.[75]

BOB in the 1940s, then, was a responsive agency, despite the "neutral competence" it embodied. But the kind of responsiveness presidents wanted changed, while the BOB's services did not, at least not as quickly. Its new brand of responsiveness, in the end, was largely imposed by outside forces rather driven by bureau leaders—a fact that only highlights the talents of Smith and Webb. Yet the story was not over. As budgetary concerns once more became paramount in the deficit politics that defined the 1980s and have continued nearly unabated, OMB regained its pride of place. Directors such as David Stockman, Richard Darman, and Leon Panetta used their own entrepreneurial energies to maneuver the agency across the new political terrain, well ahead of the pack. Fiscalism changed form, but continued to benefit OMB. Indeed, without the policy consensus that marked earlier eras, OMB was, if anything, more valuable to presidents, enabling it to deploy its expertise on many fronts of the "budget wars" against Congress.[76]

The structure of the executive office, then, from OMB to the White House policy staff, reflects the decisions made by, and about, BOB some sixty years ago, even where it reflects a presidential rejection of those choices. Smith's and Webb's vision of what made for a strong presidency, and thus "good government," largely lives on in OMB. Where presidents have sought more personal and partisan responsiveness than OMB can offer, they have added on to the institutional presidency Smith and Webb helped invent. In so doing, presidents may have helped themselves. It is perhaps less clear that they have helped the polity.

Chapter 16

Robust Action and the Strategic Use of Ambiguity in a Bureaucratic Cohort: FDA Officers and the Evolution of New Drug Regulations, 1950–70

Daniel P. Carpenter and Colin D. Moore

The stories Americans hear of "leadership," and "entrepreneurship" in politics are, by and large, stories of individuals. Their positions and roles may differ, from presidents (George Washington, Abraham Lincoln), to movement leaders (William Lloyd Garrison, Susan B. Anthony, Martin Luther King, Jr.), to legislators (Henry Clay, George Frisbee Hoar, Newt Gingrich), to bureaucrats (Gifford Pinchot, Harvey Wiley, David Lilienthal). But the stories (including many in this volume) essentially pivot on the agency of one person. The problem is that politics is shot through with organization—with parties, networks, bureaucracies, professions, unions, interest groups, and clubs. On this account, our most familiar stories often get it wrong. They assign *all* of the power and agency to the individual, when in fact the individual's success is highly dependent on his or her organizational context.

But how can an organization be entrepreneurial? If organization is required for successful political action, how does entrepreneurial action issue from organizations, which are fraught with disagreement, with collective action problems, and with uncertainty? This problem is only accentuated in government bureaucracies, which are complex, highly formalized organizations. Even though it is now widely agreed that public bureaucrats can and do take autonomous and entrepreneurial political action, the easy consensus on this question belies a harder problem that analysts of public organization have yet to tackle.[1] How do bureaucratic organizations become "entrepreneurial," politically robust, autonomous? An answer, we think, lies in two related concepts: the concept of a *bureaucratic cohort*, or an organizational "generation"—and the strategic use of ambiguity.

As in many complex organizations (corporations, legislatures, universities), bureaucratic change often occurs when a new and different cohort of members arrives to the agency and stays for a while.[2] Such a new cadre may simply displace an older generation, or (more commonly) the arrival of "new blood" will engender conflicts over control of organizational agendas and resources. Cohorts provide a minimal level of coordination based on shared experiences, education, and professional norms of the individual members. This is why, for instance, we expect a group of similarly situated cops or forest rangers to approach similar problems in nearly identical ways, even though their behavior is not explicitly coordinated. Members of a cohort, however, will certainly not see eye to eye on everything, and the small, but significant, individual differences in outlook and preferences will result in a certain degree of organizational ambiguity even where none is intended.

Whether undertaken by individuals or organizations, crucial political action is often highly ambiguous. At the time of their occurrence, the same events accrue different (sometimes inconsistent) interpretations from different audiences. In many cases this ambiguity is a direct and intended product of speech and action. As a pattern of behavior, organizational ambiguity can arise in several ways. If a cohort of organizational members is committed to a certain policy change or outlook, some individuals may be strategically ambiguous in the sense that they only partially or vaguely disclose their intentions and plans or communicate through a limited set of viscous metaphors or parables. They may wish to remain ambiguous so as to leave themselves multiple courses of future action, or they may wish to avoid a situation where their different audiences could "run with" what they say and use their words for other ends. In other cases ambiguity is less "strategic" and more a product of norms governing behavior. Officials may speak noncommittally and ambiguously because they fear doing the "wrong thing" by saying something contentious, explosive, inappropriate, or unapproved. Or, even without any individual variability at all, ambiguity can emerge from the "noise" and multidimensionality induced by lumpy, chaotic aggregation of voices and actions. Perfectly clear and forthcoming individuals may not be "on the same page."

Ambiguity, we think, can be strategic in two ways. First, a certain measure of ambiguity facilitates political success. Ambiguity allows diverse members of a cohort to share general visions of policy, even when they have substantive disagreements about particulars. Over time, ambiguity preserves coalitions and keeps open future courses of action. Second, ambiguity may be a behavioral pattern in organizations that is stable without being designed or intentional. In other words, *what appears to be centrally planned and coordinated entrepreneurship may in reality be a series of unintentional and adaptive actions that only look entrepreneurial in retrospect.* As a result, entrepreneurship in politics can be de facto as well as de jure; adaptive and stable as well as consciously strategic and intentional.

In this chapter, we explore patterns of ambiguity by examining one of the most important formative acts in the history of U.S. regulation: the evolution and elaboration of the new drug regulations of the 1950s and 1960s. Rule-making is one of the most consequential yet least individualized activities in which federal agencies engage. Autonomous and entrepreneurial activity happen readily in these contexts, but not (usually or entirely) through the actions of a single individual. Moreover, the in-depth, micro-level analysis of rule-making is, in political science and administrative law, one of the weakest features of contemporary scholarship. A narrative focus on the evolution of new and highly consequential federal rules can illuminate some of the uniquely political and bureaucratically autonomous features of the rule-making process. In this respect, the new drug regulations are useful because they were the result not of any one individual, but of several dozen FDA officials who began to dominate the agency in the 1950s.

As formative acts, the regulations of 1963 were especially significant. It is difficult to point to a more consequential set of federal rules in recent U.S. political and economic history; as a comparison, perhaps, consider the Environmental Protection Agency's National Ambient Air Quality Standards (NAAQS). The Investigational New Drug (IND) regulations of 1963 (and the ensuing rule-making) established new baselines for modern medical progress. They transformed science, creating the modern clinical trial industry. Terms that are taken for granted today—such as "Phase III clinical trials" and "bioequivalence"—were not the result of purely scientific dialogue and evolution; they were explicit, conscious, and political creations of federal regulation. The 1963 rules spelled the deathblow for thousands of existing and pipelined quack medications and treatments. They fundamentally transformed pharmaceutical firms, making R&D houses out of bulk manufacturers. Commentators ranging from Peltzman to Hilts have argued that, for better or worse, the IND regulations shifted tens of billions of dollars in economic, medical, and scientific activity.[3]

The IND rules are continually relevant to contemporary politics, with some actors (Michael Milken and many libertarians) suggesting that the rules should be relaxed, while others (Sidney Wolfe, many medical researchers, and many consumer activists) arguing that they should be strengthened. With the rising cost of health care an increasingly visible issue in American politics, with new ethical issues (embryonic stem-cell research, human subjects protection, fetal personhood) suffusing medicine and medical research, and with the safety of the nation's pharmaceutical supply coming under question in response to recent trends as well as fears of bioterrorism, federal rules governing clinical research touch on numerous and weighty political matters.

We elaborate our argument and our narrative as follows. First we define and discuss robust action and the strategic use of ambiguity. Then we relate the narrative of regulatory transformation at the FDA. We first describe changes in pharmacology, the pharmaceutical industry, and the FDA in the

1940s and 1950s that set an essential context for development. After review-ing the thalidomide tragedy of 1959–61, we discuss the evolution of the new drug regulations of 1963, focusing particularly on the action of a co-hort of officers at the FDA. We conclude the essay discursively, by suggest-ing cases for comparison and alluding to important limitations of our study, limitations that create a persuasive rationale for more extensive analysis of ambiguity in the politics of regulation and organizations.

Concepts: Cohorts, Robust Ambiguity, and Formative Action

As ironic as it is true, entrepreneurial political activity often depends on a degree of ambiguity for its success. A useful portrait of the strategic use of ambiguity emerges from the careful historical and theoretical scholarship of political scientists John Padgett and Chrisopher Ansell, who ask why Cosimo de Medici was able to rise to unprecedented political, economic, and social power in fifteenth-century Florence while remaining "in-scrutable" and "sphinxlike" in his rhetorical demeanor and personal style. Cosimo's wishes were always met, even as they were always unspoken or vaguely defined.

The answer lies in a logic of political legitimacy. Ambiguity allowed Cosimo to hold title to an identity of benevolence, disinterest, and neutral-ity. In part this was because his words were so few; observers and contem-poraries could not easily attribute specific motives, interests, resentments, emotions, or passions to Cosimo. This is not to say that Cosimo was dissem-bling or lying. Entrepreneurial action requires a degree of ambiguity, though that ambiguity need not be intentional. (Nor is it clear that Cosimo's style was consciously cultivated.) Rather, the sphinxlike character of Cosimo de Medici may have been part of his "personality." Cosimo also presented a personage of few words and even fewer expressions of prefer-ence, except for the granting of favors to numerous and diverse suppli-cants.

The model of Cosimo de Medici in Padgett and Ansell's work is not that of an individual who maximizes use of the formal authorities at his disposal or is able to stir audiences through impassioned homily. It is instead that of an individual positioned uniquely and securely at the interstices of multi-ple, cross-cutting networks. In Florentine political society, networks of kin-ship and patrimony, networks of neighborhood (*gonfalone*), and emergent networks of financial exchange were constitutive of identity and interest. Identifiable membership in one or more of these networks was sufficient to pin down an individual's preferences in the Florentine political economy.[4] What empowered Cosimo was his unique position at the *intersection* of these networks, or equivalently, the inability of any observer to infer his patterns of interest from his social affiliations and patterns of exchange.

Two features of this notion merit discussion. First, the prevalence of ambiguity stands in deliberate contrast to the predictions of many game-theoretic models, that under conditions of uncertainty, the most "powerful" players will have preferences that are well known, even extreme (for example, why it took a Richard Nixon to normalize relations with China; or that the best mediator in international conflict will be a known and biased agent).[5] These predictions are undoubtedly right in some cases. We might accord more trust to those with whom we vehemently disagree, because we know where they stand and we know that when they express moderation it is probably sincere. In many other political situations, however, known extremity of preferences poorly equips a political actor for leadership. In many situations where political audiences (voters, professionals, worshippers) demand legitimacy and credibility, known bias can only detract from an individual's ability to lead. Just as important, we witness many political and social scenarios in which individuals deliberately maintain ambiguity on issues. Nominees for federal judgeships and administrative positions often speak in general and noncommittal terms to the U.S. Senate. New members of a voting body (a faculty committee, a state legislature) often refrain from expressing strong views initially, building "political capital" that they can deploy later on. Accuracy in description and explanation of the political world, then, requires attention to ambiguity.

Second, the strategic use of ambiguity is not necessarily maximal ambiguity or deliberate obfuscation. In some cases, ambiguity is better served by refusal to articulate one's position than by flip-flopping or attempting to create confusion. Ambiguous agents are often described as "hard to read," their intentions emerging only after action and even then being subject to alternative interpretations after the fact. Often the course of robust political action is to make one's preferences known slowly, at first symbolically, and only later programmatically.

Ambiguity underlies pivotal agency not just in fifteenth-century Florence but also in numerous other contexts. In the making of twentieth-century New York City, urban planner Robert Moses participated in numerous and diverse networks of governance and power. And as his career is narrated in Robert Caro's *The Power Broker*, Moses maintained a highly inscrutable personal style, including thorough secrecy in administrative affairs. Ambiguity allowed Moses to move from one controversial project to another, and to retain a reputation as "money honest" even as he rewarded friends with contracts and punished enemies with their absence. He received broad applause for his planning abilities as "prudent," "practical," "businesslike," and "efficient" even as he wasted tens of millions of dollars.[6]

Rule-making provides an institutionalized venue for the strategic use of ambiguity. Ambiguity allows the politically astute bureaucrat to voice general principles without making a commitment to specific (and objectionable) programs and rules. Ambiguity may also allow for healthy discretion in future decision making, as pronouncements about how the agency "will rule" on a particular question may only hem in the ability of officials to translate their preferences into regulatory outcomes. Of course the institutional procedures of rule-making are fraught with political constraints and opportunities for the strategic participation of organized interests.[7] Yet it is also true that rule-making allows the most ensconced of federal officials the ability to mandate broad changes in social and economic activity. If rule-making officials (or cohorts) are able to secure public legitimacy, are able to assemble coalitions of "strange bedfellows" behind their activities, and are able to capitalize on political opportunities, they can achieve the translation of divergent bureaucratic goals into policy while bypassing entirely the legislative process.

With Cosimo de Medici and Robert Moses as canonical examples, our scholarly aim is to reinsert concepts from organizational theory into stories of political entrepreneurship. How could the politics of ambiguity be practiced by a loosely coordinated set of federal officials over a period of many years? In the making of rules governing the modern pharmaceutical economy, we see more than just organizations characterized by great leaders. Something broader was going on.

The Emergence of a Reform Cohort at the FDA

Important changes were taking place in medicine and in clinical research in the 1940s and 1950s, and chief among these was the advent of institutionalized research pharmacology. Originally a European import, pharmacology had begun to swell in popularity and power in the early twentieth century, particularly at the University of Michigan School of Medicine and Johns Hopkins University, under the quiet leadership of Dr. John Jacob Abel. Central to the pharmacological enterprise was the planning and execution of controlled clinical trials, usually with animals as subjects, later (in "clinical pharmacology") with humans. Important studies linking brain function to serotonin, the action of sulfanomides on bacteria, and introducing and assaying new antibiotics such as streptomycin, had been published in the 1940s and 1950s. What was central to these studies was not simply the chemical analysis of new compounds, but the experimental analysis (with human subjects) of the efficacy and safety of those compounds in medical therapeutics.[8]

At the FDA's Bureau of Medicine, a pivotal event was the arrival in 1950 of Ralph G. Smith, M.D., Ph.D., who left his position as professor and chair of Pharmacology at Tulane to join the Food and Drug Administration. Smith had spent time at Michigan as an associate professor of Pharmacology and was widely respected in research circles. Once Smith took over the New Drug Division of the Bureau of Medicine, a premium on training in clinical pharmacology was attached to bureau hiring decisions. Some had received Ph.D.s in pharmacology, and some (including Francis I. Kelsey and Frances Oldham Kelsey from the University of South Dakota) were established names in the field. Many others who descended on the bureau did so from university medical centers and pharmacology faculties, as Smith and his associates established active patterns of recruitment and solicitation from medical faculties where modern clinical research was most advanced.

The cohort of significance at the FDA was not restricted to the Bureau of Medicine but also populated other offices. A. J. Lehman, M.D., headed the FDA's Division of Pharmacology and frequently consulted on new drug applications in the 1950s. F. H. Wiley headed the Division of Pharmaceutical Chemistry and also took an increasingly active consultant-like role in new drug approval. San Francisco physician Ralph Weilerstein, M.D., who became a thorn in the side of organized pharmaceutical companies, was actively calling for investigations of pharmaceutical research and promotion before 1950. In the enforcement bureaus and the Commissioner's Office, John Harvey, William Goodrich, and J. Kenneth Kirk (who later penned many of the 1963 draft rules) joined an increasingly activist force of inspectors who launched an "anti-quackery" initiative. Many inspectors and district chemists of note in the cohort resided in one of the FDA's sixteen "districts," including George Daughters (chief, Chicago District) and E. C. Boudreaux (chief, New Orleans District). The new FDA cohort was not only both medical and pharmacological but also statistical and legal. It was populated by a generation of men who arrived to the agency in the aftermath of World War II and the expansionary era of the later Roosevelt Administration.

The emergence of a reform cohort at the 1950s FDA was *not* designed, requested, or anticipated by Congress, the White House, or other FDA clientele. The Citizens' Advisory Commission, for instance, was concerned mainly about aggregate staffing levels, not about what professional sorts of staff ought to be hired.[9] The Eisenhower Administration paid little attention to the FDA, and only later in the decade (after the cohort had arrived, crystallized, and cemented itself) did Senator Estes Kefauver of Tennessee play a significant oversight role in pharmaceutical regulation.

Rule-Making in the 1950s: The Rise of Efficacy Standards

Even before the Ralph Smith became the director of the Bureau of Medicine (BOM) in 1950, officials in the BOM were pushing for different and more stringent standards in pharmaceutical research. In a February 1949 speech to the American Pharmaceutical Manufacturers' Association (APMA), Erwin E. Nelson, chief of the New Drug Section of the BOM, provided one of the first clear indications of the FDA's symbolic push for more sophisticated research and basic efficacy requirements:

We believe that an application should contain a sound pharmacological study. The type and method of action in animals usually will have been determined in the screening tests which led to the selection of the drug for further investigation. . . . Besides observations in these early studies on efficacy and toxicity, the clinical trials must at an early stage define the procedures to be employed in more extensive studies by those who are chiefly interested in therapeutic efficacy. . . . While the fundamental concern of the new drug application is with the evidence for safety, the law also has a requirement to the effect that direction for use must be supplied. And these will have to do with both the safest and the most efficacious way of using the drug. In other words, the reports of the clinical trials will properly include not only observations on freedom from untoward reactions, but also evaluations of efficacy. As a matter of fact few investigators are willing to make studies of safety alone. *Safety without efficacy is of little significance.*[10]

Nelson's speech is significant not only for the rather radical language he employed, but for the indirect way that it approached the concept of efficacy. The 1938 Food, Drug, and Cosmetic Act had authorized the FDA to assess a drug's safety before approving it for interstate marketing; there was no mention of efficacy in the law, and attempts by legislators (Rep. Owen Harris, Sen. Estes Kefauver) to insert efficacy provisions in the 1940s and 1950s failed repeatedly.[11] For Nelson and the cohort that followed him, safety *implied* efficacy. This same philosophy was echoed by Ralph G. Smith, who wrote, "Safety and efficacy are the basic considerations in the introduction of a new drugs."[12] Smith articulated this idea again in a presentation to the staff of the Albert Einstein Medical Center on April 8, 1959. As he wrote, "Clinical studies with controls are received all too infrequently. Such experiments are useful in an evaluation not only of efficacy but of safety and side effects." Even Commissioner George Larrick, a man thought by many to be intimidated by the pharmaceutical industry, declared, in a 1957 address to the Annual Meeting of the APMA, "We are a scientific and technical agency. We are committed to progress but, gentlemen, it must be real progress. Since safety and efficacy are so intimately related, it follows that if the evidence for a new use justifies a major promotional effort, it should also be sufficient for a supplemental application."[13]

The new cohort's first tangible product—the July 25, 1956 new drug regulations, published in the *Federal Register*—provides evidence of the FDA's move to require more stringent scientific standards. Receiving input from Smith, Larrick, Medical Director William Kessenich, Assistant Commissioner John Harvey, and General Counsel William Goodrich, the 1956 rules were the most far-reaching amendments to U.S. pharmaceutical regulation since the 1938 Food, Drug, and Cosmetic Act. These rules were also the first to specify what should be included in a full clinical report:

An application may be incomplete or may be refused unless it includes full reports of adequate tests by all methods reasonably applicable to show whether or not the drug is safe for use as suggested in the proposed labeling. The reports ordinarily should include detailed data derived from appropriate animal and other biological experiments in which the methods used and the results obtained are clearly set forth. Reports of all clinical tests by experts, qualified by scientific training and experience to evaluate the safety of drugs, should be attached and ordinarily should include detailed information pertaining to each individual treated, including age, sex, conditions treated, dosage, frequency of administration, duration of administration of the drug, results of clinical and laboratory examinations made, and a full statement of any adverse effects and therapeutic results observed.[14]

The older rules that these regulations replaced concentrated almost exclusively on labeling issues and the purity of the chemical compounds in the drugs. These new rules, however, did not just require clinical trials, but actually suggested the use of animal tests, as well as mandated the use of "experts, qualified by scientific training and experience." Although often overlooked by contemporary commentators on the FDA, these regulations codified a new standard for pharmaceutical testing. While they do not go so far as to require actual *efficacy* tests, they do demonstrate the increasingly elaborate scientific practices demanded by the FDA in the 1950s. The 1956 rules, however, are as interesting for what they leave ambiguous as for what they make explicit. Our story of the push for higher efficacy standards is about a cohort's strategic use of ambiguity rather than bureaucratic autonomy. In no way do we wish to imply that the FDA was loudly and heroically flouting the law to demand tests of efficacy from pharmaceutical companies. Something much more interesting was happening.

The strategic use of ambiguity allows bureaucrats to voice principles and philosophical shifts, often while purposely refusing to articulate an exact policy. Specifically, this can be done by suggesting that new rules or philosophies seamlessly comport with established rules and practices, or by issuing many statements that leave requirements ambiguous, allowing bureaucrats to have maximum leverage without being held to specific, and in this case, illegal rules. It is plausible, then, that throughout the 1950s, regulations were *kept* unclear because this ambiguity allowed bureaucratic actors maximum discretion in their push for further efficacy. Yet it would be a step too far to claim that *all* of the ambiguity *was* intentional and rationalized ahead of time; the very concept of "efficacy" in medicine and pharmacology was ill-defined and subject to debate in the 1950s and 1960s, just as it is today. Whether intentional or not, the pattern of ambiguity allowed the FDA's cold war cohort to maintain legitimacy in multiple audiences and avoid a congressional backlash, while furthering the cohort's reform goals.

The evidence for this is especially rich. In one particularly revealing speech to the Antibiotic Symposium in 1959, William H. Kessenich, medical director for the Bureau of Medicine discussed the contemporary requirements for clinical investigations:

The investigations made are ordinarily expected to include full reports of adequate tests by all methods reasonably applicable. They should contain detailed data derived from appropriate animal or other biological experiments in which the methods used and the results obtained are clearly set forth. This usually means pharmacologic studies in animals and subsequent clinical investigations. . . . We can control claims for the efficacy of the drug only inasmuch as they directly involve safety. If, for example, a completely innocuous drug were to be offered for the treatment of a potentially fatal disease and the drug were shown to be worthless, we would have to express the opinion that to rely on such a drug would indeed be hazardous for the patient. . . . While we cannot prevent a new dug application from becoming effective on the basis of unsubstantiated claims unless such can be directly related to safety, the drugs when marketed are subject to the other provisions of the Federal Food, Drug, and Cosmetic Act.[15]

In this speech Kessenich acknowledges that his hands are tied with respect to efficacy standards, and yet leaves no doubt that the FDA will try, within legal limits, to enforce a certain standard of efficacy, perhaps through prosecution of improper labeling, or as he says in a classically ambiguous phrase, through the use of "other provisions of the Federal, Food, Drug, and Cosmetic Act." In other words, while Kessenich leaves no doubt in the minds of his audience members that the FDA would like to require efficacy tests, he also engages in some apt backpedaling.

Kessenich, it seems, was quite accustomed to this behavior. In response to a letter from Dr. Frederick Wolff, assistant professor of Medicine at Johns Hopkins, Kessenich acknowledges, "In the Food, Drug, and Cosmetic Act and the regulations thereunder there is no definition of what constitutes a qualified investigator and we have not established any criteria that must be met to be considered an expert capable of evaluating a drug." That said, however, Kessenich goes on to hint that, even if the FDA has no authority, "We do evaluate these studies to determine if safety has been demonstrated and we do give greater or lesser weight to a study depending on its quality. In making this evaluation we do attempt to consider all the factors which go to make up the value of a study, including such things as the design and accomplishment of the protocol, the thoroughness with which the study was carried out, the completeness with which it is reported, and the training and stature of the investigator and the clinical facilities available to the investigator."[16] In this expertly phrased letter, Kessenich both acknowledges the fact that the FDA cannot issue specific regulations for what does and does not qualify as a clinical test, but at the same time describes how the FDA does bring such information to bear on application evaluations.

The language of the new regime—notions of "therapeutic value," "safety-in-use," and "efficacy"; broad-based examination of drugs and their makers; and concern for the specification of standards for animal and clinical trials—also suffused the writings and addresses of district personnel, showing that the ideological cohort extended to the district level of the agency's organization. In speeches to state pharmacy associations, public health audiences, and industry representatives, FDA district chiefs like George Daughters (chief of the Chicago District) and E. C. Boudreaux (chief of the New Orleans District) brought new language and terms to their listeners and readers. Speaking at the (Michigan) Governor's Committee on Public Health in September 1956, Daughters said that the FDA's enforcement patterns guaranteed the "quality" of drugs, and gave as the standard for regulation that drugs, like other products, were "pure and wholesome, safe to use, made under sanitary conditions, and truthfully labeled." In listing his agency's responsibilities, drug-related items were the top two items mentioned in a list of nine "responsibilities." In Boudreaux's speeches, to university officials and pharmacists' meetings alike, he disclosed that problems of "health" dominated those of "sanitary conditions" and "economic fraud" in the district offices' ranking of priorities. Boudreaux also emphasized the novelty of his agency's new "equivalence" standard, such that the FDA was charged with determining "that each batch of the new drug is of identical composition." (Aside from antibiotics, no equivalence standard had yet been formulated for new drugs in federal law.) FDA chemist Horace Allen, in delivering a "public relations talk" to the 1956 Washington State Pharmacists' Postgraduate Refresher Course, described the task of his agency as the assurance of "safe, effective drugs," a responsibility that imposed a tradeoff on the agency's drug reviewers in Washington. Drugs could be approved for marketing only when the New Drug Division staff was "convinced through evaluation of the manufacturer's tests that their potentiality for good *far outweighed* the possibility of injury from their use."[17]

Back in Washington, officials outside the Bureau of Medicine helped elaborate the new structure and principles for regulation of new drugs. Associate Commissioner John Harvey and General Counsel William Goodrich outlined new principles and blankly stated that, what authority Congress was slow to give the FDA would accrue to the agency anyway through rule-making as an a form of administration. In other words, rule-making was separate from legislation, not delegated to the agency but rather a constitutional duty of the FDA as it administered existing law (that is, the 1938 Act). Harvey and Goodrich, and later General Counsel Kenneth Kirk, read broad new principles out of the 1938 legislation, including a general mandate for economic "fairness" to "the ultimate consumer for whom in a final sense we all work." Administrators in the Division of Antibiotics issued new rules that gave control over all antibiotic labeling to FDA medical officers. When new legislation was passed in 1963, many of these officials acted quickly to ensure that regulation of clinical development and efficacy was the foremost official consideration of numerous FDA offices, including inspection offices, the Division of

New Drugs, the Bureau of Biological and Physical Sciences, and the general counsel's office.[18]

All in all, the reach of the cohort lay far beyond what we can describe here. The importance of the "cohort" (as opposed to a collection of individuals) lies in the frequency with which these individual officers communicated with one another and cooperated on matters of general policy and public relations. Table 1 offers a summary (though incomplete) portrait of this cohort.

TABLE 1. SELECTED MEMBERS OF THE REFORM COHORT AT THE U.S. FOOD AND DRUG ADMINISTRATION, 1955–63

Division/Bureau of Medicine	Ralph G. Smith, M.D. (director) Albert "Jerry" Holland, M.D. (medical director) Ernest Q. King, M.D. (medical director before Holland) William Kessenich, M.D. (medical director after Holland) Irvin Kerlan, M.D. (medical officer, and head of Drug Reference Branch) Eugene M. K. Geiling, M.D., Ph.D. (consultant and medical officer, 1959–63) Barbara Moulton, M.D. (medical officer) Bert Vox, M.D., Ph.D. (medical officer, 1957– ; student of Geiling) Frances Oldham Kelsey, M.D., Ph.D. (medical officer, 1960– ; student of Geiling)
Bureau of Field Administration	Kenneth Milstead (chief, BFA) George T. Daughters (chief, Chicago District) E.C. Boudreaux (chief, New Orleans District) Ralph Weilerstein, M.D. (San Francisco District)
Bureau of Pharmacology	Robert S. Rose, Ph.D. (director) Geoffrey Woodard, Ph.D. (pharmacologist) M.R. Woodard, Ph.D. (pharmacologist) Francis I. Kelsey, M.D., Ph.D. (pharmacologist, 1960–)
Commissioner's Office, and General Counsel's Office	John L. Harvey (associate commissioner) William Goodrich (general counsel) Kenneth Kirk (general counsel)
Bureau of Biological and Physical Sciences	Robert S. Roe, Ph.D. (director)
Division of Antibiotics	Henry Welch, M.D. (director)

See Notes for archive sources from which these positions and associations were drawn and verified.

By 1961, two years before the Kefauver-Harris Amendments were approved, the culture in the FDA had become so infused with the language of efficacy that a field investigator named Harold O'Keefe sent a rather remarkable question to Ralph Smith. O'Keefe, it seems, was confused about whether efficacy was a requirement for new drugs, and wanted to know if he could prosecute a field violation under that standard. As he wrote, "First we should like to know if the New Drug Branch has now established a firm policy or requiring proof of efficacy before making effective any new-drug application. We wish to know if you will require proof of efficacy for each of the conditions mentioned for this product before making an application effective."[19] While Smith's response has either been lost or was never recorded, the very fact that the investigator felt the need to clarify this fact shows just how far the philosophy of efficacy had spread by 1961.

Yet these episodes also underscore the genuine ambiguity of the efficacy movement within the FDA. By 1960, it was clear to every interested observer in Washington that "the Administration's regulations [had] gone far beyond the exact words of the 1938 Act." When Tennessee Senator Estes Kefauver held hearings on issues of drug safety before his Subcommittee on Antitrust and Monopoly for the Senate Judiciary Committee, no one doubted that organizational practice at the FDA had stepped well beyond statutory concept of "safety." Kefauver introduced S. 1552, a radical measure that would have required FDA officials to make a determination of efficacy in new drug applications. A very diverse set of witnesses at Kefauver's hearings that year—Physicians' Council President Julius Richmond, Cornell's Walter Modell, *Pediatrics* editor Charles May, Rochester's Louis Lasagna, the AMA's Howard Hussey, University of Illinois' Harry Dowling, University of Utah's Louis Goodman, Massachusetts General Hospital's Allan Butler, Harvard's Maxwell Finland, and George Larrick himself—could all agree on one thing: Bureau of Medicine decisions were actively and necessarily incorporating "efficacy" considerations already. Yet none of these individuals could clearly decipher the meaning of efficacy in FDA regulations.[20]

In the statements of the wider cohort of cold war FDA officials—Smith, Kessenich, Nelson, John Harvey, Robert Roe, and Larrick—we see the emergence of a language of efficacy, but it was a language that was still highly ambiguous and differed substantially across individuals in the 1950s. Such ambiguity belies the notion that strategic individuals or clearly coordinated political action were necessary to spread efficacy standards—there are no secret meetings and smoke-filled rooms in this story. Rather, the movement toward increased scientific controls and efficacy standards resulted from the shared training and education of this cohort. This "cohort effect" allowed a degree of coordination, but the ambiguity of each official's statements resulted in a surprisingly effective strategy to spread the gospel of strict scientific standards and drug efficacy.

Thalidomide, Frances Kelsey, and the New Law

In March 1960 the Richard Merrell Corporation submitted its application for thalidomide (trade name Kevadon) to the FDA. Merrell expected an easy approval, and so (at first) did the FDA. The new drug application was assigned to Frances Kelsey, the newest member of the pharmacological and reform cohort. It was Kelsey's first application, and as was customary during this period, a detail from the company visited her several weeks after the submission of the application.[21]

Thalidomide was originally manufactured by Chemie Grunenthal and had already been sold under the trade name Contergan in Germany. At the time of its submission to U.S. regulators, an estimated one million West Germans were taking Contergan nightly as a sedative. The widespread use of thalidomide in Europe provided reassurance (at least to Merrell officials) that it was safe as prescribed for use and that FDA approval would be quickly and fluidly forthcoming.

From the very start, however, it was clear that Frances Kelsey's standards for a sound new drug application differed from the previous norm. Kelsey wrote her first official reply to the Kevadon application on November 10, 1960. As the Insight Team of the *Sunday London Times* summarized her response, "Everything about the application seemed to her to be inadequate," including the details of the animal and clinical (human) studies, the incompleteness of chronic toxicity and stability data, and dismissal of evidence for genuine and worrisome side effects.[22]

The crucial adverse event for the thalidomide application occurred when the *British Medical Journal* published a physician's report of peripheral neuropathy (loss of sensation in the limbs and extremities) associated with thalidomide. Kelsey had noticed this report in the *British Medical Journal*,[23] and she was quite concerned that Merrell had not alerted her of this report before she had chanced to read it. She was also concerned that peripheral neuropathy might be linked to a teratogenic effect (inducement of birth defects). When she confronted Merrell officials about the report, they said that they were aware of the reports but had not conveyed the information to the FDA because the events were of negligible incidence and the effects were reversible. Kelsey said nothing at the time, but the episode convinced her that Richardson-Merrell officials were not reporting truthfully: "I had the feeling . . . that they were at no time being wholly frank with me and that this attitude has obtained in all our conferences etc. regarding this drug."[24]

Merrell officials continued to press Kelsey for approval. They correctly noted that while doctors had reported associations between thalidomide and peripheral neuropathy, no one had yet established a causal link. But in one of the strongest demonstrations of the new culture at the FDA—a demonstration that came well before thalidomide's teratogenicity was established and a full year before the Kefauver-Harris Amendments of 1962, Kelsey argued that the burden of proof in new drug applications rested with the sponsor, not with the FDA. She also argued that clinical studies supporting safety needed to test for any and all side effects or toxicities that had been noticed in clinical practice. In essence, Kelsey was floating a new rule, an interpretation of previous regulations.

We have taken appropriate note of your contention that it has not been proved that Kevadon tablets actually cause peripheral neuritis, and the fact that the labelling of the drug proposed in your letter of March 29, 1961, fails to make a frank disclosure that the drug has been found to cause peripheral neuritis. *In the consideration of an application for a new drug, the burden of proof that the drug causes side effects does not lie with this Administration. The burden of proof that the drug is safe—which must include adequate studies of all the manifestations of toxicity which medical or clinical experience suggest—lies with the applicant.*[25]

Kelsey never got the chance to officially reject the Kevadon application. Independently, the physicians William G. McBride of Sydney, Australia, and Widukind Lenz of Germany began to associate thalidomide with severe deformities in newborn children. Richardson-Merrell officials contacted Kelsey on November 30, 1961, to inform her that the drug was being withdrawn from the European market, and the Kevadon application was soon withdrawn. In the end, over eight thousand children born to mothers in Europe and Asia had birth defects traceable to thalidomide, many being born as limbless trunks, bereft of arms and legs. The thalidomide tragedy had become a worldwide phenomenon.[26]

Two features of the thalidomide tragedy—its historical conjunction and cultural distillation—enhanced the opportunities for bureaucratic opportunism. First, the incidents occurred as the Senate Judiciary Committee, chaired by Senator Estes Kefauver of Tennessee, was conducting investigations of the pharmaceutical industry. Kefauver's investigations, it is useful to recall, focused not on pharmaceutical safety but on the perceived high price of prescription pharmaceuticals. After the publication of the thalidomide episode and Frances Kelsey's rise to heroine status, a senatorial investigation into pharmaceutical pricing was diverted to an investigation (with subsequent lawmaking) on premarket approval.

The second and crucial feature of the thalidomide episode was its distillation and reinterpretation in the national media. The key story was written by Morton Mintz, a *Washington Post* staff reporter, and it appeared on the front page of the Sunday *Post*, on July 15, 1962. The day after the story was published, Senator Kefauver rose on the Senate floor to call upon President Kennedy to award Kelsey a National Civilian Medal of Honor, the highest award that a president could then bestow upon a U.S. civilian. With the press coverage, and with the Kennedy ceremony, Kelsey soon became a household name and a reluctant media celebrity. The FDA played an important role in this transformation, not least by sponsoring numerous trips for Kelsey.[27]

The legislation that became the 1962 amendments, and that was passed by a unanimous Senate vote, was drafted in the Department of Health, Education, and Welfare. While we cannot at present say with certainty whether Kelsey and other FDA officials in fact drafted the legislation, it seems highly likely that they played a significant role in the writing process.[28] Among many provisions, the law added an efficacy standard to the 1938 Food, Drug, and Cosmetic Act, requiring companies to prove efficacy as well as safety before new drug approval. And in one of the most important phrases of the new legislation, Congress required "adequate and well-controlled clinical studies" for proof of efficacy and safety.

The Cold War Cohort and the 1963 Rules

For two reasons, rule-making was high on the FDA's agenda very early in 1963. First and formally, Congress had called upon the FDA to promulgate rules for the administration and enforcement of the 1962 legislation. Second, and likely more important, FDA officials wanted to seize the political momentum and the agency's favorable reputation to cement their regulatory agenda as quickly as possible.

The proposed rules were first published in the *Federal Register* on February 14, 1963. The power of the new rules was literally buried in the fine print. The crucial provisions regulating clinical research came not directly, but as attached to the newly minted form of a drug application. By spelling out provisions for clinical research in its new "Form FD-356," FDA officials were explicitly using the agency's gatekeeping authority to regulate clinical research.

a. An application may be incomplete or may be refused unless it contains full reports of adequate tests by all methods reasonably applicable to show whether or not the drug is safe and effective for use as suggested in the proposed labeling and includes all the following:
   i. Detailed reports of the preclinical investigations, including studies made on laboratory animals, in which the methods used and results obtained are clearly set forth. . . .
   ii. Reports of all clinical tests by experts should be attached. These reports should include adequate information concerning each subject treated with the drug or employed as a control, including age, sex, conditions treated, dosage, frequency of administration of the drug, results of all relevant clinical observations and laboratory examinations made, full information concerning any other treatment given previously or concurrently, and a full statement of adverse effects and useful results observed. . . . Ordinarily, the reports of clinical studies will not be regarded as adequate unless they include reports from more than one independent, competent investigator who maintain adequate case histories of an adequate number of subjects, designed to records observations and permit evaluation of any and all discernible effects attributable to

the drug in each individual treated and comparable records on any individuals employed as controls. Except where the disease for which the drug is being tested does not occur in the United States, some of the investigations should be performed by competent investigators within the United States.

iii. All information pertinent to an evaluation of the safety and effectiveness of the drug available to the applicant from any source, including information derived from other investigations or commercial marketing (for example, outside the United States), or reports in the scientific literature. . . .

b. An application may be incomplete or may be refused unless it includes substantial evidence consisting of adequate and well-controlled investigations, by experts qualified by scientific training and experience to evaluate the effectiveness of the drug involved, on the basis of which it could fairly and responsibly be concluded that the drug will have the effect it purports or is represented to have under the conditions of use prescribed.[29]

The small type and specificity of these rules concealed their sheer weight. Full reports of clinical studies meant that extensive, exhaustive, and massive documentation of research would now be required. Section 130.4, (c) 1.a.ii, now required that sponsors and researchers separately and individually document every single human subject in clinical trials whose results were submitted as part of a new drug application.[30] Other provisions required that at least some of the research be conducted in the United States and that any information available in medical journals or even from casual observation in foreign markets be included. The FDA could reject a new drug application if just one of these standards was not met or under the more general standard of "insufficient information to determine whether such drug is safe for use under such conditions."[31]

FDA officials took a mixed and very flexible approach in their call for new regulation. On the one hand, FDA officials argued that the lessons of thalidomide pointed starkly to the need for new regulation, indeed a whole new approach. On the other hand, thalidomide did not offer new information as much as it confirmed FDA thinking that had previously crystallized. In a public address wherein she defended the new regulations in 1963, Kelsey offered this historical portrait of the evolution of the new rules.

The thalidomide incident was a major factor leading to the enactment of the Kefauver-Harris Amendments of 1962. This has led to the conclusion by some that the law, and our investigational drug regulations, were hastily drawn and thus must have been poorly drawn. This is not correct. The Department's proposed legislation, which served as the basis for most of the provisions in the law as enacted which relate to drug testing, was very carefully drafted by experts and widely studied within the Executive Branch of the Government before it was sent to the Congress by our Secretary. Similarly the proposed investigational drug regulations were carefully prepared on the basis of many years of experience with the new drug law before the thalidomide situation came to public attention. Rapid developments in drug research and in promotional methods for drugs necessitated evaluation of the effectiveness of new drugs as well as their safety. Furthermore, the need for greater control and surveillance over the distribution and clinical testing of investigational drugs became apparent as abuses began to appear.[32]

Kelsey's frank statement about the evolution of the IND rules is remarkable for several reasons. First, she admits to the very fact that we have discussed in this chapter, namely, that the new federal rules were in the making long before thalidomide (and long before the 1962 statutory amendments) was ever in the picture. Second, her statement is unapologetic. Kelsey gives no ground to critics of the Amendments, and she forcefully argues that changes in science, in medicine, and in the pharmaceutical economy "necessitated" new regulatory approaches.

We also pause to note here that yet another crucial act of regulation in American history was authored within the federal bureaucracy. In this respect, the IND rules of 1963 echo the Comstock laws of 1873 and 1890; the Pure Food and Drugs Act of 1906; the Forest Reserves Transfer Act of 1905; and the Food, Drug, and Cosmetic Act of 1938.[33] The other remarkable feature of Kelsey's statement is that the Kefauver legislation itself was drawn up in the "Department," meaning within the FDA. We have not as yet been able to ascertain the individual authorship of the Kefauver-Harris Amendments, but evidence suggests that such authorship resided in the very federal bureaucracy that wrote up the rules accompanying the new legislation. This implies a very expansive reach of bureaucratic power.

Perhaps the pivotal event in the evolution of the IND rules was a public forum held on February 15, 1963. One month after the publication of the FDA's Notice of Proposed Rule-Making for the IND regulations, the agency convened a public meeting at which interested parties could voice their concerns, their suggestions, and even their confusion with respect to the new rules. At that forum, two things were evident. First, it was abundantly clear that FDA staffers and not Commissioner George Larrick were behind the investigational new drug regulations. When the investigational new drug regulations were presented to the audience, it was Kelsey and Arthur Ruskin (then acting director of the Division of New Drugs in the Bureau of Medicine) who made the presentation and fielded questions. Behind the new advertising regulations stood not Larrick, but Morris Yakowitz, director of the Division of Advisory Opinions for the Bureau of Enforcement.[34]

It was never clearly stated that Kelsey had been behind the IND regulations, but her presence and platform at the March 1963 forum indicated to all present that she must have been involved in their writing. She casually but authoritatively described the evolution of the rules. She also interpreted their meaning, albeit with considerable ambiguity. She offered rationales for many of the specific provisions. In discussing the FDA's new restrictions on promotion during the investigational new drug stage, she was plain as to her agency's intentions.

Three sections are intended to curb the occasional instances of commercialism before the drug has been released: i.e. those dealing with the sale of investigational drugs, with the dissemination of promotional material representing the investigational drug to be safe or useful for the purposes for which it is under investigation: and with the time limit placed on the unduly prolonged distribution of investigational drugs.[35]

In other cases, Kelsey was stern and rather paternalistic with her audience. She dismissed as unfounded and normatively unscientific concerns about the requirements for detailing clinical trials on paper and for protecting human subjects.

It is difficult to understand why any conscientious and experienced clinical investigator would object to supplying detailed reports of his work. It is to be presumed that he would keep such reports for the protection of his patient, and, it is assumed that as a scientist he would want the optimum benefits to come from his work.

It is also somewhat surprising that objections should have been made to the provision that patients or persons used as controls, or their representatives be informed that investigational drugs are being used and that their consent be obtained before they serve as experimental or control subjects. These provisions are embodied in the Code of Ethics of the American Medical Association and have been upheld in civil courts.[36]

Kelsey continued this disciplinary tone in her summary of the IND rules:

In conclusion, the 1962 Kefauver-Harris Amendments of the Federal Food, Drug and Cosmetic Act, and the 1963 regulations for investigational drugs stress the need for improved procedures in the clinical testing of new drugs for safety and efficacy. Fears have been expressed that the additional requirements will discourage clinicians from testing drugs. However, it is acknowledged that the current status of drug evaluation leaves much to be desired. Much of this is due to the lack of adequately trained and experienced clinical investigators. It is hoped that the new requirements for improved testing procedures will give added stature to the field of drug testing and that recent steps taken to provide fellowships and training programs in clinical pharmacology will be accelerated.

Beyond this, the pattern of FDA participation at this conference showed that an inversion of hierarchy had taken place. Larrick's role at the conference was exceedingly passive. He sat and read written questions submitted by audience members to the assembled panel of FDA officials. It was as if Larrick no longer spoke for the agency, and Kelsey, Yakowitz, Ruskin, and other careerists and reformers did. At no time did Larrick defend either his agency or the new rules. All the rationales, all the apologia, and all the blunt rhetoric were coming from career scientists and regulators.

Ambiguity and Persuasion: The FDA Sells the New Rules

The rhetorical pattern emerging from FDA appearances and public hearings, from Ruskin, Yakowitz, and others as well as from Kelsey, evinced a blunt, paternalistic, even castigating tone. Beyond this, and perhaps more important from the vantage of regulatory politics, was a measured ambiguity in discussing the potential applications of the rules in FDA enforcement. In response to repeated questions and the rehearsal of detailed scenarios involving advertisements, new labeling, new indications, and new product approval submissions, FDA officials refused to commit themselves to specifics or promises.

Examples abound in the public hearing of February 15, 1963. Ruskin, in describing the general program of new drug review, refused to offer commitment on the subject of what defined a clinical investigator.

Q [read by Commissioner Larrick]: The definition of a new drug in section 201(p) says: "Recognized among experts qualified by scientific training and experience." What is the Administration's definition of "experts" who meet these "qualifications"?

Dr. Ruskin: Well, experts will have to be considered obviously in regard to their own training and experience, and in particular in regard to the subject involved. An expert in obstetrics and gynecology will not be considered an expert on cancer, and vice versa. . . . Each case would have to be evaluated on its own merits, each investigator.[37]

Kelsey, speaking after Ruskin, also showed her proficiency at rhetorical hedging.

Q: What constitutes a qualified clinical investigator? How specific will FDA be in this area?

Dr. Kelsey: I believe this question was answered earlier. Again the nature of the investigator's background and training, publications, and so on will be taken into consideration, particularly though as they bear in the area of the drug being investigated.

Q: Where does the bona fide clinical investigation stop and the efforts become free-marketing commercialization of the new drug?

Dr. Kelsey: Well, we simply have to examine the facts in each case as it comes up. I don't believe it will be too difficult to determine this when the occasion arises.

Q: What is considered sufficiently alarming to warrant immediate discontinuance of the investigation?

Dr. Kelsey: We think the "sufficiently alarming" will actually vary with use of the drug. We would tolerate a good deal more severe effects in a drug, say used in the treatment of cancer, than one used to relieve headache. I think in all these cases it will be a question of the investigational drug branch and a sponsor getting together and exchanging information and views before a decision, and I don't believe this will be too difficult.[38]

An important feature of the political process by which new regulations were adopted, then, was their occluded presentation to the public and to organized communities by the Food and Drug Administration. This happened both formally and informally. Formally, it occurred during the conference on the proposed rule-making in 1963, as well as at other events. Informally, this presentation occurred during the frequent travels of FDA officials in 1962 and 1963, and the discussions that arose in specific cases where the new rules and the amendments were being applied.

Among institutions active in clinical research, some apprehension about the rules and their application was in evidence. In many cases, such institutions invited Kelsey and other FDA officials to speak publicly and meet with interested and affected personnel. At the Mayo Clinic in Rochester, Minnesota, leadership actively courted Kelsey for a visit in 1963 and issued strong messages to Mayo doctors and researchers to attend meetings with the FDA heroine.

Tentative plans for the December 4–5 visit of Dr. F. O. Kelsey, Chief of Investigational Drug Branch of the Department of Health, Education and Welfare were formulated. Final plans will be made when Dr. Kelsey's arrival and departure plans are known.

Tentative plans include a luncheon on Wednesday noon, December 4, to include members of the Clinic and hospital staffs concerned with the medical and legal aspects of the use of investigational drugs. On Wednesday evening a dinner at the Foundation House before the Staff meeting should be arranged to include members of the Research and Laboratory Committee and a number of staff men currently engaged in or with present interests in problems of drug investigation and clinical research. On Thursday morning either a late coffee meeting or an early luncheon will be planned to include as many as possible of those currently engaged in the use of investigational drugs and/or interested in discussing the new drug laws with Dr. Kelsey.

Plans for tours of Clinic and hospital facilities will be adjusted to Dr. Kelsey's period in Rochester as soon as this is known.

It is hoped that as many as possible who are carrying out clinical investigation and who will have to work with the FDA will meet Dr. Kelsey. To this end special notices and invitations to attend the Staff Meeting will be sent to representative staff investigators.[39]

Interested observers and critics were well aware of the FDA's rhetorical patterns. The ambiguous nature of FDA pronouncements was a subject of frequent (though politically inconsequential) lamentation. Carl Pfeiffer, a research physician from Chicago, was among the agency's fiercest critics.

At the very least, the Food and Drug Administration has been remiss in not clarifying the interpretation it will choose to place on the law in this respect. This College [the American College of Clinical Pharmacology and Chemotherapy] could perform a valuable service to all investigators, as well as to the public and industry, and even to the Food and Drug Administration itself, by prodding these authorities to take a stand. Until now, its flabby practice has been to avoid committing itself to any stand while always maintaining the possibility of saying "nay." This refusal often comes in serial form, so that an IND may have to be submitted in as many as five revisions only to be rejected each time by a new reviewer. These dilatory tactics may safeguard them from criticism by anyone who is interested only in status quo, as is typically true of bureaucrats.[40]

Whatever their appreciation of or frustration with the FDA, observers could agree that the new rules specified much greater power for the FDA. Lowell T. Coggeshall, vice president of the University of Chicago and chairman of the federal Commission on Drug Safety, plainly acknowledged that FDA scientists in the Bureau of Medicine were full participants.

The second equally obvious lesson is that scientists of the Food and Drug Administration are going to have to become part of the scientific process to a much greater degree than before. Rather than remaining apart to maintain judicial independence, they are going to have to become more involved as participating scientists, fully aware of the ramifications, providing perceptive understanding of the decisions that must be made if progress is to continue. They bear a responsibility in helping make them succeed. I am reassured that this is presently the aim and plan of their leaders in the FDA.[41]

The Possibility of Comparison

Does the narrative elaborated here have any echo in other stories of bureaucratic development in American politics? Looking at the evidence, and in light of the alternative model presented here, it seems that Carpenter's 2001 narratives may have overemphasized the entrepreneurial activity of *individuals* such as Harvey Wiley and Gifford Pinchot and may have underemphasized the reliance of these men on others in their agency. If this is true, then to what degree is the sort of narrative elaborated here valuable for studying other agencies?

From Carpenter's 2001 study, it would appear that several cases of organizational generations in the late nineteenth-century Post Office Department (the Armstrong generation and the Bangs generation were politically consequential).[42] At the Department of Agriculture, the cohort of individuals in the Bureau of Forestry (later the Forest Service), the Bureau of Plant Industry, and the Bureau of Chemistry provided crucial support to the "entrepreneurs" who receive more official political credit for lasting and enduring policy changes.

Yet this only raises further questions. If we looked hard enough, would we find evidence of cohort-structured action in other politically consequential agencies in American political development? Would we find them at the Social Security Administration? At the Environmental Protection Agency? In selected state-level agencies such as Robert Moses's Triborough Authority? It will be interesting for researchers in political science, public policy, public administration, history, and administrative law to focus on bureaucratic cohorts. A more immediate question is how any of these cohorts confronted and used the ambiguity involved in the regulatory process to further their agency's mission. We hope that by identifying some of the key characteristics of the strategic use of ambiguity in one crucial episode, our chapter can serve as a partial guide to future research.

Conclusions and Qualifications

We intend to couch our conclusions in appropriate circumspection. It should be remarked that our analysis has been purely narrative, that this narrative lacks some "transitional fossils," and that other analytic tools (statistical analysis, comparison with other agencies or other sets of rules, examination of cases where political ambiguity may have failed) have not been employed here. Along these lines, there is some key evidence lacking for our account: a pattern of meetings between FDA scientists, politicians, and other professional authorities at which new rules were discussed. Perhaps such meetings, if they ever took place, were not documented. Still, the evidence is fairly compelling that something other than the standard story of rule-making following legislation, and "efficacy" standards following thalidomide, occurred.

We close by offering some tentative lessons from our narrative about the strategic use of ambiguity by a bureaucratic cohort.

1. In the strategic use of ambiguity, whether or not it is intended, a symbolic expression of vision precedes the programmatic expression of vision. FDA officials first discussed symbolic aims (efficacy), without discussing specific programmatic details or defining what that concept meant. Only at the moment of decisive opportunity did they pin down what they really wanted, and even then their messages retained significant ambiguity.
2. Ambiguity was the essential rhetorical tool used by FDA officials both to persuade the interested public of the validity of the new regulations and to avoid any commitment to a particular form of administration. The rehearsal of efficacy rhetoric kept the term alive, even to the point of establishing the concept by 1960 as an accepted standard that no one could clearly define.
3. The audience for robust ambiguity is crucial. Multiple, cross-cutting networks support strategic ambiguity, and in general, aggregations of specific audiences (professions, subspecialties, business groups) outweigh nonaggregated, general ones ("the public"). The "aggregation" in ambiguity is in part "endogenous," a part of the very story in which ambiguity is used by politically robust bureaucrats.[43]
4. Uncertainty can be used to support ambiguity and, at the same time, an aggressive public stance. This differentiates the FDA's Kelsey, Ruskin, Smith, and others from Padgett and Ansell's Cosimo de Medici, whose tone appears to have been much more patrimonial and gentle.[44]
5. In observing rhetorical and behavioral patterns such as bureaucratic ambiguity, students of politics must consider the possibility that a good portion of the observed behavior is not intentional or strategic, but occurs "naturally" or "typically" to the individual, results from coordination problems, or may be undertaken for normative (value-laden) purposes.

Chapter 17
Retrospective: Formative Action and Second Acts

Elisabeth Clemens

Political history has long been dominated by the deeds of kings, generals, and other commanding types. Such narratives embody the belief that individual action makes a difference, that doing or not doing can decisively change the course of events. But by using the concept "formative acts," this powerful literary convention can be restated as a provisional claim about cause and effect. Certain kinds of action appear to result in durable changes in social practices and organization, including political practices and institutions. This claim generates key questions: How do actions make a difference? When and why is some action formative?

To these questions, popular commentary and scholarly analysis offer different answers. Popular political history is dominated by biography and narrative, which often focus on the character or skills of individual actors. The genre itself assumes that action is formative, that deeds make a difference. Scholarly analysts, in contrast, have highlighted the ways in which durable institutions constrain and shape action or, from a different theoretical vantage point, the extent to which political outcomes can be explained as the aggregate product of a great many individual choices and behaviors. From either of these theoretical vantage points, biography appears as hagiography, historical narrative as anecdote. Consequently, a serious theoretical challenge can be found in every best-selling biography of a founding father, in every excoriation of the moral failings of a particular politician or celebration of inspired leadership or commemoration of a decisive act in a critical moment. How and when does action matter?

The essays in *Formative Acts* take up this challenge, not as a unified program but as the opening for a rich conversation that begins to establish the conceptual frameworks necessary for linking the actions of individuals—or groups and networks—to durable transformations in the organization of governance. The opening theoretical chapters discuss three modalities of action—agency, leadership, and entrepreneurship—but many of the essays that follow document how these actions are shaped by the complex and multitiered contexts in which political action plays out. Many of the authors emphasize the importance of decoupling action from the presumption of change. A great deal of what is done in politics serves to maintain or reproduce existing institutions and principles of order. Change, from this perspective, may be the product of a failure to act as much as of intentional projects (or unintentional acts) of transformation. In addition, the formative consequences of action may vary both by the character of the action and its context or setting. Taken together, these discussions provide a rich sense of the multidimensional factors that shape the connection of action to formative and transformative outcomes.

Inevitably, all these complications, distinctions, and taxonomies threaten to overwhelm more general argument. The path out of bewildering complexity lies in carefully identifying the different types of combinations and interactions that sometimes produce transformation and sometimes do not. From the chapters in this volume, a set of middle-range propositions emerges: acknowledged failure can contribute more to the achievement of one's goals than near success; actors can advance their interests by serving those of others; sometimes a split within a movement is just the thing to secure success. More such propositions can be found, but the resulting imagery differs markedly from the standard template of effective leadership, the durable capacity to rally support in pursuit and achievement of some intended goal. The chapters instead make clear some of the many reasons why it is so difficult to generate change, particularly change that produces the intended results. They also suggest why it has been so difficult to explain how change happens. Narratives of effective, commanding leadership may not comport with the way in which events actually unfold, but they are much easier to write and more compelling to read.

Nowhere are the challenges of sustaining effective action more evident than in the successful leaders who were failures in their youth, in the failures later found to have had lasting impact, in the inspired political operators who continually fail to achieve for a second time. Andrew Johnson, labeled as ineffective and impeached by a Congress hostile to the easy reincorporation of the Confederate states, nevertheless shaped the political alignments that in time consolidated southern power in national politics (Tulis and Mellow). Alice Paul, the dynamic leader of the more radical supporters of woman suffrage, forces President Wilson to lend support to the cause, but sees victory on the terms of the more moderate suffragists and then fails in the subsequent effort to extend women's right to vote to an equal rights amendment (Tichenor). Lyndon B. Johnson, "master of the Senate" and extraordinary political operator, secures passage of pathbreaking civil rights legislation and yet declines to run for reelection, his capacity for leadership undercut by the same allies he had cultivated in other political projects (Milkis). This litany of bittersweet political careers could be expanded on at length, but the point should be clear. In American political development, formative acts appear as distinctive conjunctures of actors and circumstances rather than as outcomes reliably produced by great men and women.

In one respect, "it depends" becomes the default answer to the question of which actions become "formative." Even biographies of leaders become intellectually indefensible as explanations of political change; only vignettes seem appropriate for such a fragmented and episodic process. Yet the apparently unpredictable, rare quality of formative acts can be illuminated by looking more systematically at the context in which political actors work to maintain or transform the political order.

The Varieties of Formative Acts

The chapters in this volume—and the conference for which they were originally written—were organized around three nouns of action: agents, leaders, and entrepreneurs. These nouns of action were linked to two other nouns: change and development. In various grammatical forms—as verbs, adverbs, adjectives, and nouns—all these terms recur through the chapters, signaling important variations in the types of action that are conducive to change, that produce significant and lasting rearrangements of governance.

Each form of action or type of actor can be linked to different constitutive relationships. For agents, the defining relationships are double, both to oneself as an autonomous actor and to the "principal" in whose name one acts. Agents are, in a paradoxical sense, the authors of their own actions but also vehicles for some greater project. As James Block argues, a conception of agency—understood as both formative and publicly oriented—distinguished American political culture from the start. Rooted in the religious beliefs of dissenting Protestantism, this understanding of the individual as responsible for his or her own community intensified as nineteenth-century revivals linked individual confession to a responsibility for the sins of the nation. The confession of faith was linked to an intense personal responsibility for the eradication of slavery, temperance, and other vices that afflicted the country.[1] William Jennings Bryan, the "godly hero," brought this style of leadership, grounded in agency to the divine, into the twentieth century (Bensel).[2] Even as the multiplication of formal institutions and bureaucratic agencies has impinged on the space for unfettered agency, this widely held belief in the responsibility and capacity of ordinary citizens to constitute a virtuous society has persisted across American political history, a durable challenge to other forms of political order.

Agency may be constituted by a particular relationship to the self (or at least to those selves who meet the requirements for citizens) and to *principle*, but agency can also be a collective act, generated by shared practices of voluntarism and aspirations for public goods. As Daniel Carpenter and

Colin Moore contend in their study of the Food and Drug Administration, entire organizations may develop a capacity for agency premised on a shared vision or set of practices. Social movements are another example of the upwellings of action that are generated not only by shared grievances but also by citizens' recognition of their own capacity to secure redress for those grievances. Although this agentic political culture has been constrained and challenged by the development of other forms of governing, it endures as a source of formative acts that may disrupt existing orders and champion changes within the organization of American politics.

If agency is potentially either individual or collective, leadership is by definition a relational concept. Leaders are defined by the existence of followers. As Max Weber observed in his discussion of charismatic authority, its "basis lies rather in the conception that it is the duty of those subject to charismatic authority to recognize its genuineness and to act accordingly. Psychologically this recognition is a matter of complete personal devotion to the possessor of the quality, arising out of enthusiasm, or of despair and hope."[3] Leadership requires deference from followers. In the context of American political culture, leadership involves at least a temporary abdication of followers' claims to agency and a presumption that the agentic properties of the leader will take precedence over those of the followers. That presumption may be established in many ways: by tradition, through charisma, on the basis of legal rules. Indeed a single individual may simultaneously exert leadership based on rules and charisma, as Lyndon Johnson did during the period when he drew on both the formal powers of office (in the Senate and then the presidency) and on his reputation as a moral leader of the civil rights movement (see Milkis). Yet, as Bruce Miroff underlines, leadership in American politics does not entail total deference. He uses the image of a "web of leadership" to highlight how leaders negotiate with and enroll followers in their projects, linking initiatives for change to shared values or presenting change as a reform or extension of existing and legitimated governing arrangements.

The competing natures of agency and leadership establish a durable tension within American political development. Those who hold formal positions of leadership must continually anticipate the upwelling of popular political agency. And, indeed, formal leaders do not themselves abdicate their own capacity to act as agents, to engage in formative acts rather than—or in addition to—fulfilling the requirements of office. Just as the multiplication of formal political institutions has limited but not eliminated the possibilities for widespread political agency, it has also constrained the actions of those in any given position of formal leadership. Even the powers of the presidency are limited by those of Congress, federal agencies, state legislators, and corporate leadership. In such a complex terrain, neither leadership alone nor in combination with agency may be sufficient for the success of formative acts.

With the establishment of ever more formal institutions and agencies of governance, the political landscape of the United States has been populated by would-be but constrained agents and leaders with competing jurisdictions and claims for deference. The sources of power are multiple and the division of authority contested. This combination of heterogeneity and ambiguity, Adam Sheingate argues, has created a context conducive to a third form of political action: entrepreneurship. Like agency, entrepreneurship is defined by the actions of individuals (or collectivities) pursing some end or promoting some value. Yet the relationship of entrepreneurs to other political actors differs importantly from the collective voluntarism that James Block found in the collaborative agency of the early Republic or the open frontier. Entrepreneurs orient themselves strategically to others, looking for opportunities and vulnerabilities, seeking to enroll the interests or ambitions of those necessary for the success of a particular initiative. Unlike leaders, entrepreneurs do not begin with assumption of deference. Other actors may follow the lead of the entrepreneur, but they do so for their own reasons, not out of acquiescence to political or charismatic authority.

Entrepreneurship is therefore fundamentally both negotiated and recombinatorial. To the extent that entrepreneurial politics generates formative acts, these are exercises in *bricolage*, in the linking or transposition of already-existing actors and resources and schemas into new governing arrangements and political outcomes.[4] This style of politics potentially crosscuts the relations of leader to follower, agent to principal, that characterize other modes of action. In response to the accumulation of executive power, Eric Schickler explains, Congress responded by exploiting its relatively underused power of investigation, particularly of executive agencies: "Rather than substitute a Congress-dominated set of arrangements for the executive-led model sought by Roosevelt, the result was a highly contested, ongoing struggle for control, in which both ideological and institutional interests were at stake. One systemic effect of this struggle was to greatly complicate bids for coherent, executive-led planning and coordination of the postwar economic order." In this case, as in others, the product of formative action was further fragmentation and ambiguity, which could be exploited by later strategic actors.[5] Consequently, entrepreneurial politics tends to reproduce, indeed intensify, its own conditions of possibility and thereby to shape the possible directions for American political development in the future.

The Changing Contexts for Political Action

Each of these basic forms of action has affinities with different contexts or settings. Thus, a stylized narrative of institutional development informs many of the discussions of political action included in this volume. As

James Block argues, the early Republic constituted a relatively open space. Colonial governing institutions lay thinly over the surface of social life which itself was organized more fully by voluntary associations, notably religious organizations. These associations constituted a matrix for action by the colonists which sustained the self-organizing of new forms of government. Yet this very accomplishment of self-organization—a concatenation of exemplary formative acts—eventually undermined the conditions of its own success.[6] Again, Weber captured the essence of this negative-feedback relationship: "It is the fate of charisma to recede before the powers of tradition or of rational association after it has entered the permanent structures of social action. This waning of charisma generally indicates the diminishing importance of individual action. In this respect, the most irresistible force is *rational discipline*, which eradicates not only personal charisma but also stratification by social groups, or at least transforms them in a rationalizing direction."[7]

The institutional elaboration of American government thus constrained the possibilities for individual (and collective) formative agency as well as for charismatic leadership. Instead, multiplying formal political organizations created alternative frameworks for the "charisma of office," the constitution of leadership through occupation of a formal organizational role. This complex and often fragmented terrain encouraged different forms of political action that centered on enrolling the support of other interested and influential actors. In the place of self-sufficient agency or uncontested leadership (with the accompanying deference of followers), entrepreneurship became a more prominent form of action. The conditions for imagining politics as a multiplayer strategic game were the product of this trajectory of political development. And, as numerous contributors have concluded, the proliferation of political entrepreneurs has fueled the lack of accountability and fracturing of authority in the American political system. In a setting where no one actor can regularly translate intentions into outcomes, no one is responsible, no one is reliable.

In such a setting, can political development be more than a random walk, driven by "contingent alignments" or "a momentary accommodation among actors normally indifferent, if not hostile, to one another" (Skowronek and Glassman)? Although contingency appears overwhelming in any given decision or contest, too tight a focus on separate episodes obscures how actions may cumulate into projects of political change. American political history provides repeated episodes in which actors—or more typically networks of actors—are able to coordinate alignments across successive decisions thereby generating a distinctive trajectory of change, at least for a while.

John Wesley Powell exemplifies this capacity to coordinate action in a fragmented institutional setting and, in the process, to contribute greatly to the expansion of government science and the autonomy of the federal bureaucracy.[8] Better known for his leadership of the first expeditions down the Colorado and through the Grand Canyon, Powell is remembered as an explorer rather than as an institution builder. Yet critically, those expeditions in the arid West produced a cadre of Powell loyalists—highly competent scientists, capable as independent political agents, yet deeply loyal to their leader, to one another, and to a vision of settlement policy informed by scientific inquiry. Mapped onto the newly founded agencies of government science, this cadre provided Powell with a source of coordination in his political contests with Congress as well as other would-be bureaucratic entrepreneurs. Similar networks or cadres appear across the chapters of this volume.[9] Miroff sketches how Newt Gingrich forged a conservative network within the U.S. House of Representatives, a cadre that eventually took control and elected Gingrich himself Speaker. Andrew Johnson pursued a similar strategy, and although he failed to secure reelection to the presidency, "the political networks and protocoalitions spawned by Johnson in the immediate aftermath of the war authorized and legitimated the Southern racial order" (Tulis and Mellow). Such coordinated action may also stem from the ascension of a new bureaucratic generation, committed to a distinctive set of principles. In their study of the Food and Drug Administration, Carpenter and Moore describe the entry of a new cohort into an established bureaucracy, a cadre without the strong personal ties of Powell's geologists but linked by a similar vision of—and sense of being the agents for—policy decisions based on rigorous scientific analysis.

It would be too simple to conclude that coordinated cadres are the key to the success of movements in shaping political outcomes. Actors in control of the powers of office, notably the president, control many of the terms on which their interests may align with those of organized movements or cadres of entrepreneurs (Sanders). As Daniel Tichenor's discussion of social movements and the presidency demonstrates, division within movements may also shape the choices that confront those in positions of institutional leadership. In the case of abolition, woman suffrage, and the labor movement of the 1930s, presidents confronted movements that were divided within themselves, committed to radical or reformist goals, suspicious and uncooperative. Yet, perhaps perversely, the inability to impose a common message on all activists created the conditions for a "radical flank effect" in which presidents found it preferable to work with the reformist wing of the movement in order to deflect demands for more radical change.

As with the cases of coordinated networks or cadres, to the extent that movements can be credited with producing change, the process appears to involve the interplay of multiple contenders, in a complex game of shifting opportunities, contingently aligned interests, and billiard shots off the bumpers. Taken as a group, these chapters do produce a stylized narrative of how action produces change, but it is radically different from the literary narrative of strong leaders committing effective acts to achieve their intentions.

Formation, Reproduction, Transformation

What is it about the character of political order that proves resistant to the type of leadership and formative action that standard historical narratives lead us to expect? Can this understanding of order lead to a more general argument about formative action? In order to understand how action produces change, it is important to consider how order is created and reproduced. For social scientists, this is the question of structure, the mutual embedding of cognitive schemas and material resources or relationships.[10] In a literally concrete fashion, order may be embedded in places, in buildings, in objects. The choice of location and layout for Washington, D.C., for example, has had durable consequences for the disruptive power of protest by ensuring that most protestors have been visitors cut off from the supporting networks of their home communities but also that any major protest has been met with the police force of a midsize city rather than a major metropolis. But the cultural template for great cities, borrowed from European modernizers of the eighteenth century, also embedded opportunities for military mobilization and control along broad avenues (Kryder). The organization of physical space structures the opportunities for individual actors, whether protestors and police, or speakers confronted by a large and noisy auditorium (Bensel). Whether the tactics of protest marches or the lung capacity of orators matters for the success of political action is shaped by institutions in this most literal sense.

Order is also embedded in practices as well as in accumulations of resources and privileges and precedents. The office of the presidency carries with it the tradition of authority linked to political leadership generally, but is also constituted by a double mandate in which "each incumbent swears *both* 'to execute the office of President of the United States,' presupposing their independent intervention in affairs *and* 'to preserve, protect and defend the Constitution of the United States,' requiring the affirmation of the existing order of things" (Milkis). In a powerful sense, the office of presidency constitutes its occupant as simultaneously agent of the nation, leader of the government and party, and entrepreneur in pursuit of change.

Other political actors, located in different positions on the political terrain, confront distinctive possibilities for contributing to the reproduction of order or enacting durable changes in governing arrangements. Endowed with the power of investigation, members of Congress were able to resist the expansion of executive powers from the New Deal through the 1950s by fashioning a vehicle for collective action that protected their institutional prerogatives (Schickler). Yet during the same decades, bureaucratic entrepreneurs in the Bureau of Budget advanced their organizational interests by aligning them with the enhancement of executive powers (Rudalevige), and a new cohort within the Food and Drug Administration deployed the authority of scientific expertise to strengthen the capacity and autonomy of that agency (Carpenter and Moore).

The image of political action as bureaucratic politics within the concrete settings of buildings, cities, and nations, however, misses something fundamental to the maintenance of order. All these actors, roles, agencies, and settings are embedded within systems of meaning or classification orders that contribute to their legitimacy (either ritually celebrated or routinely taken for granted) as well as to the potential for the repair or regeneration of order. The same constitution that imposes a dual mandate on the presidency also encompasses core categories of liberal political theory, embedded relations between public and private, between men and women, deeply within the fundamental grammar of American politics. Thus what might seem like an incremental reform—extending the franchise to women—actually required engagement with the cultural categories that defined citizenship in terms of the productive capacity of citizens assumed to be male and heads of households (McDonagh). Thus, much of the action in reproducing or disrupting political order lies in the work of reinforcing associations of categories or creating new chains of association. In the wake of the Civil War, President Andrew Johnson "was able to position the 'dispossessed' South on the side of the Constitution" by presenting himself as defender against a Congress bent on Reconstruction at all costs, no matter what the constraints of constitutional law (Tulis and Mellow). Decades later, the Dixiecrats engaged in similar work forging new chains of association. Linking the racial order of the midcentury South to states' rights and to respect for constitutional constraints, these ideological innovators drove a wedge between Southern Democrats in Congress and their party, laying the foundations for the dissolution of the Solid South when confronted with a project of racial liberalism championed by a president from the South, Lyndon Johnson (Hattam and Lowndes).

Political order is, in sum, profoundly multidimensional, sutured in many different ways, each of which provides opportunities—and obstacles—to potentially formative acts. Some decisions embed destabilizing tendencies deep within the political order (for example, Tulis and Mellow on presidential hypocrisy as the "design flaw" in the constitution). Other orderings generate stabilizing feedbacks,[11] counteracting possible disruptions and challenges. Arrayed against any candidate committed to a novel strategy are a host of consultants, donors, media commentators, and others just as ready to declare that such a thing cannot be done (and to withdraw the funds, legitimacy, and enthusiasm required for a successful strategy in the first place). Established categories of meaning and classification work to contain novel combinations, to buffer existing practices against challenge or unintended deviations from standard procedures.

Upsurges of popular activism also confront entrenched mechanisms that deflate challenges to existing elites and governing arrangements. As Daniel Kryder explains, the location and spatial organization of the nation's capital, as well as the performance of policing activities, work to contain protest and thereby to delimit one potential source of destabilizing action. Thus the initial set of decisions about the site and layout of the capital—the rejection of options that would have located the national legislature in a major commercial or industrial city, exposed to popular protest—has dampened one possible source of disruption. Given the multiple bulwarks that defend existing practices, just how can action produce durable political change? If order is multiply defended, effective formative action must proceed along multiple dimensions, generating parallel disruptions and new sets of mutually reinforcing arrangements.

Finding the Formative Action in Events

Formative events can be recognized by the production of discontinuities; upticks in the organization of social power as theorized by Michael Mann, changes in governing arrangements as explicated by Karen Orren and Stephen Skowronek in their manifesto for the study of American political development.[12] At root, formative acts involve transformation. They either create new configurations from scratch, or as is more likely in a world that is always already densely organized, they recombine and reconfigure the relations among ideas, institutions, actors, and interests.

The puzzle is how this happens, a question that directs attention to the relationships between events and structures. If action is a sort of event—or "happening"—how is it that acts become formative?[13] William Sewell explores this theoretical question through the case of the fall of the Bastille. How did a mob attack on a physical manifestation of the French regime produce a new linkage of "the people" with claims for political virtue and a new basis for political legitimacy? Like Hattam and Lowndes, he has argued that the answers lie in applying the tools of cultural analysis to the explanation of institutional change.[14] In a moment charged with political uncertainty and emotional intensity, the taking of the Bastille—and the events of the subsequent days—produced a significant realignment of the categories of political actors and political virtues. Le peuple was established as a foundation for the legitimacy of a new political order.

Can this theoretical lens illuminate how formative acts contribute to American political development? Let us begin with the most eventlike episode discussed in the contributions to this volume: William Jennings Bryan's "Cross of Gold" speech to the 1896 Democratic Convention. What did Bryan as individual actor make happen in the setting? How did it generate durable transformations that are the hallmark of effective formative acts?

As reconstructed by Richard Bensel, Bryan came to the convention as a decidedly dark horse for the party's presidential nomination. Working within the established rules for sequencing decisions and performances, Bryan secured a key position as the last speaker on the issue of monetarizing silver. The potential significance of this position was shaped by a set of decisions about earlier performances: The opening prosilver speech by Ben Tillman of South Carolina proved to be both ineffective as oratory and potentially threatening in its effort to forge a chain of associations between silver and regional hostilities. Tillman was followed by two more competent speakers who argued in favor of gold as the sole basis for currency. Thus the convention audience—including the delegates who were numerically in favor of monetarizing silver—were placed in a position of uncertainty infused with anxiety. Judging the oratory alone, they saw their case in danger. Combining his position on the program with his exceptional talents as a speaker, Bryan presented himself as the champion of silver, rescuing the cause of the majority from rhetorical defeat (even as its victory in the actual balloting on the platform was already secured). His performance fused in his person the silver cause and a claim for its virtue rooted in Christian imagery rather than the regional imagery of the Civil War offered by Tillman. In Bensel's recounting of this episode, Bryan is quite cognizant of the strategy required to enact this realignment of person with case and category. On the evening before the speech, still very much a minor contender for the nomination that would be decided days later, Bryan declared at dinner that "I am the only man who can be nominated. I am what they call 'the logic of the situation'" (Bensel).

What had been required to create this situation within which Bryan took such decisive action? At a minimum, Bryan had to perform at a level that would *confirm* the reputation as an exceptional orator that he had acquired during his then relatively short political career.[15] His speeches on the tariff and on silver given in the U.S. House of Representatives had created an expectation—at least within the press and among delegates who knew of his reputation—of an outstanding performance. Beyond this, the more prominent candidates for the nomination had to fail to generate comparably effective action. Representative Richard Bland of Missouri, arguably the leading contender for the nomination prior to the convention, followed the tradition of not actively campaigning and remained on his farm while events unfolded in Chicago. Bland's lack of effective action may be compared to President Andrew Johnson's long-term success in neutralizing the intendedly formative—indeed extraconstitutional—initiatives of the post-Civil War Congress bent on thoroughgoing reconstruction of the former Confederacy (Tulis and Mellow). Bland left an undefended opening for a creative, ambitious actor; Johnson aggressively preempted the actions of a Congress bent on a wholesale reconfiguration of the defeated South.

Although this narrative highlights the importance of strategic action by political elites, the focus on what happened at the convention obscures a different sort of formative act: the political agency of the thousands of members of the Farmers Alliance and various populist parties who had constituted silver as the preferred solution to agricultural depression and had made themselves into a formidable faction within the Democratic party. Here the rich political culture of agency and voluntarism, discussed by James Block, created the preconditions for the individual strategizing so evident in Bryan's approach to the 1896 convention. Years of organizing agricultural cooperatives had generated a powerful movement with a demonstrated capacity to intervene in elections at the local and state level—the work of linking agricultural grievances to the monetary system had been accomplished long before Bryan's speech by cohorts of activists and editors and orators.[16] Like the Dixiecrats discussed by Hattam and Lowndes, the work of the movement had forged new chains of association that sustained widespread political mobilization.

So how can we understand the relationship between this broad upwelling of collective political agency and the strategic performance by Bryan at the 1896 convention? In Lawrence Goodwyn's influential analysis, the conjuncture of the populist movement and party politics was fundamentally an act of hijacking. The articulated grievances of farmers were effectively disembedded from a movement culture of cooperatives and linked to the delimited "solution" of monetarized silver. Nebraska, home to both Bryan and what Goodwyn describes as the "shadow movement," was the key site for this political alchemy. From a different vantage point, however, this capture of the movement may be seen as a willing act of deference, a process by which political agents voluntarily become followers. Just as civil rights activists courted Martin Luther King, Jr., as their leader (see Miroff), so too some populists found in Bryan the leader that they sought. As one Omaha lawyer wrote to Bryan immediately after the 1894 election, "You are the first man in politics whom I have fully and completely trusted. . . . I would stake my life on your honor, sincerity and love of our country."[17]

At a minimum, therefore, the "formative" quality of Bryan's famous speech rested on the prior agency of thousands of organized farmers and aggrieved citizens as well as on the routine performance of Representative Bland, who failed to see in the 1896 convention a set of opportunities that could be seized in novel ways. But if these other actions were preconditions for Bryan's performance, what was necessary to embed the consequences of that performance in a way that produced durable changes in the organization of governing and the categories of political life in the United States? As Bensel describes, the received rules for conducting conventions translated—although not with certainty—Bryan's performance into the party's nomination. But that nomination also irreversibly activated schisms within the party, sending the gold Democrats over to the Republican side and consolidating business opposition to populism. As with Senator George Frisbie Hoar's championing of federal enforcement of voting laws in the former Confederacy (Vallely), *near* success had the effect of significantly strengthening the opposition.[18] Both acts, because of the very efficacy of their performance, had effects diametrically opposed to those intended by the central actors.

But near success also cemented support for Bryan within the party in ways that both secured his influence on American politics for the decades that followed and limited the possibilities of enacting the policies central to his explicit agenda. As Michael Kazin has argued, the weakness of the 1896 campaign lay in its lack of direct appeal to industrial workers. Even when Bryan was renominated in 1900, his commitment to bimetallism limited his strategic options to appeal to this constituency by reframing opposition to big business around the trust problem rather than the monetarization of silver.[19] At the same time, however, by championing the linkage of agrarian grievances to a federal solution (the monetarization of silver) Bryan contributed to a durable recategorization of government as a political remedy rather than a political threat. This reframing shaped processes of state-building throughout the decades of Republican dominance that followed and established a durable tradition of populist support for expansion of the federal government that would resurface powerfully during the New Deal.[20] As the acknowledged leader of the broad reform tendency within the Democratic party, Bryan retained sufficient influence to shape decisions at subsequent conventions. In 1912, he threw his support to the governor of New Jersey, Woodrow Wilson, as the better bet for a reform agenda. Rewarded with appointment as secretary of state, Bryan served in a time when the United States edged into World War I against all his antiwar commitments. In Bryan's case, therefore, the capacity for leadership that might be expected to flow from occupying one of the most prominent positions in government instead eroded his standing as the moral leader of populists and reformers.

How does this expanded sketch of the "event" of Bryan's convention speech illuminate our understanding of the interplay of agency, leadership, and entrepreneurship in American political development? Above all, it suggests the dangers of equating any of the central nouns of action—agent, leader, entrepreneur—with single individuals. The translation of an action into a formative event appears to rest on complex combinations of diverse prior acts. This combinatorial quality of formative action reflects the multidimensional character of political order. Disruption and recombination must proceed along multiple dimensions simultaneously in order to overcome the powerful feedbacks that contribute to the repair and restoration of dominant political relationships.

The need for a combination of a skilled actor with conducive circumstances also helps to explain why narratives of sustained leadership become so scarce in American political history after the founding generation. In the ever more complex and fragmented terrain of American politics, the masterful actor who takes center stage at one moment is frequently unable to repeat the performance. William Jennings Bryan was brilliant in securing the Democratic nomination for president, but unable to win the office itself. Alice Paul, another forceful figure who shows up repeatedly in the preceding chapters, is credited as an exceptional leader of the woman suffrage movement, but she met with regular defeat and disappointments in her efforts to follow this victory with advances toward an equal rights amendment. Lyndon Johnson earned his title as "master of the Senate" with extraordinarily creative entrepreneurship, discovering opportunities and linking preferences of diverse constituencies in unexpected ways. Yet he left office, declining to run again for the presidency, stymied by the political landscape with his powers undercut by some of the bargains he had made in pursuit of earlier political goals (Milkis).

Even for such masters of political action, genuinely formative action is not easily accomplished, particularly if we restrict such cases to those where the resultant change roughly matches the intended outcome. Whether operating in the mode of leadership or entrepreneurial politics, effective action can be difficult to sustain from one situation to the next. In a context where the organization of governance is relatively unified, there may be sufficient deference to leaders to sustain those elites across a mix of failures and formative actions. As commander of the Continental Army, after all, George Washington oversaw military defeats and brilliant campaigns, as well as showing genius in retreat when the army escaped from Brooklyn to Manhattan under cover of fog, surviving to fight again, be defeated again, and fight yet again. Consequently, as instrumental and entrepreneurial modes of political action become more prevalent, the benefits of cultivating the charisma of office and deference to leadership may increase proportionately.[21]

The legitimacy of leadership, however, rests in the established order, on ties of deference which once given may be withdrawn. Therefore, it is dangerous and difficult for acknowledged leaders to bring about formative change. Success in such a transformative endeavor would threaten the foundations of their very leadership—a situation sure to be challenged if there are any other bases of leadership, any other concentrations of political power or networks to be mobilized. Transformative change is infrequent not least because those with the greatest political resources will seek to preserve and enhance their political control (Sanders). Not surprisingly, then, the telling of formative action in contemporary politics is likely to feature trickster figures, relatively less powerful actors who find ways to leverage networks or align the interests of others in order to secure some durable rearrangement of governance and authority, or leaders who risk their position by sharing power to enroll allies who may then withdraw their deference. In either mode, the execution of a formative act may consume the authority or the newly discovered leverage that made success possible. So while formative action is difficult to carry out, second acts are harder still.

Notes

Chapter 2. The Terrain of the Political Entrepreneur

1. Adam D. Sheingate, "Political Entrepreneurship, Institutional Change, and American Political Development," *Studies in American Political Development* 17 (2003): 185–203.

2. Nelson W. Polsby, *Political Innovation in America: The Politics of Policy Initiation* (New Haven, Conn.: Yale University Press, 1984).

3. Charles M. Cameron, "Bargaining and Presidential Power," in Robert Y. Shapiro, Martha Joynt Kumar, and Lawrence R. Jacobs, eds., *Presidential Power: Forging the Presidency for the Twenty-First Century* (New York: Columbia University Press, 2000), 47 (emphasis in original).

4. John F. Padgett and Christopher K. Ansell, "Robust Action and the Rise of the Medici, 1400–1434," *American Journal of Sociology* 98 (1993): 1263.

5. Joseph A. Schumpeter, *Capitalism, Socialism, and Democracy* (New York: Harper, 1942); John W. Kingdon, *Agendas, Alternatives, and Public Policies*, 2nd ed. (New York: HarperCollins, 1995), 124.

6. Kingdon, *Agendas*, 182.

7. James G. March and Johan P. Olsen, "The New Institutionalism: Organizational Factors in Political Life," *American Political Science Review* 78 (1984): 734, 749.

8. Israel M. Kirzner, *Discovery and the Capitalist Process* (Chicago: University of Chicago Press, 1985), 65.

9. William E. Connolly, *The Ethos of Pluralization* (Minneapolis: University of Minnesota Press, 1995), 163.

10. David C. King, *Turf Wars: How Congressional Committees Claim Jurisdiction* (Chicago: University of Chicago Press, 1997), 126–36.

11. William H. Sewell, Jr., "A Theory of Structure: Duality, Agency, and Transformation," *American Journal of Sociology* 98 (1992): 1–29.

12. Elisabeth S. Clemens and James M. Cook, "Politics and Institutionalism: Explaining Durability and Change," *Annual Review of Sociology* 25 (1999): 453.

13. Elisabeth S. Clemens, *The People's Lobby: Organizational Innovation and the Rise of Interest Group Politics in the United States, 1890–1925* (Chicago: University of Chicago Press, 1997).

14. Karen Orren and Stephen Skowronek, *The Search for American Political Development* (Cambridge: Cambridge University Press, 2004), 17.

15. Frank Lantz and Eric Zimmerman, "Rules, Play and Culture: Towards an Aesthetic of Games," *Merge Magazine*, n.d., http://www.ericzimmerman.com/texts/RulesPlayCulture.htm, 3

16. Ibid.

17. For presidential expenditures, see http://www.opensecrets.org/presidential/index.asp. In constant 2000 dollars, spending grew from $184 million in 1976

to $658 million in 2004, an increase of 258 percent. To put this in some perspective, over the same period, real GDP per capita increased 77 percent, real federal outlays increased 105 percent and real federal discretionary spending increased 61 percent.

18. Frank J. Sorauf, "Adaptation and Innovation in Political Action Committees," in Allan J. Cigler and Burdett A. Loomis, eds., *Interest Group Politics*, 4th ed. (Washington, D.C.: CQ Press, 1995), 176.

19. Frank J. Sorauf, "Power, Money, and Responsibility in the Major American Parties," in John C. Green and Paul S. Herrnson, eds., *Responsible Partisanship? The Evolution of American Political Parties since 1950* (Lawrence: University Press of Kansas, 2002), 87–89.

20. For figures on 527 expenditures, see http://www.opensecrets.org/527s/527cmtes.asp

21. Robert C. Lieberman, *Shaping Race Policy: The United States in Comparative Perspective* (Princeton, N.J.: Princeton University Press, 2005), 158–63.

22. J. David Greenstone, "Political Culture and American Political Development: Liberty, Union, and the Liberal Bipolarity," *Studies in American Political Development* 1 (1986): 48.

23. Frank Dobbin, J. Meyer, and W. R. Scott, "Equal Opportunity Law and the Construction of Internal Labor Markets," *American Journal of Sociology* 99 (1993): 397.

24. Lauren B. Edelman, "Legal Ambiguity and Symbolic Structures: Organizational Mediation of Civil Rights Law," *American Journal of Sociology* 97 (1992): 1545.

25. Hokyo Hwang and Walter W. Powell, "Institutions and Entrepreneurship," in Sharon A. Alvarez, Olav Sorenson, and Rajshree Agarwal, eds., *Handbook of Entrepreneurship: Disciplinary Perspectives* (New York: Springer Verlag, 2005), 186.

26. Frank Dobbin and John R. Sutton, "The Strength of a Weak State: The Rights Revolution and the Rise of Human Resources Management Divisions," *American Journal of Sociology* 104 (1998): 443.

27. Ibid., 442.

28. Robert A. Kagan, *Adversarial Legalism: An American Way of Law* (Cambridge, Mass.: Harvard University Press, 2001).

29. Erin L. Kelly, "The Strange History of Employer-Sponsored Child Care: Interested Actors, Uncertainty, and the Transformation of Law in Organizational Fields," *American Journal of Sociology* 109 (2003): 606-49.

30. Ibid., 615–16.

31. Samuell Kernell, *Going Public: New Strategies of Presidential Leadership*, 3rd ed. (Washington, D.C.: CQ Press, 1997); William G. Howell, *Power Without Persuasion: The Politics of Direct Presidential Action* (Princeton, N.J.: Princeton University Press, 2003).

32. Bert A. Rockman, "Entrepreneur in the Constitutional Marketplace: The Development of the Presidency," in Peter F. Nardulli, ed., *The Constitution in American Political Development: An Institutional Perspective* (Urbana: University of Illinois Press, 1992).

33. Ralph Ketcham, *Presidents Above Party: The First American Presidency, 1788–1829* (Chapel Hill: University of North Carolina Press, 1984).

34. Stephen Skowronek, *Building a New American State: The Expansion of National Administrative Capacities, 1877–1920* (Cambridge: Cambridge University Press, 1982).

35. Sidney Milkis, *The President and the Parties: The Transformation of the American Party System Since the New Deal* (Oxford: Oxford University Press, 1993).

36. Kenneth R. Mayer and Thomas J. Weko, "The Institutionalization of Power," in Shapiro et al., *Presidential Power*.

37. Paul Pierson, *Politics in Time: History, Institutions, and Social Analysis* (Princeton, N.J.: Princeton University Press, 2004).

38. Thomas E. Cronin and Michael A. Genovese, *The Paradoxes of the American Presidency*, 2nd ed. (Oxford: Oxford University Press, 2004).

39. Robert H. Salisbury and Kenneth Shepsle, "U.S. Congressman as Enterprise," *Legislative Studies Quarterly* 6 (1981): 559–76.

40. Barbara Sinclair, *The Transformation of the U.S. Senate* (Baltimore: Johns Hopkins University Press, 1989), 14-18, 57-69.

41. Burdett A. Loomis, *The New American Politician: Ambition, Entrepreneurship, and the Changing Face of Political Life* (New York: Basic Books, 1988), 13.

42. Eric Schickler, *Disjointed Pluralism: Institutional Innovation and the Development of the U.S. Congress* (Princeton, N.J.: Princeton University Press, 2001).

43. Stanley Bach and Steven S. Smith, *Managing Uncertainty in the House of Representatives: Adaptation and Innovation in Special Rules* (Washington, D.C.: Brookings Institution Press, 1988), 13.

44. Ibid., 36, 74.

45. Ibid.

46. C. Lawrence Evans and Daniel Lapinski, "Obstruction and Leadership in the U.S. Senate," in Lawrence C. Dodd and Bruce I. Oppenheimer, eds., *Congress Reconsidered*, 8th ed. (Washington, D.C.: CQ Press, 2005), 231.

47. Nelson W. Polsby, *Consequences of Party Reform* (Oxford: Oxford University Press, 1983).

48. Theda Skocpol, *Diminished Democracy: From Membership to Management in American Civic Life* (Norman: University of Oklahoma Press, 2003), 139.

49. Frank R. Baumgartner and Beth L. Leech, "Issue Niches and Policy Bandwagons: Patterns of Interest Group Involvement in National Politics," *Journal of Politics* 63 (2001): 1191–1213.

50. Jeffrey M. Berry, *The New Liberalism: The Rising Power of Citizen Groups* (Washington, D.C.: Brookings Institution, 1997).

51. Robin Kolodny and David A. Dulio, "Political Party Adaptation in US Congressional Campaigns: Why Parties Use Coordinated Expenditures to Hire Political Consultants," *Party Politics* 9 (2003): 729–46.

52. John F. Bibby, "Party Organizations, 1946–1996," in Byron E. Shafer, ed., *Partisan Approaches to Postwar American Politics* (New York: Chatham House, 1998).

53. Richard M. Skinner, "Do 527s Add Up to a Party: Thinking About the 'Shadows' of Politics," *The Forum* 3, 3 (2005), http://www.bepress.com/forum/vol3/iss3/art5

54. Robin Kolodny, *Pursuing Majorities: Congressional Campaign Committees in American Politics* (Norman: University of Oklahoma Press, 1998).

55. Bibby, "Party Organizations," 156.

56. James A. Thurber, Candice J. Nelson, and David A. Dulio," Portrait of Campaign Consultants," in Thurber and Nelson, eds., *Campaign Warriors: The Role of Political Consultants in Elections* (Washington, D.C.: Brookings Institution, 2000).

57. James Sterling Young, *The Washington Community, 1800–1828* (New York: Columbia University Press, 1966).

58. Nelson W. Polsby, "Institutionalization of the House of Representatives," *American Political Science Review* 62 (1968): 144–68.

59. Hugh Heclo, "Issue Networks and the Executive Establishment," in Anthony King, ed., *The New American Political System* (Washington, D.C.: American Enterprise Institute, 1978).

60. Paul C. Light, *The True Size of Government* (Washington, D.C.: Brookings Institution, 1999).

61. David Osbourne and Ted Gaebler, *Reinventing Government: How the Entrepreneurial Spirit is Transforming the Public Sector* (Reading, Mass.: Addison-Wesley, 1992).

62. Bryan D. Jones and Frank R. Baumgartner, *The Politics of Attention: How Government Prioritizes Problems* (Chicago: University of Chicago Press, 2005).

63. Orren and Skowronek, *Search for American Political Development*, 123.

64. Kernell, *Going Public*, 27.

65. Ibid.

66. For a similar view, see R. Shep Melnick, "Governing More But Enjoying It Less," in Morton Keller and Melnick, eds., *Taking Stock: American Government in the Twentieth Century* (Washington, D.C.: Woodrow Wilson Center, 1999).

67. George C. Edwards III, "Building Coalitions," *Presidential Studies Quarterly* 30 (2000): 47–78.

68. Peri Arnold, "One President, Two Presidencies: George W. Bush in Peace and War," in Steven E. Schier, ed., *High Risk and Big Ambition: The Presidency of George W. Bush* (Pittsburgh: University of Pittsburgh Press, 2004).

69. John J. Coleman, "Resurgent or Just Busy? Party Organizations in Contemporary America," in John C. Green and Danial M. Shea, eds., *The State of the Parties: The Changing Role of Contemporary American Parties*, 2nd ed. (Lanham, Md.: Rowman and Littlefield, 1996).

70. Skocpol, *Diminished Democracy*, 153–54.

71. Ibid.

72. Matt Bai, "Who Lost Ohio?" *New York Times*, November 21, 2004, Magazine section.

73. Ibid.; Matt Bai, "The Multi-Level Marketing of the President," *New York Times*, April 25, 2004, Magazine section.

74. Bruce Miroff, "Entrepreneurship and Leadership," *Studies in American Political Development* 17 (2003): 204–11.

Chapter 3. Leadership and American Political Development

I received much valuable feedback on this project from participants in the conference on "Political Action and Political Change: Leaders, Entrepreneurs, and Agents in American Political Development," Yale University, October 2004. Thanks also to Peter Breiner, Adam Sheingate, and Steve Skowronek for their dialogue with me on leadership and entrepreneurship.

1. See Daniel P. Carpenter, *The Forging of Bureaucratic Autonomy: Reputations, Networks, and Policy Innovation in Executive Agencies, 1862–1928* (Princeton, N.J.: Princeton University Press, 2001) and Eric Schickler, *Disjointed Pluralism: Institutional Innovation and the Development of the U.S. Congress* (Princeton, N.J.: Princeton University Press, 2001).

2. Joseph A. Schumpeter, *The Theory of Economic Development* (New Brunswick, N.J.: Transaction Publishers, 1983).

3. John W. Kingdon, *Agendas, Alternatives, and Public Policies*, 2nd ed. (New York: Longman, 1995), esp. 122–25, 179–83.

4. Robert A. Dahl, *Who Governs? Democracy and Power in an American City* (New Haven, Conn.: Yale University Press, 1961).

5. Eugene Lewis, *Public Entrepreneurship: Toward a Theory of Bureaucratic Political Power* (Bloomington: Indiana University Press, 1980), 94–155.

6. Carpenter, *The Forging of Bureaucratic Autonomy*.

7. Schumpeter, *Theory of Economic Development*, 75.

8. For example, see Adam D. Sheingate, "Political Entrepreneurship, Institutional Change, and American Political Development," *Studies in American Political Development* 17 (Fall 2003): 185.

9. Joseph A. Schumpeter, *Capitalism, Socialism, and Democracy*, 3rd ed. (New York: Harper and Row, 1950), 132.

10. Schumpeter, *Theory of Economic Development*, 65.

11. Kingdon, *Agendas*, 180–81.

12. Bruce Miroff, "Entrepreneurship and Leadership," *Studies in American Political Development* 17 (Fall 2003): 204.

13. Dahl, *Who Governs?* 121.

14. Carpenter, *Forging of Bureaucratic Autonomy*, 275–88.

15. Lewis, *Public Entrepreneurship*, 104–23.

16. Dahl, *Who Governs?* 134.

17. Robert C. Tucker, *Politics as Leadership* (Columbia: University of Missouri Press, 1981), 15.

18. James MacGregor Burns, *Leadership* (New York: Harper and Row, 1978), 19.

19. John Gardner, *On Leadership* (New York: Free Press, 1990), 1.

20. Burns, *Leadership*, 19–20.

21. For examples, see Kingdon, *Agendas* and Schickler, *Disjointed Pluralism*.

22. Stephen Skowronek, *The Politics Presidents Make: Leadership from John Adams to Bill Clinton* (Cambridge, Mass.: Harvard University Press, 1997), 24.

23. Howard Gardner, *Leading Minds: An Anatomy of Leadership* (New York: Basic Books, 1995), 43.

24. Young quoted in Howell Raines, *My Soul Is Rested: Movement Days in the Deep South Remembered* (New York: Penguin, 1983), 425.

25. Rustin quoted in David J. Garrow, *Bearing the Cross: Martin Luther King, Jr., and the Southern Christian Leadership Conference* (New York: Vintage, 1988), 72.

26. Taylor Branch, *Parting the Waters: America in the King Years, 1954–63* (New York: Simon and Schuster, 1988), 346.

27. King quoted in Branch, *Parting the Waters*, 352.

28. Data from Jeane Kirkpatrick, *The New Presidential Elite: Men and Women in National Politics* (New York: Sage, 1976), 84.

29. See Ruth Rosen, *The World Split Open: How the Modern Women's Movement Changed America* (New York: Penguin, 2001), 143–260.

30. Bella Abzug with Mim Kelber, *Gender Gap: Bella Abzug's Guide to Political Power for American Women* (Boston: Houghton Mifflin, 1984), 21.

31. Interview with Jane Pierson, July 29, 2003.

32. Byron Shafer, *Quiet Revolution: The Struggle for the Democratic Party and the Shaping of Post-Reform Politics* (New York: Sage, 1983), 460–91.

33. Theda Skocpol, *Protecting Soldiers and Mothers: The Political Origins of Social Policy in the United States* (Cambridge, Mass.: Harvard University Press, 1992).

34. David Plotke, *Building a Democratic Political Order: Reshaping American Liberalism in the 1930s and 1940s* (New York: Cambridge University Press, 1996) and Julian E. Zelizer, *On Capitol Hill: The Struggle to Reform Congress and Its Consequences, 1948–2000* (New York: Cambridge University Press, 2004).

35. Shafer, *Quiet Revolution*, 474–76.

36. Ibid., 470.

37. Interview with Phyllis Segal, July 8, 2003.

38. Susan and Martin Tolchin, *Clout: Womanpower and Politics* (New York: Coward, McCann & Geoghegan, 1974), 31–59; Segal interview.

39. Interview with Doris Meissner, October 3, 2003.

40. Pierson interview.

41. Newt Gingrich, *Lessons Learned the Hard Way: A Personal Report* (New York: HarperCollins, 1998), 106.

42. Peter J. Boyer, "Good Newt, Bad Newt," *Vanity Fair,* July 1989.

43. Ibid.

44. Ronald M. Peters, Jr., "Institutional Context and Leadership Style: The Case of Newt Gingrich," in Nicol C. Rae and Colton C. Campbell, eds., *New Majority or Old Minority? The Impact of Republicans on Congress* (Lanham, Md.: Rowman and Littlefield, 1999), 50.

45. Ibid.

46. Katherine Q. Seelye, "He's Top Man in the House, But Not in the Nation," *New York Times,* March 19, 1995.

47. David Maraniss and Michael Weisskopf, *"Tell Newt to Shut Up!"* *Prizewinning Washington Post Journalists Reveal How Reality Gagged the Gingrich Revolution* (New York: Simon and Schuster, 1996), 146–77.

48. Ibid.

Chapter 4. Agency and Popular Activism in American Political Culture

1. Louis Hartz, *The Founding of New Societies* (New York: Harcourt, Brace, 1964), 10; Eric Foner, *The Story of American Freedom* (New York: Norton, 1998), xiv; Seymour Martin Lipset, *The First New Nation* (Garden City, N.Y.: Doubleday, 1967), 2.

2. Daniel T. Rodgers, "Exceptionalism," in Anthony Molho and Gordon S. Wood, eds., *Imagined Histories: American Historians Interpret the Past* (Princeton, N.J.: Princeton University Press, 1998), 31, 35; George M. Fredrickson, *The Comparative Imagination: On the History of Racism, Nationalism, and Social Movements* (Berkeley: University of California Press, 1997), 49, 51, 50, 58, 53.

3. Fredrickson, *Comparative Imagination,* 65.

4. Samuel Huntington, "The Democratic Distemper," *Public Interest* 41 (Fall 1975).

5. Gordon S. Wood, "Founders & Keepers," *New York Review of Books,* July 14, 2005, 34. The story of the Revolutionary leaders' campaign against popular meddling is told in James E. Block, *A Nation of Agents: The American Path to a Modern Self and Society* (Cambridge, Mass.: Harvard University Press, 2002), chap. 7.

6. Alexis de Tocqueville, *Democracy in America* (New York: New American Library, 1956), 194.

7. Paul Rich, "American Voluntarism, Social Capital, and Political Culture," in *Civil Society and Democratization, Annals of the American Academy of Political and Social Science* 565 (1999): 16; Clarence Y. H. Lo, "Communities of Challengers in Social Movement Theory," in Aldon D. Morris and Carol McClurg Mueller, eds., *Frontiers in Social Movement Theory* (New Haven, Conn., Yale University Press, 1992), 228; Francis Fukuyama, quoted in John S. Robey, "Civil Society and NAFTA: Initial Results," in *Civil Society and Democratization,* 114.

8. James Luther Adams, *On Being Human Religiously* (Boston: Beacon Press, 1976), 60; Weber quoted in same volume, 60. William Ellery Channing, "Remarks on Associations, in *Works of William E. Channing* (Boston: American Unitarian Association, 1874), 1: 281–83.

9. Tocqueville, *Democracy in America,* 198, 95.

10. Louis Hartz, *The Liberal Tradition in America* (New York: Harcourt Brace, 1955), 17, 9, 11; Thomas Jefferson, "Inaugural Address—March 4, 1801," in *The Life and Selected Writings of Thomas Jefferson,* ed. Adrienne Koch and William Peden (New York: Modern Library, 1944), 323.

11. Jan Elster, "Introduction," in Elster, ed., *Rational Choice* (New York: New York University Press, 1986), 23; Kristen Renwick Monroe, "The Theory of Rational Action," in Monroe, ed. *The Economic Approach to Politics: A Critical Assessment of the Theory of Rational Action* (New York: HarperCollins, 1991), 4; Barry Hindess, *Choice, Rationality, and Social Theory* (London: Unwin Hyman, 1988), 16.

12. Myra Marx Ferree, "The Political Context of Rationality," in Morris and Mueller, *Social Movement Theory*, 31.

13. Ralph H. Turner and Lewis M. Killian, "The Field of Collective Behavior," in Russell L. Curtis, Jr., and Benigno E. Aguirre, eds., *Collective Behavior and Social Movements* (Boston: Prentice Hall, 1993), 6, 7; Neil J. Smelser, "The Nature of Collective Behavior," in the same volume, 25.

14. Lo, "Communities of Challengers," 224; Margit Mayer, "Social Movement Research in the United States: A European Perspective," in Stanford M. Lyman, ed., *Social Movements* (New York: New York University Press, 1995), 175.

15. Ferree, "Political Context of Rationality," 34; Pamela E. Oliver and Gerald Marwell, "Mobilizing Technologies for Collective Action," in Morris and Mueller, *Social Movement Theory*, 252; Jean L. Cohen, quoted in William A. Gamson, "The Social Psychology of Collective Action," in the same volume, 54.

16. Margit Mayer, "Social Movement Research and Social Movement Practice: The U.S. Pattern," in Dieter Rucht, ed., *Research on Social Movements* (Boulder, Colo.: Westview Press, 1991), 198.

17. Mayer, "European Perspective," 185; Mayer, "U.S. Pattern," 55; Gamson, "Collective Action," 62; Oliver and Marwell, "Mobilizing Technologies," 252.

18. Aldon D. Morris, "Political Consciousness and Collective Action," in Morris and Mueller, *Social Movement Theory*, 352; Mayer, "European Perspective," 184; Mayer, "U.S. Pattern," 54. The corporate idea is present in Locke's theory of revolution, the French regicides for whom "Louis must die because the nation must live" (Robespierre, in *Regicide and Revolution*, ed. Michael Walzer [Cambridge: Cambridge University Press, 1974]), early European worker movements, and Tocqueville's description of the feudal citizen who is "closely attached" to many "fellow citizens" (Tocqueville, *Democracy in America*, 193).

19. Carol McClurg Mueller, "Building Social Movement Theory," in Morris and Mueller, *Social Movement Theory*, 3, 22; Gamson, "Collective Action," 55; Mayer, "U.S. Pattern," 98.

20. Gamson, "Collective Action," 55; Mayer, "U.S. Pattern," 97; Marc Howard Ross, "Substance and Method in Cultural and Crosscultural Political Psychology: Commentary," in Stanley A. Renshon and John Duckitt, eds., *Political Psychology* (New York: New York University Press, 2000), 68, 73.

21. Mayer, "U.S. Pattern," 54; Turner and Killian, "Field of Collective Behavior," 18; Mueller, "Building Social Movement Theory," 8.

22. Gamson, "Collective Action," 65; Ferree, "Political Context of Rationality," 33; Turner and Killian, "Field of Collective Behavior," 13.

23. Robert Putnam, "Bowling Alone: America's Declining Social Capital," *Journal of Democracy* 6 (January 1995): 65.

24. Ross, "The Relevance of Culture for the Study of Political Psychology," in Renshon and Duckitt, *Political Psychology*, 41; Michael Walzer, "The Concept of Civil Society," in Walzer, ed., *Toward a Global Civil Society* (Providence, R.I.: Berghahn, 1998), 7; Robert C. Post and Nancy L. Rosenblum, "Introduction," in Rosenblum and Post, eds., *Civil Society and Government* (Princeton, N.J.: Princeton University Press, 2002), 18; Michael Walzer, "Equality and Civil Society," in Simone Chambers and Will Kymlicka, eds., *Alternative Conceptions of Civil Society* (Princeton, N.J.: Princeton University Press, 2002), 35.

25. Michael Walzer, "Introduction," in Walzer, *Global Civil Society*, 1. For an extended discussion of the concept of social capital, see, e.g., Bob Edwards, Michael W. Foley, and Mario Diani, eds., *Beyond Tocqueville: Civil Society and the Social Capital Debate in Comparative Perspective* (Hanover, N.H.: University Press of New England, 2001).

26. Theda Skocpol, *Diminished Democracy: From Membership to Management in American Civic Life* (Norman: University of Oklahoma Press, 2003), 36.

27. Tocqueville, *Democracy in America*, 116, 303.

28. Rhys H. Williams, "From the 'Beloved Community" to 'Family Values': Religious Language, Symbolic Repetoires, and Democratic Culture," in David S. Meyer, Nancy Whittier, and Belinda Robnett, eds., *Social Movements* (Oxford: Oxford University Press, 2002), 250.

29. Stephen Darwall, *The British Moralists and the Internal "Ought": 1640–1740* (Cambridge: Cambridge University Press, 1995), 16; John Macmurray, *The Self as Agent* (London: Faber, 1957), 134.

30. See, e.g., Elster, *Rational Choice*, 27 (rational choice); Philip Pettit, *Republicanism* (Oxford: Clarendon Press, 1999), 53 (republicanism); Charles Taylor, *Modern Social Imaginaries* (Durham, N.C.: Duke University Press, 2004), 21 (communitarianism); James Youniss, Jeffrey A. McLellan, and Miranda Yates, "A Developmental Approach to Civil Society" in Edwards et al., *Beyond Tocqueville*, 243–43 (democratic theory); Stuart Hampshire, *Freedom of the Individual* (Princeton, N.J.: Princeton University Press, 1975), 112 (contemporary moral philosophy).

31. Andrew Greeley, "Coleman Revisited: Religious Structures as a Source of Social Capital," in Edwards et al., *Beyond Tocqueville*, 240; see also Mark R. Warren, "Power and Conflict in Social Capital," 173, and Richard L. Wood, "Political Culture Reconsidered," both in Edwards et al., *Beyond Tocqueville*, 260; Lo, "Communities of Challengers," 241.

32. Stanford M. Lyman, "Social Theory and Social Movements: Sociology as Sociodicy," in Lyman, *Social Movements*, 397; Williams, "Religious Language," 247; Perry Miller, *The Life of the Mind in America from the Revolution to the Civil War* (New York: Harcourt, Brace, 1965), 7, 6; James Madison, "No. 10," in Alexander Hamilton, James Madison, and John Jay, *The Federalist Papers* (New York: Signet, 1961), 79; George Washington, "The Farewell Address," in Merle Curti, Willard Thorpe, and Carlos Baker, eds., *American Issues: The Social Record* (Chicago: Lippincott, 1960), 141.

33. Walzer, "Concept," 20; Martin E. Marty, "Where the Energies Go," in *Religion in the Nineties, Annals of the American Academy of Political and Social Science* 525 (May 1993): 15, 16; Adams, *On Being Human Religiously*, 64–65.

34. Philip F. Gura, *A Glimpse of Sion's Glory: Puritan Radicalism in New England, 1620-1660* (Middletown, Conn.: Wesleyan University Press, 1984), 121, 125; see also 155.

35. Richard L. Bushman, *From Puritan to Yankee: Character and the Social Order in Connecticut, 1690-1765* (New York: Norton, 1970), 59; Isaac Backus, quoted in William G. McLoughlin, *Isaac Backus* (Boston: Little, Brown, 1967), 31; McLoughlin, *Isaac Backus*, 45, 43; Patricia U. Bonomi, *Under the Cope of Heaven: Religion, Society and Politics in Colonial America* (New York: Oxford University Press, 1986), 186.

36. Bushman, *From Puritan to Yankee*, 71.

37. Charles Brockwell, quoted in C. C. Goen, *Revivalism and Separatism in New England, 1740–1800* (Middletown, Conn.: Wesleyan University Press, 1987), 30; Philemon Robbins, quoted in Bushman, *From Puritan to Yankee*, 211.

38. Elisha Williams, quoted in Bushman, *From Puritan to Yankee*, 227.

39. See Rhys Isaac, *The Transformation of Virginia, 1740–1790* (New York: Norton,

1988); Gary B. Nash, *The American Revolution: The Unruly Birth of Democracy and the Struggle to Create America* (New York: Viking, 2005).

40. Alan Taylor, *William Cooper's Town* (New York: Knopf, 1995); Isaac, *Transformation of Virginia*, 321.

41. J. Hector St. John de Crèvecoeur, *Letters from an American Farmer* (New York: E.P. Dutton, 1957), 34; Stanley Elkins and Eric McKitrick, "A Meaning for Turner's Frontier," *Political Science Quarterly* (September 1954): 339, 330; T. Scott Miyakawa, *Protestants and Pioneers: Individualism and Conformity on the American Frontier* (Chicago: University of Chicago Press, 1964), 230.

42. Nathan O. Hatch, *The Democratization of American Christianity* (New Haven, Conn.: Yale University Press, 1989), 222, 5; Jon Butler, *Awash in a Sea of Faith: Christianizing the American People* (Cambridge, Mass.: Harvard University Press, 1990), 2; Miller, *Life of the Mind*, 8; "Declaration and Address of the Christian Association of Washington," quoted in Hatch, *Democratization*, 162; Angelina Grimke Weld, quoted in Whitney R. Cross, *The Burned-Over District* (New York: Harper, 1965), 286.

43. Paul E. Johnson, *A Shopkeeper's Millennium: Society and Revivals in Rochester, New York, 1815-1837* (New York: Hill and Wang, 1978), 9; Hatch, *Democratization*, 7.

44. Brick Church Session Minutes, quoted in Johnson, *Shopkeeper's Millennium*, 110; Mary P. Ryan, *Cradle of the Middle Class* (Cambridge: Cambridge University Press, 1981), 72; David Harrowar, quoted in Ryan, *Cradle*, 69.

45. Robert H. Abzug, *Cosmos Crumbling: American Reform and the Religious Imagination* (New York: Oxford University Press, 1994), vii; Ralph Waldo Emerson, "New England Reformers," in *Ralph Waldo Emerson: Selected Prose and Poetry*, ed. Reginald L. Cook (New York: Holt, Rinehart, 1950), 144–46.

46. Stanton, quoted in Page Smith, "From Masses to Peoplehood," *Historical Reflections/Reflexions Historiques* 1 (June 1974): 119; Jama Lazerow, *Religion and the Working Class in Antebellum America* (Washington, D.C.: Smithsonian Institution Press, 1995), 12. See also William R. Sutton, *Journeymen for Jesus: Evangelican Artisans Confront Capitalism in Jacksonian Baltimore* (University Park: Pennsylvania State University Press, 1998).

47. Hannah Arendt, "Civil Disobedience," in Crises of the Republic (New York: Harcourt Brace Jovanovich, 1972), 98, 99; Emerson, "Politics," in *Selected Prose*, 199; Henry D. Thoreau, "Civil Disobedience," in Hugo Adam Bedau, ed., *Civil Disobedience: Theory and Practice*, (New York: Pegasus, 1969), 28, 38, 32, 30, 40.

48. Louis S. Gerteis, *Morality and Utility in American Antislavery Reform* (Chapel Hill: University of North Carolina Press, 1987), 47; Edward H. Madden, *The Disobedience and Moral Law in Nineteenth-Century American Philosophy* (Seattle: University of Washington Press, 1968), 10; Michael Walzer, "The Obligation to Disobey," in Walter, *Obligations: Essays on Disobedience, War, and Citizenship* (Cambridge, Mass.: Harvard University Press, 1970), 10, 17; Arendt, "Civil Disobedience," 96. See also Peter Brock, *Radical Pacifists in Antebellum America* (Princeton, N.J.: Princeton University Press, 1968); Edward Needles Wright, *Conscientious Objectors in the Civil War* (Philadelphia: University of Pennsylvania Press, 1931).

49. Frederick Jackson Turner, *Frontier and Section: Selected Essays of Frederick Jackson Turner* (Englewood Cliffs, N.J., Prentice-Hall, 1961), 62, 76, 38, 61, 38, 63.

50. David Hollinger, "The Problem of Pragmatism in American History," *Journal of American History* 67 (June 1980): 105.

51. Stephen M. Tipton, *Getting Saved from the Sixties: Moral Meaning in Conversion and Cultural Change* (Berkeley: University of California Press, 1982), 27, 29; Huntington, "Democratic Distemper," 15.

52. Wade Clark Roof, *A Generation of Seekers: The Spiritual Journeys of the Baby Boom Generation* (San Francisco: Harper, 1993), 249; Stephen C. Craig, *The Malevolent*

Leaders: Popular Discontent in America (Boulder, Colo.: Westview Press, 1993), 78; Walzer, "Obligation," 20.

53. Rebecca E. Klatch, "The Counterculture, the New Left, and the New Right," in Marcy Darnovsky, Barbara Epstein, and Richard Flacks, eds., *Cultural Politics and Social Movements* (Philadelphia: Temple University Press, 1995), 83; Alan Wolfe, *Moral Freedom* (New York: Norton, 2001), 195; Wade Clark Roof and William McKinney, *American Mainline Religion* (New Brunswick, N.J.: Rutgers University Press, 1987), 43.

54. Stephanie Coontz, *Marriage, a History* (New York: Viking, 2005), 2, 4; Harry C. Boyte, *Community Is Possible* (New York: Harper and Row, 1984), 210, 218.

55. Marty, "Energy," 15; Donald E. Miller, "Postdenominational Christianity in the Twenty-First Century," in *Americans and Religions in the Twenty-First Century, Annals of the American Academy of Political and Social Science* 558 (1998), 196. See also William McKinney, "Mainline Protestantism 2000," in the same volume.

56. Roof, "Modernity, The Religious, and the Spiritual," in *Americans and Religions*, 222; Roof, *Generation*, 5, 251.

57. Ron Pagnucco, "A Comparison of the Political Behavior of Faith-Based and Secular Peace Groups," in Christian Smith, ed., *Disruptive Religion: The Force of Faith in Social-Movement Activism* (New York: Routledge, 1996), 206; Barbara Epstein, *Political Protest and Cultural Revolution* (Berkeley: University of California Press, 1991), 1.

58. Wolfe, *Moral Freedom*, 195, 196, 14; Roof, *Generation*, 114, 108.

59. Christian Smith, *Christian America? What Evangelicals Really Want* (Berkeley: University of California Press, 2002), 18, 46, 95, 109, 103, 96, 95, 49, 52, 117, 54.

60. Smith, *Christian America*, 59, 57; Miller, "Postdenominational Christianity," 197, 204.

61. Thomas Franks, *What's the Matter with Kansas? How Conservatives Won the Heart of America* (New York: Henry Holt, 2005), 95, 109, 133.

62. Rhys H. Williams and Jeffrey Blackburn, "Many Are Called But Few Obey: Ideological Commitment and Activism in Operation Rescue," in Smith, ed., *Disruptive Religion*, 181, 184. Franks, *What's the Matter*, 226, 5, 247, 68, 7, 9.

63. Franks, *What's the Matter*, 196. See also Mike Dorning, "Religious Right Wants Its Due from Bush, GOP," *Chicago Tribune*, July 17, 2005, 1, 1.

64. Keith Whittington, "Revisiting Tocqueville's America," in Edwards et al., *Beyond Tocqueville*, 31; Ken Thompson, *From Neighborhood to Nation: The Democratic Foundations of Civil Society* (Hanover, N.H.: University Press of New England, 2001), 2; "Editors' Introduction," in Edwards et al., *Beyond Tocqueville*, 17.

65. Iris Young, "Activist Challenges to Deliberative Democracy," *Political Theory* 29 (October 2001): 670; Walzer, "Equality," 39.

Chapter 5. A Calculated Enchantment of Passion: Bryan and the "Cross of Gold" in the 1896 Democratic National Convention

The author would like to thank the participants in the conference on Political Action and Political Change for their comments and advice, particularly David Mayhew and Stephen Skowronek. In addition, Ayse Banu Bargu carefully read the essay and corrected all the errors now missing from this text.

1. *New York Tribune*, July 10, 1896.
2. Richard Bensel, "A Cross of Gold, a Crown of Thorns: Preferences and Decisions in the 1896 Democratic National Convention," in Ira Katznelson and Barry R.

Weingast, eds., *Preferences and Situations: Points of Intersection Between Historical and Rational Choice Institutionalism* (New York: Sage, 2005). For an extended analysis of how monetary preferences shaped the convention, see Richard Franklin Bensel, *Passion and Preferences: Demonstrations and Decisions in the 1896 Democratic National Convention* (in preparation).

3. Michael Suk-Young Chwe, *Rational Ritual: Culture, Coordination, and Common Knowledge* (Princeton, N.J.: Princeton University Press, 2001).

4. Richard Franklin Bensel, *The Political Economy of American Industrialization, 1877–1900* (New York: Cambridge University Press, 2000), chap. 6.

5. Edward B. Dickinson, *Official Proceedings of the Democratic National Convention* (Logansport, Ind.: Wilson, Humphreys, 1896), 251.

6. *Atlanta Constitution*, July 10, 1896.

7. *Detroit Free Press*, July 10, 1896.

8. "Applause" (*Chicago Tribune, Memphis Commercial Appeal*, July 10, 1896); "cheers" (*Atlanta Constitution, New York Tribune*, July 10, 1896).

9. "Applause" (*Atlanta Constitution, New York Tribune*, July 10, 1896); "great applause and cheering" (*Chicago Tribune, Memphis Commercial Appeal*, July 10, 1896).

10. "Applause" (*Atlanta Constitution, New York Tribune*, July 10, 1896); "continued cheering" (*Chicago Tribune*, July 10, 1896); "continued cheers" (*Memphis Commercial Appeal*, July 10, 1896).

11. "Cheers" (*Atlanta Constitution, New York Tribune*, July 10, 1896).

12. "Great cheering" (*Atlanta Constitution, New York Tribune*, July 10, 1896).

13. "Loud applause" (*Chicago Tribune*, July 10, 1896).

14. "Great applause and confusion in the silver delegations" (*Chicago Tribune, Memphis Commercial Appeal*, July 10, 1896).

15. "Cheers" (*Atlanta Constitution, New York Tribune*, July 10, 1896).

16. "Cheering" (*Chicago Tribune*, July 10, 1896); "cheers" (*Memphis Commercial Appeal, New York Tribune*, July 10, 1896).

17. *Chicago Tribune*, July 10, 1896.

18. "Great applause" (*Atlanta Constitution*, July 10, 1896); "loud applause" (*Chicago Tribune, Memphis Commercial Appeal*, July 10, 1896); "great cheering" (*New York Tribune*, July 10, 1896).

19. Figure 1 appeared in the *Chicago Tribune* on July 5, 1896.

20. *Chicago Tribune*, July 9, 1896; *Boston Globe*, July 9, 1896.

21. William Jennings Bryan and Mary Baird Bryan, *The Memoirs of William Jennings Bryan* (Philadelphia: John C. Winston, 1925), 109.

22. William Jennings Bryan, *The First Battle: A Story of the Campaign of 1896* (Chicago: W.B. Conkey, 1896), 206. Also see Louis W. Koenig, *Bryan: A Political Biography of William Jennings Bryan* (New York: Putnam, 1975), 189–90.

23. *Atlanta Constitution*, July 11, 1896.

24. *Boston Globe*, July 9, 1896; Bryan and Bryan, *The Memoirs of William Jennings Bryan*, 103–4; Paolo E. Coletta, *William Jennings Bryan*, vol. 1, *Political Evangelist, 1860–1908* (Lincoln: University of Nebraska Press, 1964), 121.

25. Bryan, *The First Battle*, 615.

26. See Koenig, *Bryan*, 187, 191–94.

27. David Mayhew, *America's Congress: Actions in the Public Sphere, James Madison Through Newt Gingrich* (New Haven, Conn.: Yale University Press, 2000), 37–38.

28. Fernand Braudel, *The Mediterranean and the Mediterranean World in the Age of Philip II*, trans. Sian Reynolds (New York: Harper and Row, 1972), 1: 20–21.

29. Jon Elster, *Making Sense of Marx* (New York: Cambridge University Press,

1985), 8; Fritz Wilhelm Scharpf, *Games Real Actors Play: Actor-Centered Institutionalism in Policy Research* (Boulder, Colo.: Westview Press, 1997), 1.

30. Greg Wawro, *Legislative Entrepreneurship in the U.S. House of Representatives* (Ann Arbor: University of Michigan Press, 2001).

31. Amartya Sen, "Behavior and the Concept of Preference," *Economica* n.s. 40, 159 (August 1973): 241–59.

32. James Morone, *Hellfire Nation: The Politics of Sin in American History* (New Haven, Conn.: Yale University Press, 2003).

Chapter 6. Organizing for Disorder: Civil Unrest, Police Control, and the Invention of Washington, D.C.

For excellent research support, I wish to thank Justin Peck, Melissa Prosky and the Gordon Center of Brandeis University. For exacting comments on earlier drafts, I thank Robert Mickey and Stephen Skowronek, and the members of my 2006 police seminar at Brandeis.

1. Ira Katznelson, "Structure and Configuration in Comparative Politics," in Mark Lichbach and Alan Zuckerman, eds., *Comparative Politics: Rationality, Culture and Structure* (New York: Cambridge University Press, 1997); Theda Skocpol, "Bringing the State Back In: Strategies of Analysis in Current Research," in Peter B. Evans, Dietrich Rueschemeyer, and Theda Skocpol, eds., *Bringing the State Back In* (New York: Cambridge University Press, 1985), 7; Stephen Skowronek, *Building a New American State: The Expansion of National Administrative Capacities, 1877–1920* (New York: Cambridge University Press, 1982), 4; William H. Sewell, Jr., "Space in Contentious Politics," in Ronald R. Aminzade, Jack A. Goldstone, Doug McAdam, and Elizabeth J. Perry, *Silence and Voice in the Study of Contentious Politics* (Cambridge: Cambridge University Press, 2001), 68–69, 58–59.

2. Gabriel A. Almond and Stephen J. Genco, "Clouds, Clocks, and the Study of Politics," *World Politics* 24, 4 (July 1977).

3. Adam D. Sheingate, "Political Entrepreneurship, Institutional Change, and American Political Development," *Studies in American Political Development* 17 (Fall 2003): 190, 197, 202.

4. Stanley Elkins and Eric McKitrick, *The Age of Federalism* (New York: Oxford University Press, 1993), 176; James E. Block, *A Nation of Agents: The American Path to a Modern Self and Society* (Cambridge, Mass.: Harvard University Press, 2002), 23, 19.

5. Block, *Nation of Agents*, 246, 251, 257.

6. Ibid., 23, 236, 235, 240.

7. Ibid., 236–37, 273, 283.

8. Ibid., 277–78, 290, 284, 284, 246, 267.

9. Elkins and McKitrick, *Age of Federalism*, 174, 182, 184.

10. James Madison, *Notes of Debates in the Federal Convention of 1787* (New York: Norton, 1966), 378–79.

11. Madison, *Notes of Debates*, 434–36, 477, 580–81, 620–21.

12. Alexander Hamilton, James Madison, and John Jay, *The Federalist Papers* (New York: Mentor Books, 1961), 198, 272–73; Elkins and McKitrick, *Age of Federalism*, 169–70.

13. Elkins and McKitrick, *Age of Federalism*, 170–71, 173, 192. New York would have been the "historically logical" choice. By the 1790s it led the nation in the value of trade, and it was America's most easily reached destination.

14. Conversely, Peter the Great imagined St. Petersburg as not only a new capital

but a robust cultural, commercial, and naval hub turning Russia toward Europe. He thus directed 1,000 of the leading noble families, 500 merchants, 500 traders, and 2,000 artisans to settle there. Fittingly, Americans chose to build their capital through real estate speculation. Elkins and McKitrick, *Age of Federalism*, 184–86.

15. Alan Lessoff, *The Nation and Its City: Politics, "Corruption," and Progress in Washington D.C., 1861–1902* (Baltimore: Johns Hopkins University Press, 1994), 5; Frederick Gutheim, *Worthy of the Nation: The History of Planning for the National Capital* (Washington, D.C.: Smithsonian Institution Press, 1977), 25.

16. Lessoff, *Nation and Its City*, 3, 17; Anthony Sutcliffe, *The Autumn of Central Paris: The Defeat of Town Planning 1850–1970* (Montreal: McGill-Queens University Press, 1971), 32; Gutheim, *Worthy of the Nation*, 27; James Sterling Young, *The Washington Community 1800–1828* (New York: Columbia University Press, 1966), 2, 7; Elkins and McKitrick, *Age of Federalism*, 180.

17. Elkins and McKitrick, *Age of Federalism*, 187–93, 177. It was so inhospitable a site that planners relied primarily on slaves for construction workers, a fact central to arguments for reparations for African Americans in our day. Randall Robinson, *The Debt: What American Owes to Blacks* (New York: Plume Books, 2001).

18. Even the new site seemed to portend social conflict to Tocqueville, who noted the pretension of the "magnificent palace" recently built to house Congress (Tocqueville, *Democracy in America*, 53–54).

19. This may refer to the New Year's Eve riot which struck New York in 1826. At least fourteen riots occurred in that city in the nineteenth century. Eric. H. Monkkonen, *Police in Urban America, 1860–1920* (New York: Cambridge University Press, 1981), 196n76.

20. Tocqueville, *Democracy in America*, 230–31, 238, 247–48, 289n1. Governors controlled state militias, he noted, and would restore public order when the public disobeyed legitimate authority.

21. Ibid., 88–92, 95, 166, 140.

22. George P. Fletcher, "Some Unwise Reflections About Discretion," Herman Goldstein, "Police Discretion: The Ideal Versus the Real," and Lawrence W. Sherman, "Experiments in Police Discretion," *Law and Contemporary Problems* 47, 4 (1984); Gordon P. Whitaker, "Managing Police Discretion: A Central Dilemma of Police Administration," *Public Administration Review* 39, 2 (1979).

23. P. A. J. Waddington, *Liberty and Order: Public Order Policing in a Capital City* (London: UCL Press, 1994), 28, 150–53.

24. John D. McCarthy and Clark McPhail, "The Institutionalization of Protest in the United States," in David S. Meyer and Sidney Tarrow, eds., *The Social Movement Society: Contentious Politics for a New Century* (New York: Rowman and Littlefield, 1998). See also Donatella Della Porta and Herbert Reiter, "Introduction," and Gary T. Marx, "Some Reflections on the Democratic Policing of Demonstrations," in Donatella Della Porta and Herbert Reiter, eds., *Policing Protest: The Control of Mass Demonstrations in Western Democracies* (Minneapolis: University of Minnesota Press, 1998).

25. In 1930, Washington, D.C., had 486,000 residents spread over 62 square miles. By comparison, New York had 6.9 million residents spread over 288 square miles and Philadelphia 1.9 million over 128 square miles. City size generally determines the scale of police resources and larger departments with greater resources will have a "greater capacity to repress." Jennifer Earl, "Protest Under Fire? Explaining the Policing of Protest," *American Sociological Review* 68 (August 2003): 585; Monkkonen, *Police in Urban America*, 55–58.

26. Barry Mackintosh, *The United State Park Police: A History* (Washington, D.C.: National Park Service, 1989). For a statutory, personnel, and funding history of the

Capitol Police Force, see Committee on House Administration, *A Statutory History of the United States Capitol Police Force* (Washington, D.C.: Government Printing Office, 1985).

27. Constance McLaughlin Green, *Washington: Village and Capital, 1800–1878* (Princeton, N.J.: Princeton University Press, 1962), 248–50; Alan Lessoff, *Nation and Its City*, 39, 116. Kenneth G. Alfers, *Law and Order in the Capital City: A History of the Washington Police, 1800–1886*, George Washington University Studies 5 (Washington, D.C.: George Washington University, 1976).

28. Robert M. Fogelson, *Big-City Police* (Cambridge, Mass.: Harvard University Press, 1977), 97, 193–95; Green, *Washington*, 253, 395, 38–39. "Slasher Has a Wife," *Washington Post* (hereafter *WP*), April 20, 1903; "Policemen Poorly Armed," *WP*, January 10, 1908. "Stamp Out Anarchy," *WP*, May 8, 1902; "Seek Government Aid," *WP*, October 23, 1905; "Police Methods Lax," *WP*, June 14, 1911.

29. "City Has 339,403," *WP*, April 30, 1908; "Police Cry for Help," *WP*, January 18, 1908; "Need More Police," *WP*, February 17, 1908; "Too Few Police at Night," *WP*, November 22, 1902; "Washington Policemen," *WP*, February 14, 1904.

30. "All Crooks Will Be Bagged," *WP*, September 24, 1902. "Trouble Makers In Town," *WP*, November 9, 1906; "No Place for Crooks," *WP*, September 30, 1902; "Preparing for Crowd," *WP*, November 15, 1908. "500 Extra Policemen," *WP*, January 28, 1909.

31. To commemorate the city's centennial, Congress convened the Senate Park Commission, known as the McMillan Commission. Its 1901 plan was faithful to L'Enfant's original design.

32. Paul and her associates had developed such disruptive techniques precisely where Jefferson would have expected it, in central London, New York, and Philadelphia. Lucy Barber, *Marching on Washington: The Forging of an American Political Tradition* (Berkeley: University of California Press, 2002), 46–49, 50–53; Christine A. Lunardini and Thomas J. Knock, "Woodrow Wilson and Woman Suffrage: A New Look," *Political Science Quarterly* 95, 4; Sally Hunter Graham, "Woodrow Wilson, Alice Paul, and the Woman Suffrage Movement," *Political Science Quarterly* 98, 4.

33. Barber, *Marching on Washington*, 71; "Women's Beauty, Grace, and Art Bewilder the Capital," *WP*, March 4, 1913; "Men in Police Attack," *WP*, March 10, 1913; "Vast Crowd 'Jolly'," *WP*, March 18, 1913; "Men in Police Attack," *WP*, March 10, 1913.

34. Barber, *Marching on Washington*, 73; "Traps Laid for Crooks," *WP*, September 22, 1915; "Public Order and Safety," *WP*, July 23, 1919. Meanwhile, war service drained a large number of policemen from the force. See Fogelson, *Big-City Police*, 86–87; Green, *Washington*, 244–45; Graham, "Woodrow Wilson," 675.

35. "Up from the Ranks," *WP*, April 20, 1920; "Arrests for Crime Soar 107 Percent Here in 10 Years," *WP*, March 2, 1924; "More Policemen to Guard Suburbs," *WP*, February 21, 1922; "Denouncing Wave of Crime Here, Officials, Ministers and Others Declare Police Are Too Few," *WP*, July 21, 1919.

36. "May Have 58 More Policemen by Fall," *WP*, July 4, 1922; "District No Place for Crooks in June," *WP*, March 11, 1923; "Sullivan Commended for Handling of Crowd," *WP*, June 5, 1923; "150,000 Will March in Big Klan Parade," *WP*, June 18, 1925; "Klan Leader Asks Parade Right of Way," *WP*, July 28, 1925; "Police, Quite Ready for Trouble, Find Parade Peaceful," *WP*, August 9, 1925.

37. "Outrage of the Public Peace," *WP*, October 20, 1925; "Spectacular Law Enforcement," *WP*, August 3, 1926; "Hesse Cites Part of Manual to Curb Gun Play by Police," *WP*, November 7, 1925. "Maj. Hesse Warns Police of Beatings," *WP*, August 20, 1926; "City Heads to Hear Police Board Plans," *WP*, September 7, 1928; "Half-

Way Police Reform," *WP*, September 8, 1928; "Maj. Hesse Wants 1,500 Police Force for War on Crime," *WP*, September 9, 1927 "Klan Seeks Permit to Parade Sept. 13," *WP*, August 13, 1926, 20; "100,000 Visitors Coming to Greet Col. Lindbergh," *WP*, June 7, 1927, 1; "Police Get Orders to Do Their Best to Protect Flier," *WP*, June 10, 1927, 3; "Capital Heads Approve Hesse Plea to Retire," *WP*, March 10, 1929; "Pratt to Urge Police School and More Men," *WP*, April 21, 1929, 20; "Pratt to Back Present Laws; Will Ask None," *WP*, April 25, 1929, 20; "Maj. Pratt's Report," *WP*, January 28, 1930.

38. "Bonus Groups Ignore Police Plea to Leave," *WP*, June 9, 1932; "Plot to Cause Riots in Bonus Parade Is Seen," *WP*, June 7, 1932; "Veterans Defy Plea of Police Chief to Leave," *WP*, June 24, 1932.

39. Green, *Washington*, 365–66; "Bonus Brigade Asks Permit for Parade," *WP*, December 13, 1931, M14; Barber, *Marching on Washington*, 81–83; "Glassford Moves to Limit Veterans' Stay to 48 Hours," *WP*, May 26, 1932, 1; "The Bonus Seekers," *WP*, June 1, 1932; "Curb on Glassford Benevolence Urged," *WP*, June 8, 1932.

40. "One Slain, 60 Hurt, as Troops Rout B.E.F. with Gas Bombs and Flames," *WP*, July 29, 1932; Barber, *Marching on Washington*, 100–101.

41. Rexford G. Tugwell, "Roosevelt and the Bonus Marchers of 1932," *Political Science Quarterly* 87, 3 (1972): 367; David M. Kennedy, *Freedom from Fear: The American People in Depression and War 1929–45* (New York: Oxford University Press, 1999), 92.

42. "Order Holds Glassford Fate," *WP*, July 31, 1932; "Sane Police Regime Pledged by Brown," *WP*, October 23, 1932; "Red Hunger March on Capital Starts," *WP*, November 15, 1932; "500 Farmers Plan March Here for Aid," *WP*, November 11, 1932; "Hunger March Bar Authority Sought," *WP*, November 18, 1932; "Civic Groups Pledge Aid to Balk Invasion," *WP*, November 26, 1932.

43. "Troops Ready for Call in Case of Trouble," *WP*, December 4, 1932; "Court Test Is Set Today on Camp Restriction," *WP*, December 5, 1932; "New Police Radio Studio, Nearer Curb on Crime," *WP*, February 6, 1933, 14; "Police Headquarters Given New Modern Switchboard," *WP*, February 20, 1933, 2; "Washington Crime at Low Ebb During Last Few Months," *WP*, June 28, 1933, 22.

44. Daniel Kryder, *Divided Arsenal: Race and the American State During World War II* (Cambridge: Cambridge University Press, 2000), 56, 62, 64–65; Barber, *Marching on Washington*, 122, 128, 130.

45. David J. Garrow, *Bearing the Cross: Martin Luther King, Jr., and the Southern Christian Leadership Conference* (New York: Harper, 1986), 272, 277; Barber, *Marching on Washington*, 149–50.

46. Garrow, *Bearing the Cross*, 280–86; Barber, *Marching on Washington*, 151–53, 160–62, 172.

47. John D. McCarthy, Jack McPhail, and Jackie Smith, "Images of Protest: Dimensions of Selection Bias in Media Coverage of Washington Demonstrations, 1982 and 1991," *American Sociological Review* 61, 3 (1996).

48. Robert A. Dahl, *How Democratic Is the American Constitution?* (New Haven, Conn.: Yale University Press, 2003).

Chapter 7. Partisan Entrepreneurship and Policy Windows: George Frisbie Hoar and the 1890 Federal Elections Bill

Dan Crofts provided invaluable comments on an early draft. A residential research fellowship at the Massachusetts Historical Society to work with the papers of George Frisbie Hoar in June 1996 allowed me to learn a great deal about Hoar.

1. Kirk H. Porter and Donald Bruce Johnson, *National Party Platforms, 1840–1956* (Urbana: University of Illinois Press, 1956), 80.

2. Gregory Wawro and Eric Schickler, *Filibuster: Obstruction and Lawmaking in the U.S. Senate* (Princeton, N.J.: Princeton University Press, 2006), chap. 3; Edward Arthur White, "The Republican Party in National Politics 1888–1891," Ph.D. dissertation, University of Wisconsin, 1941, 492–96.

3. Porter and Johnson, *National Party Platforms*, 86, 93–94.

4. *Repeal of Federal Election Laws*, 53rd Congress, 1st Sess., 1893, H. Rep. 18, 7.

5. Theda Skocpol, *Boomerang: Clinton's Health Security Effort and the Turn Against Government in U.S. Politics* (New York: Norton, 1996).

6. Richard Welch, "The Federal Elections Bill of 1890: Postscripts and Prelude," *Journal of American History* 52 (December 1965): 511–26, and Thomas Adams Upchurch, *Legislating Racism: The Billion Dollar Congress and the Birth of Jim Crow* (Lexington: University Press of Kentucky, 2004).

7. John W. Kingdon, *Agendas, Alternatives, and Public Policies* (Boston: Little, Brown, 1984).

8. Richard E. Welch, Jr., *George Frisbie Hoar and the Half-Breed Republicans* (Cambridge, Mass.: Harvard University Press, 1971), chap. 4.

9. Richard Franklin Bensel, *The Political Economy of American Industrialization, 1877–1900* (New York: Cambridge University Press, 2001).

10. Eric Schickler, Terri Bimes, and Robert Mickey, "Safe at Any Speed: Legislative Intent, the Electoral Count Act of 1887, and *Bush v. Gore*," *Journal of Law and Politics* 16 (Fall 2000): 717–64, at 731n57, 734.

11. Quotations from George F. Hoar, *Autobiography of Seventy Years* (New York: Scribner's, 1903), 1: 256, 2: 158–59. See also Welch, *George Frisbie Hoar*, intro. and chap. 2, and Jonathan Chu, "George Frisbie Hoar and Chinese Exclusion: The Political Construction of Race," in Reed Ueda and Conrad Edick Wright, eds., *Faces of Community: Immigrant Massachusetts 1860–2000* (Boston: Massachusetts Historical Society, 2003), 89–114.

12. Among others, see C. Vann Woodward, *Reunion and Reaction: The Compromise of 1877 and the End of Reconstruction* (Boston: Little, Brown, 1951), and Michael W. McConnell, "The Forgotten Constitutional Moment," *Constitutional Commentary* 11 (1994): 115–44.

13. Woodrow Wilson, *Congressional Government: A Study in American Politics*, 2nd ed. (Boston: Houghton Mifflin, 1885), 27.

14. See Steven P. Erie, *Rainbow's End: Irish-Americans and the Dilemmas of Urban Machine Politics, 1840–1985* (Berkeley: University of California Press, 1988), 35–38; Robert Anderson Horn, "National Control of Congressional Elections," Ph.D. dissertation, Princeton University, 1942, 141–47, 189–99; Jerome Mushkat, *The Reconstruction of the New York Democracy 1861–1874* (Rutherford, N.J.: Fairleigh Dickinson University Press, 1981), 145–46, 163–65, 167–68; *Congressional Quarterly's Guide to U.S. Elections* (Washington, D.C.: CQ, 1985), 337.

15. Xi Wang, *The Trial of Democracy: Black Suffrage and Northern Republicans, 1860–1910* (Athens: University of Georgia Press, 1997), app. 2, 275–77. See also Horn, "National Control," 144; John I. Davenport, *The Election Frauds of New York City and Their Prevention* (New York: n.p., 1881), 1: 107–344.

16. Wang, *Trial of Democracy*, app. 3, 278–87, and James Lowell Underwood, *The Constitution of South Carolina*, vol. 4, *The Struggle for Political Equality* (Columbia: University of South Carolina Press, 1994), 138–39.

17. Kenneth C. Martis and Gregory A. Elmes, *The Historical Atlas of State Power in*

Congress, 1790–1990 (Washington D.C.: CQ, 1993), 163, table 3–11, "High-Density House Districts in Relation to Total House Districts, 1870–1930."

18. Wang, *Trial of Democracy*, app. 5, 292–93.

19. *Ex parte Siebold*, decision for the Court by Justice Bradley, quotations at 382, 386–88, 394, 395–96.

20. The supposedly unconstitutional sections of the Revised Statutes were Sections 5508 (formerly Section 6 of the First Federal Elections Act of May 31, 1870) and Section 5520 (a piece of Section 2 of the Third Federal Elections Act—the Ku-Klux Act—of April 20, 1871). Wang, *Trial of Democracy*, app. 6, 294–99, "Sections from the Enforcement Acts in the *Revised Statutes*, Their Repeals, and Amendments." These numbers refer both to the first and second editions of the Revised Statutes; the first edition was published in 1875, the second in 1878.

21. See *United States v. Hiram Reese and Matthew Foushee*, 92 U.S. 214 (1876); *United States v. Cruikshank*, 92 U.S. 542 (1876); *United States v. Harris*, 106 U.S. 629 (1883). Robert M. Goldman, *Reconstruction & Suffrage: Losing the Vote in* Reese & Cruikshank (Lawrence: University Press of Kansas, 2001); C. Peter Magrath, *Morrison R. Waite: The Triumph of Character* (New York: Macmillan, 1963), chap. 7, and William Gillette, "Anatomy of a Failure: Federal Enforcement of the Right to Vote in the Border States during Reconstruction," in Richard O. Curry, ed., *Radicalism, Racism, and Party Realignment: The Border States During Reconstruction* (Baltimore: Johns Hopkins University Press, 1969), 265–304, esp. 286–89.

22. *Ex parte Yarbrough*, 110 U.S. 651 (1884) (sometimes referred to as "The Ku Klux Cases"); quotations from 657–58, 659, 660, 661–62, 664, 665, 667.

23. *Ex parte Coy*, 127 U.S. 731 (1888).

24. Welch, *George Frisbie Hoar*, 133.

25. Daniel Wallace Crofts, "The Blair Bill and The Elections Bill: The Congressional Aftermath to Reconstruction," Ph.D. dissertation, Yale University, 1968, 233.

26. Ibid., 252–55; White, "Republican Party," 374–37; Hoar, *Autobiography*, 2: 151.

27. Hoar, *Autobiography*, 2: 151–52, quotation at 152. Crofts, "Blair Bill and Elections Bill," 239–40.

28. Crofts, "Blair Bill and Elections Bill," 252–63; Upchurch, *Legislating Racism*, chap. 4; Wang, *Trial of Democracy*, 232–41.

29. Hoar, *Autobiography*, 2: 151–53.

30. Russell R. Wheeler, "Origins of the Elements of Federal Court Governance" (Federal Judicial Center, 1992), 1–3, 5–12; www.fjc.gov/public/pdf.nsf/lookup/?governce.pdf/?$File/?governce.pdf

31. Wang, *Trial of Democracy*, 236–37. See also Crofts, "Blair Bill and Elections Bill," 299–300; Horn, "National Control," 259–69; Hoar, *Autobiography*, vol. 2, chap. 13.

32. Martis and Elmes, *Historical Atlas of State Power*, table 3-11, 163.

33. Kingdon, *Agendas*, 99–105, 177–78; Kenneth C. Barnes, *Who Killed John Clayton? Political Violence and the Emergence of the New South, 1861–1893* (Durham, N.C.: Duke University Press, 1998), chap. 3; Upchurch, *Legislating Racism*, 110–11.

34. Bensel, *Political Economy*, chap. 3, esp. 168–74, sources listed at 112–13; Vernon Lane Wharton, *The Negro in Mississippi 1865–1890*, foreword by A. R. Newsome, James Sprunt Studies in History and Political Science (Chapel Hill: University of North Carolina Press, 1947), 209. On Chalmers and Chandler, see Crofts, "Blair Bill and Elections Bill," 230.

35. Bensel, *Political Economy*, 168–74.

36. Steven Hahn, *A Nation Under Our Feet: Black Political Struggle in the Rural South from Slavery to the Great Migration* (Cambridge, Mass.: Harvard University Press, 2003).

37. Edward Ayers, *The Promise of the New South: Life After Reconstruction* (New York: Oxford University Press, 1992), 51.

38. Stanley B. Parsons, William W. Beach, and Michael J. Dubin, *United States Congressional Districts and Data, 1843 to 1883* (Westport, Conn.: Greenwood Press, 1986), 146–223.

39. U.S. Senate, *Petition of Ezra Hill for the Passage of a National Election Law*, Misc. Document No. 244, 51st Congress, 1st Sess., Box 11, George Frisbie Hoar Papers, Massachusetts Historical Society.

40. Upchurch, *Legislating Racism*, 120.

41. Jeffery A. Jenkins, "Partisanship and Contested Election Cases in the House of Representatives, 1789–2002," *Studies in American Political Development* 18 (Fall 2004): 112–35, and Matthew N. Green, "Reconsidering Contested Elections: Race, Party, and Institutional Development," http://faculty.cua.edu/greenm/research.htm.

42. Jenkins, "Partisanship and Contested Elections Cases," table 9, "The South and Contested Election Cases, 1867–1911"; Jerrold G. Rusk, *A Statistical History of the American Electorate* (Washington, D.C.: CQ Press, 2001), 219.

43. Jenkins, "Partisanship and Contested Elections Cases," 132–33.

44. Upchurch, *Legislating Racism*, 66–67.

45. Ibid., 71–73.

46. Kenneth C. Martis, *The Historical Atlas of Political Parties in the United States Congress 1789–1989* (New York: Macmillan, 1989), 143–45; White, "Republican Party," chap. 15.

47. See Voteview for Windows, v. 3.0.3, roll-calls 384–426, Senate, 51st Congress, passim.

48. Wawro and Schickler, *Filibuster*, chap. 3; Homer E. Socolofsky and Allan B. Spetter, *The Presidency of Benjamin Harrison* (Lawrence: University Press of Kansas, 1987), 64.

49. Upchurch, *Legislating Racism*, 162.

50. Crofts, "Blair Bill and Elections Bill," 332–37, 340–41.

51. See Edward G. Carmines and James A. Stimson, *Issue Evolution: Race and the Transformation of American Politics* (Princeton, N.J.: Princeton University Press, 1989), 56–57.

52. Lawrence Grossman, *The Democratic Party and the Negro: Northern and National Politics, 1868–92* (Urbana: University of Illinois Press, 1976), chaps. 3, 5.

53. Wang, *Trial of Democracy*, 254–59.

54. Hoar, *Autobiography*, 2: 157 (emphasis added).

55. Ibid., 158 (emphasis added).

56. Skocpol, *Boomerang*.

57. Welch, *George Frisbie Hoar*, 161; Crofts, "Blair Bill and Elections Bill," ix; Upchurch, *Legislating Racism*; Ayers, *The Promise of the New South*, 50–51.

58. Kingdon, *Agendas*, 92, 93.

59. Ibid., 68.

Chapter 8. Andrew Johnson and the Politics of Failure

Valuable research assistance for this project was provided by Jacob Eisler, and made possible by the financial support of the Ursula Prescott Fund and the Williams College Political Science Department. We would also like to thank colleagues who commented on earlier drafts of this chapter, especially the editors of this volume, and Marc Landy, Mariah Zeisberg, Mark Graber, Richard Valelly, Bruce

Ackerman, Richard Bensel, Jacob Hacker, Elizabeth Clemmens, James Morone, and Bryan Garsten.

1. Our focus in this chapter is Reconstruction, but it is worth noting that Johnson's leadership style and his defense against impeachment also reveal the pattern of immediate political failure followed by lasting influence. Johnson invented the political practice of "going public" and was ridiculed as a demagogue. Indeed, one of the articles of impeachment was for his demagogic rhetoric. That charge was dropped when Johnson successfully framed the impeachment process as a legal rather than political matter. One hundred fifty years later, "going public" is a prescribed norm, not a deviant exercise, and the legalistic understanding of impeachment has also prevailed over the political interpretation.

2. Southern elites believed that only the right to secession and slavery had been lost, not the rights to manage race and class relations as they saw fit. Former Confederate leaders, including Jefferson Davis, prophesied that the "Southern cause" would find new form and a new time. And as Southern historian Edward Pollard, writing contemporaneously, describes, Andrew Johnson was just the man for the job. In *The Lost Cause: A New Southern History of the War of the Confederates* (New York: E.B. Treat, 1866), 745, Pollard writes that Johnson "saw before him a part in American history second only to that of George Washington; he left behind him the ambitions and resentments of mere party; he rose as the man who has been secretly, almost unconsciously, great. . . . The man who had been twitted as a tailor and condemned as a demagogue, proved a statesman, measuring his actions for the future, insensible to clamour and patient for results."

3. See John Milton Cooper, *Breaking the Heart of the World: Woodrow Wilson and the Fight for the League of Nations* (Cambridge: Cambridge University Press, 2001); Jeffrey K. Tulis, *The Rhetorical Presidency* (Princeton, N.J.: Princeton University Press, 1987), 147–61.

4. As Pollard describes it, "the new President was sprung from a low order of life, and was what Southern gentlemen called a 'scrub.' In qualities of mind it was generally considered that he had the shallowness and fluency of the demagogue; but in this there was a mistake." Pollard, *Lost Cause*, 744.

5. Albert Castel, *The Presidency of Andrew Johnson* (Lawrence: Regents Press of Kansas, 1979), 18–23; Eric McKitrick, *Andrew Johnson and Reconstruction* (Chicago: University of Chicago Press, 1960), 105.

6. Radical optimism stemmed from a misinterpretation of the intent behind some of Johnson's first comments after assuming the presidency, including telling a group of Radical congressmen that, "Treason must be made infamous, and traitors must be impoverished." Raised in poverty in the mountains of Tennessee, Johnson disliked the white planter elites who dominated Southern politics before the war and who had led the rebellion. He had also recently been the target of an assassination attempt. The combination fueled his interest in punishing treason; it did not, as Radicals believed, extend to a principled commitment to Radical ideas. Castel, *Presidency of Andrew Johnson*, 20.

7. Johnson preferred the term "restoration" to "reconstruction" because it implied a return to the status quo ante, which was more or less how he envisioned the postwar settlement. On the use of the terms, see Glenna R. Schroeder-Lein and Richard Zuczek, *Andrew Johnson: A Biographical Companion* (Santa Barbara, Calif.: ABC-CLIO, 2001), 239.

8. Heather Cox Richardson, *The Death of Reconstruction: Race, Labor, and Politics in the Post-Civil War North, 1865–1901* (Cambridge, Mass.: Harvard University Press, 2001), 16.

9. Cotton production, for example, fell from 5 million bales in 1860 to just 300,000 bales in 1865. Castel, *Presidency of Andrew Johnson*, 14.

10. In 1865, Northern Democrats held a quarter of the seats in Congress.

11. From Andrew Johnson's "Washington's Birthday Address," February 22, 1866. *The Papers of Andrew Johnson*, ed. Paul H. Bergeron, vol. 10, *February–July 1866* (Knoxville: University of Tennessee Press, 1992).

12. For example, in replying to an African American delegation's request for Black suffrage in 1866, Johnson said, "Each community is better prepared to determine the depository of its political power than anybody else, and it is for the legislature . . . to say who shall vote, and not the Congress of the United States." Charles Ernest Chadsey, *The Struggle Between President Johnson and Congress over Reconstruction* (New York: Columbia University, 1896), 65.

13. Castel, *Presidency of Andrew Johnson*, 50–51.

14. Chadsey, *Struggle Between President Johnson and Congress*, 44–45; Michael Les Benedict, *The Fruits of Victory: Alternatives in Restoring the Union, 1865–1877* (Philadelphia: Lippincott, 1975), part 2, document 4.

15. Richardson, *Death of Reconstruction*, 17.

16. Johnson even went so far as to manipulate information on conditions in the South, most notably early in the promotion of his policy, when he dispatched a more sympathetic General Grant to survey the South after receiving an unfavorable report by General Schurz. See Richardson, *Death of Reconstruction*, 17–20.

17. Again, Pollard is instructive here. He warned: "The people of the South have surrendered in the war what the war has conquered; but they cannot be expected to give up what was not involved in the war, and voluntarily abandon their political schools . . . a 'war of ideas' is what the South wants and insists upon perpetrating." *Lost Cause*, 750.

18. During this time and even earlier, when Johnson was promoting his Restoration agenda, moderate lawmakers repeatedly made overtures to him with strategies designed to build a consensus around modified versions of Johnson's own policies. He rebuffed every one of these efforts.

19. As evidence of this, Johnson's first veto at this time was of an extension and expansion of the Freedman's Bureau. Lawmakers accepted this veto but consistently overrode subsequent vetoes, including another piece of legislation that accomplished almost all the goals laid out in the original, vetoed bill. Also, as moderates moved toward the agenda of leading Radicals, they embraced proposals of Black suffrage and civil rights and asserted the need for military oversight to ensure this, but never fully embraced the Radical idea of confiscating and redistributing rebel land to former slaves. See Eric Foner, *Politics and Ideology in the Age of the Civil War* (New York: Oxford University Press, 1980), 130–37.

20. Martin E. Mantell, *Johnson, Grant, and the Politics of Reconstruction* (New York: Columbia University Press, 1973), 22; Castel, *Presidency of Andrew Johnson*, 103–5; McKitrick, *Andrew Johnson and Reconstruction*, 467–71.

21. Mantell, *Johnson, Grant, and the Politics of Reconstruction*, chap. 2.

22. Mantell, *Johnson, Grant, and the Politics of Reconstruction*, chap. 4 and p. 98. Assessing the 1867 election outcomes, *The Nation* declared, "It would be vain to deny that the fidelity of the Republican party to the cause of equal rights . . . has been one of the chief causes of its heavy losses." Quoted in Eric Foner, *A Short History of Reconstruction, 1863–1877* (New York: Harper and Row, 1990), 136.

23. Richard Valelly's insightful analysis of the failure of Congressional Reconstruction provides support for this claim. Valelly argues that Congressional Reconstruction failed, in part, because the speed with which Northern Republicans expanded their coalition to include Southern African Americans made for unstable

party building and ultimately led to incomplete institutionalization. According to Valelly, this attempt at "crash party building" was a direct response to the threat from President Johnson's actions, both prior to and after enfranchising Blacks. Our contention is that, had Johnson not precipitated this political frenzy, it is feasible that an alternative, enduring coalition building and reconstruction might have taken place. As Richard Bensel points out, Republican difficulties in maintaining their coalition stemmed in part from the fact that none of the party's dominant economic interests were especially vested in Radical Reconstruction. Northern finance capital was most interested in scuttling the Radicals' plan. For a number of immediate and long-term economic reasons, including most notably Reconstruction's interference with the resumption of cotton production and exports, finance capitalists remained loyal to Johnson long after other Northern Republicans had deserted him. Here, too, we see Bensel's argument about the role played by the finance community in ending Reconstruction as complementary to our argument. Moderate proposals, that satisfied a majority of Republicans and that would have more quickly returned the South's cotton fields to production, were abandoned in Congress after Johnson rejected them (see note 18 above). By hardening and prolonging Radical response, Johnson's actions served to wedge apart the Republican coalition (separating out the Johnson sympathizing finance capitalists from others); and in fueling a key division in the North, his actions helped to close the window of opportunity that Radicals had to enact their agenda. See Richard Valelly, *The Two Reconstructions: The Struggle for Black Enfranchisement* (Chicago: University of Chicago Press, 2004); Richard Bensel, *Yankee Leviathan: The Origins of Central State Authority in America, 1859–1877* (New York: Cambridge University Press, 1990), 348–63.

24. Mantell, *Johnson, Grant, and the Politics of Reconstruction,* 75–77.

25. Ibid., 134–36.

26. Johnson's tolerance, and even perhaps encouragement, of violence to suppress black political organization was not new. The most notorious incident occurred in the summer of 1866 when Unionists in Louisiana, dissatisfied with the largely former Confederate government, organized a convention in New Orleans. Local authorities tried to prevent the assembly and asked if Johnson would interfere with their actions. Not only did the president indicate that he would not interfere, he gave them permission to request military aid in support of their actions. While troops ultimately were not deployed to break up the convention, the encouragement from Johnson was seen by many at the time as facilitating the violent riot that ensued, in which local white citizens and police killed and injured scores of primarily black convention-goers. Not only did Johnson fail to condemn the action, he blamed the riot on the actions of Radical members of Congress. It was the New Orleans riot that turned many Northerners against Johnson's Union party in 1866 and convinced Congress of the need to increase their reconstructive efforts. For a more detailed chronology of events, see Schroeder-Lein and Zuczek, *Andrew Johnson,* 209.

27. Foner, *Politics and Ideology,* 122–25.

28. Castel, *Presidency of Andrew Johnson,* 20.

29. Ibid., 42–43.

30. Mantell, *Johnson, Grant, and the Politics of Reconstruction,* 18–20; Castel, *Presidency of Andrew Johnson,* 78–79.

31. Benedict, *Fruits of Victory,* 61.

32. For other economic and political considerations in the election outcome, see C. Vann Woodward, *Reunion and Reaction: The Compromise of 1877 and the End of Reconstruction* (Boston: Little, Brown, 1951); Keith Ian Polakoff, *The Politics of Inertia: The Election of 1876 and the End of Reconstruction* (Baton Rouge: Louisiana State University Press, 1973).

33. Joel Williamson, *The Crucible of Race: Black-White Relations in the American South Since Emancipation* (New York: Oxford University Press, 1984), 132–35 and chap. 7.

34. From Andrew Johnson's "Washington's Birthday Address."

35. Ibid.

36. Castel, *Presidency of Andrew Johnson,* 56–57; Mantell, *Johnson, Grant, and the Politics of Reconstruction,* 20.

37. Pollard, *Lost Cause,* 748.

38. Ibid., 750

39. While Southern elites used race to trump class concerns and establish the loyalty of poor and middle-class whites, they simultaneously argued to Northern audiences that much of the mob violence in their region was at the hands of poor whites, whom they could best control. Stephen Kantrowitz, "One Man's Mob Is Another Man's Militia: Violence, Manhood, and Authority in Reconstruction South Carolina," in Jane Dailey, Glenda Elizabeth Gilmore, and Bryant Simon, eds., *Jumpin' Jim Crow: Southern Politics from Civil War to Civil Rights* (Princeton, N.J.: Princeton University Press, 2000).

40. Richardson, *Death of Reconstruction,* 203.

41. The argument was not a difficult one to make, especially when it came to laws that effectively segregated the races. Even during Reconstruction, the North had not been insistent on enforcing antisegregation laws, and *Plessy v. Ferguson,* of course, gave national constitutional legitimacy to "separate but equal." Williamson, *Crucible of Race,* 249–55.

42. Ibid., 209–10.

43. Richard Henry Dana, "Grasp of War," in Benedict, *Fruits of Victory,* part 2, document 7.

44. Foner, *Politics and Ideology,* 127.

45. Alexis de Tocqueville, *Democracy in America,* trans. Harvey C. Mansfield and Delba Winthrop (Chicago: University of Chicago press, 2000), 469–72.

Chapter 9. Forging a New Grammar of Equality and Difference: Progressive Era Suffrage and Reform

1. William Blackstone, *Commentaries on the Laws of England* (1765; Chicago: University of Chicago Press, 1979), bk. 1, 430.

2. William J. Crotty, *Political Reform and the American Experiment* (New York: Thomas Crowell, 1977), 20.

3. Linda K. Kerber, *Women of the Republic: Intellect and Ideology in Revolutionary America* (Chapel Hill: University of North Carolina Press, 1980); Kerber, *No Constitutional Right to Be Ladies: Women and the Obligations of Citizenship* (New York: Hill and Wang, 1998).

4. Theda Skocpol, *Protecting Soldiers and Mothers: The Political Origins of Social Policy in the United States* (Cambridge, Mass.: Harvard University Press, 2000).

5. Suzanne Mettler, *Soldiers to Citizens: The G.I. Bill and the Making of the Greatest Generation* (Cambridge: Oxford University Press, 2005); Andrea Campbell, *How Policies Make Citizens: Senior Political Activism and the American Welfare State* (Princeton, N.J.: Princeton University Press, 2005); Robert C. Lieberman, *Shaping Race Policy: The United States in Comparative Perspective* (Princeton, N.J.: Princeton University Press, 2005); Jacob S. Hacker, *The Divided Welfare State: The Battle over Public and Private Social Benefits in the United States* (New York: Cambridge University Press, 2002).

6. Mettler, *Soldiers to Citizens.*

7. I am indebted to Mary Katzenstein and Stephen Skowronek for suggesting the

language of representative state performance. For a more complete treatment, see Eileen McDonagh, *State-Building and the Political Meaning of Gender: Is Democratization Progress for Women?* (Chicago: University of Chicago Press, forthcoming).

8. Laura Jensen, *Patriots, Settlers, and the Origins of American Social Policy* (Cambridge: Cambridge University Press, 2003).

9. Theda Skocpol, *Protecting Soldiers and Mothers*, 102.

10. Eleanor Flexner, *Century of Struggle: The Woman's Rights Movement in the United States*, rev. ed. (Cambridge, Mass.: Harvard University Press, 1975), 71.

11. Flexner, *Century of Struggle*, 72–73.

12. Paula S. Rothenberg, *Race, Class, and Gender in the United States*, 2nd ed. (New York: St.Martin's Press, 1992), 266–69.

13. *Congressional Globe*, Senate, 40th Congress, 3rd Sess., February 26, 1869, p. 1630.

14. *Congressional Globe*, Senate, 39th Congress, 2nd Sess., December 11, 1866, p. 56.

15. *Congressional Globe*, House, 40th Congress, 3rd Sess., Feb. 20, 1869, p. 1426.

16. *Congressional Globe*, Senate, 40th Congress, 3rd Sess., February 17, 1869, p. 1301.

17. *Congressional Globe*, Senate, 39th Congress, 2nd Sess., December 10, 1866, p. 55.

18. Paula Baker, *Gender and the Transformation of Politics: Public and Private Life in New York, 1870–1930* (New York: Free Press, 1989).

19. Elisabeth S. Clemens, *The People's Lobby: Organizational Innovation and the Rise of Interest Group Politics in the United States, 1890–1925* (Chicago: University of Chicago Press, 1997); Michael McGerr, *The Decline of Popular Politics: The American North, 1865–1928* (New York: Oxford University Press, 1988), 1–8

20. Sonya Michel and Seth Koven, "Womanly Duties: Maternalist Politics and the Origins of the Welfare State in France, Germany, Great Britain and the United States, 1880–1920," *American Historical Review* 95 (1990): 1076–1108; Seth Koven and Sonya Michel, *Mothers of a New World: Maternalist Politics and the Origins of Welfare States* (New York: Routledge, 1993).

21. Quoted in Michel and Koven, "Womanly Duties"; see also Katheryn Kish Sklar, "Hull House in the 1890s: A Community of Women Reformers," *Signs* 10, 4 (1985): 658–77.

22. Skocpol, *Protecting Soldiers and Mothers*.

23. Aileen S. Kraditor, *The Ideas of the Woman Suffrage Movement, 1890–1920* (New York: Columbia University Press, 1965).

24. Alexander Keyssar, *The Right to Vote: The Contested History of Democracy in the United States* (New York: Basic Books, 2000).

25. Ellen Carol Du Bois, *Harriot Stanton Blatch and the Winning of Woman Suffrage* (New Haven, Conn.: Yale University Press, 1997).

26. Skocpol, *Protecting Soldiers and Mothers*.

27. J. Stanley Lemons, *The Woman Citizen: Social Feminism in the 1920's* (Urbana: University of Illinois Press, 1973).

28. Susan Lehrer, *Origins of Protection Labor Legislation for Women, 1905–1925* (Albany: State University of New York Press, 1987), 38.

29. *Lochner v. New York*, 198 U.S. 45 (1905).

30. *Lochner v. New York*, cited in Leslie Friedman Goldstein, *The Constitutional Rights of Women: Cases in Law and Social Change* (Madison: University of Wisconsin Press, 1989), 10–11.

31. *Muller v. Oregon*, 208 U.S. 412 (1908).

32. Cited in Goldstein, *Constitutional Rights of Women*, 21–22.

33. Christine A. Lunardini, *From Equal Suffrage to Equal Rights: Alice Paul and the National Woman's Party, 1910–1928* (New York: New York University Press, 1986).

34. Carrie Chapman Catt, speech, "Mount Rushmore National Memorial and the Lack of Representation of Women, 1917, folder 2, p. 1, Schlesinger Library, Harvard University.

35. Catt, speech, "An Appeal for Liberty," 1915, p. 1, Schlesinger Library, Harvard University.

36. Catt, article, "The Widow's Mite," c. 1919, p. 1, Schlesinger Library, Harvard University.

37. Catt, article, "Women and the Presidency," 1916, p. 1, Schlesinger Library, Harvard University.

38. Catt, article, "God and the People," 1915, pp. 15–16, Schlesinger Library, Harvard University; Catt, speech, "The Nation Calls: An Address to the Jubilee Convention of the National American Woman Suffrage Association," 1919, p. 2, Schlesinger Library, Harvard University.

39. Catt, "Nation Calls" and "Widow's Mite."

40. Catt, "Women and the Presidency," 1.

41. Catt, "Advance Notes of Speech by Mrs. Catt at Albany Suffrage Convention," 1918, folder 1, p. 1, Schlesinger Library, Harvard University.

42. Catt, untitled speech about World War I, 1916, p. 4, Schlesinger Library, Harvard University.

43. Catt, speech, "An Address to the Congress of the United States," 1918, p. 3, Schlesinger Library, Harvard University.

44. See Sidney Milkis, forthcoming book on the Progressive Party.

45. Jane Addams, speech, "Miss Addams at Smith College," p. 1, Schlesinger Library, Harvard University.

46. Addams, "The Ballot for Health and Beauty," p. 1, Schlesinger Library, Harvard University.

47. See articles 30, 31, and 45.

48. Addams, "Jane Addams on Suffrage Cause," p. 1, Schlesinger Library, Harvard University.

49. Addams, "War's Debasement of Women," p. 1, Schlesinger Library, Harvard University.

50. Ibid.

51. Addams, "Some of the Larger Aspects of the Votes for Women Movement," p. 2, Schlesinger Library, Harvard University.

52. Addams, "The Workingwoman's Need of the Ballot," p. 1, Schlesinger Library, Harvard University.

53. Addams, "Women, War, and Suffrage," p. 1, Schlesinger Library, Harvard University.

54. Nancy F. Cott, *The Grounding of Modern Feminism* (New Haven, Conn.: Yale University Press, 1987), 123.

55. Ibid.

56. Ibid., 120.

57. Ibid.

58. Kristi Andersen, *After Suffrage: Women in Partisan and Electoral Politics Before the New Deal* (Chicago: University of Chicago Press, 1996), 44.

59. Ibid., 45.

60. Ibid, 54–55.

61. T. H. Marshall, *Citizenship and Social Class* (London: Pluto Press, 1987).

62. *Reed v. Reed*, 404 U.S. 71 (1971).

63. *Roe v. Wade*, 410 U.S. 113 (1973) and *Doe v. Bolton*, 410 U.S. 179 (1973).

64. R. Darcy, Susan Welch, and Janet Clark, *Women, Elections and Representation*, 2nd ed. (Lincoln: University of Nebraska Press, 1994); Pippa Norris "The Impact of the Electoral System on Election of Women to National Legislatures," in Marianne Githens, Pippa Norris, and Joni Lovenduski, eds., *Different Roles, Different Voices: Women and Politics in the United States and Europe* (New York: HarperCollins, 1994); Pippa Norris, ed., *Passages to Power: Legislative Recruitment in Advanced Democracies* (Cambridge: Cambridge University Press, 1997).

65. Skocpol, *Protecting Soldiers and Mothers*, 527–28.

Chapter 10. The Ground Beneath Our Feet: Language, Culture, and Political Change

1. See Karen Orren and Stephen Skowronek, "Beyond the Iconography of Order: Notes for a 'New Institutionalism'," in Lawrence C. Dodd and Calvin Jillson, eds., *Dynamics of American Politics: Approaches and Interpretations* (Boulder, Colo.: Westview Press, 1994); Karen Orren and Stephen Skowronek, *The Search for American Political Development* (New York: Cambridge University Press, 2004); Rogers Smith, *Civic Ideals: Conflicting Visions of Citizenship in U.S. History* (New Haven, Conn.: Yale University Press, 1997); and Adam D. Sheingate, "Political Entrepreneurship, Institutional Change, and American Political Development," *Studies in American Political Development* 17, 2 (Fall 2003): 185–203. See Louis Hartz, *The Liberal Tradition in America* (New York: Harcourt, 1955); Walter Dean Burnham, *Critical Elections and the Mainsprings of American Politics* (New York: Norton, 1971); Clifford Geertz, *Interpretation of Cultures* (New York: Basic Books, 1973); Robert Wiebe, *The Search for Order, 1877–1920* (New York: Hill and Wang, 1966).

2. See Denise Riley, *"Am I That Name": Feminism and the Category of "Women" in History* (Minneapolis: University of Minnesota Press, 1988); Judith Butler, *Gender Trouble: Feminism and the Subversion of Identity* (New York: Routledge, 1990).

3. Cherríe Moraga and Gloria Anzaldúa, eds., *This Bridge Called My Back: Writings by Radical Women of Color* (New York: Kitchen Table/Women of Color Press, 1984); Barbara Smith, ed., *Home Girls: A Black Feminist Anthology* (New York: Kitchen Table/Women of Color Press, 1983).

4. Butler, *Gender Trouble*; Diana Fuss, ed., *Inside/Out: Lesbian Theories, Gay Theories* (New York: Routledge, 1991); William E. Connolly, *The Ethos of Pluralization* (Minneapolis: University of Minnesota Press, 1995); Michael Warner, *The Trouble with Normal: Sex, Politics, and the Ethics of Queer Life* (Cambridge, Mass.: Harvard University Press, 1999); and José Esteban Muñoz, *Disidentifications: Queers of Color and the Performance of Politics* (Minneapolis: University of Minnesota Press, 1999).

5. See Bruce Miroff, "Entrepreneurship and Leadership," *Studies in American Political Development* 17 (Fall 2003): 204–11.

6. Orren and Skowronek, *Search for American Political Development*, chaps. 1, 4, pp. 120, 123.

7. See Michael Foucault, *Discipline and Punish: The Birth of the Prison*, 2nd ed. (New York: Vintage, 1995).

8. Ernesto Laclau, *Emancipation(s)* (New York: Verso, 1996); Victoria Hattam, *In the Shadow of Race: Jews, Latinos and Immigrant Politics in the United States* (Chicago: University of Chicago Press, forthcoming 2007), chap. 1.

9. Arjun Appadurai, *Modernity at Large: Cultural Dimensions of Globalization* (Minneapolis: University of Minnesota Press, 1996), 51.

10. We draw on a wide range of theorists, including Judith Butler, *Bodies That Matter: On the Discursive Limits of Sex* (New York: Routledge, 1991); Anne Norton, *Reflections on Political Identity* (Baltimore: Johns Hopkins University Press, 1988); Slavoj

Îiĭek, *The Sublime Object of Ideology* (New York: Verso, 1989); Yannis Stavrakakis, *Lacan and the Political* (New York: Routledge, 1999). For attention to the historicity of language, see J. G. A. Pocock, *Politics, Language, and Time: Essays on Political Thought and History* (Chicago: University of Chicago Press, 1989); J. G. A. Pocock, *The Machiavellian Moment: Florentine Political Thought and the Atlantic Republican Tradition* (Princeton, N.J.: Princeton University Press, 1975); Quentin Skinner, "Meaning and Understanding in the History of Ideas," *History and Theory* 8, 1 (1969): 3–53; and Bernard Bailyn, *The Ideological Origins of the American Revolution* (Cambridge, Mass.: Harvard University Press, 1967). For genealogical analysis of key words, see Raymond Williams, *Keywords: A Vocabulary of Culture and Society* (New York: Oxford University Press, 1985).

11. See Miroff, this volume.

12. See Jonathan Rieder, *Canarsie: The Jews and Italians of Brooklyn Against Liberalism* (Cambridge, Mass.: Harvard University Press, 1985); Thomas Edsall and Mary Edsall, *Chain Reaction: The Impact of Race, Rights, and Taxes on American Politics* (New York: Norton, 1992); and E. J. Dionne, *Stand Up, Fight Back: Republican Toughs, Democratic Wimps, and the Politics of Revenge* (New York: Simon and Schuster, 2004).

13. Papers of Charles Wallace Collins, Archives and Manuscripts Department, University of Maryland Libraries, "Guide to the Papers," 1; *National Cyclopedia of American Biography* 51: 296–98.

14. Charles Collins, *Whither Solid South: A Study in Politics and Race Relations* (New Orleans: Pelican Press, 1947).

15. Collins, *Whither Solid South*, chaps. 7-14; see also Joseph Lowndes, *The Southern Origins of Modern Conservatism* (New Haven, Conn.: Yale University Press, forthcoming 2008).

16. V. O. Key, *Southern Politics in State and Nation*, new ed. (Nashville: University of Tennessee Press, 1984), 73.

17. Collins, *Whither Solid South*, 181

18. Ibid., 241.

19. Ibid., 227.

20. Ibid., 257; Kevin Philips, *The Emerging Republican Majority* (New York: Arlington House, 1969).

21. Robert Garson, *The Democratic Party and the Politics of Sectionalism, 1941–1948* (Baton Rouge: Louisiana State University Press, 1974), 233.

22. Kari Fredrickson, *The Dixiecrat Revolt and the End of the Solid South, 1932–1968* (Chapel Hill: University of North Carolina Press, 2001), 141.

23. Ibid., 174–75.

24. Ibid., 175.

25. Numan A. Bartley, *The New South, 1945–1980* (Baton Rouge: Louisiana State University Press, 1995), 36.

26. Collins, letter to Gibson, November 8, 1948, "Dixiecrat Correspondence Series," Dixon Papers, ADAH.

27. Ibid.

28. "Report of the Jackson Meeting—National States Rights Committee, Jackson, Mississippi, May 10, 1949," Dixon Papers, LPR 33, Box 2, Folder 11; "Constitution and Declaration of Principles, National States Rights Committee," Papers of J. Strom Thurmond, Special Collections, Clemson University Libraries, Clemson, S.C.

29. John Temple Graves, *The Fighting South* (University: University of Alabama Press, 1985); see also John Egerton, *Speak Now Against the Day: The Generation Before the Civil Rights Movement* (New York: Knopf, 1994), 492.

30. Fredrickson, *Dixiecrat Revolt*, 191.

31. Collins to Graves, June 27, 1951, Collins Papers, Series 11, Box 3.

32. Margaret E. Armbrester, "John Temple Graves II: A Southern Liberal Views the New Deal," *Alabama Historical Review* 32, 3 (July 1979): 204–5.

33. *Jackson Daily News*, April 18, 1951, Karl E. Mundt Archives, Dakota State University, Madison, S.D., 57042, Record Group VII, Document Box 1116, Folder 3, 1951.

34. Fredrickson, *Dixiecrat Revolt,* 227.

35. For the original notification of Directive 15, see *Federal Register* 43, 87 (May 4, 1978): 19269–70.

36. "Standards for the Classification of Federal Data on Race and Ethnicity," *Federal Register* 59, 110 (June 9, 1994): 29834–35.

37. For Flores, see Daryl Fears, "The Roots of 'Hispanic': 1975 Committee of Bureaucrats Produced Designation." *Washington Post,* October 15, 2003, A 21; Juanita Tamayo Lott, interview by Victoria Hattam, June 23, 2004.

38. See Hattam, *In the Shadow of Race.*

39. Horace Kallen, "Beyond the Melting Pot: A Study of American Nationality," *The Nation* 100 (February 18, 1915): 190–94; (February 25, 1915): 217–20.

40. Ibid., 191 (emphasis original).

41. Ibid., 192.

42. I. B. Berkson, "A Community Theory of American Life," *Menorah Journal* 6, 6 (December 1920): 311–21; I. B. Berkson, "The Jewish Right to Live: A Defense of Ethnic Loyalty," *Menorah Journal* 7, 1 (February 1921): 41–51; Julius Drachsler, "The Blending of Immigrant Cultures," *Menorah Journal* 6, 2 (April 1920): 80–88; Julius Drachsler, "Americanization and Race Fusion," *Menorah Journal* 6, 3 (June 1920): 131–38; and A. L. Kroeber, "Are the Jews a Race?" *Menorah Journal* 3, 5 (December 1917): 290–94.

43. Daniel Kryder, *Divided Arsenal: Race and the American State During World War II* (New York: Cambridge University Press, 2000); Mary Dudziak, *Cold War Civil Rights: Race and the Image of American Democracy* (Princeton, N.J.: Princeton University Press, 2002); and Stephen Skowronek, "The Reassociation of Ideas and Purposes: Racism, Liberalism, and the American Political Tradition," *American Political Science Review* 100, 3 (August 2006): 385-401.

44. Steve Weisman, "At Memorial Ceremony in Alabama, Rice Pays Homage to Young Victims of Church Bombing," *New York Times,* October 23, 2005.

45. Remarks by National Security Advisor Condoleezza Rice, Vanderbilt University, May 13, 2004, Press Release, Office of the Press Secretary, May 17, 2004.

46. Ibid., emphasis added.

47. See Rice with Straw, interview by Orndorff, parenthetical referent added.

48. Ibid.

49. See Rice, interview by Weisman.

50. "RNC Chairman Ken Mehlman Addresses African Methodist Episcopal (AME) Church Convention," Houston, Texas, July 26, 2005, http://www.gop.com/News/Read.aspx?ID=5679

51. RNC Chairman Ken Mehlman Remarks to the National Association of Black Journalists 30th Anniversary Convention, August 4, 2005, http://www.gop.com/News/Read.aspx?ID=5710

52. Nancy Wadsworth, "Reconciliation Politics: Conservative Evangelicals and the New Race Discourse," *Politics & Society* 25, 3 (September 1997): 341–76.

53. Anne Norton, *95 Theses on Politics, Culture and Method* (New Haven, Conn.: Yale University Press, 2004), esp. 1–37.

54. Chester I. Barnard, *The Functions of the Executive* (1938; Cambridge, Mass.: Harvard University Press, 1968); Rogers Smith, "If Politics Matters: Implications for a

'New Institutionalism'," *Studies in American Political Development* 6 (Spring 1992): 1–36; and Timothy Mitchell, "The Limits of the State: Beyond Statist Approaches and Their Critics," *American Political Science Review* 85, 1 (March 1991): 77–95.

55. George W. Stocking, Jr., "Lamarckianism in American Social Science," in Stocking, *Race, Culture, and Evolution: Essays in the History of Anthropology* (Chicago: University of Chicago Press, 1968); Raymond Seidelman, *The Disenchanted Realists: Political Science and the American Crisis, 1884–1984* (Albany: State University of New York Press, 1985); David Ricci, *The Tragedy of Political Science: Politics, Scholarship, and Democracy* (New Haven, Conn.: Yale University Press, 1887); Dorothy Ross, *The Origins of Social Science* (New York: Cambridge University Press, 1992); Ira Katznelson and Helen V. Milner, eds., *Political Science: State of the Discipline*, Centennial Edition (New York: Norton, 2002), introduction; and Robert Vitalis, "Birth of a Discipline," in David Long and Brian Schmidt, eds, *Imperialism and Internationalism in the Discipline of International Relations* (Albany: State University of New York Press, 2005), chap. 7.

Chapter 11. Presidents and Social Movements: A Logic and Preliminary Results

I would like to thank Meredith Levine, Brian Schartz, Michelle Krohn-Friedson, and David Gartenberg for their invaluable research assistance with this project.

1. Elizabeth Sanders, *Roots of Reform: Farmers, Workers, and the American State 1877–1917* (Chicago: University of Chicago Press, 1999).

2. Doug McAdam, *Political Process and the Development of Black Insurgency* (Chicago: University of Chicago Press, 1982); William E. Gamson, *The Strategy of Social Protest*, 2nd ed. (Belmont, Calif.: Wadsworth, 1990).

3. William E. Grover, *The President as Prisoner: A Structural Critique of the Carter and Reagan Years* (Albany: State University of New York Press, 1989), 15–61.

4. See the war count in John M. Collins with Frederick Hamerman and James P. Seevers, *America's Small Wars: Lessons for the Future* (Washington, D.C.: Brassey's US, 1991).

5. Quoting Russell L. Riley, *The Presidency and the Politics of Racial Inequality* (New York: Columbia University Press, 1999), 3..

6. This is a definition I have adapted from that of Charles Tilly.

7. Theda Skocpol, *Diminished Democracy: From Membership to Management in American Civic Life* (Norman: University of Oklahoma Press, 2003).

8. Theda Skocpol, Ziad Munson, Andrew Karch, and Bayliss Camp, "Patriotic Partnerships," in Ira Katznelson and Martin Shefter, eds., *Shaped by War and Trade: International Influences in American Political Development* (Princeton, N.J.: Princeton University Press, 2002), 135.

9. William E. Gamson, *The Strategy of Social Protest*, 2nd ed. (Belmont: Wadsworth, 1990).

10. Sanders, *Roots of Reform*, 149–53. For the contemporary national organization see www.nfu.org

11. For membership figures, see Carl C. Taylor, *The Farmers' Movement, 1670–1920* (Westport, Conn.: Greenwood Press, 1953), 349–50.

12. Jack L.Walker, "The Origins and Maintenance of Interest Groups in America," *American Political Science Review* 77 (1983): 390–406.

13. Anne N. Costain, *Inviting Women's Rebellion: A Political Process Interpretation of the Women's Movement* (Baltimore: Johns Hopkins University Press, 1992), perceives

the existence of a women's movement in the early 1960s, contained in "a multitude of groups, organizations, and individuals" (3), but her title is revealing.

14. J. Brooks Flippen, *Nixon and the Environment* (Albuquerque: University of New Mexico Press, 2000).

15. Skocpol et al., "Patriotic Partnerships," 134–80.

16. On the Wilson-Gompers collaboration, see Sanders, *Roots of Reform*, chap. 10, and Joseph A. McCartin, *Labor's Great War: The Struggle for Industrial Democracy and the Origins of Modern American Labor Relations, 1912-1921* (Chapel Hill: University of North Carolina Press, 1997), 73–81.

17. Sanders, *Roots of Reform*; Eleanor Flexnor, *Century of Struggle: The Women's Rights Movement in the United States* (Cambridge, Mass.: Harvard University Press, 1975), 276.

18. Theodore Lowi, *The Personal President: Power Invested, Promise Unfulfilled* (Ithaca, N.Y.: Cornell University Press, 1984).

19. Skocpol et al., "Patriotic Partnerships."

20. "McKinley and the GAR. He Rides at the Column's Right with Gov. Black in the Buffalo Parade. Over 45,000 Veterans in Line. Flying Flags, Music, and Cheers," *New York Times* (hereafter *NYT*). August 7, 26, 1917.

21. *NYT*, November 11, 17, 1917.

22. Sanders, *Roots of Reform*, chap. 10; Flexnor, *Century of Struggle*, 294–99.

23. *NYT*, March 18, 1913; July 4, 1914; December 15, 1915. On labor legislation, in which Wilson considerably lagged behind his party, see Sanders, *Roots of Reform*, chap. 10.

24. *NYT*, July 31, 1918.

25. On emancipation and Lincoln's war strategy, see David Herbert Donald, *Lincoln* (New York: Simon and Schuster, 1995), 379. Almost a century later, presidents saw denial of citizenship rights to Southern Blacks as a liability in the cold war competition with the Soviet Union. Mary Dudziak, *Cold War Civil Rights: Race and the Image of American Democracy* (Princeton, N.J.: Princeton University Press, 2002).

26. Eileen McDonagh, this volume.

27. Sanders, *Roots of Reform*, chap. 10.

28. Ibid.; *NYT*, June 24, 1913.

29. *NYT*, October 12, 1916; Sanders, *Roots of Reform*, 403–4.

30. *NYT*, August 3, 18, 1913.

31. *NYT*, July 27, 1918.

32. *NYT*, February 29, 1920.

33. On the peace efforts of women's groups, see *NYT*, October 21, 1921, also May 11, 1921, August 4, 1921.

34. *NYT*, September 4, 1921.

35. *NYT*, January 22, 1929; December 22, 1925, January 7, 1926 (on the Railway Labor Act).

36. Sanders, *Roots of Reform*, 264–66; *NYT*, March 20, 1921, January 6, 1922, January 13, 1923.

37. *NYT*, December 13, 1923.

38. *NYT*, October 7, 1925. This speech would appear rather cold-hearted but for its remarkable turn to a plea for peace, through "fair dealings with other nations" and cutting the armaments budget. Perhaps peace simply appealed to Coolidge as far less costly than war to the government, but his many speeches in this vein suggest a sincere belief in the value of peace. His words would have been well received by the American Legion in this era, which was itself deeply antiwar.

39. *NYT*, May 20, 1924.

40. *NYT*, October 5, 1926. On Taft and the Red Cross, see *NYT*, November 10, 1900.

41. John Gerring, *Party Ideologies in America, 1829–1996* (Cambridge: Cambridge University Press, 2001), 14–20. Though Gerring locates the GOP transformation from a Whiggish statism to neoliberalism in 1928, Coolidge, whose portrait hung in Ronald Reagan's Cabinet Room, would seem to lie on the neoliberal side.

42. *NYT*, February 26, 1927, May 24, 1928.

43. *NYT*, September 2, 1924. Coolidge seemed remarkably unworried about the 1924 competition of Progressive Robert La Follette, who was making a concerted attempt to woo labor. In the end, LaFollette carried only Wisconsin.

44. *NYT*, January 2, 1929.

45. *NYT*, September 22, 1924, October 7, 1925.

46. See *NYT*, October 27, 1921, on Harding's southern strategy.

47. *NYT*, April 20, 22, 1929; June 16, 1929; February 16, 1930; July 16, 1930.

48. See, e.g., *NYT*, August 2, 1930, August 21, 1931, on appointments of large numbers of group leaders to different advisory committees.

49. Arthur Stanley Link, *Wilson*, vol. 2, *The New Freedom* (Princeton, N.J.: Princeton University Press, 1956), 458–59.

50. Kenneth S. Davis, *FDR: The New Deal Years, 1933–1937* (New York: Random House, 1986), 400–404, 456.

Chapter 12. Leaders, Citizenship Movements, and the Politics Rivalries Make

1. James M. Jasper, *The Art of Moral Protest: Culture, Biography, and Creativity in Social Movements* (Chicago: University of Chicago Press, 1997), 7.

2. Russell Riley, "The Presidency and the Politics of Racial Inequality," Ph.D. dissertation, University of Virginia, 1995, 46–47.

3. William Sherman Savage, *The Controversy over the Distribution of Abolition Literature, 1830–1860* (Washington, D.C.: Association for the Study of Negro Life and History, 1938), 14–15.

4. Elizabeth Cady Stanton, *History of Woman Suffrage* (1881–1922; New York: Source Book Press, 1970), 3: 118.

5. Roosevelt is quoted in C. Allen Foster, *Votes for Women* (New York: Criterion Books, 1966), 138–39.

6. James Morone, *The Democratic Wish: Popular Participation and the Limits of American Government* (New York: Basic Books, 1990), 148.

7. Samuel Gompers, "The Lessons of the Recent Strikes," *North American Review* (August 1894): 201–6; Lindsey Almont, *The Pullman Strike* (Chicago: University of Chicago Press, 1942); Nick Salvatore, *Eugene V. Debs: Citizen and Socialist* (Urbana: University of Illinois Press, 1982).

8. Frances Fox Piven and Richard Cloward, *Poor People's Movements: Why They Succeed, How They Fail* (New York: Vintage, 1978).

9. Ann-Marie Szymanski, *Pathways to Prohibition* (Durham, N.C.: Duke University Press, 2003).

10. See especially Sidney Tarrow, "'The Very Excesses of Democracy': State Building and Contentious Politics in America," in Anne Costain and Andrew McFarland, eds., *Social Movements and American Political Institutions* (New York: Rowman and Littlefield, 1998), 20–37; Harold Haines, *Black Radicals and the Civil Rights Mainstream, 1954–1970* (Knoxville: University of Tennessee Press, 1988).

11. For example, see Sidney Tarrow, *Power in Movement: Social Movements and Con-

tentious Politics (New York: Cambridge University Press, 1998); and Jasper, *The Art of Moral Protest.*

12. Robert Beisner, *Twelve Against Empire: The Anti-Imperialists, 1989–1900* (New York: McGraw-Hill, 1968); Daniel Schirmer, *Republic or Empire* (Cambridge, Mass.: Schenkman, 1972); Philip Foner and Richard Winchester, eds., *The Anti-Imperialism Reader* (New York: Holmes and Meier, 1984).

13. Ben Gilbert, *Ten Blocks from the White House* (New York: Praeger, 1968); Milton Viorst, *Fire in the Streets* (New York: Simon and Schuster, 1979); Clayborn Carson et al., eds., *The Eyes on the Prize Civil Rights Reader* (New York: Penguin, 1991).

14. Joyce Kornbluh, *Rebel Voices: An IWW Anthology* (Ann Arbor: University of Michigan Press, 1964); Patrick Renshaw, *The Wobblies: The Story of Syndicalism in the United States* (Garden City, N.Y.: Doubleday, 1967); Melvyn Dubofsky, *"Big Bill" Haywood* (New York: St. Martin's Press, 1987).

15. David H. Bennett, *The Party of Fear: From Nativist Movements to the New Right in American History* (Chapel Hill: University of North Carolina Press, 1988); James Coates, *Armed and Dangerous: The Rise of the Survivalist Right* (New York: Hill and Wang, 1987); Kenneth Stern, *A Force upon the Plain: The American Militia Movement and the Politics of Hate* (New York: Simon and Schuster, 1996).

16. Alan Brinkley, *The End of Reform: New Deal Liberalism in Recession and War* (New York: Knopf, 1995), 201–26.

17. Ibid., 212.

18. Gilbert Hobbs Barnes, *The Antislavery Impulse, 1830–1844* (New York: Harcourt, Brace, 1964), 71–89.

19. Ibid.

20. Wendell Phillips, *Review of Lysander Spooner's Essay on the Unconstitutionality of Slavery* (Boston, 1847); William Wiecek, *The Sources of Antislavery Constitutionalism in America, 1760–1848* (Ithaca, N.Y.: Cornell University Press, 1977).

21. Richard Sewell, *Ballots for Freedom: Antislavery Politics in the United States, 1837–1860* (New York: Oxford University Press, 1976), ch. 2.

22. Quoted in Lillie Buffum Chace Wyman and Arthur Crawford Wyman, *Elizabeth Buffum Chace, 1806–1899* (Boston: W.B. Clarke, 1914), 1: 83.

23. Quoted in Irving Bartlett, *Wendell and Ann Phillips: The Community of Reform, 1840–1880* (New York: Norton, 1979), 151.

24. *The Liberator,* May 16, 1845.

25. David Potter, *The Impending Crisis, 1848–1861* (New York: Harper and Row, 1976), 143.

26. "Lincoln's Inaugural Address," in James D. Richardson, ed., *Messages and Papers of the Presidents* (New York: Harper and Row, 1897), 7: 3206.

27. Ibid., 3210.

28. See Hans L. Trefousse, *The Radical Republicans: Lincoln's Vanguard for Racial Justice* (New York: Knopf, 1969), 228.

29. Quoted in Gerald Sorin, *Abolitionism: A New Perspective* (New York: Praeger, 1972), 150.

30. Quoted in Richard Hofstadter, *The American Political Tradition* (New York: Vintage, 1973), 184.

31. See Philip Foner, *Frederick Douglass* (New York: Citadel Press, 1964), 201–5.

32. Hofstadter, *American Tradition,* 196.

33. Sorin, *Abolitionism,* 151; Oscar Sherwin, *Prophet of Liberty: The Life and Times of Wendell Phillips* (New York: Bookman Associates), 452.

34. Foner, *Frederick Douglass,* 197, 200.

35. Included in *The Collected Works of Abraham Lincoln,* ed. Roy Basler (New Brunswick, N.J.: Rutgers University Press, 1953), 5: 420.

36. David Herbert Donald, *Lincoln* (NewYork: Simon and Schuster, 1995) 345.

37. T. Harry Williams, *Lincoln and the Radicals* (Madison: University of Wisconsin Press, 1941), 64.

38. Donald, Lincoln, 343.

39. Sorin, *Abolitionism*, 154.

40. Hans Trefousse, *Lincoln's Decision for Emancipation* (Philadelphia: Lippincott, 1975), 18–23.

41. *Collected Works of Abraham Lincoln*, 5: 144–46.

42. Sherwin, *Prophet of Liberty*, 458.

43. *Collected Works of Abraham Lincoln*, 5: 318–19.

44. Foner, *Frederick Douglass*, 200–201.

45. Trefousse, *The Radical Republicans*, 203–4.

46. Williams, *Lincoln and the Radicals*, 157–67.

47. Sherwin, *Prophet of Liberty*, 464–65.

48. Quoted in Benjamin P. Thomas, *Abraham Lincoln* (New York: Knopf, 1952), 342–43.

49. Donald, *Lincoln*, 362–69; see also Sherwin, *Prophet of Liberty*, 464–65.

50. Trefousse, *Radical Republicans*, 203–4.

51. James M. McPherson, *Battle Cry of Freedom: The Civil War Era* (New York: Oxford University Press, 1988), 558; John Hope Franklin, *Emancipation Proclamation* (Washington, D.C.: National Archives and Records Service, 1994), 61–62.

52. Philip Foner, ed., *The Life and Writings of Frederick Douglass* (New York: International Publishers, 1955), 4: 316.

53. Sarah Hunter Graham, *Woman Suffrage and the New Democracy* (New Haven, Conn.: Yale University Press, 1996), 7–9.

54. Quoted in Foster, *Votes for Women*, 138–39.

55. Ibid., 142–44; Carrie Chapman Catt, *Woman Suffrage and Politics* (New York: Scribner's, 1926), 237–38.

56. See, e.g., Anna Howard Shaw, "The Nonpartisan View," quoted in Aileen Kraditor, *The Ideas of the Woman Suffrage Movement, 1890–1920* (New York: Columbia University Press, 1965), 247; Sidney Milkis and Daniel J. Tichenor, "Direct Democracy and Social Justice: The Progressive Party Campaign of 1912," *Studies in American Political Development* (Fall 1994).

57. Catt explains this strategic political reasoning in her account of the suffrage campaign in *Woman Suffrage and Politics*, chap. 16.

58. Ibid., 227.

59. Ibid.

60. Frank Parker Stockbridge, "How Woodrow Wilson Won His Nomination," *Current History* 20 (July 1924): 567. See also Milkis and Tichenor, "Direct Democracy," 311–14.

61. Stockbridge, "Woodrow Wilson," 567–69.

62. Daniel Tichenor, "The Presidency, Social Movements, and Contentious Change: Lessons From the Woman's Suffrage and Labor Movements," *Presidential Studies Quarterly* 29, 1 (March 1999): 16.

63. Christine Lunardi and Thomas Knock, "Woodrow Wilson and Woman Suffrage: A New Look," *Political Science Quarterly* 95 (Winter 1980–81): 659.

64. Christine A. Lunardini, *From Equal Suffrage to Equal Rights: Alice Paul and the National Woman's Party, 1910-1928* (New York: New York University Press, 1986), 32–49.

65. Catt, *Woman's Suffrage and Politics*, chap. 16.

66. See Kraditor, *Ideas of the Woman Suffrage Movement*, 235–36.

67. "Speech of President Woodrow Wilson Before the 48th Conference of the Na-

tional American Woman Suffrage Association," Atlantic City, N.J., September 8, 1916, Records of the National Association of the American Woman Suffrage Association, Library of Congress, Manuscript Division (hereafter Records of NAWSA), microfilm reel no. 55.

68. Catt, *Woman's Suffrage and Politics*, 280.

69. Graham, *Woman Suffrage and the New Democracy*, 111.

70. Ibid., 110–12.

71. "Report for 1916," National Woman's Party Papers, 1913–1929 (Microfilms Corporation of America, 1979), microfilm reel no. 2.

72. National Woman's Party to Mrs. Davis Ewing, August 20, 1917, National Woman's Party Papers, microfilm reel no. 2.

73. Lunardi and Krock, 667.

74. Carrie Chapman Catt to Woodrow Wilson, September 29, 1918, Records of NAWSA, microfilm reel no. 21.

75. "President Woodrow Wilson's Message to the United States Senate Urging Passage of the Suffrage Amendment to the Constitution," September 30, 1918, National Woman's Party Papers, microfilm reel no. 2.

76. Piven and Cloward, *Poor People's Movements*, 115–19.

77. Melvyn Dubofsky and Warren Van Tine, *John L. Lewis* (Urbana: University of Illinois Press, 1986), 132–35.

78. Morone, *Democratic Wish*, 160.

79. See, for instance, Melvyn Dubofsky and Warren Van Tine, "John L. Lewis," in Melvyn Dubofsky and Warren Van Tine, eds., *Labor Leaders in America* (Urbana: University of Illinois Press, 1987), 193–94.

80. William Leuchtenburg, *Franklin Roosevelt and the New Deal* (New York: Harper and Row, 1963), 106–7; Morone, *Democratic Wish*, 162–63; Piven and Cloward, *Poor People's Movements*, 113–15.

81. Dubofsky and Van Tine, "John L. Lewis," 195–97; Morone, *Democratic Wish*, 165; Daniel J. Tichenor, "The Presidency, Social Movements, and Contentious Change," *Presidential Studies Quarterly* 29 (March 1999): 20.

82. Piven and Cloward, *Poor People's Movements*, 120–25.

83. Dubofsky and Van Tine, "John L. Lewis," 196.

84. Leuchtenburg, *Franklin Roosevelt*, 82.

85. Bruce Miroff, *Icons of Democracy* (New York: Basic Books, 1993), 260–62.

86. Ibid., 262.

87. Alonzo Hamby, *Liberalism and Its Challengers* (New York: Oxford University Press, 1992), 25.

88. Leuchtenburg, *Franklin Roosevelt*, 49.

89. Ibid.

90. Robert H. Zieger, *John L. Lewis: Labor Leader* (Boston: Twayne, 1988), 105–6.

91. Ibid., 109.

92. Marc Landy, "FDR and John L. Lewis," in Marc Landy, ed., *Modern Presidents and the Modern Presidency* (Lexington, Mass.: D.C. Heath, 1985), 105.

Chapter 13. The Presidency in the Vanguard: Lyndon Johnson and the Civil Rights Insurgency

1. Sidney M. Milkis, "Lyndon Johnson, the Great Society, and the Twilight of the Modern Presidency," in Milkis and Jerome Mileur, eds., *The Great Society and the High Tide of Liberalism* (Amherst: University of Massachusetts Press, 2005).

2. Richard Goodwin, *Remembering America: A Voice from the Sixties* (Boston: Little, Brown, 1988), 275.

3. Paul Conkin, *Big Daddy from the Pedernales: Lyndon Baines Johnson* (Boston: Twayne, 1986), 164.

4. Memos, Rowe to Johnson, December 22, 1960, March 6, 1962, James Rowe Papers, Box 100, Folders: LBJ (1960-1961), LBJ (1962-1963), Franklin D. Roosevelt Library, Hyde Park, New York.

5. Conkin, *Big Daddy from the Pedernales*, 164.

6. Remarks of Vice President Lyndon B. Johnson, Memorial Day, Gettysburg, Pennsylvania, May 30, 1963, www.lbjlib.utexas.edu

7. Telephone conversation between Lyndon Johnson and Ted Sorenson, June 3, 1963, George Reedy Office Files, Johnson Library.

8. Lyndon B. Johnson, "Remarks at a Breakfast of the Georgia Legislature," May 8, 1964, *Public Papers of the Presidents: Lyndon B. Johnson, 1963–1964* (Washington, D.C.: Government Printing Office, 1965-70), 1: 648.

9. Ibid., 649.

10. Editorial, "LBJ's Challenge," *Washington Post*, May 9, 1964, A8.

11. *Washington Post*, May 9, 1964, A1.

12. *Richmond Times Dispatch*, May 9, 1964, 1, 11.

13. Editorial, "With South in His Tongue and Heart, LBJ Sounds Call for Justice for All," *Atlanta Constitution*, May 9, 1964, 4.

14. Dirksen cited in Byron Hulsey, *Everett Dirksen and His Presidents: How a Senate Giant Shaped American Politics* (Lawrence: University Press of Kansas, 2000), 196. Johnson's power over Congress had become so great by the summer of 1964 that he was able to pressure Republican minority leader, Charles Halleck, to support a rule that enabled Congress to act on the president's poverty legislation. See telephone conversation between Lyndon Johnson and Charles Halleck, June 22, 1964, White House Tapes.

15. Johnson telephone conversation with Roy Wilkins, head of the NAACP, July 2, 1964, Johnson Tapes.

16. Johnson telephone conversation with Martin Luther King, Jr., January 15, 1965, Johnson Tapes.

17. Nick Kotz, *Judgment Days: Lyndon Baines Johnson, Martin Luther King, Jr., and the Laws That Changed America* (Boston: Houghton Mifflin, 2005), 267.

18. Lyndon B. Johnson, "Special Message to Congress: The American Promise," March 15, 1965, www.lbjlib.utexas.edu

19. Conkin, *Big Daddy from the Pedernales*, 216.

20. Kotz, *Judgment Days*, 312.

21. Interview with Harry McPherson, July 30, 1985.

22. Goodwin, *Remembering America*, 316; telephone conversation between Lyndon Johnson, Bill Moyers, and McGeorge Bundy, November 3, 1964, Johnson Tapes.

23. See Paul Hope, "New Faces Mark Victory of Republicans," *Washington Star*, November 9, 1966; Richard M. Scammon and Ben J. Wattenberg, *The Real Majority* (New York: Coward-McCann, 1970), 29, 209–10.

24. Memorandum, Ervin Duggan to Douglas Cater, November 9, 1966, Henry Wilson Papers, Johnson Library.

25. McPherson interview, July 30, 1985.

26. On King's Chicago campaign, see Kotz, *Judgment Days*, 363–67.

27. Ibid, 312.

28. Memorandum, Bill Moyers to LBJ, June 21, 1965, Office Files of Bill Moyers.

29. Memoranda, Hayes Redmon to Bill Moyers, November 27, 1965, 30, 1965.

30. Johnson, telephone conversation with Martin Luther King, August 20, 1965, Johnson Tapes.

31. Oral History Interview, Lee White, by Joe B. Frantz, March 2, 1971, Johnson Library, 20.

32. Kotz, *Judgment Days*, 353.

33. Richard Goodwin, speech draft, May 1965, White House Central File: SP 3-93, Box 172, Johnson Library; Johnson, telephone conversation with King, August 20, 1965, Johnson tapes; Lyndon Johnson, "Commencement Address at Howard University: 'To Fulfill These Rights'," June 4, 1965, *Public Papers of the Presidents: Lyndon B. Johnson, 1965*, 2: 636.

34. Johnson, telephone conversation with King, August 20, 1965.

35. Ibid.

36. Memorandum, Lee C. White to the President, July 23, 1965, White House Central Files, SP 3-93, Box 172, Johnson Library.

37. David Charles Carter, "Two Nations: Social Insurgency and National Civil Rights Policymaking in the Johnson Administration, 1965–1968," Ph.D. dissertation, Duke University, 2001, 320.

38. Robert Mann, *The Walls of Jericho: Lyndon Johnson, Hubert Humphrey, Richard Russell, and the Struggle for Civil Rights* (New York: Harcourt, Brace, 1996), 480.

39. Bruce Miroff, "Presidential Leverage over Social Movements: The Johnson White House and Civil Rights," *Journal of Politics* 43 (1981): 14.

40. Because LBJ's efforts were sub rosa, direct evidence of his efforts to influence the civil rights leadership is lacking, but leaders of the major organizations convened on July 29, and issued statements that conformed to LBJ's immediate political objectives. See *New York Times*, July 30, 1964, 12; and Miroff, "Presidential Leverage," 10–11. Martin Luther King implied that the civil rights leadership had done the White House's bidding in calling for a moratorium when he asked for Johnson's cooperation in resolving the Mississippi Freedom Democratic Party controversy that threatened to disrupt the national Democratic Convention, which was held a month later in Atlantic City, New Jersey. As White House aide Lee White wrote in a memorandum to LBJ, King "expressed the thought that those leaders who had signed the moratorium were in a difficult situation. They needed to be supported." Memorandum, Lee C. White to the President, August 13, 1964, White House Central Files, Ex & Gen PL, Johnson Library.

41. Written communication from Sherwin Markman, a Johnson White House aide, who was heavily involved in the resolving the MFDC controversy. January 13, 2004.

42. "Text of Statement by Negro Leaders," printed in *New York Times*, July 30, 1964, 12.

43. Memorandum, White to Johnson, August 13, 1964.

44. Johnson also was concerned, even at this early stage of his presidency, that an unruly convention might open the door to a Robert Kennedy candidacy. Markman, written communication.

45. Johnson, telephone conversation with Walter Reuther, August 9, 1964, Johnson tapes.

46. Johnson, telephone conversation with Hubert Humphrey and Walter Reuther, August 25, 1964, Johnson tapes; memorandum, Marvin Watson to LBJ, April 19, 1967, Marvin Watson Files, Johnson Library; Sidney M. Milkis, *The President and the Parties: The Transformation of the American Party System Since the New Deal* (New York: Oxford University Press, 1993), 210–16.

47. Kotz, *Judgment Days*, 285–96.

48. Memorandum, Harry McPherson to Lyndon Johnson, September 12, 1966, Office Files of Harry McPherson, Johnson Library.

49. Memorandum, Nicholas de B. Katzenbach to Harry McPherson, September 17, 1966, ibid.

50. See James R. Jones to Marvin Watson, September 15, 1967, Marvin Watson Files, Johnson Library; memorandum, Bill Graham to the President, May 18, 1967, White House Central File: We9, Johnson Library.

51. The term *extraordinary isolation* is Woodrow Wilson's. See Wilson, *Constitutional Government in the United States* (New York: Columbia University Press, 1908), 69.

52. Memorandum, Sherwin Markman for the President, February 1, 1967, White House Central File, We9, Johnson Library.

53. Markman, written communication.

54. For a primary account of the ghetto visits, see the Oral History of Sherwin J. Markman, Tape 1, May 21, 1969, interview by Dorothy Pierce McSweeney, 24–36, Johnson Library. The most detailed account of the ghetto visits is Carter, "'Two Nations'," chap. 5.

55. Sherwin J. Markman, "American Ghettos: Our Challenge and Response," April 5, 1967, White House Central File, We9, Johnson Library; memorandum, Markman to the President, February 1, 1967, ibid.

56. Memorandum, Markman to the President, February 17, 1968, ibid.; White House Fellow, Thomas E. Cronin, who visited Baltimore, spoke of the "*absence of proud men.*" Memorandum: Cronin to LBJ, May 11, 1967 (emphasis in original).

57. See Oral History of Sherwin Markman, 28; and Notes of a Meeting with Peter Lisigor, of the Chicago Daily News, August 4, 1967, Tom Johnson's Notes of Meetings, May 1968, Meetings with Correspondents; and memorandum, Tom Johnson to the President, August 10, 1967, and attached notes of meeting with labor leaders, ibid., Box 1. Although Johnson did not refer directly to the ghetto reports in a meeting with labor leaders, his discussion of the riots was certainly informed by it.

58. *Public Papers of the Presidents: Lyndon B. Johnson, 1967,* 1: 721, 723.

59. Memorandum, James Rowe to the President, June 29, 1965, White House Central File: Aides, Moyers, Johnson Library..

60. Frances Fox Piven and Richard Cloward, "The Politics of the Great Society," in Milkis and Mileur, *The Great Society and the High Tide of Liberalism.*

61. Memorandum, Sherwin Markman to the President, March 14, 1967, White House Central File, We9, Johnson Library.

62. *The Administrative History of the OEO,* Special Files, Johnson Library, 35–36. .

63. Economic Opportunity Act of 1964, Title 2, Part A, Section 202 (a).

64. Glazer cited in *Administrative History of the OEO,* 18.

65. Daniel Patrick Moynihan, *Maximum Feasible Misunderstanding: Community Action in the War on Poverty* (New York: Free Press, 1970), 139.

66. Task Force on Government Organization, Memorandum to the President, December 15, 1966, *White House Central File;* and "A Final Report By the President's Task Force on Government Organization," June 15, 1967, 18–20, Outside Task Forces, Johnson Library.

67. Nicolau cited in Moynihan, *Maximum Feasible Misunderstanding,* 139.

68. On Johnson and the National Youth Administration, see Conkin, *Big Daddy from the Pedernales,* 74–79; Robert Dallek, *Lone Star Rising: Lyndon Johnson and His Times, 1908–1960* (New York: Oxford University Press, 1991), 123–44; and Robert A. Caro, *The Years of Lyndon Johnson: The Path to Power* (New York: Vintage, 1981), chap. 19.

69. *National Resources Development Report of 1943*, part 2, "Security, Work, and Relief Policies" (Washington, D.C.: Government Printing Office, 1943), 486.

70. Ibid., 394–95.

71. *Task Force Report on Intergovernmental Program Coordination*, December 22, 1965, I, Outside Task Forces, Johnson Library.

72. Lyndon B. Johnson, *The Vantage Point: Perspectives of the Presidency, 1963–1969* (New York: Holt, Rinehart, 1971), 81. David Welborn and Jesse Burkhead, *Intergovernmental Relations in the Administrative State* (Austin: University of Texas Press, 1989), 56–76; Gareth Davies, *From Opportunity to Entitlement: The Transformation and Decline of Great Society Liberalism* (Lawrence: University Press of Kansas, 1996), 194–97.

73. Lillian B. Rubin, "Maximum Feasible Participation: The Origins, Implications, and Present Status," *The Annals* 385 (September 1969): 17.

74. *Examination of the War on Poverty*, prepared for the Subcommittee on Employment, Manpower and Poverty of the Committee on Labor and Public Welfare, U.S. Senate (Washington, D.C.: Government Printing Office, 1967), 5: 1238, 1241–42. For this quotation and many of the ideas expressed in the discussion of the Community Action Program, I am indebted to James A. Morone, *The Democratic Wish: Popular Participation and the Limits of American Government* (New Haven, Conn.: Yale University Press, 1998), ch. 6.

75. Memorandum, Sherwin Markman, for the President, February 1, 1967; Kotz, *Judgment Days*, 395.

76. Memorandum, Harry McPherson to the President, March 12, 1965, White House Diary Backup, Johnson Library.

77. Wilson Carey McWilliams, "Great Societies and Great Empires," in Milkis and Mileur, *The Great Society and the High Tide of Liberalism*, 222-23.

78. "Creative Federalism," Speech Notes prepared by Harry McPherson, n.d., Aides: McPherson, Box 55; Memorandum, Fred Panzer to Harry McPherson, February 21, 1968, White House Central File, EX-SP.

79. W. W. Rostow, Memorandum of Conversation, Participants: The President; the Vice President; Charles Murphy; W. W. Rostow, April 5, 1968, White House Famous Names, Box 6, Folder: Robert F. Kennedy, 1968 Campaign, Johnson Library.

Chapter 14. Entrepreneurial Defenses of Congressional Power

1. Samuel Huntington, "Congressional Responses to the Twentieth Century," in David B. Truman, ed., *Congress and America's Future* (Englewood Cliffs, N.J.: Prentice-Hall, 1965).

2. Barry R. Weingast and Mark J. Moran, "Bureaucratic Discretion or Congressional Control? Regulatory Policymaking by the Federal Trade Commission," *Journal of Political Economy* 91 (1983): 765–800.

3. See Terry Moe, "The Presidency and the Bureaucracy: The Presidential Advantage," in Michael Nelson, ed., *The Presidency and the Political System*, 6th ed. (Washington, D.C.: CQ Press, 2000).

4. Ibid., 451.

5. Ibid.

6. Ibid., 452.

7. William Howell, *Power Without Persuasion: The Politics of Direct Presidential Action* (Princeton, N.J.: Princeton University Press, 2003), 111.

8. Ibid., 112.

9. See James Sundquist, *The Decline and Resurgence of Congress* (Washington, D.C.: Brookings Institution, 1981).

10. Eric Schickler, *Disjointed Pluralism: Institutional Innovation and the Development of the U.S. Congress* (Princeton, N.J.: Princeton University Press, 2001).

11. Ibid., 251.

12. See, e.g., Kirk Victor, "Congress in Eclipse," *National Journal,* April 5, 2003.

13. See, e.g., *Congressional Record,* June 10, 1946, 6558; July 25, 1946, 10039; June 8, 1946, 6531; see also Joseph Cooper, *Congress and Its Committees* (1960; New York: Garland, 1988), 187.

14. Stephen Skowronek, *The Politics Presidents Make: Leadership from John Adams to George Bush* (Cambridge, Mass.: Harvard University Press, 1993).

15. Lead sponsors from the minority party would typically be named to the special committee.

16. See David R. Mayhew, *Divided We Govern: Party Control, Lawmaking, and Investigations, 1946–1990* (New Haven, Conn.: Yale University Press, 1993); Mayhew, *America's Congress: Actions in the Public Sphere, James Madison Through Newt Gingrich* (New Haven, Conn.: Yale University Press, 2002).

17. Schickler, *Disjointed Pluralism,* chap. 4.

18. David Rosenbloom, *Building a Legislative-Centered Public Administration: Congress and the Administrative State, 1946–1999* (University: University of Alabama Press, 2002).

19. See David Epstein and Sharyn O'Halloran, *Delegating Powers: A Transaction Cost Politics Approach to Policy Making Under Separate Powers* (New York: Cambridge University Press, 1999); John D. Huber and Charles R. Shipan, *Deliberate Discretion: The Institutional Foundations of Bureaucratic Autonomy* (New York: Cambridge University Press, 2002).

20. James E. Brazier, "An Anti-New Dealer Legacy: The Administrative Procedure Act," *Journal of Policy History* 8 (1996): 206–26.

21. Ira Katznelson, Kim Geiger, and Daniel Kryder, "Limiting Liberalism: The Southern Veto in Congress, 1933–1950," *Political Science Quarterly* 108 (1993): 283–306.

22. Telford Taylor, *Grand Inquest: The Story of Congressional Investigations* (New York: Simon and Schuster, 1954).

23. Joseph P. Harris, *Congressional Control of Administration* (Washington, D.C.: Brookings Institution, 1964), 264.

24. Ibid., 261.

25. Ibid., 265.

26. Mayhew, *America's Congress,* 82.

27. Walter Goodman, *The Committee: The Extraordinary Career of the House Committee on Un-American Activities* (New York: Farrar, Straus, Giroux, 1968).

28. Edward V. Schneier, "The Politics of Anti-Communism: A Study of the House Committee on Un-American Activities and Its Role in the Political Process," Ph.D. dissertation, Claremont Graduate School, 1963.

29. *Congressional Record,* April 27, 1938, 5881–82; May 26, 1938, 7583–84.

30. William Leuchtenburg, *Franklin D. Roosevelt and the New Deal, 1932–1940* (New York: Harper and Row, 1963), 280–81.

31. *Congressional Record,* January 24, 1939, 733–35.

32. Stewart Henderson Britt and Seldon C. Menefee, "Did the Publicity of the Dies Committee in 1938 Influence Public Opinion?" *Public Opinion Quarterly* 3 (1939): 449–57.

33. *New York Times,* January 8, 1939, 70.

34. August Raymond Ogden, *The Dies Committee* (Washington, D.C.: Catholic University of America Press, 1944), 109.

35. See Goodman, *Committee.*

36. William Gellerman, *Martin Dies* (New York: John Day, 1944).

37. D. A. Saunders, "The Dies Committee: First Phase," *Public Opinion Quarterly* 3 (1939): 223–38.

38. *New York Times,* January 4, 1939, 4.

39. Porter, *Waning of the New Deal.*

40. See Porter, *Waning of the New Deal,* 79–80; *New York Times,* March 17, 1939, 1; March 21, 1939, 1.

41. *Washington Post,* March 23, 1939, 2.

42. *New York Times,* April 4, 1939, 18.

43. *New York Times,* April 19, 1939, 1; May 2, 1939, 1; June 13, 1939, 1; June 26, 1940, 25.

44. *New York Times,* June 26, 1940, 25.

45. Porter, *Waning of the New Deal; New York Times,* May 3, 1939, 1; May 23, 1939, 1.

46. *New York Times,* June 13, 1939, 1.

47. Woodrum's attack on the WPA attracted wide attention, especially following an expensive "swing" production of the *Mikado.* The *Times* noted that Woodrum was being described as the "Lord High Executioner" of the WPA (April 4, 1939, 18).

48. *New York Times,* July 16, 1939, 1, 9; July 21, 1939, 1, 4.

49. See, e.g., *New York Times,* December 12, 13, 14, 15, 17, 19, 20, 23, 1939; January 9, 10, 27, 1940; February 2, 3, 15, 22, 27, 1940; March 7, 8, 1940.

50. See Schickler and Pearson, "Agenda Control."

51. See Roland Young, *Congressional Politics in the Second World War* (New York: Columbia University Press, 1956), 227. Nonetheless, Allan Bogue, *The Congressman's Civil War* (Cambridge: Cambridge University Press, 1989) and Liam Schwartz, "Friend and Foe: Congressional Development in a System of Separated Power," Working Paper, Harvard University, 2005, show that investigations during the Civil War were far reaching. With respect to World War I, more investigations were launched *after* hostilities ended.

52. Floyd M. Riddick, "The Second Session of the Seventy-Seventh Congress," *American Political Science Review* 37 (1943): 300.

53. See also Floyd M. Riddick, *The United States Congress: Its Organization and Procedure* (Manassas, Va.: National Capitol Publishers, 1949), 27.

54. These counts treat each separate Congress in which an investigation is authorized as a separate investigation.

55. See *Washington Post,* March 12, 1943; January 24, 1944, 1.

56. See Donald Riddle, *The Truman Committee: A Study in Congressional Responsibility* (New Brunswick, N.J.: Rutgers University Press, 1964); Theodore Wilson, "The Truman Committee, 1941," in Arthur M. Schlesinger, Jr., and Roger Bruns, eds., *Congress Investigates: A Documentary History, 1792-1974* (New York: Chelsea House, 1975).

57. See Riddle, *Truman Committee,* 51, 159–60; Wilson, "Truman Committee, 1941."

58. Bruce J. Dierenfield, *Keeper of the Rules: Congressman Howard W. Smith of Virginia* (Charlottesville: University Press of Virginia, 1987), 102.

59. *Time,* February 22, 1943, 22.

60. Schickler, *Disjointed Pluralism,* 158–59.

61. Dierenfield, *Keeper of the Rules,* 103–4.

62. Young, *Congressional Politics in the Second World War,* 107.

63. This count is from a Proquest online search specifying that the front-page story include the words (a) "investigation," "inquiry," or "investigate"; (b) "House,"

"Senate," "Congress," or "congressional"; and (c) "executive," "agency," "bureau," "Roosevelt," or "Truman." Stories were eliminated if they did not relate to an actual or proposed congressional investigation.

64. The numbers for front-page stories discussing investigations that fit this description in each year are 23 (1941), 40 (1942), 40 (1943), 20 (1944), and 57 (1945).

65. See Cooper, *Congress and Its Committees*, 190, 206–8; Riddick, *United States Congress: Organization and Procedure*, 152.

66. Cooper, *Congress and Its Committees*, 203–5.

67. Joint Committee on the Organization of Congress. *Organization of Congress: Hearings, 79th Congress, 1st Session* (Washington, D.C.: Government Printing Office, 1945), 40.

68. Ibid., 25.

69. Ibid., 259–60, 308–9, 236–29.

70. Ibid., 304.

71. See Harris, *Congressional Control*; Mayhew, *Divided We Govern*.

72. *Congressional Record*, July 26, 1946, 10045.

73. See Terry Moe, "The Politicized Presidency," in John Chubb and Paul E. Peterson, eds., *New Directions in American Politics* (Washington, D.C.: Brookings Institution Press, 1985).

74. See Louis Fisher, *The Politics of Shared Power: Congress and the Executive* (Washington, D.C.: CQ Press, 1981), chaps. 2 and 3.

75. Mayhew, *Divided We Govern*.

Chapter 15. Inventing the Institutional Presidency: Entrepreneurship and the Rise of the Bureau of the Budget, 1939–49

1. Shelley Lynne Tomkin, *Inside OMB: Politics and Process in the President's Budget Office* (Armonk, N.Y.: M.E. Sharpe, 1998), 3; John Hart, *The Presidential Branch*, 2nd ed. (Chatham, N.J.: Chatham House, 1995).

2. Roger W. Jones quoted in Daniel Biederman, "Harold Smith and the Growth of the Bureau of the Budget," Senior Thesis, Department of Politics, Princeton University, 1975, 11.

3. Wayne Coy, "Federal Executive Reorganization Re-Examined: Basic Problems," *American Political Science Review* 40 (December 1946): 1134.

4. Ira Katznelson and Bruce Pietrykowski, "Rebuilding the American State: Evidence from the 1940s," *Studies in American Political Development* 5 (Fall 1991): 301-39; Katznelson and Pietrykowski, "On Categories and Configurations: Further Remarks on Rebuilding the American State," *Studies in American Political Development* 9 (Spring 1995): 213–21; Katznelson, Kim Geiger, and Daniel Kryder, "Limiting Liberalism: The Southern Veto in Congress, 1933–1950," *Political Science Quarterly* 108 (Summer 1993): 283–307.

5. Larry Berman, *The Office of Management and Budget and the Presidency* (Princeton, N.J.: Princeton University Press, 1979); W. Henry Lambright, *Powering Apollo: James E. Webb of NASA* (Baltimore: Johns Hopkins University Press, 1995).

6. Richard P. Nathan, *The Administrative Presidency* (New York: Macmillan, 1983); Andrew Rudalevige, "The 'M' in OMB: Presidential Management of the Executive Branch, 1939–2003," paper presented at the 2003 Annual Meeting of the American Political Science Association.

7. Adam D. Sheingate, "Political Entrepreneurship, Institutional Change, and American Political Development," *Studies in American Political Development* 17 (Fall 2003): 191, 188; and see Sheingate's chapter in this volume.

8. Katznelson and Pietrykowski, "Rebuilding the American State," 317.

9. See, e.g,. Hart, *Presidential Branch*; John Burke, *The Institutional Presidency*, 2nd ed. (Baltimore: Johns Hopkins University Press, 1999); Matthew J. Dickinson, *Bitter Harvest* (New York: Cambridge University Press, 1997).

10. "1/19/50 Staff Meeting Items Checklist," Lawton papers, BOB—Staff Meetings, Harry S Truman Library (hereafter HSTL).

11. Staff Memo, "Executive Branch Teamwork in the Critical Days Ahead," April 7, 1948, Webb papers, BOB: Organization of the Executive Branch of the Government, Commission on, HSTL.

12. For Smith, see the interviews in John Warren Ramsey, "The Director of the Bureau of the Budget as a Presidential Aide, 1921–1952; With Emphasis on the Truman Years," Ph.D. dissertation, University of Missouri, 1967, 92; Smith's diary, here quoting the entry of October 21, 1939, is housed in the Franklin D. Roosevelt Library (FDRL). For Webb, see Lambright, *Powering Apollo*, 5, 7–9; Lambright, "James Webb and Administrative Power," in Jameson W. Doig and Erwin C. Hargrove, eds., *Leadership and Innovation* (Baltimore: Johns Hopkins University Press, 1987), 176–78. See also Webb's comments in the Joint Oral History Interview: The Truman White House, HSTL, 1–2, 8–11.

13. Smith to the President, June 29, 1944, Smith papers, White House Memoranda—1944, FDRL; Smith diary, October 13, 1939, March 1, 1940. On Smith's "vision of administrative planning," see Katznelson and Pietrykowski, "Categories and Configurations," 217. For Webb, see Lambright, *Powering Apollo*, 216; "Webb," 200.

14. Testimony of Franklin D. Roosevelt to the Select Committee of the Budget of the House of Representatives, October 1, 1919, RG 51, Series 21.6a, The Presidency, National Archives (hereafter NA).

15. Donald Wilhelm, "The Presidential Handicap," *The Independent*, March 26, 1921. On the Budget Act, see Peri E. Arnold, *Making the Managerial Presidency*, 2nd rev. ed. (Lawrence: University Press of Kansas, 1998), chaps. 2–3.

16. Roger Jones 1969 oral history, HSTL, 11; Stephen Skowronek, *Building a New American State* (New York: Cambridge University Press, 1982), 206–8; Dawes, *The First Year of the Budget of the United States* (New York: Harper, 1923); Dawes to Rep. Martin Madden, July 22, 1921, RG 51, Series 21.1, *Budget, General-1-13*, NA.

17. For detail on the 1921–39 period, see Matthew Dickinson and Andrew Rudalevige, "'Worked Out in Fractions': Neutral Competence, FDR, and the Bureau of the Budget," *Congress and the Presidency* (Spring 2007). See also Berman, *OMB*, 7–8, 17; Alfred Dick Sander, *A Staff for the President: The Executive Office, 1921–1952* (Westport, Conn.: Greenwood, 1989), 16–18.

18. Frederick C. Mosher, *A Tale of Two Agencies* (Baton Rouge: Louisiana State University Press, 1984), 35.

19. Lester G. Seligman and Elmer E. Cornwell, Jr., eds., *New Deal Mosaic: Roosevelt Confers with His National Emergency Council, 1933–1936* (Eugene: University of Oregon Books, 1965), 492–93.

20. Brownlow memorandum for the record, March 4, 1936, Document A-II-7, PCAM files, FDRL.

21. Dickinson, *Bitter Harvest*, chap. 3; Patrick J. Wolf, "Neutral and Responsive Competence: The Bureau of the Budget, 1939–1948, Revisited," *Administration and Society* 31 (March 1999): 148–49. E.O. 8248 also placed a tiny Liaison Office for Personnel Management and the Office of Government Reports in the EOP.

22. Stephen Skowronek, *The Politics Presidents Make: Leadership from John Adams to George Bush* (Cambridge, Mass.: Harvard University Press, 1994), 318–19.

23. Meeting of February 8, 1946, Harold Smith Papers, Conferences with President Truman (1946), FDRL.

24. See Berman, *OMB*, 22.

25. Matthew J. Dickinson and Andrew Rudalevige, "Presidents, Responsiveness, and Competence: Revisiting the 'Golden Age' at the Bureau of the Budget," *Political Science Quarterly* 119 (Winter–Spring 2004–5): 642; Smith to President, December 8, 1943, PSF, Bureau of the Budget: December 1939–45, FDRL.

26. For BOB's wartime responsibilities, see Berman, *OMB*, 28–30; Bureau of the Budget, *The United States at War* (Washington, D.C.: Government Printing Office, 1946); Smith's "Statement of Support of Estimates of Appropriations for 1943," RG51, Series 39.28, Bureau of the Budget Annual Budget Estimates, NA. On impoundment, see Norman M. Pearson, "The Budget Bureau: From Routine Business to General Staff," *Public Administration Review* 3 (Spring 1943): 126–49.

27. Francis H. Heller, ed., *The Truman White House* (Lawrence: Regents Press of Kansas, 1980), 116.

28. For specific examples, see Dickinson and Rudalevige, "Fractions." More generally see Terry Moe, "The Politics of Bureaucratic Structure," in John Chubb and Paul Peterson, eds., *Can the Government Govern?* (Washington, D.C.: Brookings Institution, 1989). Webb quoted in Lambright, *Powering Apollo*, 42.

29. See Smith diary, entries of May 23, 1939, and May 25, 1939; Smith to President, February 21, 1942, White House Memoranda, 1942, FDRL. Herring quoted in Bureau of the Budget, *United States at War*, v.

30. Bureau of the Budget, *United States at War*; John D. Millett, *The Division of Administrative Management in the Federal Bureau of the Budget* (New York: Institute of Public Administration, 1948); Mosher, *Two Agencies*, 70, 104–7.

31. "Toward Better Management in the Federal Government," August 1950, RG 51, Entry 9-B, B2–11 Gov't Management and Organization, general, NA; see also Bureau Circular A-8 and Bulletin 50-2 (August 1, 1949).

32. Charles O. Jones, ed., *Preparing to Be President: The Memos of Richard E. Neustadt* (Washington, D.C.: AEI/Brookings Institution, 2000), 62.

33. Katznelson and Pietrykowski, "Rebuilding the American State," 318.

34. For examples, see Dickinson and Rudalevige, "Fractions"; Sander, *Staff for the President*, 46.

35. For clearance statistics, see Richard E. Neustadt, "Presidency and Legislation: The Growth of Central Clearance," *American Political Science Review* 48 (September 1954): 641–71; notes of February 8, 1946, Smith papers, Conferences with President Truman, HSTL; Don K. Price, "Staffing the Presidency," *American Political Science Review* 40 (December 1946): 1160–61. On pressures from the White House see Smith diary, especially regarding his discussions with Tommy Corcoran during May–July 1939. But Smith did sometimes urge dubious bills be signed because of "the temper of Congress . . . and the Congressional and political commitments" already made. Smith to President, "To Accompany . . . SJ Res 60," May 22, 1941, White House Memoranda, 1941, Smith papers, FDRL.

36. Andrew Rudalevige, *Managing the President's Program: Presidential Leadership and Legislative Policy Formulation* (Princeton, N.J.: Princeton University Press, 2002), ch. 3.

37. Division of Administrative Management, Government Organization Branch, "The Functioning of the Executive Office of the President," 1945, RG 51, Series 39.32, E2-15/50.1, NA.

38. Smith diary, September 27, 1939, and May 25, 1940; Ramsey, *Presidential Aide*, 99.

39. Ramsey, *Presidential Aide*, 152–57; Staats in Heller, *Truman White House*, 227.

40. Stowe and Murphy in Truman White House oral history, HSTL, 4, 23–25; Murphy oral history, HSTL.

41. Neustadt, "Central Clearance," 669.

42. Webb, White House oral history, HSTL, 12; Edward S. Flash, Jr., *Economic Advice and Presidential Leadership: The Council of Economic Advisers* (New York: Columbia University Press, 1965), 19; Lambright, *Powering Apollo*, 41.

43. Katznelson, Geiger, and Kryder, "Limiting Liberalism."

44. See Sander, *Staff for the President*, 20–23, 47–49; Marion Clawson, *New Deal Planning: The National Resources Planning Board* (Baltimore: Johns Hopkins University Press, 1981), ch. 1.

45. Clawson, *New Deal Planning*, 12, 202–3, 225–26; Patrick D. Reagan, *Designing a New America* (Amherst: University of Massachusetts Press, 1995), 239; Philip W. Warken, *A History of the National Resources Planning Board, 1933–1943* (New York: Garland, 1979), 248–49.

46. In February 1943, even as budget disaster loomed for NRPB, the president's reply to a request for a meeting with the Board was brief: "No, sorry." Clawson, *New Deal Planning*, 9, 239; Warken, *National Resources Planning Board*, 227.

47. Reagan, *Designing a New America*, 227; Warken, *National Resources Planning Board*, 242.

48. Philip White, quoted in Clawson, *New Deal Planning*, 236, see 214–22 in same volume; Reagan, *Designing a New America*, 228, 246. For testimony see Smith diary, 12/19/39, and "Statement of Support of Estimates of Appropriations" for 1943 and 1944, RG 51, Series 39.28, Bureau of the Budget Annual Budget Estimates, NA.

49. This counterfactual is of course particularly relevant to entrepreneurship; see Clawson, *New Deal Planning*, 50ff.

50. E.O. 9347; "War Mobilization and Reconversion Act of 1944," no author given, on "the problems of interrelationship between BOB and OWMR." RG 51, Office Files of Harold D. Smith, Box 2, NA. See also V. O. Key, Jr., "The Reconversion Phase of Demobilization," *American Political Science Review* 38 (December 1944): 1137–53; Herman Miles Somers, *Presidential Agency: OWMR* (Cambridge, Mass.: Harvard University Press, 1950). The legislative act followed earlier executive orders charging OWM with the disposition of surplus property from the war effort as well as postwar retraining policy.

51. George A. Graham, "The Presidency and the Executive Office of the President," *Journal of Politics* 12 (November 1950): 608; Key, "Reconversion Phase," 1152. See also Price, "Staffing the Presidency," 1163.

52. Price, "Staffing the Presidency," 1164. See also Somers, *Presidential Agency*, 67–70; Neustadt, "Central Clearance," 657.

53. Notes of February 8, 1946, and February 28, 1946, Smith Papers, Conferences with President Truman, FDRL; Berman, *OMB*, 34; Neustadt to Jim Rowe, July 11, 1942, Rowe papers, Neustadt, Richard, FDRL.

54. Ken Hechler, *Working with Truman* (New York: Putnam, 1982), 160; Wolf, "Neutral and Responsive Competence," 162; White House oral history, HSTL, 7. See also Somers, *Presidential Agency*, 95–100; Roger Jones, oral history, HSTL, 89, 90.

55. Somers, *Presidential Agency*, 75.

56. David Bell oral history, HSTL, 3–4; Clifford to Webb, January 8, 1947, Webb papers, Box 8, BOB: Clark Clifford, HSTL.

57. Murphy, Webb, quoted in Truman White House oral history, 7, 14; Lambright, *Powering Apollo*, 35. More broadly, see Somers, *Presidential Agency*, 100; Sander, *Staff for the President*, 98.

58. Key, "Reconversion Phase," 1152; Gulick, "War Organization of the Federal Government," *American Political Science Review* 38 (December 1944): 1174.

59. Lester Seligman, "Presidential Leadership," *Journal of Politics* 18 (August 1959): 410–26. See also Stephen Bailey, *Congress Makes a Law* (New York: Columbia

University Press, 1950); Flash, *Economic Advice*, 14–25; Katznelson and Pietrykowski, "Building," 325; Roger Porter, "Presidents and Economists: The Council of Economic Advisers," *AEA Papers and Proceedings* 87 (May 1997): 103–6.

60. Katznelson and Pietrykowski point out their essential congruence: see "Building," 325–27.

61. Smith papers, December 17, 1945, and February 8, 1946, diary entries; Smith to FDR, November 9, 1944, PSF, *BOB: December 1939–45*, FDRL; Sander, *Staff for the President*, 116–21.

62. Neustadt to Staats and Carey, "Bureau-Council Relationships," memo of November 22, 1946, RG 51, Series 39.28, *CEA*—General Administration, NA; Webb notes on conference with Truman, September 5, 1946, Webb papers, HSTL.

63. See the series of memos by Neustadt, who as budget examiner for the EOP was able to spy on Council developments: among others, Neustadt to Staats and Carey, "Housekeeping Services for the Council of Economic Advisers," August 12, 1946, HSTL; to Staats and Heun, "Miscellany on the Council of Economic Advisers," August 29, 1946, HSTL; to Staats, "Crisis for Next Month on CEA," January 30, 1947, NA; to Staats, "Activity on the Staffing Front in the Council of Economic Advisers," March 12, 1947, NA. HSTL memos are in the Neustadt papers; NA papers are in RG 51, Series 39.28, CEA—General Administration.

64. Sander, *Staff for the President*, 149; Neustadt to Staats and Carey, "Ideas on the Development of Program Review," November 27, 1946, NA; J. Weldon Jones to Neustadt, "Your Memorandum of November 27," December 9, 1946, NA; Neustadt to Marx, December 12, 1946, "Tentative Questions and Answers on Bureau-Council Relations," NA; Neustadt to Jones, "Bureau Procedure for Utilizing Agency Legislative Programs Submitted Under Sec. 86," September 6, 1949, RG 51, Series 39.39, Legislative Program—81st Congress, 2nd session, NA.

65. Neustadt to Staats, "Legislative Progress Reporting for the President," memo of November 23, 1948, Neustadt papers, Chron. Files, May–Dec. 1948, HSTL; Neustadt to Jones, "Weekly Reports on Anticipated Congressional Schedules," memo of May 15, 1950, RG 51, Series 39.39, Legislative Program—82nd Congress, 1st Sess., NA; Staats to Director, "Some Immediate Issues in Relation to the President's Legislative Program for the Forthcoming Session," November 12, 1948, Neustadt papers, Addendum: Budget Policy and Legislative Program, 1948–49, HSTL.

66. Charles Murphy, quoted in Heller, *Truman White House*, 90; Staats to Stauffacher, Martin, and J. W. Jones, "Review of Legislative Proposals prior to Convening of 81st Congress," December 6, 1948, Neustadt papers, Addendum: Budget Policy and Legislative Program, 1948–49, HSTL; Dickinson and Rudalevige, "Golden Age," 641–42; Neustadt, "Planning the President's Program," *American Political Science Review* 49 (December 1955), 1003–7.

67. Smith to Division Chiefs, August 24, 1945, RG 51, Series 39.27a, *Correspondence—1945*, NA; Roger Jones to Frank Pace, "Budget Bureau Problems and Relationships with the 81st Congress on Legislation," November 19, 1948, Series 39.39, Legislative Program—81st Congress, 1st Sess., NA.

68. Notes of February 8, 1946, Smith papers, Conferences with President Truman, 1946, FDRL.

69. Webb in Truman White House oral history, HSTL, 59, and see 51–59; Sander, *Staff for the President*, 128–30; Dickinson and Rudalevige, "Golden Age."

70. Staff Meeting Minutes of September 29, 1948, Lawton papers, BOB—Staff Meetings, HSTL.

71. Neustadt, "Planning the President's Program," 1000, 1014–15; Rudalevige, "'M' in OMB."

72. Ash, "Draft—Opening Statement," August 5, 1969, (EOP—August 1969, 2 of 2), Box 28, White House Central Files: President's Advisory Council on Executive Organization, Nixon Presidential Materials Staff; Nathan, *Administrative Presidency*; OMB, *The President's Management Agenda, Fiscal Year 2002* (Washington, D.C.: Government Printing Office, 2001); Sheingate, this volume.

73. Price, "Staffing the Presidency," 1164; Dickinson and Rudalevige, "Golden Age," 650; Larry Berman, "The OMB That Almost Wasn't," *Political Science Quarterly* 92 (Summer 1977): 281–303; Hugh Heclo, "The Office of Management and Budget and the Presidency: The Problem of Neutral Competence," *Public Interest* 38 (Winter 1975): 80–98.

74. Berman, "OMB That Almost Wasn't"; William R. Thomas, 3rd, to Office and Division Chiefs, "Draft Roles and Missions Paper," April 17, 1967, Working Papers of the Steering Group, April–June 1967, Box 146, Entry 161, NA; Dickinson and Rudalevige, "Presidents, Responsiveness, and the Creation of the Office of Management and Budget," paper presented at the Annual Meeting of the Midwest Political Science Association, April 2005.

75. Samuel Kernell, *Going Public*, 3rd ed. (Washington, D.C.: CQ Press, 1997); Sidney Milkis. *The President and the Parties* (New York: Oxford University Press, 1993).

76. Allen Schick with Felix LoStracco, *The Federal Budget: Politics, Policy, Process* (Washington, D.C.: Brookings Institution, 2000).

Chapter 16. Robust Action and the Strategic Use of Ambiguity in a Bureaucratic Cohort: FDA Officers and the Evolution of New Drug Regulations, 1950–70

We acknowledge Bruce Ackerman, Matt Glassman, Stephen Skowronek, and Wayne Thornton for helpful comments. Special thanks for archival assistance to Marjorie Ciarlante (National Archives, College Park), John Swann (FDA), Laura Carroll (AMA, Chicago), and staff members at the Mayo Foundation, Chesney Medical Archives at Johns Hopkins University, Seeley Mudd Manuscript Library (Princeton), Mandeville Special Collections Library (UCSD), UCSF Special Collections Library, and Countway Medical Library (Harvard Medical School). We thank Sarah Burg for excellent archival research for some of the materials employed here.

1. Daniel Carpenter, "State-Building Through Reputation Building: Policy Innovation and Cohorts of Esteem at the Post Office, 1883–1912," *Studies in American Political Development* 14, 2 (Fall 2000): 121–55; Carpenter, *The Forging of Bureaucratic Autonomy: Reputations, Networks, and Policy Innovation in Executive Agencies, 1862–1928* (Princeton, N.J.: Princeton University Press, 2001); Adam D. Sheingate, "Political Entrepreneurship, Institutional Change, and American Political Development," *Studies in American Political Development* 17 (2003): 185–203; Clayton A. Coppin and Jack C. High, *The Politics of Purity: Harvey Washington Wiley and the Origins of Federal Food Policy* (Ann Arbor: University of Michigan Press, 2000).

2. Herbert Kaufman, *The Forest Ranger: A Study in Administrative Behavior* (Washington, D.C.: Resources for the Future, 1960); Martha Derthick, *Policymaking for Social Security* (Washington, D.C.: Brookings Institution Press, 1979); Carpenter, *Forging of Bureaucratic Autonomy.*

3. Philip J. Hilts, *Protecting America's Health: The FDA, Business, and One Hundred Years of Regulation* (New York: Knopf, 2003); Sam Peltzman, "Toward a More General Theory of Regulation," *Journal of Law and Economics* 19 (1976): 211-40.

4. John F. Padgett and Christopher K. Ansell, "Robust Action and the Rise of the Medici, 1400-1434," *American Journal of Sociology* 98 (1993): 1259-1319; John F. Pad-

gett and Paul McLean, "Organizational Invention and Elite Transformation: The Birth of Partnership in Renaissance Florence," *American Journal of Sociology* 111 (2006): 1463-1568.

5. Kenneth A. Schultz, *Democracy and Coercive Diplomacy* (New York: Cambridge University Press, 2001; Andrew Kydd, "Which Side Are You On? Bias, Credibility and Mediation," *American Journal of Political Science* 47, 4 (October 2003): 597–611.

6. Robert A. Caro, *The Power Broker: Robert Moses and the Fall of New York* (New York: Vintage, 1975), 17–18, 715–22.

7. Cornelius M. Kerwin, *Rulemaking: How Government Agencies Write Law and Make Policy*, 3rd ed. (Washington, D.C.: CQ Press, 2003).

8. See B. Holmstedt and G. Liljestrand, eds., *Readings in Pharmacology* (New York: Macmillan, 1963).

9. Report of the Citizens' Advisory Committee on the U.S. Food and Drug Administration, copy in Archives of the American Medical Association, Bureau of Investigation Files, Folder "Special Data, 1955," 0272-8.

10. Erwin Nelson, February 1949 speech to the American Pharmaceutical Manufacturers' Association (emphasis added); Records of the U.S. Food and Drug Administration, RG 88, National Archive (heareafter NA).

11. John Swann, "Sure Cure: Public Policy on Drug Efficacy before 1962," in Gregory J. Higby and Elaine C. Stroud, eds., *The Inside Story of Medicines: A Symposium* (Madison, Wis.: American Institute for the History of Pharmacy, 1997). For another interesting example of drug review where considerations related to "efficacy" were of central significance, see Suzanne White-Junod and Lara Marks, "Women's Trials: The Approval of the First Oral Contraceptive Pill in the United States and Great Britain," *Bulletin of the History of Medicine* 57 (April 2002): 117–60.

12. "Problems Raised by New Drugs," *Association of Food & Drug Officials of the United States* 19, 4 (October 1955): 144.

13. George Larrick at the Annual Meeting of the American Pharmaceutical Manufacturers Association, May 29, 1957, FDA Records, RG 88, NA.

14. *Federal Register* (July 25, 1956). One of the most important institutional transformations in the 1950s was the institutional competition over drug evaluation. From midcentury onward, AMA was involved in making efficacy judgments, and the overall result of the 1960s was the displacement of the AMA by the FDA in this role. This is one reason why the AMA may have been opposed to the Kefauver-Harris Amendments and the IND regulations in the early 1960s. Hilts, *Protecting America's Health*, 126–27. See also AMA archival records.

15. William H. Kessenich, medical director, Bureau of Medicine, speech presented at the Antibiotic Symposium, November 4, 1959, FDA Records, RG 88, NA.

16. William H. Kessenich to Frederick Wolff, n.d., 1961; FDA Records, RG 88, NA.

17. George T. Daughters, "The Food and Drug Administration Program," presented to the Governors Committee on Public Health, Ann Arbor, Mich., September 8, 1956; Memo from E. C. Boudreaux to Administration, "Annual Contention of Mississippi State Pharmaceutical Association at Jackson, Miss.," June 16, 1955; Boudreaux, "The Food and Drug Administration and What It Does," delivered before the Institute of Industrial Relations, Loyola University, New Orleans, March 3, 1955, DF 505, RG 88, NA; Horace Allen to Chief, Seattle District, re "Public Relations Talk," April 20, 1956; Allen, "The Relationship of the Food and Drug Administration to Retail Pharmacists," delivered at Postgraduate Refresher Course, State College of Washington College of Pharmacy, Pullman, Wash., April 19, 1956, DF 040.5, RG 88, NA (emphasis added).

18. John L. Harvey, "A Look at Rule-Making," statement for delivery at the An-

nual Meeting of the Food, Drug and Cosmetic Law Section of the American Bar Association, Los Angeles, Calif., August 26, 1958; Harvey, "Progress and Problems," delivered at the annual meeting of the Division of Food, Drug and Cosmetic Law of the American Bar Association, Dallas, Texas, August 28, 1956, DF 505, RG 88, NA. For discussion of developments after passage of the Kefauver-Harris legislation, see the following: Robert S. Roe, "Drug Amendments of 1962—Certification of Antibiotics," October 17, 1962, DF 051.11, RG 88, NA; Ralph G. Smith, Memo on "New Drug Policies—Supplements," to Division of New Drugs and Division of Veterinary Medicine, January 16, 1963, DF 505.5, RG 88, NA; K. L. Milstead (Bureau of Field Administration) to Directors of Districts, Memo re "New Drug Investigation," October 12, 1962, DF 505.7 (652), RG 88, NA.

19. Harold F. O'Keefe to Ralph Smith, June 29, 1961, FDA Records, RG 88, NA.

20. U.S. Senate, *Drug Industry Antitrust Act*, Hearings before the Subcommittee on Antitrust and Monopoly of the Committee on the Judiciary, 87th Congress, 1st Session (Washington, D.C.: GPO, 1961), esp. the remarks of Hussey (54), Howard (75), Goodman (213), Lasagna (283, 288), Butler (351–52), Richmond (373), Finland (436), Larrick (78, 80–81, 86), and Kefauver himself (82, 88, 421).

21. The thalidomide episode has been narrated in much greater detail by the Insight Team of the *Sunday Times* of London in *Suffer the Children: The Story of Thalidomide* (New York: Viking, 1979). See also Hilts, *Protecting America's Health*, and Daniel Carpenter, *Reputation and Power: Organizational Image and Pharmaceutical Regulation at the FDA* (forthcoming).

22. Insight Team, *Suffer the Children*.

23. A. Leslie Florence letter, "Is Thalidomide to Blame?" *BMJ* 2 (December 31, 1960): 1954. See also related correspondence in *BMJ* (January 14, 1961). In conversations with John DeAngelis, M.D., Professor of Psychiatry at Johns Hopkins, it was suggested that in fact the original notification came not from Kelsey's perusal of the *BMJ* but from notification of the FDA librarian, whose name is not remembered by our interview subjects. We cannot at present verify this report.

24. Kelsey, "Summary of Substance of Contact" and "Memo of Interview," March 30, 1961, Thalidomide NDA File, FOK Papers, Manuscript Division, Library of Congress (emphasis added).

25. Insight Team, *Suffer the Children*, 78–79 (emphasis added).

26. Widukind Lenz (Universitäts-Kinderklinik, Hamburg-Eppendorf, Germany), "Thalidomide and Congenital Abnormalities," *Lancet* (Letters) 1 (January 1962): 45; See also article by R. A. Pfieffer and W. Kosenow (also from the Universitäts-Kinderklinik) in the same issue. More generally, see "Sleeping Pill Rouses Germans," *Medical World News* 3 (February 2, 1962): 80–81.

27. "Heroine of FDA Keeps Bad Drug off Market," *Washington Post*, July 15, 1962, A1. Subsequent coverage included the following: "Dr. Kelsey's Stubborn Triumph," *Good Housekeeping*, November 1962; "Doctor and the Drug," *Newsweek* 60 (July 30, 1962): 70; "Thalidomide Disaster," *Time* 80 (August 10, 1962): 32; J. Mulliken, "Woman Doctor Who Would Not be Hurried," *Life* 53 (August 10, 1962): 82–89; "Inside Story of a Medical Tragedy: Interview," *U.S. News* 53 (August 13, 1962): 54–55; D. Wolfle, "Thalidomide Lesson," *Science* 137 (August 17, 1962): 497; "Vigilant Doctor Gets a Medal," *U.S. News* 53 (August 20, 1962): 13; W. Jonathan, "Feminine Conscience of FDA: Dr. Frances Oldham Kelsey," *Saturday Review* 45 (September 1, 1962): 41–43; "Parent's Magazine Honors Dr. Frances Oldham Kelsey for Outstanding Service to Family Health," *Parent's Magazine* 37 (October 1962): 64; Morton Mintz, "Doctor Kelsey Said No," *Reader's Digest* 81 (October 1962): 86–89; "Toward Safer Drugs," *Consumer Reports* 27 (October 1962): 509–11; J. Lear, "Reward," *Saturday Review* 46 (February 2, 1963): 47;

"Thalidomide Heroine Seeks New Culprits," *Scientific Digest* 53 (May 1963): 32; "Lady Cop," *Newsweek* 61 (June 24, 1963): 100.

28. For some general and suggestive evidence, see Richard Harris, *The Real Voice* (New York: Macmillan, 1964), 190–206. For more on this question, see Carpenter, *Gatekeeper.*

29. *Federal Register* 23, 32 (February 14, 1963): 1449-57.

30. These "case reports" now account for hundreds of thousands of pages of new drug submissions to the FDA. For current regulation embodying this principle, see 21 CFR, chap. 1, sec. 314.50 (f), "Case Report Forms and Tabulations."

31. For current regulations on "adequate and well-controlled studies," see 21 CFR, chap. 1, sec. 314.126.

32. Frances Oldham Kelsey, "Problems Raised for the FDA by the Occurrence of Thalidomide Embryopathy in Germany, 1960–1961," pre-script of speech presented at the 91st Annual Meeting of the American Public Health Association, Kansas City, November 14, 1963, Frances Oldham Kelsey Papers, Manuscript Division, Library of Congress.

33. See Carpenter, *Forging of Bureaucratic Autonomy,* for a discussion of these other examples.

34. Arthur Ruskin, M.D., "New Drug Procedures," statement delivered to FDA conference on Kefauver-Harris Drug Amendments and Related Regulations, February 15, 1963, DF 051.155 (1963), RG 88, NA.

35. Proceedings, FDA Conference on the Kefauver-Harris Drug Amendments and Proposed Regulations, February 15, 1963 (Washington, D.C.: U.S. Department of Health, Education and Welfare, Food and Drug Administration).

36. Proceedings, FDA Conference.

37. Ibid., 24.

38. Ibid., 34–35.

39. Minutes of the Committee on the Safety of Therapeutic Agents (CSTA), Mayo Clinic, November 21, 1963, Records of the CSTA, Mayo Clinic Archives, Rochester, Minn.

40. Carl C. Pfeiffer, "Problems in Drug Development as they Relate to the Clinical Investigator," *Journal of New Drugs* (November–December 1964): 299–305, presented at a symposium on "Problems in the Development of New Drugs" at the First Annual Meeting of the American College of Clinical Pharmacology and Chemotherapy, New York, October 29–30, 1964.

41. L. T. Coggeshall, M.D., "The University and the Food and Drug Administration," presented at the Joint Food and Drug Administration—Food Law Institute Conference, Washington, D.C., December 2, 1963 (Commission on Drug Safety, 221 N. LaSalle Street, Chicago, Ill.), Frances Oldham Kelsey Papers, Manuscript Division, Library of Congress.

42. Carpenter, *Forging of Bureaucratic Autonomy,* 90, table 3.1.

43. See Carpenter, *Forging of Bureaucratic Autonomy.*

44. Peltzman, "Toward a More General Theory of Regulation"; Hilts, *Protecting America's Health.*

Chapter 17. Retrospective: Formative Action and Second Acts

1. Michael Young, "Confessional Protest: The Religious Birth of U.S. Social Movements," *American Sociological Review* 67 (October 2002): 660–88.

2. Michael Kazin, *A Godly Hero: The Life of William Jennings Bryan* (New York: Knopf, 2006).

3. Max Weber, *Economy and Society*, ed. Guenther Roth and Claus Wittich (Berkeley: University of California Press, 1978), 1: 243.

4. William Sewell, Jr., "A Theory of Structure: Duality, Agency and Transformation." *American Journal of Sociology* 98, 1 (1992): 1–29.; Elisabeth S. Clemens and James M. Cook, "Politics and Institutionalism: Explaining Durability and Change," *Annual Review of Sociology* 25 (1999): 441–66.

5. Further fragmentation is not inevitable, however. As Rudalevige demonstrates in his study of the Bureau of the Budget, the entrepreneurial politics of agency directors led to a greater consolidation of political power in the agency as it became more closely aligned with the interests of the office of the presidency.

6. On decline of republicanism, see Gordon Wood, *The Radicalism of the American Revolution* (New York: Vintage, 1991).

7. Weber, *Economy and Society*, 2: 1148–49.

8. Wallace Stegner, *Beyond the Hundredth Meridian: John Wesley Powell and the Second Opening of the West* (New York: Penguin, 1953).

9. The history of the U.S. Post Office was similarly transformed by cadres of Civil War veterans. Daniel Carpenter, "State-Building Through Reputation Building: Policy Innovation and Cohorts of Esteem at the Post Office, 1883–1912," *Studies in American Political Development* 14, 2 (Fall 2000): 121–55.

10. Sewell, "The Duality of Structure."

11. James Mahoney, "Path Dependence in Historical Sociology," *Theory and Society* 29 (2000): 507–48.

12. Michael Mann, *The Sources of Social Power: A History of Power from the Beginning to A.D. 1760* (New York: Cambridge University Press, 1986), 1: 3; Karen Orren and Stephen Skowronek, *The Search for American Political Development* (New York: Cambridge University Press, 2004).

13. George Kubler, *The Shape of Time: Remarks on the History of Things* (New Haven, Conn.: Yale University Press, 1962).

14. William Sewell, "Three Temporalities: Towards an Eventful Sociology," in Terrence McDonald, ed., *The Historic Turn in the Human Sciences* (Ann Arbor: University of Michigan Press, 1996), 245–80. For a more general discussion of this theoretical turn in historical explanation see Julia Adams, Elisabeth S. Clemens, and Ann Shola Orloff, eds., *Remaking Modernity: Politics, History, and Sociology* (Durham, N.C.: Duke University Press, 2005).

15. For the broader context of the Bryan speech and his political career, see Kazin, *Godly Hero.*

16. Lawrence Goodwyn, *The Populist Moment: A Short History of the Agrarian Revolt in America* (New York: Oxford University Press, 1978).

17. Quoted in Kazin, *A Godly Hero*, 43–44.

18. Joseph Gerteis, "Populism, Race, and Politican Interest in Virginia," *Social Science History* 27, 2 (2003): 197–227.

19. Kazin, *Godly Hero*, 68–69.

20. Elizabeth Sanders, *Roots of Reform: Farmers, Workers, and the American State, 1877–1917* (Chicago: University of Chicago Press, 1999); Alan Brinkley, *Voices of Protest: Huey Long, Father Coughlin and the Great Depression* (New York: Vintage, 1982), 161–65.

21. Edgar Kiser and Justin Baer, "The Bureaucratization of States: Toward an Analytical Weberianism," in Adams, Clemens, and Orloff, *Remaking Modernity.*

Contributors

Richard Bensel is Professor of Government at Cornell University. He is the author of four books: *Sectionalism and American Political Development, 1880–1980; Yankee Leviathan: The Origins of Central State Authority in America, 1859–1877; The Political Economy of American Industrialization, 1877–1900;* and *The American Ballot Box in the Mid-Nineteenth Century.* His current research includes a book-length manuscript, *Passion and Preferences in the 1896 Democratic National Convention,* and a new project, *The Material Construction of Courage: The Political Economy of Violence in the American South, 1865–1900.*

James Block teaches political theory and American political culture at DePaul University. In addition to numerous articles, he is the author of *A Nation of Agents: The American Path to a Modern Self and Society,* and the forthcoming *The Crucible of Consent: American Child Rearing and the Forging of a Liberal Society.*

Daniel P. Carpenter is Professor of Government at Harvard University. He is the author of *The Forging of Bureaucratic Autonomy.* He is an expert on the politics of disease prevention and is current working on a book about the Food and Drug Administration.

Elisabeth Clemens is Associate Professor of Sociology at the University of Chicago. Building on organizational theory and political sociology, her research has addressed the role of social movements and voluntary organizations in processes of institutional change. Her first book, *The People's Lobby: Organizational Innovation and the Rise of Interest Group Politics in the United States, 1890–1925,* received the Max Weber Award for organizational sociology and the award for the best book in political sociology. She is also coeditor of *Private Action and the Public Good* and *Remaking Modernity: Politics, History and Sociology.* Her current research addresses the relations between formal state institutions and private organizations in American political development.

Matthew Glassman is a Ph.D. candidate in political science at Yale University. His dissertation examines the development of the political structure of the western United States as a process of institutional change.

Victoria Hattam received her Ph.D. from MIT and teaches at the New School for Social Research. Her first book, *Labor Visions and State Power,* explored nineteenth-century working-class formation. She has recently completed a book on ethnic and racial politics in the U.S. entitled *In the Shadow of Race: Jews, Latinos and Immigrant Politics in the Twentieth Century United States.*

Daniel Kryder is Associate Professor of Politics at Brandeis University. His book *Divided Arsenal* investigated patterns of racial conflict and policy response in industry, agriculture, and the Army during World War II. His current scholarship concerns the relationship between policing and politics in American history; the relationship of war to presidents and reform; and qualitative and historical methods.

Joseph Lowndes is Assistant Professor of Political Science at the University of Oregon. He completed his Ph.D. in political science at the New School for Social Research in 2003. His interests are in American political history and political theory, and he currently teaches courses on racial politics, political culture, and the presidency. His research concerns the construction of political identities through discourse and institutions. His book, *The Southern Origins of Modern Conservatives*, will be published in 2008. He has taught at the City University of New York and Eugene Lang College.

Eileen McDonagh is Professor of Political Science at Northeastern University and visiting scholar at the Institute for Quantitative Social Science at Harvard University. She is the 2004–6 recipient of the American Association of University Women (AAUW) Scholarship Award to complete her book *Gendering the State: Women's Political Leadership in Democracies*. She has written extensively on gender and political issues from institutional and historical perspectives. She is the author of *Breaking the Abortion Deadlock: From Choice to Consent*, and the forthcoming *Playing with the Boys: Separate Is Not Equal in Sports* (coauthored with Laura Pappano). Her work has appeared in major journals, including *Studies in American Political Development* and *American Political Science Review*.

Nicole Mellow teaches political science at Williams College. She has published articles and book chapters on elections, parties, education policy, and gender and politics. She is currently completing the provisionally titled *Unfinished Nation: Regional Coalitions and Party Conflict in Postwar America*, which examines the regional sources of partisanship.

Sidney M. Milkis is White Burkett Miller Professor and Chair of the Department of Politics and codirector of the American Political Development Program at the Miller School of Public Affairs at the University of Virginia. His books include *The President and the Parties: The Transformation of the American Party System Since the New Deal; Political Parties and Constitutional Government: Remaking American Democracy; Presidential Greatness*, coauthored with Marc Landy; and *The American Presidency: Origins and Development, 1776–2002*, 4th edition, coauthored with Michael Nelson. He is the coeditor, with Jerome Mileur, of three volumes on twentieth-century political reform: *Progressivism and the New Democracy; The New Deal and the Triumph of Liberalism);* and *The Great Society and the High Tide of Liberalism.*

Bruce Miroff is Professor and former Chair of Political Science at the State University of New York, Albany. His books include *The Democratic Debate*, 4th ed. (with Raymond Seidelman and Todd Swanstrom); *Icons of Democracy: American Leaders as Heroes, Aristocrats, Dissenters, and Democrats;* and *Pragmatic Illusions: The Presidential Politics of John F. Kennedy*. His new book, *The Liberals' Moment: The McGovern Insurgency and the Identity Crisis of the Democratic Party*, will be published in fall 2007.

Colin D. Moore is a Ph.D. candidate in American Politics at Harvard University. His work focuses on bureaucratic politics and the development of the American state.

Andrew Rudalevige is Associate Professor of Political Science at Dickinson College. A graduate of the University of Chicago and Harvard University, he is the author of *Managing the President's Program: Presidential Leadership and Legislative Policy Formulation*, which won the Richard E. Neustadt Award, and *The New Imperial Presidency: Renewing Presidential Power after Watergate*. In other recent research he has explored presidential management of the executive branch, especially through the Office of Management and Budget.

Elizabeth Sanders is Professor in the Cornell University Government Department. She has published articles on American political development, economic regulation, the impact of black voting in the South, the New Deal, presidential politics and governance, the determinants of voter choice in presidential elections, antitrust policy, and agrarian movements. Her book on the politics of energy regulation won the Kammerer Prize of the APSA for the best book on American public policy in 1982. Her book *Roots of Reform: Farmers, Workers, and the American State 1877–1911* was awarded the 2000 Greenstone Prize of the Politics and History Association of APSA.

Eric Schickler is Professor of Political Science at the University of California, Berkeley. He is the author of *Disjointed Pluralism: Institutional Innovation and the Development of the U.S. Congress*, which received APSA Richard F. Fenno Award. He is coauthor (with Donald Green and Bradley Palmquist) of *Partisan Hearts and Minds* and (with Gregory Wawro) of *Filibuster: Obstruction and Lawmaking in the U.S. Senate*. He has authored articles in *American Political Science Review, American Journal of Political Science, Legislative Studies Quarterly, Comparative Political Studies, Polity, Public Opinion Quarterly*, and *Social Science History*.

Adam Sheingate teaches political science at Johns Hopkins University. He is the author of *The Rise of the Agricultural Welfare State: Institutions and Interest Group Power in the United States, France, and Japan*, and has published articles in *Governance, Studies in American Political Development, Social Science History*, and *British Journal of Political Science*.

Stephen Skowronek is Peletiah Perit Professor of Political and Social Science at Yale University. He is the author of *Building a New American State: The Expansion of National Administrative Capacities 1877–1920; The Politics Presidents Make: Leadership from John Adams to Bill Clinton;* and coauthor of *The Search for American Political Development*. His is also a managing editor of the journal *Studies in American Political Development*.

Daniel J. Tichenor is Associate Professor in the Political Science Department and at the Eagleton Institute of Politics at Rutgers University. He received the APSA 2003 Kammerer Award for his book on immigration policy making in American Political Development, and the Jack Walker and Mary Parker Follett awards for new research on interest groups and social movements. He is currently researching and writing a book on wartime presidents and civil liberties.

Jeffrey K. Tulis has taught at the University of Texas at Austin for the past fifteen years. His work explores issues at the juncture of American politics and political theory, including such topics as outsiders' perspectives on American politics, slippery-slope rhetoric and policy, and constitutional pathologies. He is author of *The Rhetorical Presidency* and is currently completing a book titled *The Politics of Deference*.

Richard M. Valelly is Professor of Political Science at Swarthmore College. He is author of *The Two Reconstructions: The Struggle for Black Enfranchisement*, which won the J. David Greenstone Book Award of the Politics and History Section of the American Political Science Association, the Ralph Bunche Book Award of the American Political Science Association, and the V. O. Key, Jr., Book Award of the Southern Political Science Association. He is also the editor of *The Voting Rights Act: Securing the Ballot*.

Index

Poage, William, 311
Police agency: concept of, 105; formative
    structure and, 105, 106; and interactions
    with protesters in Washington, D.C., 105,
    106–8, 114–22; types of uncertainty
    created by, 114
Police/policing, Tocqueville on, 113. *See also*
    Metropolitan Police Department
Police-protester interactions: dynamics of,
    114; formative structure and, 105, 114–15;
    in Washington, 105–8, 114–22
Policy windows, 1890 Federal Elections Bill
    and, 128, *129*
Political action, context and, 367–70
Political Action Committees (PACs), 17
Political change: in relationship to order,
    201–3; language and culture as locus of,
    203–5
Political citizenship, 171, 174–75. *See also*
    Women's political citizenship
Political entrepreneurs/entrepreneurship,
    13, 21–28, 319; Bureau of the Budget
    and, 319–22, 336; Congress and, 29–30,
    293–95, 312; congressional investigations
    and, 367; consequences of, 28–31; 1896
    Democratic National Convention and,
    102; innovations and, 39; institutional
    complexity and, 13, 14–20; interest
    groups and, 25–26; persuasion and, 38;
    political change and, 34–35; presidential
    campaign of 2004 and, 30–31
Political innovation, institutional complexity
    and, 15–20
Political networks/networking, 44; change
    and, 368–69. *See also* Networks
Political order: and change, 201–3;
    formation, reproduction and
    transformation of, 370–72. *See also* Order
Political parties: entrepreneurial politics
    and, 25–27; resurgence of party
    organizations, 26
Political professionals, 27
Pollard, Edward, 166, 397n2
Poor People's Campaign, 246–47
Popular activism: abolitionist movement
    and, 67; civic culture and, 58–59;
    conservatism and, 72–73
Popular agency, 73–74
Post-War Economic Policy Committee, 303
Potter, David, 252
Powell, John Wesley, 368–69
The Power Broker (Caro), 344
Power Without Persuasion (Howell), 293

"The Prayer of Twenty Millions" (Greeley), 256
Presidency: Bureau of the Budget and,
    320–21, 335–36, 338–39; modern
    dilemma in, 29
Presidential campaign of 2004, 30–31
Presidential power: entrepreneurial politics
    and, 21–23, 29; notions of institutional
    complexity and, 15; rationalist notions of,
    14–15
Presidents, social movements and, 223–26,
    230–32, 233–39, 241–43, 249–50, 267
President's Management Agenda (2001),
    319, 337
President's Management Program (1949), 326
President-social movement interaction study,
    223–26; data and methodology, 233;
    defining and delineating social
    movements, 226–29; findings, 233–40;
    modes of interaction, 230–32
Price, Don K., 332
The Process of Government (Bentley), 2
Progress for America, 26
Progressive era: grammar of equality and
    difference in, 173–74; mother's pensions,
    181; social policies and creation of
    citizenship, 174–75; women's rights
    movement and, 196–97; women's social
    involvement and, 179–80
Progressive Party, 258
Progressive political activism, 71
Prohibition, 239
Protestantism, 61–68
Protest(s): agency and, 109; Montgomery
    bus boycott, 41, 42; Selma, 275. *See also*
    Marches and demonstrations; Police-
    protester interactions
Public interest groups, 25
Pullman, Raymond W., 117
Pullman strike, 244
Pyramid marketing scheme, 31

Racial classifications, 20, 210–14
Racial politics: Dixiecrat Revolt and, 205–10;
    Lyndon Johnson and, 271–77; post-
    Reconstruction South and, 163–64, 166–68
Railway Labor Act of 1926, 236
Ramspeck, Robert, 311
Randolph, A. Philip, 120, 121, 280
Rankin, Jeannette, 181
Rational choice theory, 55
Rauh, Joseph, 280
Rayburn, Sam, 300
Reagan, Ronald, 276

Snyder, John, 321, 332–33
Social benefits, 175–76
Social movement analysis (SMA), 56–57
Social movements, 226; distinguishing from
interest groups, 226–27; list, *228–29*;
presidents and, 223–26, 230–39, 241–43,
249–50; of 1960s, 70. *See also* Citizenship
movements; President-social movement
interaction study
Social theory, on mass action, 55–56
Sorauf, Frank, 17
Sorenson, Theodore, 272
South: end of Reconstruction and, 163–64;
Andrew Johnson's support for, 164–68;
Andrew Johnson's policies, 159–62;
Andrew Johnson's "restoration plan" for,
155–59; Redemption governments, 163
Southern Christian Leadership Conference
(SCLC), 274
Spanish-American War, 246
Special Committee on Un-American
Activities, 299–300
Spooner, John Coit, 137
Staats, Elmer, 335
Stanford, Leland, 145
Stanton, Edwin, 163
Stanton, Elizabeth Cady, 67, 176, 243
Stanton, Henry B., 176
State performance: affecting women,
197–98; creation of citizens and, 175;
nineteenth century, 175–76; Progressive
era, 181–82; women's political citizenship
and, 175, 190–96
States' rights, 157–58
Steelman, John, 329
Stewart, William, 145, 147
Stone, Donald, 326
Stowe, David, 329
Stowe, Harriet Beecher, 251
Strategic ambiguity, 341, 343–44; FDA and,
348–52, 358–62; Cosimo de Medici and,
343; rule-making and, 344–45
Straw, Jack, 214
Strikes, 263–64
Structure-agency framework, Bryan's "Cross
of Gold" speech and, 99–100
Student Nonviolent Coordinating
Committee (SNCC), 276–77, 279–80
Sullivan, Daniel, 118
Sumner, Charles, 251, 253–57, 267
Supreme Court: federal electoral regulation,
131–36;women's rights and benefits, 182,
189

Sutton, John, 19
Sylvester, Richard, 115–17
Szymanski, Ann-Marie, 245

Taft, William Howard, 258
Taft-Hartley Act, 302
Talmadge, Herman, 273
Tammany Hall, 130
Tarrow, Sidney, 245
Teapot Dome scandal, 298
Ten percent plan, 155
Thalidomide, 353–55
Thirteenth Amendment, 257
Thompson, Fred, 313
Thoreau, Henry David, 67
Thurmond, J. Strom, 205, 207–9
Tichenor, Daniel, 235, 269
Tillman, Benjamin ("Pitchfork"), 85, 86, 97,
98, 373
Title IX (Education Act of 1972), 189
Title VII (Civil Rights Act of 1964), 18
Tocqueville, Alexis de, 54, 55; on cities, 113;
on criminal justice and policing, 113; on
history and historians, 168; on tyranny of
the majority, 59
Towner, Horace, 181
"Transactional leadership," 38
Treason, 397n6
Treasury Department, 322
Truman, Harry S., 207, 303, 329, 332
Truman Committee, 303
Tucker, Robert C., 35
Tugwell, Rexford, 119
Turner, Frederick Jackson, 68

Unanimous Consent Agreements, 25
Uncle Tom's Cabin (Stowe), 251
United Auto Workers (UAW), 265
United Mine Workers (UMW), 262–63, 265

Valelly, Richard, 398n23
Values, political leadership and, 38
Vander Jagt, Guy, 26–27
Veterans, Bonus Expeditionary Force, 108,
118–19
Vietnam War, 278, 288
Vilas, William, 85, 86
Volunteerism, 54–55, 179–80
Voorhis, Jerry, 311
Voting rights: debate during Reconstruction,
177–78; historical exclusions to, 172. *See
also* Federal Elections Bill; Women's
suffrage movement